Web Data Mining and the Development of Knowledge-Based Decision Support Systems

G. Sreedhar
Rashtriya Sanskrit Vidyapeetha (Deemed University), India

A volume in the Advances in Data Mining and
Database Management (ADMDM) Book Series

www.igi-global.com

Published in the United States of America by
IGI Global
Information Science Reference (an imprint of IGI Global)
701 E. Chocolate Avenue
Hershey PA, USA 17033
Tel: 717-533-8845
Fax: 717-533-8661
E-mail: cust@igi-global.com
Web site: http://www.igi-global.com

Library of Congress Cataloging-in-Publication Data

Names: Sreedhar, G., 1974- editor.
Title: Web data mining and the development of knowledge-based decision
  support systems / G. Sreedhar, editor.
Description: Hershey, PA : Information Science Reference, [2017] | Includes
  bibliographical references and index.
Identifiers: LCCN 2016046936| ISBN 9781522518778 (hardcover) | ISBN
  9781522518785 (ebook)
Subjects: LCSH: Data mining. | Decision support systems. | Semantic web. |
  Machine learning. | Expert systems (Computer science)
Classification: LCC QA76.9.D37 W43 2017 | DDC 006.3/12--dc23 LC record available at https://lccn.loc.gov/2016046936

This book is published in the IGI Global book series Advances in Data Mining and Database Management (ADMDM) (ISSN: 2327-1981; eISSN: 2327-199X)

British Cataloguing in Publication Data
A Cataloguing in Publication record for this book is available from the British Library.

All work contributed to this book is new, previously-unpublished material. The views expressed in this book are those of the authors, but not necessarily of the publisher.

For electronic access to this publication, please contact: eresources@igi-global.com.

Advances in Data Mining and Database Management (ADMDM) Book Series

David Taniar
Monash University, Australia

ISSN:2327-1981
EISSN:2327-199X

MISSION

With the large amounts of information available to organizations in today's digital world, there is a need for continual research surrounding emerging methods and tools for collecting, analyzing, and storing data.

The **Advances in Data Mining & Database Management (ADMDM)** series aims to bring together research in information retrieval, data analysis, data warehousing, and related areas in order to become an ideal resource for those working and studying in these fields. IT professionals, software engineers, academicians and upper-level students will find titles within the ADMDM book series particularly useful for staying up-to-date on emerging research, theories, and applications in the fields of data mining and database management.

COVERAGE

- Customer Analytics
- Profiling Practices
- Educational Data Mining
- Web-based information systems
- Data Warehousing
- Data Analysis
- Database Security
- Web mining
- Text Mining
- Data Mining

IGI Global is currently accepting manuscripts for publication within this series. To submit a proposal for a volume in this series, please contact our Acquisition Editors at Acquisitions@igi-global.com or visit: http://www.igi-global.com/publish/.

Titles in this Series

For a list of additional titles in this series, please visit: www.igi-global.com

Emerging Trends in the Development and Application of Composite Indicators
Veljko Jeremic (University of Belgrade, Serbia) Zoran Radojicic (University of Belgrade, Serbia) and Marina Dobrota (University of Belgrade, Serbia)
Information Science Reference • copyright 2017 • 402pp • H/C (ISBN: 9781522507147) • US $205.00 (our price)

Web Usage Mining Techniques and Applications Across Industries
A.V. Senthil Kumar (Hindusthan College of Arts and Science, India)
Information Science Reference • copyright 2017 • 424pp • H/C (ISBN: 9781522506133) • US $200.00 (our price)

Social Media Data Extraction and Content Analysis
Shalin Hai-Jew (Kansas State University, USA)
Information Science Reference • copyright 2017 • 493pp • H/C (ISBN: 9781522506485) • US $225.00 (our price)

Collaborative Filtering Using Data Mining and Analysis
Vishal Bhatnagar (Ambedkar Institute of Advanced Communication Technologies and Research, India)
Information Science Reference • copyright 2017 • 309pp • H/C (ISBN: 9781522504894) • US $195.00 (our price)

Effective Big Data Management and Opportunities for Implementation
Manoj Kumar Singh (Adama Science and Technology University, Ethiopia) and Dileep Kumar G. (Adama Science and Technology University, Ethiopia)
Information Science Reference • copyright 2016 • 324pp • H/C (ISBN: 9781522501824) • US $195.00 (our price)

Data Mining Trends and Applications in Criminal Science and Investigations
Omowunmi E. Isafiade (University of Cape Town, South Africa) and Antoine B. Bagula (University of the Western Cape, South Africa)
Information Science Reference • copyright 2016 • 386pp • H/C (ISBN: 9781522504634) • US $210.00 (our price)

Intelligent Techniques for Data Analysis in Diverse Settings
Numan Celebi (Sakarya University, Turkey)
Information Science Reference • copyright 2016 • 353pp • H/C (ISBN: 9781522500759) • US $195.00 (our price)

Managing and Processing Big Data in Cloud Computing
Rajkumar Kannan (King Faisal University, Saudi Arabia) Raihan Ur Rasool (King Faisal University, Saudi Arabia) Hai Jin (Huazhong University of Science and Technology, China) and S.R. Balasundaram (National Institute of Technology, Tiruchirappalli, India)
Information Science Reference • copyright 2016 • 307pp • H/C (ISBN: 9781466697676) • US $200.00 (our price)

DISSEMINATOR of KNOWLEDGE

www.igi-global.com

701 E. Chocolate Ave., Hershey, PA 17033
Order online at www.igi-global.com or call 717-533-8845 x100
To place a standing order for titles released in this series, contact: cust@igi-global.com
Mon-Fri 8:00 am - 5:00 pm (est) or fax 24 hours a day 717-533-8661

Table of Contents

Section 3
Developing Efficient Knowledge based Systems

Section 4
Developing Social Media based Mining Systems

Section 5
Developing Data and Text Mining Systems

Detailed Table of Contents

Section 1
Developing Decision Support Systems

Chapter 1
    G. Sreedhar, Rashtriya Sanskrit Vidyapeetha (Deemed University), India
    A. Anandaraja Chari, Rayalaseema University, India

The management of web sites imposes a constant demand for new information and timely updates due
to the increase of services and content that site owners wish to make available to their users, which in
turn is motivated by the complexity and diversity of needs and behaviours of the users. Such constant
labour intensive effort implies very high financial and personnel costs. The growth of World Wide Web
and technologies has made business functions to be executed fast and easier. E-commerce has provided
a cost efficient and effective way of doing business. Web mining is usually defined as the use of data
mining techniques to automatically discover and extract information from web documents and services.
Also, web data mining is commonly categorized into three areas: web content mining that describes the
discovery of useful information from content, web structure mining that analyses the topology of web
sites, and web usage mining that tries to make sense of the data generated by the navigation behaviour
and user profile.

Chapter 2
    Carlos Alberto Ochoa Ortiz Zezzatti, Juarez City University, Mexico

This study combines Fuzzy Logic and multicriteria TOPSIS method for the selection, from three different
alternatives, which machines of high productivity is more convenient to a construction company. The
evaluation of each alternative is made through group decision making which identifies the most important
criteria according to the requirements presented by the company. To assess the selected criteria in the
TOPSIS method is weighted by a group of experts who, based on their experience and knowledge of
this type of machinery, assess the relevance of these in the operation and functioning of the hydraulic
excavator. Both qualitative and quantitative studies are used in this work, however the experts evaluate,

through surveys based on Likert scale all the criteria in which they want to measure the perception. Data provided from the surveys is used for the construction and association of the groups of expert's opinion through the use of fuzzy sets to avoid ambiguity problems of the linguistic variables.

Chapter 3

Decision Supports Systems (DSS) are computer-based information systems designed to help managers to select one of the many alternative solutions to a problem. A DSS is an interactive computer based information system with an organized collection of models, people, procedures, software, databases, telecommunication, and devices, which helps decision makers to solve unstructured or semi-structured business problems. Web mining is the application of data mining techniques to discover patterns from the World Wide Web. Web mining can be divided into three different types – Web usage mining, Web content mining and Web structure mining. Recommender systems (RS) aim to capture the user behavior by suggesting/recommending users with relevant items or services that they find interesting in. Recommender systems have gained prominence in the field of information technology, e-commerce, etc., by inferring personalized recommendations by effectively pruning from a universal set of choices that directed users to identify content of interest.

Chapter 4

This chapter explains the overview of Intelligent Decision Support Systems (IDSSs); the overview of Enterprise Information Management (EIM); the IDSS techniques for EIM in terms of Expert System (ES), Multi-Agent System (MAS), Fuzzy Logic (FL), Artificial Neural Network (ANN), Evolutionary Computation (EC), and Hybrid System (HS); and the multifaceted applications of IDSSs in EIM. IDSS techniques are rapidly emerging as the modern tools in information management systems and include various techniques, such as ES, MAS, FL, ANN, EC, and HS. IDSS techniques can increase the sensitiveness, flexibility, and accuracy of information management systems. IDSS techniques should be implemented in modern enterprise in order to gain the benefits of using the decision-making process concerning EIM. The chapter argues that utilizing IDSS techniques for EIM has the potential to increase organizational performance and reach strategic goals in global operations.

Section 2
Developing Web Mining Systems

Chapter 5

Web data mining for extracting meaningful information from large amount of web data has been explored over a decade. The concepts and techniques have been borrowed into the education sector and the new research discipline of learning analytics has emerged. With the development of web technologies, it has been a common practice to design online collaborative learning activities to enhance learning. To apply learning analytics techniques to monitor the online collaborative process enables a lecturer to make instant and informed pedagogical decisions. However, it is still a challenge to build strong connection between learning analytics and learning science for understanding cognitive progression in learning. In this connection, this chapter reports a study to apply learning analytics techniques in the aspect of web usage mining and clustering analysis with underpinning Bloom's taxonomy to analyze students' performance in the online collaborative learning process. The impacts of intermediate interventions are also elaborated.

Chapter 6

The Web can be defined as a depot of varied range of information present in the form of millions of websites dispersed around us. Often users find it difficult to locate the appropriate information fulfilling their needs with the abundant number of websites in the Web. Hence multiple research work has been conducted in the field of Web Mining so as to present any information matching the user's needs. The application of data mining techniques on web usage, web content or web structure data to find out useful data like users' way in patterns and website utility statistics on a whole can be defined as Web mining. The main cause behind development of such websites was to personalize the substance of a website on user's preference. New methods are developed to deal with a Web site using a link hierarchy and a conceptual link hierarchy respectively on the basis of how users have used the Web site link structure.

Chapter 7

In recent days, Internet technology has provided a lot of services for sharing and distributing information across the world. Among all the services, World Wide Web (WWW) plays a significant role. The slow retrieval of Web pages may lessen the interest of users from accessing them. To deal with this problem, Web caching and Web pre-fetching are the two techniques used. Web proxy caching plays a key role in improving Web performance by keeping Web objects that are likely to be used in the near future in the proxy server which is closer to the end user. It helps in reducing user perceived latency, network bandwidth utilization, and alleviating loads on the Web servers. Thus, it improves the efficiency and scalability of Web based system. This chapter gives an overview of Web usage mining and its application on Web and discusses various approaches for improving the performance of Web.

Chapter 8

This chapter explains the multi-agent system for effective information retrieval using information scent in query log mining. The precision of search results is low due to difficult to infer the information need of the small size search query and therefore information need of the user is not satisfied effectively. Information Scent is used for modeling the information need of user web search session and clustering is performed to identify the similar information need sessions. Hyper Link-Induced Topic Search (HITS) is executed on clusters to generate the Hubs and authorities for web page recommendations to users who search with similar intents. This multi-agent system based on clustered query sessions uses query operations like expansion and recommendation to infer the information need of user search queries and recommends Hubs and authorities for effective web search.

Section 3
Developing Efficient Knowledge based Systems

The World Wide Web (WWW) is global information medium, where users can read and write using computers over internet. Web is one of the services available on internet. The Web was created in 1989 by Sir Tim Berners-Lee. Since then a great refinement has done in the web usage and development of its applications. Semantic Web Technologies enable machines to interpret data published in a machine-interpretable form on the web. Semantic web is not a separate web it is an extension to the current web with additional semantics. Semantic technologies play a crucial role to provide data understandable to machines. To achieve machine understandable, we should add semantics to existing websites. With additional semantics, we can achieve next level web where knowledge repositories are available for better understanding of web data. This facilitates better search, accurate filtering and intelligent retrieval of data. This paper discusses about the Semantic Web and languages involved in describing documents in machine understandable format.

As the speed of information growth exceeds in this new century, excessive data is making great troubles to human beings. However, there are so much potential and highly useful values hidden in the huge volume of data. Big Data has drawn huge attention from researchers in information sciences, policy and decision makers in governments and enterprises. Data analytic is the science of examining raw data with the purpose of drawing conclusions about that information. Data analytics is about discovering knowledge from large volumes data and applying it to the business. Machine learning is ideal for exploiting the opportunities hidden in big data. This chapter able to discover and display the patterns buried in the data using machine learning.

Data mining extracts novel and useful knowledge from large repositories of data and has become an effective analysis and decision means in any organization. The resource of the World Wide Web is almost infinite. The growing importance of electronic media for storing and disseminating text documents has created an urgent need for tools and techniques that assist users in finding and extracting relevant and previously unknown information from massive collection of documents available in the web. Thus the development of techniques for mining unstructured, semi-structured, and fully structured textual data has become quite important in both academia and industry. Information management of well organized databases has been a focus of the Data mining research. When to specify too many attributes, system will slow down thus exclude irrelevant or weakly relevant attributes. The general idea behind attribute relevance analysis is to compute some measure that is used to quantify the relevance of an attribute with respect to a given class or concept.

Chapter 12

The hotlinks are the special links introduced in the website to reduce the time to access certain webpages in a webpage that is present in the deeper levels of the topology. Hotlinks selection mechanism plays a vital role in quick access of webpages. The problem is to decide which webpage should be having hotlinks and where the hotlinks should be placed in the website tree topology. We have proposed a methodology which starts by finding the frequent webpage access pattern of visitors of the website. The frequent pattern is found using Associative mining, Apriori algorithm or Frequent Pattern Tree algorithm. Then the frequent patterns are passed through page ranking mechanism. We find the pattern which is having the highest priority. Then the hotlinks are created for the members (webpages hyperlinks) of the pattern. Thus, the work is about assigning hotlinks for a set of pages which are frequently visited. Thus, by updating the topology by introducing hotlinks we can reduce the time to access the web pages.

Section 4
Developing Social Media based Mining Systems

Chapter 13

Social media mining is the process of representing, analyzing, and extracting actionable patterns and trends from raw social media data. Social media is favored by many users since it is available to individuals without any limitations to share their opinions, educational learning experiences and concerns via their status. Twitter API, twitter4j, is processed for searching the tweets based on the geo location. Student's posts on social network offers us a stronger concern to take decisions concerning the particular education system's learning method of the system. Evaluating knowledge in social media is sort of a difficult method. Bayes classifier are enforced on deep-mined knowledge for analysis purpose to urge the deeper understanding of the information. It uses multi label classification technique as every label falls into completely different classes. Label based measures are mostly taken to research the results and comparing them with the prevailing sentiment analysis technique.

Chapter 14

Bapuji Rao, iNurture Education Solutions Private Limited, India
Sasmita Mishra, IGIT, India
Saroja Nanda Mishra, IGIT, India

The retrieval of sub-graph from a large graph in structured data mining is one of the fundamental tasks for analyze. Visualization and analyze large community graph are challenging day by day. Since a large community graph is very difficult to visualize, so compression is essential. To study a large community graph, compression technique may be used for compression of community graph. There should not be any loss of information or knowledge while compressing the community graph. Similarly to extract desired knowledge of a particular sub-graph from a large community graph, then the large community graph needs to be partitioned into smaller sub-community graphs. The partition aims at the edges among the community members of dissimilar communities in a community graph. Sometimes it is essential to compare two community graphs for similarity which makes easier for mining the reliable knowledge from a large community graph. Once the similarity is done then the necessary mining of knowledge can be extracted from only one community graph rather than from both which leads saving of time.

Chapter 15

Balamurugan Balusamy, VIT University, India
Vegesna Tarun Sai Varma, VIT University, India
Sohil Sri Mani Yeshwanth Grandhi, VIT University, India

Today, social networks are major part of everyone's lives. They provide means to communicate with people across the globe with ease. As of July 2016, there are over 1.71 billion monthly active Facebook users. They generate significant amount of data, which if analysed well will provide us with valuable information. This can be done by analysing the log data collected at the respective social networking service. This chapter focuses on extraction and analysis of Facebook data since it is presently the most used social network. The result of analysis can be used in building decision support systems for an organization to help with the decision making process.

Section 5
Developing Data and Text Mining Systems

Chapter 16

Sathiyamoorthi V, Sona College of Technology, India

It is generally observed throughout the world that in the last two decades, while the average speed of computers has almost doubled in a span of around eighteen months, the average speed of the network has doubled merely in a span of just eight months! In order to improve the performance, more and more researchers are focusing their research in the field of computers and its related technologies. Data Mining is one such research area. It extracts useful information the huge amount of data present in the database. The discovered knowledge can be applied in various application areas such as marketing, fraud detections and customer retention. It discovers implicit, previously unknown and potentially useful information out of datasets. Recent trend in data mining include web mining where it discover knowledge from web based information to improve the page layout, structure and its content.

Chapter 17

Kijpokin Kasemsap, Suan Sunandha Rajabhat University, Thailand

This chapter reveals the overview of text mining; text mining, patent analysis, and keyword selection; text mining and sentiment analysis in modern marketing; text mining applications in the biomedical sciences; and the multifaceted applications of text mining. Text mining is an advanced technology utilized in business, marketing, biomedical sciences, education, and operations. Text mining offers a solution to many problems, drawing on techniques concerning information retrieval, natural language processing, information extraction, and knowledge management. Through text mining, information can be extracted to derive summaries for the words contained in the documents. Text mining has the potential to increase the research base available to business and society and to enable business to utilize the research base more effectively. Economic and societal benefits of text mining include cost savings, productivity gains, innovative new service development, new business models, and new medical treatments.

Preface

This book presents recent investigations and enhancements in the field of Decision Support Systems, Web Data Mining, web engineering, with specific emphasis on development of Decision Support Systems based on web applications. Today, web is a major information resource and is becoming an obvious automated tool in various applications. Due to increased growth and popularity of WWW, one needs to be very cautious in designing the website as per standard and norms. An estimated 90% of websites from projected growth of 196 million websites severely suffered with usability and accessibility issues. Web Engineering must be explored in a systematic, disciplined way for development, operation and maintenance of web based applications using certain guidelines. The data on World Wide Web are available in three different formats: web content, web structure and web usage. Web mining is usually defined as the use of data mining techniques to automatically discover and extract information from web documents and services. Web mining is the application of data mining techniques to extract knowledge from web data, i.e. web content, web structure, and web usage data. A decision support system is a computer-based information system that supports business and organizational decision-making activities.

The book comprises of the ideas of various researchers, scholars, website design experts and others to develop and evaluate decision support systems based on web data mining. Web Data Mining focuses on Web content which includes text, HTML pages, images, audio, videos etc. Also Web Data Mining investigates the linkages and relationships among web pages based on website structure. Further Web Data Mining extracts web data by web server to track various types of transactions through website and web usage is mainly focuses for decision making. The book is organized in five sections that cover the main concepts and studies for the development of decision support system through web data mining. The Section 1 consists of chapters which describe the development of decision support systems. The Section 2 deals with development of web mining systems. The Section 3 covers details about the development of knowledge based systems from web mining process. The Section 4 provides research insights of various authors about mining aspects of social media, graph mining techniques and aspects of social network web mining. Finally, Section 5 introduces the importance of data mining and text mining aspects of various authors' contributions. The present book is an attempt to investigate various solutions for the development of decision support systems through web data mining. In this book, all areas of web data mining, decision support systems, knowledge based systems, social media mining and text mining are thoroughly discussed for finding desired solutions for the web data mining and the development of decision support systems for knowledge representation. The book is a step forward towards presenting recent studies for decision support systems and web data mining and serves the purpose for the present trend in web engineering. Hence the book focuses important aspects of web designing process to improve the business intelligence through web mining.

Acknowledgment

I am very much happy and thankful to IGI global for giving me the opportunity to produce my second *Web Data Mining and the Development of Knowledge-Based Decision Support Systems*, which is very much necessary in the present internet world. I express a deep sense of gratitude to the Jan Travers, David J Perreault, Eleana Wehr, Joshua Herring, Kayla Wolfe, and other members of IGI global who supported either directly or indirectly during book project development.

I am thankful to all authors who contributed their valuable efforts and ideas in the form of chapters in the book. I would like to express my sincere thanks to Prof. A. Anandaraja Chari for his continuous support and encouragement in my career.

I am thankful to vice chancellor, registrar and other faculty members of Rashtriya Sanskrit Vidyapeetha, Tirupati for their support and kindness in completing the book.

Finally, I am very much thankful to my parents and family members for their support and encouragement in achieving this target goal in my academic career.

Section 1
Developing Decision Support Systems

Chapter 1
Development of Efficient Decision Support System Using Web Data Mining

G. Sreedhar
Rashtriya Sanskrit Vidyapeetha (Deemed University), India

A. Anandaraja Chari
Rayalaseema University, India

ABSTRACT

The management of web sites imposes a constant demand for new information and timely updates due to the increase of services and content that site owners wish to make available to their users, which in turn is motivated by the complexity and diversity of needs and behaviours of the users. Such constant labour intensive effort implies very high financial and personnel costs. The growth of World Wide Web and technologies has made business functions to be executed fast and easier. E-commerce has provided a cost efficient and effective way of doing business. Web mining is usually defined as the use of data mining techniques to automatically discover and extract information from web documents and services. Also, web data mining is commonly categorized into three areas: web content mining that describes the discovery of useful information from content, web structure mining that analyses the topology of web sites, and web usage mining that tries to make sense of the data generated by the navigation behaviour and user profile.

INTRODUCTION

Over the last few years there has been a remarkable increase in use of the World Wide Web (WWW) for a wide and variety of purposes. There was also a fast growth in its applications. This led the Internet users to realize the importance and the benefits gained from a globally interconnected hypermedia system. On the other hand, it causes a larger number of useless, meaningless and badly designed websites on the Internet world causing unwanted additional traffic; this is all because of an unorganized, non-planned websites development processes. Due to the unceasing growth of web sites and applications, developers and evaluators have interesting challenges not only from the development but also from the quality assurance

DOI: 10.4018/978-1-5225-1877-8.ch001

point of view. Today, web is not only an information resource but also it is becoming an automated tool in various applications. The management of web sites imposes a constant demand for new information and timely updates due to the increase of services and content that site owners wish to make available to their users, which in turn is motivated by the complexity and diversity of needs and behaviours of the users. Such constant labour intensive effort implies very high financial and personnel costs.

BACKGROUND: WEB MINING

The data on World Wide Web are available in three different formats: web content, web structure and web usage. Web mining is usually defined as the use of data mining techniques to automatically discover and extract information from web documents and services. The authors of O.Etzioni (1996) and R. Cooley (1997) discuss in their research that web data mining can be defined in two distinct forms: first, it is defined as chain of order tasks and second, it is defined considering type of web data used in web data mining process. Web mining is the application of data mining techniques to extract knowledge from web data, i.e. web content, web structure, and web usage data. Web Data Mining extracts and analyses useful information from huge amounts of data stored in different data sources to provide additional information and knowledge that are crucial of decision making process. A decision support system is a computer-based information system that supports business and organizational decision-making activities. According to J. Srivastava et al. (2002) also web data mining is commonly categorized into three areas. They are:

1. Web content mining
2. Web structure mining
3. Web usage mining

Web Content Mining

Web content data is web pages content availed to users to satisfy their needs of information. This can be in the form of text, HTML pages, images, audio, video etc. In this category, the HTML pages are common and more familiar form of web content data. The author S.Nestorov et al. (1998) discuss in their research that HTML documents are often considered as semi structured as different elements of documents are not designed according to specific schema. In HTML, elements are tagged in a way to enable designing layout of document. Generally, HTML elements are of two types: first concerns with way of displaying documents in browser and second concerns with information about document itself like title and other document relationship. XML document is another known form of web content data which enables storing and transporting information. It is having structured information and includes contents and information about contents. Each XML document has specific structure and XML is a mark-up language which allows identifying document structure and adding the information. In XML, there are no predefined tags and it is language to describe and add mark-up to documents using XML specification. The applications processing XML document or the style sheets decide the semantics of XML document. Another type of web content data is dynamic server pages which are processed by the web server and generated result is sent to web browser. In contrast, without any change, the static contents are sent to browser. Some of familiar dynamic server page contents are like JSP (Java Server Page), ASP (Active Server Page) and PHP (Pre-Hypertext Processor). The author Manoj Pandia et al. (2011) said that Web Content Mining is the task of extracting knowledge from the content of documents on World Wide Web. The web documents may consists of text, images, audio, video or structured records like tables and lists. Web Content Mining is a form of text data mining applied to the web domain, and has to do with finding the content of documents, classifying documents, and clustering documents. HTML documents are semi structured data. Others like data in tables and databases, generated HTML pages are the more structured data and most of the data is unstructured text data. Due to this unstructured nature, web content mining becomes more complex. Web content mining focuses on automatic search of information resources online. Mining can be applied on the web documents as well the results pages produced from a search engine. There are two types of approach in content mining called agent based approach and database based approach. The agent based approach concentrate on searching relevant information using the characteristics of a particular domain to interpret and organize the collected information. The database approach is used for retrieving the semi-structure data from the web.

Web Structure Mining

Web structure data represents linkage and relationship of web contents to others. Two types of structure namely intra-page and inter-page structure can be considered. In specific web page, information about arrangement of different HTML tags is intra page structure information. The pages are connected with other pages using hyperlinks. This is inter-page structure information. Hyperlinks of web pages collectively form a graph called web graph and it describes the whole structure of the web site. Web graph is a common way of showing the links from one web page to another in whole site and depicts overall structure. The author M. Gandhi et al. (2004) said that that it is a representation of WWW for specific site describing structure of links and relationship to the HTML documents. Web document is depicted as a node in graph and edge is HTML link connecting one page with another. In two different ways, the edges of the graph are presented. A hyperlink stopping at related page is presented as outgoing arcs and hyperlinks using which related page can be found is presented as incoming arcs. Web graph can be used in some applications like web searching, indexing and web communities detection (Murat Ali Bayir, n.d.). Web Structure Mining focuses on discovering structure information from the Web to identify relevant documents. It describes the connectivity in the Web subset based on the given collection of interconnected Web documents. The goal of the Web Structure Mining is to generate the structural summary about the Web site and Web page. It tries to discover the link structure of the hyperlinks at the inter-document level. The structure of a typical Web graph consists of Web pages as nodes, and hyperlinks as edges connecting related pages. Based on the topology of the hyperlinks, Web Structure mining will categorize the Web pages and generate the information like similarity and relationship between different Web sites. This type of mining can be performed at the document level (intra-page) or at the hyperlink level (inter-page). It is important to understand the Web data structure for Information Retrieval. Mining the site structure and Web page structure can help to guide the classification and clustering of pages to find authoritative pages to improve retrieval performance. Web Structure Mining is the process of discovering structure information from the web. Another task of web structure mining is to discover the nature of the hierarchy or network of hyperlink in the web sites of a particular domain. This may help to generalize the flow of information in Web sites that may represent some particular domain; therefore the query processing can be performed easier and more efficient. Web structure mining has a strong relation with the content mining.

Web Usage Mining

Web usage data involves log data collected by web server and application server which is the main source of data. When user interacts with web site, web log data is generated on web server in form of web server log files. Application Server Data is common in commercial application servers. The importance of these data types comes from their feature to track various types of business events and log them in application server logs. Application Level Data is another source for web usage data. With this type of data it is possible to record various kinds of events in an application. These data are used for generating histories about selected special events. The data in this category can be divided into three categories based on the source of its collection: onthe server side, the client side, and the proxy side. Other additional data sources are demographic data, site files, cookies etc. Generally, web server is assigned a domain name and has IP address. When user sends request for page to web server through browser, request is processed by server and page is sent to user. As a result of user interaction with web site and server, data are generated on server and resource request, success, error etc information are recorded into server log files. Different types of usage log files are created on server such as access log, error log, referrer log, agent log. Information stored in web access log includes IP Address, username, date and time, request. Error information like file not found, no data, aborted transmission etc. are recorded into Error logs. The information about browser, its version and operating system of user making request is stored into Agent logs. Different server log file formats are available such as Common Log file Format and Extended Log file Format. The Common Log file Format includes IP Address, date, time, login name of a user, bytes transferred, status code, URL requested. Extended Log file Format includes IP Address, bytes sent and received, request query, server name, port, requested service name, time elapsed for transaction to complete, version of transfer protocol used, user agent showing browser used for request, cookie ID, and referrer. Using web traffic analyser software, log files of web server can be analysed and a useful information can be derived which helps to improve structure of web site. Web Usage Mining which is also known as web log mining aims to find out interesting and frequent user access patterns from web browsing data that are stored in web server log. Such discovered knowledge is useful in analysing how the web pages are accessed or what are seeking for by the users. According to Srivastava. J (2000) for the task of applying data mining techniques, information from web data is extracted in order to understand and better serve the needs of users navigating on the web. Web usage mining focuses on techniques that could predict user behaviour while the user interacts with the web. Usage analysis includes straightforward statistics, such as page access frequency, as well as more sophisticated form of analysis such as finding the common traversal paths through a Website. Web Usage Mining is the process of applying data mining techniques to discover interesting patterns from Web usage data. Web usage mining provides better understanding for serving the needs of Web-based applications. Web Usage data keeps information about the identity or origin of Web users with their browsing behaviour in a web domain. Web Usage Mining is the process of extracting useful information from the secondary data derived from the interactions of the user while surfing on the Web. It extracts data stored in server access logs, referrer logs, agent logs, client-side cookies, user profile and Meta data. The authors G. Chang et al. (2001) discuss in their research that web usage mining is the application of data mining techniques to discover interesting usage patterns from web usage data, in order to understand and better serve the needs of web-based applications. The web log files on the web server are major source of data for Web Usage Mining. When user requests resources of web server, each request is recorded in the web log file on web server. As a consequence, users browsing behaviour is recorded into the web log file. In Web Usage Mining, data can be collected from server log files that include web server access logs and application server logs. The data collected in web log file is incomplete and not suitable for mining directly. Pre-processing is necessary to convert the data into suitable form for pattern discovery. Pre-processing can provide accurate, concise data for data mining. Data pre-processing, includes data cleaning, user identification, user sessions identification, path completion and data integration.

E-COMMERCE WEB APPLICATIONS

E-commerce websites have the advantage of reaching a large number of customers regardless of distance and time limitations. The advantage of e-commerce over traditional businesses is the faster speed and the lower expenses for both e-commerce website owners and customers in completing customer transactions and orders. Because of the above advantages of e-commerce over traditional businesses, a lot of industries in different fields such as retailing, banking, medical services, transportation, communication, and education are establishing their business in the web. But creating a successful online business can be a very difficult and costly task if not taking into account e-commerce website design principles, web engineering techniques, and what e-commerce is supposed to do for the online business. Unfortunately, to most companies, web is nothing more than a place where transactions take place. All the e-commerce sites have high traffic. People surf the sites very often but the income is not always very high. So, the web data mining appeared and also nowadays much attention is paid to it. It is very important to apply web data mining to e-commerce in order to gather knowledge about users and rank data accordingly. It is advance successful technology through which information is filtered easier. So, web data mining became a publicly accessible source that gives promising results. With the use of e-commerce through internet, companies find a new and better way to do business. After developing the web site thought companies get benefits, they have to implement Web mining systems to understand their customers' profiles and to identify their own strength and weakness of their E-marketing efforts on the web through continuous improvements. Internet is a gold mine, but only for those companies who realize the importance of Web mining and adopt a Web mining strategy now. Web mining technology has many important roles that should be mentioned. It can automatically find, extract information from the variety web resources. The authors Etnoteam S. et al (2000) said that web mining develops, improves and enhances the quality and the efficiency of search engines, determines web pages or files, makes classifications. It can also generate large-scale real-time data. Web data mining discovers useful information from the Web hyperlink and page content. It has already changed the face of many business functions in a modern competitive enterprise. It is obviously easier to make right business decisions or understand the information that came from customers with the help of web data mining. It helps e-commerce to understand how to improve its services for special groups of customers and clients, and what tasks to realize. The e-commerce site can increase the exposure of its product pages and so average order size can be increased. Companies can save percentage of its budget per month owing to knowledge that was received from web mining analysis. Web data mining gathers implicit knowledge about clients and instructs e-commerce in every aspect. Then, it extracts valuable and comprehensible information from huge web resources to instruct e-commerce. It also gathers the information in an automated way and builds models used to predict customer purchasing decisions. Web mining is very precious to the company in the fields of understanding customer behaviour, improving customer services and relationship, launching target marketing campaigns, measuring the success of marketing efforts, and so on.

Attractiveness of the site depends on its reasonable design of content and organizational structure. The author TIAN Meirong et al (2010) described that Web Mining can provide details of user behaviour, providing web site designers basis of decision making to improve the design of the site. E-Commerce generally refers to a new business model, where consumer makes online shopping, online transactions between merchants and online electronic payments and a variety of business activities, trading activities, financial activities and related integrated services activities, buyers and sellers are not met to conduct various business activities based on browser/server application mode.

INTERNET OF THINGS (IOT)

Internet of Things (IoT) is a network which is composed with Radio Frequency Identification (RFID), infrared sensors, global positioning systems, laser scanners, gas sensors and other information sensing device, according to the agreed protocol, any goods is connected with the Internet for information exchange, communication, IoT is used to make intelligent identification, positioning, tracking, monitoring and management. The schematic diagram IoT is shown in the following Figure 1.

With the rapid development of e-commerce, its technology requirements will also increase on all aspects of future e-commerce. Firstly, the e-commerce applications are combined with IoT development and IoT technologies are applied in three important aspects of e-commerce, such as inventory, logistics and payment. An e-commerce system includes inventory, logistics, electronic payment and other important aspects, if IoT technology is used in various aspects of e-commerce, e-commerce will greatly improve the efficiency of the system. The diagram of E-Commerce with combined IoT is shown in the Figure 2.

Figure 1. Schematic diagram of Internet of Things

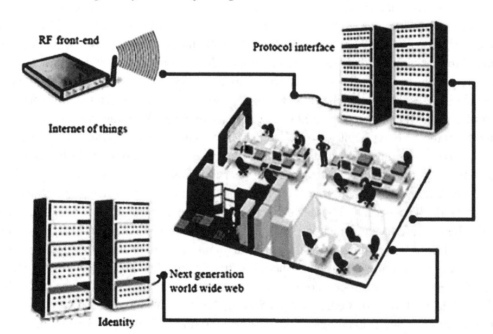

Figure 2. E-Commerce Web application with Internet of Things

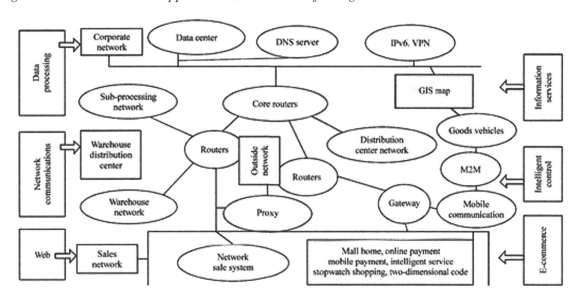

ANALYZING PERFORMANCE OF E-COMMERCE WEB APPLICATIONS

The procedure for analysing performance of e-commerce website initially starts with a web program. The program consists of two parts: extracting components of website with download time and download time performance grades. In the web program, all the components of website with corresponding downloading time are extracted using a web tool namely Web Page Analyser (Figure 3). The Download

Figure 3. Website analysis

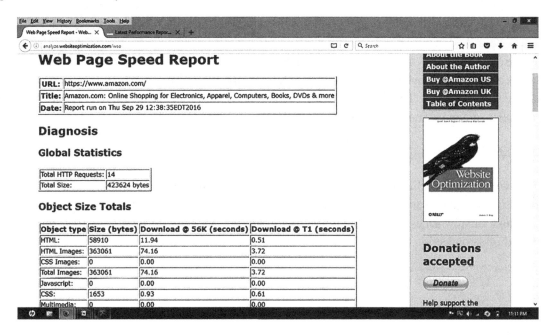

Figure 4. Performance of e-commerce website

Table 1. Description of web application performance grades

Web Application Performance Grade	Description
A	Very Good
B	Good
C	Better than Average
D	Average
E	Poor
F	Very Poor

time performance grade is obtained using the web tool GTMetrix (Figure 4). The GTMetrix web tool analyses the website download time and evaluates the download time performance in A, B, C, D, E and F grades as described in Table 1.

The size of a web page is measured considering all its images, sounds, videos and textual components. For each page, the size in bytes can be obtained. The size of pages is an important issue in order to appreciate the site efficiency. The download time (T) is related with the size of a page (τ) and the speed in the established connection line (c) and this relation is shown in Equation 1.

$$T_{Download} = f(\tau, c)...$$
(1)

This download time is directly proportional to the page size and inversely proportional to the speed of a given connection line and it is shown in Equation 2. A function may be created in order to classify pages as quick or slow access pages, according to a minimum threshold of time (e.g. 10 seconds) for a given speed of a connection line.

$$g(T_{Download}) = \begin{matrix} QuickAccess & T_{Download} < T_{\max} \\ SlowAccess & T_{Download} \geq T_{\max} \end{matrix}$$
(2)

The authors Glover, E et al (2002), Zheng Chen et al (2003) verified that website size is dependent on various components of the website. These components include Images Size, Documents size, Media Size, Programs or Scripts Size, CSS Size and other objects. As the components sizes increase then automatically the size of website is also increases. The relation between website size and web components is shown in Equation 3.

$$WEBSIZE = f(IMAGESIZE, DOCSIZE, MEDIASIZE, CSSSIZE, SCRIPTSIZE, OTHEROBJSIZE) \dots \tag{3}$$

Where

WEBSIZE = Website Size
IMAGESIZE = Images Size
DOCSIZE = Documents Size
MEDIASIZE = Multimedia Size
SCRIPTSIZE = Scripts or Programs Size
CSSSIZE = Cascading Style Sheet Size
OTHEROBJSIZE = Other Objects Size like Active X Control Objects, Applets etc.

A regression analysis is carried out to analyse the relationships among these variables. The analysis is carried out through the estimation of a relationship using equation. The results serve the following two purposes:

- Answer the question of how much web size changes with changes in each of the web component's size
- Forecast or predict the value of web size based on the values of the web component's size

In analyzing the download time performance of the websites, the websites of 10 e-commerce websites are considered in evaluation process. The download time of each e-commerce website is analyzed using web program and the corresponding download time performance grade is derived using GTMetrix web tool. The performance of e-commerce websites is shown in Table 2.

Table 2. Performance of e-commerce web applications

S.No.	E-Commerce Website	Download time (in secs)	Web page Size (in M.B)	Performance Grade
1	http://goidirectory.nic.in/ministries_departments_view.php	18.3	1.76	F
2	http://goidirectory.nic.in/state_departments.php?ou=AP.	4.3	0.5	F
3	http://www.amazon.com	5.8	4.89	A
4	http://www.flipkart.com	4.7	1	A
5	http://fitness.reebok.com/international	10.4	2.78	A
6	http://www.spyder.com	5	2.31	B
7	http://www.apple.com	1.8	1.25	B
8	http://ebay.com	4.2	2.49	B
9	http://myspace.com	7.3	5.98	C
10	http://www.hp.com	5.2	4.01	C

CONCLUSION

The main objective of the chapter is how to understand the performance of the system. In this paper the importance of e-commerce web applications and how Internet of Things is related to e-commerce is well discussed. In end user perspective the performance of e-commerce application is mainly connected to the web application design and services provided in the e-commerce website. In this paper a focused approach has been made to identify all possible parameters in the web design with specific reference to some of the major e-commerce websites. The performance of each e-commerce web application is measured in terms of web page speed and loading time of the website. Hence performance evaluation of web applications is very much necessary to fulfill the need of online user and web developer can enhance the features based on the performance report of e-commerce website.

REFERENCES

Analyzing Website Speed. (n.d.). Retrieved from www.GTMetrix.com

Chang, G., Healy, M. J., McHugh, J. A. M., & Wang, J. T. L. (2001). *Mining the World Wide Web: An Information Search Approach*. Kluwer Academic Publishers. doi:10.1007/978-1-4615-1639-2

Chen, Liu, Liu, Pu, & Ma. (2003). *Building a Web Thesaurus form Web Link Structure*. SIGIR 2003, Toronto, Canada.

Cooley, R., Mobasher, B., & Srivastava, J. (1997). Web Mining: Information and Pattern Discovery on the Word Wide Web.*Proceedings ICTAI*. doi:10.1109/TAI.1997.632303

Etzioni, O. (1996). The World Wide Web: Quagmire or Gold Mine. *Communications of the ACM*, *39*(11), 65–68. doi:10.1145/240455.240473

Gandhi, M., Jeyebalan, K., Kallukalam, J., Rapkin, A., Reilly, P., & Widodo, N. (2004). *Web Research Infrastructure Project Final Report*. Cornell University.

Glover, E., Tsioutsiouliklis, K., Lawrence, S., Pennock, D., & Flake, G. (2002). Using Web Structure for Classifying and Describing Web Pages.*Proceedings of WWW2002*. doi:10.1145/511446.511520

Meirong, T., & Xuedong, C. (2010). Application of Agent-based Web Mining in E-business. *Second International Conference on Intelligent Human-Machine Systems and Cybernetic*. Retrieved from http://www.websiteoptimization.com

Murat Ali Bayir. (n.d.). *A New Reactive Method for Processing Web Usage Data*. Retrieved from http://etd.lib.metu.edu.tr/upload/12607323/index.pdf

Nestorov, S., Abiteboul, S., & Motwani, R. (1998). Extracting Schema from Semistructured Data. In ACM SIGMOD. doi:10.1145/276305.276331

Page, L., Brin, S., Motwani, R., & Winograd, T. (1998). *The Page Rank Citation Ranking: Bring Order to the Web. Technical Report*. Stanford University.

Pandia, Pani, & Padhi, Panigrahy, & Ramakrishna. (2011). A Review of Trends in Research on Web Mining. *International Journal of Instrumentation Control and Automation*, *1*(1), 37–41.

Purandare, P. (2002). Web Mining: A Key to Improve Business On Web.*IADIS European Conference Data Mining*.

Srivastava, J., Cooley, R., Deshpande, M., & Tan, P. N. (2000). Web Usage Mining: Discovery and Applications of Usage Patterns from Web Data. *ACM SIGKDD Explorations Newsletter*, *1*(2), 12–23. doi:10.1145/846183.846188

Srivastava. Desikan, J. P., & Kumar, V. (2002). Web Mining: *Accomplishments and Future Directions. National Science Foundation Workshop on Next Generation Data Mining*.

KEY TERMS AND DEFINITIONS

E-Commerce Websites: E-commerce websites have the advantage of reaching a large number of customers regardless of distance and time limitations. The advantage of e-commerce over traditional businesses is the faster speed and the lower expenses for both e-commerce website owners and customers in completing customer transactions and orders.

Web Mining: Web mining is the application of data mining techniques to extract knowledge from web data, i.e. web content, web structure, and web usage data. Web Content Mining: Web Content Mining is a form of text data mining applied to the web domain, and has to do with finding the content of documents, classifying documents, and clustering documents.

Web Structure Mining: The goal of the Web Structure Mining is to generate the structural summary about the Web site and Web page. It tries to discover the link structure of the hyperlinks at the inter-document level. The structure of a typical Web graph consists of Web pages as nodes, and hyperlinks as edges connecting related pages. Based on the topology of the hyperlinks, Web Structure mining will categorize the Web pages and generate the information like similarity and relationship between different Web sites.

Web Usage Mining: Web Usage Mining which is also known as web log mining aims to findout interesting and frequent user access patterns from web browsing data that arestored in web server log. Such discovered knowledge is useful in analysing how theweb pages are accessed or what are seeking for by the users.

Chapter 2
Improving Decision–Making in a Business Simulator Using TOPSIS Methodology for the Establishment of Reactive Stratagem

Carlos Alberto Ochoa Ortiz Zezzatti
Juarez City University, Mexico

ABSTRACT

This study combines Fuzzy Logic and multicriteria TOPSIS method for the selection, from three different alternatives, which machines of high productivity is more convenient to a construction company. The evaluation of each alternative is made through group decision making which identifies the most important criteria according to the requirements presented by the company. To assess the selected criteria in the TOPSIS method is weighted by a group of experts who, based on their experience and knowledge of this type of machinery, assess the relevance of these in the operation and functioning of the hydraulic excavator. Both qualitative and quantitative studies are used in this work, however the experts evaluate, through surveys based on Likert scale all the criteria in which they want to measure the perception. Data provided from the surveys is used for the construction and association of the groups of expert's opinion through the use of fuzzy sets to avoid ambiguity problems of the linguistic variables.

INTRODUCTION

The use of technology in business in a way helps a lot in making decisions, i.e. approaches to reality, figuring that we can have different scenarios, identifying the complexity of daily work that occurs in organizations within which can be found: industrial organizations, trade organizations for goods and services, public organizations, educational organizations, the nonprofit organizations. It is important and helpful to rely on a certain part in an organized and generally focused on the events that occur in

DOI: 10.4018/978-1-5225-1877-8.ch002

business (Barnes, 1984). Thus the use of simulation as a system created to streamline decision-making and delineate the scenarios we can test and company information is certainly an advantage for employers who do business and turn all seeking profitability. A business simulator is a decisive intelligent tool, usually using Artificial Intelligence, which allows playback and feedback of a system. The simulators reproduce sensations and experiences that in reality may come to pass. A simulator is intended to play both physical sensations (speed, acceleration, perception of the environment) and the behavior of the machine equipment that is meant to simulate.

TOPSIS METHODOLOGY TO IMPROVE A BUSINESS SIMULATOR

Business Simulator is a learning tool and modeling which allows the entrepreneurial experience of creating and managing own business in an environment that does not risk money, a special situation which don't occurs in the real life. This will help you acquire the necessary experience to learn to distinguish the important from the unimportant when it comes to managing a business. Business Simulator can learn without risk –an important and transcendental factor in the real situations-, but empirically, it should not be done and what cannot be left to do. This is a systemic game in which the entrepreneur enters a simulator that behaves autonomously. Our actions affect others and those of others influence us. The entrepreneur must meet all the needs of your business: finance, marketing, sales, production, human resources, tax, competition, marketing positional and quality of services or products. An entrepreneur must learn to make decisions in a fog of uncertainty, should know to take advantage of the moments when all men doubt to gain competitive advantage. An entrepreneur must learn to calibrate each decision to understand the effect of short, medium and long term as in our Business simulator. See Figure 1. The chosen Alternative should have the shortest distance from the ideal solution and the farthest from the negative-ideal solution. It is very difficult to justify the selection of A_1 or A_2. Each Attribute in the Decision Matrix takes either monotonically increasing or monotonically decreasing utility, a Set

Figure 1. Intelligent selection of stratagems using TOPSIS Methodology

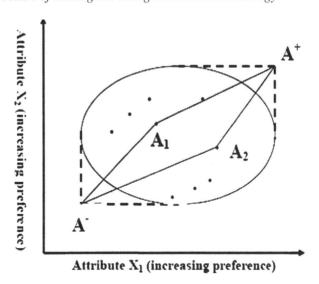

of Weights for the Attributes is required to Any Outcome which is expressed in a non-numerical way, should be quantified through the appropriate scaling technique and rank the preference order specify a set of alternatives can now be preference ranked according to the descending order of $ci*$.

Learn that ill-considered decisions are priced and that the right decisions with calculated risk and it can lead to success. In the game simulation the entrepreneur will get to know how hard it is to get funding. Even so, many resources have so longed for necessary capital to implement their project. Each has its advantages and disadvantages. Inside should address both manage their employees, equipment, processes purchase, production, in another. - As sales and advertising campaigns. The user should pay attention to the fees, investment in Research & Development, quality and even overall competition because this simulator, not playing alone. And the actions of others affect us about with their decisions. In an uncertainty world, make a large and specific decisions naturally requires a team. It is expected that a virtual company to begin operations within the simulator is managed by one person. For this reason, is very important begins with the formation of real teams of entrepreneurs who are virtually your company and begin to make their business operations, technology, production and finance, in competition with other teams. The simulator is an experience not individually but collectively. No one individual plays against a preset machine but real teams play against other real equipment. So there a specific date that begin and ends the game. In the simulated environment, each quarter equals one week in the real environment. Therefore, for each company to compete for a minimum period of two years (where introduce new products on the market, will expand its workforce will require new investments, media advertisings and market implications). The business simulator requires a minimum of eight weeks of real time (Salem, 2005). This is the time we spend on each new edition of the simulator. Go ahead, if you feel the entrepreneurial vein, no issues and learn how to run a business preserving your money for when you're really ready. Participate in an exciting take of decisions to a real world where success is measured by profit and failure goes straight to oblivion. We propose the development of a model according at specifications to a small company, we propose that the final users can adequate the actual equipment to our necessities using the same software development on the real equipment but making a computer run more conventional (and therefore cheaper). The latter option is known as "Rehosted Software" (Sundin & Braban-Ledoux, 2001). The more complex simulators are evaluated and qualified by the competent authorities using a Lickert scale and a grand model prix based on evaluation of components. As shown in Figure 2, this simulator business so far consists of four modules: Visual Marketing Module, Marketing under uncertainty, Decisions under uncertainty, Detail Marketing Module and Financial Module.

IMPLEMENTATION OF AN INTELIGENT APPLICATION

The simulator provides this data to the simulator, so users will have information that allows them to have some knowledge of the market they will face and make decisions for the current stage (Klayman, & Schoemaker, 1993). Once all this is well defined, we can start with the dynamic part. They must decide which products to implement in the shelves on the first week of the simulation. After that, during the course of the simulation, shall be presented, week after week, different situations related to marketing variables and in these situations, the user must take several decisions that can impact both positively and negatively in the business. The simulator will give the user to know the event or situation itself and three different possible options to choose from, each of which would cause a different result, affecting either sales or income consumers directly (Laudon & Laudon, 2002). Each answer leads to three pos-

Figure 2. Prototype of our Business simulator

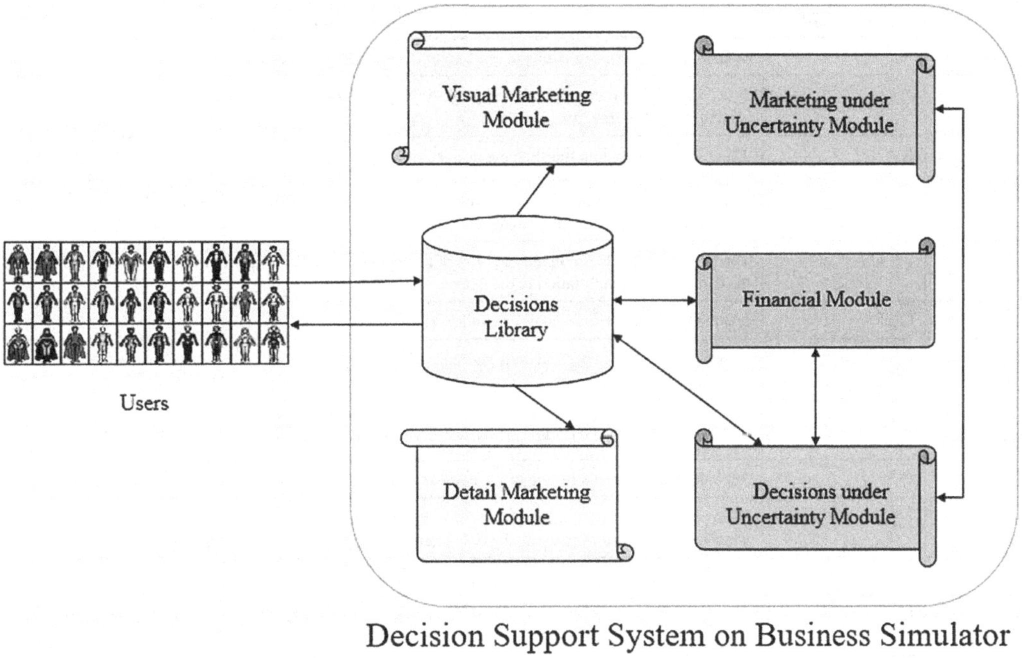

Decision Support System on Business Simulator

sible scenarios: one positive, one negative and one neutral. The positive scenario is the result of having made the right choice of the three that the simulator given a choice to the user, this leads to an increase in sales or profits earned. The negative scenario is the result of poor decision-making to the situation (Pretorius, 2008). The third scenario, the neutral, when will choose the remaining option, which does not impact or a negative or positive result, leaving the sales or profits of a similar way as they were in the previous week, although this is the least risky option, the user can represent a loss because they may overlook potential growth opportunities stagnating business development and ending with a poor result at the end of the simulation (Kanooni, 2009). In addition to weekly decisions, it must decide which products will replenish the stock to avoid the lack of these in case of high demand from consumers, since the lack of stock of a product represents dissatisfaction customers, resulting in a lower turnover. Based on the decisions taken either increase the simulator input to business customers or demand for certain products, forcing the user to adapt their future decisions on the possible scenarios that could happen. At the end of each period the business simulator, based on the information you have about the products on sale, price, promotions, stock there and each assessment or demand that consumers have of each, throw a turnover which, minus the cost of sales will result in net profits, which, along with the decisions taken at each stage, determine user performance in the simulation. The variables used in these five modules are enlisted in Table 1. The Table 2 describes the variables which are result of a specific process in the business simulator.

Table 1. Input variables

Variable	Nomenclature	Definition
Advertising	A_D*	Spending on advertising media to reach more consumers and to position our company in a wider market.
Quantity	C*	Is the number of products purchased for sale. This decision requires planning because they buy products to be used in the next period and the present.
Functional strategies and differentiation strategies	E_D*	These variables contain the strategic evaluations, ie, strengths and opportunities presented, as well as the weaknesses and threats, within the internal approach will have what are the strengths and weaknesses, and external focus within the opportunities and threats, this SWOT based model. The results will enable functional and differentiation strategies.
Competitive Strengths	F*	This group of variables contains a group of competitive strength measurements. Evaluation of how relevant is the company's differentiation in the market.
Retained earnings	G_A*	It is the sum of net earnings over periods.
Inventory management	G_I*	Is measured existing physical units and sales in the period.
Uncertainty in marketing decision	G_P*	Also assess the economic performance of the company in the period.
Income	I*	Regardless of the market share of the company will assess the income that they generate.
Uncertainty support decisions	I_M*	These variables measure the scenarios in which the answers are given to the uncertainty that is generated when making decisions, making the only alternative approach to marketing.
Marketing	M*	The monetary value allocated to expenditure on advertising the product.
Market and competitors position	M_C*	This set of variables contains all the parameters evaluating the position which deals in the market, as well as the position of competitors.
Target Marketing	M_M*	These variables are related to the market which requires reaching, ie the focus and function of the business simulator is based on the market that is contemplated. Which gives results of different scenarios of possible markets.
Market Share	M_P*	The percentage occupied by the sales joint venture in relation to other companies and the overall market.
Financial Impact	N*	How will translate the monetary costs and benefits of this option in the final results by means net present value and what will be the opportunity of this result.
Prices and discounts	P_D*	The selling price of each product and the discounts can encourage increased consumption.
Product mix	P_M*	The products will be available for sale on the shelves during simulation.
Place	P_L*	The visual improvement of point of sale and special markings may have certain products.
Budgets and projections	P_P*	This group of variables contains all projections, budgets and objectives to be used in the strategy.
Price	P_R*	Is the value at which the product will be marketed has an acceptance range is defined in part by the system and in part by the administrator to take decisions.
Human Resources	R_H*	Personal optimal to operate the company
Gifts and promotions	R_P*	Spurs made to motivate consumers may be discounts on products or a gift attached to a product for sale as a gift.
Suppliers	S_P*	Managing the various suppliers, the difference in product quality, price and credit management between them.
Return Time	T_I*	The time that it takes for the return of the investment.
Time	T_P*	These variables refer to the time that the business targeted, this in order that business life is given in medium and long term.
Units in stock	U_S*	The amounts of stock we have of each product and the same weekly refill.
Evaluation of the company's current strategy	Ve*	This group of variables contains all the information for the indicators of current strategy fro company in terms of visual communication and advertising. (Budget applied, means used creative type, frequency and period Post exposure, existence and use of logo and corporate identity).
Competitive forces evaluation	V_F*	This group of variables is composed by competitive forces facing the market Knowing how the competition is conformed and how it behaves. Within this group can be found evaluating substitute products, buyers, degree of influence on each of them. Considering the actions of competitors regarding measures within commercial visual communication. Relative distance from the market leader.

continued on following page

Table 1. Continued

Variable	Nomenclature	Definition
Expansion	X^*	This group contains all the parameters that evaluate the position it occupies in the market as well as the position of competitors. Based on a forward-looking approach (leadership).
Visual Advertising Budget	X_C^*	In this group of variables includes today's budget spent for the purposes of advertising and visual communication company's business SMEs.
Budget	X_T^*	These variables are related to the investment you have in an SME (small budget) and prices that exist in the different marketing strategies that can be implemented, taking into account what can be used economically on investment SME (as intended for this module).
Identification of strengths, weaknesses, opportunities and threats.	Y^*	This group of variables contain the evaluation of the strengths and weaknesses of the resources of a company, its business opportunities and external threats to their future welfare. An example of this group of variables are SWOT indicators.

Table 2. Output variables

Variable	Nomenclature	Definition
Implementation of corrective actions	A'	In the simulator has the advantage of having alternatives, ie you can play with the different decisions before implementing an SME, therefore, to correct, to get the expected result (optimal).
Competition	Cp'	Strategies and behaviors implemented by competition for greater market share and response to take to avoid losing our consumers.
Effectiveness of strategy applied	E_A'	Sales Generation: Incremental sales as a result of advertising stimuli. * Remembrance of advertising. * Willingness to purchase. * Generate leads or leads.
Economic environment	E_E'	Changes in the general economic environment where the business simulation and the possible actions and reactions to face these changes with the least possible reduction in the profit margin.
Proposed Strategy	E_P'	This output shall make recommendations to the administrative leader through various strategies proposed to be included in the projections about advertising goals. Each strategy suggest advertising media, public choice you target, ad frequency, period and amount of investment publication.
Risks	R'	What kind of risks associated this alternative? e.g., Could cause loss of profits or competitive advantage? How competition respond? Since the risk and uncertainty are essentially the same, what information would reduce this uncertainty?
Follow up marketing strategies	S_E'	This variable grant support marketing strategies, ie, does the implementation of these are contributing? Does it add value?
Monitoring marketing results	S_M'	In this variable is intended to grant a balance of the results obtained, ie really worked as intended? It has made the right decisions in this module? In short, you get a feedback.
Costs	T'	How much will cost the alternative? Will result in cost savings now or long term? Can additional costs arise on the way? Is the alternative in the budget?
Viability	W'	Can be implemented alternative really?, Can be an obstacle to be overcome? If the alternative is implemented, what resistance could be from inside to outside the organization?

DESIGN OF EXPERIMENTS

We determine and evaluate using TOPSIS Methodology with four different scenarios:

Weight 0.1 0.4 0.3 0.2
Style Business Reliability Financial Economics Cost of operation
Scenario A 7 9 9 8
Scenario B 8 7 8 7
Scenario C 9 6 8 9
Scenario D 6 7 8 6
After Calculate $(\Sigma x^2_{ij})^{1/2}$ for each column and divide each column by that to get r_{ij}
Style Business Reliability Financial Economics Cost of operation
Scenario A 0.46 0.61 0.54 0.53
Scenario B 0.53 0.48 0.48 0.46
Scenario C 0.59 0.41 0.48 0.59
Scenario D 0.40 0.48 0.48 0.40

After multiply each Column by w_j to get V_{ij}.

Style Business Reliability Financial Economics Cost of operation
Scenario A 0.046 0.244 0.162 0.106
Scenario B 0.053 0.192 0.144 0.092
Scenario C 0.059 0.164 0.144 0.118
Scenario D 0.040 0.192 0.144 0.080

Determine Ideal Solution A*.

A* = {0.059, 0.244, 0.162, 0.080}
Style Business Reliability Financial Economics Cost of operation
Scenario A 0.046 0.244 0.162 0.106
Scenario B 0.053 0.192 0.144 0.092
Scenario C 0.059 0.164 0.144 0.118
Scenario D 0.040 0.192 0.144 0.080

Find Negative Ideal Solution A-.

A- = {0.040, 0.164, 0.144, 0.118}
Style Business Reliability Financial Economics Cost of operation
Scenario A 0.046 0.244 0.162 0.106
Scenario B 0.053 0.192 0.144 0.092
Scenario C 0.059 0.164 0.144 0.118
Scenario D 0.040 0.192 0.144 0.080

Determine Separation From Ideal Solution

A* = {0.059, 0.244, 0.162, 0.080} S_i^* = [(vj*– vij)2] ½ for each row j
Style Business Reliability Financial Economics Cost of operation
Scenario A **(.046**-.059)² **(.244**-.244)² **(0)² (.026)²**
Scenario B **(.053**-.059)² **(.192**-.244)² **(-.018)² (.012)²**
Scenario C **(.053**-.059)² **(.164**-.244)² **(-.018)² (.038)²**
Scenario D **(.053**-.059)² **(.192**-.244)² **(-.018)² (.0)²**

Determine Separation From Ideal Solution S_i^*

Σ (vj*–vij)2 S_i^* = [Σ(v_j*– v_{ij})2] ½
Scenario A **0.000845** 0.029
Scenario B **0.003208** 0.057
Scenario C **0.008186** 0.090
Scenario D **0.003389** 0.058

Determine Separation From Negative Ideal Solution **Si-**

Σ (vj-–vij)2 Si- = [Σ(v_j-– v_{ij})2]½
Scenario A **0.006904** 0.083
Scenario B **0.001629** 0.040
Scenario C **0.000361** 0.019
Scenario D **0.002228** 0.047

Calculate the relative closeness to the ideal solution C_i^* = S_i/ (S_i^* +S_i)

S_i/(S_i*+ S_i) Ci*
Scenario A **0.083/0.112** 0.74 ¬ BEST
Scenario B **0.040/0.097** 0.41
Scenario C **0.019/0.109** 0.17 ¬ WORSE
Scenario D **0.047/0.105** 0.45

Finally we generate a "narrative guide" to explain each relevant aspect to support a specific scenario and will be include our reactive stratagems.

CONCLUSION AND FUTURE RESEARCH DIRECTION

Each business simulation modules comprising the customization process of filling information or input variable data, analysis, decision making and finally the simulation of such decisions. As a first step it is necessary to enter into the module the company's information that will be assessed in this way to create real conditions today and to make more accurate prognosis and create visual advertising strategy that best suits the needs of the user and business goals. Through the design of this tool can find a support, which is of paramount importance because, when making decisions under uncertainty speaking specifically about marketing strategies, gives SMEs an advance and improve the development of strategies to be implemented, taking into account the limited budget that account. It is very important to have the display functions such strategies in the medium and long term, and make corrections at the right time, because the simulator is achieved through trial and error decisions. The results of the periods set offer a competitive advantage to SMEs that are within the same niche. Concluding about the decision making under uncertainty module, can be said that the decision making as an experience is a key element, and that decisions should be taken on a reality that in many cases is complex because there are many variables involved, both within the organization and in the outside. Accumulating experience is over (for the time that you learn) and expensive (make mistakes), considering that the more you gain experience is the consequence of errors. Therefore, to achieve a high level of experience in the workplace can have very high costs. The role of a simulator business, specifically in the form of decision making, is that the immediate consequences of all the experience you can gain without the effects that might result from a wrong decision or simply a non-optimal decision, will be welcomed and cheaper, whatever the cost. Precisely the risk is that we do not know if it has made a good decision, not knowing whether an idea will work or not, and exactly a bad decision taken what leads to success or failure of a company. The marketing module will place the user in detail simulator business in an environment where they can become familiar with the development and design strategies, with the variables to consider in any election relating to products and services offered by a company using a safe method where not risk economic resources and increasing experience in business management. Utilities that can be given to this module are varied, ranging from an educational perspective to prepare for a future business, in a dynamic and fun way, preparing the user to deal with different situations that occur in the world of sales detail

REFERENCES

Barnes, J. (1984). Cognitive Biases and Their Impact on Strategic Planning. *Strategic Management Journal*, *5*(2), 129–137. doi:10.1002/smj.4250050204

Kanooni, A. (2009). *Organizational factors affecting business and information technology alignment: A structural equation modeling analysis* (Ph.D. dissertation). Capella University.

Klayman, J., & Schoemaker, P. (1993). Thinking about the future: A cognitive perspective. *Journal of Forecasting*, *12*(2), 161–186. doi:10.1002/for.3980120208

Laudon, K., & Laudon, J. (2002). Management Information Systems Managing the Digital Firm (7th ed.). Pearson Prentice-Hall.

Pretorius, M. (2008). When Porters generic strategies are not enough: Complementary strategies for turnaround situations. *The Journal of Business Strategy*, *29*(6), 19–28. doi:10.1108/02756660810917200

Salem, M. (2005). The Use of Strategic Planning Tools and Techniques in Saudi Arabia: An Empirical study. *International Journal of Management*, *22*(3), 376-395, 507.

Sundin, S., & Braban-Ledoux, C. (2001). Artificial Intelligence–Based Decision Support Technologies in Pavement Management. *Computer-Aided Civil and Infrastructure Engineering*, *16*(2), 143–157. doi:10.1111/0885-9507.00220

ADDITIONAL READING

Peyrefitte, J., Golden, P., & Brice, J. Jr. (2002). Vertical integration and economic performance: A managerial capability framework. *Management Decision*, *40*(3), 217–226. doi:10.1108/00251740210420165

Philip, G. (2007). IS Strategic Planning for Operational Efficiency. *Information Systems Management*, *24*(3), 247–264. doi:10.1080/10580530701404504

Porter, M. (1998). *Estrategia Competitiva: Técnicas para el Análisis de los Sectores Industriales y de la Competencia*. México: Continental.

KEY TERMS AND DEFINITIONS

Business Simulator: It is an intelligent tool to simulate the decisions to diverse scenarios in a small or medium company.

TOPSIS Methodology: Is a model to represent correct decisions in a multi-criteria decisions problem.

Chapter 3
DSS for Web Mining Using Recommendation System

Varaprasad Rao M
Anurag Group of Institutions, India

Vishnu Murthy G
Anurag Group of Institutions, India

ABSTRACT

Decision Supports Systems (DSS) are computer-based information systems designed to help managers to select one of the many alternative solutions to a problem. A DSS is an interactive computer based information system with an organized collection of models, people, procedures, software, databases, telecommunication, and devices, which helps decision makers to solve unstructured or semi-structured business problems. Web mining is the application of data mining techniques to discover patterns from the World Wide Web. Web mining can be divided into three different types – Web usage mining, Web content mining and Web structure mining. Recommender systems (RS) aim to capture the user behavior by suggesting/recommending users with relevant items or services that they find interesting in. Recommender systems have gained prominence in the field of information technology, e-commerce, etc., by inferring personalized recommendations by effectively pruning from a universal set of choices that directed users to identify content of interest.

INTRODUCTION: DECISION SUPPORT SYSTEM

A decision support system (DSS) is a computer-based information system that supports business or organizational decision-making activities. DSSs serve the management, operations, and planning levels of an organization (usually mid and higher management) and help people make decisions about problems that may be rapidly changing and not easily specified in advance. i.e. Unstructured and Semi-Structured decision problems. Decision support systems can be either fully computerized, human-powered or a combination of both. While academics have perceived DSS as a tool to support decision making process, DSS users see DSS as a tool to facilitate organizational processes (Keen, 1980). Some authors have ex-

DOI: 10.4018/978-1-5225-1877-8.ch003

tended the definition of DSS to include any system that might support decision making. Sprague (1980) defines DSS by its characteristics:

- DSS tends to be aimed at the less well structured, underspecified problem that upper level managers typically face.
- DSS attempts to combine the use of models or analytic techniques with traditional data access and retrieval functions.
- DSS specifically focuses on features which make them easy to use by non-computer people in an interactive mode.
- DSS emphasizes flexibility and adaptability to accommodate changes in the environment and the decision making approach of the user.

DSSs include knowledge-based systems. A properly designed DSS is an interactive software-based system intended to help decision makers compile useful information from a combination of raw data, documents, and personal knowledge, or business models to identify and solve problems and make decisions. The common thread of articles published in *Decision Support Systems* is their relevance to theoretical and technical issues in the support of enhanced decision making. The areas addressed may include foundations, functionality, interfaces, implementation, impacts, and evaluation of decision support systems (DSSs). Manuscripts may draw from diverse methods and methodologies, including those from decision theory, economics, econometrics, statistics, computer supported cooperative work, data base management, linguistics, management science, mathematical modeling, operations management, cognitive science, psychology, user interface management, and others. However, a manuscript focused on direct contributions to any of these related areas should be submitted to an outlet appropriate to the specific area [Elsevier]. Examples of research topics that would be appropriate for *Decision Support Systems* include the following:

1. DSS Foundations
   a. Principles, concepts, and theories of enhanced decision making; formal languages and research methods enabling improvements in decision making
   b. It is important that theory validation be carefully addressed.
2. DSS Functionality
   a. Methods, tools, and techniques for developing the functional aspects of enhanced decision making; solver, model, and/or data management in DSSs; rule formulation and management in DSSs; DSS development and use in computer supported cooperative work, negotiation, research and product
3. DSS Interfaces
   a. Methods, tools, and techniques for designing and developing DSS interfaces; development, management, and presentation of knowledge in a DSS; coordination of a DSS's interface with its functionality
4. DSS Implementation
   a. Experiences in DSS development and utilization; DSS management and updating; DSS instruction/training
   b. A critical consideration must be how specific experiences provide more general implications.
5. DSS Evaluation and Impact
   a. Evaluation metrics and processes; DSS impact on decision makers, organizational processes and performance

Typical information that a decision support application might gather and present includes: inventories of information assets (including legacy and relational data sources, cubes, data warehouses, and data marts),comparative sales figures between one period and the next, projected revenue figures based on product sales assumptions. DSSs are often contrasted with more automated decision-making systems known as Decision Management Systems (Taylor, 2012).

WEB MINING

Web is a collection of inter-related files on one or more Web servers. Web mining (R. Cooley, B. Mobasher & J. Srivastava, 1997) is the application of data mining techniques to extract knowledge from Web data. Web data is Web content –text, image, records, etc. Web structure –hyperlinks, tags, etc. Web usage –http logs, app server logs, etc. Web mining (R. Cooley, 2000) is the application of data mining techniques to discover patterns from the World Wide Web. Web mining can be divided into three different types – Web usage mining, Web content mining and Web structure mining. Web Content Mining is the process of extracting useful information from the contents of Web documents. Content data corresponds to the collection of facts a Web page was designed to convey to the users. It may consist of text, images, audio, video, or structured records such as lists and tables. Research activities in this field also involve using techniques from other disciplines such as Information Retrieval (IR) and Natural Language Processing (NLP). Data Mining (sometimes called data or knowledge discovery) is the process of analyzing data from different perspectives and summarizing it into useful information - information that can be used to increase revenue, cuts costs, or both. The more basic and popular data mining techniques include:

- Classification
- Clustering
- Associations

The other significant ideas are:

- Topic Identification, tracking and drift analysis
- Concept hierarchy creation
- Relevance of content

Relevance can be measured with respect to any of the following criteria:

1. Document Relevance
   a. Measure of how useful a given document is in a given situation
   b. Commonly seen in the context of queries -results are ordered by some measure of relevance
   c. In general, a query is not necessary to assign a relevance score to a document
2. Query Based Relevance
   a. Most common
   b. Well established in Information Retrieval
   c. Similarity between query keywords and document is calculated
   d. Can be enhanced through additional information such as popularity (Google) or term positions (AltaVista)

3. User Based Relevance
   a. Often associated with personalization
   b. Profile for a particular user is created
   c. Similarity between a profile and document is calculated
   d. No query is necessary
4. Role/Task Based Relevance
   a. Similar to User Based Relevance
   b. Profile is based on a particular role or task, instead of an individual
   c. Input to profile can come from multiple users

Web Content Mining

Applications are given as follows:

- Identify the topics represented by Web Documents
- Categorize Web Documents
- Find Web Pages across different servers that are similar
- Applications related to relevance
- Queries – Enhance standard Query Relevance with User, Role, and/or Task Based Relevance
- Recommendations – List of top "n" relevant documents in a collection or portion of a collection.
- Filters – Show/Hide documents based on relevance score

RECOMMENDER SYSTEMS

Recommender systems (RS) aim to capture the user behavior by suggesting/recommending users with relevant items or services that they find interesting in. Recommender systems have gained prominence in the field Recommender systems or recommendation systems (sometimes replacing "system" with a synonym such as platform or engine) are a subclass of information filtering system that seek to predict the 'rating' or 'preference' that a user would give to an item (Ricci et al, 2011 & TIME.com, 2015) of information technology, e-commerce, etc., by inferring personalized recommendations by effectively pruning from a universal set of choices that directed users to identify content of interest. In recent years, Recommender systems has received more attention and have become an integral part of a number of e-commerce applications which include recommending movies, books, news, research articles, social tags, etc., Moreover, new research works on Recommender systems also predicted for experts (Buettner et al, 2014 & H. Chen et al, 2015), collaborators (H. Chen, 2011), jokes, restaurants, financial services (Felfernig, 2007), persons (online dating), life insurance and Twitter followers (Pankaj Gupta et al). Recommender systems are mainly categorized into two types: Collaborative Filtering and Content Based Recommender system (Jafarkarimi, 2012). Content Based Recommender system recommend items similar to the ones the user liked in the past (R. J. Mooney & L. Roy, 1999). Collaborative Filtering Recommender systems are based on the similarity of users. It builds a model from user's past behavior and decisions made by similar users. The model then predicts items that the target user might be interested in (Prem Melville & Vikas Sindhwani). Combining both content based and collaborative based results in Hybrid Recommender systems. Recommender systems is an alternative to search algorithms as they help users in discovering items or services they might not have found by themselves. More often

Recommender systems are implemented using search engines by indexing non-traditional data. There are many approaches in recommendation systems:

- Collaborative filtering
- Content-based filtering
- Hybrid based Recommender system
- Knowledge Based Recommender System
- Graph Based Recommended Systems
- Case based RS
- Constraint RS
- Non-Independent and Identically Distributed Recommended systems
- Expert Based Recommender System
- Group Recommender System
- Context Aware Recommender System
- Multi-Criteria Recommender Systems
- Risk-Aware Recommender Systems
- Mobile Recommender Systems

These collaborative and content based filtering techniques are the most widely used in suggesting recommendations to user or system.

Collaborative Filtering

Collaborative filtering (Breese, Heckerman & Kadie, 1998) is one of the most widely used technique of Recommender system. The main idea of a Collaborative based technique is based on finding and analyzing users past behavior, such as ratings for an item and then it predicts the items to the target user based on the ratings of like-minded users. The main advantage of using Collaborative filtering is that it is machine independent analyzable content and is therefore capable of recommending complex items such as movies, news, etc., accurately without having an item "understanding". For instance, the most commonly used similarity measures in measuring similarity of items or users are the k-nearest neighbor (k-NN) approach (Sarwar, Karypis, Konstan, & Riedl, 2000) and the Pearson Correlation as first implemented by (Allen R.B). Collaborative filtering basic underlying assumption is that the people who have similar preferences in the past will agree to have similar preferences in the future. Collaborative based techniques often face certain limitations: cold start, sparsity and scalability (Lee, Yang & Park, 2007).

- **Cold Start:** This refers to new item or new user. It is difficult to recommend to a new user as he/she has not yet rated any item and as such there exists very less information about the users. Similarly, new item recommendation is also difficult.
- **Scalability:** As there are millions of users and products over the Internet, Recommender systems are facing great challenges in handling huge amount of information. Thus computations to calculate recommendations grow exponentially, become expensive and sometimes lead to inaccurate results.
- **Sparsity:** Most users do not involve in rating most of the items, thus making rating matrix usually sparse and making hard to find similar users.

A low-rank matrix approximation technique (Markovsky, 2012), scalability (Takács, Pilászy, Németh and Tikk, 2009) and matrix factorization (Rennie & Srebro, 2005) is used by a particular type of collaborative filtering algorithm. Collaborative filtering techniques can be essentially classified as memory-based and model based collaborative filtering. Memory based collaborative filtering makes use of database of user-item in order to predict the ratings. Neighborhood based methods and user based algorithms (in microsoft.com) used memory based collaborative filtering. Model based collaborative filtering makes use of ratings to learn the user preferences model and is then used to predict the ratings. Kernel-Mapping Recommender, Bayesian classifiers and cluster based collaborative filtering use model-based collaborative filtering.

Content-based Filtering

Content based Recommender system work with user profiles which consists of user preferences for an item (Brusilovsky, 2007). It compares the item list and attempts to recommend items that are most similar to the ones user preferred in the past. It mostly uses keywords, tags and weights to describe the items. This technique has its roots in information filtering research and information retrieval. An item presentation algorithm is applied to abstract the features of the item in the system. To abstract the features of the items in the system, an item presentation algorithm is applied. Tf–idf representation (also called vector space representation) is a widely used algorithm. Content based Recommender system often suffer from the following issues:

- **Limited Content Analysis**
  - i.e., if the content is not enough, it is difficult to provide accurate recommendations.
- **Overspecialization**
  - Restricts users to items similar to the ones defined in their respective profiles and thus new items and other options are not discovered. For instance, to illustrate the differences between content based Recommender system and collaborative based Recommender system, the following two popular music Recommender systems Pandora and Last.fm are shown:
    - **Collaborative Filtering Example:** Last.fm makes a "station" of recommended songs by recording what bands and tracks the user has listened to regularly and comparing them against other users listening behavior. Last.fm play tracks that match with similar users' interests.
    - **Content Based Approach Example:** Pandora makes use of the properties of a song or an artist (a subset of the 400 attributes provided by the Music Genome Project) in order to recommend music which have similar properties. User feedback refines the results by emphasizing and deemphasizing certain attributes of a song by "likes" and "dislikes" respectively.

EXISTING METHODS

There are many kinds of DSS such as Data-Driven, Model-Driven, Knowledge-based, Document-Driven and Group based DSS. The first generic type of DSS is a *Data-Driven DSS*. These systems include file drawer and management reporting systems, data warehousing and analysis systems, Executive Information

Figure 1. Elements of problem solving process

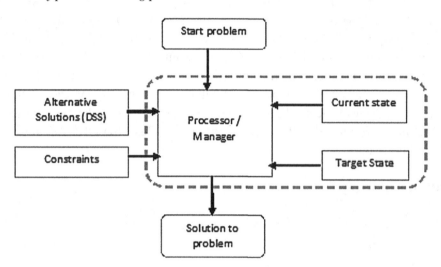

Systems and Spatial DSS. Data-Driven DSS emphasize access to and manipulation of large databases of structured data and especially a time-series of internal company data and sometimes external data. Relational databases accessed by query and retrieval tools provide an elementary level of functionality. Data warehouse systems that allow the manipulation of data by computerized tools tailored to a specific task and setting or by more general tools and operations provided additional functionality. Data-Driven DSS with Online Analytical Processing (OLAP) provide the highest level of functionality and decision support that is linked to analysis of large collections of historical data is explained in Figure 1.

A second category, *Model-Driven DSS*, includes systems that use accounting and financial models, representational models, and optimization models, and optimization models. Model-Driven DSS emphasize access to and manipulation of a model. Simple statistical and analytical tools provide an elementary level of functionality. Some OLAP systems that allow complex analysis of data may be classified as hybrid DSS providing modeling, data retrieval, and data summarization functionality. Model-Driven DSS use data and parameters provided by decision-makers to aid them in analyzing a situation, but they are not usually data intensive. Very large databases are usually not needed for Model-driven DSS as follows in Figure 2.

Knowledge-Driven DSS or Expert Systems can suggest or recommend actions to managers. These DSS are human-computer systems with specialized problem-solving expertise. The expertise consists of knowledge about a particular domain, understanding of problems within that domain, and skills at solving some of these problems (AI algorithms and solutions can be used). A related concept is data mining. It refers to a class of analytical applications that search for hidden patterns in a database. Data mining is the process of sifting through large amounts of data to produce data content relationships. Tools used for building Knowledge-Driven DSS are sometimes called Intelligent Decision Support methods.

Document-Driven DSS are evolving to help mangers retrieve and manage unstructured documents and Web pages. A Document-Driven DSS integrates a variety of storage and processing technologies to provide complete document retrieval and analysis. WWW provides access to large document databases including databases of hypertext documents, images, sounds and video. Examples of documents that would be accessed by Document-Driven DSS are policies and procedures, product specifications, catalogs,

Figure 2. Main components of DSS   *Figure 3. Web enabled DSS*

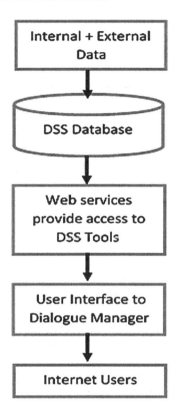

and corporate historical documents, including minutes of meetings, corporate records, and important correspondence. Search engines are powerful decision-aiding tools associated with Document-Driven DSS in the following Figure 3.

Group DSS (GDSS) came first, but now a broader category of Communications-Driven DSS or groupware can be identified. These DSS includes communication, collaboration and related decision support technologies. These are hybrid DSS that emphasize both the use of communications and decision models to facilitate the solution of problems by decision-makers working together as a group. Groupware supports electronic communication, scheduling, document sharing, and other group productivity and decision support enhancing activities.

DSS FOR WEB MINING USING RS

A new model named as *"DSS for Web Mining using RS"* proposed for targeting at improving features of an existing model must not risk or threaten other important features of the current model. The proposed model is used to take a decision on any web information (Masand, Piliopoulou, Srivastava & Zaiane, 2002) in support of recommender system for generating a gist/summary to the required customer and is explained in Figure 4.

Figure 4. Problem solving and learning with knowledge objects

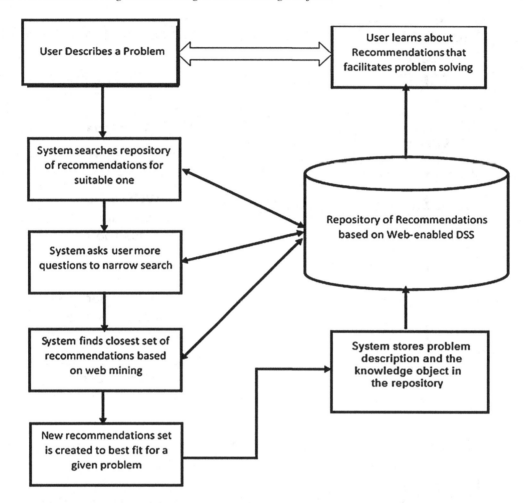

Description: RS Distinguishes Two Kinds of Learning Methods

The first kind is based on coupling new information to previously acquired knowledge. The second kind is based on digging useful regularity out of data; a practice often refers as data mining. Expert systems primarily capture the tacit knowledge of individual experts, but organizations also have collective knowledge and expertise that they have built up over the years. This organizational knowledge can be captured and stored using case-based RS (CBR). In CBR description of the past experiences of human specialists, represented as cases, are stored in a database for the later retrieval when the user encounters a new case with similar parameters. The system searches for stored cases with problem characteristic similar to the new one, finds the closest fit, and applies the solution of the old case to the new case. Successful solutions are tagged to the new case and both are stored together with the other cases in the knowledge base. Unsuccessful solutions are also appended to the case database along with explanations as why the solutions did not work. Problem-based learning (PBL) is (along with active learning and cooperative/collaborative learning) one of the most important developments in contemporary higher education. PBL is based on the assumption that human beings evolved as individuals who are motivated to solve problems, and that problem solvers will seek and learn whatever knowledge is needed for successful problem solving. PBL is a typical example of an application of the first type of filtering technique.

CONCLUSION

Recommendation systems are a complex phenomenon, and there are many aspects to the process of managing knowledge. The new set of recommendations are generated from expert systems by utilizing the sources of web mining algorithms, DSS, Repository Management System and collaborative filtering method to a web site which enables RS. This chapter discusses Web-enabled DSS, Web mining, related to knowledge repositories, and Repository Management Systems that facilitate the problem solving and learning. This approach to the knowledge representation allows considering contemporary DSS as integrated parts of the corresponding Repository Management Systems.

ACKNOWLEDGMENT

Words cannot express my gratitude to Editor Prof. G Sreedhar for his assistance in polishing this manuscript. Thanks to all the technical reviewers who reviewed this chapter and made me in strengthen the chapter not only by catching mistakes but also by suggesting those additions. I thank to one and all, who directly or indirectly, have lent their hand in this completion of the chapter. I would like to express my sincere gratitude to my advisor Prof. B Vishnu Vardhan for the continuous support to complete this chapter, for his patience, motivation, and immense knowledge. Also I thank Prof. G Vishnu Murthy to his continuous encouragement and standing behind in completion of this work in time. I take this opportunity to express gratitude to all of the Department faculty members, Prof. V Vijaya Kumar, Dean CSE, Prof. K S Rao, Director, and Dr P Rajeshwar Reddy, Chairman, Anurag Group of Institutions for their help and continuous support. I'd like to thank my parents for allowing me to follow my ambitions throughout my childhood. This chapter would not have been possible without the support, motivation and encouragement of my wife, Mrs. PV Prajwala. For understanding my long nights at the computer, I'd like to thank my children, Karthikeya and Harshith. Finally, my sincere thanks to IGI Publisher to publish the chapter/book.

REFERENCES

Allen, R. B. (1990). *User Models: Theory, Method, Practice. International J. Man-Machine Studies.*

Berners-Lee, T., Weitzner, D. J., Hall, W., OHara, K., Shadbolt, N., & Hendler, J. A. (2006). A Framework for Web Science. *Foundations and Trends in Web Science, 1*(1), 1–130. doi:10.1561/1800000001

Boreisha, Y. (2001). Internet-Based Data Warehousing. *Proceedings of SPIE Internet-Based Enterprise Integration and Management, 4566*, 102–108. doi:10.1117/12.443132

Boreisha, Y. (2002). Database Integration Over the Web. *Proceedings of the International Conference on Internet Computing, IC'02*.

Boreisha, Y., & Myronovych, O. (2003). Data-Driven Web Sites. *WSEAS Transactions on Computers*, *2*(1), 79–83.

Boreisha, Y., & Myronovych, O. (2005a). Knowledge Navigation and Evolutionary Prototyping in E-Learning Systems. *Proceedings of the E-Learn 2005 World Conference on E-Learning in Corporate, Government, Healthcare, and Higher Education*.

Boreisha, Y., & Myronovych, O. (2005b). Web Services-Based Virtual Data Warehouse as an Integration and ETL Tool. *Proceedings of the 2005 International Symposium on Web Services and Applications, ISWS'05*.

Boreisha, Y., & Myronovych, O. (2007). Web-Based Decision Support Systems in Knowledge Management and Education. *Proceedings of the 2007 International Conference on Information and Knowledge Engineering, IKE'07*.

Breese, J. S., & Heckerman, D. (1998). Empirical analysis of predictive algorithms for collaborative filtering. In *Proceedings of the Fourteenth conference on Uncertainty in artificial intelligence (UAI'98)*.

Brusilovsky, P. (2007). *The Adaptive Web*. doi:10.1007/978-3-540-72079-9

Buettner, R. (2014). A Framework for Recommender Systems in Online Social Network Recruiting: An Interdisciplinary Call to Arms. *47th Annual Hawaii International Conference on System Sciences*. Big Island, HI: IEEE. doi:10.1109/HICSS.2014.184

Chen, Ororbia II, & Giles. (2015). *ExpertSeer: a Keyphrase Based Expert Recommender for Digital Libraries*. in arXiv preprint 2015.

Chen, H., Gou, L., Zhang, X., & Giles Collabseer, C. (2011). A search engine for collaboration discovery. In *ACM/IEEE Joint Conference on Digital Libraries (JCDL)*.

Cooley, R. (2000). *Web Usage Mining: Discovery and Usage of Interesting Patterns from Web Data* (Ph.D. Thesis). University of Minnesota, Computer Science & Engineering.

Cooley, R., Mobasher, B., & Srivastava, J. (1997). Web Mining: Information and Pattern Discovery on the World Wide Web. In *Proceedings of the 9th IEEE International Conference on Tools With Artificial Intelligence (ICTAI '97)*. doi:10.1109/TAI.1997.632303

Deitel, P. J., & Deitel, H. M. (2008). *Internet and World Wide Web. How to Program* (4th ed.). Prentice Hall.

Felfernig, A., & Isak, K. (2007). The VITA Financial Services Sales Support Environment. In AAAI/IAAI 2007, (pp. 1692-1699).

French, S., & Turoff, M. (2007). Decision Support Systems. *Communications of the ACM*, *50*(3), 39–40. doi:10.1145/1226736.1226762

Ghazanfar, PrüGel-Bennett, & Szedmak. (n.d.). Kernel-Mapping Recommender system algorithms. *Information Sciences*, *208*, 81–104. doi:10.1016/j.ins.2012.04.012

Gupta, Goel, Lin, Sharma, Wang, & Zadeh. (n.d.). WTF: The who-to-follow system at Twitter. In *Proceedings of the 22nd International Conference on World Wide Web*.

Jafarkarimi, Sim, & Saadatdoost. (2012, June). A Naïve Recommendation Model for Large Databases. *International Journal of Information and Education Technology*.

Keen, P. (1980). Decision support systems: a research perspective. Cambridge, MA: Center for Information Systems Research, Alfred P. Sloan School of Management. Retrieved from http://hdl.handle.net/1721.1/47172

Laudon, K. C., & Laudon, J. P. (2006). *Management Information Systems. In Managing the Digital Farm* (pp. 428–508). Prentice Hall.

Lee, Yang, & Park. (2007). *Discovery of Hidden Similarity on Collaborative Filtering to Overcome Sparsity Problem*. Discovery Science.

Markovsky, I. (2012). *Low-Rank Approximation: Algorithms, Implementation, Applications*. Springer. doi:10.1007/978-1-4471-2227-2

Masand, Spiliopoulou, Srivastava, & Zaiane. (Eds.). (2002). *Proceedings of WebKDD 2002 – Web Mining for Usage Patterns and User Profiles*. Retrieved from http://db.cs.ualberta.ca/webkdd02/

McLeod, R., & Schell, G. (2006). *Management Information Systems* (10th ed.). Prentice Hall.

Melville & Sindhwani. (2010). Recommender Systems. In Encyclopedia of Machine Learning. Academic Press.

Mooney, R. J., & Roy, L. (1999). Content-based book recommendation using learning for text categorization. In *Workshop Recom. Sys. Algo. and Evaluation*.

Rennie, J., & Srebro, N. (2005). Fast Maximum Margin Matrix Factorization for Collaborative Prediction (PDF).*Proceedings of the 22nd Annual International Conference on Machine Learning*. ACM Press.

Sarwar, B., Karypis, G., Konstan, J., & Riedl, J. (2000). *Application of Dimensionality Reduction in Recommender System: A Case Study*. Academic Press.

Sprague, R. (1980). A Framework for the Development of Decision Support Systems. *Management Information Systems Quarterly*, *4*(4), 1–25. doi:10.2307/248957

Supyuenyong, V., & Islam, N. (2006). Knowledge Management Architecture: Building Blocks and Their Relationships. *Technology Management for the Global Future*, *3*, 1210–1219.

Takács, G., Pilászy, I., Németh, B., & Tikk, D. (2009, March). Scalable Collaborative Filtering Approaches for Large Recommender Systems. *Journal of Machine Learning Research*, *10*, 623–656.

Taylor, J. (2012). *Decision Management Systems: A Practical Guide to Using Business Rules and Predictive Analytics*. Boston, MA: Pearson Education.

Winston, P. H. (1992). *Artificial Intelligence*. Addison-Wesley.

Yu. (2004). A Web-Based Consumer- Oriented Intelligent Decision Support System for Personalized E-Services. ACM International Conference Proceeding Series, 60, 429-437.

KEY TERMS AND DEFINITIONS

Collaborative Filtering: Collaborative based technique is based on finding and analyzing users past behavior.

Content Based Filtering: Content based Recommender system work with user profiles which consists of user preferences for an item.

Data Mining: Data Mining (sometimes called data or knowledge discovery) is the process of analyzing data from different perspectives and summarizing it into useful information - information that can be used to increase revenue, cuts costs, or both.

Decision Support System: A decision support system (DSS) is a computer-based information system that supports business or organizational decision-making activities.

E-Commerce: Electronic commerce, is the trading or facilitation of trading in products or services using computer networks.

Information Retrieval: Information Retrieval (IR) is the activity of obtaining information resources relevant to an information need from a collection of information resources.

Information Technology: Information Technology (IT) is the application of computers and internet to store, retrieve, transmit, and manipulate data or information.

Natural Language Processing: Natural Language Processing (NLP)enabling computers to derive meaning from human or natural language input.

Recommender Systems: Recommender systems (RS) aim to capture the user behavior by suggesting/recommending users with relevant items or services that they find interesting in.

Web Content Mining: is the process of extracting useful information from the contents of Web documents.

Web Mining: Web is a collection of inter-related files on one or more Web servers.

Chapter 4
Mastering Intelligent Decision Support Systems in Enterprise Information Management

Kijpokin Kasemsap
Suan Sunandha Rajabhat University, Thailand

ABSTRACT

This chapter explains the overview of Intelligent Decision Support Systems (IDSSs); the overview of Enterprise Information Management (EIM); the IDSS techniques for EIM in terms of Expert System (ES), Multi-Agent System (MAS), Fuzzy Logic (FL), Artificial Neural Network (ANN), Evolutionary Computation (EC), and Hybrid System (HS); and the multifaceted applications of IDSSs in EIM. IDSS techniques are rapidly emerging as the modern tools in information management systems and include various techniques, such as ES, MAS, FL, ANN, EC, and HS. IDSS techniques can increase the sensitiveness, flexibility, and accuracy of information management systems. IDSS techniques should be implemented in modern enterprise in order to gain the benefits of using the decision-making process concerning EIM. The chapter argues that utilizing IDSS techniques for EIM has the potential to increase organizational performance and reach strategic goals in global operations.

INTRODUCTION

The evolution of information technology (IT) applications makes the enterprise an absolute commitment on behalf of the decision makers to constantly make the best decisions in the shortest possible time (Jantan, Hamdan, & Othman, 2010). Decision support system (DSS) is a technology that assists managerial decision makers to utilize business data and models toward solving the semi-structured and unstructured problems (Qian, Huang, & Chan, 2004), used to support the complex decision-making and problem-solving processes in modern organizations (e.g., Arnott & Pervan, 2008; Shim et al., 2002; Turban, Aronson, & Liang, 2005). Problem solving ability develops over a long period of time and grows with experience in solving a wide variety of problems in many different ways (Kasemsap, 2017a). Although the development of DSS has been executed for over 40 years, DSS suffers from many limitations, such

DOI: 10.4018/978-1-5225-1877-8.ch004

as poor maintainability, poor adaptability, and less reusability (Janjua & Hussain, 2012). Information plays an important role in modern enterprise (Kahraman, Kaya, & Cevikcan, 2011).

Many IDSSs have been developed to support decision making for modern enterprises (Kahraman et al., 2011). Regarding global competition, enterprises are increasingly employing IT to electronically conduct business (Kahraman et al., 2011). The information sector in modern business is the most energetic segment (Rehman & Marouf, 2004). Those various transaction data can be transformed into information and knowledge by using business intelligence tools. Business intelligence involves creating any type of data visualization that provides insight into a business for the purpose of making a decision or taking an action (Kasemsap, 2016a). Enterprise-related decision makers make better business decisions using IDSSs (Wu, 2010).

Enterprise resource planning (ERP) is useful in providing the management team with the types of information necessary for making critical decisions (Kasemsap, 2015a). Decision making is the cognitive process resulting in the selection of a course of action among several scenarios (Kasemsap, 2016b) and is based on different data sources obtained from information systems, such as ERP, supply chain management, human resource management, financial management, and customer relationship management (CRM). The focus on the role of IS within business architecture and their impact on business performance by utilizing IT based on the practical application of IT, technical alignment, IS capabilities, and IS effectiveness is to connect people, processes, and technology for the purpose of maximizing corporate IT, technical alignment, and information systems capabilities to enhance business performance and reach organizational goals in the digital age (Kasemsap, 2015b).

The applications of IDSSs in EIM are discussed in this chapter in order to obtain a successful business strategy in enterprise. EIM systems in modern organizations have been developed following the requirements obtaining from administration, control, reporting, and transaction management in the global competitive environments. The focus of EIM must be shifted from general management to the development of business solutions to enable the operational integration of cross-functional teams, key business processes, performance management, information, and knowledge in order to increase the profitable market share in modern organizations.

Background

Computer applications can be used to provide proper and consistent decisions, thus increasing the effectiveness of decision-making process (Palma-dos-Reis & Zahedi, 1999). DSS is the key application in the field of software engineering (Vinodh & Kumar, 2012). The origin of DSS is in the early 1970s (Marakas, 2003). The continued forms are web-based DSS, group DSS, and executive support system (e.g., Laudon & Laudon, 2004; Power & Sharda, 2007). Swanepoel (2004) developed the DSS for the real-time control system of manufacturing processes. Laudon and Laudon (2004) created the DSS for supply chain management and CRM. CRM becomes one of the most important business strategies in the digital age, thus involving organizational capability of managing business interactions with customers in an effective manner (Kasemsap, 2015c).

A definition of intelligence, which is important in the fields of artificial intelligence (AI) and computational intelligence, has only rarely been provided (Kahraman et al., 2011). Many AI models (e.g., ANN, FL, and genetic algorithms) are the prominent research subjects, since they can deal with the complicated engineering problems which are difficult to solve by classical methods (Konar, 2005). These techniques have been favorably used in analyzing the enterprise problems (e.g., Hadavandi, Ghanbari, Shahanaghi, & Abbasian, 2011; Wang, 2010).

Dey (2001) developed the DSS for making objective decisions in project management using analytic hierarchy process and decision tree analysis framework. The analytic hierarchy process is a broadly recognized method that can take into account many criteria at the same time in enterprise (Kahraman, Oztaysi, Sari, & Turanoglu, 2014). van de Water and van Peet (2006) developed the DSS to make decision in manufacturing concerning analytic hierarchy process. The traditional functions of DSS are applied to enhance managerial decision makers in semi-structured and unstructured decision situations for enlarging their enterprise capabilities but not to replace their judgment (Turban, Aronson, Liang, & Sharda, 2007). The leading intelligent decision support techniques are applicable in designing an intelligent system application (Jantan et al., 2010).

The DSS applications which are embedded with intelligent decision support components can improve the traditional DSS concerning the processes of learning and reasoning in AI (Jantan et al., 2010). IDSSs describe DSS, thus making the broad use of AI techniques (Kahraman et al., 2011). The adoption of AI techniques in management information system (MIS) has a long history regarding knowledge-based system executed in IDSS applications (e.g., Quintero, Konare, & Pierre, 2005; Waiman, Leung, & Tam, 2005). IDSSs have been used since the early 1980s to illustrate the component of management systems (Holsapple & Whinston, 1987). The flexible manufacturing systems can be the meaningful examples of IDSSs in modern manufacturing (Chan, Jiang, & Tang, 2000).

IMPORTANT ASPECTS OF INTELLIGENT DECISION SUPPORT SYSTEMS

This section emphasizes the overview of IDSSs; the perspectives on EIM; the IDSS techniques for EIM in terms of ES, MAS, FL, ANN, EC, and HS; and the multifaceted applications of IDSSs in EIM.

Overview of Intelligent Decision Support Systems

Intelligent decision support systems (IDSSs) are based on ES (Matsatsinis & Siskos, 1999), a well-established type of knowledge-based system that encode the cognitive behaviors of human experts utilizing logic rules and have been shown to perform better than the original human experts in some conditions (e.g., Baron, 1998; Turban, Volonio, McLean, & Wetherbe, 2009). IDSSs behave like a human consultant, thus supporting decision makers, indicating problems, proposing possible courses of action, and evaluating the proposed actions in an effective manner. The aims of AI techniques are to enable tasks to be achieved by a computer and to imitate human capabilities as closely as possible (Kahraman et al., 2011).

IDSS is developed to help decision makers during various phases of decision making by synchronizing business tools and human knowledge for providing total control to the user regarding information acquisition and evaluation toward better decision (Jantan et al., 2010). IDSSs are the important tools to assist the decision-making process where uncertainty or incomplete information exists and where decisions must be made using human judgment and preferences (Jantan et al., 2010). IDSS is an interactive system, particularly developed to support the solution of a non-structured management problem for the improved decision making (Quintero et al., 2005). IDSS is the cognitive system in enterprise (Malhotra et al., 2003).

The aims of IDSS are to support the solution of a non-structured management and to enable knowledge processing with communication capabilities (e.g., Qian et al., 2004; Quintero et al., 2005). IDSS can consolidate specific knowledge and accomplish some types of intelligent decision support behaviors (e.g., learning and reasoning) in order to support decision-making processes (e.g., Qian et al., 2004; Viademonte & Burstein, 2006). Jantan et al. (2010) stated that IDSS applications are developed in various fields (e.g., product development, product planning, management decisions, enterprise, manufacturing, and services). Many IDSS applications are specific to problem domains. For example, in business services sector, IDSS is used for sales prediction (Baba & Suto, 2000), stock trading forecasting (Kuo, Chen, & Hwang, 2001), and financial investment (Palmados-Reis & Zahedi, 1999).

Guerlain et al. (2000) identified six characteristics of IDSS (i.e., interactivity, representation aiding, event and change detection, error detection and recovery, information extraction, and predictive capability). Interactivity is the interaction between the system and user. IDSS is expected to support interactivity, in which user can exhibit the input and receive the output as the feedback (Ishak, Ku-Mahamud, & Morwawi, 2011). The intelligent capability should be intelligent enough to detect and adapt the changes in user input or the surroundings which might influence the transaction or the processes in the decision-making system. The major components of the IDSS are the information extraction and predictive capability. Information extraction is the capability to extract the helpful information from the plenty of information. This information will serve as the input to IDSS or to be represented to the user in a relevant format. The IDSS-related predictive capability categorizes the information into a pattern, thus representing a direction of the IDSS occurrence (Ishak et al., 2011).

Perspectives on Enterprise Information Management

A critical element of enterprise information management (EIM) is related to the techniques to organize and control the internal data for modern enterprises (Rehman & Marouf, 2004). Conversion of data into meaningful information is the function of techniques of data mining, data warehousing, indexing, organizing, packaging, and database management (Rehman & Marouf, 2004). Data mining is the process of applying these computational methods in showing unknown data formats in large data sets (Kasemsap, 2015d). Cheng and Chang (1998) explained the potential applications in order to turn the existing information within organization into a business advantage through data warehousing and data mining. The information can be retrieved, summarized, and delivered to decision makers, business analysts, and other key personnel people (Rehman & Marouf, 2004). Bergeron (1996) stated that the information and organizational resources help organization improve productivity, competitiveness, and overall business performance.

Bergeron (1996) focused on the concept of information resource management in both public and private sectors. The character of information professionals in modern organizations is changing fast (Rehman & Marouf, 2004). Organizations manage the risk of suboptimal information utilization and the risk of information destruction due to the absence of professionals. Despite end users' capability to search for information, an abundant amount of information can be overlooked because the apprentices cannot consider into the information query as the professionals do (Rehman & Marouf, 2004). Heckman (1998) studied about the skill problems found in a virtual information management organization, and highlighted the particular skills required in the modern organizations. Organizations require the tactical human resource planning for enabling organizations to effectively deploy knowledge and skills and to create a systematic environment where the discretionary collaborations among distributed business units are encouraged.

The systems for EIM should control, approve, and measure the flow of information (Best, 2010). Best (2010) indicated that the practices of EIM include performance level setting (by which targets for different parameters of information management may be created); positive and negative feedback (by which information can be provided to the information manager which enables people to change the completion of the systems under their control); dynamic equilibrium (by which the information manager may maintain the accomplishment of the systems within the changing limits); bounded autonomy (by which the information manager can describe the extent to which individual information systems may independently act); and self organization (by which the tendency of systems of all types to form new groupings which serve local purposes).

INTELLIGENT DECISION SUPPORT SYSTEM TECHNIQUES FOR ENTERPRISE INFORMATION MANAGEMENT

In this section, the techniques of IDSSs for EIM (i.e., ES, MAS, FL, ANN, EC, and HS) are demonstrated.

Expert System

Expert system (ES) is a computer system that emulates the decision-making ability of a human expert obtained from a branch of AI (Jackson, 1998). ES is defined as a computer program that exhibits a degree of expertise in solving problem. ES utilizes human expert knowledge concerning decision capability of human expert regarding routine tasks (Durkin, 1994) and is a part of strategic change for organizations as a result of the strategic IT plan (Coakes, Merchant, & Lehaney, 1997). ES exploits the reasoning mechanisms in order to apply knowledge for solving the given problems (Jayaraman & Srivastava, 1996). ES plays a significant role as a meaningful tool to enhance organizational productivity, improve quality, and increase profits while minimizing costs and capturing expertise in the global business environments.

ES is extensively applied in the modern business world with positive impacts (Nwankwo, Obidigbo, & Ekwulugo, 2002). ES is correlated with various areas, such as business process reengineering (Guimaraes, Yoon, & Clevenson, 1997), human resource management (e.g., Berry, 1997; Grandon, 1996), and public service contexts (Berry, Berry, & Foster, 1998). ES can provide information on demand to improve the effectiveness and efficiency of organizational decision-making processes of non-experts (Motiwalla & Fairfield-Sonn, 1998).

ES is sometimes called "knowledge management (KM)" or "diagnostic systems" (Nwankwo et al., 2002). ES utilizes the systematic algorithms to estimate the human knowledge and expertise in the specialized areas (Nwankwo et al., 2002). KM has become one of the most significant trends across the globe (Pandey & Dutta, 2013). Organizations that embed KM practices across a range of organizational innovation activities create a boundary spanning culture, which links various organizational disciplines in the knowledge-based economy (Kasemsap, 2016c). Lifelong learning and KM become a valuable origin of competitive advantage in the information age (Kasemsap, 2016d). Successful KM efforts are focused on ideal outcomes that help organizations meet critical business objectives in global business (Kasemsap, 2016e).

Multi-Agent System

Multi-agent system (MAS) is a type of intelligent decision support techniques that are applied in IDSS applications (Kwon, Yoo, & Suh, 2005). The theory of MAS can be viewed as an evolution of AI in order to achieve the autonomous and computational systems (Kahraman et al., 2011). The MAS is considered as a coupled network of agents that work together to find answers to problems beyond the individual capabilities or knowledge of each agent (Flores-Mendez, 1999). Agent environments can be organized according to various properties, such as accessibility (if it is possible to gather complete information about the environment), determinism (if an action performed in the environment causes a definite effect), dynamics (whether the entities influence the environment), discreteness (whether the number of possible actions in the environment is finite), episodicity (whether agent actions in certain time periods influence other periods) (Russell & Norvig, 2003), and dimensionality (whether spatial characteristics are the significant factors of the environment and the agent considers space in its decision making (Salamon, 2011).

Wooldridge (2002) stated that the agents in the MAS system have three characteristics (i.e., autonomy - the agents are at least partially independent, self-aware, and autonomous; local views - no agent has a full global view of the system, or the system is too complex for an agent to make practical use of such knowledge; and decentralization - there is no designated controlling agent). Cerrada et al. (2007) stated that the important characteristics of MAS system include autonomy, communication, reactivity, intelligence, and mobility. Topics of research in MAS involve various tasks (e.g., the agent-oriented software engineering, beliefs, coordination, organization, communication, negotiation, distributed problem solving, multi-agent learning, scientific communities, dependability, and robotics).

Although the definition of MAS has been discussed into the researchers' association of the distributed AI area, the autonomy in the MAS system is the main characteristic toward accomplishing tasks and reaching practical objectives without assistance (Kahraman et al., 2011). Each agent in the MAS system has properties as autonomy, mobility, rationality, sociability, and reactivity. Intelligent agents have the functional method, such as the object-oriented programming. The intelligent agents have the built-in beliefs, desires, and intentions (Kahraman et al., 2011). The actions of agent in the AI environment are typically mediated through an appropriate middleware. The middleware of MAS offers the first-class consideration for MAS, thus providing the means to control the access of organizational resources and the arrangement of agent (Weyns, Omicini, & Odell, 2007).

Fuzzy Logic

Fuzzy logic (FL) has gained much importance for its applications in DSS where the final user needs an intelligible system based on clear rule bases (Pota, Exposito, & de Pietro, 2014). FL aims at modeling the complex reasoning capability that plays an important role in the human ability to make rational decisions in an environment of uncertainty and imprecision (Crunk & North, 2007). FL has been used in conjunction to the ES to increase its reasoning capability, thus improving the quality of decisions (Kildisas, 2001). FL is an alternative method of interpretation based on fuzzy sets (Zadeh, 1965) rather than numbers (Zadeh, 1973). Zadeh published the first paper, called "fuzzy sets," on the theory of FL in 1965. Zadeh (1973) provided a methodology for computing the data and information that are uncertain and imprecise. Zadeh (1996) defined FL as a methodology for computing the intelligent decision support words. FL approach has its origin based on the human logic that takes advantage of conceptual knowledge without borderlines (Vinodh & Kumar, 2012).

The applications of FL include fuzzy sets, linguistic variables, and probability distribution. Researchers in qualitative environment suffer from the unclearness in which case data is not shown as the exact numbers (Yang & Li, 2002). The evaluation of linguistic variables is recommended instead of numerical values (Beach, Muhlemann, Price, Paterson, & Sharp, 2000). Linguistic variables are defined by words or sentences instead of numbers (Zadeh, 1975). FL continues to be implemented in the design of system controllers (Kobbacy & Vadera, 2011). Andujar and Barragan (2005) utilized FL in order to design a nonlinear multivariate controller that is enough to handle the adoption of FL functions.

Ababneh et al. (2009) explained the utilization of the Takagi-Sugeno fuzzy model to design the digital controller for a chaotic system. There are several applications of FL in ecodesign methodology (Kobbacy & Vadera, 2011). Vakili-Ardebili and Boussabaine (2007) showed the difficulties of designing eco-friendly products since social and environmental impacts can be uncertain. Vakili-Ardebili and Boussabaine (2007) took advantage of FL ability to design the imprecise factors and deduce an indication of the extent to which a pattern is eco-efficient. Kuo et al. (2009) stated that although several organizations have designed the eco-friendly products, these aspects have not been as successful as anticipated because their designs ignore cost and customer requirements. Kuo et al. (2009) proposed the use of FL to estimate the customer requirements and eco-friendly requirements in an endeavor to produce better balanced designs.

Artificial Neural Network

Artificial neural network (ANN) is a flexible computing framework for modeling a broad range of nonlinear problems (Shahrabi, Hadavandi, & Esfandarani, 2013). A neural network is an algorithm that dynamically inherits human neuron information processing capability (Coley, 1999) and imitates the human brain in terms of learning a meaningful concept (Ozmutlu & Cavdur, 2005). Haykin (1994) defined a neural network as a largely distributed processor that has a natural tendency for storing experiential knowledge and making it available for use. Haykin (1994) stated that a neural network resembles the brain in two aspects. Firstly, knowledge is acquired by the network through a learning process. Secondly, interneuron connection strengths called "synaptic weights" are used to store the knowledge.

ANN is a collection of simple processors that are interconnected to form a mathematical representation of the relationship embedded in any set of data (Park & Kim, 2011). ANN is helpful when it is difficult to determine the exact relationship between input and output variables for the system (Ozmutlu & Cavdur, 2005). ANN has been found to be a useful tool to solve many problems in the field of geotechnical engineering. For example, many researchers have utilized the ANN to predict the uplift capacity of suction caisson, the pre-consolidation pressure of clay soils, the residual shear strength of cohesive soils, the bearing capacity of strip footing, and other areas (e.g., Celic & Tan, 2005; Kaya, 2009). ANN is a type of intelligent decision support techniques applied in IDSS applications (Sajjad & Slobodan, 2006).

ANN is an optimization algorithm used in the variety of applications with great success. The models of ANN take inspiration from the basic framework of the brain. The main parts of a neuron are cell body, axon, and dendrites. An ANN consists of many nodes and synapses (Fu, 1994). Nodes operate in parallel and communicate with each other through the connecting synapses. ANN is effectively used for pattern recognition and regression. Solving the complex nonlinear problems and conducting the high computation rate are the important features in ANN. In addition, there is no requirement for the assumptions in ANN (Pal & Mitra, 1992).

Evolutionary Computation

Evolutionary computation (EC) concept has received considerable attention during the last two decades based on Darwin's evolution theory by applying the biological principle of natural evolution to artificial systems for the solution of optimization problems (Back, Hammel, & Schwefel, 1997). The scope of EC involves the study of the foundations and the applications of computational techniques based on the principles of natural evolution (Kahraman et al., 2011). The algorithms of EC employ the design philosophy to find solutions to the hard problems from various domains, optimization, automatic programming, circuit design, machine learning, economics, ecology, and population genetics. EC for solving optimization has the substantial advantages in the modern enterprise (Kahraman et al., 2011).

Hybrid System

The effective system solutions can be obtained while utilizing the combination of hybrid system (HS) techniques (Kahraman et al., 2011). Each combination of HS techniques has an aim to decrease the limitation of one method. For example, genetic algorithm has been used to improve the performance of ANN. Another example is the use of fuzzy inference with other computational intelligence techniques. A fuzzy inference system can take linguistic information from human experts and also adapt itself using numerical data to achieve better performance. Using HS provides the synergy to the resulting system in the advantages of the constituent techniques, thus avoiding the shortcomings in the system (Jang & Sun, 1995).

MULTIFACETED APPLICATIONS OF INTELLIGENT DECISION SUPPORT SYSTEMS IN ENTERPRISE INFORMATION MANAGEMENT

Chang et al. (2011) listed the criteria that affect supplier selection, and established the strategy map among the criteria using the theory of fuzzy set. The strategy map reveals interdependencies among the criteria and the strengths. Chen et al. (2010) introduced fuzzy trust evaluation method for sharing knowledge gained from the activities of a virtual enterprise and the interactions among allied enterprises, including collaborative relations. Chen and Lin (2009) proposed a fuzzy linguistic performance index based on the flow network model to evaluate the performance of the system of ERP regarding the linguistic grades of the ERP examination in modern business. Tai and Chen (2009) proposed a suitable model for intellectual capital performance evaluation by combining the 2-tuple fuzzy linguistic approach with the multiple criteria decision-making (MCDM) applications. Karsak and Ozogul (2009) used the quality function deployment (QFD), fuzzy linear regression (FLR), and zero-one goal programming (ZOGP) by integrating them in ERP.

Xirogiannis et al. (2008) described an enterprise approach to designing a decision modeling tool, which evaluates the effect of contemporary practices of human resource management toward the shareholders' value and satisfaction. Cerrada et al. (2007) proposed a model for managing faults in the manufacturing processes. The model has a generic framework that uses MAS for the distributed control system (DCS).

The system manages the faults with feedback control process and decides about the scheduling of the preventive maintenance tasks, thus conducting preventive and corrective maintenance tasks. Monteiro et al. (2007) emphasized a hierarchical architecture to integrate the individual planner agent, negotiator agent, and mediator agent with a decentralized control toward achieving the flexibility of the supply chain networks. Supply chain networks are the integrated patterns of processes utilized within a facility and over distribution connections, adding value to customers by improving the delivery and manufacturing of products (Kasemsap, 2016f). Qiu et al. (2006) stated that workflow management technology promotes the automation of enterprise business processes.

Lee et al. (2011) examined how AI techniques and radio frequency identification technology (RFID) can enhance the responsiveness of the logistics workflow. RFID solutions can be utilized to reduce the operating costs through decreasing labor costs, enhancing automation, improving tracking and tracing, and preventing the loss of materials (Kasemsap, 2015e). The proposed system determines the correct replenishment strategy by automatically classifying the distribution patterns within the complex demand and supply chain. Zhao and Yu (2011) introduced a reasoning framework for supplier selection in petroleum enterprises. Lopez-Ortega and Villar-Medina (2009) utilized the feedforward neural network, embedded in a machine agent with the purpose of determining the suitable machine in order to fulfill clients' requirements. Emphasizing the importance of both geographic information system (GIS) and the Internet on the bridge maintenance management, Liu and Itoh (2001) applied the genetic algorithm for the rehabilitation plan of bridge decks with the purpose of minimizing rehabilitation cost and deterioration degree.

Lu et al. (2010) presented a risk management model for virtual enterprise, a constructional distributed decision-making model where the situation of information symmetry between owner and partners is considered. Lu et al. (2010) recognized the various risks for virtual enterprise, due to the virtual enterprise's agility and the diversity of its members and its distributed characteristics. Lu et al. (2010) proposed a multi-swarm particle swarm optimization to solve the optimization problem in modern enterprise. Gao et al. (2009) indicated that the wide range of mapping enterprise capabilities of ANN and the global search ability of particle swarm optimization are combined to find the global optimal solution during the training process of ANN. Niu and Gu (2007) established a hybrid genetic particle swarm optimization algorithm for a material purchase and storage optimization for electric power plants to minimize the cost based on its characteristic of raw material stock.

FUTURE RESEARCH DIRECTIONS

The classification of the extensive literature in the domains of IDSSs will provide the potential opportunities for future research. Future research direction should develop an integrated framework for the application of IDSS technologies in various EIM processes and should broaden the perspectives in the implementation of IDSSs in enterprise. Another research challenge is to develop methods to measure EIM benefits from the utilization of IT. Practitioners and researchers should consider the applicability of a more multidisciplinary approach toward research activities in implementing IDSSs. It will be useful to bring the additional disciplines (e.g., human-robot interaction, brain-machine interfaces, the Internet of Things, and cloud computing) to support a more holistic examination of IDSSs in order to transfer the existing theories and approaches to inquiry in this area.

Information retrieval is the process of obtaining relevant information from a collection of informational resources (Kasemsap, 2017b). Effective information system can encourage the processes of information integration and information sharing toward enhancing entrepreneurial success, increasing business growth, and gaining customer satisfaction in global supply chain (Kasemsap, 2017c). Social media allows organizations to improve communication and productivity by disseminating information among the different groups of employees in a more efficient manner (Kasemsap, 2017d). Business process management enables organizations to align business functions with customer needs and helps executives determine how to deploy, monitor, and measure the organizational resources (Kasemsap, 2017e). An examination of linkages among IDSSs, information retrieval, information system, social media, and business process management would seem to be viable for future research efforts.

CONCLUSION

This chapter highlighted the overview of IDSSs; the perspectives on EIM; the IDSS techniques for EIM in terms of ES, MAS, FL, ANN, EC, and HS; and the multifaceted applications of IDSSs in EIM. The role of IDSSs in EIM is important to obtain a successful business strategy. IDSS techniques are rapidly emerging as the modern tools in information management systems and include various techniques, such as ES, MAS, FL, ANN, EC, and HS. IDSSs are a form of support systems focusing on the provision of internal data to aid decision making in modern business. The goal of IDSSs is to make management more efficient and effective, particularly with ad hoc and discretionary decisions (versus routine or programmatic ones that require little judgment).

IDSSs do not attempt to make the decision themselves, but rather present information in a manner that is conducive to making an informed and efficient decision. IDSS techniques can increase the sensitiveness, flexibility, and accuracy of information management systems. There are many benefits of using IDSS techniques in EIM, such as time savings, cost reduction, enhanced effectiveness, improved interpersonal communication, increased decision maker satisfaction, promoted learning, and increased organizational control. IDSS techniques should be implemented in modern enterprise in order to gain the benefits of using the decision-making process concerning EIM. Utilizing IDSS techniques for EIM has the potential to increase organizational performance and reach strategic goals in global operations.

REFERENCES

Ababneh, M., Almanasreh, A. M., & Amasha, H. (2009). Design of digital controllers for uncertain chaotic systems using fuzzy logic. *Journal of the Franklin Institute*, *346*(6), 543–556. doi:10.1016/j.jfranklin.2009.02.002

Andujar, J. M., & Barragan, A. J. (2005). A methodology to design stable nonlinear fuzzy control systems. *Fuzzy Sets and Systems*, *154*(2), 157–181. doi:10.1016/j.fss.2005.03.006

Arnott, D., & Pervan, G. (2008). Eight key issues for the decision support systems discipline. *Decision Support Systems*, *44*(3), 657–672. doi:10.1016/j.dss.2007.09.003

Baba, N., & Suto, H. (2000). Utilization of artificial neural networks and the TD-learning method for constructing intelligent decision support system. *European Journal of Operational Research*, *122*(2), 501–508. doi:10.1016/S0377-2217(99)00250-7

Back, T., Hammel, U., & Schwefel, H. P. (1997). Evolutionary computation: Comments on the history and current state. *IEEE Transactions on Evolutionary Computation*, *1*(1), 3–17. doi:10.1109/4235.585888

Baron, J. (1998). *Thinking and deciding*. Cambridge, UK: Cambridge University Press.

Beach, R., Muhlemann, A. P., Price, D. H. R., Paterson, A., & Sharp, J. A. (2000). A review of manufacturing flexibility. *European Journal of Operational Research*, *122*(2), 41–57. doi:10.1016/S0377-2217(99)00062-4

Bergeron, P. (1996). Information resources management. *Annual Review of Information Science & Technology*, *31*, 263–300.

Berry, F. (1997). Explaining managerial acceptance of expert systems. *Public Productivity and Management Review*, *20*(3), 323–335. doi:10.2307/3380981

Berry, F., Berry, W., & Foster, S. (1998). The determinants of success in implementing an expert system in state government. *Public Administration Review*, *58*(4), 293–305. doi:10.2307/977559

Best, D. P. (2010). The future of information management. *Records Management Journal*, *20*(1), 61–71. doi:10.1108/09565691011039834

Celic, S., & Tan, O. (2005). Determination of preconsolidation pressure with artificial neural network. *Civil Engineering and Environmental Science*, *22*(4), 217–231. doi:10.1080/10286600500383923

Cerrada, M., Cardillo, J., Aguilar, J., & Faneite, R. (2007). Agents-based design for fault management systems in industrial processes. *Computers in Industry*, *58*(4), 313–328. doi:10.1016/j.compind.2006.07.008

Chan, F. T. S., Jiang, B., & Tang, N. K. H. (2000). The development of intelligent decision support tools to aid the design of flexible manufacturing systems. *International Journal of Production Economics*, *65*(1), 73–84. doi:10.1016/S0925-5273(99)00091-2

Chang, B., Chang, C. W., & Wu, C. H. (2011). Fuzzy DEMATEL method for developing supplier selection criteria. *Expert Systems with Applications: An International Journal*, *38*(3), 1850–1858. doi:10.1016/j.eswa.2010.07.114

Chen, S. G., & Lin, Y. K. (2009). On performance evaluation of ERP systems with fuzzy mathematics. *Expert Systems with Applications: An International Journal*, *36*(3), 6362–6367. doi:10.1016/j.eswa.2008.08.078

Chen, T. Y., Chen, Y. M., Lin, C. J., & Chen, P. Y. (2010). A fuzzy trust evaluation method for knowledge sharing in virtual enterprises. *Computers & Industrial Engineering*, *59*(4), 853–864. doi:10.1016/j.cie.2010.08.015

Cheng, P. S., & Chang, P. (1998). Transforming corporate information into value through data warehousing and data mining. *Aslib Proceedings*, *50*(5), 109–113. doi:10.1108/eb051492

Coakes, E., Merchant, K., & Lehaney, B. (1997). The use of expert systems in business transformation. *Management Decision*, *35*(1), 53–57. doi:10.1108/00251749710160197

Coley, D. A. (1999). *An introduction to genetic algorithms for scientists and engineers.* Singapore: World Scientific Publishing. doi:10.1142/3904

Crunk, J., & North, M. M. (2007). Decision support systems and artificial intelligence technologies in aid of information systems based marketing. *International Management Review*, *3*(2), 61–67.

Dey, P. K. (2001). Decision support system for risk management: A case study. *Management Decision*, *39*(8), 634–649. doi:10.1108/00251740110399558

Durkin, J. (1994). *Expert systems: Design and development.* New York, NY: Prentice Hall.

Flores-Mendez, R. A. (1999). Towards a standardization of multi-agent system frameworks. *Crossroads*, *5*(4), 18–24. doi:10.1145/331648.331659

Fu, L. (1994). *Neural networks in computer intelligence.* New York, NY: McGraw–Hill.

Gao, Y., Gu, Y., & Li, T. (2009). *Evaluation approach on enterprise integrated business efficiency based on ANN-QPSO.* Paper presented at the 2nd International Conference on Information Management, Innovation Management and Industrial Engineering (ICIII 2009), Xi'an, China. doi:10.1109/ICIII.2009.398

Grandon, G. (1996). Expert systems usage: Task challenge and intrinsic motivation. *Management Information Systems Quarterly*, *20*(3), 301–329. doi:10.2307/249658

Guerlain, S., Brown, D. E., & Mastrangelo, C. (2000). *Intelligent decision support systems.* Paper presented at the 2000 IEEE International Conference on Systems, Man, and Cybernetics (SMC 2000), Nashville, TN.

Guimaraes, T., Yoon, Y., & Clevenson, A. (1997). Empirically testing ES success factors in business process reengineering. *International Journal of Production Economics*, *50*(2/3), 245–259. doi:10.1016/S0925-5273(97)00044-3

Hadavandi, E., Ghanbari, A., Shahanaghi, K., & Abbasian, S. (2011). Tourist arrival forecasting by evolutionary fuzzy systems. *Tourism Management*, *32*(5), 1196–1203. doi:10.1016/j.tourman.2010.09.015

Haykin, S. (1994). *Neural networks: A comprehensive foundation.* Englewood Cliffs, NJ: Prentice Hall.

Heckman, R. (1998). Planning to solve the "skill problem" in the virtual information management organization. *International Journal of Information Management*, *18*(1), 3–16. doi:10.1016/S0268-4012(97)00036-4

Holsapple, C., & Whinston, A. (1987). *Business expert systems.* New York, NY: McGraw–Hill.

Ishak, W. H. W., Ku-Mahamud, K. R., & Morwawi, N. M. (2011). Conceptual model of intelligent decision support system based on naturalistic decision theory for reservoir operation during emergency situation. *International Journal of Civil & Environmental Engineering*, *11*(2), 6–11.

Jackson, P. (1998). *Introduction to expert systems.* Harlow, UK: Addison–Wesley.

Jang, J. S. R., & Sun, C. T. (1995). Neuro-fuzzy modeling and control. *Proceedings of the IEEE, 83*(3), 378–406. doi:10.1109/5.364486

Janjua, N. K., & Hussain, F. K. (2012). Web@IDSS: Argumentation-enabled web-based IDSS for reasoning over incomplete and conflicting information. *Knowledge-Based Systems, 32*, 9–27. doi:10.1016/j.knosys.2011.09.009

Jantan, H., Hamdan, A. R., & Othman, Z. A. (2010). Intelligent techniques for decision support system in human resource management. In G. Devlin (Ed.), *Decision support systems: Advances* (pp. 261–276). Rijeka, Croatia: InTech. doi:10.5772/39401

Jayaraman, V., & Srivastava, R. (1996). Expert systems in production and operations management: Current applications and future prospects. *International Journal of Operations & Production Management, 16*(12), 27–44. doi:10.1108/01443579610151742

Kahraman, C., Kaya, I., & Cevikcan, E. (2011). Intelligence decision systems in enterprise information management. *Journal of Enterprise Information Management, 24*(4), 360–379. doi:10.1108/17410391111148594

Kahraman, C., Oztaysi, B., Sari, I. U., & Turanoglu, E. (2014). Fuzzy analytic hierarchy process with interval type-2 fuzzy sets. *Knowledge-Based Systems, 59*, 48–57. doi:10.1016/j.knosys.2014.02.001

Karsak, E. E., & Ozogul, C. O. (2009). An integrated decision making approach for ERP system selection. *Expert Systems with Applications: An International Journal, 36*(1), 660–667. doi:10.1016/j.eswa.2007.09.016

Kasemsap, K. (2015a). Implementing enterprise resource planning. In M. Khosrow-Pour (Ed.), *Encyclopedia of information science and technology* (3rd ed., pp. 798–807). Hershey, PA: IGI Global. doi:10.4018/978-1-4666-5888-2.ch076

Kasemsap, K. (2015b). The role of information system within enterprise architecture and their impact on business performance. In M. Wadhwa & A. Harper (Eds.), *Technology, innovation, and enterprise transformation* (pp. 262–284). Hershey, PA: IGI Global. doi:10.4018/978-1-4666-6473-9.ch012

Kasemsap, K. (2015c). The role of customer relationship management in the global business environments. In T. Tsiakis (Ed.), *Trends and innovations in marketing information systems* (pp. 130–156). Hershey, PA: IGI Global. doi:10.4018/978-1-4666-8459-1.ch007

Kasemsap, K. (2015d). The role of data mining for business intelligence in knowledge management. In A. Azevedo & M. Santos (Eds.), *Integration of data mining in business intelligence systems* (pp. 12–33). Hershey, PA: IGI Global. doi:10.4018/978-1-4666-6477-7.ch002

Kasemsap, K. (2015e). The role of radio frequency identification in modern libraries. In S. Thanuskodi (Ed.), *Handbook of research on inventive digital tools for collection management and development in modern libraries* (pp. 361–385). Hershey, PA: IGI Global. doi:10.4018/978-1-4666-8178-1.ch021

Kasemsap, K. (2016a). The fundamentals of business intelligence. *International Journal of Organizational and Collective Intelligence, 6*(2), 12–25. doi:10.4018/IJOCI.2016040102

Kasemsap, K. (2016b). The fundamentals of neuroeconomics. In B. Christiansen & E. Lechman (Eds.), *Neuroeconomics and the decision-making process* (pp. 1–32). Hershey, PA: IGI Global. doi:10.4018/978-1-4666-9989-2.ch001

Kasemsap, K. (2016c). The roles of knowledge management and organizational innovation in global business. In G. Jamil, J. Poças-Rascão, F. Ribeiro, & A. Malheiro da Silva (Eds.), *Handbook of research on information architecture and management in modern organizations* (pp. 130–153). Hershey, PA: IGI Global. doi:10.4018/978-1-4666-8637-3.ch006

Kasemsap, K. (2016d). The roles of lifelong learning and knowledge management in global higher education. In P. Ordóñez de Pablos & R. Tennyson (Eds.), *Impact of economic crisis on education and the next-generation workforce* (pp. 71–100). Hershey, PA: IGI Global. doi:10.4018/978-1-4666-9455-2.ch004

Kasemsap, K. (2016e). The roles of e-learning, organizational learning, and knowledge management in the learning organizations. In E. Railean, G. Walker, A. Elçi, & L. Jackson (Eds.), *Handbook of research on applied learning theory and design in modern education* (pp. 786–816). Hershey, PA: IGI Global. doi:10.4018/978-1-4666-9634-1.ch039

Kascmsap, K. (2016f). Encouraging supply chain nctworks and customer loyalty in global supply chain. In N. Kamath & S. Saurav (Eds.), *Handbook of research on strategic supply chain management in the retail industry* (pp. 87–112). Hershey, PA: IGI Global. doi:10.4018/978-1-4666-9894-9.ch006

Kasemsap, K. (2017a). Advocating problem-based learning and creative problem-solving skills in global education. In C. Zhou (Ed.), *Handbook of research on creative problem-solving skill development in higher education* (pp. 351–377). Hershey, PA: IGI Global. doi:10.4018/978-1-5225-0643-0.ch016

Kasemsap, K. (2017b). Mastering web mining and information retrieval in the digital age. In A. Kumar (Ed.), *Web usage mining techniques and applications across industries* (pp. 1–28). Hershey, PA: IGI Global. doi:10.4018/978-1-5225-0613-3.ch001

Kasemsap, K. (2017c). Advocating information system, information integration, and information sharing in global supply chain. In G. Jamil, A. Soares, & C. Pessoa (Eds.), *Handbook of research on information management for effective logistics and supply chains* (pp. 107–130). Hershey, PA: IGI Global. doi:10.4018/978-1-5225-0973-8.ch006

Kasemsap, K. (2017d). Mastering social media in the modern business world. In N. Rao (Ed.), *Social media listening and monitoring for business applications* (pp. 18–44). Hershey, PA: IGI Global. doi:10.4018/978-1-5225-0846-5.ch002

Kasemsap, K. (2017e). Mastering business process management and business intelligence in global business. In M. Tavana, K. Szabat, & K. Puranam (Eds.), *Organizational productivity and performance measurements using predictive modeling and analytics* (pp. 192–212). Hershey, PA: IGI Global. doi:10.4018/978-1-5225-0654-6.ch010

Kaya, A. (2009). Residual and fully softened strength evaluation of soils using artificial neural networks. *Geotechnical and Geological Engineering, 27*(2), 281–288. doi:10.1007/s10706-008-9228-x

Kildisas, V. (2001). Intelligent decision support system for environmental management. *Environmental Research, Engineering and Management, 2*(16), 69–75.

Kobbacy, K. A. H., & Vadera, S. (2011). A survey of AI in operations management from 2005 to 2009. *Journal of Manufacturing Technology Management, 22*(6), 706–733. doi:10.1108/17410381111149602

Konar, A. (2005). *Computational intelligence: Principles, techniques and applications.* Berlin, Germany: Springer–Verlag. doi:10.1007/b138935

Kuo, R. J., Chen, C. H., & Hwang, Y. C. (2001). An intelligent stock trading decision support system through integration of genetic algorithm based fuzzy neural network and artificial neural network. *Fuzzy Sets and Systems, 118*(2), 21–45. doi:10.1016/S0165-0114(98)00399-6

Kuo, T. C., Wu, H. H., & Shieh, J. I. (2009). Integration of environmental considerations in quality function deployment by using fuzzy logic. *Expert Systems with Applications: An International Journal, 36*(3), 7148–7156. doi:10.1016/j.eswa.2008.08.029

Kwon, O., Yoo, K., & Suh, E. (2005). UbiDSS: A proactive intelligent decision support system as an expert system deploying ubiquitous computing technologies. *Expert Systems with Applications*: An International Journal, *28*(1), 149–161. doi:10.1016/j.eswa.2004.08.007

Laudon, K. C., & Laudon, J. P. (2004). *Management information system.* Upper Saddle River, NJ: Prentice Hall.

Lee, C. K. M., Ho, W., Ho, G. T. S., & Lau, H. C. W. (2011). Design and development of logistics workflow systems for demand management with RFID. *Expert Systems with Applications: An International Journal, 38*(5), 5428–5437. doi:10.1016/j.eswa.2010.10.012

Liu, C., & Itoh, Y. (2001). Information technology applications for bridge maintenance management. *Logistics Information Management, 14*(5/6), 393–400. doi:10.1108/EUM0000000006251

Lopez-Ortega, O., & Villar-Medina, I. (2009). A multi-agent system to construct production orders by employing an expert system and a neural network. *Expert Systems with Applications: An International Journal, 36*(2), 2937–2946. doi:10.1016/j.eswa.2008.01.070

Lu, F. Q., Huang, M., Ching, W. K., Wang, X. W., & Sun, X. L. (2009). *Multi-swarm particle swarm optimization based risk management model for virtual enterprise.* Paper presented at the 1st ACM/SIGEVO Summit on Genetic and Evolutionary Computation (GEC 2009), Shanghai, China. doi:10.1145/1543834.1543886

Lu, F. Q., Huang, M., & Wang, X. W. (2010). *Partners' risk level considered CDDM model for risk management of virtual enterprise.* Paper presented at the 4th International Conference on Management and Service Science (MASS 2010), Wuhan, China. doi:10.1109/ICMSS.2010.5577219

Malhotra, P., Burstein, F., Fisher, J., McKemmish, S., Anderson, J., & Manaszewicz, R. (2003). *Brest cancer knowledge on-line portal: An intelligent decision support system perspective.* Paper presented at the 14th Australasian Conference on Information Systems (ACIS 2003), Perth, Australia.

Marakas, G. M. (2003). *Decision support systems in the 21st century.* Upper Saddle River, NJ: Prentice Hall.

Matsatsinis, N. F., & Siskos, Y. (1999). MARKEX: An intelligent decision support system for product development decisions. *European Journal of Operational Research*, *113*(2), 336–354. doi:10.1016/S0377-2217(98)00220-3

Monteiro, T., Daniel, R. B., & Anciaux, D. (2007). Multi-site coordination using a multi-agent system. *Computers in Industry*, *58*(4), 367–377. doi:10.1016/j.compind.2006.07.005

Motiwalla, L., & Fairfield-Sonn, J. (1998). Measuring the impact of expert systems. *Journal of Business and Economic Studies*, *4*, 10–17.

Niu, D., & Gu, X. (2007). *Application of HGPSOA in electric power system material purchase and storage optimization.* Paper presented at the 16th International Conference on Service Systems and Service Management (ICSSSM 2007), Chengdu, China. doi:10.1109/ICSSSM.2007.4280283

Nwankwo, S., Obidigbo, B., & Ekwulugo, F. (2002). Allying for quality excellence: Scope for expert systems in supplier quality management. *International Journal of Quality & Reliability Management*, *19*(2), 187–205. doi:10.1108/02656710210413516

Ozmutlu, S., & Cavdur, F. (2005). Neural network applications for automatic new topic identification. *Online Information Review*, *29*(1), 34–53. doi:10.1108/14684520510583936

Pal, S. K., & Mitra, S. (1992). Multilayer perception, fuzzy sets, and classification. *IEEE Transactions on Neural Networks*, *3*(5), 683–697. doi:10.1109/72.159058 PMID:18276468

Palma-dos-Reis, A., & Zahedi, F. M. (1999). Designing personalized intelligent financial support systems. *Decision Support Systems*, *26*(1), 31–47. doi:10.1016/S0167-9236(99)00027-5

Pandey, S. C., & Dutta, A. (2013). Role of knowledge infrastructure capabilities in knowledge management. *Journal of Knowledge Management*, *17*(3), 435–453. doi:10.1108/JKM-11-2012-0365

Park, H. I., & Kim, Y. T. (2011). Prediction of strength of reinforced lightweight soil using an artificial neural network. *Engineering Computations: International Journal for Computer-Aided Engineering and Software*, *28*(5), 600–615. doi:10.1108/02644401111141037

Pota, M., Exposito, M., & de Pietro, G. (2014). Fuzzy partitioning for clinical DSSs using statistical information transformed into possibility-based knowledge. *Knowledge-Based Systems*, *67*, 1–15. doi:10.1016/j.knosys.2014.06.021

Power, D. J., & Sharda, R. (2007). Model-driven decision support systems: Concepts and research directions. *Decision Support Systems*, *43*(3), 1044–1061. doi:10.1016/j.dss.2005.05.030

Qian, Z., Huang, G. H., & Chan, C. W. (2004). Development of an intelligent decision support system for air pollution control at coal-fired power plants. *Expert Systems with Applications*: An International Journal, *26*(3), 335–356. doi:10.1016/j.eswa.2003.09.005

Qiu, R. G., Tang, Y., & Xu, Q. (2006). Integration design of material flow management in an e-business manufacturing environment. *Decision Support Systems*, *42*(2), 1104–1115. doi:10.1016/j.dss.2005.10.005

Quintero, A., Konare, D., & Pierre, S. (2005). Prototyping an intelligent decision support system for improving urban infrastructures management. *European Journal of Operational Research*, *162*(3), 654–672. doi:10.1016/j.ejor.2003.10.019

Rehman, S., & Marouf, L. (2004). Human resources for information management operations in Kuwaiti corporate companies. *Information Management & Computer Security*, *12*(2), 191–201. doi:10.1108/09685220410530825

Russell, S. J., & Norvig, P. (2003). *Artificial Intelligence: A modern approach*. Upper Saddle River, NJ: Prentice Hall.

Sajjad, A., & Slobodan, P. S. (2006). An intelligent decision support system for management of floods. *Water Resources Management*, *20*(3), 391–410. doi:10.1007/s11269-006-0326-3

Salamon, T. (2011). *Design of agent-based models*. Repin, Czech Republic: Bruckner Publishing.

Shahrabi, J., Hadavandi, E., & Esfandarani, M. S. (2013). Developing a hybrid intelligent model for constructing a size recommendation expert system in textile industries. *International Journal of Clothing Science and Technology*, *25*(5), 338–349. doi:10.1108/IJCST-04-2012-0015

Shim, J. P., Warkentin, M., Counrtney, J. F., Power, D. J., Sharda, R., & Carlsson, C. (2002). Past, present, and future of decision support technology. *Decision Support Systems*, *33*(2), 111–126. doi:10.1016/S0167-9236(01)00139-7

Swanepoel, K. T. (2004). Decision support system: Real-time control of manufacturing processes. *Journal of Manufacturing Technology Management*, *15*(1), 68–75. doi:10.1108/09576060410512338

Tai, W. S., & Chen, C. T. (2009). A new evaluation model for intellectual capital based on computing with linguistic variable. *Expert Systems with Applications: An International Journal*, *36*(2), 3483–3488. doi:10.1016/j.eswa.2008.02.017

Turban, E., Aronson, J. E., & Liang, T. P. (2005). *Decision support systems and intelligent systems*. Upper Saddle River, NJ: Prentice Hall.

Turban, E., Aronson, J. E., Liang, T. P., & Sharda, R. (2007). *Decision support and business intelligence systems*. Upper Saddle River, NJ: Prentice Hall.

Turban, E., Volonio, L., McLean, E., & Wetherbe, J. (2009). *Information technology for management: Transforming organizations in the digital economy*. New York, NY: John Wiley & Sons.

Vakili-Ardebili, A., & Boussabaine, A. H. (2007). Application of fuzzy techniques to develop an assessment framework for building design eco-drivers. *Building and Environment*, *42*(11), 3785–3800. doi:10.1016/j.buildenv.2006.11.017

van de Water, H., & van Peet, H. P. (2006). A decision support model based on the analytic hierarchy process for the make or buy decision in manufacturing. *Journal of Purchasing and Supply Management*, *12*(5), 258–271. doi:10.1016/j.pursup.2007.01.003

Viademonte, S., & Burstein, F. (2006). *From knowledge discovery to computational intelligence: A framework for intelligent decision support systems*. London, UK: Springer–Verlag.

Vinodh, S., & Kumar, C. D. (2012). Development of computerized decision support system for leanness assessment using multi grade fuzzy approach. *Journal of Manufacturing Technology Management*, *23*(4), 503–516. doi:10.1108/17410381211230457

Waiman, C., Leung, L. C., & Tam, P. C. F. (2005). An intelligent decision support system for service network planning. *Decision Support Systems*, *39*(3), 415–428. doi:10.1016/j.dss.2003.09.007

Wang, W. P. (2010). A fuzzy linguistic computing approach to supplier evaluation. *Applied Mathematical Modelling*, *34*(10), 3130–3141. doi:10.1016/j.apm.2010.02.002

Weyns, D., Omicini, A., & Odell, J. (2007). Environment as a first-class abstraction in multiagent systems. *Autonomous Agents and Multi-Agent Systems*, *14*(1), 5–30. doi:10.1007/s10458-006-0012-0

Wooldridge, M. (2002). *An introduction to multiagent systems*. New York, NY: John Wiley & Sons.

Wu, J. Y. (2010). *Computational intelligence-based intelligent business intelligence system: Concept and framework*. Paper presented at the 2nd International Conference on Computer and Network Technology (ICCNT 2010), Bangkok, Thailand. doi:10.1109/ICCNT.2010.23

Xirogiannis, G., Chytas, P., Glykas, M., & Valiris, G. (2008). Intelligent impact assessment of IIRM to the shareholder value. *Expert Systems with Applications: An International Journal*, *35*(4), 2017–2031. doi:10.1016/j.eswa.2007.08.103

Yang, S. L., & Li, T. F. (2002). Agility evaluation of mass customization product manufacturing. *Journal of Materials Processing Technology*, *129*(1/3), 640–644. doi:10.1016/S0924-0136(02)00674-X

Zadeh, L. A. (1965). Fuzzy sets. *Information and Control*, *8*(3), 338–353. doi:10.1016/S0019-9958(65)90241-X

Zadeh, L. A. (1973). Outline of a new approach to the analysis of complex systems and decision processes. *IEEE Transactions on Systems, Man, and Cybernetics*, *3*(1), 28–44. doi:10.1109/TSMC.1973.5408575

Zadeh, L. A. (1975). The concept of a linguistic variable and its application to approximate reasoning. *Information Sciences*, *8*(3), 199–249. doi:10.1016/0020-0255(75)90036-5

Zadeh, L. A. (1996). Fuzzy logic equals computing with words. *IEEE Transactions on Fuzzy Systems*, *4*(2), 103–111. doi:10.1109/91.493904

Zhao, K., & Yu, X. (2011). A case based reasoning approach on supplier selection in petroleum enterprises. *Expert Systems with Applications: An International Journal*, *38*(6), 6839–6847. doi:10.1016/j.eswa.2010.12.055

ADDITIONAL READING

Ahmed, Z., Noor, R. A. M., & Zhang, J. (2009). Multiple neural networks modelling techniques in process control: A review. *Asian Pacific Journal of Chemical Engineering*, *4*(4), 403–417. doi:10.1002/apj.213

Aksoy, A., Ozturk, N., & Sucky, E. (2012). A decision support system for demand forecasting in the clothing industry. *International Journal of Clothing Science and Technology*, *24*(4), 221–236. doi:10.1108/09556221211232829

Altiparmak, F., Gen, M., Lin, L., & Karaoglan, I. (2009). A steady-state genetic algorithm for multi-product supply chain network design. *Computers & Industrial Engineering*, *56*(2), 521–537. doi:10.1016/j. cie.2007.05.012

Asadi, S., Hadavandi, E., Mehmanpazir, F., & Nakhostin, M. (2012). Hybridization of evolutionary Levenberg-Marquardt neural networks and data pre-processing for stock market prediction. *Knowledge-Based Systems*, *35*, 245–258. doi:10.1016/j.knosys.2012.05.003

Bakhrankova, K. (2010). Decision support system for continuous production. *Industrial Management & Data Systems*, *110*(4), 591–610. doi:10.1108/02635571011039043

Bottani, E. (2009). A fuzzy QFD approach to achieve agility. *International Journal of Production Economics*, *119*(2), 380–391. doi:10.1016/j.ijpe.2009.02.013

Calabuig, D., Monserrat, J. F., Gomez-Barquero, D., & Lazaro, O. (2008). An efficient dynamic resource allocation algorithm for packet-switched communication networks based on Hopfield neural excitation method. *Neurocomputing*, *71*(16/18), 3439–3446. doi:10.1016/j.neucom.2007.10.009

Chang, I. C., Hwang, H. G., Liaw, H. C., Hung, M. C., Chen, S. L., & Yen, D. C. (2008). A neural network evaluation model for ERP performance from SCM perspective to enhance enterprise competitive advantage. *Expert Systems with Applications: An International Journal*, *35*(4), 1809–1816. doi:10.1016/j. eswa.2007.08.102

Chang, P. C., Fan, C. Y., & Dzan, W. Y. (2010). A CBR-based fuzzy decision tree approach for database classification. *Expert Systems with Applications: An International Journal*, *37*(1), 214–225. doi:10.1016/j. eswa.2009.04.062

Chen, W. S., & Du, Y. K. (2009). Using neural networks and data mining techniques for the financial distress prediction model. *Expert Systems with Applications: An International Journal*, *36*(2), 4075–4086. doi:10.1016/j.eswa.2008.03.020

Cheng, J., Chen, H., & Lin, Y. (2010). A hybrid forecast marketing timing model based on probabilistic neural network, rough set and C4.5. *Expert Systems with Applications: An International Journal*, *37*(4), 1814–1820. doi:10.1016/j.eswa.2009.07.019

Ding, L., & Matthews, J. (2009). A contemporary study into the application of neural network techniques employed to automate CAD/CAM integration for die manufacture. *Computers & Industrial Engineering*, *57*(4), 1457–1471. doi:10.1016/j.cie.2009.01.006

Doraid, D., & Bataineh, O. (2009). A fuzzy logic approach to the selection of the best silicon crystal slicing technology. *Expert Systems with Applications: An International Journal*, *36*(2), 3712–3719. doi:10.1016/j.eswa.2008.02.020

Engin, O., Celik, A., & Kaya, I. (2008). A fuzzy approach to define sample size for attributes control chart in multistage processes: An application in engine valve manufacturing process. *Applied Soft Computing*, *8*(4), 1654–1663. doi:10.1016/j.asoc.2008.01.005

Guo, Z. X., Wong, W. K., Leung, S. Y. S., & Fan, J. T. (2009). Intelligent production control decision support system for flexible assembly lines. *Expert Systems with Applications: An International Journal*, *36*(3), 4268–4277. doi:10.1016/j.eswa.2008.03.023

Hadavandi, E., Shavandi, H., & Ghanbari, A. (2011). An improved sales forecasting approach by the integration of genetic fuzzy systems and data clustering: Case study of printed circuit board. *Expert Systems with Applications: An International Journal*, *38*(8), 9392–9399. doi:10.1016/j.eswa.2011.01.132

Hanafizadeh, P., & Sherkat, M. H. (2009). Designing fuzzy-genetic learner model based on multi-agent systems in supply chain management. *Expert Systems with Applications: An International Journal*, *36*(6), 10120–10134. doi:10.1016/j.eswa.2009.01.008

Irani, Z., Sharif, A. M., & Love, P. E. D. (2009). Mapping knowledge management and organizational learning in support of organizational memory. *International Journal of Production Economics*, *122*(1), 200–215. doi:10.1016/j.ijpe.2009.05.020

Kahraman, C., Kaya, I., & Cinar, D. (2010). Computational intelligence: Past, today and future. In D. Ruan (Ed.), *Computational intelligence in complex decision systems* (pp. 1–46). Paris, France: Atlantis Press. doi:10.2991/978-94-91216-29-9_1

Kalogirou, S., Lalot, S., Florides, G., & Desmet, B. (2008). Development of a neural network-based fault diagnostic system for solar thermal applications. *Solar Energy*, *82*(2), 164–172. doi:10.1016/j.solener.2007.06.010

Kaya, I. (2009). A genetic algorithm approach to determine the sample size for control charts with variables and attributes. *Expert Systems with Applications: An International Journal*, *36*(5), 8719–8734. doi:10.1016/j.eswa.2008.12.011

Kazemi, S. M. R., Hadavandi, E., Mehmanpazir, F., & Nakhostin, M. (2013). A hybrid intelligent approach for modeling brand choice and constructing a market response simulator. *Knowledge-Based Systems*, *40*, 101–110. doi:10.1016/j.knosys.2012.11.016

Lam, C. H. Y., Choy, K. L., & Chung, S. H. (2011). A decision support system to facilitate warehouse order fulfillment in cross-border supply chain. *Journal of Manufacturing Technology Management*, *22*(8), 972–983. doi:10.1108/17410381111177430

Lau, H. C. W., Ho, G. T. S., Zhao, Y., & Chung, N. S. H. (2009). Development of a process mining system for supporting knowledge discovery in a supply chain network. *International Journal of Production Economics*, *122*(1), 176–187. doi:10.1016/j.ijpe.2009.05.014

Lin, R. H., Chuang, C. L., Lion, J. J. H., & Wu, G. D. (2009). An integrated method for finding key suppliers in SCM. *Expert Systems with Applications: An International Journal*, *36*(3), 6461–6465. doi:10.1016/j.eswa.2008.07.078

Liu, Q., Sun, S. X., Wang, H., & Zhao, J. (2011). A multi-agent based system for e-procurement exception management. *Knowledge-Based Systems*, 24(1), 49–57. doi:10.1016/j.knosys.2010.07.004

Nan, C., Khan, F., & Iqbal, M. T. (2008). Real-time fault diagnosis using knowledge-based expert system. *Process Safety and Environmental Protection*, 86(1), 55–71. doi:10.1016/j.psep.2007.10.014

Pham, H. V., Tran, K. D., & Kamei, K. (2014). Applications using hybrid intelligent decision support systems for selection of alternatives under uncertainty and risk. *International Journal of Innovative Computing, Information, & Control*, 10(1), 39–56.

Salehi, M., & Tavakkoli-Moghaddam, R. (2009). Application of genetic algorithm to computer-aided process planning in preliminary and detailed planning. *Engineering Applications of Artificial Intelligence*, 22(8), 1179–1187. doi:10.1016/j.engappai.2009.04.005

Shehab, T., & Farooq, M. (2013). Neural network cost estimating model for utility rehabilitation projects. *Engineering, Construction, and Architectural Management*, 20(2), 118–126. doi:10.1108/09699981311302991

Stubbings, P., Virninas, B., Owusu, G., & Voudouris, C. (2008). Modular neural networks for recursive collaborative forecasting in the service chain. *Knowledge-Based Systems*, 21(6), 450–457. doi:10.1016/j.knosys.2008.03.021

Verlinden, B., Duflou, J. R., Collin, P., & Cattrysse, D. (2008). Cost estimation for sheet metal parts using multiple regression and artificial neural networks: A case study. *International Journal of Production Economics*, 111(2), 484–492. doi:10.1016/j.ijpe.2007.02.004

Vinodh, S., & Balaji, S. R. (2011). Fuzzy logic based leanness assessment and its decision support system. *International Journal of Production Research*, 49(13), 4027–4041. doi:10.1080/00207543.2010.492408

Vosniakos, G. C., Galiotou, V., Pantelis, D., Benardos, P., & Pavlou, P. (2009). The scope of artificial neural network metamodels for precision casting process planning. *Robotics and Computer-integrated Manufacturing*, 25(6), 909–916. doi:10.1016/j.rcim.2009.04.018

Xiong, N., Yang, L. T., & Li, Y. (2009). ODMCA: An adaptive data mining control algorithm in multicarrier networks. *Computer Communications*, 32(3), 560–567. doi:10.1016/j.comcom.2008.08.026

Yuan, F. C. (2009). The use of a fuzzy logic-based system in cost-volume-profit analysis under uncertainty. *Expert Systems with Applications: An International Journal*, 36(2), 1155–1163. doi:10.1016/j.eswa.2007.11.025

Yun, Y., Moon, C., & Kim, D. (2009). Hybrid genetic algorithm with adaptive local search scheme for solving multistage-based supply chain problems. *Computers & Industrial Engineering*, 56(3), 821–838. doi:10.1016/j.cie.2008.09.016

Zammori, F. A., Braglia, M., & Frosolini, M. (2009). A fuzzy multi-criteria approach for critical path definition. *International Journal of Project Management*, 27(3), 278–291. doi:10.1016/j.ijproman.2008.03.006

KEY TERMS AND DEFINITIONS

Artificial Intelligence: The branch of computer science that develops intelligent machines and software.

Artificial Neural Network: The computational system of interconnected neurons that can compute values from inputs by feeding information through the network.

Decision Support System: The computer system designed to provide the assistance in determining and evaluating the alternative courses of action.

Enterprise Information Management: The particular field of interest within information technology about finding solutions for the optimal use of information within organizations.

Evolutionary Computation: The subfield of artificial intelligence that involves the continuous optimization and combinatorial optimization problems.

Fuzzy Logic: The type of reasoning based on the recognition that logical statements are not only true or false but can also range from "almost certain" to "very unlikely" condition.

Intelligent Decision Support Systems: The decision support systems that make extensive use of artificial intelligence techniques.

Multi-Agent System: The computerized system composed of multiple intelligent agents within an organization.

Section 2
Developing Web Mining Systems

Chapter 5
Web Data Mining in Education:
Decision Support by Learning Analytics with Bloom's Taxonomy

Wing Shui Ng
The Education University of Hong Kong, Hong Kong

ABSTRACT

Web data mining for extracting meaningful information from large amount of web data has been explored over a decade. The concepts and techniques have been borrowed into the education sector and the new research discipline of learning analytics has emerged. With the development of web technologies, it has been a common practice to design online collaborative learning activities to enhance learning. To apply learning analytics techniques to monitor the online collaborative process enables a lecturer to make instant and informed pedagogical decisions. However, it is still a challenge to build strong connection between learning analytics and learning science for understanding cognitive progression in learning. In this connection, this chapter reports a study to apply learning analytics techniques in the aspect of web usage mining and clustering analysis with underpinning Bloom's taxonomy to analyze students' performance in the online collaborative learning process. The impacts of intermediate interventions are also elaborated.

INTRODUCTION

Techniques for web data mining has been developed over a decade. It aims to extract large amount of data collected over the web for further analysis to obtain useful information. Based on the purposes and natures, an analysis is usually categorized into one of the three aspects of web data mining, namely web content mining, web structure mining and web usage mining (Sakthipriya et al., 2015). Applications of web data mining can be found in different areas such as e-commerce (Verma et al., 2015), social networking (Russell, 2013) and health care (Lai & Shi, 2015). Enlightened by the impacts of web data mining, related concepts and techniques have been borrowed to the eduation sector since 2011 and the new research area of learning analytics has emerged. Baker and Inventado (2014) suggested that educational data mining is concerned with the analysis of large scale educational data using data mining methods.

DOI: 10.4018/978-1-5225-1877-8.ch005

In the first International Conference on Learning Analytics and Knowledge held in 2011, learning analytics was defined as "the measurement, collection, analysis and reporting of data about learners and their contexts, for purposes of understanding and optimizing learning and the environments in which it occurs". It is a newly emerging research discipline rooted from business intelligence and web analytics which focuses on handling large amount of data collected from websites using computer technologies (Siemens, 2012; Ferguson, 2012). As emphasized by Larusson and White (2014), learning analytics is an ideal strategy to look into the learning process. Results obtained can be fed back into the learning and teaching process for making decisions to adapt subsequent pedagogy for further enhancing teaching effectiveness. The U.S. Department of Education (2012) also stated that it is important to ensure that key decisions about learning are informed by data. The learning analytics, therefore, helps understand the learning system and supports decision making in an educational setting.

With the development of web technologies, it has been a common practice to integrate online collaborative learning activities in designing courses in higher education (e.g. Lai & Ng, 2011, Brindley et al., 2009). The educational benefits of online collaborative learning have been confirmed in numerous studies (Chiong & Jovanovic, 2012). However, in the development of assessing online collaborative learning, most previous studies incorporated measurement on learning only after the collaborative activities by filling out a self-report questionnaire, reviewing the products, interviewing participants for collecting feedback and carrying out after collaboration observation (Gress et al., 2010). The lecturer was hard to provide instant feedback to learners and almost impossible to make decisions to adapt teaching strategies. Few research can be found to monitor and assess the online collaborative process. Actually, researchers has raised the importance to look into the online learning process for making decisions to adapt teaching strategies for enhancing students' learning (Lera-Lopez et al., 2010). This rationale aligns with the purpose of assessment for learning. Under the rationale of assessment for learning, the first priority of assessment design and practice is to serve the purpose of pupils' learning (Black & Wiliam, 2003). The collected evidence is used to adapt the learning and teaching strategies so as to meet the learning needs (Black & Wiliam, 1998). However, to analyze online learning process can be regarded as highly complicated (Gress et al., 2010). It is also very labor intensive to process large amount of data when the class size is large and participation is high (Persico et al., 2010; Brookhart et al. 2010; MacPhail & Halbert, 2010). Since the main purpose of learning analytics is to analyze large amount of data, related concepts and techniques can be considered as a possible solution to analyze the online learning process so as to make further decisions on pedagogy.

However, the development of research on learning analytics is still in an early stage. One of the challenges of learning analytics is to build strong connection with the area of learning sciences (Ferguson, 2012). Although some researchers attempted to suggest methods to analyze the online learning process (Mazzoni & Gaffuri, 2010; Lera-Lopez et al., 2010; Pantaleon & Saiz, 2010; Trentin, 2009), learning theory was seldom incorporated in the framework of analysis. The measurement of learning progression was mainly based on students' performance in different points of evaluation. The inadequacy is that the methods suggested in previous studies cannot evaluate at which cognitive level of learning the student achieved. It is therefore not easy to make decisions on the way forward for improvement. Therefore, although related measurement and assessment strategies helps to track students' participations in online learning environment and different reports or charts may provide some reference information, the design of an analysis that based on sound learning theory for understanding cognitive progression to make informed decisions is still a challenge.

In this chapter, the author reports a case study of web data mining in education, and elaborates how analyses were carried out and how instructional decisions were made in the process. The design of learning activities and the analytical framework were based on Bloom's (1956) taxonomy of learning. According to Bloom's (1956) taxonomy, learning is classified into six progressive levels, namely knowledge, comprehension, application, analysis, synthesis and evaluation. The author applied learning analytics techniques in the aspect of web usage mining to analyze students' performance in the online learning process. Intervention decisions were made based on the analysis of participation records retrieved from the wiki platform together with the Bloom's taxonomy. The author also conducted clustering analysis to evaluate students' performance between groups. This chapter also reports how students improved in their performance after applying some intermediate interventions in the learning process.

In the following sections, the benefits and challenges of assessing online collaboration process are discussed. The author then elaborates a case study of online collaborative learning designed based on Bloom's taxonomy. It is followed by the introduction of the assessment framework with the concepts of learning analytics. The interpretation of analytical results will then be presented. At the end of this chapter, the contributions of this study will be systematically summarized.

Benefits of Online Collaborative Learning

Collaborative learning has been recognized as an effective pedagogy in education and related research have been developed across different disciplines (O'Donnell & Hmelo-Silver, 2013). Roschelle and Teasley (1995) considered collaborative learning as the co-construction of shared understanding while Littleton and Hakkinen (1999) supplemented that collaboration not only involves the construction of meaning through interaction with others but it can also be characterized by a joint commitment to a shared goal. The underlying rationale of collaborative learning is rooted in the epistemology of constructionism which stresses that truth, or meaning, comes into existence in and out of our engagement with the realities in our world. This school of thought advocates that meaning is not discovered, but constructed and no meaning exists without a mind. Subject and object emerge as partners in the generation of meaning (Crotty, 1998). The rationale of collaborative learning is also underpinned by the socio-cultural perspective of learning suggested by Vygotsky (1978). In Vygotsky's perspective, education and cognitive development are regarded as cultural processes. Knowledge is not only possessed by individuals but it is also shared amongst the communities. People jointly construct understandings by their involvement and interactions in the events which are shaped by cultural and historical factors. From the socio-cultural perspective, learning occurs in the mental process of social interaction and dialogue. Students thereby can learn by negotiating and collaborating with others (McLoughlin & Marshall, 2000). Fernandez et al. (2001) further suggested that students are able to proceed to the "Intermental Development Zone" (IDZ) by collaborative processes. The IDZ is considered as a characteristic of dialogical phenomenon, created and maintained between people with similar status or abilities in interaction. They claimed that any joint, goal-directed task must involve the creation and maintenance of a dynamic, contextual basis of shared knowledge and understanding.

With the development of web technologies, web-based collaborative learning or sometimes called online collaborative learning has become practical with high potential for knowledge acquisition (Hron &Friedrich, 2003). Web-based technologies support both synchronous and asynchronous collaboration. The asynchronous mode of web-based collaboration allows participants to engage in collaborative tasks anytime, anywhere which is most suitable for distributed learning. Actually, rich research on different aspects of online collaborative learning can be found in the literature in recent years. For example, a Web 2.0 tool was used in the collaborative learning processes for training early childhood student teachers (Lai & Ng, 2011). Gress and his colleagues (2010) conducted a meta-analysis of research on measurement and assessment in computer-supported collaborative learning. Brindley with his research team (2009) focused on creating effective collaborative learning groups in an online environment. So and Brush (2008) also reported a study to explore student perceptions of collaborative learning, social presence and satisfaction. Actually, the educational benefits of online collaborative learning have been confirmed in numerous studies (Chiong & Jovanovic, 2012).

Challenges of Monitoring and Assessing Online Collaborative Process

Notwithstanding the benefits of online collaborative learning have been advocated, certain challenges are still to be tackled for maximizing its effectiveness. As mentioned by Lera-Lopez and his colleagues (2010), it is important to monitor the learning process since various educational benefits can be obtained. The practice of monitoring learning process helps to identify at-risk students who are not willing to participate in learning activities and aware possible unbalanced assignment of tasks within a group. These information allows lecturer to improve the instructional strategies to achieve better learning outcomes. Students can also have better learning motivation and performance since timely feedback could be provided by the lecturer. In traditional education with little application of technologies in learning, it was very hard for a lecturer to understand and monitor the collaborative process when students engaged in a group project since the process of collaboration was a black box and it was difficult to gather process data for analysis. In addition, when the class size is large and participation is high, it is a very labor intensive task for lecturers to gather evidence of students' learning for analysis and hard to provide instant feedback (Persico et al., 2010; Brookhart et al. 2010; MacPhail & Halbert, 2010). When the collaborative process is supported by computer equipment, the analysis of collaborative learning process becomes relatively feasible since computer systems usually incorporate features to log participants' online activities and afford the potential for collaborative process analysis. In the current status of software development, student-tracking capabilities are typically included in online learning systems (Ferguson, 2012).

Despite the value of analyzing online collaborative process has been recognized, some researchers raised their concerns on the measurement and assessment in computer-supported collaborative process (Gress et al., 2010; Pantaleon & Saiz, 2010). As stressed by Gress and his colleagues (2010), analysis of collaborative process is highly complex and challenging since it involves:

- The measurement of cognitive progression of individuals and the whole group.
- The measurement of individual differences.
- A meaningful assessment for the process.
- An analytical method for understanding the process.

This is why most previous studies incorporated measurement on learning only after the collaborative activities by self-report questionnaires, products, interview, feedback and after collaboration observation (Gress et al., 2010).

To tackle the challenges, some researchers attempted to propose methods to assess the online collaborative process with analytical method to identify individual differences. In the study by Mazzoni and Gaffuri (2010), a quantitative model for monitoring activity in e-learning based on web tracking and social network analysis was proposed. The data collected by web tracking was used to analyze individuals' actions within a web environment while the social network analysis was applied to analyze the roles of members during collaborative activities. Some researchers (Lera-Lopez et al., 2010; Pantaleon & Saiz, 2010) proposed a set of reports and charts for tracking and assessing students' performance in online learning activities. In another study by Trentin (2009), data was extracted in a wiki platform to evaluate individual contribution to a collaborative project. Students' participations were put into different categories. The evaluation of individual contribution was based on a formula with different weighting assigned to different categories of participations. Different tables and charts were generated accordingly for analysis.

In recent years, some researchers attempted to apply learning analytics techniques to evaluate students' performance in online collaborative learning process. For example, Xing and his colleagues (2014, 2015) suggested to integrate activity theory in learning analytics to assess individual and group learning performance during online collaborative process. The analysis was based on the values of six indicators in the activity theory, namely subject, object, rules, division of labor, tools and community. In the study conducted by Fidalgo-Blanco and her colleagues (2015), they applied a learning analytics system to improve teamwork assessment. Results showed that timely information provided by the learning analytics system enable preventing problems, carrying out corrective measures and making decisions to improve collaborative learning process. Moreover, Leeuwen and his colleagues (2015) attempted to use learning analytics for teacher regulation of cognitive activities during students' collaborative process. Results suggested that, with the assistance of learning analytics software, teacher were not better at detecting problematic groups. However, teachers were more confident to offer more support in general and students could thereby benefit.

In the aforementioned studies, it is undeniable that related statistical reports or charts and proposed analytical model enable a lecturer to have better understanding on students' performance in the online learning process. However, certain limitations exist in these studies. Related proposed models or evaluation methods attempt to integrate data from different dimensions into analysis. Although relatively detailed analyses on the collaborative learning process can be obtained, the proposed models or the evaluation process are inevitably complicated from educational practitioners' point of view. It affects the feasibility on actual application of the evaluation models. Moreover, the evaluation method suggested by Trentin (2009) largely depends on the qualitative analysis of contents data. The analysis becomes impossible when students' participation is high and many online learning activities are included in the process since human interpretation of contents is inevitably involved. In addition, related suggested analyses mainly focus on identifying individual differences. Few research can be found to propose strategies to measure cognitive progression of individuals and the whole group. In these studies, learning theory was seldom incorporated in the framework of analysis and the measurement of learning progression was mainly based on performance in different points of evaluation. The inadequacy is that these proposed methods for assessing online collaborative process cannot evaluate at which level of learning the student achieved. It is therefore not easy to figure out the way forward for improvement. Therefore, although related measurement and assessment strategies suggested in previous studies helps to track students' participations in online collaborative environment and different reports or charts provides some reference information, the analysis based on sound learning theory for understanding cognitive progression is still a challenge. This perspective was also stressed by Ferguson (2012) as one of the future challenges for the development of learning analytics.

TAXONOMY OF LEARNING TO MEASURE COGNITIVE PROGRESSION

In order to measure cognitive progression in learning, there must be a tool to classify the mastery of learning into different levels. In the literature, two different systems of taxonomy of learning are suggested for reference, which are the Bloom's taxonomy (Bloom, 1956) and the structure of the observed learning outcome (SOLO) taxonomy (Biggs & Collis, 1982). These systems of taxonomy enable a lecture to design learning activities in different cognitive levels and serve as frameworks to evaluate students' cognitive progression during learning process.

Bloom's Taxonomy

According to Bloom (1956), the mastery of learning can be categorized into 6 levels. The lowest level of learning is "Knowledge". It includes those behaviors and test situation which emphasize the remembering of ideas, materials or phenomena. Student is expected to store some information in his mind and recall related information in an occasion later. Student may not actually understand related information. The next higher level of learning suggested by Bloom is "Comprehension". The focus is the understanding on the materials during communication. Materials may be in oral or written form and it can be presented in verbal, pictorial or symbolic form on paper. Students who developed comprehension are able to translate the communication into other language, into other terms or into another form of communication. They are also able to demonstrate the behaviors of interpretation by reordering ideas into new configuration in the mind and the behaviors of extrapolation by making estimates or prediction based on understanding. The next higher level of learning in Bloom's taxonomy is "Application". A student reaches the application level of learning if he can correctly use his knowledge or the abstraction under an appropriate situation in which no mode of solution is specified. To advance beyond application, the next higher level of learning is "Analysis". According to Bloom (1956), the process of analysis "emphasizes the breakdown of the material into its constituent parts and detection of the relationships of the parts and of the way they are organized" (p. 144). The skill in comprehending the interrelationships among the ideas in a passage and the ability to infer the author's point of view or concept of philosophy are examples of analytical skills. To proceed further in the level of learning, Bloom (1956) suggested the level of "Synthesis" which requires a student to put together elements and parts so as to form a whole. It involves the combination of parts of previous experience with new material and to reconstruct it into a new and well-integrated whole. In Bloom's taxonomy, the highest level of learning is "Evaluation". Evaluation, according to Bloom, is defined as "the making of judgments about the value, for some purposes, of ideas, works, solutions, methods, material, etc" (p. 185). It involves the use of criteria and standards for assessing to what extent a piece of work is accurate, effective, economical or satisfying. Figure 1 illustrates different levels of learning suggested by Bloom (1956).

SOLO Taxonomy

In SOLO taxonomy, Biggs and Collis (1982) considered learning as a cyclic pattern with 5 progressive levels. The lowest level of learning in this taxonomy is "prestructural". A student in this level attempts to engage in a task. However, he or she is distracted or misled by irrelevant previous knowledge or experiences. The next higher level is "unistructural". A learner in this level of learning is able to focus on the relevant domain and picks up one aspect to work with. To advance in the mastery of learning,

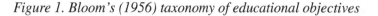
Figure 1. Bloom's (1956) taxonomy of educational objectives

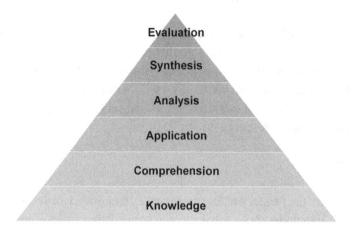

a learner is required to proceed to the next higher level of "multistructural". The learner achieved this level is able to deal with more than one relevant features of a specific domain. However, he or she cannot integrate various features at this stage. To obtain further improvement in learning, a learner is required to proceed to the "relational" level. In this level, the learner is able to integrate different parts together to form a coherent structure with particular meaning. The highest level of learning in SOLO taxonomy is "extended abstract". The learner is able to generalize the structure and integrate new and more abstract features so as to represent a new and higher mode of operation.

A main difference between Bloom's taxonomy and SOLO taxonomy is that the SOLO taxonomy was developed based on the cognitive development of school age children while the Bloom's taxonomy was developed in a more general educational context. Since the participants of this study were undergraduates, the learning theory of Bloom's taxonomy was considered more appropriate and was applied to underpin the analysis of students' performance in this study so as to investigate students' cognitive progression in the online collaborative learning process.

Context of the Study

The researcher is a teacher trainer in The Education University ofHong Kong for training and assessing pre-service and in-service teachers. This study was implemented in the course Information Technology in Education taught by the researcher. Four classes of first year pre-service kindergarten teachers taking the Higher Diploma in Early Childhood Education Programme with class size of about 40 and a total of 173 students were included in this study. The participants involved 170 females and 3 males. The course was designed to provide pre-service teachers with foundation knowledge on IT tools, multimedia and Internet technologies, and critical understanding of the application of information and communication technology to the solution of instructional problems from the perspective of related learning theories in the pre-primary school settings. Upon graduation, students were expected to work as kindergarten teachers in Hong Kong.

A major focus of the course is to explore the role of information technology in early childhood education. Actually, academics such as Yelland (2005), Clements and Nastasi (1992) had initiated vigorous debate about the role of technology in early childhood. They were concerned whether:

- Young children are physically and cognitively ready to use computers.
- The use of computers may inhibit children socio-emotional development.
- Computers can help develop problem-solving ability.
- The use is developmentally appropriate for young children (Clements & Nastasi, 1992).

Despite the existence of advocators' views, some early childhood educators opined that young children should not use computers. According to the literature review conducted by Yelland (2005), computers were deemed to be too abstract. It minimized the role of teachers and did not assist children to work collaboratively. As reflected by the literature, the issue of using information technology in early childhood education is found to be highly controversial.

In order to assist students to study the controversial issues, students were required to form groups by themselves with about 7 students in each group to carry out online collaborative learning activities. Six groups were formed in each class and a total of 24 groups were form in all four classes. Students in each group were required to critically discuss one of the following three controversial issues on using information and communication technology in early childhood education. Each discussion issue was assigned to two groups in each class for discussion. At the end of the learning activity, each group was required to submit a group report in Chinese of about 1000 words to elaborate their understanding on related issue.

Issues

1. A child's development in terms of creative thinking capability is inhibited by using information and communication technology.
2. A child's development in terms of social communication ability is inhibited by using information and communication technology.
3. Children are not secure when using the Internet.

All of these issues emphasize that information and communication technology is adverse to a child's development. The students were free to choose their own stances, either for or against the issue, in discussing these topics.

Instructional Design Underpinned by Bloom's Taxonomy

During the learning process, students were expected to have cognitive progression on the understanding of the controversial issue. Weekly online collaborative learning activities were designed as scaffolding for escalating the level of learning. The overall framework of the instructional design was based on the taxonomy of educational objectives suggested by Bloom (1956). In this case study, since the participants were students of tertiary level, all of them were assumed with the ability to achieve the lowest level of learning, "Knowledge", which focuses on recalling materials. After the researcher elaborated some fundamental materials concerning those controversial issues in week 1 of the course, students were instructed to carry out online collaborative learning at a wiki platform in the following weeks so as to develop more in-depth understanding on related issues. The scaffolding strategies were designed for escalating students to higher levels of learning. The instructional design for cognitive progression, including the descriptions of scaffolding strategies, its duration and the target level of learning, is elaborated in Table 1.

Table 1. Instructional design of online collaborative learning activities for cognitive progression

Duration	Scaffolding Strategies (Students were required to …)	Level of Learning
1 week	• Write their fundamental understanding on the controversial issue at the wiki platform. • Think about some keywords related to the controversial issue.	Comprehension
1 week	Apply their understanding of the controversial issue to search related learning resources and post it on the wiki platform.	Application
2 weeks	• Read at least 2 papers, identify main points or arguments and write a short summary for each paper. • Post the summaries on the wiki platform for sharing.	Analysis
2 weeks	Write a group report on their understanding of the controversial issue and post it on the wiki platform.	Synthesis
2 weeks	Carry out anonymous peer assessment to two peer reports of the same discussion issue in another class based on a set of provided rubric which adapted from that used in Xiao and Lucking's (2008) study.	Evaluation

Analysis of Online Collaborative Learning Process

The analysis of online collaborative process is a complicated task. Even though contents record and students' activities logging function is integrated in the wiki leaning platform, to achieve a meaningful analysis of data for monitoring cognitive progression is still a great challenge. In this case study, the students were required to carry out collaborative learning activities at a wiki platform. The wiki platform provides functions to record two main categories of participative information. The first category of information is the contents directly entered into the wiki page and the comments area. This type of information is contents-based which is related to the discussion of the controversial issue. The functions provided by wiki are for consolidating ideas. Another category is logging information of students' participation. A participation record includes the name of student, the date and time of updating wiki page contents or writing comments. Related information can be retrieved by the page revision history and comments log functions. Figure 2 and Figure 3 are examples of wiki page revision history and comments log respectively.

Although qualitative data such as page contents and comments allow a lecturer to obtain better understanding on students' learning, the efforts paid in qualitative data analysis are highly demanding since human judgments are inevitably involved. An example of research is that conducted by Trentin (2009) to evaluate individual contribution in a collaborative learning project using wiki. The proposed evaluation methods largely depend on the analysis of qualitative data. It is almost impossible to complete the analytical tasks when there are large number of participants and lots of collaborative activities. With this consideration, techniques of web usage mining were applied on the data obtained from the activities logging functions provided by the wiki platform as shown in Figure 2 and Figure 3.

Web Usage Mining

Web usage mining is a subcategory of web data mining to analyze data from log record on a web page to obtain meaningful information. A log record of a web usage usually consists of user identity, and the date and time of accesses (Bari & Chawan, 2013). The first step of web usage mining is data collection.

Figure 2. Example of wiki page revision history

Figure 3. Example of comments log

In this study, the user log information provided by the wiki platform was collected. Related information was extracted and put into spreadsheet software for further analysis. The required workload was considered affordable since similar processes were conducted every week to deal with limited information. The analytic process can be regarded as feasible. After obtaining web usage data, data cleaning is required to eliminate irrelevant items. In this study, the researcher only concerned the date of modifying a wiki page or writing a comment. It was required to remove the information regarding the time of access. In addition, the researcher required to convert the format of the date information so as to carry out further analysis. The next step of data preprocessing is user identification. In the wiki platform, the user identity information has already been included in the usage log. It was easy to identify the record of a particular user. After preparing the whole set of web usage data, analysis can be carried out to explore meaningful information for making further decisions. Related analyses conducted and intervention decisions made in this study are reported in the Results section.

Online Participation as Online Learning

The analyses in this study for evaluating students' learning were based on the quantity of students' participation in the online collaborative learning process. Actually, to evaluate students' performance based on participation has been supported by literature. For example, participation has been argued to be an intrinsic part of learning (Wenger, 1998). Barab and Duffy (2012) pointed out that the quantity of participation can be regarded as an important indicator of knowledge construction. According to the literature review conducted by Hrastinski (2009), more participations in the learning process create better learning effectiveness and result in positive impact on learning outcomes. Hrastinski (2009) further stressed that online participation drives online learning. Furthermore, participation also positively influences learner satisfaction (Alavi & Dufner, 2005) and knowledge retention (Rovai, 2002).

In addition to quantity of participation, the nature of participation is also a critical factor in the online collaborative learning process. To understand the nature of participation, Hrastinski (2008) classified 6 categories of participation with progressive level of engagement:

1. The fundamental level is simply to measure how many times a learner accesses an e-learning environment. No information can be shown on whether the learner has written or read any contents.
2. The second level is the participation as writing. A learner is more active when he or she writes some messages on the learning platform.
3. The third level is the participation as quality writing. The learner demonstrates active participation by providing high quality writing.
4. The fourth level involves participation as writing and reading. It is believed that the more reading and writing, the better the participation.
5. The fifth level is the participation as actual and perceived writing. A learner has deeper engagement in online collaborative tasks if he or she writes many messages that are perceived of importance.
6. The sixth level, which is the highest level, is the participation as taking part and joining in a dialogue.

In this study, students were required to take part in revising wiki pages and to participate in dialogues by sharing opinions in the comments area. It demonstrated the practice of high level of participation. In that connection, the definition of participation, "taking part and joining in a dialogue for engaged and active learning. Participation is more than the total number of student postings in a discussion forum." (p.

214), provided by Vonderwell and Zachariah (2005) was adopted in this study. In addition, the students were instructed to use their first language in online discussion. Research suggested that the students allowed to use first language in the learning process are able to work collaboratively in a more balanced and coherent manner. The learning performances, such as reading, thinking and other subsequence actions, are also better when first language is used in the learning process (Scott & Fuente, 2008). Therefore, although the evaluation of students' learning in this study was based on the number of participations in the online learning process, it is anticipate that reliable analysis could be achieved since related online learning activities involved high level of participations using first language.

RESULTS

On the basis of the instructional design, this section reports how analyses of web usage mining were conducted and how respective intervention decisions were made in the process. The impacts on students' learning performance are also elaborated.

Overall Participation Analysis

The first analysis concerning students' overall participation is shown in Figure 4. During the entire online collaborative learning process, all participants (173) generated a total of 1,537 records of participation. A critical difference of this analysis compared with that in other studies is the application of Bloom's taxonomy. Based on different stages of online learning activities as mentioned in Table 1, records of participation were grouped into different levels of learning suggested by Bloom. By using the Bloom's taxonomy, an overall understanding on students' cognitive progression can be achieved.

Actually, no absolute participation count could serve as a reference since the number of participation largely depends on the nature of the activities. As shown in Figure 4, the participation in the early "Comprehension" stage was relatively low. There were only 79 numbers of participation count generated from a total of 173 students. It implied that less than 50% of students participated in the online learning activities at this early stage. This unsatisfactory situation raised a signal to the researcher. However, it should be noted that results obtained from learning analytics only showed a picture of the actual situation. It did not reveal the underlying causes. The researcher was required to explore the reasons that lead to the happening of such results. Based on the researcher's observation and experiences of teaching in tertiary education, since all participants were first year students who newly joined the tertiary institute, it was believed that the students required to adapt to the learning style in tertiary education that expects students to behave as active learners. In addition, it took time for them to develop collaborative relationship. With these considerations, the researcher explained to the students the expectation of active learning in tertiary education in the next lesson and encouraged their collaboration. An immediate effect of this intervention was that students' participation increased to a great extent in the later "Application" and "Analysis" stages. This reflected that students had recognized the rationales of online collaborative learning and began to actively engage in the process. Intra-group momentum started to drive students' participation. In the "Synthesis" stage, the participation count was 288. It appeared that there was a significant decline in participation. A reasonable judgment of the situation was that the learning activities in these stages were mainly on group-based to prepare a group report and particular group members were responsible to update contents for the whole group. At the same time, students might engage in offline face-to-face discussion in which no participation records could be obtained. Since there were 24 groups of students engaged in online learning activities, the average participation count per group in that stage was 12. This could be considered as satisfactory and no action was deemed required. In the final "Evaluation" stage, the total participation count dropped to 85 and that was considered as unsatisfactory. As reported by the students, they were busy in dealing with assignments of other courses and the participation of online learning activities inevitably declined. As it had come to the end of the online learning activities, no further action was taken by the researcher.

Class-based Participation Analysis

Apart from obtaining an overall picture of students' participation, clustering analysis was conducted to look into the participation of each class so as to understand inter-class students' learning performance. Clustering analysis is to group the data of similar attributes or characteristics for further analysis (Sakthipriya et al., 2015). As shown in Figure 5, very low participation was found in Class D in the "Comprehension" stage. It raised the researcher's concern and actions were required to investigate the situation. After discussed with students, it was found that students in Class D did not fully understand the rationales of online collaborative learning strategy to enhance learning. The researcher then took immediate actions

Figure 4. Students' overall participation in different stages of online collaborative learning

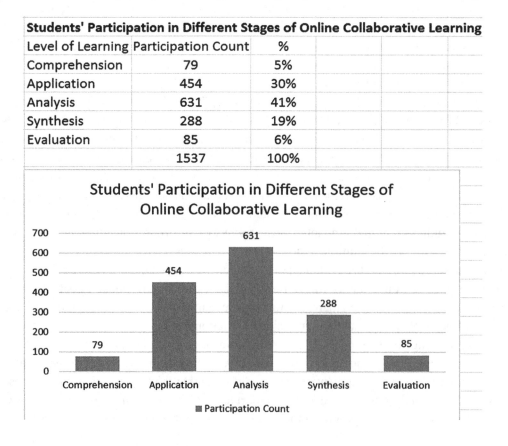

Students' Participation in Different Stages of Online Collaborative Learning		
Level of Learning	Participation Count	%
Comprehension	79	5%
Application	454	30%
Analysis	631	41%
Synthesis	288	19%
Evaluation	85	6%
	1537	100%

Figure 5. Class-based students' participation in different levels of online collaborative learning

Class-based Students' Parcitipation in Different Stages of Online Collaborative Learning					
Level of Learning	Class A	Class B	Class C	Class D	Total
Comprehension	35	20	20	4	79
Application	192	115	55	92	454
Analysis	168	180	104	179	631
Synthesis	73	80	63	72	288
Evaluation	22	38	20	5	85
	490	433	262	352	1537

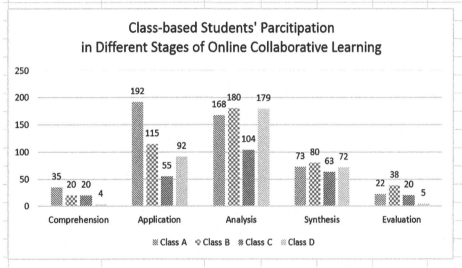

to reiterate the educational benefits of the instructional strategy to students in Class D again. With this reinforcement, students' participation in Class D improved in the following stages of learning.

Individual Participation Analysis

To obtain more in-depth understanding on the learning process, individual student's learning report could be generated after activities corresponding to each level of learning in Bloom's taxonomy. A lecturer could considered to rank all the students based on their participation counts, and look into those at risk students who had low participation. As shown in Figure 6, this student demonstrated satisfactory participation in "Comprehension", "Application", "Analysis" and "Synthesis" stages compared with the average participation of all students. However, no participation was found in the highest "Evaluation" stage. By conducting these analyses, the researcher was able to evaluate the depth of students' learning. As reflected in this example, it was believed that the student achieved the synthesis level of learning in Bloom's taxonomy but failed to escalate to the highest "Evaluation" level. It means that the student was able to compile a report to elaborate her understanding on the discussion issue. However, this student was not competent enough to evaluation the quality of a report. Apart from the purpose of making intermediate intervention, this analysis also enabled the researcher to allocate a justified assessment mark to students based on their participation in the online collaborative learning process.

Figure 6. Individual student's participation in different stages of online collaborative learning

Individual Student's Participation Report

Student	S...	
Class	C	
Group	D	
Discussion Issue	2	

Level	Student Participation Count	Average Particiation Count
Comprehension	3	0.5
Application	6	2.6
Analysis	6	3.6
Synthesis	11	1.7
Evaluation	0	0.5

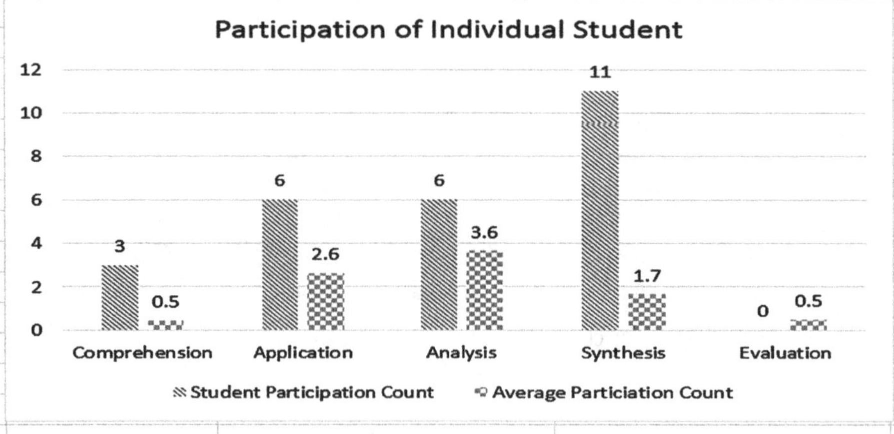

Participation of Individual Student

CONCLUSION

With the development of technology and the emphasis of investigating the learning process, learning analytics has emerged as a new research discipline. The development of learning analytics is still in its early stage and it demands academics' further efforts to explore its beneficial impacts in learning. Learning analytics is borrowed from the area web analytics which aims to process relatively large set of data obtained over the web. The purpose is to generate productive information to inform further pedagogical actions to improve learning and teaching. Enlightened by this newly emerged area of practice, this study introduced an instructional strategy which applied the rationales of learning analytics to analyse students' performance in the process of online collaborative learning.

As stressed by Gress and his colleagues (2010), the analysis of collaborative process is highly complicated and challenging. This study contributes to the field by tackling related challenges. First of all, it has been considered very hard to measure the cognitive progression of individuals and the whole group. In this study, individual (Figure 6) and class-based (Figure 5) progression reports are suggested to understand respective performance. More importantly, by using the Bloom's Taxonomy as a framework for analysis, reference information concerning students' cognitive progression, from surface to deep learning, can be obtained. The second challenge of assessing online collaboration is the difficulty on measuring individual differences. In this study, the report to compare individual participation and the average participation is suggested to explore individual difference (Figure 6). At the same time, a report of individual participation ranking can also be generated to identify at-risk students. In addition, Gress and his colleagues (2010) pointed out that it is a challenge to propose a meaningful analytical strategy for the process. In this study, students' participation counts was selected as an indicator on students' learning in the online collaborative process. As mentioned in previous section, evidence support that participation can serve as an important indicator of knowledge construction and it drives online learning (Barab & Duffy, 2012; Hrastinski, 2009; Rovai, 2002; Wenger, 1998). The setting in this study provoked meaningful discussion using first language in the form of taking part and joining in a dialogue. The quality of discussion could be maintained. The last challenge mentioned by Gress and his colleagues (2010) is the difficulty to identify an analytical method for understanding the process. In this connection, this study proposed to apply analyses in the aspect of web usage mining and clustering analysis with underpinning learning theory of Bloom's taxonomy. With this framework, lecturer can understand students' cognitive progression during the process from low level of learning, "Comprehension", to high level of learning, "Evaluation".

Since learning analytics mainly developed from the computer science discipline with main focus on the application of technologies, a main challenge is to build strong connections between learning analytics and learning science (Ferguson, 2012). In this study, a well-integrated design of instructional strategy and assessment framework using Bloom's taxonomy was proposed for the implementation of learning analytics. The Bloom's taxonomy of learning was developed in 1956 and it has obtained wide recognition regarding its understanding on learning. The application of Bloom's taxonomy in this study provided a strong connection among learning analytics and learning science. It enables a lecturer to make judgment on the level of learning of a particular student and to make early intervention.

Another merit of the strategy proposed in this study is that the whole instructional design can be regarded not complicated. The analytical process requires reasonable efforts to assess online collaborative learning process. It greatly enhances the feasibility of application from practitioners' point of view. The analysis of the online learning process allows a lecturer to provide timely feedback, and enables a lecturer to adapt instructional strategies to further improve students' learning. The results obtained from the analyses can also be served as a good reference for the allocation of assessment marks towards students' performance in the online collaborative process. With full elaborations of the instructional strategy in this study, it is believed that more understanding on students' learning performance in the online collaborative process can be achieved and appropriate interventions could be applied to further enhance learning effectiveness.

REFERENCES

Alavi, M., & Dufner, D. (2005). Technology-mediated collaborative learning: A research perspective. In S. R. Hiltz & R. Goldman (Eds.), *Learning together online: Research on asynchronous learning networks* (pp. 191–213). Mahwah, NJ: Lawrence Erlbaum.

Baker, R. S., & Inventado, P. S. (2014). Educational data mining and learning analytics. In J. A. Larusson & B. White (Eds.), *Learning analytics: from research to practice* (pp. 61–75). New York: Springer.

Barab, S. A., & Duffy, T. (2012). From practice fields to communities of practice. In D. Jonassen & S. Land (Eds.), *Theoretical foundation of learning environments* (pp. 29–65). New York: Routledge.

Bari, P., & Chawan, P. M. (2013). Web usage mining. *Journal of Engineering. Computers & Applied Sciences, 2*(6), 34–38.

Biggs, J. B., & Collis, K. F. (1982). *Evaluating the quality of learning: The SOLO taxonomy (Structure of the Observed Learning Outcome)*. London: Academic Press.

Black, P., & Wiliam, D. (1998). *Inside the black box: raising standards through classroom assessment.* London: GL Assessment.

Black, P., & Wiliam, D. (2003). In praise of educational research: Formative assessment. *British Educational Research Journal, 29*(5), 623–637. doi:10.1080/0141192032000133721

Bloom, B. S. (1956). *Taxonomy of educational objectives*. London: Longman.

Brindley, J. E., Walti, C., & Blaschke, L. M. (2009). Creating effective collaborative learning groups in an online environment. *The International Review of Research in Open and Distributed Learning, 10*(3), 1–18. doi:10.19173/irrodl.v10i3.675

Brookhart, S. M., Moss, C. M., & Long, B. A. (2010). Teacher inquiry into formative assessment practices in remedial reading classrooms. *Assessment in Education: Principles, Policy & Practice, 17*(1), 41–58. doi:10.1080/09695940903565545

Chiong, R., & Jovanovic, J. (2012). Collaborative learning in online study groups: An evolutionary game theory perspective. *Journal of Information Technology Education: Research, 11*, 81–101.

Clements, D. H., & Nastasi, B. K. (1992). Computers and early childhood education. In M. Gettinger, S. N. Elliott, & T. R. Kratochwill (Eds.), *Preschool and early childhood treatment directions* (pp. 187–246). London: Lawrence Erlbaum Associates.

Crotty, M. (1998). *The foundations of social research: meaning and perspective in the research process.* London: Sage.

Ferguson, R. (2012). Learning analytics: Drivers, developments and challenges. *International Journal of Technology Enhanced Learning, 4*(5-6).

Fernandez, M., Wegerif, R., Mercer, N., & Drummond, S. R. (2001). Re-conceptualizing "scaffolding" and the zone of proximal develoopment in the context of symmetrical collaborative learning. *Journal of Classroom Interaction, 36*(2), 40–54.

Fidalgo-Blanco, A., Sein-Echaluce, M. L., Garcia-Penalvo, F. J., & Conde, M. A. (2015). Using learning analytics to improve teamwork assessment. *Computers in Human Behavior, 47*, 149–156. doi:10.1016/j. chb.2014.11.050

Gress, C. L., Fior, M., Hadwin, A. F., & Winne, P. H. (2010). Measurement and assessment in computer-supported collaborative learning. *Computers in Human Behavior, 26*(5), 806–814. doi:10.1016/j. chb.2007.05.012

Hrastinski, S. (2008). What is online learner participation? A literature review. *Computers & Education*, *51*(4), 1755–1765. doi:10.1016/j.compedu.2008.05.005

Hrastinski, S. (2009). A theory of online learning as online participation. *Computers & Education*, *52*(1), 78–82. doi:10.1016/j.compedu.2008.06.009

Hron, A., & Friedrich, H. F. (2003). A review of web-based collaborative learning: Factors beyond technology. *Journal of Computer Assisted Learning*, *19*(1), 70–79. doi:10.1046/j.0266-4909.2002.00007.x

Lai, K. K., & Shi, J. (2015). An intelligence system based on social web mining and its application in health care in Hong Kong.*AFIN 2015: The Seventh International Conference on Advances in Future Internet* (pp. 42-46). Venice, Italy: IARIA.

Lai, Y. C., & Ng, W. S. (2011). Nurturing information literacy of early childhood teachers through web-based collaborative learning activities. *Hong Kong Journal of Early Childhood*, *10*(1), 77–83.

Larusson, J. A., & White, B. (2016). *Learning analytics: from research to practice*. New York: Springer.

Leeuwen, A., Janssen, J., Erkens, G., & Brekelmans, M. (2015). Teacher regulation of cognitive activities during student collaboration: Effects of learning analytics. *Computers & Education*, *90*, 80–94. doi:10.1016/j.compedu.2015.09.006

Lera-Lopez, F., Faulin, J., Juan, A. A., & Cavaller, V. (2010). Monitoring students' activity and performance in online higher education: A European perspective. In A. A. Juan, T. Daradoumis, F. Xhafa, S. Caballe, & J. Faulin (Eds.), *Monitoring and assessment in online collaborative environments: Emergent computational technologies for e-learning support* (pp. 131–148). New York: Information Science Reference. doi:10.4018/978-1-60566-786-7.ch008

Littleton, K., & Hakkinen, P. (1999). Learning together: Understanding the processes of computer-based collaborative learning. In P. Dillenbourg (Ed.), *Collaborative learning: cognitive and computational approaches* (pp. 20–30). Oxford: Elsevier.

MacPhail, A., & Halbert, J. (2010). We had to do intelligent thinking during recent PE: Students and teachers experiences of assessment for learning in post-primary physical education. *Assessment in Education: Principles, Policy & Practice*, *17*(1), 23–39. doi:10.1080/09695940903565412

Mazzoni, E., & Gaffuri, P. (2010). Monitoring activitiy in e-learning: A quantitative model based on web tracking. In A. A. Juan, T. Daradoumis, F. Xhafa, S. Caballe, & J. Faulin (Eds.), *Monitoring and assessment in online collaborative environments: Emergent computational technologies for e-learning support*(pp. 111–130). New York: Information Science Reference. doi:10.4018/978-1-60566-786-7.ch007

McLoughlin, C., & Marshall, L. (2000). Scaffolding: A model for learner support in an online teaching enviornment. In A. Herrmann & M. M. Kulski (Eds.), *Flexible futures in tertiary teaching.Proceedings of the 9th Annual Teaching Learning Forum*. Perth: Curtin University of Technology.

O'Donnell, A. M., & Hmelo-Silver, C. E. (2013). Introduction: What is collaborative learning? An overview. In *The international handbook of collaborative learning* (pp. 1–15). New York: Routledge.

Pantaleon, M. E., & Saiz, E. E. (2010). Proposal of a set of reports for students' tracking and assessing in e-learning platforms. In A. A. Juan, T. Daradoumis, F. Xhafa, S. Caballe, & J. Faulin (Eds.), *Monitoring and assessment in online collaborative environments: Emergent computational technologies for e-learning support* (pp. 235–261). New York: Information Science Reference. doi:10.4018/978-1-60566-786-7.ch013

Persico, D., Pozzi, F., & Sarti, L. (2010). A model for monitoring and evaluating CSCL. In A. A. Juan, T. Daradoumis, F. Xhafa, S. Caalle, & J. Faulin (Eds.), *Monitoring and assessment in online collaborative environments: Emergent computational technologies for e-learning support* (pp. 149–170). Hershey, PA: Information Science Reference. doi:10.4018/978-1-60566-786-7.ch009

Roschelle, J., & Teasley, S. D. (1995). The construction of shared knowledge in collaborative problem solving. In *Computer-supported collaborative learning* (pp. 69–97). Berlin: Springer. doi:10.1007/978-3-642-85098-1_5

Rovai, A. (2002). Building sense of community at a distance. *International Review of Research in Open and Distance Learning*, *3*(1), 1–16. doi:10.19173/irrodl.v3i1.79

Russell, M. A. (2013). *Mining the social web: Data mining Facebook, Twitter, LinkedIn, Google+, GitHub, and more*. O'Reilly Media.

Sakthipriya, C., Srinaganya, G., & Sathiaseelan, J. G. (2015). An analysis of recent trends and challenges in web usage mining applications. *International Journal of Computer Science and Mobile Computing*, *4*(4), 41–48.

Scott, V. M., & Fuente, M. (2008). Whats the problem? L2 learners use of the L1 during consciousness-raising, form-focused tasks. *Modern Language Journal*, *92*(1), 100–103. doi:10.1111/j.1540-4781.2008.00689.x

Siemens, G. (2012). Learning analytics: envisioning a research discipline and a domain of practice. *Proceedings of the 2nd International Conference on Learning Analytics and Knowledge* (pp. 4-8). New York: ACM. doi:10.1145/2330601.2330605

So, H.-J., & Brush, T. A. (2008). Student perceptions of collaborative learning, social presence and satisfaction in a blended learning environment: Relationships and critical factors. *Computers & Education*, *51*(1), 318–336. doi:10.1016/j.compedu.2007.05.009

Trentin, G. (2009). Using a wiki to evaluate individual contribution to a collaborative learning project. *Journal of Computer Assisted Learning*, *25*(1), 43–55. doi:10.1111/j.1365-2729.2008.00276.x

U.S. Department of Education, Office of Educational Technology. (2012). Enhancing teaching and learning through educational data mining and learning analytics: An issue brief. Washington, DC: Author.

Verma, N., Malhotra, D., Malhotra, M., & Singh, J. (2015). E-commerce website ranking using semantic web mining and neural computing. *Procedia Computer Science*, *45*, 42–51. doi:10.1016/j.procs.2015.03.080

Vonderwell, S., & Zachariah, S. (2005). Factors that influence participation in online learning. *Journal of Research on Technology in Education*, *38*(2), 213–230. doi:10.1080/15391523.2005.10782457

Vygotsky, L. S. (1978). *Mind in Society: The development of higher psychological processes*. Cambridge, MA: Harvard University Press.

Wenger, E. (1998). *Communities of practice: Learning, meaning, and identity.* Cambridge, UK: Cambridge University Press. doi:10.1017/CBO9780511803932

Xiao, Y., & Lucking, R. (2008). The impact of two types of peer assessment on students performance and satisfaction within a wiki environment. *The Internet and Higher Education, 11*(3-4), 186–193. doi:10.1016/j.iheduc.2008.06.005

Xing, W., Wadholm, B., & Goggins, S. (2014). Learning analytics in CSCL with a focus on assessment: an exploratory study of activity theory-informed cluster analysis. *LAK '14 Proceedings of the Fourth International Conference on Learning Analytics and Knowledge* (pp. 59-67). New York: ACM.

Xing, W., Wadholm, R., Petakovic, E., & Goggins, S. (2015). Group learning assessment: Developing a theory-informed analytics. *Journal of Educational Technology & Society, 18*(2), 110–128.

Yelland, N. (2005). The future is now: A review of the literature on the use of computers in early childhood education (1994-2004). *AACE Journal, 13*(3), 201–232.

KEY TERMS AND DEFINITIONS

Clustering Analysis: Techniques focuses on grouping data of similar attributes for conducting further analyses.

Instant Feedback: Timely information on the performance of an individual.

Learning Progression: The development of low-level and surface learning to high-level and in-depth learning.

Web Data Mining: A set of concepts and techniques for collecting, processing, analyzing, interpreting and reporting a large set of data collected from the web to generate meaningful information.

Web Usage Mining: A subcategory of web data mining that focuses on analyzing web usage data. A typical web usage record includes user's identity, date and time of web access.

Chapter 6
Discover Patterns from Web-Based Dataset

Raghvendra Kumar
LNCT College, India

Priyanka Pandey
LNCT College, India

Prasant Kumar Pattnaik
KIIT University, India

ABSTRACT

The Web can be defined as a depot of varied range of information present in the form of millions of websites dispersed around us. Often users find it difficult to locate the appropriate information fulfilling their needs with the abundant number of websites in the Web. Hence multiple research work has been conducted in the field of Web Mining so as to present any information matching the user's needs. The application of data mining techniques on web usage, web content or web structure data to find out useful data like users' way in patterns and website utility statistics on a whole can be defined as Web mining. The main cause behind development of such websites was to personalize the substance of a website on user's preference. New methods are developed to deal with a Web site using a link hierarchy and a conceptual link hierarchy respectively on the basis of how users have used the Web site link structure.

INTRODUCTION

Navigation and search can be considered as the two primary models to find appropriate data on the web. Most Web users often use the web browser to find their way through a Web site either by beginning through home page or a Web page found through a search engine or linked from another Web site. This is then succeeded by hyperlinks relevant in the starting page and the subsequent pages, until they reach the appropriate information. Usually the search option provided on the Web site is used to speed up searching of data by author Agarwal, C. C. (2004). In case of Web site that pertaining huge number of Web pages and hyperlinks between them, such maneuvers do not justify users need to piece of information. None the less, the fleetness in the information explosion in the Web is not without consequences.

DOI: 10.4018/978-1-5225-1877-8.ch006

Users have many websites that are static in nature and provide the purpose of relaying information to get hold of correct data to quench their needs with no official governance on websites. Static websites have certain advantages and disadvantages. The advantages can be counted as follows that, they are cheap and easy to create and often developed to supply the developers need rather than the user. The biggest disadvantage of the websites is the information contained in them is fixed upon publishing and cannot be changed until the developer decides to publish a newer version of the website which needs professional skill hence increasing the maintenance cost. Furthermore, different users will have dissimilar preferences on the piece of data in a website. Thus increasing the necessity of smart websites to meet user expectations to find appropriate information.

The application of data mining techniques on web resources to find patterns in the Web is called as web mining by author Altingovde, I. S. and Ulusoy, O. (2004). Web resources available are mainly of three kinds, namely usage data, content data and structure data. Web Mining can be categorized into three main parts first is web usage mining; second one is web content mining and last is web structure mining. A common source of usage data is web server logs which are textual data brought together by servers and are enriched with information on users browsing behavior and website usage statistics. It is a huge warehouse of users' activities in a website tracked by the web server. Web usage mining applies data mining techniques on this repository to discover useful knowledge about user behavior in a website. This understanding of web applications can be used to find a way through the website and signify popular links to users. Web content data consists of document's textual information which is highly unstructured and varying in websites. On the other hand, web logs have a fixed set of data fields that are utilized to interpret the data, however no such accurate indication enclosure is offered to represent a document's content. Data mining techniques suggested by author Ansari, S., Kohavi, R., Mason, L. and Zheng, Z. (2001), when applied to the content of a document to ascertain information such as topical relations between documents in a website is via means of web content mining. This piece of information can further be utilized to generate a topical hierarchy of the documents in a website so as to recognize and identify documents equivalent to user's need. Web structure data means hyperlinks interconnecting the group of documents in a website where each a number of outgoing and incoming hyperlinks have. A link between two documents in a website suggests that the documents may be related and may contain relevant information. Data mining techniques are implemented on web structure mining in the network of hyperlinks structure to extort information utilized for various purposes, for example web crawling.

The most primitive move towards intelligent websites was customization suggested by author BBC(2005) and Berendt, B., Mobasher, B., Nakagawa, M. and Spiliopoulou, M. (2002)., which involved altering the interface and contents of a website to go with a user's need. Categorization is done by asking the users to choose from a set of predefined interest categories by manually filling up a form e.g.: Yahoo. The drawback of this approach is that it is time consuming and needs to keep user profiles up-to-date, else they will remain static. Website personalization addresses this restraint via automated user profiling which is understanding of user profiling methods to secure a user's predilection in a website. On the other hand Personalization utilizes web mining techniques to involuntarily build a user's profile from web logs to convert information into a user's document. This was followed by recommender systems gives an idea by author Brickell, J., Dhillon, I. S. and Modha, D. S. (2007), which are web applications that make use of web usage mining techniques on web logs to come up with personalized recommendations on appealing information in a website. These recommendations can be straight forward as signifying popular links in a website or may be complex approaches like proposing links to documents that are related to a user need. Bulk of the tribulations faced by Web users are the inability to find the appropriate documents or may be the complexity in navigating a website. These are caused by either a poor website design or because of an unforeseen way that violates its original design function. The authors challenged the AI community to deal with this problem by emerging adaptive websites which can be defined as sites that involuntarily recover their organization and arrangement by gaining knowledge from visitor's access patterns. This brought about the commencement of expansion of adaptive websites that focus on modeling the website based on user need instead of smart websites that model the users. The key to creating such adaptive websites is the transformation approach which involves in making changes to the basics of a website design using the information obtained from web logs by author Catledge, L. D. and Pitkow, J. E. (1995).

Association Rules

At present, there are many competent algorithms that handle well-linked and computationally expensive task of association rule mining being one of data mining techniques. Concisely an association rule is defined as an expression $X \rightarrow Y$, where X and Y are sets of items. The denotation of such rules is fairly instinctive: Given a database D of transactions where each transaction $T \in D$ is association rules. In brief, an association rule is an expression $X \rightarrow Y$ expresses that whenever a transaction T contains X than T probably contains Y also. The probability or rule confidence is defined as the percentage of transactions containing Y in addition to X with regard to the overall number of transactions containing X. that is, the rule confidence can be understood as the conditional probability $p(Y \subseteq T | X \subseteq T)$.

Web Server Log

To ascertain adequate bandwidth and server capacity on their organizations website by authors Chakrabarti, S., Dom, B. and van de Berg, M. (1999)., IT administrators were inspired to emerge with web log file analysis thus ending up into priceless imminence into web site usage. It represents the commotion of many users, over long period of time, compared to a limited number of users for an hour or two each.

Significance of the Study

The conclusions drawn from this study grant us a summary of the usage pattern of website Portal by author Cooley, R., Mobasher, B. and Srivastava, J. (1999). This study also shows use of Generalized Association Rules in Web Usage Mining. The results of this study can be utilized by the System administrator as instructions enhancing the use of website.

VISUALIZING WEB SITE LINK STRUCTURES FOR USER NAVIGATION

The prime concern of this is to envisage a Web site in a hierarchical order to respond to the first two navigation questions by author Cooley, R., Tan, P.-N. and Srivastava, J. (2000)., i.e. Where am I now? Where have I been? In the hierarchy built, the Web site link structure produced by the designer has been modified according to the reviews of users in using the Web site link structure, hence showing users view for the web site. This hierarchy assists users appreciate the association between the Web pages they have visited by helping them gain control over their navigation and not just confining themselves to the hyperlinks in each page. They can understand their current locations in the context of different levels of pages in the hierarchy. It also assists users gain knowledge of their current location in the matter within the pages in the hierarchy.

Link Prediction for User Navigation

The second concern of this is how to foresee a user, Web navigation in the pages visited by the user on the Web site so as to know the response to the third navigation question, i.e., where can I go next? We can tackle this issue by mounting a two-step process of modeling and prediction. By using a collaborative approach, a user model can be constructed utilizing the data from a set of users, to make assumptions about a new user in the deficiency of information about him/her to predict his next request.

Two prime methodologies suggested for finding information on the Web are navigation and keyword-based search. Keyword-based search by author Crescenzi, V., Merialdo, P. and Missier, P. (2005) is admired because of its swiftness in recognizing pages containing precise information. On the contrary, navigation search is utilized when keyword-based search is uneasy to be carried out due to various reasons e.g., the user is not specific in his search and needs options as a guideline whereas some have complex information-searching tasks which are difficult to be presented into keywords. Hence we can conclude by saying that neither methodology is sufficient for complex information searching tasks as navigation is not a proficient method of locating specific information, as users must constantly direct themselves towards browsing cues: textual and graphical indications of the content accessible via a hyperlink whereas Searching, on the other hand, gives improper results and loses the significant context present in the pages guiding towards the search result. Therefore, by combining navigation with searching paradigms and facilitating transition between them, users can find the preferred information corresponding to their search of complex information successfully.

Previous Issue and Challenges

The research community has taken it as a challenge to search through the disorganized World Wide Web for valuable knowledge after analyzing the navigation patterns of website users. The users of the web have addressed their needs for web data as well as by those who have business built around the web. For example, users nag about the poor presentation of the websites which makes it uneasy for the users to achieve their desired objective. This occurs either because of bad site structure or mismatches between site design and user needs. On the other hand problems like lack of standards in the design and its implementation in its web pages make it difficult for data mining techniques to web data.

The server log is the chief source of data for analyzing user course-plotting patterns which contains the information collected by Web servers. Now several kinds of access pattern mining can be done depending on the analyst needs. One of the ways suggested to get the server logs processed is by utilizing web mining techniques so as to gain information about web usage. Hence promoting varied web mining techniques to assist web administrator in indulging himself into user's site usage patterns. Upon analyzing the server access logs and user registration data one can get useful information about a better structure of a website so as to create effectual presence for the organization. Also such data helps business organizations to get the customer's cross-marketing strategies across products and efficacy of promotional campaigns amongst all other things.

INFORMATION IN WEBSITE AND WEB SERVER LOGS

Software engineers aim to serve excellence in their products to their user's which is of the similar concern in case of Web sites. As a matter of fact, web sites keep on enlarging in number of subpages and hyperlinks thus provoking web experts to constantly assess the web site quality factors. Not only in order to improve quality, but also to make sure that structure or design changes do not lower the web site quality. High quality of the web site is important for the owners from the market benefit point of view. This improves the quality of the structure of the web site, regardless of the role of the web site in an organization, the success of the business organization, requires its quality.

By means of this, we are trying to present how data mining techniques can be utilized for the appraisal of the web sites. Also we will make an attempt to respond to a sub question that if the web designer can trust the changes suggested by the mining outcome suggested by author Etzioni, O. and Perkowitz, M. (1997).

All Around the Website

Frequent review of the hyperlinks is significant both for the business benefits and unspecified web site goals. We can conclude by saying "Dead links means no business", hence solutions that make routine through the hyperlink validation process can help save both time and money on task improvements. Thus website complexity can be dealt by scrutinizing users' behavior essential for structures improvements.

Web site can be defined as a finite set of the web pages, where these create a web of connected web pages. Hence the terminology website should be clearly specified o the reader so as to utilize the hyperlink evaluation to improve web site design. Graphical representation of the web site defines the traversed structure suggesting finest traversal practice such as three-click navigation does not assure user contentment.

In order to fulfill users' navigational needs the web site responds in different web structures. Theoretically to show traversing through the web site easy the designer can upload the links to all pages on the main page. This will be denoted in the form of a star shaped structure on a web site, which is characterized by paths spread from root web page in various directions.

Apart from radiation structure, two basic structure types have been described:

1. First, waterfall type where the path way through the web pages has only one direction leading to defy the restructuring of web and adjudicate amongst all which pages be placed deeply in the web structure. But the chief snag to the last page is its long path. On the contrary, situations arise when displaying pages in the succession is vital:
   a. Portraying a story
   b. First signing contracts, and then displaying download page for the program
2. The second one is an interconnected structure. Here each page in the web site is straight forwardly linked to all the other web pages within the same web site and hence this type of structures can only be effective in small web sites.

Plotting a course through the web site is probable due to the hyperlinks which connect the web pages together. Designers often place the hyperlinks to help their users search through the web site or guide them to their desired information. A hyperlink can be described with the following features from a user's perspective as suggested by author Etzioni, O. and Perkowitz, M. (2000):

1. Source URL (Web Page Where the Hyperlinks is Placed)
2. Target URL (Web Page That the Hyper Link Leads to)
3. Label (e.g. for a textual hyperlink, the text used for the link name)
4. Type of Graphic (text, figure)
5. Place (where in the layout of the web page link is placed

Data Used for Website Evaluation

While performing hyperlink assessment appropriate data is required. Transactional data required in executing association rules mining is received from the log files, and actions performed by the web site users are recorded. The log files supply history of the user's behavior on a specific web site to the software engineers with data which is utilized for the analysis and further website development. Hence, making it feasible to retrieve sessions of usage from these log files. Thus providing probability to mine for the association rules between the pages on the basis of user behavior. Considering the web site structure as an input, portraying the goals of a web designer, along with actual usage of the web site, the analyst can determine the gap between designer assumptions and user's behavior inclination. Since these hyperlinks help plot the course throughout the web, history of their usage is utilized as the user's feedback about website's structure and functioning.

The Web Site as an Input

The web site structure information can be redeemed in many ways either by taking assistance of website expert who can devote all the existing hyperlinks in the web site structure which can augment structure information with proposed navigational user's behavior. The other convenient way is practice of automatic tools such as web crawlers or web spiders. These tools function to collect web pages interconnected to the starting web page by addressing the URL which follows the existing links on the first page so as to redeem connection to the web pages. Hence in this manner the web site can be downloaded and the website structure can be reclaimed. Moreover, the web site structure can also be redeemed from in hand database connected to the content management system. From the above database we are able to reclaim information about placement of a hyperlink and to which web pages it leads along with its time of recreation and dismiss making it the most convenient method that does not need additional computations as in the case of the web spiders.

Once data is collected about the web site's hyperlinks we have accomplished the first step of determining the navigational structure of a web site which is a set of links to construct a navigational path through the web site. The significance of the web site structure is shown in the utility of web site, indicating why assessment of hyperlinks utility can be seen as usability assessment of the web site, or particular web page. The existing hyperlinks on the web pages show the designer intention to direct the web site users about the anticipated navigational paths required for justification of the web site usability. Nonetheless information collected shows not only web designer's intentions, but the actual state of the web site suggested by authors Facca, F. and Lanzi, P. (2005).

The Web Site's Traffic Log

A Web server when properly configured, can record every click that users make on a Website. The server will add information to the log file about user request with every single click in the visited path. The data on the server will be assembled by the logs in the form of files of specific format. Such dealings contain information about the usage of web site by keeping footage of how users visit the web site and how active they are. Based on the structure of log format diverse data is stored. Usually logs contain data such as: client's IP address, URL of the page requested, time when the request was send to the server etc. This data is used later as the basis of usage behavior discovery. Based on server settings log files format vary. The form of web logs files standard changes over years as there was more requirements for the web log processing.

Acquaintance gathered about the used web browser becomes of prime importance when the web sites provide services by performing various web applications. This forms the basis for platforms tests of the web site which become crucial in making configurations which can be tested later in the project. After professing when the server has the highest number of requests helps to identify periods in which maintenance activities or shutting the server down has the lowest possibility to 'disappoint' its users.

Information in Web Server Logs

These days since many organizations consider the Web as an essential component of their operations and exterior communications, a curiosity has been generated in the measurement and evaluation of Web site usage. Server logs are used to garner an assured sum of quantitative usage information which is then compiled and interpreted properly to provide a baseline of statistics indicating utility levels as well as support and growth comparisons amongst parts of a site. Scrutinizing the above also gives some technical information about the server load, strange movements, or failed requests, along with assistance in marketing and site development and management activities. In vibrant systems like the Internet, at times recording samples of activity is a general practice which is then utilized to exemplify the activity in the system and for assessment of new mechanisms to be used in this system. This is certainly true of HTTP traffic.

Web Server logs are plain text (ASCII) files, that is independent from server platform. There are some differences between server software, but traditionally there are four types of server logs:

1. Access log
2. Agent log
3. Transfer log
4. Error log
5. Referrer log

Transfer and Agent log files are standard. The referrer and agent logs may or may not be "turned on" at the server or may be added to the transfer log file to create an "extended" log file format. Each HTTP protocol transaction, weather completed or not, is recorded in the logs and some transactions are recorded in more than one log by author Fan, L., Cao, P., Lin, W. and Jacobson, Q. (1999).

Access Log

Below is an example of a single line in a common transfer log collected from a Portal. This typically displays as one log line of ASCII text, separated by tabs and spaces.

```
2003-11-23 16:00:13 210.186.180.199 - CSLNTSVR20 202.190.126.85 80 GET/tutor/
images/icons/fold. Gif- 304 140 470 0 HTTP/1.1 www.tutor.com.my
Mozilla/4.0+ (compatible; +MSIE+5.5; +Windows+98; +win+9x+4.90) ASPSESSIONINCS
TSBQDC=NBKBCPIBBJHCMMFIKMLNNKFD; +browser=done; +ASPSESSI ONIDAQPPCQCC=LBDGBPI
BDFCOKHMLHNKFBN http://www.tutor.com.my/
```

There are 19 attributes in above as:

1.   Date – The date from GMT are recorded for each hit.
2.   Time – The time of transaction.
3.   Client IP Address – Client IP is the number of computer who access or request the site.
4.   User Authentication – Some web sites are set up with a security feature that requires a user to enter username and password. Once a user logs on to a website, that user's "username" is logged in the fourth field of the log file.
5.   Server Name – Name of the server.
6.   Server IP Address – Server IP address is a static provided by Internet Service Provider. This IP will be a reference for access the information from the server.
7.   Server Port – This is used for data transmission, usually port 80.
8.   Server Method (HTTP Request) – The word request refers to an image, movie sound, pdf, txt, HTML file and more. Currently, there are three formats that Web servers send information in GET, POST, and Head.
9.   URI Stem – URI Stem is path from the host. It represents the structure of the websites.
10. Server URI Query – URI-Query usually appears after sign "?". This represents the type of user request and the value usually appears in the Address Bar.
11. Status – This is the status code returned by the server. There are four classes of codes:
     1.   Success (200 series)
     2.   Redirect (300 series)
     3.   Failure (400 series)
     4.   Server Error (500 series)
12. Bytes Sent – Amount of data returned by the server, not counting the header line.
13. Bytes Received – Amount of data sent by the client to the server.
14. Time stamp – It is used to determine how long a visitor spent on a given page.
15. Protocol Version – HHTP protocol being used.
16. Host – It is either the IP address or the corresponding host name of the remote user requesting the page.
17. User Agent – It is reported by the remote user's browser. Typically is the string describing the type and version of browser software being used.
18. Cookies – It can be used to track individual users thus make the sessionizer task easier.

19. Referrer – The referring page, if any, as reported by the remote user's browser. It is possible to analyze the following variables in the access log:
    1. Domain Name or Internet Protocol (IP number)
    2. Date and Time
    3. Item accessed

The data from Access Logs provides a broad view of a Web servers and users. Such analysis enables server administrators and decision makers to characterize their server's audience and usage patterns.

Agent Log

The agent log provides data on a user's browser, browser version, and operating system. This is the significant information, as the type of browser and operating system determines what a user is able to access on a site. A sample is presented below:

```
Mozilla/3.0(Win 95; 1)
```

- **Browser:** The type of browser used to access a website. There are several different Web browsers on the market today, each of which has different viewing capabilities.
- **Browser Version:** Each browser has its own capabilities.
- **Operating System:** The type of computer and operating system used to determine the Graphical User Interface (GUI) of a website depending on the computer platform.

The Agent log information is essential for the design and development of Websites. Without such information, server administrator could design sites that require viewing capabilities that vast majority of the site's users do not possess. This could lead to wasted effort by the server administrators. Worst still, this can lead to improperly displayed web content, thus effectively rendering the site useless to the user.

Error Log

The average Web user will receive an "Error 404 File Not Found" message several times a day. When a user encounters this message, an entry is made in the Error Log. A sample is presented below:

```
2003-11-23 16:00:13 210.186.180.199 - CSLNTSVR20 202.190.126.85 80 GET/tutor/
images/icons/fold. Gif- 304 141 404 0 HTTP/1.1www.tutor.com.my
Mozilla/4.0+ (compatible; +MSIE+6.0; +Windows+NT+5.1) SPSESSION DCSTSBQDC=NLKB
CPIBNAHCLLMNEJLCIHLC; +browser=done http://www.tutor.com.my/
```

- **Error 404:** The error log tells a server administrator the time, domain name of the user, and page on which a user received the error. These error messages are critical to Web server administration activities, as they inform server administrators of problematic and erroneous links on their servers.
- **Stopped Transmission:** This informs a server administrator of a user-interrupted transfer. For example, a user clicking on the "stop" button would generate a "stopped transmission" error message.

The analysis of Error log data can provide important server information such as missing files, erroneous links, and aborted downloads. This information can enable server administrators to modify and correct server content, thus decreasing the number of errors users encounter while navigating a site.

Referrer Log

The referrer log indicates what other sites on the Web link to a particular server. Each link made to a site generates a Referrer Log entry, a sample of which is below:

http://search.yahoo.com/search?p=utusan&ei=UTF-8&fr=fp-tab-web-t&cop=mss&tab=_

In this particular example, the referrer was AltaVista, indicating that user entered the Web site after performing a search using the AltaVista search facility.

If a user is on a site, and clicks on a link to another site, then another entry will receive an entry in their Referrer Log. The log will show that the user came to the other site via first link. Through the analysis of the four log files, Web service providers can begin the process of assessing and evaluating their networked information services. Current Web usage statistics generally center on the analysis of the Access Log, thus limiting the ability of Web-mounted service extensiveness measures. There are however, means to analyze the Agent, Error, and Referrer log files. Such techniques can provide important additional insight into the use of Web-based services by users.

Preparation of Data

Procedure for the hyperlinks utility assessment is not hidden from all today. All we need to know is how to discover the information. The preparatory process is of vital significance as the dependability of the data mining process depends on the superiority of the pre-processing. The higher quality of the preparation the more reliable outcome will be. After we have recognized data sources, it is prepared for later usage. Data cleaning has been defined as removing invalid data, whereas data processing has been addressed as transforming data into appropriate format. Starting from the web site structure this section contains information what needs to be done in order to make the evaluation process possible. As was said before web site structure is available in the web site itself. Nevertheless, for further computation it needs to be presented in a more adjustable form. Data preparation for the web site structure will in most cases be simplified to the data pre-processing. Of course, depending on the source of information the data cleaning can be unavoidable.

After defining the web site structure source, the data preparation can vary, making it convenient to convert tables from content management systems than to redeem information about the structure from raw codes of web pages. However, if the obligatory information about web site structure is cut down to the least of the target and source page, data preparation becomes a smaller issue. Log files however contain quite useful data hence require more effort to be processed.

In order to conduct association rules discovery on the web site's usage history, the behavior recognition of each visitor's activities is essential. Before beginning this process, logs are cleaned from records which have requirement for sources of particular type (like images) or web resources that are out of the evaluation interests. Various kinds of agents which contain information from the World Wide Web manipulate the log files and in this way they can change the concluding comprehension discovery from this source.

This being the prime reason; as to why data cleaning process is essential before initializing information discover including removal of web site usage records by the software agents (e.g. web crawlers).

DATA MINING FOR THE WEB SITES

Data mining techniques provide assessment methods along with, specification of type of data input necessary for association rules discovery, determining which measures to be under taken. The likelihood of appraising hyperlink is based on the supposition that every preexisting hyperlink is meant to be utilized. This conjecture makes it feasible for the analysts to deduce results and thus offer suggestions by author Festa, P. (2003) such as:

1. Adding new hyperlinks
2. Removing
3. Changing existing hyperlinks

One of the prime concerns of data discovery usefulness is to determine information that is insignificant. In mining for association rules one desires to discover rules that bring to the filed new information.

Data mining techniques utilize pre-collected data, without additional interface between the web site users. The choice to utilize data mining techniques for the hyperlink assessment is made via use of the existing analytical techniques. Complex computation is required to handle pre-collected data. The size of pre-collected data depends on the assessed system, yet traffic seen on the website and recorded on the log files growths to giant sizes. Here the dilemma is how to extort information in a well-organized way.

On Combination of existing algorithms and processes we can endeavor for the finest solution to assess website's hyperlinks and upon utilizing this assessment conclusion as a feedback to the website design.

What is Web Mining?

An imperative expansion of data mining, Web mining is defined as an incorporated technology of a variety of research fields including computational linguistics, statistics, informatics, artificial intelligence and information detention. Web mining can be classified into three categories as seen in Figure 1: Web Content Mining, Web Structure Mining, and Web Usage Mining.

Web Content Mining involves mining web data contents ranging from the HTML based document and XML-based documents found in the web servers to the mining of data and knowledge from the data source. Content mining consists of two domain areas: Web Page Content Mining and Search Mining result. Content data corresponds to the collection of facts from a Web page that was designed to convey information to the users. It may consist of text, images, audio, video or structured records such as lists and tables. Web structure mining used to discover the model underlying the link structures of the Web. This type of mining can be further divided into two types based on the structural data used:

*   **Hyperlinks:** A hyperlink is a structural unit that connects a Web page to different location, either within the same Web page or to a different Web page. A Hyperlink that connects to a different part of the same Web page is called Intra-Document Hyperlink, and a hyperlink that connects two different pages is called Inter-Document Hyperlink.

Figure 1. Nomenclature of web mining

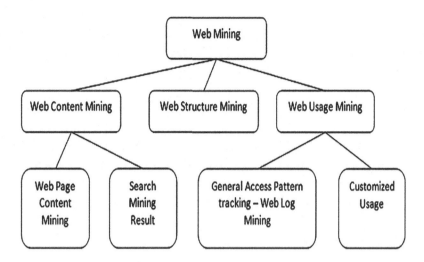

- **Document Structure:** In addition, the content within a Web page can also be organized in a tree structure format, based on the various HTML and XML tags within the page.

While content mining and structure mining utilize the real or primary data on the web, Web usage Mining focuses on discovery of meaningful patterns from data generated from client-server transitions on one or more web server in order to study the navigation behavior and access patterns of website visitors. Web usage data includes data from web server access logs, proxy server logs, browser logs, user profiles; registration files user sessions or transactions, mouse clicks and scrolls, and any other data generated by the interaction of users and the web.

The web usage mining process could be classified into two commonly used approaches:

1. The first approach maps usage data of the Web Server into relational tables before an adapted data mining techniques is performed.
2. The second approach uses the log data directly by utilizing special preprocessing techniques. Mining behavior patterns from web log data needs data cleaning, user identification, session identification and path completion.

Web Mining in Learning

Web mining is used as a means to improve line instructions. Web site course's form a key component of online learning, which acts as a virtual classroom of the course providing admittance to dynamic learning materials and enables students to interact with the learning materials, with the teaching staff and within themselves.

Since online teaching needs a considerable investment of rational and monetary efforts, it is quite significant to assess its pedagogical efficacy. Although, to know the efficacy of a teaching method; is a complex issue affected by many interconnected variables.

Web Usage Mining

Web usage mining is an explorative field that focuses on the expansion of techniques and tools to gain knowledge about user's web navigation behavior. Considering the visitor's course plotting preferences is of vital significance in studying the quality of an electronic commerce site. Actually on indulging in the most common access patterns of the users permits the service provider to modify and become accustomed to the site's interface for that particular user to recover the site's static structure contained in the underlying hypertext system.

Whenever web users interrelate within a site, data noting their behavior is accumulated in web server logs which may also have precious information comprising of the users experience in the site. On top of this, since in a medium size site log files amount to several megabytes a day, it becomes obligatory of the techniques and tools to help take benefit of their content.

Web Usage Mining Procedure

At present, many commercial log analysis tools have existed but they do have limitation that is their analytical capabilities produce results such as summary statistics and rate of recurrence of page visits. Statistical analysis can be considered as a widespread method to extort knowledge about the visitors to a Web site to know the various descriptive statistical analyses on variables such as page views, viewing time and length of navigational path. For generation of index pages involuntarily from the log data, i.e. pages containing collections of links, which the user navigation behavior suggests, are related. Graph creation in which the node corresponds to a page and a link gives the possibility of the interconnected between the two pages occurs in the same session. An algorithm is anticipated which utilizes the graph to find for a small number of clusters of pages that come up together in a session. These clusters are actually the candidate's index pages, utilized to modify a web site to suit the user's needs. A model based clustering approach can be utilized where users with like course plotting patterns are assembled into the same cluster. One such example is Markov model which shows the behavior of the users contained in each cluster.

For the time being the research community has been occupied with keen observation of studying techniques to take complete gain of the information contained in log files so that much more relevance of such techniques is presented. Many techniques have been brought together in web usage mining like adaptive neural network to envisage the Website usage patterns which then support the recognition of clusters of Web page that are recurrently visited together by users. Rule categorization itself is utilized to categorize new data items that are attached to the database. The technique used to manage inductive learning algorithms such as decision tree classifiers, Bayesian classifier, K-nearest neighbor classifier and support vector machine. The sequential patterns were used to predict user visit patterns. Clustering analysis is technique to assemble together a set of items having like characteristics. There are two kinds of fascinating clusters to be revealed: usage clusters and page clusters. Usage cluster permits one to group together clients or data items that have like characteristics on the other hand page cluster will determine groups of pages having related content.

Mogul (1996) proposed a method where a reliable graph is directed and vigorously reorganized as the server receives requests. Every requested page has been designated a node, and an arc between two nodes exists if the target node was requested within x accesses after the source node; the weight of an arc is proportional to the number of such requests. The simulations carried out with log data show that a reduction in the reclamation latency can be accomplished. But this method does not guarantee alterations only between consecutive requests.

Drott (1998) suggested many ways of manipulating the log files in designing the site to decrease the file size and respond to specific questions such as those engaged in tracking links, searches, paths, and initial contact by the user. This research study also brings into notice the limitations of the data existing within the log files, giving essential suggestions on how to view the data while Stout in 1997 gave suggestions on how to design website molded according to specific user audiences. Wong in 2001 gave a new methodology on the basis of case based interpretation approach to find user patterns by mining unclear association rules from the historical web log data. Association rules means sets of pages that gain admittance together with a support value surpassing some specified threshold. This engages the support and confidence for each transaction that consists of a set of item in the database.

Many techniques have been suggested for building association-rule based prediction models utilizing the web logs which have been proposed and empirically tested on real web logs. Although, systematic studies on the relative merits of these methods has not been performed yet. While Borgelt & Kruse illustrated an execution of the well-known Apriori algorithm for the initiation of association rules which works on the concept of a prefix tree. Web mining using Association rules is amongst the popular techniques utilized so far. Since this study is self-explanatory in its character, the association rules technique is utilized.

Usage of Data Mining Techniques

The powerful tool of data mining techniques proves its possibilities in many business and research fields. The goal is to expand its usage and use its power to maximum, with growing hardware capabilities algorithms that were used in theory can now be tested and implemented in the real world. Growing interest in software qualities expands the size of the filed in which data mining can be used.

Analysis of Web Usage Behavior

El-Ramly and Strulia during their research explored and focused web site in the aspect of sequential-pattern mining to forecast web-usage behavior. By mining for the sessions in the log files they found recurring patterns with one goal in mind; to provide recommendations at run time. El-Ramly and Strulia suggested usage of found patterns mentioning usability problems. The longer the discovered paths, more complex it becomes with the usability of the web site. Their interpretation was based on the fact that users want to reach resources in shorter time. The chief use of mining for the web sites in their case study was production of hyperlinks to the web site that might be the choice of a new user. The list generated via their research is based on the pre-used patterns of web site. In the experimental assessment of their assumption they investigated the log files from the web site of an undergraduate course at the Computing Science Department, University of Alberta. The efficacy of the maneuver was quantified by how many times the proposed url occurs in three next pages once the user has visited the pages after recommendation.

Post-research conduction they found out a tradeoff between discovering more patterns (with high level of errors permission) with more suggested urls, and discovering less patterns (less errors allowed) with smaller but much more focused number of suggested urls. During their research they concluded that in focused web sites the tasks employed by the assessed web site impact the users' behavior. This implies that data mining can be fruitful in fulfillment of web site designer's goals along with this provide a better understanding to the users about their required information.

Navigational Structure Mining

Chui & Li recommended a hyperlink recurrent items extraction algorithm, permitting involuntary extortion of navigational structures without executing textual analysis. The structure mining was the term addressed by them for extortion of structures from web site. Utilizing recurrent item-sets data mining algorithms and Adaptive Window Algorithm Chui & Li extorted so called near-identical hyperlinks patterns. They addressed these near-identical hyperlinks patterns as to widespread situations where navigational structure does not differ much between web pages. For example, any two web pages can have the same near-identical hyperlinks pattern if fewer links are indifferent (removed etc.). Chui & Li conducted several experiments on the usability of three computer science department web sites after conducting remodeling the hyperlink graph and discovery of navigational structure. They then concluded that the organization of the navigation structure can be utilized as forward planner for the user performance in using the web site.

Negative Association Mining for the Web Site

Pilarczyk with the help of this presents the utilization of the negative association rules mining for the web pages on a particular selected web site. This methodology is based on the mining of association rules derived from HTTP server logs. Pilarczyk during his research work found out both positive and negative association between pages and made efforts to assess the hyperlink usability. He concluded that mining process is positive association between pages as good usability of the hyperlinks, but when links between associated pages is nonexistent the positive rule provides suggestion for adding new link. The negative association between pages is utilized for providing judgment in removal of the hyperlinks. The complexity found in his research was building up of the thresholds for the rule discovery. By setting the low level of support threshold 0,00075 more links is identified as negative, and more links is suggested to add.

Traps of Data Mining

The data mining techniques provide proposal and solutions to perform computation but they cannot be considered as bullet proof answers for the analysis problems. Analysis of the resultant by the researcher, as well as providing knowledge about faults of used method is his responsibility. Certain well-known issues are considering early stage of data pre-processing along with advanced stage of information discovery. As already discussed before reconstructing visits on the web site no bullet proof solution preexists. Due to the web browser identified web spiders, the discovered transactions used for the rules mining can contain invalid data. On discovering association rule mining, analytics require to set thresholds for the rules factors. A relationship between items is tested whether it passes the requirements of a rule or not by setting a threshold level. Higher the level of threshold more dependable is the outcome along with the risk of discarding all possible associations in the terms of the rule. But if many aspects are utilized to identify association rule, all should be incorporated in the measure of the rule strength. One of the aspects that depicts association rule is its confidence, however we risk accuracy if we validate rules only on the basis of this factor. The implication which should always be considered is: "rules having a high level of confidence but little support should be interpreted with caution". But this seems to be easily forgotten as the support of the rule is time and again utilized as choice if the investigated pair (precursor and subsequent) is taken into consideration for further assessment. This dilemma could be rectified by verifying if there subsists link (navigation path) to every webpage from assessed website starting from the main page. This along with, assumption related, traps research can fall into while utilizing data mining outcome for the system's analysis. On further discussing data mining techniques we should also bear in mind that these are costly and time-consuming tasks.

PATTERN ANALYSIS USING ASSOCIATION RULE MINING

In this, we shall be describing the methodology and implementation in this study. This chapter also describes the steps engaged in the server log process and analysis. The chapter further discusses the preprocessing of the server logs and pattern mining. On top of this, the algorithm of generalized association rules is also presented. It will also discuss about the algorithm, tools utilized to reproduce the results. In this study, the methodology consists of the following phases in Figure 2.

Raw Log File

The log files in the form of text files range in size from 1KB to 100MB, depending on the traffic at a given website. What the log files are counting and tracking is needed in determining the amount of traffic a site receives during a specified period of time. Particularly, there is a critical distinction between a hit and access:

1. A hit is downloadable file in the form of text document, image, movie, or a sound file. In case of downloading a web page consisting of 6 images on it, then that user "hit" the web site seven times (6 images = 1 text page).
2. An access, which is sometimes called a page hit, is an entire page downloaded by a user regardless of the number of images, sounds, or movies. In this case downloading a web page having 6 images, means accessing one page of the site.

Figure 2. Methodology of the study

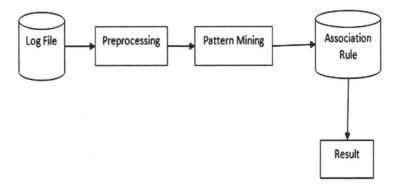

In this study, raw log files were collected from Tutor.com. This portal focuses on education and provides more information related to education purposes such as tutorials, Question Banks, Teaching Guidelines, and etc. for the analysis purposes, data dated on 24 November that consists of 82 683 records was retrieved from the server and needed to be preprocessed.

The raw log files consists of 19 attributes such as Date, Time, Client IP, Auth User, Server Name, Server IP, Setver Port, Request Method, URI-Stem, URI-Query, Protocol Status, Time Taken, Bytes Sent, Bytes Received, protocol Version, Host, User AGENT, Cookies, Referer. One of the main problems encountered when dealing with the log files is the amount of data needs to be preprocessed.

Preprocessing

Web usage mining is the application of data mining techniques to usage logs of large data repositories. Site's content can be improved and optimized via the results produced. In this phase, the starting point and critical point for successful log mining is data preprocessing. The required tasks are data cleaning, user identification and session identification. An entry of web server log contains the time stamp of a traversal from a source to a target page, the IP address of the originating host, the type of request (GET and POST) and other data, many entries that are considered uninteresting for mining were removed from the data files. The filtering is an application dependent. While in most cases accesses to embedded content such as image and scripts are filtered out. However, before applying data mining algorithm, data preprocessing must be performed to convert the raw data into data abstraction necessary for the further processing.

Pattern Mining

On completion of preprocessing, pattern mining can be performed in order to find the useful patterns that can be used to improve the sites. Pattern mining will return several findings:

1. **General Statistics:** The summary of the whole log file. Usually it provides the Total Hits, Page Views, and Total Visitor.
2. **Access Statistics:** Provides information such as Most Popular Access Page and Most Downloaded Files.
3. **Visitors Information:** Provides the information such as the most active country which accesses the website.
4. **Referrer:** Provides information such as the most used search engines and phrases, and keyword used.
5. **Error:** Important for the system administrator's website in order to improve the site as well as to reduce the error such as "404 file not found".

Generalized Association Rules

In this phase, Generalized Association Rules is used to mine the data in order to obtain the support and confidence for each rule. Generalized association rule is one of the commonly used web usage mining technique. Concept hierarchy is used to illustrate the relation between options provided by Tutor.com.

Concept hierarchy shows the set of relationship between different items, generalized association rules allow rules at different levels. From the log file, a structure of the web site shown in Figure 3.

Figure 3 depicts the hierarchy structure for Portal. The structure was captured from the Server logs. This study only expands the structure until level 3, specifically focusing on Question Banks and Tuition which have been selected for applying Generalized Association Rules. Since the tuition modules are updated daily, it is not possible to apply the generalized association rules because these modules are based on URI query and access to data is from separate database. Due to this problem, only Question Banks were selected for mining the patterns using Generalized Association Rules. Small simulator program was written using Active Server Pages in order to mine the rules and to calculate the support and confidence. When applying generalized association rules, any unused transaction from the database such as images access (e.g..gif,.jpg), scripts (e.g..css,.jis) were removed.

1. **Support Counting:** To generate support counting from the system, the following formula is applied
   Support= ($\sum$Transaction {X, Y})/ ($\sum$ Transaction in BD) x 100
2. **Confidence Counting:** To generate confidence from the system, the following formula is applied
   Confidence= ($\sum$ Transaction {X, Y})/ ($\sum$ Transaction {X}) x 100

Results

The results of web log processing are described in two ways. The general description about the access patterns, Access statistic, Visitors, Referrer, Error will be displayed using charts. In addition, the support and confidences of different levels of server portal accessed will be illustrated using bar charts. The system administrator could make a decision from the result illustrated in order to improve or enhance the content, link, site navigation and facilities.

Figure 3. Hierarchy structure for portal

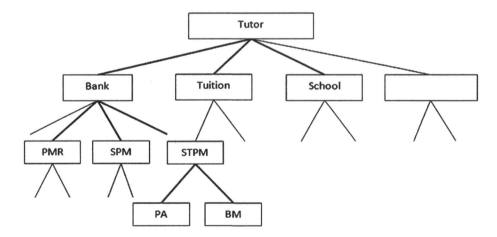

Read Server Logs

In order to perform pattern mining and generalized association rules, a tool was written using C#.Net to perform preprocessing techniques. The algorithm for preprocessing is explained below:

```
1.          Const ForReading = 1;
2.          Const ForWriting = 2;
3.              Sub ReadLog (Physical-Path, ModeFile-1, TypeOfLog, ModeFile
2,StrTypeOfFormat)
4.                              RecordCounter = 0;
5.                          Set LogReader = Server.CreateObject("IISLog");
6.                          LogReader.OpenLogFile LogFilePath, ModeFile-1,
7.                          TypeOfLogFile, ModeFile-2, StrTypeOfLogFormat;
8.                           LogReader.ReadLogRecord;
9.                          While NOT LogReader.EndOfLogRecord
10.                            Retrieve Log Attributes;
11.                    ... ...
12.                  ... ...
13.                RecordCounter = RecordCounter + 1;
14.                Log Reader.ReadLogRecord;
15.                Loop
16.                 LogReader.CloseLogFile;
17.          End Sub
```

Transfer Server Logs to Database

After reading the files, several attributes are ignored because they were considered not important for the analysis. The read logs records will be stored in a database. Figure 4 shows the database to store the data.

The algorithm that implements this function is written as:

```
1.          Declare Variables;
2.           Set DB =  Server.CreateObject("ADODB.Connection");
3.           Set RS = Server.createObject("ADODB.Recordset");
4.           ConnStr = {MsAccess Driver};
5.          DB.Open ConnStr;
6.          RS.Open TableName,ActiveConnection,
7.                  Add Data;
8.              ... ...
9.            ... ...
10.               RS.Update;
11.          Set Rs = Nothing;
12.          DB.Close;
```

Figure 4. After data is transferred to database

Sno	DateTime	ServerIp	Method	URIStem	Port	ClientIp
1	2012-05-23 00:0...	69.10.57.50	GET	/MAHindi.aspx	80	100.43.83.146
2	2012-05-23 00:1...	69.10.57.50	GET	/DeptofElectro...	80	66.249.71.162
3	2012-05-23 00:4...	69.10.57.50	GET	/robots.txt	80	207.46.13.114
4	2012-05-23 00:4...	69.10.57.50	GET	/Labs.aspx	80	207.46.13.114
5	2012-05-23 00:4...	69.10.57.50	GET	/Labs.aspx	80	207.46.199.33
6	2012-05-23 00:5...	69.10.57.50	GET	/AboutUs.aspx	80	66.249.71.162
7	2012-05-23 00:5...	69.10.57.50	GET	/DeptofMusic.a...	80	180.76.5.177
8	2012-05-23 01:0...	69.10.57.50	GET	/DeptofPhy.aspx	80	66.249.71.162
9	2012-05-23 01:0...	69.10.57.50	GET	/robots.txt	80	124.115.6.13
10	2012-05-23 01:1...	69.10.57.50	GET	/Images/banne...	80	66.249.71.162
11	2012-05-23 01:2...	69.10.57.50	GET	/robots.txt	80	180.76.5.171
12	2012-05-23 01:5...	69.10.57.50	GET	/academic.aspx	80	66.249.71.162
13	2012-05-23 02:2...	69.10.57.50	GET	/mscmicro.aspx	80	66.249.71.1
14	2012-05-23 03:0...	69.10.57.50	GET	/images/Admis...	80	66.54.75.248
15	2012-05-23 03:0...	69.10.57.50	GET	/Images/Admis...	80	66.54.75.245
16	2012-05-23 03:0...	69.10.57.50	GET	/images/Admis...	80	66.54.75.243
17	2012-05-23 03:1...	69.10.57.50	GET	/robots.txt	80	65.52.104.26
18	2012-05-23 03:1...	69.10.57.50	GET	/General.aspx	80	65.52.104.26
19	2012-05-23 03:1...	69.10.57.50	GET	/General.aspx	80	207.46.199.30
20	2012-05-23 03:4...	69.10.57.50	GET	/IGNOU.aspx	80	180.76.5.87
21	2012-05-23 04:1...	69.10.57.50	GET		80	117.200.154.34
22	2012-05-23 04:1...	69.10.57.50	GET	/home.aspx	80	117.200.154.34
NULL	NULL	NULL	NULL	NULL	NULL	NULL

The algorithm to perform data transferring from flat file (Original log file) to database. Once the data already in database, mining task can be performed to produce the useful patterns.

Pattern Mining

Pattern mining is implemented using the C#. The algorithm to perform General Statistics is as:

```
Integer Hits = 0;
While (OledbDataReader.Read())
{
        Hits = Hits+1;
OledbDataReader.Next();
}
```

The algorithm to calculate the total number of hits. Generally, the total number of hits is equal to the total number of transaction in database. The algorithm to calculate the total page views below:

```
PageViewCount = 0;
While (OledbDataReader.Read())
{
        If (Right(Rs("URI-Stem"),4) = extension of pages)
```

```
        {
                PageViewCount = PageViewCount + 1;
        }
        OledbDataReader.Next();
}
```

The algorithm used to determine the number of page viewed through the server logs. In this algorithm, only file extension such as *.hrm, *.html and *.asp will be recognized for calculating the Page View options. URI-Stem is applied to check the file being accessed by the user.

```
DownloadFileCounter = 0;
Do While not RS.EOF
        If Right(Rs("URI-Stem"),4) = extension of download file
                DownloadFileCounter = DownloadFileCounter +1;
        End If
        RS.MoveNext;
Loop;
```

An algorithm to determine the number of downloaded files through the server logs. The number of downloaded files could be identified through the extensions such as Ms Word Document (*.doc), Adobe Acrobat (*.pdf), Ms Excel (*.xls), Zipped Files (*.zip), Postscript (*.ps). These extensions are the most common used for downloading purposes.

Generalized Association Rules

Once pattern mining analysis has been successfully executed, generalized association rules were applied to mine the useful patterns using support and confidence counting. From the server logs, hierarchy of the websites is determined. To perform this task, generalized association rules is applied until level 3. Comparing with the standard association rules, generalized association rules allow rules at different levels. Generalized association rules were also used to tackle the data diversity problems. To perform generalized association rules, server logs must be cleaned or filtered. Many entries that were considered uninteresting for mining were removed. In the entries such as images (e.g. *.gif, *.jpg) and scripts (*.css, *.js) are removed. An algorithm for cleaning the entries of server logs is presented below:

```
Read record in database
For each record in database
        Read fields (URI-Stem)
        If fields = {*.gif, *.jpg,*.css} then
                Remove records;
        Else
                Save records;
        End if
        Next record;
```

Counting Occurrence Algorithm

Before support and confidence for each is determined, number of occurrence for each rule must be calculated. An algorithm for counting the number of occurrence is shown below:

```
Read record in database
For each record in database
        if Filter item_Level1 ∩Item_lever2 <> 0 then
                Counter = Counter + 1;
        End if
        Next record;
```

An algorithm for calculating the number of occurrence based on the rules for each record and level. The implementation of this algorithm is as follows.

```
From level 1:
        Identify child from parent
        For example: Tutor →QuestionBank
        Tutor (parent node)
        QuestionBank (child node in level 1)
        Combine parent and node using AND operator then fit in Filter
        Function
```

Algorithm for Support

Support measure how often the rules occur in database. To determine the support for each rules produced, several arguments have been identified in calculating the support such as Total Transaction in database and number of occurrence for each rules. The formula for support is shown below:

```
Input:-          Total Transaction in DB
                 No. of occurrences each item {x,y}
```

$$Support = \frac{\text{Number of occurrences} \{x, y\}}{\text{Total Transaction in DB}}$$

An example of calculation of support from the mined rules is shown below:

Total Transaction in Database=38524 (After cleaning process)
Total occurrence for Tutor →Estidotmy = 310
Support (Tutor → Estidotmy) = (310/38524) * 100
Support (Tutor →Estidotmy) = 0.80

The support for rules Tutor → Estidotmy has a value 0.80 percent. This means the probability the Tutor → Estidotmy occur in database is 0.80%.

Algorithm for Confidence

Based on the examples, support measures how often the rules occur in database while confidence measures strength of the rules. Typically, large confidence values and a smaller support are used. Formula for calculating the confidence value is shown below:

```
Input:-
        Total occurrence for item X
        Total occurrence for item X and Y
```

$$Confidence = \frac{Total\ occurence\ for\ item\ X\ and\ Y}{Total\ occurence\ for\ item\ X}$$

The example of calculation of confidence value from rules produced:

Calculating confidence for rules Tutor →Estidotmy
Number of occurrence for Tutor = 21179
Number of occurrence for Tutor → Estidotmy
Confidence (Tutor → Estidotmy) = (310/21179) * 100
Confidence (Tutor → Estidotmy) =1.46

Since the confidence from the above calculation shows that Confidence > Support, it means the rules for Tutor → Estidotmy are interesting rules.

RESEARCH DIRECTION

The collaborative efforts brought forward in this research have attempted to present advancements in adaptive websites with the chief goal of improving users' task of navigating in a website. Although, this research work is far away from a finished work in particular consideration to its long term goal of improving a website's organization involuntarily. Also via this particular section, we will take a glimpse of the limitations of the work addressed here, discover ways of addressing them and finally confer possible expansion to this research's scope.

Data Acquisition from Web Logs

Data acquisition from web logs has a chief role to play in usage mining as it affects the knowledge discovered from it. Via means of this during the web logs filtration task we presume that calls for documents other than HTML as inappropriate and filtered them out. But this is regardless of the fact that the possibility of these non-html files can be of user's choice in the website. Often this becomes tremendously intricate to decide whether such non-html files are of any significance or not based on the information available from web logs alone. The previously revealed presumptions did not relentlessly affect the conclusion, most likely due to the possibility that users could visit HTML documents pertinent to links to such non-html files. Although this issue could be used to address additional website structure information, to know if these non-html files are an element of a HTML document or a document by themselves. ON keeping a track in the crawler logs elimination task, we utilized illustrations that had a combined approach utilizing a list of known crawlers IP addresses and the Robots Exclusion Standard to filter out crawler logs from web logs. In spite of its ease, the experiment stated in this demonstrated the efficacy of the combined approach in determining bulk of crawler's requests in the web logs. Still, the Robots Exclusion Standard is not controlled by a qualified body and crawler's conformity to it is questionable. Besides this, publicly accessible record of popular crawlers IP addresses is not exhaustive. Hence, if a crawler is not registered it does not comply with the Robots Exclusion Standard, and shall be recognized as an authentic user instead of a crawler. This could be addressed by employing a more sophisticated method of detecting a crawler's requests such as in (Tan and Kumar, 2002).Lastly, in the sessionization task, one chief aspect confronted was the omission of the document requests pertaining to the internal users made through the school's proxy server which comprised of approximately 65% of the original dataset and could be considered as making the conclusion of this research a biased one. However, the research defers fairly good results mainly because the remaining 35% of the dataset constituted both internal and external users' document requests. Still, this case may not be true in case of other websites. Hence one of the methods to address these document requests linked to proxy servers could be to utilize the proxy logs to differentiate between requests made by other users.

Limited Background Information

Our work depends exclusively on the knowledge discerned from the web logs. However, enhanced with information on users' access patterns and website usage statistics, we would like to call attention into the type of information that could be gathered from the CLF web logs are still limited. This established suspicion in the approaches utilized to recognize the end of a user's session and target documents from the website and hence brings our research work in role by being a time based approach where a threshold is used to identify both from the web logs. Though, this needs the information of the actual time the users have spent in each document they had visited while browsing the website, but the drawback of our web logs used in our research work does not capture such information. Consequently, the date and time stamp of subsequent document requests appearing in the web logs show the approximate time spent by a user on a document. Similar uncertainty persists in making out the end of a user's session and hence time thresholds were set to specify this on the basis of the TI distribution of users' logs which has also been utilized to generate the distribution. This drawback can be dealt with the use of customized cookies written to allocate a session ID for each visit made by a user to the website so as to note the time spent on each document visited by him in the session.

Dynamic Websites

The effort presented via this is based on a single website, which is the RGU's School of Computing website which chiefly comprises of documents with static information in them and did not have any dynamic features. Thus the relevance and performance of our approach on other websites such as dynamic websites still remain largely unknown.

Grouping Similar Paths Together

In our research work the measures help to determine the resemblance between two paths which focused on the number of co-occurring documents between them immaterial of their sequence. Hence in mere future we could look into grouping the paths based on the sequence. Besides this our work depended on K-means algorithm to cluster similar paths together. Also we can engage into a conceptual based clustering technique such as COBWEB and compare the performances of these two algorithms in grouping similar paths together which can form the basis for future research work.

Qualitative Evaluation

On assessing our approach utilizing a qualitative method and confer the scenario's in which the shortcuts can be utilized in shortening user's navigational paths. Our maneuvers also provides us with the knowledge that how useful the shortcuts could be in supporting the users to reach their target documents. But a quantitative method is required to estimate the utility of these shortcuts.Use of historical web logs can be used to obtain an approximation of the usefulness of the suggested shortcuts by dividing our main data set into training and test data, which then generates a set probable shortcut from the training data. Collection of users' paths from the test data is then obtained on the basis of the target documents recognized in the training data. After this each path discovered from the test data could be used to calculate the number of original clicks a user requires to reach a specific target document. We can then recalculate the number of clicks a user could have saved from using the new shortcuts for each path discovered in the test data allowing us to gain quantitative approximation of the utility of the suggested shortcuts in shortening navigational paths adopted by the users to reach their target documents.

Automated Adaptation of Website's Organization

Also via means of this, we have suggested shortcuts based on the way posts identified from recurrent travelled users' paths. Although, our extended goal is to expand this work, so that these projected shortcuts could be involuntarily included into the website. Hence involving development of such a tool that mechanizes website transformation thus permitting a webmaster to monitor and manipulate the changes made to the website's organization. Above all, we intend to look into means of adding the generated shortcuts to the website by dealing with quite a lot of issues related with how, where and should the generated shortcuts be executed into the website. A way forward with the first two issues would be to acquire the dedicated dialogue box adaptation method introduced in. In this method, given a shortcut to be added between two documents A and B, a dedicated dialogue box with restricted space is placed in A to promote the hyperlink to B. New shortcuts are added into the dialogue box as they are suggested and unpopular shortcuts will be removed to make way for the new ones. Upon addressing the third issue as to whether a shortcut should be added or not, it could be easily solved using the hyperlinks structure information of the website. In addition to this labeling the shortcuts is equally important to adding them to the website as improperly labeled shortcuts are detrimental. Hence, we can also look into utilizing content mining techniques to generate significant labels for the shortcuts before adding them to the website.

CONCLUSION

This chapter has scrutinized the concept of hash table in websites and brought forward an advancement serving as navigational shortcuts utilized to bring about a progression in a website's organization. The methodology implemented in this work is superior to the preceding one in terms of time consumed by a file of certain Mb when supplied as input. Web usage mining is a characteristic of data mining that has become popularized in past few years. Commercial companies along with academic researchers have an expanded array of tools that functionalize several data mining algorithms on log files coming from web servers so as to discover user behavior on a particular web site. Execution of such an investigation on the web site can generate information that can be utilized to better accommodate the user's needs. Today numerous applications such as business and finance E-commerce, information retrieval and Academic and Industry use web usage mining. In this study, generalized association rules have been applied to web server log from Education site. Also we should not forget to mention that mostly attempts have relied on comparatively simpler techniques which can prove to be insufficient for real user profile data since noise in the data has to be dealt first. Thus, bringing about a necessity for robust methods that assimilates different intelligent techniques that are free of any suppositions about the noise contamination rate.

REFERENCES

Agarwal, C. C. (2004). On leveraging user access patterns for topic specific crawling. *Data Mining and Knowledge Discovery*, *9*(2), 123–145. doi:10.1023/B:DAMI.0000031633.76754.d3

Altingovde, I. S., & Ulusoy, O. (2004). Exploiting interclass rules for focussed crawling. *IEEE Intelligent Systems*, *19*(6), 66–73. doi:10.1109/MIS.2004.62

Ansari, S., Kohavi, R., Mason, L., & Zheng, Z. (2001). Integrating e-commerce and data mining: Architecture and challenges.*Proceedings of the 2001 IEEE International Conference on Data Mining*. IEEE Computer Society. doi:10.1109/ICDM.2001.989497

BBC. (2005). *Web enjoys year of biggest growth, Online*. Accessed on 05/2008 from *http://news.bbc.co.uk/2/hi/technology/4325918.stm

Berendt, B., Mobasher, B., Nakagawa, M., & Spiliopoulou, M. (2002). The impact of site structure and user environment on session reconstruction in web usage analysis.*Proceedings of the 4th WebKDD 2002 Workshop, at the ACMSIGKDD Conference on Knowledge Discovery in Databases*.

Brickell, J., Dhillon, I. S., & Modha, D. S. (2007). *Adaptive website design using caching algorithm. Advances in Web Mining and Web Usage Analysis* (Vol. 4811, pp. 1–20). Springer. doi:10.1007/978-3-540-77485-3_1

Catledge, L. D., & Pitkow, J. E. (1995). Characterizing browsing strategies in the World Wide Web. *Computer Networks and ISDN Systems*, *27*(6), 1065–1073. doi:10.1016/0169-7552(95)00043-7

Chakrabarti, S., Dom, B., & van de Berg, M. (1999). Focussed crawling: A new approach to topic specific web resource discovery.*Proceedings of the 8th World Wide Web Conference*. Elsevier.

Cooley, R., Mobasher, B., & Srivastava, J. (1999). Data preparation for mining World Wide Web browsing patterns. *Knowledge and Information Systems*, *1*(1), 5–32. doi:10.1007/BF03325089

Cooley, R., Tan, P.-N., & Srivastava, J. (2000). *Discovery of interesting usage patterns from web data. Web Usage Analysis and User Profiling* (Vol. 1836, pp. 163–182). San Diego, CA: Springer. doi:10.1007/3-540-44934-5_10

Crescenzi, V., Merialdo, P., & Missier, P. (2005). Clustering Web pages based on their structures. *Data & Knowledge Engineering*, *54*(3), 279–299. doi:10.1016/j.datak.2004.11.004

Etzioni, O., & Perkowitz, M. (1997). Adaptive websites: An AI challenge. *Proceedings of the 15th International Joint Conference on Artificial Intelligence*. Morgan Kaufmann.

Etzioni, O., & Perkowitz, M. (2000). Towards adaptive web sites: Conceptual framework and case study. *Artificial Intelligence*, *118*(1-2), 245–275. doi:10.1016/S0004-3702(99)00098-3

Facca, F., & Lanzi, P. (2005). Mining interesting knowledge from weblogs: A survey. *Data Mining and Knowledge Discovery*, *53*(5), 225–241.

Fan, L., Cao, P., Lin, W., & Jacobson, Q. (1999). Web prefetching between low- bandwidth clients and proxies: Potential and performance. *Proceedings of the ACM SIGMETRICS International Conference on Measurement and Modeling of Computer Systems*. ACM Press. doi:10.1145/301464.301557

Festa, P. (2003). *Personalized websites are driving customers away*. Accessed on 03/2007 from *http://networks.silicon.com/webwatch/0,39024667,10006394,00.htm

Godoy, D., & Amandi, A. (2006). *Modeling user interests by conceptual clustering, Information Systems* (Vol. 31). Elsevier Science Ltd.

Goker, A., & He, D. (2000a). Analysing Web search logs to determine session boundaries for user-oriented learning. *Proceedings of the International Conference on Adaptive Hypermedia and Adaptive Web-based Systems*. doi:10.1007/3-540-44595-1_38

Goker, A., & He, D. (2000b). Detecting session boundaries from Web user logs. *Proceedings of the 22nd Annual Colloquium on Information Retrieval Research*, (pp. 57–66).

Goker, A., He, D., & Harper, D. (2002). Combining evidence for automatic web session identification. *Information Processing & Management*, *38*(5), 727–742. doi:10.1016/S0306-4573(01)00060-7

Good, N., Schafer, B., Konstan, J., Borchers, A., Sarwar, B., Herlocker, J., & Riedl, J. (1999). Combining collaborative filtering with personal agents for better recommendation. *Proceedings of the 16th National Conference on Artificial Intelligence*. American Association for Artificial Intelligence.

Jiang, X.-M., Song, W.-G., & Zeng, H.-J. (2005). *Applying associative relationship on the clickthrough data to improve web search. Advances in Information Retrieval* (Vol. 3408, pp. 475–486). Springer.

Langley, P. (1999). User modeling in adaptive interfaces. *Proceedings of the 7th International Conference on User Modeling. Springer New York, Inc.*

Lee, J.-H., & Shiu, W.-K. (2004). An adaptive website system to improve efficiency with web mining techniques. *Advanced Engineering Informatics*, *18*(3), 129–142. doi:10.1016/j.aei.2004.09.007

Lieberman, H. (1995). Letizia: An agent that assists Web browsing.*Proceedings of the International Joint Conference on Artificial Intelligence.* Morgan Kaufmann.

Lieberman, H., Dyke, N. V., & Vivacqua, A. S. (1999). Let's Browse: A collaborative Web browsing agent. *Proceedings of the 1999 International Conference on Intelligent User Interfaces.* ACM Press. doi:10.1145/291080.291092

Lourenco, A., & Belo, O. (2006). Catching web crawlers in the act. *Proceedings of the 6th International Conference on Web Engineering.* ACM.

Masseglia, F., Poncelet, P., & Teisseire, M. (2003). Using data mining techniques on Web access logs to dynamically improve hypertext structure. *SIGWEB Newsletter, 8*(3), 13–19. doi:10.1145/951440.951443

McGovern, G. (2003). *Why personalization hasn't worked.* Accessed on 03/2007 from http://www.gerrymcgovern.com/nt/2003/nt 2003 10 20 personalization.htm

Mitchell, T., Joachims, T., & Freitag, D. (1997). Web watcher: A tour guide for the world wide web. *Proceeding of the 15th International Joint Conference on Artificial Intelligence.* Morgan Kaufmann.

Mobasher, B., Cooley, R., & Srivastava, J. (1999). Creating adaptive web sites through usage-based clustering of URLs.*Proceedings of the 1999 Workshop on Knowledge and Data Engineering Exchange.* IEEE Computer Society.

Mobasher, B., Cooley, R., & Srivastava, J. (2000). Automatic personalization based on web usage mining. *Communications of the ACM, 43*(8), 142–151. doi:10.1145/345124.345169

Netcraft. (2008). *Web server survey.* Accessed on 05/2008 from http://news.netcraft.com/archives/web server survey.html

Page, L., Brin, S., Motwani, R., & Winograd, T. (1998). *The PageRank citation ranking: Bringing order to the web.* Technical report. Stanford Digital Library Technologies Project. Accessed from citeseer.ist. psu.edu/page98pagerank.html

Pavlov, D., Manvoglu, E., Giles, L., & Pennock, D. (2004). Collaborative filtering with maximum entropy. *IEEE Intelligent Systems, 19*(6), 40–48. doi:10.1109/MIS.2004.59

Perkowitz, M., & Etzioni, O. (1997). *Adaptive sites: Automatically learning from user access patterns. Technical report.* Department of Computer Science and Engineering, University of Washington.

Pirolli, P., Pitkow, J., & Rao, R. (1996). Silk from a sow's ear: Extracting usable structures from the Web.*Proceedings of the 1996 Conference on Human Factors in Computing Systems (CHI-96).* doi:10.1145/238386.238450

Pitkow, J. (1997). *In search of reliable usage data on the WWW. In Computer Networks and ISDN Systems* (Vol. 29, pp. 1343–1355). Santa Clara, CA: Elsevier Science.

Rangarajan, S., Phoha, V., Balagani, K., Selmic, R., & Iyengar, S. (2004). Adaptive neural network clustering of Web users. *Computer, 37*(4), 34–40. doi:10.1109/MC.2004.1297299

Shardanand, U., & Maes, P. (1995). Social information filtering: malgorithms for automating "word of mouth". *Proceedings of ACM Conference on Human Factor in Computing Systems*. ACM Press. doi:10.1145/223904.223931

SPSS. (2008). *Predictive web analytics*. Accessed on 04/2008 from http://www.spss.com/pwa/index.html

Srikant, R., & Yang, Y. (2001). Mining web logs to improve website organization.*Proceedings of the 10th international conference on World Wide Web*. ACM Press. doi:10.1145/371920.372097

Srivastava, J., Cooley, R., Deshpande, M., & Tan, P.-N. (2000). Web usage mining: Discovery and applications of usage patterns from web data. *SIGKDD Explorations*, *1*(2), 12–23. doi:10.1145/846183.846188

Tan, P.-N., & Kumar, V. (2002). Discovery of web robot sessions based on their navigational patterns. *Data Mining and Knowledge Discovery*, *6*(1), 9–35. doi:10.1023/A:1013228602957

WebTrend. (2008). *Webtrends visitor intelligence*. Accessed on 04/2008 from http://www.webtrends.com/Products/WebTrendsVisitorIntelligence.aspx

Wexelblat, A., & Maes, P. (1999). Footprints: History-rich tools for information foraging.*Proceedings of the SIGCHI Conference on Human Factors in Computing Systems*. ACM Press.

Chapter 7
Web Usage Mining:
Improving the Performance of Web–Based Application through Web Mining

Sathiyamoorthi V
Sona College of Technology, India

ABSTRACT

In recent days, Internet technology has provided a lot of services for sharing and distributing information across the world. Among all the services, World Wide Web (WWW) plays a significant role. The slow retrieval of Web pages may lessen the interest of users from accessing them. To deal with this problem, Web caching and Web pre-fetching are the two techniques used. Web proxy caching plays a key role in improving Web performance by keeping Web objects that are likely to be used in the near future in the proxy server which is closer to the end user. It helps in reducing user perceived latency, network bandwidth utilization, and alleviating loads on the Web servers. Thus, it improves the efficiency and scalability of Web based system. This chapter gives an overview of Web usage mining and its application on Web and discusses various approaches for improving the performance of Web.

INTRODUCTION

It is generally observed throughout the world that in the last two decades, while the average speed of computers has almost doubled in a span of around eighteen months, the average speed of the network has doubled merely in a span of just eight months! In order to improve the performance, more and more researchers are focusing their research in the field of computers and its related technologies. Internet is one such technology that plays a major role in simplifying the information sharing and retrieval. World Wide Web (WWW) is one such service provided by the Internet. It acts as a medium for sharing of information. As a result, millions of applications run on the Internet and cause increased network traffic and put a great demand on the available network infrastructure. The rapid growth of the WWW and Web development has been the result of many innovative advances in Web technology. Web works with arrays of technologies for better communication with the Internet user, but the inconveniences to users still persistent among the users. A possible solution for this problem is, to add a new resource and distribute

DOI: 10.4018/978-1-5225-1877-8.ch007

the network traffic across one or more resources. Web caching is one such method which is widely used to reduce the network traffic by storing Webpages to a location nearer to the client (Pallis et al 2008). A proxy server is responsible for Web caching which acts as a mediator between the Web server and the Web client and thus reduces latency in retrieving the pages. This proxy-based Web caching system can still be improved to control the performance of the Web. This chapter thus focuses on a methodology for improving the proxy-based Web caching system. It uses Web Usage Mining (WUM) to optimize the performance of the Web based system through Web caching and pre-fetching.

Basic Terminologies

The word cache means, fastest memory. Caching refers to the storage of recently or frequently retrieved information for future access (Wessels & Duane 2001). It reduces latency in accessing Webpages and also improves the performance of Web-based systems. The most important terms used in cache memory references are: i) cache hit and ii) cache miss. If the user requested object is not present in the cache, then it is called a cache miss else if it is present then it is called a cache hit. The hit rate also known as hit ratio (HR) is the percentage of user's requests served from the cache. The byte hit rate (BHR) also known as byte hit ratio is the percentage of bytes served from the cache. Thus, caching saves bandwidth utilization and byte hit rate used to measures it. Byte hit rate is used to measure network performance whereas hit rate used to measure the user satisfaction. Client is the program that makes a request for some resources or objects from the server. Server is a service provider for the client. It is the storage of multiple heterogeneous resources that are accessed by multiple clients. Each server has a unique name or identifier through which a client can refer the server and make requests for some resources. This unique identifier is called URL. Usually, communication can take place only between clients which initiates the communication by sending a request and the server which processes the user request and sends response. Web-based system is an example for client server system environment. In this, the most commonly used client is Web browser. A proxy server lies in between clients and servers and reduces latency. It acts as a client when interacting with a Web server and acts as a server when interacting with a browser. Web documents might be classified into either dynamic or static documents. Dynamic documents are generated by the server when a request arrives and is dependent on time of user's request whereas static documents are produced independent of any user's request. These documents are identified based on file extensions such as.jsp,.asp,.html,.xml and so on. The interaction between client and server is initiated by the protocol called Hypertext Transfer Protocol (HTTP). The response header of HTTP protocol contains information that is originally requested by the user and control information which includes size, type and various cache control directives. Response header also contains status code which tells about the success or failure of the user request. The commonly exchanged status codes are 200 (OK), 404 (Not Found) (Wessels & Duane 2001). The other codes exchanged between proxy server and Web server is 304 (Freshness). Cache has limited space. So when a new object arrives and no space has been left for the incoming object, then it must remove some objects from the cache. To do this, a cache replacement policy has been designed. It assigns a priority value to each object in the cache by using some heuristic technique and removes the least expensive objects based on priority value. It depends on the cache replacement policies used for replacement. Different heuristic techniques have been adapted by various replacement policies. Some of these standard policies include LRU, LFU, and FIFO. A user session is interaction between a client and a server during particular time period or visits. During this session, user might have accessed large number of Web pages. Web pages are piece of information present in a

Website which is managed by Web server and accessed by several clients. Web pages are always associated with some Websites. Hence Websites are collection of highly homogeneous information linked by hyperlinks. Hyperlinks are logical connection between Web pages which contains similar information. It might be in the same Web page called intra link or in another Web page called inter link. The rest of this chapter is organized as follows: The next section gives the introduction of web mining, data mining and web usage mining then followed by related works on Web caching and Web Pre-fetching and then last section presents the conclusions, findings and suggestion for future research.

BACKGROUND

As the Internet continues to grow in size and popularity, Web traffic and network problems are the major issues in the Internet world. The continued increase in demand for objects on the Internet causes ruthless overloads on many Websites and network links. The internet users have no patience to wait even for few seconds for downloading a Webpage. Web traffic reduction techniques are necessary for accessing the Websites efficiently with the existing network facility. Web caching with Web pre-fetching techniques reduces the Web latency that we normally face on the internet (Sathiyamoorthi & Murali Bhaskaran 2010a). Research in Web caching and Web pre-fetching is considered to be very important due to the issues and challenges exist and arise in the following dimensions:

- Ever increasing bandwidth cost and demand
- Non-uniform bandwidth across network
- Non-uniform latencies across network
- Increase in Network distances
- High bandwidth demands from users

There are many factors that affect the performances of Web including variations in network connectivity, distance between nodes and congestion in networks or servers due to unpredicted demand. Web caching and Web pre-fetching are the methodologies that help to increase the performance of the Web (Sathiyamoorthi & Murali Bhaskaran 2012). Further improvement in the performance of Web application can be achieved through data mining techniques (Bamshad 2007) widely known as Web mining. The following subsections give an overview of some of these techniques.

Data Mining

Data Mining, also known as the Knowledge Discovery in Databases (KDD), is the nontrivial extraction of implicit, previously unknown and potentially a useful information from the raw data present in the large database. Data mining techniques can be applied upon various data sources to improve the value of existing information system (Sathiyamoorthi & Murali Bhaskaran 2010b). When implemented on high performance client and server system, data mining tools can analyze large databases to deliver highly reliable results. It is also described that the data mining techniques can be coupled with relational database engines (Jiawei et al 2006). Data mining differs from the conventional database retrieval in the fact, that it extracts hidden information or knowledge that is not explicitly available in database, whereas database retrieval extracts the data that is explicitly available in the databases. Based on the fact that, a certain degree of intelligence is incorporated in the system, data mining could further be viewed as a branch of artificial intelligence and thus, data mining could be treated as an intelligent database manipulation system. Dunham et al (2006) have explained that data mining is an interdisciplinary field that incorporates concepts from several disciplines such as statistics, neural networks and machine learning in the process of knowledge discovery.

Basic Steps in Data Mining

It is described that data mining can be viewed as a crucial step in knowledge discovery process. It is composed of various phases such as:

- Pre-processing
- Data Mining
- Pattern Extraction
- Pattern Evaluation
- Knowledge Presentation

The data preprocessing phase devises the data to be in a format that are suitable for further data mining operations. Data cleaning removes noise, inconsistent data, and irrelevant data that are present in the data sources. Since the input database could be composed of data that arrives from multiple sources, data integration is employed to integrate data from those sources. Data mining phase identifies the specific data mining tasks that employs intelligent methods and extracts knowledge. The resulting knowledge or patterns are evaluated for usability in the pattern evaluation phase. The last step of KDD process is the presentation of discovered knowledge in a user friendly and user understandable format referred to as the knowledge presentation phase (Jiawei et al 2006). Data mining techniques such as Classification, Prediction, Association Rule Mining, Trend Analysis, etc. are present so as to choose the suitable technique depending upon the nature of data mining application. The technique chosen in this chapter is clustering.

Clustering

Dunham et al (2006) highlight in their work that clustering is a process of dividing the given objects into groups of similar objects based on some similarity. It is also known as unsupervised learning process. In general, it is described as follows: Given a set of data objects, each having a set of attributes and a similarity measure among them, find clusters such that objects within the clusters are highly similar to one another and dissimilar to objects of other clusters. Different similarity measure can be employed based on the type of attributes involved in distance calculation. For example, if attributes are continuous in nature then the distance calculated is a Euclidean distance. The ultimate goal of clustering is to segregate objects into k-subsets called clusters. Usually, subsets do not intersect and their union is equal to a full data set. Representing data by fewer clusters necessarily loses at least some fine details, but achieves simplification or reduction. Clustering represents many data objects into fewer clusters. K-Means and K-Medoids are some of the standard algorithms used in clustering (Jiawei et al 2006).

Web Mining

In today's Internet scenario, WWW plays a significant role in retrieving and sharing information. Hence, WWW becomes a huge repository of data. As a result, it is difficult for data analyst or end users to analyze the entire data and to discover some useful information. To overcome these troubles, data mining can be applied for knowledge discovery in WWW. To discover knowledge from Web, Web mining is used. Web mining is broadly categorized into three major areas such as Web Content Mining; Web Structure Mining and Web Log Mining or Web Usage Mining Srivastava et al 2000, Zaiane 2000). Web Content Mining is the part of Web Mining which focuses on the raw information available in Web pages (Kosala & Blockeel 2000). Data source mainly consists of textual data present in the Web pages. Mining is based on content categorization and content ranking of Web pages. Web Structure Mining is a Web Mining task which deals with the structure of the Websites. The data source consists of structural information present in Webpages that are hyperlinks. The mining includes link-based categorization of Webpages, ranking of Webpages through a combination of content and structure (Brin & Pange 1998), and reverse engineering of Website models. Web Usage Mining (WUM) is another Web Mining task which describes knowledge discovery from Web server log files (Sathiyamoorthi & Mural Bhaskaran 2011a). The source data mainly consist of the raw text file that is stored in Web server when a user accesses the Webpage. It might be represented either in Common Log Format (CLF) or in Extended Common Log Format (ECLF). It includes Web personalization, adaptive Websites, and user modeling. This chapter discusses the WUM to optimize the existing Web caching and pre-fetching technique.

WEB USAGE MINING

It is noted that research in Web Usage Mining started in late 1990's according to Srivastava et al (2000), Mobasher et al (2002), Cyrus et al (1997), Feng et al (2009). Web Usage Mining (WUM) is also known as Web log mining wherein it relies on the information present in the Web log file produced by the Web servers. Web log files are raw text file which needs certain preprocessing methods before applying the data mining techniques. The basic steps involved in WUM are:

- Data Collection
- Data Preprocessing
- Pattern Extraction
- Pattern Analysis and Visualization
- Pattern Applications

Data Sources for Web Usage Mining

Data sources used for WUM can be collected from three different locations (Srivastva et al 2000) as is shown in Figure 1.

1. **Server-Level** : It stores data about the requests that are activated by different clients. It keeps track of multiple users' interest on a single Website. The main drawback is that log files must be

secured since it contains some sensitive information about the users. Further, it does not contain information about cached pages.

2. **Client-Level**: The browser itself will send some information to a repository regarding the user's access. This is achieved by using an adhoc browsing application or through client-side applications that can run on standard Web browsers. It requires the design team to develop special software and deploy it along with the end users' browsers.

3. **Proxy-level** : It collects the information about user's browsing behavior and recorded at proxy server log. It keeps track of multiple users' interest on several Websites. It is used only by the users whose requests are passed through the proxy.

The following information can be gathered from the Web log file (Sathiyamoorthi & Murali Bhaskaran 2011b):

1. General summary information regarding user and page access.
2. Statistical information about Web pages hit.
3. From where user is accessing the Web pages?
4. Is Browser used by the users to access the Webpages?
5. Success or failure code for each page access.
6. Report based on page size, type and so on.
7. How often user's visit each Webpage?
8. When a Web page has been accessed?
9. Who is interested in which pages?
10. What is the access frequency of each Webpage?
11. Which pages are accessed frequently and recently?

Figure 1. Data sources for web usage mining

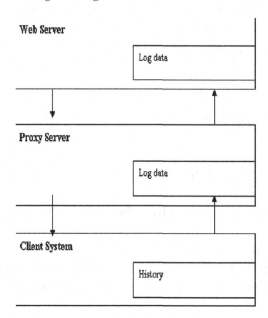

Web Caching

Web caching is a technique which is used for caching as many Webpages in the cache to improve the network performance. The main component is its page replacement policy. When a new document arrives, the replacement policy has to make critical decision in replacing an existing Webpage from the cache. In this research work WUM is used to modify the existing Web cache page replacement policy for better performance (Sathiyamoorthi 2016). The next section gives an overview of various replacement algorithms.

Web Pre-Fetching

Web pre-fetching or pre-loading is a technique which pre-fetches Webpages into the cache before the actual request for that page arrives (Sathiyamoorthi & Murali Bhaskaran 2013). There are two approaches used:

1. **Short-term Pre-Fetching:** In short-term pre-fetching, Webpages are pre-fetched into the cache by analyzing the recent access history of the Web cache (Chen et al 2002).
2. **Long-term Pre-Fetching:** In this technique, the probability of accessing Webpages are identified and pre-fetched by analyzing the global access pattern (Lee et al 2009).

The authors Loon and Bhargavan (1997) have presented a pre-fetching technique based on user profiles which are represented through a weighted directed graph where the nodes represent Uniform Resource Locators (URL) and the edges represent the access paths. The weight of a node represents the access frequency of URLs and the weight of an edge represents the access frequency of one URL after another. Ibrahim and Xu (2000) have presented a technique that uses an artificial neural network for predicting the next user request. Fan et al (1999) investigated an approach to reduce Web latency, by pre-fetching between caching proxies and browsers. This approach has used the Prediction by Partial Match (PPM) algorithm for pre-fetching. The authors Markatos et al (1998) have presented a Top-10 approach for pre-fetching. In their approach, the ten most popular Webpages are pre-fetched and cached. Also Padmanabhan and Mogul (1996) have presented a pre-fetching scheme in which the server computes the likelihood that a particular Webpage will be accessed and conveys the information to the client. The upcoming section gives the overview of Web pre-fetching and their research work.

Integration of Web Caching and Web Pre-Fetching

Web caching and Web pre-fetching schemes have been presented in (Podlipnig & Boszormenyi 2003; Teng et al 2005; Balamash & Krunz 2004). They state that integration of these two techniques would perform better. An additional improvement to traditional cache replacement policies used in the proxy server's cache is explained in Pallis et al (2008) which are based on the clustering-based pre-fetching scheme using dependency graph. In this work, the authors have used traditional algorithm to measure the performance of pre-fetching technique. Caching and pre-fetching have often been studied as separate tools for reducing the latency observed by the users in accessing the Web. Less work has been done on integration of caching and pre-fetching techniques. Kroeger et al (1997) have studied the combined effect of caching and pre-fetching on end user latency. Lan et al (2000) have proposed a Rule-Assisted

Pre-fetching in Web server caching. Yang et al (2004) have proposed a method for Mining Web Logs to obtain a prediction model and then using the model to extend the well-known GDSF caching policy.

RESEARCH PROGRESS IN WEB CACHING USING WEB LOG MINING

One key factor for civilizing the performance of Web-based applications is Web caching. Caching anticipates the popular objects that are likely to be accessed in the near future and hence they should be kept in a location nearer to the client. Thus, it helps in reducing the network traffic over the Internet and apart from that, the server load ultimately improves the scalability of the Web-based system. Wong (2006), Wang (1999) have reviewed and discussed about various Web cache replacement algorithms that were carried out in the past. Venketesh and Venkatesan (2009) have proposed an intelligent Web caching approach which is based on neural network and evolutionary techniques. Web caching provides the following paybacks to users such as clients, network administrators and content providers (Acharjee et al 2006):

- The user delay in accessing a Webpage is reduced i.e., Latency Reduction
- Efficiency in using network bandwidth
- Reduction in the loads on the Web server
- Network traffics reduction

Types of Web Caching

Web caching is a means that keeps the Web objects in a location nearer to the end users. As seen in Figure 2, on the basis of location, Web caching system is classified into browser cache, proxy cache, and server cache:

- **Browser Cache:** This type of cache is located at the client side helping the users to access the pages that have been accessed recently or visited already. Some of the modern browsers that support Web caching are Internet Explorer, Mozilla and Google chrome. This is useful when user presses the 'Back' button to view the previous page or clicks a link that was accessed already in the current Website or session. It focuses on one single user only (Chen 2007; Krishnamurthy & Rexforrd 2001).
- **Proxy Cache:** It is located at the proxy server which acts as an intermediate storage of Web objects between the clients and the servers. Its major role is to reduce the latency in accessing a Web page and serves the need of the user groups. It differs from browser cache and deals with single user. When a client request arrives, the proxy intercepts it and checks it in local cache. If the requested object is found then it sends the object back to the client. If the requested object is not found, then proxy will fetch it from origin server, store it in the cache and sends back to the client (Chen 2007; Krishnamurthy & Rexforrd 2001).
- **Server Cache:** In this category, a server side cache is employed eventually for storing the pages which will reduce the server work load. Thus, the redundant computation at the server side can be reduced. This is also known as Reverse Proxy Cache. (Chen 2007; Krishnamurthy & Rexforrd 2001).

Figure 2. Web caching locations

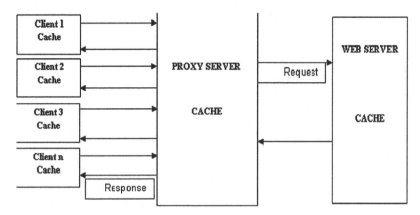

Among the above three approaches, a proxy-based Web caching is widely used by the computer network administrators, content providers, and business firms to reduce user delays and network traffic (Kaya et al 2009; Kumar 2009; Kumar & Norris 2008). The basic steps involved in processing a user request includes:

1. Client makes a request for an object which is passed through proxy server
2. Proxy checks its local cache for the requested object
3. If the requested object is found, then it revalidates it to make sure that it is fresh and sends it to the client
4. If the requested object is not found then the proxy fetches it from the origin server, stores it in a local cache and then sends it back to the client.

Working Principles of Proxy-based Web Caching

Basic proxy-based Web caching algorithm is shown in Figure 3. In this system, an object might be cached based on information present in the HTTP response header. Web server can also control objects caching by using Cache-Control directories. They are:

- **No-Store:** An object cannot be cached.
- **Private:** It can only be accessed by the person who originally requested it.

Some heuristics methods are applied in order to identify dynamic Web objects. There are file names ending with.cgi,.asp, or.jsp or path names containing cgi-bin or servlet categorized as dynamic Web objects. Hence caching them is not useful. The problem with Web caching is staleness of objects present in the cache. If the cache size is too large to store Webpages then they often stale. Such objects need to be refreshed or revalidated before sending it to client. This is accomplished using If-Modified-Since (IMS) query.

Figure 3. Basic proxy cache algorithms

```
If (Page is in the Cache)
If (Page is expired or stale)
              Validate it //if-modified-since (IMS Query)
              If (Page is not modified)//IMS Query Response
                    Serve from cache
              Else
                        Get from server and serve
    Else
              Serve from cache
    Else
    Get from server and serve
```

Web pre-fetching can resolve staleness issue. By predicting which object will be requested next and revalidate it if it is already in cache else adds them into the cache. Pre-fetching can further reduce latency in retrieving Web objects. Figure 4 shows the initial Web object request.

If a requested object is present in the cache, then it must be revalidated to make sure that it is fresh copy. This is achieved by sending IMS query along with the timestamp of the cached objects in the request. If the object has changed then the server response might contain the status code 200 (OK) and an updated version of the object is sent as the message body in response header which is shown in Figure 5.

Figure 4. Initial web object retrieval

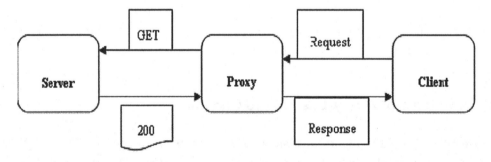

Figure 5. Validation of web object if it has changed

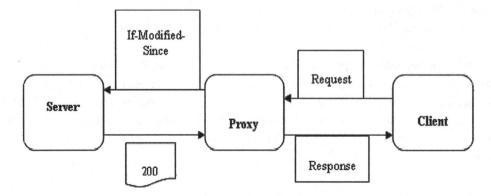

Figure 6. Validation of web object if it has not changed

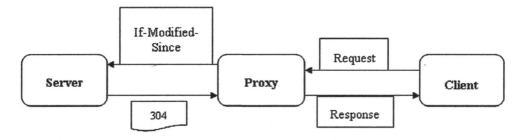

Figure 7. Web Object Validation using Expire Information

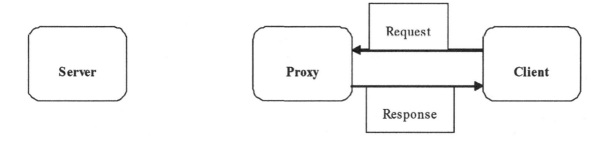

If the object has not changed then the server's response contains the status code 304 (Not Modified) and no body part which is shown in Figure 6.

If response header contains Expires information, it shows that the object will not change before the specified timestamp. Then no validation is necessary before this time period. Figure 7 shows the validation using Expire information present in the cached Web objects.

Basically Web caching and Web pre-fetching yields the following benefits.

1. Web pages are retrieved faster, reducing latency
2. Network bandwidth is utilized efficiently
3. Web server load and network traffic gets reduced

Intelligent Web Caching Policies

Cache replacement policy, being the heart of Web caching makes critical decision when cache is full on arrival of new documents. This is because cache has limited space and hence efficient cache replacement policy must be adapted to manage the cached objects. Web caching and traditional memory caching is different since the former deals with the variable sized objects whereas the later deals with fixed sized page (Koskela et al 2003). The following are some of the important features of Web objects that must be considered while making decisions (Chen et al 2003; Podlipnig & Boszormenyi 2003; Vakali 2002):

*   **Recency:** Last access time, on accessing a Web object
*   **Frequency:** Number of times an object is accessed since it is in the cache
*   **Size:** Size of an object in bytes

- **Cost:** Cost to fetch an object from server into the cache

Depending on these factors, the replacement policies can be further classified into five classes (Waleed et al 2011) which are given in Table 1. Ali and Shamsuddin (2009) have proposed an intelligent Web Caching called Intelligent Client side Web Caching Scheme (ICWCS). The Web objects have been classified into either cacheable or un-cacheable objects. They have used neuro-fuzzy system to predict Web objects that are likely to be accessed in the near future. A trained neuro-fuzzy system with LRU has been employed. The simulation results show that ICWCS would provide better Hit Rate (HR) but it provides low Byte Hit Rate (BHR) since it ignored the factors such as cost and size of the objects in the cache replacement process. This client side implementation poses other issues like the training process which requires longer time and higher computational cost.

The Authors Cobb and ElAarag (2008), Elaarag and Romano (2009) have used an Artificial Neural Network (ANN) in making cache replacement decision which classifies Web objects into different classes. However, objects that belong to the same classes are removed without any precedence between them. Moreover they have considered only conventional algorithm. Tian et al (2002) have proposed an adaptive Web cache access predictor using neural network. They have presented an intelligent predictor design that uses back propagation neural network algorithm to improve the performance of Web catching by predicting the most likely re-accessed objects and then keeping these objects in the cache for future access. However, they have ignored recency factor in Web objects removal policy. Even though the above methods are better than traditional algorithms, practically it is difficult as it is time consuming and moreover it does not consider the objects cost and size in the cache replacement process.

WEB PRE-FETCHING

Pre-fetching or Pre-loading is a technique adopted in order to reduce the latency problem and also to boost up the Web caching system performance. It uses intelligent algorithms to predict the Webpages

Table 1. Replacement policies merits and demerits (Waleed et. al)

Classes	Description	Example Policies	Demerits
Recency	It uses the recency or aging factor to remove objects from the cache	LRU, LRU-threshold	It does not consider access frequency, size and downloads latency of Web objects
Frequency	These policies use object access frequency to remove Web object	LFU, LFU-Aging	It does not consider recency, size and download latency of Web objects
Size	These policies use object size for removing Web object	SIZE, Partitioned Caching	It does not consider recency, frequency and downloads latency of objects
Function	These policies assign a priority value to each cached object which is calculated based on some functions	GDS, GDSF	Assigning weight factors is a difficult task and the cost of fetching Web object is dynamic and it differs time to time
Randomized	These policies use randomized decisions for object removal policy	RAND, LRU-C, LRU-S	It is inaccurate and difficult to evaluate

expected to be accessed in the near future before the actual user request. Then, the predicted objects are fetched from the server and stored in a location close to the client. Thus, it helps in increasing the cache hit rate and reduces the latency in accessing Webpages.

Types of Web Pre-Fetching

Similar to Web caching, Web pre-fetching can also be implemented on server side, proxy side and client side. Table 2 summarizes the merits and demerits of pre-fetching based on its location (Waleed et al 2011). It is inferred from (Zhijie et al 2009) that the client-based pre-fetching only deals with access behavior of a single user while sever-based pre-fetching deals with access behavior of all the users to a single Website. The proxy-based pre-fetching deals with access behavior of user group segments which reflect a common interest for user's community. Hence, proxy-based pre-fetching is the most widely used method as it is more and more useful and accurate to predict the pages of many Websites (Pallis et al 2008; Domenech et al 2010).

Related Work on Web Pre-Fetching

Web pre-fetching techniques can be categorized into two main classes. They are:

- Content-based approach
- History-based approach

The former pre-fetching analyses the current Webpage contents and identifies hyperlinks that are likely to be visited. The prediction is carried out using ANN mechanism depending on keywords in URL (Ibrahim and Xu 2000). It is suitable for client side pre-fetching technique. At the server side, it negatively affects the server performance due to high overhead involved in parsing every Webpage by affecting the server service time with an increase in the server load (Domenech et al 2010). According

Table 2. Types of pre-fetching based on location (Waleed et. al)

Pre-fetching Location	Data Sources	Merits	Demerits
Client Side	User historical request	It is easy to partition user sessions and useful in user centered pre-fetching	It does not share pre-fetching content among users and it needs a lot of network bandwidth
Proxy Side	Proxy Log file	It shares the common interests of a group of users. It shares pre-fetching content from different servers among users	It does not reflect common user interests for a single Website from all users Privacy information is ignored
Server Side	Web Server Log file	It records single Website access information from all users and reflects their common interests	It does not reflect the users actual browsing behavior and so difficult to identify user session. It needs additional communications cost between clients and servers for deciding pre-fetching content

to Zhijie et al (2009), in history-based pre-fetching, prediction is done based on the historical page access recorded in the Web log file. It is mainly used in server side pre-fetching techniques where user's history of accesses is recorded in the form of server log. Pre-fetching can be done using any one of the approaches given below:

- Graph based approach
- Markov model approach
- Cost based approach
- Data mining approach

Dependency Graph based Pre-Fetching Approach

According to Padmanabhan and Mogul (1996), pre-fetching technique can be based on Dependency Graph (DG). The DG consists of nodes representing Webpages, and links representing access sequence from one page to other. Weight associated with each of the links represents the probability of accessing the target node from the current node. Domenech et al (2010) have presented a pre-fetching approach based on Double Dependency Graph (DDG). DDG is used to predict inter and intra Webpage access. The main drawbacks of DG are that it is controlled by the threshold value and it will predict only one page at a time which will increase the server load and the network traffic when multiple users are accessing the server (Nanopoulos et al 2003).

Markov Model based Pre-Fetching Approach

Pre-fetching approach based on Markov model is more appropriate to predict user's next request by comparing the user's current access with the user's past access sequences that are recorded in Web log file (Pitkow & Pirolli 1999). This approach follows different order that is either the first order Markov model or the higher order Markov model which are discussed below.

A user access sequence consists of sequence of pages of the form:

$x_1 \rightarrow x_2 \rightarrow .... x_{k-1}$ where $k \geq 2$ (Palpanas & Mendelzon 1999).

In the first-order Markov model, also known as low-order Markov model, the next page access x_k depends only on current page x_{k-1}. If the access of x_k depends on consecutive two access of the form $x_{k-2} \rightarrow x_{k-1}$, then it is called a second-order Markov model. In general, if next page access depends on set of K previously accessed Webpages then it is called a Kth higher-order Markov model (Palpanas & Mendelzon 1999; Pitkow & Pirolli 1999). In the low-order Markov model, the prediction accuracy is very low, since it considers only the current Web page access. Therefore, Pitkow and Pirolli (1999) have proposed higher-order Markov model to improve the prediction accuracy. In this, predictions are carried out first using the higher- order Markov model. If there is no match then predictions is done by using lower-order Markov model. The order of Markov is decreased until the state is covered. The problem with higher-order Markov model is that it involves higher complexity in constructing probability matrix. Palpanas and Mendelzon (1999) have proposed pre-fetching based on Prediction-by-Partial-Match which depends on higher-order Markov model where prediction is done based on Markov decision tree that is constructed from the past access sequence of the users. The main drawback is, the tree size is increased based on number of past requests of user. The researchers Pitkow and Pirolli 1999, Chen et al (2002) have proposed different methods to control the tree size. The PPM based pre-fetching approach is not suitable for proxy side because proxy server can receive requests for pages on different server instead of a single Web server (Liu 2009).

Cost based Pre-Fetching Approach

This approach uses a cost function to pre-fetch the Web objects into the cache based on some factors including page popularity and its lifetime. According to Markatos and Chronaki (1998), 'pre-fetch by popularity' predicts and keeps top ten popular Webpages in cache. It is also known as Top-10 approach. The other work presented by (Jiang et al 2002) is called 'Pre-fetch by Lifetime' where the 'n' objects are selected based on their lifetime minimizing the bandwidth consumption.

Data Mining based Pre-Fetching Approach

The data mining based pre-fetching approach is classified based on the two data mining techniques: association rules and clustering.

Association Rules based Pre-Fetching Approach

In association rule, the prediction is done using the set of rules revealed from different user sessions which is segregated using Web log file. These sessions describe the sequence of Webpages accessed by a single user during some period of time. In association rules, support measure is used to identify frequent pages whereas confidence measure is used to discover rules from these frequent pages (Yang et al 2004). Yang et al (2001) have proposed an N-gram based pre-fetching approach which is based on association rule. The problem in this approach is that too many useless rules are produced from the user's session which makes incorrect predictions, especially when the dataset is large. Hence, the predictions become inaccurate (Khalil et al 2009; Xiao et al 2001). The research progress in association rule mining is given below. Jianhan (2002) have used the Markov model to predict the user's next access. In their work, they have applied a transition matrix to predict Webpages based on past visitor behavior which makes the user find information more efficiently and accurately. An improved Apriori algorithm proposed by Wang and Pi-lian (2005) consumes less time and space complexity than the original algorithm. It adds an attribute called 'userid' during each and every step of producing the candidate set. It can decide whether an item in the candidate set should be added into the large set which will be used to produce the next candidate set or not. This makes the algorithm widely and aptly useful in Web mining. Two common data mining approaches such as FP Growth and PrefixSpan in sequential data mining have been presented by Hengshan et al (2006). It helps in Web content personalization and user navigation through pre-fetching and caching. It also uses the Maximum Forward Path (MFP) in Web usage mining model. Sandeep (2010) has proposed a custom-built Apriori algorithm based on the traditional Apriori algorithm, to find the effective pattern. They have tested the proposed work in educational log file. This algorithm helps the Website developer in making effective decisions to improve the efficiency of the Website. Navin et al (2011) have proposed a recommendation methodology based on correlation rules where Association rules are generated from log data using FP Growth algorithm. Further the cosine measure is used for generating correlation rules.

Clustering based Pre-Fetching Approach

All the methodologies employed in previous section covers only a single object pre-fetching which will increase network traffic and server load when multiple users are accessing the server. In order to overcome these problems clustering-based pre-fetching techniques can used. Clustering is the process of grouping the users based on similarity present in the user session. The objects present in the same clusters are highly similar whereas objects present in different clusters are highly dissimilar. An effective clustering algorithm should minimize the intra-cluster distance and maximize inter-cluster distance. Many research works have been carried out related to clustering (Papadakis et al 2005; Cadez et al 2003; Adami et al 2003). Clustering can be either Webpage clustering or user session clustering (Khalil et al 2009). The Webpage clustering is achieved by grouping the pages into different clusters based on the content similarity (Tang & Vemuri 2005; Xu et al 2006). In session-based clustering technique, users are grouped based on the similarity between different user sessions. Clustering-based approach is widely used in fields like Webpage prediction, personalization and Web pre-fetching. Pallis et al (2008) have proposed an algorithm called ClustWeb for clustering inter-site Webpages in proxy servers based on DG and association rule. The problem with this approach is that the high complexity involved in construction of DG and moreover it is pruned by support and confidence measures. As per Paola (2007), Self Organized Maps (SOM) is a kind of artificial neural network, in the process of WUM to detect user patterns. The authors have stated that, in order to identify the common patterns in Websites, SOM is better than K-means. Mehrdad (2008) have proposed an approach that was based on the graph partitioning for modeling user navigation patterns. In order to perform mining on user navigation patterns, they have established an undirected graph based on connectivity between each pair of the Webpages. They have also proposed novel formula for assigning weights to edges of the graph. Another clustering-based pre-fetching approach has been proposed by Rangarajan et al (2004), based on ART1 neural network. It includes grouping the users' access patterns and pre-fetch the prototype vector of each group. In their experiment they have focused only on the pre-fetching and did not address the issues related to interaction between Web caching and pre-fetching. In recent years data mining approaches have been widely used in Web pre-fetching area (Huang & Hsu 2008; Pallis et al 2008). Sujatha and Iyakutty (2010) have proposed a new framework to improve the cluster quality from k-means clustering using genetic algorithm. The above discussed works were found to be inefficient because they use association rules for pre-fetching Web objects which ultimately leads to inaccuracy due to the prediction of a particular page depending on the patterns observed from all the user's preferences (Khalil et al 2009; Xiao et al 2001). Furthermore, these approaches employed traditional replacement algorithms that are not suitable for clustering-based pre-fetching environment. Table 3 gives the literature support for forming the research problem.

PERFORMANCE MEASURES FOR WEB CACHING AND WEB PRE-FETCHING

The most commonly used metrics to measure the performance of Web caching and Web pre-fetching systems are given below (Koskela et al 2003; Cobb & ElAarag 2008; Wong 2006):

- Hit Ratio (HR) also known as Hit Rate
- Byte Hit Ratio (BHR) also known as Byte Hit Rate

Table 3. Literature support for formulation of research problem

S. No.	Base papers	Authors	Issue and Inference
1	Web user clustering and its application to pre-fetching using ART neural networks	Rangarajan et al (2004)	It presents a pre-fetching approach based on ART1 neural network. It does not address the issues while integrating Web caching and Web pre-fetching
2	Integrating Web caching and Web pre-fetching in Client-Side Proxies	Teng et al (2005)	Have proposed pre-fetching approach based on association rule. They have proposed an innovative cache replacement policy called (Integration of Web Caching and Pre-fetching (IWCP). They have categorized Web objects into implied and non-implied objects.
3	A clustering-based pre-fetching scheme on a Web cache environment	Pallis et al (2008)	Proposed a graph-based pre-fetching technique. Have used DG for pre-fetching. It is based on association rule and it is controlled by support and confidence. Moreover they have used traditional policies in Web cache environment and didn't address issues while integrating these two.
4	Intelligent Client-side Web Caching Scheme Based on Least Recently Used Algorithm and Neuro-Fuzzy System	Ali & Shamsuddin (2009)	It uses the neuro-fuzzy system to classify a Web object into cacheable or un-cacheable objects. It has LRU algorithm in cache to predict Web objects that may be re-accessed later. Training process requires long time and extra computational cost. It ignored the factors such as cost and size of the objects in the cache replacement policy
5	A survey of Web cache replacement strategies	Podlipnig & Böszörmenyi (2003)	The authors have reviewed and presented an overview of various page replacement policies. It is observed that GDSF perform better in Web cache environment. They also have presented merits and demerits of various page replacement policies.
6	A Keyword-Based Semantic Pre-fetching Approach in Internet News Services	Ibrahim & Xu (2004)	It predicts users' future access based on semantic preferences of past retrieved Web documents. It is implemented on Internet news services. The semantic preferences are identified by analyzing keywords present in the URL of previously accessed Web. It employs a neural network model over the keyword set to predict user future requests.
7	A Survey of Web Caching and Pre-fetching	Waleed et al (2011)	The authors have discussed and reviewed various Web caching and Web pre-fetching techniques. It is observed that most of the pre-fetching techniques discussed here were focusing on single user which will ultimately reduce server performance if number of users increase. Moreover, in recent years data mining plays a major role in Web pre-fetching areas and most of the data mining-based approach uses association rule mining.

HR is the percentage of user requests that are served from the cache. That is HR is the ratio of total number of cache hit to the total number of user requests while BHR is the ratio of total bytes served from the cache to the total bytes requested by user. The mathematical representation is:

Let N be the total number of user requests (objects) and $\delta_i = 1$, if the requested object 'i' is in the cache (Cache Hit), and $\delta_i = 0$ otherwise (Cache Miss). Equation 1 mathematically represents HR while Equation 2 mathematically represents BHR

$$HR = \frac{\sum_{i=1}^{N} \delta i}{N} \qquad (1)$$

whereas BHR is as follows

$$BHR = \frac{\sum_{i=1}^{N} bi\delta i}{\sum_{i=1}^{N} bi} \tag{2}$$

Here b_i= size of the ith requested object.

The most commonly used metrics to measure the performance of Web pre-fetching (Huang & Hsu 2008; Domenech et al 2010) are given in Equations 3 and 4 below.

- **Precision (Pc):** The ratio of pre-fetch hits to the total number of objects pre-fetched.

$$Pc = \frac{No.\ of\ Prefetch\ Hits}{No.\ of\ Objects\ Prefetched} \tag{3}$$

- **Recall (Rc):** The ratio of pre-fetch hits to the total number of objects requested by users.

$$Rc = \frac{No.\ of\ prefetch\ Hits}{No.\ of\ User\ Requests} \tag{4}$$

FUTURE RESEARCH DIRECTIONS

The above discussed works were found to be inefficient because they use association rules for pre-fetching Web objects which ultimately leads to inaccuracy due to the prediction of a particular page depending on the patterns observed from all the user's preferences (Khalil et al 2009; Xiao et al 2001). Also, most of the existing approaches are based on the association rule mining which will increase the number of rules and only focusing on single object pre-fetching which intern increases number of objects to be pre-fetched when users get increased. Furthermore, these approaches employed traditional replacement algorithms that are not suitable for clustering-based pre-fetching environment. As the user datasets containing the privacy information should not be exposed to the outside world, privacy preserving data mining techniques can be applied in order to hide personal information about the users. Also, evolutionary optimization techniques can be applied in order to optimize the system further. A session-based approach can also be adopted to improve bandwidth utilization. Moreover, a hybrid approach out of the existing algorithms can be tried out for cache replacement process. This system can also be implemented to extend the performance of Content Distribution Network (CDN) server and Enterprise Resource Planning (ERP) system for effective content distribution and decision making process. This system can also be used in the application areas where Web search, access and retrieval are involved, such as Predicting user purchase pattern of commodities in E-Commerce Website, Redesigning of a site according to user interest.

CONCLUSION

The vast amount of literature studied and reported so far in this chapter has yielded the need of new Web caching and pre-fetching approach to improve scalability of the Web-based system. The literature also points out the importance of Web caching and pre-fetching using data mining and Web mining techniques as important findings which stood as the base for the formulation of research problem, which are tabulated and presented in Table 3. The survey also reviews and summarizes the work related to Web caching and pre-fetching techniques. From this, it is also observed that both the techniques would improve the performance by reducing server load and latency in accessing Web pages. However, if the Web caching and pre-fetching approaches are integrated inefficiently then this might cause huge network traffic; increase in Web server load in addition to the inefficient use of cache space (Waleed et al 2011). Hence, the pre-fetching approach should be designed carefully in order to overcome the above said limitations. Therefore, the importance of Web usage mining to optimize the existing Web cache performance has been realized.

REFERENCES

Acharjee, U. (2006). *Personalized and Artificial Intelligence Web Caching and Pre-fetching* (Master thesis). University of Ottawa, Canada.

Ali, W., & Shamsuddin, S. M. (2009). Intelligent Client-Side Web Caching Scheme Based on Least Recently Used Algorithm and Neuro-Fuzzy System. *The Sixth International Symposium on Neural Networks (ISNN 2009)*, (LNCS). Springer-Verlag Berlin Heidelberg.

Balamash, A., & Krunz, M. (2004). An Overview of Web Caching Replacement Algorithms. *IEEE Communications Surveys and Tutorials*, 6(2), 44–56. doi:10.1109/COMST.2004.5342239

Bamshad, M. (2007). *Data Mining for Web Personalization*. Heidelberg, Germany: LCNS, Springer-Verleg Berlin.

Brin, S., & Pange, L. (1998). The Anatomy of a Large-scale Hyper Textual Web Search Engine. *Computer Networks and ISDN Systems*, 30(1-7), 107–117. doi:10.1016/S0169-7552(98)00110-X

Chen, T. (2007). Obtaining the Optimal Cache Document Replacement Policy for the Caching System of an EC Website. *European Journal of Operational Research*, 181(2), 828–835. doi:10.1016/j.ejor.2006.05.034

Chen, X., & Zhang, X. (2002). Popularity-based PPM: An effective Web pre-fetching technique for high accuracy and low storage. In *Proceedings of the International Conference on Parallel Processing*, (pp. 296-304). doi:10.1109/ICPP.2002.1040885

Cobb, J., & ElAarag, H. (2008). Web Proxy Cache Replacement Scheme based on Back-Propagation Neural Network. *Journal of Systems and Software*, 81(9), 1539–1558. doi:10.1016/j.jss.2007.10.024

Cyrus, S., Zarkessh, A. M., Jafar, A., & Vishal, S. (1997). Knowledge discovery from Users Web Page Navigation. In *Workshop on Research Issues in Data Engineering*.

Domenech, J., Pont-Sanju, A., Sahuquillo, J., & Gil, J. A. (2010). *Evaluation, Analysis and Adaptation of Web Pre-fetching Techniques in Current Web. In Web-Based Support Systems* (pp. 239–271). London: Springer.

Dunham, M. H. (2006). *Data Mining Introductory and Advanced Topics* (1st ed.). Pearson Education.

ElAarag, H., & Romano, S. (2009). Improvement of the neural network proxy cache replacement strategy. *Proceedings of the 2009 Spring Simulation Multiconference.*

Fan, L., Cao, P., & Jacobson, Q. (1999). Web Pre-fetching between Low-Bandwidth Clients and Proxies: Potential and Performance. In *Proceedings of the Joint International Conference on Measurement and Modeling of Computer Systems (SIGMETRICS'99).*

Feng, W., Man, S., & Hu, G. (2009). *Markov Tree Prediction on Web Cache Pre-fetching. In Software Engineering, Artificial Intelligence (SCI)* (Vol. 209, pp. 105–120). Berlin: Springer-Verlag.

Hengshan, W., Cheng, Y., & Hua, Z. (2006). Design and Implementation of a Web Usage Mining Model Based on FPgrowth and Prefixspan. Communications of the IIMA, 6(2).

Huang, Y. F., & Hsu, J. M. (2008). Mining Web Logs to Improve Hit Ratios of Pre-fetching and Caching. *Knowledge-Based Systems*, *21*(1), 62–69. doi:10.1016/j.knosys.2006.11.004

Ibrahim, T. I., & Xu, C. Z. (2000). Neural Nets based Predictive Pre-fetching to Tolerate WWW Latency. In *Proceedings of the 20th International Conference on Distributed Computing Systems.* IEEE.

Ibrahim, T. I., & Xu, C. Z. (2004). A Keyword-Based Semantic Pre-fetching Approach in Internet News Services. *IEEE Transactions on Knowledge and Data Engineering*, *16*(5), 601–611. doi:10.1109/TKDE.2004.1277820

Jianhan, Z. (2002). Using Markov Chains for Link Prediction in Adaptive Web Sites. *SoftWare* 2002. *LNCS*, *2311*, 60–73.

Jiawei, H., Micheline, K., & Jian, P. (2006). *Data Mining Concepts and Techniques.* Pearson Education.

Kaya, C. C., Zhang, G., Tan, Y., & Mookerjee, V. S. (2009). An Admission-Control Technique for Delay Reduction in Proxy Caching. *Decision Support Systems*, *46*(2), 594–603. doi:10.1016/j.dss.2008.10.004

Khalil, F., Li, A. J., & Wang, H. (2009). Integrated Model for Next Page Access Prediction. Int. *J. Knowledge and Web Intelligence*, *1*(2), 48–80. doi:10.1504/IJKWI.2009.027925

Koskela, T.J., Heikkonen & Kaski, K. (2003). Web cache optimization with nonlinear model using object feature. *Computer Networks Journal, 43*(6), 805-817.

Krishnamurthy, B., & Rexforrd, J. (2001). *Web Protocols and Practice: HTTP/1.1, Networking Protocols, Caching and Traffic Measurement.* Addison-Wesley.

Kroeger, T. M., Long, D. D. E., & Mogul, J. C. (1997). Exploring the Bounds of Web Latency Reduction from Caching and Pre-fetching. *Proceedings of the USENDC Symposium on Internet Technology and Systems*, (pp. 13-22).

Kumar, C., & Norris, J. B. (2008). A New Approach for a Proxy-level Web Caching Mechanism. *Decision Support Systems, Elsevier, 46*(1), 52–60. doi:10.1016/j.dss.2008.05.001

Lan, B., Bressan, S., Ooi, B. C., & Tan, K. L. (2000). Rule-Assisted Pre-fetching in Web-Server Caching. In *Proceedings of the 9th International Conference on Information and Knowledge Management*.

Lee, H. K., An, B. S., & Kim, E. J. (2009). Adaptive Pre-fetching Scheme Using Web Log Mining in Cluster-Based Web Systems.*IEEE International Conference on Web Services (ICWS)*, (pp. 903-910).

Liu, Q. (2009). *Web Latency Reduction with Pre-fetching* (Ph.D Thesis). University of Western Ontario, London, Canada.

Loon, T. S., & Bharghavan, V. (1997). Alleviating the Latency and Bandwidth Problems in WWW Browsing. In *Proceedings of the USENIX Symposium on Internet Technologies and Systems (USITS)*.

Markatos, E. P., & Chronaki, C. E. (1998). A Top-10 Approach to Pre-fetching on the Web. In *Proceedings of INET Geneva*.

Mehrdad, J. (2008). Web User Navigation Pattern Mining Approach Based on Graph Partitioning Algorithm. *Journal of Theoretical and Applied Information Technology*.

Mobasher, B., Cooley, R., & Srivastava, J. (2000). Automatic Personalization Based on Web Usage Mining. *Communications of the ACM, 43*(8), 142–151. doi:10.1145/345124.345169

Mobasher, B., Dai, H., Luo, T., & Nakagawa, M. (2002). Discovery and Evaluation of Aggregate Usage Profiles for Web Personalization. *Data Mining and Knowledge Discovery, 6*(1), 61–82. doi:10.1023/A:1013232803866

Nanopoulos, A., Katsaros, D., & Manolopoulos, Y. (2003). A Data Mining Algorithm for Generalized Web Pre-fetching. *IEEE Transactions on Knowledge and Data Engineering, 15*(5), 1155–1169. doi:10.1109/TKDE.2003.1232270

Navin, K., Tyagi, & Solanki, A.K. (2011). Analysis of Server Log by Web Usage Mining for Website Improvement. *International Journal of Computer Science Issues, 7*(4).

Padmanabhan, V. N., & Mogul, J. C. (1996). Using Predictive Pre-fetching to Improve World Wide Web Latency. *ACM Computer Communication Review, 26*(3), 23–36. doi:10.1145/235160.235164

Pallis, G., Vakali, A., & Pokorny, J. (2008). A Clustering-Based Pre-Fetching Scheme on A Web Cache Environment. ACM Journal Computers and Electrical Engineering, 34(4).

Palpanas, T., & Mendelzon, A. (1999). Web Pre-fetching using Partial Match Prediction. In *Proceedings of the 4th International Web Caching Workshop*.

Paola, B.c(2007). Web Usage Mining Using Self Organized Maps. *International Journal of Computer Science and Network Security, 7*(6).

Pei, C., & Irani, S. (1997). Cost-Aware WWW Proxy Caching Algorithms. In *Proceedings of the USENIX Symposium on Internet Technologies and Systems*, (pp. 193-206).

Pitkow, J., & Pirolli, P. (1999). Mining Longest Repeating Subsequences to Predict World Wide Web Surfing.*Proceedings USENIX Symposium on Internet Technologies and Systems* (USITS).

Podlipnig, S., & Boszormenyi, L. (2003). A Survey of Web Cache Replacement Strategies. *ACM Computing Surveys, 35*(4), 374–398. doi:10.1145/954339.954341

Rangarajan, S. K., Phoha, V. V., Balagani, K., Selmic, R. R., & Iyengar, S. S. (2004). *Web User Clustering and its Application to Pre-fetching using ART Neural Networks*. IEEE Computer.

Sandeep, S. (2010). Discovering Potential User Browsing Behaviors Using Custom-Built Apriori Algorithm. *International Journal of Computer Science & Information Technology, 2*(4).

Sathiyamoorthi, V. (2016). A Novel Cache Replacement Policy for Web Proxy Caching System Using Web Usage Mining. *International Journal of Information Technology and Web Engineering, 11*(2), 1–12. doi:10.4018/IJITWE.2016040101

Sathiyamoorthi, V., & Murali Bhaskaran, V. (2010a). Data Preparation Techniques for Mining World Wide Web through Web Usage Mining-An Approach. *International Journal of Recent Trends in Engineering, 2*(4), 1–4.

Sathiyamoorthi, V., & Murali Bhaskaran, V. (2010b). Data mining for intelligent enterprise resource planning system. *International Journal of Recent Trends in Engineering, 2*(3), 1–4.

Sathiyamoorthi, V., & Murali Bhaskaran, V. (2011a). Improving the Performance of Web Page Retrieval through Pre-Fetching and Caching. *European Journal of Scientific Research, 66*(2), 207–217.

Sathiyamoorthi, V., & Murali Bhaskaran, V. (2011b). Data Pre-Processing Techniques for Pre-Fetching and Caching of Web Data through Proxy Server. *International Journal of Computer Science and Network Security, 11*(11), 92-98.

Sathiyamoorthi, V., & Murali Bhaskaran, V. (2012). Optimizing the Web Cache performance by Clustering Based Pre-Fetching Technique Using Modified ART1. *International Journal of Computers and Applications, 44*(1), 51–60.

Sathiyamoorthi, V., & Murali Bhaskaran, V. (2013). Novel Approaches for Integrating MART1 Clustering Based Pre-Fetching Technique with Web Caching. *International Journal of Information Technology and Web Engineering, 8*(2), 18–32. doi:10.4018/jitwe.2013040102

Srivastava, J., Cooley, R., Deshpande, M., & Tan, P. N. (2000). Web Usage Mining: Discovery and Applications of Usage Patterns from Web Data. *SIGKDD Explorations, 1*(2), 12–23. doi:10.1145/846183.846188

Sujatha, N., & Iyakutty, K. (2010). Refinement of Web usage Data Clustering from K-means with Genetic Algorithm. *European Journal of Scientific Research, 42*(3), 464-476.

Teng, W., Chang, C., & Chen, M. (2005). Integrating Web Caching and Web Pre-fetching in Client-Side Proxies. *IEEE Transactions on Parallel and Distributed Systems, 16*(5), 444–455. doi:10.1109/TPDS.2005.56

Tian, W., Choi, B., & Phoha, V. V. (2002). An Adaptive Web Cache Access Predictor Using Neural Network. *Proceedings of the 15th international conference on Industrial and engineering applications of artificial intelligence and expert systems: developments in applied artificial intelligence*, (LNCS). Springer-Verlag. doi:10.1007/3-540-48035-8_44

Venketesh, P., & Venkatesan, R. (2009). A Survey on Applications of Neural Networks and Evolutionary Techniques in Web Caching. *IETE Technical Review*, *26*(3), 171–180. doi:10.4103/0256-4602.50701

Waleed, A., Siti M.S. & Abdul S.I. (2011). A Survey of Web Caching and Prefetching. *Int. J. Advance. Soft Comput. Appl.*, *3*(1).

Wang, G. T., & Pi-lian, H. E. (2005). *Web Log Mining by an Improved AprioriAll Algorithm* (Vol. 4). World Academy of Science, Engineering and Technology.

Wang, J. (1999). A Survey of Web Caching Schemes for the Internet. *ACM Comp. Commun. Review*, *29*(5), 36–46. doi:10.1145/505696.505701

Wessels & Duane. (2001). Web Caching. O'Reilly Publication.

Wong, A. K. Y. (2006). Web Cache Replacement Policies: A Pragmatic Approach. *IEEE Network*, *20*(1), 28–34. doi:10.1109/MNET.2006.1580916

Xiao, J., Zhang, Y., Jia, X., & Li, T. (2001). Measuring Similarity of Interests for Clustering Web-users.*12th Australasian Database Conference (ADC)*, (pp. 107-114).

Xu, L., Mo, H., Wang, K., & Tang, N. (2006). Document Clustering Based on Modified Artificial Immune Network. Rough Sets and Knowledge Technology, 4062, 516-521.

Yang, Q., Li, T., & Wang, K. (2004). Building Association-Rule Based Sequential Classifiers for Web-Document Prediction. *Journal of Data Mining and Knowledge Discovery*, *8*(3), 253–273. doi:10.1023/B:DAMI.0000023675.04946.f1

Yang, Q., Zhang, H., & Li, T. (2001). Mining Web Logs for Prediction Models in WWW Caching and Pre-Fetching. *Proceedings of the 7th ACM International Conference on Knowledge Discovery and Data Mining*, (pp. 473-478).

Zaiane, O. (2000). Web Mining: Concepts, Practices and Research. In *Proc. SDBD, Conference Tutorial Notes*.

Zhijie, B., Zhimin, G., & Yu, J. (2009). A Survey of Web Pre-fetching. *Journal of Computer Research and Development*, *46*(2), 202–210.

KEY TERMS AND DEFINITIONS

Bandwidth: Amount of data transferred per unit time or Capacity of the communication link that is used for transferring data between client and Server.

Clustering: It is the process of grouping objects based on similarity between them. It is also known as unsupervised learning. Each cluster contains objects that are similar to each other and highly dissimilar with objects present in the other cluster.

Data Mining: it is also known as knowledge discovery in database. It is the process of discovering novel, previously unknown and implicit information present in the database.

Internet: Interconnection of computers across the world is called as Internet. Each computer is identified using URL accessed through HTTP protocol.

Proxy Server: It acts as an inter-mediatory between client and server and contains caching mechanism for storing web objects for future access.

Web Caching: It provides temporal locality of a Web object i.e. most popular web objects are stored here for future access.

Web Client: Client is a machine that request some information from web server through HTTP Request protocol.

Web Pre-Fetching: It provides spatial locality of a Web object i.e. Pages that are closer to each other are considered for future reference.

Web Server: It is a machine that processes the user request and provides resources to the client machine through HTTP Response protocol.

Chapter 8

Multi-Agent-Based Information Retrieval System Using Information Scent in Query Log Mining for Effective Web Search

Suruchi Chawla
Shaheed Rajguru College Delhi University, India

ABSTRACT

This chapter explains the multi-agent system for effective information retrieval using information scent in query log mining. The precision of search results is low due to difficult to infer the information need of the small size search query and therefore information need of the user is not satisfied effectively. Information Scent is used for modeling the information need of user web search session and clustering is performed to identify the similar information need sessions. Hyper Link-Induced Topic Search (HITS) is executed on clusters to generate the Hubs and authorities for web page recommendations to users who search with similar intents. This multi-agent system based on clustered query sessions uses query operations like expansion and recommendation to infer the information need of user search queries and recommends Hubs and authorities for effective web search.

INTRODUCTION

Information on the web is huge and the retrieval of web documents relevant to a user information need is a big challenge. Search engines are used for web information retrieval and retrieves large collection of documents for a given query. The user query issued for web search contains few keywords therefore difficult to infer information need of the user. This is because of small size user query, the search engine retrieves large collection of documents out of which few are relevant. There is the need for personalizing the web search to the information need of the user by retrieving more and more relevant documents in search results. The data mining techniques have been applied to web usage data to get knowledge of web user's browsing pattern for effective information retrieval. The search engines store the search history of web users in query log which contains the search query and its associated clicked URLs (Broder,

DOI: 10.4018/978-1-5225-1877-8.ch008

2002; Jansen & Spink, 2006). There are four broad categorization of personalization techniques based on various factors such as context, behavior, location and history. In Saravanakumar and Deepa (2011), WordNet 3.1 is used to find different synonyms of query keywords to form alternate queries. In Gulati and Sharma (2010), the context of query is applied to retrieve the document containing the synonyms of user query which is otherwise missed in traditional search system. Personalization system based on capturing the behavior of user such as short term and long term interest has been proposed in Gao, Xi, and Im (2013). History based personalization has been proposed in Rastafari and Shamsuddin (2010), which uses the factors such as user query logs history, pages visited by user, action performed on that page, time spent on that page etc. Google generates the customized search result based on user search activity linked to cookie saved in browser. In Sethi and Dixit (2015), the personalized search system is proposed based on user previous history. The user behavior on the web like surfing pattern, search queries submitted and some explicitly collected information is used to re–rank the search results. In Li, Yang and Kitsuregawa (2009) and Morris, Teevan and Bush (2008), search engine search results are re-ranked based on user preferences. In Carman et al. (2010) and Lv et al. (2006), user implicit feedback is used to fine-tune the search results. In Stermsek, Strembeck, and Neumann (2007) and Ghosh and Dekhil (2009), web search personalization is based on user profile built from different resources, but it ignores the vocabulary problem and involves users in maintaining the profile. In location based personalization, a model for web personalization is proposed based on current location of users in (Mokbel et al., 2011). In Leung, Lee and Lee (2010); Bouidghaghen, Tamine, and Boughanem (2011) and Weber and Castillo (2010), personalized search techniques are proposed based on user's geographical location. In Moawad et al. (2012), multiagent system is proposed that uses profile and WordNet ontology for web search personalization. In Lieberman (1995) and Turner et al. (2001), software agent track the user browsing and generates the user profile in order to assist the user web search. In Menczer (2003) and Wei, Moreau and Jennings (2003), auction protocol and reward techniques are used for collaboration among agents in order to answer single and multiple queries. In Blanzieri et al. (2001); Chau et al. (2003) and Yu and Singh (2002), personal agents collaborate with another in order to improve the user browsing where users were asked to specify the areas of interest or analyze the similar search results. In Birukov, Blanzieri, and Giorgini (2005), agent system is used to generate the personalized search results using collaborative approach and generates the suggestions from the members of the community in addition to search engine results. In comparative analysis of personalized search techniques such as context, behaviour, location and history oriented. In context oriented technique synonyms and polysemy of keywords are used for context disambiguation with no user involvement. In behavior oriented, the user interest area is tracked using explicit or implicit involvement of user. In location oriented, geographic location is inferred automatically by the system but sometimes generates the misleading results. In history oriented, the user's clicks, action and time spent during web surfing is tracked implicitly and provides the relevant results. Google generates the personalized search results based on context, behavior, location and history. Yahoo uses the behavior approach and Bing generates the results based on user behavior and history (Mittal & Sethi, 2015). There are issues related to personalized search techniques such as there are many techniques but all are not applicable to all users at the same time. It is realized that hybrid of personalized search techniques can generate better results than any individual techniques. Thus the system proposed in this chapter provides the hybrid solution to various issues associated with effective information retrieval in one system. It uses query expansion and related queries recommendation for context of user input query and builds the user profile based on search behavior. At the same time web structure mining is used to identify the high quality content(Authorities) and resource web pages(Hubs) for web page recommendations and personalize the web search effectively. This chapter describes multi agent based information retrieval system in Bedi and Chawla (2010), which personalizes the web search based on Hubs & Authorities recommendations using information scent and HITS (Hyper linked Induced Topic search) in query sessions mining. The information scent is used in query log mining to generate the clusters of similar information need web user search sessions. The clusters are processed using HITS to generate hubs and authorities. Hubs are high quality resource web pages which point to many good authorities and good authorities are high quality content web pages pointed by many good hub web pages. During web search, the cluster is selected to generate the hubs and authorities for recommendation to the users who search with similar intent as that of user sessions in clusters. The recommendation of hubs and authorities according to user search pattern on the web continues till search is personalized to the information need of the user. This multi agent Information retrieval system contains user agent, interface agent, related queries generator agent, query sessions miner agent using information scent and high scent hubs and authorities recommender agent. The entire processing is divided into two phases:

1. Phase I (Offline Processing)
    a. In Phase I query session miner agent generates the clustered query sessions data set mined using information scent. Hubs and authorities agent execute HITS algorithm on clustered query sessions database to generate the Hubs and authorities.
2. Phase II (Online Processing)
    a. In Phase II user agent, interface agent, related queries generator agent and hubs authorities' agent interact with each other to recommend the hubs and authorities(web pages) relevant to the information need of the user and personalizes the web search effectively.

Initially, the query issued for web search goes to the user agent that disambiguates the context of query with the help of interface agent and related queries generator agent. The final processed user query is given to hubs and authorities agent for the recommendations of hubs and authorities. The experiment was performed to evaluate the effectiveness of the multiagent system on the data of web query sessions collected in three domains namely Academics, Entertainment and Sports. The results show that average precision of personalized search results is improved due to effective Information Retrieval. The chapter is organized as follows: background explains the basic concepts related to the theme of chapter and their literature survey is discussed. Review of related work in the field of Personalized Web Search is discussed explaining the various issues, problems related to effective Information Retrieval(IR) and their proposed solutions. Then the multiagent system using information scent in query log mining is explained for personalization of web search. The future scope is discussed based on using soft computing techniques in web data mining to deal with imprecise and vague nature of data for effective Information Retrieval. Finally, the chapter ended with the conclusion giving the overall coverage.

BACKGROUND: INFORMATION RETRIEVAL SYSTEM

A user searches for information on search tool to satisfy his information, need. The user enters a query in the search tool and passed on to a query processing system. The query processing system retrieves a result by executing a search on the web and displays the ranked results. The classical approach to information retrieval as shown in Figure 1 uses the query formulation techniques to generate the final query.

Figure 1. Classical approach to information retrieval

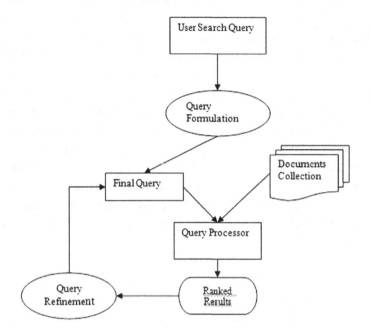

The final query is processed using query processor along with the document collection to generate the ranked results and user response to ranked results is further used for query refinement (Buckland & Plaunt, 1994).

HITS ALGORITHM

The Hypertext Induced Topic Selection (HITS) algorithm of Kleinberg calculates Hubs and Authorities scores based on the principle of mutual reinforcement that is – any high-quality authority has a large number of in-links from many high-quality hubs and vice versa. The HITS algorithm works on that part of the web graph which is query dependent. It uses keyword search for web information retrieval and the link structure of the relevant web pages is analyzed. The entire process is called topic distillation (Kleinberg, 1999). There is a great deal of self-organization in the web's complex network of hyper-links. It is stated in Kleinberg and Lawrence (2001) that the pages and links on the web are created by content authors with particular interests, and pages with similar topics tend to cluster together in natural "community" structures. Web pages in these communities are defined as either Hubs or Authorities. A Hub is a page that points to one or more authority pages. Hubs offer a guide to a certain topic or some resource list on the given topic. Authorities are high quality content web pages and are pointed by hubs.

SEARCH ENGINES

Web search engines have come a long way from the erstwhile 'near classic IR systems' such as AltaVista and Excite to the modern day advanced search engines such as Google, Direct Hit etc. The modern day search engines are based on click through data, link analysis and anchor text. In *AltaVista* full text documents is indexed and have a spider (called Scooter) that crawls the web and Usenet newsgroups. In *Excite* the URLs submitted to indexer for indexing generates the index terms and also a short document summary. DirectHit is based on click-through data and it works on the assumption that for a topic, web sites that have the highest hits from the search engine results should have the highest relevance for that topic. Google uses the path breaking search algorithm that put the highest weight age on link analysis for ranking. In Google search engine, the Googlebot is used for web crawling, an indexer is used for building the gigantic index of words found in all crawled web pages and a query processor is used for recommending the ranked documents relevant for a search query (Broder, 2002).

QUERY LOGS

Search query logs consist of logs of searches made by users of search engines. These logs are usually collected at the search engine servers. The log consists of: user identity (ip address or anonymous id etc), search queries, corresponding click through made by the user and click information. The client side query logs are captured on the user's computers. The click through data collected in query logs captures user context for user modeling (Wen, Nie, & Zhang, 2002). In web browsing history for the past N number of days is used for personalizing the web search (Sugiyama, Hatano, & Yoshikawa, 2004). It was found that relevance of the web results when using web browsing history is at par with the relevance of search results obtained using relevance feedback. Speretta and Gauch (2005) also used users search history to build user profiles. Several other works have made use of past queries mined from the query logs to improve search effectiveness (Raghavan & Sever, 1995; Yun, Wen, & Zhang, 2002; Fitzpatrick & Dent, 1997; Glance, 2001).

WEB MINING

Web mining is a data mining technique that is applied on the web data to dig out information. In Etzioni (1996), web mining is broken down into the following subtasks:

- Resource Discovery
- Information Extraction
- Generalization and Analysis
  In Cooley (2000), Web data is classified as:
    - Content data
    - Structure data
    - Usage data (Web log)
    - User profile data

Current and most popular types of web data mining are web content mining, web structure mining, and web usage mining (Borges & Levene, 2000). The classification is based on what type of web data to mine and is categorized to web usage mining, content mining and structure mining as depicted in Figure 2.

Figure 2. Web mining techniques

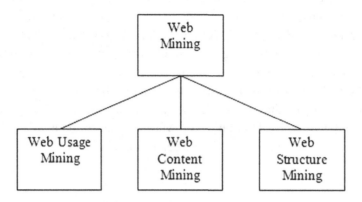

Web content mining is an application of data mining technique to web data and discover useful information from web content (Kosala & Blockeel, 2000). There are two main approaches for web content mining: Agent based approach and Database approach. In Agent based approach there are intelligent search agents, information filtering agent and personalized web agents. In Database approach the data is stored in database with well- defined schema and attributes associated with the domains (Inamdar & shinde, 2008; Dunham, 2006). Text mining mines data from different text sources to extract the unknown information. (Pol, Patil, Patankar, & Das, 2008). In Yang, Hsu, and Hung (2006), web content mining has been used for content suggestion in distance learning. In Singh and Singh (2010), web content mining is used for image retrieval. In Guo, Keselj, and Gao (2005), web content mining is used with web usage mining for clustering web pages accessed in logs. The clusters obtained from web log file and integrated data file are used for summarization using Apriori association rule mining algorithm. In Taherizadeh and Moghadam (2012), the content of web pages are extracted and are used in association with web server logs for understanding the association rule of user's behavior. In Gedov, Stolz, Neuneier, Skubacz, and Seipel (2004), content of web page is combined with information based on structure of web site to form the context based description. Web Structure mines the hyperlink structure of the web. The algorithm like Page Rank and HITS uses web structure to identify the web page rank (Page, Brin, Motwani, & Winograd, 1999). In Bianchini, Gori, and Scarselli (2005), it is found that HITS and PageRank have been used as starting points for new solutions and their extensions. In Tyagi and Sharma (2012), the web structure is used for calculating the importance of web page based on number of different pages linking to it called as backlinks. In Huang and Li (2011), weighted page rank algorithm is proposed which assign large score to the important page rather than dividing the rank score of a given page equally among its outlinks. Web usage mining analyzes the web usage data for discovering the user web usage pattern. There are three major phases of web usage mining (Srivastava, Cooley, Deshpande, & Tan, 2000):

- Preprocessing (data cleaning, data integration, data transformation and data reduction)
- Pattern recognition
- Pattern analysis

The patterns have been analyzed for various purposes such as personalization, system improvement, site modification, business intelligence and usage characterization (Chen & Sycara, 1998; Hong, Heer, Waterson, & Landay,2001; Pierrakos, Paliouras, Papatheodorou, & Spyropoulos, 2003; Eirinaki &

Vazirgiannis, 2003). In Baraglia and Silvestri (2007), the user sessions clusters are formed based on user activity recorded in user log. During web search the current user sessions is classified to existing clusters to identify the pages for recommendations. The system has the scalability problem. In Mobasher, Cooley and Srivastava (2000), web personalizer is presented which generates the dynamic recommendation of hypertext links to users based on web usage and structure of the site.

INFORMATION SCENT

Information Scent is derived from Information theory and it is based on the assumption that user behavior in the Information environment is guided by Information Scent (Pirolli & Card, 1999; Pirolli & Fu, 2003). Information Scent is determined from the perception of the value and cost of the Information with respect to the goal of the user. The theory of Information Scent assumes that navigational choices made by the user are not random but has been made rationally. There are two approaches Web User Flow by Information Scent (WUFIS) and Inferring user information need using Information Scent (IUNIS). Web User Flow by Information Scent (WUFIS) uses a combination of information retrieval and spreading activation for predictive modeling. For a given user information need WUFIS uses the probability a given page will be accessed by the user and simulate the path of web pages accessed as shown in Figure 3 (Pirolli, Card, & Van Der Wege, 2003; Pirolli, 2006; Chi, Pirolli, Chen, & Pitkow, 2001; Chi et al., 2003).

Figure 3 shows the flowchart of the WUFIS process. Thus the input to the WUFIS algorithm is a weighted vector of keywords that describes the user information need, and the output is the list of documents predicted to be visited by the users. In Inferring User Need by Information Scent (IUNIS) a method is used to infer the information need of the user given the user access pattern of web pages as shown in Figure 4. During web search user has expressed interest in various pieces of information. Information need of the user is modeled using keyword vector formed based on the content and Information Scent of web pages.

Figure 3. Simulation of the web usage given the user goal

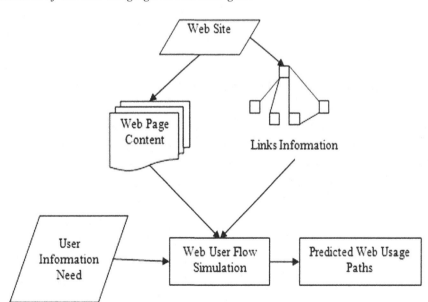

Figure 4. Inferring user need from observed path

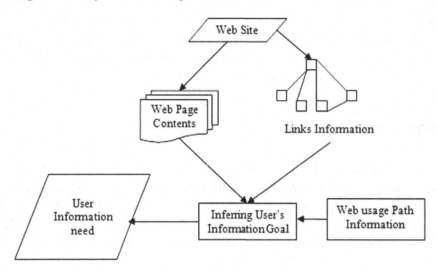

During information need modeling, certain heuristics for Information Scent can be applied to better approximate the information need of the user such as more weight age can be given to most recently visited documents, content pages and use of PF.IPF(Page Frequency Inverse Page Frequency) page access. Thus the path containing the web pages accessed by the user provides an idea of information the user is seeking and provides the huge predicted utility for simulating web usage (Heer & Chi, 2001, 2002). In the study conducted by Olston and Chi (2003), a surf-along tool is used to suggest pages to Web users based on their interest profile. In Chi, Pirolli, and Pitkow (2000), it is found that understanding the information goal of web users help the web site analyst to identify the how well the website is satisfying the information goal of user. This insight to the design of web site is used to better organize the website to increase its usability and cater to the information need of the user effectively. In Pirolli (1997), ACT-R is extended to ACT-IF (Information foraging). ACT-IF uses a formal model of Information Scent for navigational decisions and predict the user's behavior to text displayed in browsers. The result shows that Information Scent proves to be effective for generating good prediction to user WWW interaction.

INFORMATION NEED MODELING OF WEB QUERY SESSIONS USING IUNIS

The user search sessions on the web are stored in query log. Information need of a user web query session is modeled using IUNIS based on information scent and content of clicked URLs. The content of page d in the query session Q_i is a P_{id} (TF.IDF Term Frequency Inverse Document Frequency weighted vector) is given below in Equation 1:

$$P_{id} = \text{Content }_d \quad \forall d \in 1..n \tag{1}$$

The content vector of a page P_{id} is a TF.IDF keyword vector $(w_{1,d}, w_{2,d}, w_{3,d}, \ldots, w_{v,d})$ where v is the number of terms in the vocabulary set V. Vocabulary V is a set of distinct terms found in all distinct clicked pages in the whole dataset relevant to a content feature.

The TF.IDF weight is a real number indicating the relative importance of a term in a given document. Term Frequency (TF) is calculated as the number of times the term appears in the document and Inverse Document Frequency (IDF) is computed as the ratio of the number of all documents to the number of documents that contain the term.

The information scent s_{id} the given clicked page, P_{id}, is calculated by using two factors i.e. PF. IPF(Page Frequency. Inverse Page Frequency) page access and Time.

$$s_{id} = PF.IPF(P_{id}) * Time(P_{id}) \forall d \in 1..n \tag{2}$$

$$PF.IPF(P_{id}) = f_{P_{id}}/\max(f_{P_{id}}) * \log(M/m_{P_{id}})$$
$$d \in 1..n \tag{3}$$

where $PF.IPF(P_{id})$ and $Time(P_{id})$ are defined as follows.

$PF.IPF(P_{id})$: PF corresponds to the page P_{id} normalized frequency $f_{P_{id}}$ in a given query session Q_i and IPF correspond to the ratio of total number of query sessions M in the whole log to the number of query sessions $m_{P_{id}}$ that contain the given page P_{id}.

$Time(P_{id})$: It is the ratio of time spent on the page P_{id} in a given session Q_i to the total duration of session Q_i. Each query session Q_i, is constructed as a linear combination of content vector of each page, P_{id} scaled by the information scent weight, s_{id}. That is

$$Q_i = \sum_{d=1}^{n} s_{id} * P_{id} \tag{4}$$

In above formula, n is the number of distinct clicked pages in the session Q_i and s_{id} (information scent) is calculated for each page P_{id} using Equations 2 and 3. Each query session Q_i is obtained as weighted vector using Equation 4. This weighted query session vector models the information need associated with the query session Q_i. Query sessions vector are clustered using Leader-Sub Leader algorithms. Leader-Sub Leaders algorithm is used for clustering query sessions keyword vector because of its good performance and better classification accuracy for large data set (Bedi & Chawla, 2008, 2009, 2010; Chawla & Bedi 2008a, 2008b, 2008c, 2008d).

AGENTS

Software Agent is a autonomous software entity which functions continuously and learn from its experience. The agents are the intelligent entity which responds to changes in the environment without human guidance or intervention. The agents inhabiting an environment with other agents cooperate and communicate with each other to accomplish a given task. The classification of agents into Reactive, Reasoning, Planning and Adaptive Agents is explained as follows (Shoham, 1997):

- **Reactive Agents:** Reactive Agents uses the stimuli response behavior to react to the changes in the environment.

- **Reasoning Agents:** Reasoning Agents are intelligent agents. The perception is interpreted and the knowledge base is used to draw the inference along with the rationale underlying the inference.
- **Planning Agents:** Planning Agents perform planned actions which is the implementation of sequence of action in order to achieve their goal.
- **Adaptive Agents:** The knowledge acquired for planning and domain learning enables the agent to carry out activities that it could not perform previously. It learns from its experience and is able to adapt its behavior as it adds experience (Rosenschein & Kaelbling, 1995; Brustoloni, 1991).

Agents have various applications such as electronic commerce (J.G. Lee & E.S. Lee, 1997; J. K. Lee & W. Lee, 1997), manufacturing (Freund & Buxbaum, 1993), interface design (Montazemi & Gupta, 1997), computer games (Kim et al., 1997; Noda, Matsubara, Hiraki, & Frank, 1998; De la Rosa, Oller, Vehi, & Puyol, 1997; Wavish, 1996), and industrial processes (Athas & Seitz, 1988; Hopgood, 1993; Rizzi, Gowdy, & Hollis, 1997; Sirola, 1996). Smith, Cypher, and Spohrer (1994) define it as "a persistent software entity dedicated to a specific purpose". Selker (1994) takes agents to be "computer programs that simulate a human relationship by doing something that another person could do for you." Janca (1995) defines an agent as "a software entity to which tasks can be delegated". Jennings (1996) says, "…the term is usually applied to describe self-contained programs which can control their own actions based on their perceptions of their operating environment". The definition by Franklin and Graesser (1996) states, "An autonomous agent is a system situated within and a part of an environment that senses that environment and acts on it, over time, in pursuit of its own agenda and so as to effect what it senses in the future". In Multi Agent systems the agents are autonomous but their interactions are coordinated and knowledge, goals, skills and plan are integrated to solve the problems. It is possible for the agents to work for achieving both a single as well as separate individual goals. Multi-agent systems are typically based on two approaches to achieve inter-agent communication. First is the actor model proposed by Hewitt that developed into concurrent languages and the second is blackboard model used in several systems (Guessoum & Dojat, 1996; Bussmann & Demazeau, 1994; Hayes-Roth et al., 1982). In actor model, message passing is used for communicating information from one actor to another. In loosely coupled multiagent systems, message-passing is efficient (Hewitt, 1977; Müller & Pischel, 1994). In blackboard model, the shared memory structure called blackboard is used for communications. Agents use the accessible information but are unaware of its source and generate information without knowing its destination. The blackboard model is used in tightly coupled multi-agent systems. Low overhead, predictability and high reliability are the desired characteristics that are offered by the shared memory communication for use in real time applications (Hassani & Stewart, 1997). In EL-Korany and Bahnasy (2009), an intelligent web based multi agent system is developed for integration, easy access and sharing of domain specific knowledge base.

REVIEW OF PERSONALIZED WEB SEARCH TECHNIQUES FOR EFFECTIVE INFORMATION RETRIEVAL

Information on the web is voluminous and extensive research has been done in personalization of user web search for effective information retrieval. The main problem related to web search is to infer the information need of the user from search query which is ambiguous due to small size. Therefore web query retrieves large number of irrelevant documents and information need of the user is not satisfied effectively. The methods have been proposed for effective information retrieval based on query recommendation, expansion, user profiling, web page re ranking, collaborative community based search (Zhu, Xu, Ren, Tian, & Li, 2007; Palleti, Karnick, & Mitra, 2007; Liu, Yu, & Meng, 2004; Biancalana & Micarelli, 2009; Smyth, 2007; Dansdan, Tsioutsiouliklis, & Velipasaoglu, 2009; Dou, Song, Wen, & Yuan, 2009; Pan, Wang, & Gu, 2007; Peng & Lin, 2006; Sieg, Mobasher, & Burke, 2007a; Xu, Jiang, & Lau, 2011). All the methods proposed so far centered on understanding the intent with which the user search on the web for retrieving more and more relevant documents. In Nauman and Khan (2007) personalized web search is used to extend the common sense and folksonomy based intelligent search systems and solve the problem of noise in search results. In Zhu et al. (2007), query expansion method is proposed for personalized web search. The user profile is generated based on user's favorite and keywords of user query are used to select the expansion words. In Palleti et al. (2007) probabilistic query expansion is used for personalized web search. In Pan et al. (2007), context based adaptive personalized web search is proposed for effective Information retrieval. In Biancalana and Micarelli (2009), social tagging is used in query expansion for personalized web search. In Smyth (2007), the suggestions of the community based search adapt the conventional search engine output for personalized web search. In Arzanian, Akhlaghian, and Moradi (2010), multiagent based meta search system is developed and uses automatic Fuzzy concept networks for personalizing the output of meta-search engine. In Matthijs and Radlinski (2011), web usage data containing the URL of page, duration of page visit, page session date, time and the length of the source HTML is collected for personalizing the web search. In Peng, Niu, Huang, and Zhao (2012), user profile is constructed based on search results used by user. In Acharyya and Ghosh (2003), a general personalization framework is proposed for conceptual modeling of user's navigation behavior using concept tree. In Sieg, Mobasher, and Burke (2007b), interest scores of the concepts based on user's ongoing behavior is kept using spread activation algorithm. In Kim, Collins-Thompson, Bennett, and Dumais (2012), probabilistic profile is used to describe users, queries or web sites. In Dansdan et al. (2009), neighborhood based method is used. In this subset of users is first selected based on similarity to active users and a weighted combination of rating is generated for active user. In Sun, Zeng, Liu, Lu, & Chen (2005), click through data is used for web search based on cubeSVD. In Daoud, Tamine-Lechani, and Boughanem (2008) method is proposed for user's intent modeling based on data mining technique like Association rules. In Collins-Thompson, Bennett, White, de la Chica, and Sontag (2011), reading proficiency of users and reading difficulty of document is modeled to improve the relevance of search results. In Xu et al. (2011) personalized re ranking method uses user's online reading or browsing activities for deriving and mining of user's dwell times. In Dou et al. (2009), search results are personalized based on two strategies first person level and group level. In person level the search results are personalized based on user's past web page clicks and in group level, the web page clicks of group of similar users are used to re rank the search results. In Pannu, Anane, and James (2013), both explicit and implicit profiles are combined to generate the hybrid profile for improving both precision and recall. In Jansen and Spink (2006), query logs have been analyzed to identify the user behavior at the query session level and query reformulation rate. In Madani and DeCoste (2005), conceptualization personalization is proposed which groups the queries based on user profile using both explicit and implicit participation of user feedback. In Gauch, Chaffee, and Pretschner (2003), it uses the approach similar to Google personal for information filtering. The profile is generated based on categories selected by the user. The user profile is used to map the web pages into similar categories for personalizing the web search results. In Koenemann and Belkin (1996), several different interface techniques have been examined which enable the users to specify how their queries should be expanded. In Teevan, Alvarado,

Ackerman, and Karger (2004), user's information need is accessed based on his previous queries, web pages already visited, documents and emails accessed. This chapter explains the multiagent system based on using information scent in query log mining for effective Information Retrieval in Bedi and Chawla (2010). The system provides the solution to various issues responsible for low precision of Information Retrieval. It contains user agent, interface agent, related queries generator agent, query sessions miner agent using information scent and high scent hubs and authorities recommender agent. These agents use query operations like recommendations, expansion for query disambiguation, models the user profile using Information Scent for better inferring the information need and generates high quality hubs and authorities for web page recommendations using HITS. The user profile changes in response to user's search behavior and personalization is performed in response to changing information need. This system is in contrast to other related work where methods have been proposed for static user's profiling and is not adaptable to changing user's need. Therefore this multiagent system claims to be the robust system including all features related to effective information retrieval for better personalization of web search.

MULTIAGENT SYSTEM USING INFORMATION SCENT IN QUERY LOG MINING FOR EFFECTIVE INFORMATION RETRIEVAL

The architecture of multiagent system using information scent in query log mining is given in Figure 5. The entire processing of the system is divided into two phases: Phase One(Off-line processing) and Phase Two(Online processing):

1. **Phase I:** During offline processing, query session miner agent preprocesses the data set to generate the query session keyword vector. The clusters of query sessions keyword vector are generated using Leader-SubLeader Algorithm to identify the community of web searchers with similar information need. Thus each cluster is associated with High Scent Clicked URLs and related user queries. Hubs and authorities Agent process the High Scent Clicked URLs associated with the cluster using HITS to generate the hubs and authorities.
   a. **Query Session Miner Agent using Information Scent:** This Agent generates the query sessions keyword vectors. Leader-SubLeaders algorithm is used for clustering query sessions keyword vector and each cluster is associated with clicked URLs. HITS algorithm is executed on high scent clicked URLs in a given cluster to generate the Hubs and Authorities associated with each cluster.
2. **Phase II:** During online processing, the user query is sent to interface and related queries recommendation agent. The related queries generator agent uses the input query to select the cluster for generating the related queries recommendations. The interface agent uses the user selected recommended query for further expansion and send it to hubs and authorities agent for hubs and authorities recommendation. The user's clicks to recommended results are tracked to update the user profile keyword vector. This keyword vector is sent to Hubs and Authorities recommender agent for further recommendations on each request of next web page. The user profiling and recommendations of hubs and authorities continues till the search is personalized to the information need of the user.
   a. **User Agent:** The User Agent is an agent representing the user who has logged on to the proposed system and track the user's response to clicked URLs in order to generate the profile.

Figure 5. Architecture of multi-agent system using INFORMATION Scent in query log mining (Bedi & Chawla, 2010)

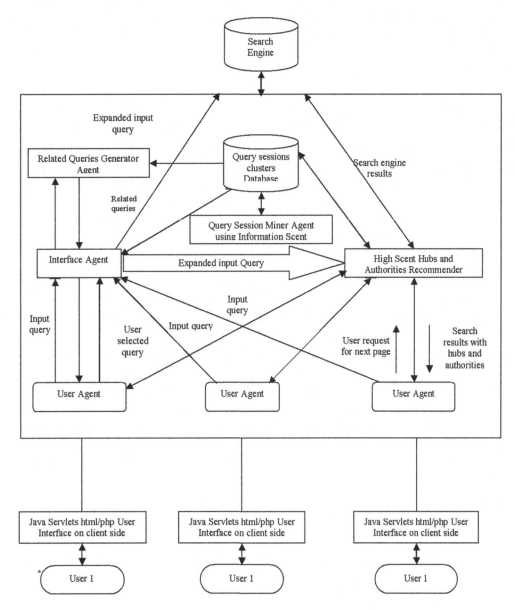

b. **Related Queries Generator Agent:** The Related Queries Generator Agent generates the related queries recommendation using the clusters of query sessions. The keywords of the input query sent by the Interface Agent are used by this agent to find the most similar cluster for related queries recommendations.

c. **Interface Agent:** The Interface Agent disambiguates the context of the input query with query expansion. The cluster most similar to user query is selected for query expansion. The selected cluster keywords which correlate best with the user selected query are then used for query expansion.

d. **High Scent Hubs and Authorities Recommender Agent:** This Agent uses the expanded input query sent by the Interface Agent to find that cluster/sub cluster most similar to expanded input query. The selected cluster/sub-cluster is used to generate the high scent hub and authorities for recommendations.

Evaluation

The experiment was performed on Pentium IV PC with 2GB RAM on Windows XP using JSP,JADE and Oracle database. The data set of query sessions was captured in three selected domains Academics, Entertainment and Sports. The number of distinct URLs in data set was 2995. The data set was preprocessed to get 595 query sessions. Cosine similarity measure was used in clustering the similar query session keyword vectors. The threshold value for Leaders computation was set to 0.5 and subthreshold value for Subleaders computation was set to 0.75. The implementation of agent was done using JADE. The system architecture was tested using Google search engine results and improvement in the precision Google search engine results was the benchmark for evaluating the effectiveness of the multiagent system using Information Scent. The test queries were chosen in selected domains in order to have wider coverage of user queries on the web. The test queries were divided into trained and untrained queries set for experimental evaluation. The trained queries had history of user sessions in the data set and untrained queries were those search queries for which there was no session in the data set. Figure 6 shows the sample of trained and untrained queries used in the experiment in the form of a table.

The performance was evaluated using the average of precision of search results generated using test queries. The precision of a given test query is measured using the fraction of relevant document retrieved in search results. The average of precision of set of test queries is computed in each domain in order to depict the performance of the proposed approach domainwise. The experimental results showing the average precision for the untrained and trained set of queries in each of the selected domains using the Google search engine results (with/without multiagent system) is given below in Figure 7 and Figure 8.

Figure 6. Sample of trained and untrained queries used in the experiment (Bedi & Chawla, 2010)

Category	Queries	
Trained Set	■ Homeloan ■ distanceeducation online ■ free pics ■ OOPS tutorial	■ how to play .vcd files ■ mpeg movies ■ dragonball ■ intranet.
Untrained Set	■ Java online tutorial ■ MovieSong ■ Spacefood ■ novels ■ magazine	■ movies ■ familyplay Games ■ movie pictures ■ India Football team ■ free software download ■ Song download

Figure 7. Impact of (with/without)multi-agent system on average precision of search results for untrained querie s(Bedi & Chawla, 2010)

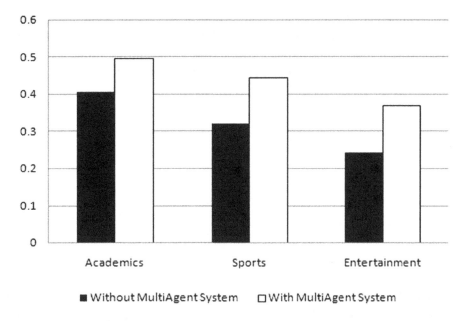

Figure 8. Impact of (with/without) multi-agent system on precision of search results for trained queries (Bedi & Chawla, 2010)

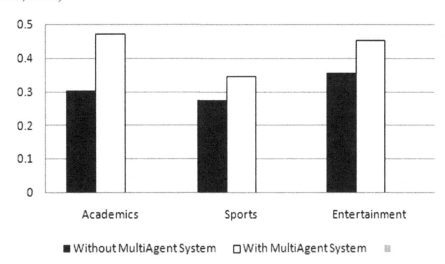

The results in Figure 7 and Figure 8 show the improvement in the average precision of the search results in each of the selected domain using the multi-agent system. It was concluded that use of Information Scent and HITS in query log mining identifies the community of web users with similar information need and recommends relevant hubs and authorities web pages for personalizing the web search to the information need of user.

FUTURE RESEARCH DIRECTIONS

Web data is vague and imprecise therefore soft computing techniques like Fuzzy Logic, genetic algorithm, neural network can be applied in query log mining to further increase the effectiveness of multi-agent system. The dimensionality reduction techniques can be used for reducing the dimensionality of clustered query sessions in order to enhance the performance of multi-agent system for effective personalized web search.

CONCLUSION

In this chapter multi-agent system is explained which is used for personalization of web search using information scent and HITS in query log mining. Information Scent and content of clicked URLs is used for modeling the information need of the web query session and clustered. The HITS algorithm uses the clustered query sessions to identify clusterwise Hubs and authorities for recommendations. The query operations like query recommendation and expansion is used for better inferring the user information need. Hubs and authorities are selected for recommendations to personalize the web search. The user's information need model changes in response to user's clicks to search results and customize the web search till the user information need is satisfied. Experimental results confirmed the effectiveness of multi-agent system for web search personalization. It proves to be robust system with common aim of identification of information need of user and retrieve relevant documents for effective Information retrieval.

REFERENCES

Acharyya, S., & Ghosh, J. (2003). Context-sensitive modeling of web- surfing behaviour using concept trees. In *Proceedings of the 5th WEBKDD Workshop*.

Arzanian, B., Akhlaghian, F., & Moradi, P. (2010). A Multi-Agent Based Personalized Meta-Search Engine Using Automatic Fuzzy Concept Networks. In *Proceedings of Third International Conference on Knowledge Discovery and Data Mining*(pp. 208- 211). Phuket, Thailand: IEEE. doi:10.1109/WKDD.2010.95

Athas, W. C., & Seitz, C. L. (1988). Multicomputers: Message-passing concurrent computers. *Computer*, *21*(8), 9–24. doi:10.1109/2.73

Baraglia, R., & Silvestri, F. (2007). Dynamic personalization of web sites without user intervention. *Communications of the ACM*, *50*(2), 63–67. doi:10.1145/1216016.1216022

Bedi, P., & Chawla, S. (2008). Improving information retrieval precision using query log mining and information scent. *Journal of Information Technology*, *6*(4), 584–588.

Bedi, P., & Chawla, S. (2009). Use of fuzzy rough set attribute reduction in high scent web page recommendations. In *Rough Sets* (pp. 192–200). Fuzzy Sets, Data Mining and Granular Computing, Springer Berlin Heidelberg. doi:10.1007/978-3-642-10646-0_23

Bedi, P., & Chawla, S. (2010). Agent based information retrieval system using information scent. *Journal of Artificial Intelligence*, *3*(4), 220–238. doi:10.3923/jai.2010.220.238

Biancalana, C., & Micarelli, A. (2009). Social tagging in query expansion: A new way for personalized web search. In *Proceedings of International Conference on Computational Science and Engineering*, (Vol 4, pp. 1060-1065), Vancouver, BC: IEEE. doi:10.1109/CSE.2009.492

Bianchini, M., Gori, M., & Scarselli, F. (2005). Inside pagerank. *ACM Transactions on Internet Technology*, *5*(1), 92–128. doi:10.1145/1052934.1052938

Birukov, A., Blanzieri, E., & Giorgini, P. (2005). Implicit: An agent-based recommendation system for web search. In *Proceedings of the fourth international joint conference on Autonomous agents and multiagent systems* (pp. 618-624). ACM.

Blanzieri, E., Giorgini, P., Massa, P., & Recla, S. (2001). Implicit culture for multi-agent interaction support. In *International Conference on Cooperative Information Systems* (pp. 27-39). Springer Berlin Heidelberg. doi:10.1007/3-540-44751-2_4

Borges, J., & Levene, M. (2000). Data mining of user navigation patterns. In *Web usage analysis and user profiling*. Springer Berlin Heidelberg.

Bouidghaghen, O., Tamine, L., & Boughanem, M. (2011, June). Personalizing mobile web search for location sensitive queries. In *12th International Conference on Mobile Data Management*, (vol. 1, pp. 110-118). IEEE. doi:10.1109/MDM.2011.52

Broder, A. (2002). A taxonomy of web search. *ACM Sigir Forum, 36*(2), 3-10.

Brustoloni, J. C. (1991). *Autonomous Agents: Characterization and Requirements*. Technical Report CMU-CS-91-204. School of Computer Science, Carnegie Mellon University.

Buckland, M., & Plaunt, C. (1994). On the construction of selection systems. *Library Hi Tech*, *12*(4), 15–28. doi:10.1108/eb047934

Bussmann, S., & Demazeau, Y. (1994). An agent model combining reactive and cognitive capabilities. In *Proceedings of the IEEE/RSJ/GI International Conference on Intelligent Robots and Systems 94* (vol. 3, pp. 2095-2102). Munich: IEEE.

Carman, M. J., Crestani, F., Harvey, M., & Baillie, M. (2010). Towards query log based personalization using topic models. In *Proceedings of the 19th ACM international conference on Information and knowledge management*, (pp.1849-1852). ACM. doi:10.1145/1871437.1871745

Chau, M., Zeng, D., Chen, H., Huang, M., & Hendriawan, D. (2003). Design and evaluation of a multi-agent collaborative Web mining system. *Decision Support Systems*, *35*(1), 167–183. doi:10.1016/S0167-9236(02)00103-3

Chawla, S., & Bedi, P. (2008a). Personalized web search using information scent. In *Innovations and Advanced Techniques in Systems, Computing Sciences and Software Engineering* (pp. 483–488). Springer Netherlands. doi:10.1007/978-1-4020-8735-6_90

Chawla, S., & Bedi, P. (2008b). Query expansion using information scent.*International Symposium on Information Technology*(vol. 3, pp 1-8). Kuala Lumpur: IEEE.

Chawla, S., & Bedi, P. (2008c). Finding Hubs and Authorities using Information Scent to Improve the Information Retrieval precision. In *Proceedings of International Conference on Artificial Intelligence* (pp. 185-191).

Chawla, S., & Bedi, P. (2008d). Improving information retrieval precision by finding related queries with similar information need using information scent. *First International Conference on Emerging Trends in Engineering and Technology* (pp 486-491). Nagpur, Maharashtra: IEEE. doi:10.1109/ICETET.2008.23

Chen, L., & Sycara, K. (1998). WebMate: A personal agent for browsing and searching. In *Proceedings of the second international conference on Autonomous agents* (pp. 132-139). New York: ACM. doi:10.1145/280765.280789

Chi, E. H., Pirolli, P., Chen, K., & Pitkow, J. (2001). Using information scent to model user information needs and actions and the Web. In *Proceedings of the SIGCHI conference on Human factors in computing systems* (pp. 490-497). New York: ACM. doi:10.1145/365024.365325

Chi, E. H., Pirolli, P., & Pitkow, J. (2000). The scent of a site: A system for analyzing and predicting information scent, usage, and usability of a web site. In *Proceedings of the SIGCHI Conference on Human Factors in Computing Systems* (pp. 161-168). New York: ACM.

Chi, E. H., Rosien, A., Supattanasiri, G., Williams, A., Royer, C., Chow, C., & Cousins, S. (2003). The bloodhound project: automating discovery of web usability issues using the InfoScentπ simulator. In *Proceedings of the SIGCHI conference on Human factors in computing systems* (pp 505-512). New York: ACM. doi:10.1145/642611.642699

Collins-Thompson, K., Bennett, P. N., White, R. W., de la Chica, S., & Sontag, D. (2011). Personalizing web search results by reading level. In *Proceedings of the 20th ACM international conference on Information and knowledge management* (pp. 403-412). New York: ACM. doi:10.1145/2063576.2063639

Cooley, R. W. (2000). *Web usage mining: discovery and application of interesting patterns from web data* (Doctoral dissertation). University of Minnesota.

Dansdan, A., Tsioutsiouliklis, K., & Velipasaoglu, E. (2009). *Web search engine metrics for measuring user satisfaction*. Retrieved from http://dasdan.net/ali/www2009/web-search-metrics-tutorial-www09-part6a.pdf

Daoud, M., Tamine-Lechani, L., & Boughanem, M. (2008). Using a graph- based ontological user profile for personalizing search. In *Proceedings of the 17th ACM conference on Information and knowledge management* (pp 1495-1496). New York: ACM. doi:10.1145/1458082.1458352

De la Rosa, J. L., Oller, A., Vehí, J., & Puyol, J. (1997). Soccer team based on agent-oriented programming. *Robotics and Autonomous Systems*, *21*(2), 167–176. doi:10.1016/S0921-8890(97)00024-9

Dou, Z., Song, R., Wen, J. R., & Yuan, X. (2009). Evaluating the effectiveness of personalized web search. *IEEE Transactions on Knowledge and Data Engineering*, *21*(8), 1178–1190. doi:10.1109/TKDE.2008.172

Dunham, M. H. (2006). *Data mining: Introductory and advanced topics*. Pearson Education.

Eirinaki, M., & Vazirgiannis, M. (2003). Web mining for web personalization. *ACM Transactions on Internet Technology*, *3*(1), 1–27. doi:10.1145/643477.643478

EL-Korany, A., & EL-Bahnasy, K. (2009). A multi-agent framework to facilitate knowledge sharing. *Journal of Artificial Intelligence*, *2*(1), 17–28. doi:10.3923/jai.2009.17.28

Etzioni, O. (1996). The World-Wide Web: Quagmire or gold mine? *Communications of the ACM*, *39*(11), 65–68. doi:10.1145/240455.240473

Fitzpatrick, L., & Dent, M. (1997). Automatic feedback using past queries: social searching? *ACM SIGIR Forum*, *31*(SI), 306-313.

Franklin, S., & Graesser, A. (1996). Is it an Agent, or just a Program?: A Taxonomy for Autonomous Agents. In *Intelligent agents III agent theories, architectures, and languages* (pp. 21–35). Springer Berlin Heidelberg.

Freund, E., & Buxbaum, H. J. (1993). A new approach to multi agent systems control in robot-based flexible manufacturing work cells. In *Proceedings of the 1993 IEEE/RSJ International Conference on Intelligent Robots and Systems* (vol. 3, pp 2015-2022). Yokohama: IEEE. doi:10.1109/IROS.1993.583909

Gao, Q., Xi, S. M., & Im Cho, Y. (2013). A multi-agent personalized ontology profile based user preference profile construction method. In *44th International Symposium on Robotics (ISR)* (pp 1-4). IEEE.

Gauch, S., Chaffee, J., & Pretschner, A. (2003). Ontology-based personalized search and browsing. *International Journal Web Intelligence and Agent Systems*, *1*(3-4), 219-234.

Gedov, V., Stolz, C., Neuneier, R., Skubacz, M., & Seipel, D. (2004). Matching web site structure and content. In *Proceedings of the 13th International World Wide Web Conference on Alternate Track Papers & Posters* (pp 286-287). New York: ACM.

Ghosh, R., & Dekhil, M. (2009, April). Discovering user profiles. In *Proceedings of the 18th international conference on World wide web* (pp 1233-1234). ACM. doi:10.1145/1526709.1526944

Glance, N. S. (2001). Community search assistant. In *Proceedings of the 6th international conference on Intelligent user interfaces* (pp. 91-96). New York: ACM.

Guessoum, Z., & Dojat, M. (1996). *A real-time agent model in an asynchronous-object environment.* Springer Berlin Heidelberg.

Gulati, P., & Sharma, A. K. (2010). Ontology Driven Query Expansion for Better Image Retrieval. *International Journal of Computers and Applications*, *5*(10), 33–37. doi:10.5120/946-1324

Guo, J., Kešelj, V., & Gao, Q. (2005). Integrating web content clustering into web log association rule mining. In *Advances in Artificial Intelligence* (pp. 182–193). Springer Berlin Heidelberg. doi:10.1007/11424918_19

Hassani, M., & Stewart, D. B. (1997). A Mechanism for Communicating in Dynamically Reconfigurable Embedded Systems. In *Proceedings of High Assurance Software Engineering Workshop*, (pp. 215-220). IEEE. doi:10.1109/HASE.1997.648069

Hayes-Roth, B., Washington, R., Ash, D., Hewett, R., Colinot, A., Vina, A., & Seiviur, A. (1982). Guardian: A Prototype Intelligent Agent for Intensive-Care Monitoring. *Artificial Intelligence in Medicine*, *4*(2), 165–185. doi:10.1016/0933-3657(92)90052-Q

Heer, J., & Chi, E. H. (2001). Identification of web user traffic composition using multi-modal clustering and information scent. In *Proceedings of the Workshop on Web Mining, SIAM Conference on Data Mining* (pp. 51-58).

Heer, J., & Chi, E. H. (2002). Separating the swarm: categorization methods for user sessions on the web. In *Proceedings of the SIGCHI Conference on Human factors in Computing Systems*(pp. 243-250). New York: ACM. doi:10.1145/503376.503420

Hewitt, C. (1977). Viewing Control Structures as Patterns of Passing Messages. *Artificial Intelligence*, *8*(3), 323–364. doi:10.1016/0004-3702(77)90033-9

Hong, J. I., Heer, J., Waterson, S., & Landay, J. A. (2001). WebQuilt: A proxy-based approach to remote web usability testing. *ACM Transactions on Information Systems*, *19*(3), 263–285. doi:10.1145/502115.502118

Hopgood, A. A. (1993). *Knowledge-based systems for engineers and scientists*. Boca Raton, FL: CRC Press, Inc.

Huang, W., & Li, B. (2011). An improved method for the computation of PageRank. In *International Conference on Mechatronic Science, Electric Engineering and Computer*(pp. 2191-2194). Jilin: IEEE. doi:10.1109/MEC.2011.6025926

Inamdar, S. A., & Shinde, G. N. (2008). An agent based intelligent search engine system for web mining. *Research, Reflections and Innovations in Integrating ICT in Education*, (pp. 1062-1065).

Janca, P. C. (1995). *Pragmatic application of information agents*. BIS Strategic Report.

Jansen, B., & Spink, A. (2006). How are we searching the web? a comparison of nine search engine query logs. *Information Processing & Management*, 42.

Jennings, N. R. (1996). Software agents. *IEEE Review*, 17-20.

Jian, Y., Wen, J.-R., & Hong-Jiang, Z. (2002). Query clustering using user logs. *ACM Transactions on Information Systems*, *20*(1), 59–81. doi:10.1145/503104.503108

Kim, J. H., Shim, H. S., Kim, H. S., Jung, M. J., Choi, L. H., & Kim, J. O. (1997). A cooperative multi-agent system and its real time application to robot soccer. In *Proceedings of IEEE International Conference on Robotics and Automation*(vol. 1, pp. 638-643). Albuquerque, NM: IEEE. doi:10.1109/ROBOT.1997.620108

Kim, J. Y., Collins-Thompson, K., Bennett, P. N., & Dumais, S. T. (2012). Characterizing web content, user interests, and search behavior by reading level and topic. In *Proceedings of the fifth ACM international conference on Web search and data mining* (pp. 213-222). New York: ACM. doi:10.1145/2124295.2124323

Kleinberg, J., & Lawrence, S. (2001). The Structure of the Web. *Science*, *294*(5548), 1849–1850. doi:10.1126/science.1067014 PMID:11729296

Kleinberg, J. M. (1999). Authoritative sources in a hyperlinked environment. *Journal of the ACM*, *46*(5), 604–632. doi:10.1145/324133.324140

Koenemann, J., & Belkin, N. J. (1996). A case for interaction: a study of interactive information retrieval behavior and effectiveness. In *Proceedings of the SIGCHI conference on human factors in computing systems* (pp. 205-212). New York: ACM. doi:10.1145/238386.238487

Kosala, R., & Blockeel, H. (2000). Web mining research: A survey. *ACM Sigkdd Explorations Newsletter, 2*(1), 1–15. doi:10.1145/360402.360406

Lee, J. G., & Lee, E. S. (1997). VEMA: Multi-Agent System for Electronic Commerce on Interne, Design of Computing Systems: Cognitive Considerations. In *Proceedings of the Seventh International Conference on Human-Computer Interaction*(vol. 1, pp. 19-22).

Lee, J. K., & Lee, W. (1997). Intelligent agent based contract process in electronic commerce: UNIK-AGENT approach. In *Proceedings of the Thirtieth Hawaii International Conference on System Sciences*(vol. 4, pp. 230-241). Wailea, HI: IEEE. doi:10.1109/HICSS.1997.663394

Leung, K. W. T., Lee, D. L., & Lee, W. C. (2010). Personalized web search with location preferences. In *26thInternational Conference on Data Engineering*(pp. 701-712). IEEE.

Li, L., Yang, Z., & Kitsuregawa, M. (2009). Rank optimization of personalized search. *Information and Media Technologies, 4*(3), 666–671.

Lieberman, H. (1995). Letizia: An agent that assists web browsing. *IJCAI, 1995*(1), 924–929.

Liu, F., Yu, C., & Meng, W. (2004). Personalized web search for improving retrieval effectiveness. *IEEE Transactions on Knowledge and Data Engineering, 16*(1), 28–40. doi:10.1109/TKDE.2004.1264820

Lv, Y., Sun, L., Zhang, J., Nie, J. Y., Chen, W., & Zhang, W. (2006). An iterative implicit feedback approach to personalized search. In *Proceedings of the 21st International Conference on Computational Linguistics and the 44th annual meeting of the Association for Computational Linguistics*(pp. 585-592). Association for Computational Linguistics. doi:10.3115/1220175.1220249

Madani, O., & DeCoste, D. (2005). Contextual recommender problems [extended abstract]. In *Proceedings of the 1st international workshop on Utility-based data mining*(pp. 86-89). New York: ACM. doi:10.1145/1089827.1089838

Matthijs, N., & Radlinski, F. (2011). Personalizing web search using long term browsing history. In *Proceedings of the fourth ACM international conference on Web search and data mining*(pp. 25-34). New York: ACM. doi:10.1145/1935826.1935840

Menczer, F. (2003). Complementing search engines with online web mining agents. *Decision Support Systems, 35*(2), 195–212. doi:10.1016/S0167-9236(02)00106-9

Mittal, A., & Sethi, S. (2015).A Review on Personalization Techniques, *Proceedings of National Conference on Innovative Trends in Computer Science Engineering (pp.*123-125).

Moawad, I. F., Talha, H., Hosny, E., & Hashim, M. (2012). Agent-based web search personalization approach using dynamic user profile. *Egyptian Informatics Journal, 13*(3), 191–198. doi:10.1016/j. eij.2012.09.002

Mobasher, B., Cooley, R., & Srivastava, J. (2000). Automatic personalization based on web usage mining. *Communications of the ACM*, *43*(8), 142–151. doi:10.1145/345124.345169

Mokbel, M., Bao, J., Eldawy, A., Levandoski, J., & Sarwat, M. (2011). Personalization, socialization, and recommendations in location-based services 2.0. In *5th International VLDB workshop on Personalized access, Profile Management and context awareness in Databases (PersDB)*.

Montazemi, A. R., & Gupta, K. M. (1997). On the effectiveness of cognitive feedback from an interface agent. *Omega*, *25*(6), 643–658. doi:10.1016/S0305-0483(97)00028-5

Morris, M. R., Teevan, J., & Bush, S. (2008). Enhancing collaborative web search with personalization: groupization, smart splitting, and group hit-highlighting. In *Proceedings of the conference on Computer supported cooperative work*, (pp. 481-484). ACM. doi:10.1145/1460563.1460640

Müller, J.-P., & Pischel, M. (1994). Modelling Reactive Behaviour in Vertically Layered Agent Architectures. In *Proceedings of the Eleventh European Conference on A* (pp. 709-713).

Nauman, M., & Khan, S. (2007). Using personalized web search for enhancing common sense and folksonomy based intelligent search systems.*International Conference on Web Intelligence*(pp. 423-426). Fremont, CA: IEEE. doi:10.1109/WI.2007.44

Noda, I., Matsubara, H., Hiraki, K., & Frank, I. (1998). Soccer server: A tool for research on multiagent systems. *Applied Artificial Intelligence*, *12*(2-3), 233–250. doi:10.1080/088395198117848

Olston, C., & Chi, E. H. (2003). ScentTrails: Integrating browsing and searching on the Web. *ACM Transactions on Computer-Human Interaction*, *10*(3), 177–197. doi:10.1145/937549.937550

Page, L., Brin, S., Motwani, R., & Winograd, T. (1999). *The PageRank citation ranking: bringing order to the web. Technical Report*. Stanford InfoLab.

Palleti, P., Karnick, H., & Mitra, P. (2007). Personalized web search using probabilistic query expansion. In *Proceedings of the 2007 IEEE/WIC/ACM International Conferences on Web Intelligence and Intelligent Agent Technology- Workshops* (pp. 83-86). Washington, DC: IEEE Computer Society.

Pan, X., Wang, Z., & Gu, X. (2007). Context-based adaptive personalized web search for improving information retrieval effectiveness.*International Conference on Wireless Communications, Networking and Mobile Computing*(pp. 5427-5430). Shanghai: IEEE. doi:10.1109/WICOM.2007.1329

Pannu, M., Anane, R., & James, A. (2013). Hybrid profiling in information retrieval.*17th International Conference on Computer Supported Cooperative Work in Design*(pp. 84-91). Whistler, BC: IEEE.

Peng, W. C., & Lin, Y. C. (2006). Ranking web search results from personalized perspective. *The 8th IEEE International Conference on E-Commerce Technology and The 3rd IEEE International Conference on Enterprise Computing, E-Commerce, and E- Services* (pp. 12-12). San Francisco, CA: IEEE.

Peng, X., Niu, Z., Huang, S., & Zhao, Y. (2012). Personalized web search using clickthrough data and web page rating. *Journal of Computers*, *7*(10), 2578–2584. doi:10.4304/jcp.7.10.2578-2584

Pierrakos, D., Paliouras, G., Papatheodorou, C., & Spyropoulos, C. D. (2003). Web usage mining as a tool for personalization: A survey. *User Modeling and User-Adapted Interaction, 13*(4), 311–372. doi:10.1023/A:1026238916441

Pirolli, P. (1997). Computational models of information scent-following in a very large browsable text collection. In *Proceedings of the ACM SIGCHI Conference on Human factors in computing systems*(pp. 3-10). New York: ACM. doi:10.1145/258549.258558

Pirolli, P. (2006). The use of proximal information scent to forage for distal content on the World Wide Web. Adaptive Perspectives on Human-Technology Interaction: Methods and Modfiles for Cognitive Engineering and Human-Computer Interaction (pp. 247-266).

Pirolli, P., & Card, S. K. (1999). Information foraging. *Psychological Review, 106*(4), 643–675. doi:10.1037/0033-295X.106.4.643

Pirolli, P., Card, S. K., & Van Der Wcgc, M. M. (2003). The effects of information scent on visual search in the hyperbolic tree browser. *ACM Transactions on Computer-Human Interaction, 10*(1), 20–53. doi:10.1145/606658.606660

Pirolli, P., & Fu, W. T. (2003). SNIF-ACT: A model of information foraging on the World Wide Web. In User modeling. Springer Berlin Heidelberg.

Pol, K., Patil, N., Patankar, S., & Das, C. (2008). A Survey on Web Content Mining and extraction of Structured and Semistructured data.*First International Conference on Emerging Trends in Engineering and Technology*(pp. 543-546). Nagpur, Maharashtra: IEEE. doi:10.1109/ICETET.2008.251

Raghavan, V. V., & Sever, H. (1995). On the reuse of past optimal queries. In *Proceedings of the 18th annual international ACM SIGIR conference on Research and development in information retrieval*(pp. 344-350). New York: ACM. doi:10.1145/215206.215381

Rastegari, H., & Shamsuddin, S. M. (2010). Web search personalization based on browsing history by artificial immune system. *International Journal of Advances in Soft Computing and Its Applications, 2*(3), 282-301.

Rizzi, A. A., Gowdy, J., & Hollis, R. L. (1997). Agile assembly architecture: An agent based approach to modular precision assembly systems. *IEEE International Conference on Robotics and Automation* (vol. 2, pp. 1511-1516). Albuquerque, NM: IEEE. doi:10.1109/ROBOT.1997.614353

Rosenschein, S. J., & Kaelbling, L. P. (1995). A Situated View of Representation and Control. *Artificial Intelligence, 73*(1-2), 149–173. doi:10.1016/0004-3702(94)00056-7

Saravanakumar, K., & Deepa, K. (2011). Alternate query construction agent for improving web search result using wordnet.*International Conference on Computational Intelligence and Communication Networks (pp.*117-120). IEEE. doi:10.1109/CICN.2011.23

Selker, T. (1994). COACH: A teaching agent that learns. *Communications of the ACM, 37*(7), 92–99. doi:10.1145/176789.176799

Sethi, S., & Dixit, A. (2015). Design of personalised search system based on user interest and query structuring. In *2nd International Conference on Computing for Sustainable Global Development* (pp. 1346-1351). IEEE.

Shoham, Y. (1997). Agent Oriented Programming: A Survey. In J. M. Bradshaw (Ed.), *Software Agents*. Menlo Park, CA: MIT Press.

Sieg, A., Mobasher, B., & Burke, R. (2007a). Web search personalization with ontological user profiles. In *Proceedings of the sixteenth ACM conference on Conference on information and knowledge management* (pp. 525-534). New York: ACM. doi:10.1145/1321440.1321515

Sieg, A., Mobasher, B., & Burke, R. (2007b). Ontological user profiles for representing context in web search. In *Proceedings of the 2007 IEEE/WIC/ACM International Conferences on Web Intelligence and Intelligent Agent Technology- Workshops* (pp. 91-94). Washington, DC: IEEE Computer Society.

Singh, B., & Singh, H. K. (2010). Web data mining research: a survey.*IEEE International Conference on Computational Intelligence and Computing Research*(pp. 1-10). Coimbatore: IEEE.

Sirola, M. (1996). A Rule-Based Agent Model for Process Automation. In *Proceedings of the IASTED/ISMM International Conference Modelling and Simulation*(pp 213-215).

Smith, D. C., Cypher, A., & Spohrer, J. (1994). KidSim: Programming agents without a programming language. *Communications of the ACM, 37*(7), 54–67. doi:10.1145/176789.176795

Smyth, B. (2007). A community-based approach to personalizing web search. *Computer, 40*(8), 42–50. doi:10.1109/MC.2007.259

Speretta, M., & Gauch, S. (2005). Personalized search based on user search histories.*IEEE/WIC/ACM International Conference on Web Intelligence*(pp. 622-628). IEEE. doi:10.1109/WI.2005.114

Srivastava, J., Cooley, R., Deshpande, M., & Tan, P. N. (2000). Web usage mining: Discovery and applications of usage patterns from web data. *ACM SIGKDD Explorations Newsletter, 1*(2), 12–23. doi:10.1145/846183.846188

Stermsek, G., Strembeck, M., & Neumann, G. (2007). User Profile Refinement Using Explicit User Interest Modeling. GI Jahrestagung, 1, 289-293.

Sugiyama, K., Hatano, K., & Yoshikawa, M. (2004). Adaptive web search based on user profile constructed without any effort from users. In *Proceedings of the 13th international conference on World Wide Web*(pp. 675-684). New York: ACM. doi:10.1145/988672.988764

Sun, J. T., Zeng, H. J., Liu, H., Lu, Y., & Chen, Z. (2005). Cubesvd: a novel approach to personalized web search. In *Proceedings of the 14th international conference on World Wide Web*(pp. 382-390). New York: ACM. doi:10.1145/1060745.1060803

Taherizadeh, S., & Moghadam, N. (2012). Integrating Web content mining into Web usage mining for finding patterns and predicting users' behaviors. *International Journal of Information Science and Management, 7*(1), 51–66.

Teevan, J., Alvarado, C., Ackerman, M. S., & Karger, D. R. (2004). The perfect search engine is not enough: a study of orienteering behavior in directed search. In *Proceedings of the SIGCHI conference on Human factors in computing systems*(pp. 415-422). New York: ACM. doi:10.1145/985692.985745

Turner, R. M., Turner, E. H., Wagner, T. A., Wheeler, T. J., & Ogle, N. E. (2001). Using explicit, a priori contextual knowledge in an intelligent web search agent. In *International and Interdisciplinary Conference on Modeling and Using Context* (pp. 343-352). Springer Berlin Heidelberg. doi:10.1007/3-540-44607-9_26

Tyagi, N., & Sharma, S. (2012). Weighted Page rank algorithm based on number of visits of Links of web page. *International Journal of Soft Computing and Engineering.*

Wavish, P. (1996). Situated action approach to implementing characters in computer games. *Applied Artificial Intelligence, 10*(1), 53–74. doi:10.1080/088395196118687

Weber, I., & Castillo, C. (2010, July). The demographics of web search. In *Proceedings of the 33rd international ACM SIGIR conference on Research and development in information retrieval* (pp. 523-530). ACM.

Wei, Y. Z., Moreau, L., & Jennings, N. R. (2003). Recommender systems: A market-based design. In *Proceedings of the second international joint conference on Autonomous agents and multiagent systems*(pp. 600-607). ACM. doi:10.1145/860575.860671

Wen, J. R., Nie, J. Y., & Zhang, H. J. (2002). Query clustering using user logs. *ACM Transactions on Information Systems, 20*(1), 59–81. doi:10.1145/503104.503108

Xu, S., Jiang, H., & Lau, F. C. M. (2011). Mining user dwell time for personalized web search re-ranking. *International Joint Conference on Artificial Intelligence, 22*(3), 2367.

Yang, C., Hsu, H., & Hung, J. C. (2006). A Web Content Suggestion System for Distance Learning. *Tamkang Journal of Science and Engineering, 9*(3), 243.

Yu, B., & Singh, M. P. (2002). An agent-based approach to knowledge management. In *Proceedings of the eleventh international conference on Information and knowledge management*(pp. 642-644). ACM.

Zhu, Z., Xu, J., Ren, X., Tian, Y., & Li, L. (2007). Query Expansion Based on a Personalized Web Search Model.*Third International Conference on Semantics, Knowledge and Grid*(pp. 128-133). Shan Xi: IEEE. doi:10.1109/SKG.2007.83

KEY TERMS AND DEFINITIONS

Agents: Agents are autonomous software entity dedicated for a specific purpose.
Authorities: High Quality content web pages in a specific domain.
Clicked URLs: The URLs clicked by the user in web search results for a given search query.
Clustering: It is the method of grouping the similar objects together and dissimilar objects in different groups.

Hubs: High quality resource pages on the web which point to high quality content web pages.

Personalize Web Search: It is the method of customizing the search to the information need of the user.

Search Engines: It is an Information Retrieval system which retrieves web search results relevant to user query.

Web Queries: It is the user search queries issued on web to retrieve the relevant information.

Section 3
Developing Efficient Knowledge based Systems

Chapter 9
Knowledge Representation Technologies Using Semantic Web

Vudattu Kiran Kumar
Dravidian University, India

ABSTRACT

The World Wide Web (WWW) is global information medium, where users can read and write using computers over internet. Web is one of the services available on internet. The Web was created in 1989 by Sir Tim Berners-Lee. Since then a great refinement has done in the web usage and development of its applications. Semantic Web Technologies enable machines to interpret data published in a machine-interpretable form on the web. Semantic web is not a separate web it is an extension to the current web with additional semantics. Semantic technologies play a crucial role to provide data understandable to machines. To achieve machine understandable, we should add semantics to existing websites. With additional semantics, we can achieve next level web where knowledge repositories are available for better understanding of web data. This facilitates better search, accurate filtering and intelligent retrieval of data. This paper discusses about the Semantic Web and languages involved in describing documents in machine understandable format.

INTRODUCTION

Internet has been perhaps the most outstanding innovation in the field of communication in the history of mankind. Now a day's most of the people surf the internet for their daily use and most of the data on internet is designed with HTML. The dream behind creating the web was to create a common information space in which people communicate by sharing information. The World Wide Web (WWW) is a collection electronic document over internet. Each electronic document is called as a webpage and it can contain text, image, video and audio etc., and the collection of such pages can be called as a Website. The WWW can be viewed as huge client-server system, where millions of servers are distributed over internet containing electronic documents. A server accepts requests from clients and transfers files / web

DOI: 10.4018/978-1-5225-1877-8.ch009

pages accordingly to client. The web was created in 1989 by Sir Tim Berners-Lee, working at CERN in Geneva, Switzerland. Since then, Tim Berners-Lee (1989) has played an active role in guiding the development of web standards starting from Web 1.0 to the present Web 3.0, which we can call it as an intelligent web or Semantic web. Generally the knowledge or information available in the World Wide Web is a collection of documents written in natural language. To make use of this knowledge, technologies such as natural language processing, information retrieval, data and knowledge mining must be applied. Semantic Web technologies follow an alternative approach by complementing web documents with explicit semantics based on formal knowledge representations, such as example ontologies. This chapter discusses about the technologies to represent the knowledge available on the web for Semantic Web. The rest of the paper is organized to give an introduction to Semantic Web and then discuss about the different technologies available on Semantic and Web.

INTRODUCTION TO SEMANTIC WEB

According to the Authors Berners-Lee, Tim; James Hendler and Ora Lassila (2008), the Semantic Web is an emerging technology intended to transform 'documents' on the World Wide Web (WWW) into *Knowledge* that can be processed by machines. The scholar Sreedhar. G (2016) in his chapter he quoted that World Wide Web Consortium (W3C) is an open source organizations and it defines various web standards for designing a website. The W3C is led by web inventor Tim Berners-Lee and CEO. The standards defined by W3C are considered as guidelines and these guidelines help in assessing the quality of website content in presenting the web content. Web mining is the process of investigating various aspects of websites. According to the World Wide Web Consortium (W3C), "The Semantic Web provides a common framework that allows data to be shared and reused across application, enterprise, and community boundaries." The term was coined by Tim Berners-Lee for a web of data that can be processed by machines. Figure 1 represents Semantic Layer with different technologies are used in designing Semantic Web applications. The primary purpose of these languages is to represent machine-understandable information and to support interoperability between applications on web. Once we add semantics to the website, we can design semantic web applications for the users to use. Uniform Resource Identifier (URI) represents any resource on the web with unique name. The key technologies include Resource Description Framework (RDF), Resource Description Framework Schema (RDFS) and Ontology Web Language (OWL).

URI REF AND NAMESPACES

A Uniform Resource Identifier (URI) is a character string that identifies an abstract (or) physical resource on the web. A URI reference (URI ref) is a URI with an optional fragment identifier attached to it and preceded by character "#". For example, the following string is a URI ref [], where "http://www.dravidianuniversity.ac.in" is a URI and "All_Genders" is a fragment identifier which was preceded by "#".

http://www.dravidianuniversity.ac.in#All_Genders_

Figure 1. Semantic layer cake

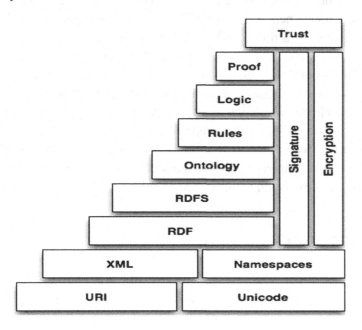

A name space is a collection of names. A name space is identified by URI ref. Names from namespaces are called as qualified names (Qnames) for example, 'p:u', where 'p' is the namespace prefix and 'u' is the local part. For example, 'rdf: description' is a qualified name where 'rdf' is namespace prefix and 'description' is a local part. This tool uses a set of namespaces, URI refs and Qnames for converting syntactic HTML table into semantic files.

TRIPLES

In RDF (Resource Description Framework) format all statements comprises with subject, a predicate (property) and an object. The subject->Predicate->Object relationship is called a triple. The subject can be an RDF URI reference or a blank node, the predicate can be RDF URI reference and an object can be an RDF URI reference, a literal or a blank node. Any statement can be represented using this triple format. For example:

"Tim Berners-Lee invented World Wide Web"
- ◦ A subject Tim Berners-Lee
- ◦ A predicate invented
- ◦ And an object World Wide Web

RDF (RESOURCE DESCRIPTION FRAMEWORK)

The World Wide Web (WWW) was originally built for human consumption, and everything on it is machine-readable, these data is not machine-understandable. The solution is to use metadata (data about data) which can be processed by machines. Resource Description Framework (RDF) is particularly intended for representing metadata about web resources, which can be processed by applications rather than being displayed to people. In February 2004, The World Wide Web Consortium released the RDF as W3C recommendation. As per the authors Trastour, David, Claudio Bartolini, and Chris Preist (2002), RDF is a general method to decompose knowledge into small pieces, having certain rules of semantics. The RDF graph for the above statement would be represented by the graph model as shown below in Figure 2.

Subject and objects are represented by nodes and predicate is represented by an arc. RDF statements may be encoded using various serialization syntaxes which include Turtle, N-Triples, N3, RDF/XML and so on. RDF/XML is sometimes simply called as RDF because it was standardized syntax as per W3C specifications. An RDF documents can contains number of RDF statements.

```
1   <rdf:RDF
2.  xmlns:rdf="http://www.w3.org/1999/02/22-rdf-syntax-ns#"
3.     xmlns:feature="http://www.example.com/clothing-features#">
4.  <rdf:Description rdf:about="http://www.example.com/clothes#t-shirt">
5.     <feature:size>12</feature:size>
6.     <feature:color rdf:resource="http://www.example.com/colors#white"/>
7.  </rdf:Description>
8.  </rdf:RDF>
```

The Line 2 in the above example shows that the RDF document uses w3.org namespace http://www.w3.org/1999/02/22-rdf-syntax-ns#. This namespace tells any machine reader that the enclosing document is an RDF document, and that the rdf:RDF tag resides in this namespace. The rdf:Description tag is mainly used to represent that a Subject is describing and it was identified by unique id http://www.example.com/clothes#t-shirt. RDF statements describe the characteristics of their subjects using properties or predicates in RDF terminology. The above RDF document contains two predicates namely size and color. The line5 explains that "The subject has a property with name feature:size which has a literal value ". Similarly the line6 shows that feature:color has another property for the same subject with ID http://www.example.com/colors#while.

The example clearly shows that http://www.example.com/clothing-features#is a Uniform Resource Identifier (URI) where 'feature' is an XML namespace. The purpose of this namespace is simply to

Figure 2. RDF graph

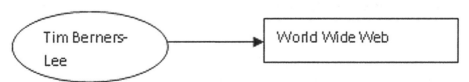

avoid name conflicts. The 'size' and 'color' are two predicates defined under the namespace http:// www.example.com/clothing-features#. RDF triples can be created for all structured, semi-structured and unstructured content. When comparing with metadata, we can create more expressive vocabularies with exact semantics using RDF. This feature makes RDF a powerful data model and language for data interoperability across datasets. As per the author T. Berners-Lee (2002), The major limitation of RDF is that it has no range or domain constraints, cardinality constraints and also lack of transitive, inverse or symmetrical properties. Hence RDF can mainly be used in describing static things or basic facts. RDFS (Resource Description Framework Schema) is the next layer in the RDF stack designed to overcome some of these basic limitations.

RDFS (RESOURCE DESCRIPTION FRAMEWORK SCHEMA)

RDF-Schema (RDF-S) was introduced and recommended by W3C in February 2004 due to the lack of defining application-specific classes and properties in RDF. In simpler terms we can say that RDF Schema is semantic extension of RDF. RDF Schema provides the framework to describe application-specific classes and properties. Classes in RDF Schema are much similar to classes in object oriented programming concept. This facilitates the user to create a resource as instance of class and subclass of a class.

1. **Class:** A class in RDF Schema is somewhat similar to 'class' in object oriented programming languages. In RDF Schema, a class is any resource having an 'rdf:type' property with the value of the resource 'rdfs:Class'. And RDF classes can be used to represent almost everything on the web.
2. **Property:** A property is any instance of the class 'rdfs: Property'. The 'rdfs:domain' property is used to indicate that a particular property applies to a designated class and 'rdfs:range' property is used to indicate that the values of a particular property are instances of a designated class (or) are instances of an XML schema data type.
3. **Instance:** An instance of a class C is a resource having an 'rdf:type' property whose value is C. A resource may be an instance of more than class.

RDF Schema can be called as lightweight language for defining a vocabulary used in RDF graphs. However RDF Schema has some limitations regarding the possibilities of formulating ontologies. For example it is not possible that Domain of a property does not contain a certain class i.e., negation of an expression. It is also not possible to define metadata of particular RDF Schema, which means that we can't provide additional information about the schema. With regard to providing relations to resources, RDF Schema was unable to provide cardinality relations. The major popular RDF vocabularies represented in RDF Schema are FOAF (Friend of a Friend), DC (Dublin Core), Simple Knowledge Organization System (SKOS) and so on.

OWL (ONTOLOGY WEB LANGUAGE)

OWL is a language for processing web information by the computers and not for being ready by people. It was built on top of RDF and was written in XML format. The three major sublanguages of OWL are OWL lite, OWL DL and OWL Full. OWL Lite supports cardinality constraints, it only permits cardinality values of 0 or 1. OWL DL supports those users who want the maximum expressiveness without losing computational completeness. OWL Full is meant for users who want maximum expressiveness and the syntactic freedom of RDF with no computational guarantees. The authors, Breitman, K.K; Truszkowski; Felicissiomo (2006) Ontology Web Language (OWL) is almost similar to RDF with respect to coding but OWL has greater machine interpretability than RDF. The next generation web i.e., Semantic Web has a vision that the information available on the web should have an explicit meaning which should understandable and automatically process able by machines. This is only possible when the information is described with OWL. To perform useful reasoning the language must go beyond the basic semantics of RDF Schema. Some ontology tools can perform automated reasoning using the ontologies and thus provide advanced services to intelligent applications such as conceptual/semantic search and retrieval, software agents, decision support, speech and natural language understanding, knowledge management, intelligent databases and electronic commerce. An ontology differs from XML Schema.XML Schema is a message format with protocol specifications where as ontology is focuses on knowledge representation. The main advantage of OWL ontologies will be the availability of tools that can reason about them. The main purpose of ontology is to classify things in terms of semantics or meaning. This is possible through classes and subclasses. An example of OWL class is as below:

```
<rdf:RDF
        xmlns:rdf="http://www.w3.org/1999/02/22-rdf-syntax-ns#"
        xmlns:rdfs="http://www.w3.org/2000/01/rdf-schema#"
        xmlns:owl="http://www.w3.org/2002/07/owl#"
        xmlns:dc="http://purl.org/dc/elements/1.1/"
        xmlns:staff="http://www.dravidianuniversity.ac.in/staff#">

<!-- OWL Class Definition - Employment Type -->
<owl:Class rdf:about="http://www.dravidianuniversity.ac.in/staff#Jobtype">
<rdfs:label>Job Category</rdfs:label>
</owl:Class>
 <!-- OWL Subclass Definition - Teaching -->
<owl:Class rdf:about="http://www.dravidianuniversity.ac.in/staff#Teaching">
<owl:Class rdf:about="http://www.dravidianuniversity.ac.in/staff#Jobtype">
 <rdfs:label>Teaching</rdfs:label>
</owl:Class>
<owl:Class rdf:about=" http://www.dravidianuniversity.ac.in/staff#NonTeaching
">
<owl:Class rdf:about="http://www.dravidianuniversity.ac.in/staff#Jobtype">
<rdfs:label>Non Teaching</rdfs:label>
</owl:Class>
 </rdf:Description>
</rdf:RDF>
```

QUERY LANGUAGE

The languages which are discussed in the previous sections are useful to describe the knowledge in machine understandable format. This section focuses on query languages which are already available for extraction of information from knowledge base. The examples of such languages are RDQL, SPARQL and so on. Normally RDF is a graph and the data is represented in triples. Each triple pattern is comprised of named variables and RDF values (URIs and literals). RDQL was first released in Jena 1.2.0. RDQL (RDF query language) has a set of constrains on those variables and a list of variables required in the answer set.

```
SELECT ?x
WHERE (?x,  <http://www.w3.org/1999/02/22-rdf-syntax-ns#type>,
                         <http://example.com/someType>)
```

This query pattern matches with all statements/triples in the graph where predicate is "http://www.w3.org/1999/02/22-rdf-syntax-ns#type" and object "http://example.com/someType". The subject "?x" will be the output in a triple format where all triples contains the predicate and object mentioned as in query. Similarly many constrains can be placed in the query to extract data from the knowledge.

SPARQL (Simple Protocol And RDF Query Language) is a W3C (World Wide Web Consortium) standard query language for RDF graph data. A SPARQL query comprises of prefix declarations, dataset definition, result clause, query pattern and query modifiers. An example query is mentioned as below:

```
PREFIX foaf:  <http://xmlns.com/foaf/0.1/>
SELECT *
WHERE {
    ?person foaf:name ?name.
    ?person foaf:mbox ?email.
}
```

This query returns all the peoples in FOAF files (Friend of a Friend) that have names and e-mail addresses as predicate and object. SPARQL is a client-server based RDF query language. It is almost similar to SQL syntax. The query language SPARQL has become standard language for querying RDF, since its standardization in 2008. SPARQL supports disjunction in the query and can process more complex queries than RDQL. It also provides optional variable binding and result size control mechanisms for real world usage. OWL Query Language (OWL-QL) is a well designed language for querying over knowledge represented in a repository. OWL-DL is an updated version of DAML Query Language (DQL). It is intended to be a candidate for query-answering dialogues among answer agents and query agents. Similarly nRQL (new RACER Query Language, an extension of RQL) is an extended query language for RACER. nRQL was constructed based on Description Logic model theory.

CONCLUSION

This chapter has given brief introduction to the Semantic Web along with different technologies. The Semantic Web is an emerging technology intended to transform 'documents' on the World Wide Web (WWW) into 'knowledge' that can be processed by machines. The major drawback of existing Web is that, the information available on Web is understandable by humans only. If the existing data is able to understand for machines, we can design number of applications on it. RDF is a language representing resources on the web, which can be processed by machines rather than just displaying them. RDF uses a general method to decompose knowledge into pieces called triples. The Web was created in 1989 by Sir Tim Berners-Lee. Since then a great refinement has done in the web usage and development of its applications. The first generation web focuses on how to connect people by designing web sites. The users can just read the web content only; the applications were designed with little bit dynamic content like submission of forms. The second generation web focuses on connecting the communities and provides access to the users to read the content as well as write content online. With the help of many authorized online tools available the users can read and write the content. Hence, applications are designed in such a way to focus social networking sites, multimedia sharing, mashup, blogs, wikis etc., The next generation web focuses on how to provide machine-understandable format and how to consider the web as database by providing semantics to the web content. Then users can design applications on the web database for the humans to reduce the burden at great extent. In this paper an attempt was made to discuss about Semantic Web and their languages to describe documents in machine understandable format.

REFERENCES

Berners-Lee, T. (2000). *Weaving the Web – The Past, Present and Future of the World Wide Web by its Inventor*. Texere.

Berners-Lee, T., Hendler, J., & Lassila, O. (2001). The Semantic Web. Scientific American Magazine; Retrieved March 26, 2008.

Breitman, K., Casanova, M., & Truszkowski, W. (2006). *Semantic Web*. Concepts.

Breitman, K. K., Truszkowski, & Felicissiomo. (2006). The automatic semantic desktop; Helping users copy with information system and complexity. In *Proceedings of IEEE International workshop*, (pp. 156-162).

Brickley, D., & Guha, R. V. (2003). *Resource Description Framework (RDF) Schema specification 1.0: RDFSchema*. W3C Working Draft.

Decker, S., & Frank, M. (2004). The social semantic desktop. In *Proceeding of the WWW 2004 Workshop Application Design, Development and Implementation Issues in the Semantic Web*.

Fikes, R; Horrocks, I. (2003). OWL-QL – A Language for Deductive Query Answering on the Semantic Web. *KSL*.

Halpin, H; Tuffield, M. (2010). *A Standards-based, Open and Privacy-aware Social Web*. W3C Social Web Incubator Group Report. W3C Incubator Group Report.

Kumar, K. (2013). Towards Web 3.0: An Application oriented approach. *IOSR Journal of Computer Engineering, 15*(5), 50-53.

Kumar, K., & Rao, R. (2009a). Semantic Extension of Syntactic table data. *International Journal of Systems and Technologies.*

Kumar, K., & Rao, R. (2009b). TBL2RDF: Html Table To RDF Translator. *International Journal of Web Applications.*

Martinez, O., & Botella, F. (n.d.). *Building E-Commerce Web Applications: Agent and Ontology-based Interface Adaptivity.* Operations Research Center, University Miguel Hernández of Elche, Avda. Universidad.

Sandahl, Z., & Sandahl, K. (2003). Potential advantages of Semantic Web for Internet commerce. In *Proceedings of the International Conference on Enterprise Information Systems (ICEIS).*

Sauermann, L., Sebastian, T., & Linux, M. (2008). Case Study: KDE 4.0 Semantic Desktop Search and Tagging. Academic Press.

Sreedhar, G. (2016). Identifying and Evaluating Web Metrics for Assuring the Quality of Web Designing. In Design Solutions for Improving Website Quality and Effectiveness (pp. 1-23). Hershey, PA: Information Science Publishing (an imprint of IGI Global).

Trastour, D., Bartolini, C., & Preist, C. (2002). Semantic web support for the business-to-business e-commerce lifecycle. In *Proceedings of the 11th international conference on World Wide Web,* (pp. 89-98). ACM. doi:10.1145/511446.511458

Williams, H., Li, F., & Whalley, J. (2000). Interoperability and electronic commerce: A new policy framework for evaluating strategic options. *Journal of Computer-Mediated Communication, 5*(3).

Chapter 10
Discovering Knowledge Hidden in Big Data from Machine- Learning Techniques

Adiraju Prashantha Rao
Anurag Group of Institutions, India

ABSTRACT

As the speed of information growth exceeds in this new century, excessive data is making great troubles to human beings. However, there are so much potential and highly useful values hidden in the huge volume of data. Big Data has drawn huge attention from researchers in information sciences, policy and decision makers in governments and enterprises. Data analytic is the science of examining raw data with the purpose of drawing conclusions about that information. Data analytics is about discovering knowledge from large volumes data and applying it to the business. Machine learning is ideal for exploiting the opportunities hidden in big data. This chapter able to discover and display the patterns buried in the data using machine learning.

INTRODUCTION

Big Data has been one of the current and future research frontiers. Big Data analytics is a broad topic, fed by a lot of other top technology trends. David Cearley (2016), vice president and Garner Fellow at Gartner Group, shared his thoughts with Information Management on the Top 10 Strategic Technology Trends that will impact IT leaders and data analytics in 2016. He noted that technology based companies such as Google, Yahoo, Face Book, Microsoft, Amazon have been collecting and maintaining data that is measured in terms of Exabyte propositions or larger. Human-sourced information is now almost entirely digitized and stored everywhere from personal computers to social networks. Data are loosely structured and often ungoverned. Internets of Things are derived from the phenomenal growth in the number of sensors and machines, used to measure and record the events and situations in the physical world. The output of these sensors is machine-generated data and from simple sensor records to complex computer logs, it is well structured. As sensors proliferate and data volumes grow, it is becoming an increasingly

DOI: 10.4018/978-1-5225-1877-8.ch010

important component of the information, stored and processed by many businesses. Its well-structured nature is suitable for computer processing, but its size and speed is beyond traditional approaches. The explosion of data sources and growing complexity of information makes manual classification and analysis, infeasible and uneconomic. "Deep Neural Nets (DNNs) automate these tasks and make it possible, to address key challenges related to the information of every trend" (Cearley, 2016). The machining learning techniques gives rise to a spectrum of smart implementation, which explores automated agents to performs all activities without human intervention. Big data refers to large volumes of data structured and unstructured, gathered from various servers and databases. Mining of information is required to extract necessary information which represents the general group of problems and techniques used for application domains that collect and maintain enormous volumes of raw data for specific domain analysis. This means big data is a collection of very huge data sets with great diversity of types which can be very difficult to process using traditional data processing techniques. So data sets are generally known to be Big Data if it is difficult to perform capture, curation, analysis, and visualization on it with current technology. So Big Data requires new forms of processing to enable enhanced decision making, insight discovery and process optimization. In many instances, science is lagging behind the real world in the capability of discovering the valuable knowledge from enormous volumes of data. There is a need to develop and create new technologies and techniques to solve the problems of big data and also enhancing the current technologies. The main contents which are presented in this chapter are, the applications of big data presented, big data definition and its challenges, big data analysis methodology and knowledge discovery from huge volume presented. Finally, the chapter concludes with its future scope.

BIG DATA APPLICATIONS

Patient Data Sensing and Clinical Records

Initially, supporting increasing potential patients in hospitals or care centers requires remote monitoring of patients as a solution, which in turn leads to difficulty in handling challenges of big data i.e. volume, velocity, variety, veracity etc. Also the full cycle of this huge data (i.e. capturing, gathering, clearing, transforming, formats, storing, analyzing and visualizing) for some patients should be covered in real time. Another data source that caters for data diversity and variety is the patient's clinical records. In all cases, data is made available for access, for all teams of doctors, nurses, administrators and social agents. So the technologies other than Hadoop like batch processing should be considered as better solutions.

Genomics

The genomics is defined as large volume of data (nearly 100 gigabytes) associated to sequencing of DNA from different biological data sources. In case of personalized genomics, number of people wants their DNA sequenced for diagnostic and prognostics purposes, leading to hundreds of thousands of peta bytes of data. Raw DNA sequences are annotated, (making intelligible and rich genomics information) further increasing the data volumes, leading to the development of efficient compression algorithms for sequencing data. The main problems encountered in this process are as follows:

- High data volumes residing at local databases as delocalization (transfer of high data at sufficiently high pace to centralized repositories) exceeds its capacity.
- Synchronization of sparsely distributed repositories given the diversity of data formats.

The main challenging issue is availability and integration among different formats and different types of data.

BIG DATA ARCHITECTURE

The Big Data definitions presented by researchers as given below:

1. The International Data Corporation's (IDC) "conservative and strict approach" defines Big Data as, "A new generation of technologies and architecture designed to economically extract value from very large volumes of wide variety of data by enabling high velocity capture, discover and/ or analysis."
2. Gartner, Inc. (2016) presented big data definition published in IT Glossary as "Big Data are high-volume, high velocity and high-variety information assets that demand cost effective, innovative forms of information processing for enhanced insight and decision making".
3. "Big Data is a massive volume of both structured and unstructured data that is so large that it's difficult to process using traditional database and software technologies" (Bloomberg, 2013).
4. "A data that exceeds the processing capacity of conventional databases systems. The data is too big, moves too fast or doesn't fit the structure of your database architectures. To gain value from this data you must chose an alternative way to process it" (Dumbill, 2013).

Based on the above definitions, the characteristics of Big Data are presented in the next section.

BIG DATA CHARACTERISTICS

There is an exponential growth of heterogeneous data that arises from different sources such as internet of things, web of things, and social media, which need to define dynamic model of 6Vs (Kune, Konugurthi, Agarwal, Rao Chillarige & Buyya, 2011). The dimension of Big Data generated from varied sources and its dimension as shown in Figure 1.

GENERAL PROPERTIES OF BIG DATA

Volume

Big Data means huge collection of data generated from different sources or databases. The huge volume of data generated by machines, networks and human interaction on the systems is massive. This enormous amount of information is produced from different sources like emails, photos, twitter messages (e.g. face book generates 10 billion massages per day), video clips, sensor data etc. This leads to forma-

Figure 1. Dimension of big data

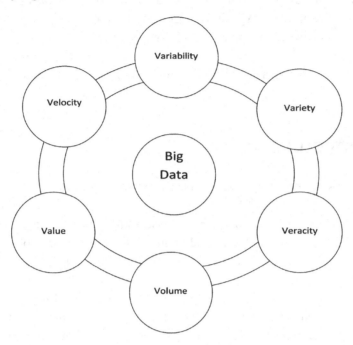

tion of different data sets which are large in number which can be stored and analyzed using big data technology with help of distributed systems, where parts of the data is scattered in different locations and brought together by software.

Variety

Variety refers to different types of data in which 80% of the world's data is unstructured which can't be put into relational data base tables easily. The big data comprises of various kinds of databases both structured and unstructured.

Velocity

Big Data Velocity deals with the speed at which the information is communicated between the processing sources (verb) and the things (noun). The processing sources like business processes, machines, networks and human interactions (things) like social media sites, mobile devices etc. The flow of data is continuous and massive, which helps researchers and businesses make more valuable decisions using big data technology.

ACQUIRED PROPERTIES OF THE BIG DATA
SYSTEM AFTER PROCESSING BEGINS

Veracity

Only faster access to a variety of big data is not enough but also production of qualitative and reliable results is needed. Big Data Veracity refers to the unfairness, noise and abnormal data being stored and mined in meaningful form using big data technology. The main issues it handles are Trust worthiness, Authenticity, Origin, Reputation, Availability and accountability.

Variability

Inconsistency of the data set can hamper handling and management of processes. The variable values change when it's executing or changing the model or linkage.

Value

The value of Big Data defines the real or bound value behind the data which represents business value, useful knowledge from it and any specific type value. This value may be used in correlation methods, statistical methods, events and it may be hypothetical value.

There is an exponential rise of big data due to advanced technologies such as Internet of things, Mobile devices, Social Networks, Cloud Computing ...etc. All such types of devices generate huge amount of data which possess a significant problem in the design of infrastructure components, solutions and processes to store, access and manage big data objects in a feasible way. The new approaches or new technologies are required to analyze and processes such big data as traditional systems cannot solve these issues. These issues, new advancement of technologies and challenges are presented by research communities presented by Jayavardhan Gubbi, Rajkumar Buyya, Slavan Marusic, and Marimuthu & Palaniswami(2013) in Generation of Computer Systems. The main challenges for handling big data rise are as follows:

- The data capture, storage, searching, sharing, analysis and visualization
- The capabilities of discovering the valuable knowledge from massive volume of data

The data is collected in an unpresented way from many applications. The state of the art techniques and technologies cannot ideally solve the real problems, especially for data analysis for real time applications. So proper tools and techniques need to be developed for analyzing the process as explained in proceeding section. The second issue states that big data techniques involve a number of disciplines which include statistics, data mining, machine learning, neural networks, Social network analysis, etc. These techniques discover the knowledge hidden in the big data. The details of these issues are presented in next section.

BIG DATA ANALYSIS PROCESS

The Big Data analysis involves multiple distinct phases and each phase introduces a new challenge, which are shown in Figure 2. These five challenges are considered as five stages of pipeline and each discussed in detail in this section.

DATA RECORDING AND ACQUISITION

The size and the number of experimental data sets available is increasing exponentially which is being gathered as ubiquitous information –sensing mobile devices, aerial sensory technologies, remote sens-

Figure 2. Phases of big data

ing, software logs, cameras, microphone, radio frequency, identification readers, and wireless sensor networks and so on. Most of the data gathered from these systems is of no interest and so appropriate filters are used to compresses the useful data. The main important challenge for data capturing system is to design the filters in such way that they do not discard useful information. For example, one sensor's reading substantially differs from that of the other sensor's reading i.e. temperature sensor reads temperature of the room while traffic sensor reads traffic at specific location. The second challenging issue is the filters automatically generating right metadata information for recording purpose. For example, in scientific experiments, consider details regarding experimental functionality to generate appropriate results. Metadata acquisition system is useful to minimize the human burden in recording metadata. The recorded information is pipelined to next stage for suitable format.

EXTRACTION AND CLEANING OF BIG DATA

The information collected from data recording and data acquisition system cannot be in proper format for data analysis purpose. For example, a health record comprises of transcribed dictations by doctors, image data such X ray, MRI report, etc. This type of a health record is in unstructured format or may not be proper for analysis purpose. The most important technical challenge is to convert the unstructured data or semi structured data into structured format suitable for analysis purpose.

DATA INTEGRATION, AGGREGATION, AND REPRESENTATION

The data sets originating from different diverse sources are differing by the structure, format, origin, access protocol and veracity. All these data should be accessed according to its nature and semantic meaning within the specified application. Data analytics is considerably more challenging than simply locating, identifying, understanding and citing such type of data. This means integrated data structure and its semantics can be expressed in the form that is computer understandable format. The main objective of the Big Data analysis process is to provide meaningful information (part of it) from large volume of data available sources or websites. The system performance decreases when it's extracting from larger volume of data due to lack of technological support. The methodologies such as hybridized content, computation are partitioning and aggregation (HCCP-A) method will resolve such performance issues in Big Data which provide the meaningful information to the cloud users. Data aggregation is the process of gathering the information from multiple sites or sources which represents it in the form of summarized report. Knowledge can be extracted from summarized report about the environment, without the need to analyse the entire content. The big data representation is expressed in terms of the dimension of the big data which is defined in characteristics of big data.

DATA ANALYSIS

The most important and challenging issue of big data as its volume increases exponentially is scalability. So, the main objectives of data analytics are as follows:

- Easy decisions made by enabling data scientists, predictive modelers and senior analytics to analyze large volumes of traction data and also other data which cannot be captured using business intelligence programs
- Usage of software tools as part of advanced analytics disciplines such as predictive analytics, data mining, text analytics and statistical analysis.
  - Data virtualization tool plays an important role for predicting future analysis
- The newer class of technologies that include Hadoop and its related tools such as YARN, MapReduce, Spark, Hive and Pig as well as NoSQL databases are used for semi structured and unstructured data.

The data analysis, organization, retrieval and modeling are functional challenges of big data.

DATA VISUALIZATION AND INTERPRETATION

The main objective of data virtualization is to effectively and efficiently communicate information via statistical graphics, plots and information graphics. Data virtualization is a process of extracting value from large data volumes efficiently, and performs intelligent caching while minimizing needless replication. The communicated information easily provides knowledge hidden in the complex and large scale data sets both in aesthetic form and functional form. The data virtualization task is very difficult for big Data applications due to their large size and high dimensionality. However, the present big data virtualization tools mostly have poor performance in terms of functionality, scalability and response time. It can also access many data source types by integrating them with traditional relational databases or from different data sources which in turn conduct combined query using these data sources. For example, a leading crop insurer has used data virtualization to expose its big data sources and integrate them with its transactional, CRM and ERP systems to deliver an integrated view of sales, forecasts and agent data to its sales team. Using data virtualization, these complex reports could be developed much faster, using fewer staff resources than in the past.

DECISION MAKING

The organization leaders make better decision and derive better performance of the system with proper understanding of the business impact of big data. The efficient algorithms developed using big data techniques which are used to analyze the data and most of these algorithms are of the type machine learning or AI techniques or may DMDW which extended in knowledge discovery techniques.

KNOWLEDGE DISCOVERY TECHNIQUES

The section presents different approaches by innovative researchers interested to match or exceed human cognitive capabilities by applying advanced machine learning algorithms and techniques from the field of artificial intelligence. The big data is growing exponentially. IMB estimates that 90% of the data in the world has been generated in the last 2 years. The aim is to extract hidden knowledge of such unprecedented volume of unstructured data collected from every conceivable source. The most powerful machines which are available in the world today are almost embarrassingly slow and limited where the best programs are running on it. Unfortunately, Big Data is almost by definition, beyond the capacity or patience of any person to manually peruse and analyze using conventional tools and queries. There is a need to design algorithms which use the big data that can teach computers to act like human being, like learning from data to perform prediction, classification and association with advances available in computational power and extracting knowledge from raw data. As a result, the field of machine learning, a branch of artificial intelligence (AI), is becoming tightly associated with big data. The main objective of using machine learning techniques in big data is to analyze data and also automatically adapt to interactive learning capability to find hidden insights without being explicitly programmed. The term iteratively capable means that system will produce reliable, repeatable decisions and results when it is exposed to new data.

Why There is Increased Interest in Machine Learning in Big Data?

1. By the growing volumes and varieties of available data, computational processing is cheaper, more powerful and leads to affordable data storage.
2. Automatically produced models that can analyze bigger, more complex data and deliver faster and more accurate results even on a very large scale are possible.
3. High value predictions can guide better decisions and smart actions in real time without human intervention.

The machine learning technique is useful when set of data elements is characterized by some unknown function but if the data is random, then there is nothing to discover from it. The system adopts learning mechanism that involves the acquisition and integration of new knowledge and also system adapts to new knowledge as the circumstance changes or due to new unseen big data. Big Data arises from sensors and sources of almost any type, from text to video, raw or organized. There are many challenges associated with mining such complex aggregations of data being resolved by machine learning. The undirected association and classification of tasks to extract knowledge and meaning from the flood of Big Data are strengths of machine learning algorithms. The next section shows discussion of the education domain application using machine learning and semantic web

Case Study: Web Based Education System using Semantic Web and Machine Learning Technique

The big data has the potential to revolutionize not only research but also education. There is a web development which generates educational activities from massive data, captured from the student's information in a university. The main objective of Choice Based Education System (CBES) is to adopt a credit dependent grading scheme for the intention of assessment of the students which will be adequate to the global universities. An effective intelligent system need to be developed for selecting different courses of student choice, allocation of resources, and curriculum preparation and generation student assessment reports. Therefore, an education application should be automatically able to communicate with different sub-systems (examination system. office management system, attendance system …, etc) and also give semantics of data. This also should provide access to different data sources for extraction of information and also knowledge for enabling auto-generation of user needs for minimizing manual work, effective storage and time. The diverse technological approach was presented by Hitzler, Krotasch and Rudolph (2009) in a foundation of semantic web technologies which is known to be a semantic web, machine learning approach presented by Anderson and Elloumi (2008) towards theory of online learning which allows a computing machine to comprehend the semantics (i.e. sense of the info). The knowledge explicitly embedded in ontology structure for integrating the information in smart way by providing semantics from texts. The learning capability provided to the system which can process without human intervention and it is automated using semantic web presented by Maedohe (2002).

OBJECTIVES OF CBCS SYSTEM

Semantic Web provides knowledge representation, organizing data and sharing knowledge of different sources in respect to machine understandable presented by Staab and Studer (2009). The main contributions are set to achieve the following:

- Form the <faculty, student> pairs and <student, choice> pairs based on the student and faculty performance.
- Propose an ontology structure for a proposed choice based education system.
- Establish relationships among the courses.
- Test and analyze the performance of proposed education system.
- Provide learning capability to the education system (i.e. auto generation reports, allocation process, etc.)

The objectives are achieved through an adaption of semantic web technology and also provide learning capability through COBWEB algorithms. The semantic web technology provides effective communication between the sub-systems:

- Examination Systems
- Office Management
- Student Management
- Faculty Management

STUDENT MODEL

The main performance factors to measure the student in an education system are as follows:

- Academic Excellence
- Placements
- Higher Studies
- Extra/Co Curriculum Activities

Based on the above performance factors, the student behavior can be measured.

STUDENT BEHAVIOR

The term student behavior refers to a student's observable response to particular area of interest in a given stream. The reports which are generated from the system act as a major input to assess the student. Using COBWEB algorithm, system can automatically compute the behavior of the student. The measurable parameter for students in terms of student assessment is explained in assessment section.

STUDENT ASSESSMENT

The choice of the core subjects is predefined in each semester and core elective and open elective selection depends upon the performance achieved in the previous semester only. The core subjects are represented in a hierarchical tree structure which shows the prerequisite for each subject and they are allocated accordingly. The core electives and open elective selection is based on its prerequisites performance if any. The purpose of our method is to map manifold agent ontology vigorously when desired. The system model tries to generate different type of semantic information between user enquiry notions and the notions in the aimed ontology's. There is a need to develop an algorithm that combines multiple agents to find suitable semantic relations. The structural similarity and rule dependent similarity are the two key groups of similarity measure. The next section presents global architecture and agent's behavior of the plotting procedure. The ontology interoperability needs to outline mapping diverse agent ontology's. In our architecture as shown in Figure 3 which divides into five levels for an education system and each level briefly presented present below.

Figure 3. Ontology spectrum

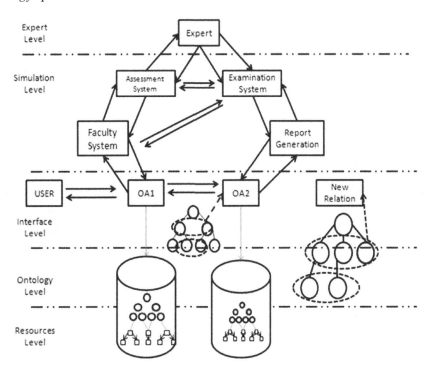

The Figure 3 combines different similarities between different agents from ontology's spectrum to measure student's performance. This algorithm can be outlined in three steps:

1. The first step produces info from the prearranged agent ontology. In order to deduce relations between concepts (convergence, divergence) of the identical ontology, it uses instance contrasts.
2. The second step examines the inference rules which are formulated to measure student performance using human experts.
3. The next step is to write a process or method using inference rules. Before relating the algorithm, we need some more descriptions and representations.

Resource Level

All available resources in an education system are inserted into the database for retrieval purpose. This faculty and student information in the university can be represented in the form of ASN.1 notation for effective retrieval.

Ontology Level

Different ontology structures such as, examination agent, faculty agent, assessment agent software are part of ontology level.

Interface Level

The interface level is an interface between the user level and ontology level. Based on the user request it connects to corresponding agent software.

Simulation Level

The different systems such as investigation system, faculty system, valuation system and report outlining system are part of this level.

MAPPING PROCEDURE IN RACBES

The simulation level contains different agents such as student's assessment agent, faculty assessment agent, schedule preparation agent and examination system agent. The behavior of each of these agents is described below. The behavior of the student assessment can be computed using following algorithm:

Algorithm1: Formation of Student Groups

```
Initialize No. of Students = n;
No. of Subjects failed= J;
//Maximum number of subjects registered in a given semester //
 For Student i =1and J =0
```

```
// J= Number subjects fialed //
Step 1: Compute Weight W_i
Extract student subject information from by calling Get Procedure Method and
compute weight i.e. mean.
Step2: Invoke COBWEB algorithm for finding    student groups
Step 3: Augment i and reiterate step 1 to 2
Step 4: Augment J
Step 5 Stop
```

The above Algorithm generates J groups and group index defines failure of subjects in a given semester. This means that the index value indicates the number of backlogs i.e. index zero means no backlogs. In each group students are arranged in subgroups based on the computed weight using COBWEB algorithm. The working principle of COBWEB is demonstrated in next section. The student clusters are generated from the well-known COBWEB algorithm. The student clusters are formed based on the credits obtained from the given semester. As stated before, the grouping utility is defined as the weighted distance utility of the attribute (i.e. credits). Weight of each student can be calculated using the Equation 1 and priorities can be assigned to students according to their weights. The current study exercises to group out all the tasks that have similar traits. The proposed task clustering algorithm can be espoused to work with numerous attribute groupings and order the weight. A bit map which represents an array type of data structure competently stores discrete bits. The value of each bit in bitmap is either high or low for a given string. In the present trial, the influence of the above attributes on the student enactment can be estimated. The bitmap String and its value are shown below:

Let w_i be the weight of student i and computation of weight using Equation 1.

$$\text{Student Weight i } w_i = \sum_{i=1}^{8} b_i c^i \text{ ------} \tag{1}$$

Where b_i = Variable and its value is either low or high.

If $b_i = 1$, it specifies that conforming attribute value is high else low.

The understanding of the above features is presented in Table 1. The Table 1 shows the attributes list which is representation in BitMap. These bits are used to measure the performance of students which is also useful information for selecting subjects of his choice in the next semester.

Table 1. Bit grouping utility order

S.No	Position in Bit String	Description	Subjects
1	6-11 bits	4 credit subjects and each bit indicate status of the particular subject. This means 1 indicates student attains required credits other zero	Core Subjects, Professional Electives, and few other subjects which have 4 credits.
2	3-5 bits	3 credits subjects and 1 in the string indicate student attains required credits otherwise zero	Open Electives, Inter disciplinary subjects and few other subjects which have 3 credits system
3	0-2 bits	2 credits system	All Lab related subjects.

These attributes are propagated in COBWEB method by means of category utility. To use COBWEB clustering method for classifying student clusters, the category utility is designated in the proposed algorithm below. The following algorithm is known as computing category utility (CCU):

Algorithm 2: Compute Category Utility

```
Begin
1. Initialize bit map array type
   // attribute required to know about the student performance
2. Propagates sequence of bits in BitMap i.e failure or pass in subjects
3. Allot student weight to each of these features depending on the credits ob-
tained.
4. Calculate the weighted sum depending on the bit map and multiplier i.e num-
ber of credits
End
```

Computation of Student Group

The COBWEB algorithm constructs a classification tree incrementally by instructing the objects (task instances) into the classification tree one by one. When inserting an object into the classification tree, the COBWEB algorithm traverses the tree top-down starting from the rest node. The COBWEB algorithm operates based on the so-called category utility function (CU) that measures clustering quality. If set of objects are classified into m clusters and CU partition function given by Equation 2:

$$CU(C_1, C_2, C_3, ...C_k) = \frac{\sum_l \Pr[C_l] \sum_i \overline{(\Pr[\tau_i \mid C_l]^2 - \Pr[\tau_i]^2}}{k} \qquad (2)$$

The Equation 3 gives instance in its own cluster:

$$\Pr[\tau_i \mid C] = \begin{cases} 1 & \tau_i = \text{actual value of instance} \\ 0 & \text{otherwise} \end{cases} \qquad (3)$$

In Equation 4, category utility function becomes:

$$CU(C_1, C_2, C_3, ...C_k) = \frac{n - \sum_i \Pr[\tau_i]^2}{k} \qquad (4)$$

The Gaussian distribution function is defined in Equation 5:

$$g(x) = \frac{1}{\sigma\sqrt{2\pi}} e^{-1/2 \left(\frac{w_i - \mu}{\sigma}\right)^2} \tag{5}$$

where $x = t_i / t_l$

The weight of new task can be computed using the CCU Task Cluster algorithm below, and this value is passed as a parameter (I) to task cluster algorithm. According Equation 1, the weight of new object (t_i) is compared with existing cluster task (t_l) weight. If it matches the new task added to corresponding cluster and likewise different clusters are formed. The computed weight of incoming task will be the input to task cluster algorithm and it generates hierarchical tree structure.

Algorithm 3: Task cluster

```
begin
        Input: Current node N in the concept hierarchy
        An unclassified Task with weight i.e. Instance I = w
                                                            i
        Output: A concept hierarchy that classify the instance I
        Function Call Cobweb (Top-node, I).
        Variables: C, P, Q and R are node variables.
        U,V,W, and X are clustering (partition) scores
        Cobweb(N, I)
        If N is a terminal node,
        Then Create-new-terminals (N, I)
        Incorporate (N, I).
        Else Incorporate (N, I).
        For each child C of node N,
        Compute the score for placing I in C.
        Let P be the node with the highest score W.
        Let Q be the node with the second highest score.
        Let X be the score for placing I in a new node R.
        Let Y be the score for merging P and Q into one node.
        Let Z be the score for splitting P into its children.
        If W is the best score,
        Then Cobweb (P, I) (place I in category P).
        Else if X is the best score,
        Then initialize R's probabilities using I's values
          (Place I by itself in the new category R).
        Else if Y is the best score,
        Then let O be Merge (P, R, N).
        Cobweb (O, I).
        Else if Z is the best score
        Then Split (P, N).
        Cobweb (N, I).
End
```

COMPUTATION OF STUDENT GROUP

A classification tree is constructed iteratively by injecting the objects i.e. student instances by the COB-WEB algorithm. The algorithm traverses the tree using top-down approach and its complexity equal to $O(\log_c nAV)$ where n is the number of students, A is characteristics of bitmap string and V is the average number of values in given characteristics. The student data extracted using get and set methods from huge data seta and these methods are implemented.

CONCLUSION

The next generation era is big data for innovation, computation, productivity, automation and trend moving towards new research area in the fields of machine learning and semantic web. In this chapter the author presented brief definition of Big Data and its challenges and its problems. The extraction of knowledge from it and techniques with its merits and demerits are presented. The semantic web techniques and machine learning techniques elaborated using choice based education system. Author encourages fundamental research towards addressing these technical challenges to meet better performance results. An Automation of Health Monitoring System is one of important future scope of big data using machine learning methods. The system analyses the patient data which in turn identifies the symptom nature and also suitable medicine for a given patient.

REFERENCES

Anderson, T., & Elloumi, F. (2008). *Theory and Practice of online Learning*. Athabasca University Digitization Portal. Retrieved from http://cde.athabascau.ca/online_book/

Bloomberg, J. (2013, January 17) *The Big Data Long Tail*. Retrieved from http://www.devx.com/blog/the-big-data-long-tail.html/

Cearley, D., Burke, B., & Walker, M. (2016). *Top 10 Strategic Technology Trends for 2016*. Gartner, Inc.

Dumbill, E. (2013). Big data, cool kids: Making sense of the hype-cycle scuffle.*Proceedings from the O'Reilly Strata Conference*.

Gartner, Inc. (2016) *What Is Big Data?* Retrieved from http://www.gartner.com/it-glossary/big-data

Gubbi, J., Buyya, R., Marusic, S., & Palaniswamia, M. (2013). *Internet of Things: A Vision, Architectural Elements and Future directions in Future Generation Computer Systems*. Cornell University. Retrieved from https://arxiv.org/ftp/arxiv/papers/1207/1207.0203.pdf

Hitzler, P; Krotzsch, M; Rudolph, S. (2009). *Foundation of Semantic Web Technologies*. CRS Press Taylor & Francis Group, A Chapman & Hall Book.

Kune, R., Konugurthi, P. K., Agarwal, A., Rao Chillarige, R., & Buyya, R. (2011). *The Anatomy of Big Data Computing*. Cornell University. Retrieved from https://arxiv.org/pdf/1509.01331

Maedche, A. (2002). *Ontology Learning for the Semantic Web*. New York: Springer Science and Business Media. doi:10.1007/978-1-4615-0925-7

Staab, S., & Studer, R. (2009). *Handbook on Ontologies*. Berlin: International Handbooks on Information Systems, Springer Science and Business Media. doi:10.1007/978-3-540-92673-3

KEY TERMS AND DEFINITIONS

BitMap: Bitmap is 8-bit string which is used to compute the weight of the student by defining variable and low value of variable indicates fail in subject otherwise weight is high.

COBWEB: It well known content based image retrieval from WEB algorithm is used to create students' classifiers (Clusters) based students' assessment parameters such commuted weight of students.

Data Visualization: Data Visualization is a general term that describes significance of data by placing it in visual context and it can viewed by many disciplines which involves the creation and study of the visual representation of data.

Knowledge Discovery: The knowledge discovery is the process of finding or extracts the knowledge in data and emphasizes the "high level application of particular data mining methods or machine learning techniques.

Chapter 11

Knowledge–Based Decision Support System for Analyzing the Relevancies of Various Attributes Based on Their Characteristics

C. Madana Kumar Reddy
Annamacharya Institute of Technology and Sciences, India

ABSTRACT

Data mining extracts novel and useful knowledge from large repositories of data and has become an effective analysis and decision means in any organization. The resource of the World Wide Web is almost infinite. The growing importance of electronic media for storing and disseminating text documents has created an urgent need for tools and techniques that assist users in finding and extracting relevant and previously unknown information from massive collection of documents available in the web. Thus the development of techniques for mining unstructured, semi-structured, and fully structured textual data has become quite important in both academia and industry. Information management of well organized databases has been a focus of the Data mining research. When to specify too many attributes, system will slow down thus exclude irrelevant or weakly relevant attributes. The general idea behind attribute relevance analysis is to compute some measure that is used to quantify the relevance of an attribute with respect to a given class or concept.

INTRODUCTION

Plato said that "necessity is the mother of invention". Data mining has attracted the attention of many researchers due to the wide availability of huge amounts of data and the need for turning such data into useful information and knowledge. Data mining is applicable to any kind of data repository like relational databases, data warehouses, transactional databases, flat files, data streams, world wide web, object-

DOI: 10.4018/978-1-5225-1877-8.ch011

relational databases and specific application-oriented databases, such as spatial databases, time-series databases, text databases, and multimedia databases. The elimination of irrelevant or weakly relevant attributes with its characterization or comparison is referred to as analytical characterization or analytical comparison respectively. We are data rich, but information poor. Data mining extracts novel and useful knowledge from large repositories of data and has become an effective analysis and decision means in any organization. The resource of the world-wide web is almost infinite. The growing importance of electronic media for storing and disseminating text documents has created an urgent need for tools and techniques that assist users in finding and extracting relevant and previously unknown information from massive collection of documents available in the web (Agrawal, 1993). Thus the development of techniques for mining unstructured, semi-structured, and fully structured textual data has become quite important in both academia and industry. Information management of well-organized databases has been a focus of the Data mining research. Data mining is defined as the process of finding useful patterns from data, which is already existed in the database, like knowledge discovery in artificial intelligence. In our daily life we receive a lot of information every day and some of them are valuable, therefore we save it in data-base for future reference. But since the information's growth is very fast, may be one week or two this data-base is become huge in size, if we don't find a way to make it easy to handle and manage, we may have a lot of trouble when we reference it later. The knowledge discovery in databases is an iterative process. Once the discovered knowledge is presented to the user the evaluation measures can be enhanced, the mining can be further refined, new data can be selected or further transformed, or new data sources can be integrated in order to get different, more appropriate results. An attribute or dimension is considered as highly relevant with respect to a given class if it is likely that the values of the attribute or dimension are used to distinguish the class from others. Class characterization includes the analysis of attribute or dimension relevance is called analytical characterization. Include pictures also as the part of the relevance of the objects, because it will give the quick idea regarding the concept what you are expressing in your way related to the context. Plato said that "Picture is worth more than thousands of words". Thus include the pictures also as the part of the attribute relevance analysis of various attributes based on their characteristics for the analysis of the data. When to specify too many attributes, system will slow down thus exclude irrelevant or weakly relevant attributes. The general idea behind attribute relevance analysis is to compute some measure that is used to quantify the relevance of an attribute with respect to a given class or concept (David Hand, 2005). The measures in the data mining are scalability, interoperability flexibility. For mining class characteristics, there is only one class to be characterized; the contrasting class is taken to be the set of comparable data in the database. Users can set attribute generalization thresholds. In general generalize dimension place to the country level. Even without explicit user instruction, a default value can be set by the data mining system, which allows each dimension to be generalized to a level that contains very few i.e., two to eight distinct values. By calculating information gain we can remove the less informative attributes by retaining the more informative attributes for use in the concept description analysis. Analytical characterization should be performed if the mined concept descriptions involve many attributes. As the part of it first remove weakly relevant or irrelevant attributes before performing the generalization. Also compute the information gain for each attribute and the result is sorted in increasing order. Users may not be interested in having a single class. Class discrimination or comparison mines descriptions that distinguish a target class from its contrasting classes. Target & contrasting classes must share similar dimensions and attributes. This chapter presents various techniques and their effectiveness with respect to the attribute relevance.

ATTRIBUTE RELEVANCE ANALYSIS

An attribute or dimension is considered as highly relevant with respect to a given class if it is likely that the values of the attribute or dimension are used to distinguish the class from others. Class characterization includes the analysis of attribute or dimension relevance is called analytical characterization. For example, the attribute color cannot be used for distinguishing least expensive vehicles from expensive vehicles but the attributes model, make, capacity, and style are likely to be more relevant attributes. Similarly, date-of-birth is unlikely to be relevant to the salary of employees. For mining class characteristics, there is only one class to be characterized; the contrasting class is taken to be the set of comparable data in the database (Daskalki et al., 2003). For example to characterize graduate students, the contrasting class can be composed of the set of undergraduate students. Users can set attribute generalization thresholds. In general generalize dimension place to the country level. Even without explicit user instruction, a default value can be set by the data mining system, which allows each dimension to be generalized to a level that contains very few (typically two to eight) distinct values. An attribute or dimension is considered as highly relevant with respect to a given class if it is likely that the values of the attribute or dimension are used to distinguish the class from others. Class characterization includes the analysis of attribute or dimension relevance is called analytical characterization. Include pictures also as the part of the relevance of the objects, because it will give the quick idea regarding the concept what you are expressing in your way related to the context. Plato said that "Picture is worth more than thousands of words". Thus include the pictures also as the part of the attribute relevance analysis of various attributes based on their characteristics for the analysis of the data.

INFORMATION GAIN IN ATTRIBUTE RELEVANCE ANALYSIS

By calculating information gain we can remove the less informative attributes by retaining the more informative attributes for use in the concept description analysis. Consider S contains si samples of class Ci, for i=1, 2,..., m. An arbitrary sample belongs to class Ci with probability si/s; here, s is the total number of samples in set S. The expected information required to classify the sample is:

$$-\sum_{i=1}^{m}\frac{s_i}{s}\log_2\frac{s_i}{s} \tag{1}$$

$$I(s_1,s_2,\ldots s_m) =$$

Let Sj contain sij samples of class Ci. The expected information based on this partitioning by A is referred as the entropy of A. It is the weighted average:

$$E(A) = \sum_{j=1}^{v}\frac{s_{1j}+\ldots+s_{mj}}{s}I(s_{1j},\ldots,s_{mj}) \tag{2}$$

The information gain by this partitioning on A is:

Gain (A) = I $(s_1, s_2,..,s_m)$ - E(A) (3)

The attribute which have the highest information gain is considered to be the most discriminating attribute in the given set. By computing the information gain ranks the attributes. This ranking can be used for relevance analysis for selecting the attributes to be used in the concept description. It is performed as follows:

1. **Collecting Data:** For the target and contrasting class collect data by using queries
2. **Preliminary Relevance Analysis:** By using conservative Attribute Oriented Induction identify the set of dimensions and attributes for which the selected relevance measure is to be applied. It is referred as the candidate relation of the mining task.
3. **Remove Weakly Relevant and Irrelevant Attributes by using the Relevance Analysis Measure:** These attributes are ranked according to their computed relevance to the data mining task.
4. **Generate the Concept Description:** Perform Attribute Oriented Induction using a less conservative set of attributes generalization thresholds.

Do not specify unnecessary are least relevant i.e., which are not of considerable relevance to your work, because when to specify too many attributes, system will slow down thus exclude irrelevant or weakly relevant attributes. The general idea behind attribute relevance analysis is to compute some measure that is used to quantify the relevance of an attribute with respect to a given class or concept. The measures in the data mining are scalability, interoperability flexibility. For mining class characteristics, there is only one class to be characterized; the contrasting class is taken to be the set of comparable data in the database.

ANALYTICAL CHARACTERIZATION

Analytical characterization should be performed if the mined concept descriptions involve many attributes (Adriaana & Zantinge, 2002). As the part of it first remove weakly relevant or irrelevant attributes before performing the generalization. For example, mining the general characteristics of graduate students. Given attributes are student name, fathers name, address, sex, branch, place of birth, date of birth, phone no, and grade.

Step 1: First collect the target class data, which includes the group of graduate students, and then collect the data for the contrasting class for performing relevance analysis.

Step 2: Apply attribute removal and generalization by using Attribute Oriented Induction with certain thresholds. The attributes student name, father's name and phone no are removed because they contain more number of distinct values. The attributes branch, address (to country) and grade can be generalized to higher abstraction levels. Resultant relations are shown in Table 1 and Table 2.

Step 3: 120 samples are belongs to class graduates. 130 samples are belonging to undergraduates. Information gain of each attribute using Equation 1 is:

$$I(s1,s2) = I(120,130) \ = -\frac{120}{250}\log_2\frac{120}{250} - \frac{130}{250}\log_2\frac{130}{250} = 0.9988 \tag{4}$$

Here, 250(120+130) is the total number of records in the target and contrasting classes. To compute the entropy of each attribute, try the branch expected information for graduate and undergraduate students:

For branch="science"

$s_n = 84\ (16+22+25+21)$

$s_2 1 = 42(18+24)$

$I\ (s11, s_2 1) = 0.9183 \tag{5}$

For branch="Mathematics"

$s12 = 36(18+18)$

$s_{22} = 46(22+24)$

$I\ (s12, s_{22}) = 0.9892 \tag{6}$

Table 1. Target class candidate relation contains graduate students

Sex	Branch	Country	Age group	Grade	Count
M	Science	Australia	21.25	Very-good	16
F	Science	India	26...30	Excellent	22
M	Mathematics	India	26...30	Excellent	18
F	Science	India	26...30	Excellent	25
M	Science	Australia	21...25	Excellent	21
F	Mathematics	Australia	21.25	Excellent	18

Table 2. Contrasting class candidate relation contains under graduate students

Sex	Branch	Country	Age_group	Grade	Count
M	Science	India	<=20	Very-good	18
F	Social	Australia	<=20	Fair	20
M	Social	Australia	<=20	Fair	22
F	Science	Australia	21...25	Fair	24
M	Mathematics	India	21...25	Very-good	22
F	Mathematics	Australia	<=20	Excellent	24

For branch="Social"

s13= 0

s_{23}= 42(20+22)

I(s13,s_{23})= 0   (7)

Calculate the expected information needed to classify a given sample using Equation 2, if the samples are partitioned according to branch is:

$$E \text{ (branch)} = \frac{126}{250} I(s_{11}, s_{21}) + \frac{82}{250} I(s_{12}, s_{22)} + \frac{42}{250} I(s_{13}, s_{23}) = 0.7873$$ (8)

Calculate the information gain from Equation 3:

Gain(branch)= I(s1,s2)-E(branch)=0.2115   (9)

Similarly, compute the information gain for each attribute and the result is sorted in increasing order:

0.0003 for sex, 0.0407 for country, 0.2115 for branch, 0.4490 for grade and 0.5971 for age group

If we use an attribute relevance threshold of 0.1 for identifying weakly relevant attributes. The information gain of the attributes sex & country are below the threshold. They are removed (because they are weakly relevant). The contrasting class is also removed, resulting is the initial target class working relation.

Step 4: Attribute Oriented Induction is applied.

MINING CLASS COMPARISONS: METHODS AND IMPLEMENTATIONS

Users may not be interested in having a single class. Class discrimination or comparison mines descriptions that distinguish a target class from its contrasting classes (Anahory & Murray, 2006). Target and contrasting classes must share similar dimensions and attributes. For example, profits in the last 3 years are comparable classes. Few classes like person, address and item are not comparable.

Procedure (Algorithm)

```
1. Collect data by using a query into a target class
2. Only highly relevant dimensions are included for subsequent analysis
3. Synchronous    (same    level)    generalization   is performed on the
target & contrasting classes.
4. Present the derived results in the form of tables, graphs  and/or rules.
The   user   can   adjust   the   comparison description by applying drill-down,
```

roll-up, and other OLAP (online analytical processing) operations on the target and contrasting classes

Example: Compare the general properties between the graduate students and the undergraduate students at J university, given attributes are student name, father's name, address, sex, branch, place of birth, date of birth, phone no and grade.

Data mining task can be expressed in DMQL as follows:

```
                    use J university DB
mine comparison "graduate undergraduate stu"
in relevance to student name, father's name, address, sex, branch, place of
birth, date of birth, phone no and grade
for "graduate-students"
where status in "graduate"
versus "undergraduate_students"
where status in "undergraduate"
analyze count%
from student
```

Table 3. Initial target class working relation (graduate student)

Student name	Father's name	Address	Sex	Branch	Date_ of birth	Date of birth	Phone no	Grade
Madhu	Kantha Reddy	Kondapeta	M	Science	Orvakal,India	8-12-76	9441105151	3.67
Raja	RavindraReddy	Yerragudi	M	Social	Gorantla,India	28-7-75	9444848333	3.70
Laxmi	LakshmiReddy	Ptc,burna	F	Physics	Seattle,wa,usa	25-8-70	9941764864	3.83
—	—	—	-	—	—	—	—	—

Table 4. Initial contrasting class working relation (undergraduate students)

Student name	Father's name	Address	Sex	Branch	Place of birth	Date of birth	Phone no	Grade
Reddy	RamiReddy	Vemana	M	Chemistry	Galg,cbi,India	10-1-78	9949075150	2.96
Nihari	RavindraRedy	Nannur	F	Biology	Slg,bc,Canada	30-3-76	9123456789	3.52
—	—	—	-	—	—	—	—	—

Step 1: Query is transformed into 2 relational queries (target and contrasting).

Step 2: Irrelevant dimensions student name, father's name, address, sex, place of birth, phone number are removed.

Step 3: Grade categorization 3.5-3.75 is good, 3.76-4.00 is very good, >4.00 is excellent

Step 4: Contrasting measure (like count%) compares the target and contrasting classes. See Table 5 and Table 6.

Example: 5.02% of graduate students with branch as science are between 26 and 30 years and good grade while only 2.32% of undergraduates have these same characteristics.

Presentation of Class Comparison Descriptions

Various forms for presentation including generalized relations, cross tabs, bar charts, pie charts, curves and rules (Nielsen, 2006). Discriminative features of the target and contrasting classes of a comparison description can be described quantitatively by a quantitative discrimination rule. Let qa be a generalized tuple covers some tuples of Cj. Cj be the target class. It is possible that qa also covers some tuples of contrasting class. The d-weight (description weight) for qa is the ratio of the number of tuples from the initial target class covered by qa to the total number of tuples in both the initial target class & contrasting class. The d-weight of q_a for the class Cj is defined as follows:

$$d\text{-weight} = count(q_a \in C_j) / \sum_{i=1}^{m} count(q_a \in C_i) \qquad (10)$$

where m is the total number of target & contrasting classes, Cj is in {C1..., Cm}, count(qaᶜ Ci) is the number of tuples of class Ci covered by qa range for the d-weight is [0.0,1.0] (i.e., 0.0 indicates0% and 1.0 indicates 100%). A high d-weight in the target class indicates that the concept represented by the generalized tuple and is basically derived from the target class (Oriezy et al., 1999). A low d-weight implies that the concept is basically derived from the contrasting classes. A threshold value is used to control the display of interesting tuples based on the d-weight.

Table 5. Basic generalized relation for the target class (graduate student)

Branch	Age group	Grade	Count%
Science	21...25	Good	5.53%
Science	26...30	Good	5.02%
Science	Over 30	Very good	5.86%
...	...	...	...
Social	Over 30	Excellent	4.68%

Table 6. Basic generalized relation for the contrasting class (undergraduate)

Branch	Age group	Grade	Count%
Science	16...20	Fair	5.53
Science	16...20	Good	4.53
Science	26...30	Good	2.32
Social	Over 30	Excellent	0.68

CONCLUSION

In this chapter, I have presented the information after a detailed examination of the things in various attributes relating to a particular problem context. The main aim of this chapter is to know which attributes are irrelevant or weakly relevant for excluding from the specification because when to specify too many attributes the former problem is that the system will slow down during the query processing. Other techniques are also there for attribute removal, such as discretization and sampling. These algorithms have their own advantages and disadvantages. Accuracy is the most important measure of efficiency for these algorithms. Over the past few years a number of research areas have been addressing various aspects of processing textual information. The advances made in these research areas are essential for approaching the problem of text mining.

REFERENCES

Adriaana, P., & Zantinge, D. (2002). *Data Mining*. Pearson Education Asia.

Agrawal, R., Imielinski, T., & Swami, A. N. (1993). Mining association rules between sets of items in large databases. In P. Buneman (Ed.), *Proceedings of the 1993 ACM-SIGMOD International Conference on Management of Data* (pp. 207–216). doi:10.1145/170035.170072

Daskalaki, S., Kopanas, I., Goudara, M., & Avouris, N. (2003). Data mining for decision support on customer insolvency in telecommunications business. *European Journal of Operational Research*, *2003*(2), 239–255. doi:10.1016/S0377-2217(02)00532-5

Han & Kamber. (n.d.). *Data Mining: Concepts and Techniques*. Morgan Kaufmann.

Han, J., Kamber, M., & Pei, J. (2011). *Data Mining: Concepts and Techniques*. New Delhi: Morgan Kaufmann.

Madana Kumar Reddy, C. (2009). Operating Systems Made easy. New Delhi: University Science Press.

Madana Kumar Reddy, C. (2016). Reliability and Scalability of Service Oriented Architecture in web services: Signature verification. IGI Global.

Nielsen, J. (1993). *Usability engineering*. London: Academic Press.

Nielsen, J. (2006). *Quantitative studies: how many users to test?*. Retrieved from http://www.useit.com

Oriezy, P., Gorlick, M. M., Taylor, R. N., Heimbigner, D., Johnson, G., Medvidovic, N., & Wolf, A. L. et al. (1999). An Architecture-Based Approach to Self-Adaptive Software. *IEEE Intelligent Systems*, *14*(3).

Pujari, R. K. (n.d.). Data mining Techniques. *Universities Press*.

Rubin, J. (1994). *Handbook of usability testing: How to plan, design, and conduct effective tests*. Wiley.

Sam Anahory, S., & Dennis Murray, D. (2006). Data Warehousing in the real World A practice; Guide for Building Decision Support Systems. Pearson Education.

Sreedhar, G. (2016). *Design solutions for improving website quality and effectiveness*. IGI Global.

KEY TERMS AND DEFINITIONS

Analytical Characterization: Classify the data based on the various characteristics of the data by doing the thorough analysis is called as analytical characterization.

Attribute Relevance: Attribute relevance is nothing but the relevance of the particular attribute in terms of various characteristics related to the context of the problem.

Class Comparison: Comparing the data qualities among the different classes.

Data Mining: Extracting the required data items from the large repository of the data ware house.

Decision: Selecting the best solution from the acquired knowledge in connection with the context of the problem.

Information Gain: Fetching the important information based on attribute relevance, comparison, etc.

Knowledge: Here knowledge in the senesce knowing the context and importance of the data based on various techniques.

Chapter 12
Website Topology Modification with Hotlinks Using Mined Webusage Knowledge

Thendral Puyalnithi
VIT University, India

Madhu Viswanatham V
VIT University, India

ABSTRACT

The hotlinks are the special links introduced in the website to reduce the time to access certain webpages in a webpage that is present in the deeper levels of the topology. Hotlinks selection mechanism plays a vital role in quick access of webpages. The problem is to decide which webpage should be having hotlinks and where the hotlinks should be placed in the website tree topology. We have proposed a methodology which starts by finding the frequent webpage access pattern of visitors of the website. The frequent pattern is found using Associative mining, Apriori algorithm or Frequent Pattern Tree algorithm. Then the frequent patterns are passed through page ranking mechanism. We find the pattern which is having the highest priority. Then the hotlinks are created for the members (webpages hyperlinks) of the pattern. Thus, the work is about assigning hotlinks for a set of pages which are frequently visited. Thus, by updating the topology by introducing hotlinks we can reduce the time to access the web pages.

INTRODUCTION

Website

A website is a collection of related web pages, including multimedia content, typically identified with a common domain name, and published on at least one web server. A web site may be accessible via a public Internet Protocol (IP) network, such as the Internet, or a private local area network (LAN), by referencing a uniform resource locator (URL) that identifies the site. All publicly accessible websites collectively constitute the World Wide Web, while private websites are typically a part of an intranet.

DOI: 10.4018/978-1-5225-1877-8.ch012

Web pages, which are the building blocks of websites, are documents, typically composed in plain text interspersed with formatting instructions of Hypertext Markup Language (HTML, XHTML). They may incorporate elements from other websites with suitable mark-up anchors. Web pages are accessed and transported with the Hypertext Transfer Protocol (HTTP), which may optionally employ encryption (HTTP Secure, HTTPS) to provide security and privacy for the user. The user's application, often a web browser, renders the page content according to its HTML mark-up instructions onto a display terminal. Hyperlinking between web pages conveys to the reader the site structure and guides the navigation of the site, which often starts with a home page containing a directory of the site web content. Some websites require user registration or subscription to access content. Examples of subscription websites include many business sites, parts of news websites, academic journal websites, gaming websites, file-sharing websites, message boards, web-based email, social networking websites, websites providing real-time stock market data, as well as sites providing various other services. There are three categories in web mining-web structure mining, web content mining, web usage mining.

Web Structure Mining

This is the process of analysing the nodes and connection structure of a website through the use of graph theory. There are two things that can be obtained from this: the structure of a website in terms of how it is connected to other sites and the document structure of the website itself, as to how each page is connected. Web structure mining is the process of using graph theory to analyse the node and connection structure of a web site. According to the type of web structural data, web structure mining can be divided into two kinds:

Extracting patterns from hyperlinks in the web: a hyperlink is a structural component that connects the web page to a different location. Mining the document structure: analysis of the tree-like structure of page structures to describe HTML or XML tag usage. PageRank algorithm is used by Google to rank search results. The name of this algorithm is given by Google-founder Larry Page. The rank of a page is decided by the number of links pointing to the target node.

Web Usage Mining

This is the process of extracting patterns and information from server logs to gain insight on user activity including where the users are from, how many clicked what item on the site and the types of activities being done on the site.

Challenges in Web Mining are:

1. **The Web is Too Huge:** The size of the web is very huge and rapidly increasing. This seems that the web is too huge for data warehousing and data mining.
2. **Complexity of Web Pages:** The web pages do not have unifying structure. They are very complex as compared to traditional text document. There are huge amount of documents in digital library of web. These libraries are not arranged according to any particular sorted order.
3. **Web is Dynamic Information Source:** The information on the web is rapidly updated. The data such as news, stock markets, weather, sports, shopping, etc., are regularly updated.

4. **Diversity of User Communities:** The user community on the web is rapidly expanding. These users have different backgrounds, interests, and usage purposes. There are more than 100 million workstations that are connected to the Internet and still rapidly increasing.
5. **Relevancy of Information:** It is considered that a particular person is generally interested in only small portion of the web, while the rest of the portion of the web contains the information that is not relevant to the user and may swamp desired results.

Methodologies for Web Usage Mining

As in the Figure 1, the models we create will be used for finding a meaningful pattern from weblog data. The models can be as follows:

1. **Classifier:** It predicts the class of objects whose class label is unknown. Its objective is to find a derived model that describes and distinguishes data classes or concepts. The Derived Model is based on the analysis set of training data i.e. the data object whose class label is well known.
2. **Predictor:** It is used to predict missing or unavailable numerical data values rather than class labels. Prediction usually refers to finding a continuous value. Regression Analysis is generally used for prediction. Prediction can also be used for identification of distribution trends based on available data.

Figure 1. Weblog pre-process and data mining

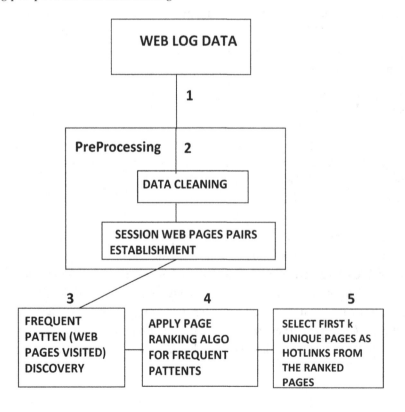

3. **Outlier Detector:** Outliers may be defined as the data objects that do not comply with the general behaviour or model of the data available.
4. **Evolution Analyser:** Evolution analysis refers to the description and model regularities or trends for objects whose behaviour changes over time.

The association among the webpages can be got from the following methods. Using the results, the hyperlinks will be moved up in the ladder in the topology tree. Thus the links that are moved up are said to be hotlinks.

BACKGROUND

Consider a website containing a collection of webpages with data such as in Yahoo or the Open Directory project. Each page is associated with a weight representing the frequency with which that page is accessed by users. In the tree hierarchy representation, accessing each page requires the user to travel along the path leading to it from the root. By enhancing the index tree with additional edges (hotlinks) one may reduce the access cost of the system. In other words, the hotlinks reduce the expected number of steps needed to reach a leaf page from the tree root, assuming that the user knows which hotlinks to take. According to O Gerstel (2007), the hotlink enhancement problem involves finding a set of hotlinks minimizing this cost. In paper Kosala et al. (2000) has done extensive survey on application of Artificial Intelligence methodologies for performing web mining. They have studied the various works on Web content mining, Web Structure mining and Web usage mining in relation to Artificial Intelligence methodologies. Their main survey is around the Text mining and they have listed the research work in the area where from the bag of words of web, they mine the key words, and they classify the web based on the key works mined. They have found out that various algorithms like Naïve bayes, Decision Trees, Support Vector machine, Hidden Markov models, Association rules, Self-Organizing maps, Statistical Analysis, Maximum entropy, Boosted Decision Trees, Neural Networks, Logistic Regression, k-Nearest Neighbor are used for web mining. The authors Hou et al. (2003) have done their work in finding the relevancy between web pages. They have used citation, co citation, latent linkage information algorithm for finding the relevancy. They have done case study too. This work is relevant to our paper in the sense that we are finding the related pages with the users' access pattern and they are finding this with citation. They are performing the content mining to find the relevant pages and we are planning to do web usage mining to find the relevant pages. Web Mining is performed on web personalization using the work of the authors Erinaki et al. (2003). They are performing user based web usage mining and they are categorizing the visitors in certain domain and each category will be having their own personalized web topology. The authors J Srivastava et al. (2000) have done their work Web usage mining. They have performed Pre-processing of web logs and they have applied clustering and classification methods to arrive at a pattern and they have analyzed the pattern. They have used Data warehouse for storing the enormous web data and pre-processing before applying data mining algorithms over it. The authors Kotsiantis et al. (2006) have performed the work of association of web pages using association rule mining. They have used Apriori, Redundant Association rules and negative association rules to associate the web pages based on the web usage log data. The authors V.V.R. Maheswara Rao et al. (2010) have proposed a framework for doing pre-processing web log data. They have doing clearing and they are imputing the data to such an extent that it will be used for efficient mining. The authors Maja Dimitrijevic et al. (2010) have done their work on pruning the association rules that are obtained from web usage data. They are of opinion based on their data analysis that the most of association rules are trivial and they have to be pruned. They have applied basic pruning methods for pruning the association rules. The authors Cyzyowicz et al. (2003) have proposed a hotlink optimizer algorithm for finding optimal number of hotlinks that can be assigned to a website. The authors Pesso A. et al. (2004) have come out with efficient algorithm for inserting hotlinks in a website whose tree architecture is having n number of nodes and m number of leaves. They have proposed an approximate algorithm that gives the complexity of O(n log m).

PROPOSED METHOD

Website Topology modification at the website maintenance end is done using the results of web usage mining. Web usage data is used to get the pattern and based on the pattern arrived, the topology of the website will be updated to give faster access to the users and to reduce the data flow in the network. The proposed algorithm is as follows:

Step 1: Extract and Pre-process of web log of various user's access for A single Website.
Step 2: Extract the list of webpages visited in a webpage by every user from the weblogs. Each record sequence is considered as a transaction.
Step 3: The records are analysed for frequent pattern using algorithms like Apriori or FP growth Tree.
Step 4: Every page in the frequent pattern found is ranked using Page Ranking algorithm.

Fitness value is found out for every frequent pattern list by summing up all the page ranks of its member pages:

$$f(\text{Pattern}) = \sum_{k=0}^{n} P\left(k\right)$$

where n is number of webpages in every pattern sequence and P(k) is the page rank of kth page.
Step 5: The frequent patterns are sorted in ascending based on the fitness value parameter.
Step 6: In every frequent pattern the web page sequence is arranged in ascending as per Page ranking values.
Step 7: First 'k' unique webpages are selected from the sorted order(where k is number of hotlinks for the website)
Step 8: The older hotlinks will be replaced by the new set of hotlinks.

Pre-Processing and Clustering of Web Log Data

The pre-processing steps are considered as the initial process of the proposed approach. Secondly the Pre-processed web logs are grouped to discover the pattern before applying the association rule mining to find the interesting measure of the web site visitors and users. Most of the researchers done their research on web usage mining as pre-processing is the initial step of their work. Later clustering techniques are applied on the pre-processed web logs to make a group for better processing of the web logs. The familiar clustering algorithms like k-means, modified k-means and Harmony k-means algorithms are usually used. The new algorithm effectively pre-processes the web logs which fit for the biological based algorithm called bird flocking algorithm. Since the web logs are growing in a rapid manner every day. So the web logs are dynamic nature. The bird flocking algorithm group the web logs in an efficient manner. The web logs from various sources like server logs, browsers logs, etc. as input to the Bird Flocking Algorithm. The aim of the proposed approach is to extract the user's interest to visit particular web pages. The web log contains the data of websites visited user, which includes URL, web session duration, date, user activity duration etc. The web logs are updates each time a user starts a new session. Initially the log file contains each and every detail regarding the user, the IP address, website name, time stamp and other details. But these details are generated based on each and every second, so to make the log files light which we obtained from different sources, some pre-processing steps are first taken into action. Extraction process of the session timing and the frequency is calculated by taking the time difference and the total number of clicks on a particular web site given in a log file. To label the Session, we have calculated the time duration between two nearby website visited by the particular user. It is calculated each and every time when a user switches from one website to another and the amount of time he spends in each website. The session is calculated as the time taken to traverse from on site to another site by the user, and the proposed approach take the whole sum of the duration of particular web site.

Frequent Pattern Analysis: Using FP Growth Tree

FP tree is a compact data structure that stores important, crucial and quantitative information about frequent patterns. FP growth algorithm generates frequent item sets from FP-Tree by traversing in bottom up fashion. It allows frequent item set discovery without candidate item set generation. It is a two-step approach algorithm:

1. **Input:** A database DB, represented by FP-tree constructed and a minimum support threshold
2. **Output:** The complete set of frequent patterns

Method

It consists of one root labelled as "root", a set of item prefix sub-trees as the children of the root, and a frequent-item header table.Each node in the item prefix sub-tree consists of three fields: item -name, count, and node-link, where item -name registers which item this node represents, count registers the number of transactions represented by the portion of the path reaching this node, and node -link links to the next node in the FP-tree carrying the same item -name, or null if there is none.

Each entry in the frequent-item header table consists of two fields:

1. Item -name
2. Head of node-link, which points to the first node in the FP-tree carrying the item -name

Second, an FP -tree-based pattern -fragment growth mining method is developed, which starts from a frequent length-1 pattern (as an initial suffix pattern), examines only its conditional -pattern base (a "sub-database" which consists of the set of frequent items co-occurring with the suffix pattern), constructs its (conditional) FP -tree, and performs mining recursively with such a tree. The pattern growth is achieved via concatenation of the suffix pattern with the new ones generated from a conditional FP -tree. Since the frequent item set in any transaction is always encoded in the corresponding path of the frequent-pattern trees, pattern growth ensures the completeness of the result.

Page Ranking using Page Ranking Algorithm

After the frequent pattern is found out the association between web pages are found out using confidence values. The associated web pages are stored in a repository which will be used for generating page raking for the pages.

The original PageRank algorithm was described by Lawrence Page and Sergey Brin in several publications. It is given by:

PR(A) = (1-d) + d (PR(T1)/C(T1) +... + PR(Tn)/C(Tn))

where

PR(A) is the PageRank of Page A
PR(Ti) is the Page Rank of pages Ti which link to Page A
C(Ti) is the number of outbound links on page Ti
d is a damping factor which can be set between 0 and 1

So, first of all, we see that PageRank does not rank web sites as a whole, but is determined for each page individually. Further, the PageRank of page A is recursively defined by the page ranks of those pages which link to page A. The PageRank of pages Ti which link to page A does not influence the PageRank of page A uniformly. Within the PageRank algorithm, the PageRank of a page T is always weighted by the number of outbound links C(T) on page T. This means that the more outbound links a page T has, the less will page A benefit from a link to it on page T. The weighted PageRank of pages Ti is then added up. The outcome of this is that an additional inbound link for page A will always increase page A's PageRank. Finally, the sum of the weighted Page ranks of all pages Ti is multiplied with a damping factor d which can be set between 0 and 1. Thereby, the extend of PageRank benefit for a page by another page linking to it is reduced. The characteristics of PageRank shall be illustrated by a small example. We regard a small web consisting of three pages A, B and C, whereby page A links to the pages B and C, page B links to page C and page C links to page A. According to Page and Brin, the damping factor d is usually set to 0.85, but to keep the calculation simple we set it to 0.5. The exact value of the damping factor d admittedly has effects on PageRank, but it does not influence the fundamental principles of PageRank. So, we get the following equations for the PageRank calculation:

PR(A) = 0.5 + 0.5 PR(C)

PR(B) = 0.5 + 0.5 (PR(A) / 2)

PR(C) = 0.5 + 0.5 (PR(A) / 2 + PR(B))

These equations can easily be solved. We get the following PageRank values for the single pages:

PR(A) = 14/13 = 1.07692308

PR(B) = 10/13 = 0.76923077

PR(C) = 15/13 = 1.15384615

It is obvious that the sum of all pages' PageRanks is 3 and thus equals the total number of web pages. As shown above this is not a specific result for our simple example. For our simple three-page example it is easy to solve the according equation system to determine PageRank values. In practice, the web consists of billions of documents and it is not possible to find a solution by inspection.

The Iterative Computation of PageRank

Because of the size of the actual web, the Google search engine uses an approximate, iterative computation of PageRank values. This means that each page is assigned an initial starting value and the PageRanks of all pages are then calculated in several computation circles based on the equations determined by the PageRank algorithm. The iterative calculation shall again be illustrated by our three-page example, whereby each page is assigned a starting PageRank value of 1. See Table 1 below.

We see that we get a good approximation of the real PageRank values after only a few iterations. According to publications of Lawrence Page and Sergey Brin, about 100 iterations are necessary to get a good approximation of the PageRank values of the whole web. Also, by means of the iterative calculation, the sum of all pages' PageRanks still converges to the total number of web pages. So the average PageRank of a web page is 1. The minimum PageRank of a page is given by (1-d). Therefore, there is a maximum PageRank for a page which is given by dN+(1-d), where N is total number of web pages. This maximum can theoretically occur, if all web pages solely link to one page, and this page also solely links to itself.

Table 1. Iterative calculation for page rank

Iteration	PR(A)	PR(B)	PR(C)
0	1	1	1
1	1	0.75	1.125
2	1.0625	0.765625	1.1484375
3	1.07421875	0.76855469	1.15283203
4	1.07641602	0.76910400	1.15365601
5	1.07682800	0.76920700	1.15381050
6	1.07690525	0.76922631	1.15383947
7	1.07691973	0.76922993	1.15384490
8	1.07692245	0.76923061	1.15384592
9	1.07692296	0.76923074	1.15384611
10	1.07692305	0.76923076	1.15384615
11	1.07692307	0.76923077	1.15384615
12	1.07692308	0.76923077	1.15384615

Finding Fitness Value for Frequent Pattern

Arrange the web pages in the frequent pattern ascending of its Page ranking. Then the summation of the page ranks gives the fitness value. See Table 2. The fitness value of a pattern is given by:

$$f(Pattern) = \sum_{k=0}^{n} P(k)$$

Where 'n' is the number of webpages in the Pattern.

P(k) is the Page rank found out for the kth webpage
Let us assume that P(A) = 2, P(B) = 4, P(C) =1, P(D) = 6, P(E) = 10, P(M) =5, P(N) = 3, P(R) = 9, P(X) = 8

If page rank is small, it's having a higher priority. Then the patterns are sorted based on its fitness value in ascending order. See Table 3. The tie can be broken by considering the size of the pattern, if the size is large, it will be having lesser priority.

Let us assume that k = 6, where k is the maximum number of hotlinks allotted for a website.

So now we have to select first 6 unique elements from patterns in the Table 3 starting from the first row.

C,A,B,R,X,D. are selected if we follow the procedure. Then the old hotlinks will be replaced by the new set of new hotlinks.

CONCLUSION

Even though there are many methods available in modifying hotlinks or finding new hotlinks are available, the above proposed method uses finds a frequent sequence of web page access. The proposed algorithm also uses Page Ranking algorithm which is mainly used for ranking the websites. The page ranking algorithm usage gives the conventional approach to the computational intelligence approach. As an enhancement to this work we can have same sized frequent patterns before finding the fitness value. We can have the frequent patterns segregated according to the sizes and then each set can be sorted based on fitness value. Collective scope value can be found for each set and the collective scope value can be used for deciding which sized pattern should be put up in the hotlinks.

Table 2. Fitness value calculation of frequent patterns

Frequent Patterns (each sorted in page rank wise)	Fitness Value
C,A,B	7
A,BD,E	22
A,N,B,M,X	22
C,A,B,R	16
X,R	17

Table 3. Sorting the frequent patterns according to fitness value

Frequent Patterns (each sorted in page rank wise)	Fitness Value (SORTED)
C,A,B	7
C,A,B,R	16
X,R	17
A,BD,E	22
A,N,B,M,X	22

REFERENCES

Cyzyowicz, J., Kranakis, E., Krizanc, D., Pelc, A., & Vargas Martin, M. (2003). Enhancing hyperlink structure for improving web performance. *Journal of Web Engineering, 1*(2), 93–127.

Dimitrijevic, & Bosnjak. (2010). Discovering interesting association rules in the web log usage data. *Interdisciplinary Journal of Information, Knowledge, and Management, 5,* 191–207.

Eirinaki, M., & Vazirgiannis, M. (2003). Web mining for web personalization. *ACM Transactions on Internet Technology, 3*(1), 1–27. doi:10.1145/643477.643478

Gerstel, O., Kutten, S., Laber, E. S., Matichin, R., Peleg, D., Pessoa, A. A., & Souza, C. (2007). Reducing human interactions in Web directory searches. *ACM Transactions on Information Systems, 25*(4), 20, es. doi:10.1145/1281485.1281491

Hou, J., & Zhang, Y. (2003). Effectively finding relevant web pages from linkage information. *IEEE Transactions on Knowledge and Data Engineering, 15*(4), 940–951. doi:10.1109/TKDE.2003.1209010

Kosala & Blockeel. (2000). Web mining research: A survey. *Newsletter of the Special Interest Group (SIG) on Knowledge Discovery and Data Mining.* ACM.

Kotsiantis, S., & Kanellopoulos, D. (2006). Association Rules Mining: A Recent Overview. *International Transactions on Computer Science and Engineering, 32*(1), 71–82.

Pessoa, Laber, & Souza. (2004). Efficient algorithms for the hotlink assignment problem: The worst case search. *Proceedings of the International Symposium on Algorithms and Computation.*

Rao & ValliKumari. (2010). An Enhanced Pre-Processing Research Framework For Web Log Data Using A Learning Algorithm. *NeTCoM 2010, CSCP 01.* Retrieved September 10, 2016 from https://en.wikipedia.org/wiki/

Srivastava, J., Cooley, R., Deshpande, M., & Tan, P. N. (2000). Web usage mining: Discovery and applications of usage patterns from web data. *SIGKDD Explorations, 1*(2), 12–23. doi:10.1145/846183.846188

KEY TERMS AND DEFINITIONS

Algorithm: Sequential steps involved in a Process.

Apriori: Prior Knowledge.

Association: Links between entities.

Classifier: Trained System which predicts a whole value.

Cluster: Group of similar entities.

Data Mining: Finding interesting and useful pattern in the Data pool.

Frequent Pattern: The mined pattern which is occurring repeatedly more than certain threshold.

Hotlinks: Shortcut links that is present near the home pages of websites which has link to deeper webpages.

Hyperlink: Active Link present in a webpage that takes you to other webpages when clicked.

Internet Protocol(IP): Connectionless data transfer protocol between two systems.

Naïve Bayes: A Data mining algorithm. Probability based.

Neural Network: A Technique in soft computing which is developed with the inspiration from brain working mechanism.

Outlier: An entity which is different from the group of other entities which are similar.

Page Ranking: The websites are ranked according to their priority.

Pattern: Useful association between data elements.

Predictor: Trained system which finds values which are continuous in nature.

Support Vector Machine: A Data mining algorithm which is vector based.

Text-Mining: Getting interesting pattern from documents. The documents can be a hypertext document.

Web Logs: The list of details about the visits happened from various visitors for a Website.

Webpage: One of the pages in a website.

Web Mining: Extracting interesting and useful information from the Web Text, Web Topology, Web Usage Data.

Website Topology: This is the structure of a website. Usually it is tree structure with home page being the root of the tree. Every web page will be a node like structure, the hyperlinks acts like edges.

Section 4
Developing Social Media based Mining Systems

Chapter 13
Mining on Social Media

Ambati Venkata Krishna Prasad
KL University, India

Venkata Naresh Mandhala
KL University, India

ABSTRACT

Social media mining is the process of representing, analyzing, and extracting actionable patterns and trends from raw social media data. Social media is favored by many users since it is available to individuals without any limitations to share their opinions, educational learning experiences and concerns via their status. Twitter API, twitter4j, is processed for searching the tweets based on the geo location. Student's posts on social network offers us a stronger concern to take decisions concerning the particular education system's learning method of the system. Evaluating knowledge in social media is sort of a difficult method. Bayes classifier are enforced on deep-mined knowledge for analysis purpose to urge the deeper understanding of the information. It uses multi label classification technique as every label falls into completely different classes. Label based measures are mostly taken to research the results and comparing them with the prevailing sentiment analysis technique.

INTRODUCTION

Social media mining is the process of representing, analyzing, and extracting actionable patterns and trends from raw social media data. Social media is the "group of internet-based applications that build on the ideological and technological foundations of Web 2.0, and that allow the creation and exchange of user-generated content|". There are many categories of social media including, but not limited to, social networking (Face book or LinkedIn), micro blogging (Twitter), photo sharing (Flickr, Photo bucket, or Picasa), news aggregation (Google reader, Stumble Upon, or Feed burner), video sharing (YouTube, MetaCafe), livecasting (Ustream or Twitch.tv), virtual worlds (Kaneva), social gaming (World of War-craft), social search (Google, Bing, or Ask.com), and instant messaging (Google Talk, Skype, or Yahoo! messenger) proposed in Jiliang and Tang, (2014). Since social media is for everyone and it became such a massive part of their life. Since it is available all over the world, social media sites had become very much popular now a day's, such as twitter, face book, YouTube, LinkedIn etc. This provides a great platform for

DOI: 10.4018/978-1-5225-1877-8.ch013

students to express their views, emotions, opinions, joy, struggle and feelings. Everyday student's discuss and share their encounters in formal and informal way on different social media sites. Student's tweets or comments on particular posts provide large amount of implicit knowledge and a whole new perspective for the educational and institutional researchers, users and practitioners to understand the student's behavior outside the controlled classroom environment. This understandings are useful for taking the decision at institutional level in taking the consideration of student's point of view for their success. Even though social media data provides a lots of opportunities to understand student's behavior, but still there are some methodological difficulties in making sense of the social media data for educational purposes (Hu, Xia, Tang and & Huan 2013). There are number of methods used by educational and institutional researchers such as surveys, focus groups, and classroom activities to collect data related to the student's behavior. These methods are usually very time-consuming and not very frequent. Considering these drawbacks of existing system, a new system was proposed. In proposed system a qualitative analysis using classification algorithm instead of the sentiment analysis is performed because sentiment analysis considers the opinion of the user about a system and categorizes it into 3 different levels namely neutral, negative or positive mood but in the proposed system, we searched the information of the student's based on the keywords such as engineer, student, campus, class, professors and labs in the twitter data as per the geo location, keyword and search id (Vorvoreanu & Q. Clark, 2010). One of the hardest task is to search keywords in twitter because of the diversity of the languages and the Internet slang used are different. By exploring more advanced information retrieval methods there are two ways of extracting data. One among them is semantic based information retrieval in which it uses semantic information to understand the documents and queries. The other method is machine learning based method which is used to reorganize Web documents such as classification and clustering. In this paper we mainly discuss on the improvement of information retrieval based on machine learning. So that we use a multi label classification algorithm which is implemented to analyze the content as per the category and the results will be reported to a decision maker which helps the person to get the overview of student's problems and their experience in learning process, so that an institution can make a proper decision making policy to improve the performance of the students as they are the future of society.

EXISTING AND PROPOSED SYSTEMS

Existing System

There are various traditional methods existing to analyze students learning process in educational system, such as surveys, interviews and questionnaires. But the major problem with these methods is they are time consuming and can't be performed more efficiently with higher frequency since the analysis has are to be performed manually. Another important problem is the data which we collect in formal way may not be genuine as the student may not convey what they feel correctly then compared to informal medium like social media (M. Ito, H. Horst, M. Bittanti, C.C 2008). In existing projects sentiment analysis is another kind of approach followed by opinion mining in which it comes under 3 class classification technique, classifies the results as positive, negative and neutral. For better understanding the tweets in deeper way this sentiment analysis is not sufficient. Thus there is a necessitate for analysis of social media data qualitatively by integrating both the workflow and algorithmic approach.

Proposed System

The proposed system is totally different from the existing system in terms of analyzing techniques of data. In proposed system, it has to perform the qualitative analysis using classification algorithm instead of sentimental analysis. Sentiment analysis consider the outlook of the user about a system and categorizes them as neutral, negative or positive mood. In the proposed system, information is searched based on the keywords such as engineer, students, campus, lab, class and professors as per the keywords and search ids (Tang; Jiliang & Liu; Huan 2014). But searching keywords in twitter is one of the hardest things because of the diversity of the languages and the Internet slang used are different. A multi-label classification algorithm is used to implement and analyze data as per the categories and the results will be reported to decision maker which helps the one to get an overview of students' problem and their experiences in learning process, so that an institution can make an appropriate decision making policy to improve the concert of the students.

LITERATURE SURVEY

The first social media website was introduced by GeoCities in 1994. It enabled users to create their own homepages without having a sophisticated knowledge of HTML coding. The first social networking site, SixDegree.com, was introduced in 1997 (D. Davidov, O. Tsur, & A. Rappoport 2010). Since then, many other social media sites have been introduced, each providing service to millions of people. These individuals form a virtual world in which individuals (social atoms), entities (content, sites, etc.) and interactions (between individuals, between entities, between individuals and entities) coexist. Social norms and human behavior govern this virtual world. By understanding these social norms and models of human behavior and combining them with the observations and measurements of this virtual world, one can systematically analyze and mine social media. Social media mining is the process of representing, analyzing, and extracting meaningful patterns from data in social media, resulting from social interactions. It is an interdisciplinary field encompassing techniques from computer science, data mining, machine learning, social network analysis, network science, sociology, ethnography, statistics, optimization, and mathematics. Social media mining faces grand challenges such as the big data paradox, obtaining sufficient samples, the noise removal fallacy, and evaluation dilemma. Social media mining represents the virtual world of social media in a computable way, measures it, and designs models that can help us understand its interactions. In addition, social media mining provides necessary tools to mine this world for interesting patterns, analyze information diffusion, study influence and homophily, provide effective recommendations, and analyze novel social behavior in social media. There are many different techniques developed for extracting the datasets through social media like Radian6 tool and Foursquare API that help for extracting the information in which data is available within the.csv,.xls file (E. Pearson, 2009). Twitter offers a group of API's for retrieving the information about its users and their communication. The theoretical foundation for the value of informal knowledge on the web may be drawn from Goffman's theory of social performance. Once student's desires to post any content on social media sites, they sometimes post what they suppose and feel at that moment. In this sense, the information collected from on-line conversations could be more authentic and unfiltered than the responses to formal research conversations. These conversations act as an outlook for student's behavior. Several studies show that social media users purposefully manage their on-line identity to look better than in reality. Different studies show that there's an absence of awareness regarding management of on-line identity among the college students, which young people usually regard social media as their personal area to hold out with peers outside the sight of parents and lecturers (K.E. Arnold & M.D. Pistilli 2012). Student's on-line conversation reveal the aspects of their behaviors that don't seem to be simply seen in formal room settings. The popular classification algorithms include Naive Bayes, Decision Tree, Maximum Entropy, Boosting, Support Vector Machine (SVM), C4.5 etc. are used to classify the social media data. Sentiment analysis is another extremely popular 3 class classification on positive, negative, or neutral emotions/opinions. Sentiment analysis is very helpful for mining client opinions on product or firms through their reviews or on-line posts. It finds wide adoption in selling and client relationship management (CRM).

DATA MINING

Data Mining is that the analysis step of the knowledge Discovery in Databases method (KDD). Data mining/Data processing is that the process exploitation analysis techniques of computer machine-controlled to extracting the knowledge from information. It's the procedure method of discovering patterns in massive datasets. The main goal of Data Mining (DM) method is to extract information from datasets and then rework or convert it into a clear format or structure for future use (Kaplan, Andreas, M, Haenlein & Michael 2010). DM Methodology is a Cross Industry Standard Process for data processing that describes commonly used approaches that data mining experts used to tackle problems. This DM methodology takes totally different stages:

1. **Business Understanding:** The main goal of the 1st stage of DM methodology is to outline objectives and the reasons of Knowledge Discovery Databases (KDD) method.
2. **Data Understanding:** This is the second stage of DM methodology which includes with the aggregation and remodeling the information into a format which will be employed by the chosen data processing tools, data description, data exploration and verification of data quality
3. **Data Preparation:** This data preparation stage is critical to organize the information. This stage is conducted through the tasks of collecting the data, data cleansing, data construction, integration, data preparation stage and data description are going to be used in an Information modelling.
4. **Modelling:** Selection of techniques is initial step of modeling stage for building a data mining model. There are totally different techniques for various issues like classification, clustering, prediction etc. These techniques are depending on information quality, time, fact.
5. **Analysis of Results:** The DM Methodology refers to the analysis of results in the context of the extent to that the model meets the business objectives and also the results generated by wrong data mining strategies so as to pick out the model that may be applied. If the results aren't satisfactory then it's necessary to come back to the previous stage of the modelling.
6. **Implementation Strategy:** The last stage of the DM Methodology is implementation strategy of the results of information mining analysis so as to improve business and its completely supports the analysis results. The main purpose and goal is to form general procedures for creating a relevant model.

Mining Twitter Data

Researchers from different fields has analyzed Twitter content to generate specific knowledge for their respective subject's domain. For example, Gaffney analyze the tweets base on their hashtag #iranElection using histograms and frequencies of top keywords. Similar study has been conducted in other fields like healthcare, marketing, athletics etc. Methods used for analysis of these studies usually include qualitative content analysis, linguistic based analysis, network based analysis, and some simple methods such as word clouds and histograms (A. Go, R. Bhayani, & L. Huang 2009). In this paper we built a classification model on inductive content analysis. This model was then applied and validated on the brand new data sets. Therefore, we put emphasis on not only the insights gained from one data set, but also the requests of the classification algorithm to other data sets for detecting students' problem.

Educational Data Mining

Educational data mining are approaches emerging in present educational systems (Baker and K. Yacef. 2009). These approaches are used to analyze data generated in educational settings for understanding students and their learning environment in order to take proper decisions by institutions. The architectural design is given below in Figure 1.

Figure 1. Architectural design

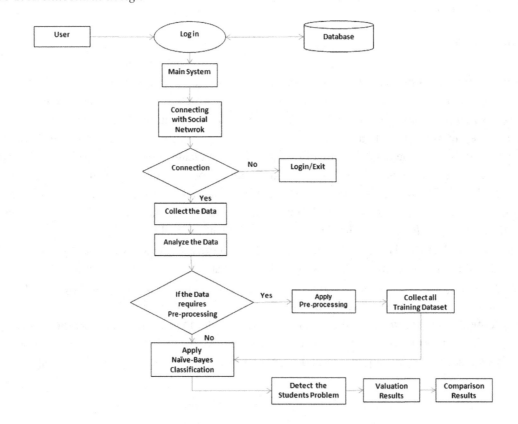

THEORETICAL ANALYSIS

Collection of Tweets

It is very challenging thing to collect data in social media, related to students' experiences since the irregularity and diversity of the languages they use. We search data using an institutional account on a commercial social media monitoring tool named WEKA. The Twitter API's are also configured to accomplish the task, which we later on use to obtain the second data set. The search process which we use is exploratory. We start our search based on different combinations of possible keywords such as engineering, exams, confusion, lack of sleep, disappointment, depression. We then expand and refine the keywords set and the combine logic iteratively. The search logic is very complicated ultimately, but the data sets we collected still contains about 35 percent noise and also the data set we collected is so small such that we have ruled out many other irrelevant tweets together with the spam and relevant tweets. As we have only limited number of relevant tweets collected, we found a Twitter hashtags such as #exams, #confusion, #lack of sleep, #disappointment, #depression occurring most frequently from the collected tweets. More than 1000 students data collected by twitter and college feedback system of 2015 batch engineering students. Students use the hashtags to post their experiences of being engineering student. This was the one of the most popular hashtag search detailed to engineering student's college life based on the data that have been retrieved using the tweets we have collected. Using WEKA tool we pre-process the tweets containing the hashtag. We also identified several other tweets with much less popular but relevant hashtags such as #lady_engineer, #engineering_majors, #switching_majors, #college_problems, and #nerdstatus. For the future work, these hashtags are also used to retrieve data which is relevant to college students' experience. See Figure 2.

After collecting the tweets database will check for three categories that is based on geo locations, keywords and search id's and are fetched under these defined categories in database that is training set. Categories like student, campus, engineering problems, college problems, sleep problems and staff will be fetched accordingly.

Figure 2. Collected tweets

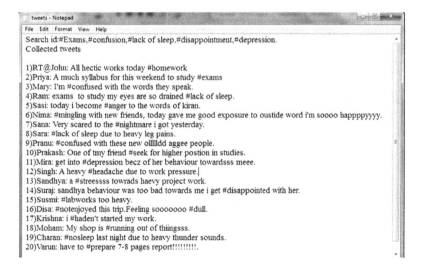

Categorization of Tweets

Since there were no pre-defined categories of the data we needed to explore what students were saying in the tweets. Therefore, first we conducted an inductive content analysis on the #engineering problems data set. Inductive content analysis is one the famous qualitative analysis method for manually analyzing text content. The tweets we used for conducting the inductive content analysis was to identify what are the major issues, worries, concerns that engineering students face in their study and their life. Initial we categories the tweets into some categories in which they include some of the keywords like: heavy_study_load, study_difficulties, imbalanced_life, future and carrier_worries, lack_of_ diversity, sleep_problems, stress, lack_of_motivation, identity_crisis, physical_health_problems, and others. These are developed in order to identify as many issues as possible. Next we write detailed descriptions of tweets along with related examples for each category and sent them to analyzers for review. Then, the analyzers discuss and subside the initial categories into 5 prominent themes, since they are the themes with relatively large number of tweets. The 5 prominent themes are: heavy_study_load, lack_of_social_engagement, negative_emotion, sleep_ problems and diversity_issues in which each of the theme reflects one issue or problem that engineering students face during their learning stages.Therefore we found that many of the tweets we collected belongs to more than one category. So one tweet is labeled with multiple categories. Since this opposed to single-label classification we use multi-label classification. The categories in which one tweet belongs to is called tweets labels or label sets. See Figure 3.

Prominent Themes

- **Heavy_Study_Load:** According to our analyses classes, homeworks, exams, and labs dominate the student's study life. Libraries and labs are most frequently visited places by the student. Such problems are catogersied into heavy_study_problems catogery.

Figure 3. Categorized tweets

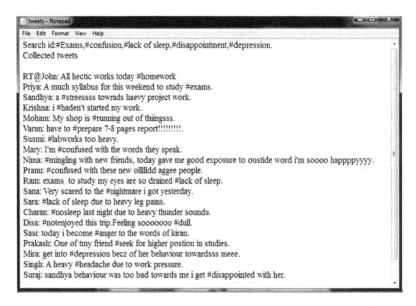

- **Lack_of_Social_Engagement:** Students who feel that they lose their freedom and the time of their enjoyment for the sake of the academic works. Such problems come under this category.
- **Negative_Emotions:** Expressing some feelings such as anger, sickness, depression and disappointment will come under category of negative_emotions.
- **Sleep_Problems:** Students frequently suffers from lack of sleep and nightmares due to heavy study load and stress. Such tweets come under this category.
- **Diversity_Issues:** Mingling with others country peoples is termed as the diversity issue. Without knowing the background all the negative issues will passed on which may cause the diversity issue. Such tweets come under this category. See Figure 4.

Pre-Processing of Data

The data which is in the form of tweets will be saved as a text file along with the database. For that, preprocessing technique should be done before using classifier. Different stages to be followed to filter the data is given below:

- All the hashtags should be removed i.e. # sign.
- Negative words having the negative emotions are identified and the words ending with "n't", none, cannot are replaced with "negtoken" since negative emotions are used in the further analysis purpose.
- Some of the special characters, punctuations and symbols are to be removed.
- The symbol RT which is used for re-tweet and all the hyperlinks should be removed.
- If any letter appears twice compress them.
  - A tweet before pre-processing:

    ```
    RT@john:Felling soooo lazzyyy due to more #Stress!!!.
    ```

  - After pre-processing:

    ```
    John feeling so lazy due to more stress.
    ```

Dataset for Collected Tweets

The data set is defined as collection of data. Mostly a data set contains the contents of a single database table or statistical data matrix, in which each column of the table represents a particular variable, and each row represents to data set member in the given question. The data set contains a list of values for each of the variables which are known as a datum. The term data set can also be used to refer to the data in a collection of closely connected tables, equivalent to a particular experiment. In the example we collect tweets, categorize them, pre-process and then form into data sets using a Weka tool.

A Weka is a tool which is a collection of machine learning algorithms for data mining techniques. The algorithms may be either applied directly for a dataset or can be called from your own Java code. It consists of tools for data pre-processing, data classification, data regression, data clustering, association rules for data, and data visualization. It is also well-matched in development of new machine learning scheme. See Figure 5.

Figure 4. Number of tweets in each category

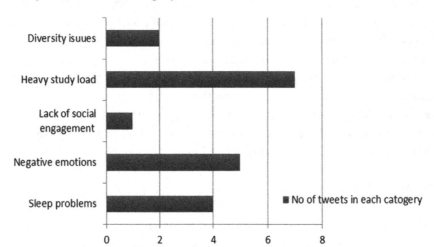

Figure 5. Dataset for collected tweets

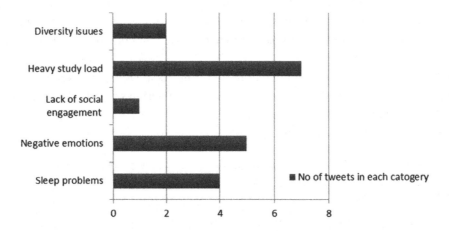

An R tool is an open source programming language and environment for statistical computing and graphics. R is an integrated suite of software facilities for data manipulation, calculation and graphical display. It includes i. an effective data handling and storage facility, ii. a suite of operators for calculations on arrays, in particular matrices, iii. a large, coherent, integrated collection of intermediate tools for data analysis, iv. graphical facilities for data analysis and display either on-screen or on hardcopy, and v. a well-developed, simple and effective programming language which includes conditionals, loops, user-defined recursive functions and input and output facilities. The steps involved to mine the twitter data are as follows:

1. Create an account @ https://apps.twitter.com/
2. Before creating an account add u r mobile number in the twitter account.
3. After filling the correct details choose "Keys and Access Tokens"
4. Copy consumer key API key and secret key

5. Then scroll down and generate access tokens.
6. Then copy access token and access token secret.
7. Consumer Key (API Key) - Iy55GlR8dDs2NqM9TLtHYcFFt
8. Consumer Secret (API Secret) - YXYX2cMd5lF6bSRJcBIjCSJB36nIw3nROIJKvyrfJ80UFe3yL5
9. Access Token - 396043722-0tNTPzyY3NMq6np1JAKSAfWTQE0Q1fNTcvEb83Cc
10. Access Token Secret - GGM5BgZmdwEoDOcv4sATpHjnLgPzcaq15JQQvWUq7rhqu
11. Install these packages: tm, twitteR, ROAuth, NLP

```
// code
setup_twitter_oauth("","","","") #use Consumer Key (API Key), Consumer Secret
(API Secret), Access Token, Access Token Secret
NBA=searchTwitter("@NBA",n=1000) # this means we are downloading the
head(NBA)
tail(NBA)
write.csv(twListToDF(NBA),file="NBA.csv") # this creates an CSV file with all
thetweets(1000)
```

Bayes Classifier

Influence of one event occurrence on the probability of another event is called as conditional probability. From the probability theory, Bayes theorem, allows us to calculate the conditional probability for given problem. Generally, in data mining Bayes theorem will be used to decide alternating suppositions. Bayes theorem for the conditional probability of **A** given B, is given below:

$$p\left(\frac{A}{B}\right) = p\left(\frac{B}{A}\right)\left(\frac{p(A)}{p(B)}\right)$$

where P (A) is prior probability P (A/B) is the posterior probability of A given B.

Naive Bayes Classifier

Suppose if there are more than one attribute then best classifier to be used is Naïve Bayes since all the attributes which are coming from different classes are independent of each other while they are mined from twitter. A simple Bayesian network is denoted as Naïve Bayesian classification making an assumption that all the attributes are independent to each other when they are represented in Bayesian network. The below Figure 6 represents Naïve bays classifier structure where the network contains only 1 parent and many child nodes in which the parent node represents which child node each object in the database should belong to.

Every attribute from $X_1 \ldots X_n$ are independent of each other and are given a class labels. The influence of an attribute has no effect over other attributes in a class since they are all independent. Initially the prior probability is determined by checking frequency of each label in the data set, in order to get the

Figure 6. Bayesian network for Naïve Bays Classifier

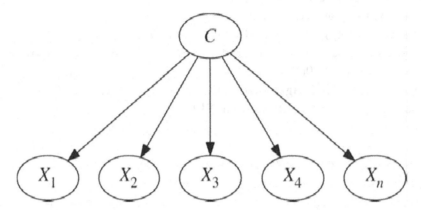

likelihood for label. The posterior probability is calculated for all classes, and the class with the highest probability will be the instance label. The Naive Bayes Classifier technique is based on the so-called Bayesian theorem and is particularly suited when the dimensionality of the inputs is high. Despite its simplicity, Naive Bayes can often outperform more sophisticated classification methods.

Suppose there are a total number of N words in the training document collection (in our case, each tweet is a document) W =w1, w2....wn, and a total number of L categories C =c1, c2:..., c_L. If a word w_n appears in a category c for $m_{wn}c$ times, and appear in categories other than c for m_{wnc} times, then based on the maximum likelihood estimation, the probability of this word in a specific category c is:

$$p\left(\frac{wn}{c}\right) = \frac{mwnc}{\sum_{n=1}^{N} mwnc)}$$

Suppose there are a total number of M documents in the training set, and C of them are in category c. Then the probability of category c is:

$$p(c) = \frac{C}{M}$$

or a document di in the testing set, there are K words $W_{di} = w_{i1}; w_{i2};...; w_{iK}$, and W_{di} is a subset of W. The purpose is to classify this document into category c or not c. We assume independence among each word in this document, and any word w_{ik} conditioned on c or c0 follows multinomial distribution. Therefore, according to Bayes Theorem, the probability that d_i belongs to category c is:

$$p\left(\frac{c}{cdi}\right) = \frac{p\left(\frac{d}{ci}\right)p(c)}{p(di)} \propto \prod_{k=1}^{K} p\left(\frac{wik}{c}\right)p(c)$$

If p(c/ d$_i$) is larger than the probability threshold T, then d$_i$ belongs to category c, otherwise, d$_i$ does belong to category c. Then repeat this procedure for each category. In our implementation, if for a certain document, there is no category with a positive probability larger than T, we assign the one category with the largest probability to this document. In addition, "Others" is an exclusive category. A tweet is only assigned to "others" when "others" is the only category with probability larger than T.

Navie Bayes Algorithm

```
1. Begin.
2. Collect the data.
3. Make a user profile.
4. Store all the data into dataset.
5. Analyze Algorithm.
6. Choose dataset.
7. Analyze the data.
        8. Data is preprocessed if required else continue.
9. Choose Naive Bayes Multi-label Classifier.
        10. Apply the formula
```

$$p\left(\frac{c}{cdi}\right) = \frac{p\left(\frac{d}{ci}\right)p(c)}{p(di)} \propto \prod_{k=1}^{K} p\left(\frac{wik}{c}\right)p(c)$$

```
11. Tokens are made.
12. Steaming is performed.
14. Go to step no 06.
15. A matching keyword is found.
16. Generate result.
```

Advantages and Disadvantages by Using Naïve Bays Classifier

Advantages:
- It is fast to train (single scan).
- Easy to classify.
- It is not sensitive to irrelevant features.
- It handles real data and discrete data.
- It handles streaming data well.
- It has a piecewise quadratic decision boundary.
- In almost all cases good result is obtained.

Disadvantage:
- It assumes independence of features.

Solution to this problem is by considering the relationship between attributes:

- Text based classification.
- Apply spam filtering.
- Hybrid recommender system:

Recommender system applies the machine learning and the data mining techniques for filtering unseen data and can be used to predict whether user would like to give resources. Online applications: Simple emotion models.

Evaluation Measures

Most commonly used procedures to assess the performance of classification models include accuracy, precision, recall, and the F1 score which is the harmonic mean between precision and recall. In case of multi-label classification, the circumstances are slightly more complicated, since each document get assigned with multiple labels. Between these labels, some are correct, and others are incorrect. Therefore, there are commonly 2 types of evaluation measures: example-based measures and label-based measures. Example-based measures are calculated for each document and then they are averaged on over all documents in the data set, but whereas label-based measure calculates measure of each label (category) and then over all labels are averaged.

Example based Evolution Measure

For a particular document d, let us suppose that true set of labels falls under Y, and the predicted set of labels falls under Z, then for this particular document, accuracy is the equal to labels having predicated numbers divided by the total number of labels i.e. union of Y and Z. Precision is equal to labels having predicated numbers divided by the total number of Z labels, while recall is equal to labels having predicated numbers divided by the number of true labels. Suppose there are a total of M documents from d_1; d_2;... ; d_M, the accuracy, precision, recall, and F1 calculated over the M documents are given in Figure 7.

Label based Evolution Measures

Among the categorized tweets, the system will show the tweets and the categorized segment. Then user will imitate based on the confusion matrix which allows visualizing the algorithm, whether they are true positive, true negative, false positive or false negative as shown below. The false positive rate (FP) is the proportion of negatives cases that were incorrectly classified as positive, the true negative rate (TN) is defined as the proportion of negatives cases that were classified correctly. The false negative rate (FN) is the proportion of positives cases that were incorrectly classified as negative. F1 represents the closeness relationship between different data sets labels when they are given to a single tweet in the harmonic manner. See Figure 8.

For a single category C accuracy is given as proposition total no of predictions, precision is given as proposition to positive predicted case which are correct and recall is given as proportion to positive cases that are correctly identified which are similar to true positive (TP).

Figure 7. The accuracy, precision, recall, and F1 calculated over the M documents

$$Accuracy\ a = \frac{1}{M} \sum_{i=1}^{M} \frac{Yi \cap Zi}{Yi \cup Zi}$$

$$Precision\ p = \frac{1}{M} \sum_{i=1}^{M} \frac{Yi \cap Zi}{Zi}$$

$$Recall\ r = \frac{1}{M} \sum_{i=1}^{M} \frac{Yi \cap Zi}{Yi}$$

$$F1 = \frac{1}{M} \sum_{i=1}^{M} \frac{2.pi.ri}{pi + ri}$$

Figure 8. Confusion matrix

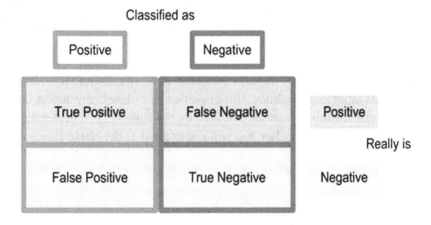

There are two commonly used measures for L categories $c_1; c_2;...\ ; c_L$ they are: micro-averaged F1 and macro-averaged F1 and they are given below in Figure 9:

In Micro-averaging all the documents are equally weighted before each per-document classification decision, while in macro-averaging it gives equal weight to each category. Therefore, micro-averaging F1 score is conquered by categories that have larger number of documents, while macro-averaged F1 score is closer to algorithm effectiveness on smaller categories. Thus micro-averaged F1 is good for classifiers which work well on large categories, whereas macro-averaged F1 is good for classifiers which work better on smaller categories.

Figure 9. Micro-averaged F1 and macro-averaged F1

$$\text{Micro-averaged } F_{1micro}$$

$$= \frac{2 \cdot \sum_{j=1}^{L} tp_{c_j}}{2 \cdot \sum_{j=1}^{L} tp_{c_j} + \sum_{j=1}^{L} fp_{c_j} + \sum_{j=1}^{L} fn_{c_j}},$$

$$\text{Macro-averaged } F_{1macro} = \frac{1}{L} \sum_{j=1}^{L} \frac{2tp_{c_j}}{2tp_{c_j} + fp_{c_j} + fn_{c_j}}.$$

COMPARISON EXPERIMENT

Support Vector Machine (SVM) is one of the most used and accurate classifiers in many machine learning tasks, but our comparison experiment shows that Naïve Bayes exceeds SVM in this study. We first implemented a linear multi-label SVM using the LibSVM library with the one-versus-all heuristic. We applied weight of loss parameters that are proportional to the inverse of the percentages of tweets in or not in each category to account for the imbalanced categories. However, with the same training and testing data sets as in the above section, this one-versus-all SVM multi-label classifier classified all tweets into not in the category for all categories. So we got empty label sets for all tweets. Then we applied the same training and testing datasets as above to an advanced SVM variation named Max Margin Multi-Label classifier. M3L is a state-of-the-art multi-label classifier. Different from the one-versus all heuristic, which assumes label independence, this classifier takes label correlation into consideration. We used the executable file of this algorithm provided by the authors. The performance is better than the simplistic one-versus-all SVM classifier, but still not as good as the Naive Bayes classifier.

CONCLUSION

Mining social media data is beneficial for researcher in an education system to identify the student learning experience. The workflow for analyzing educational content in the social media helps to overcome the limitations of the large data mining and manual quality analysis of user generated textual content in social media as in depth qualitative mining is performed in this system. This chapter presents an analysis on Twitter in order to understand engineering students 'experiences, integrating both qualitative and quantitative methods in data mining techniques. In our observation, through a qualitative content analysis, we state that engineering students are largely struggling with the heavy study load, and are not able to manage it successfully. Heavy study load leads to many consequences including lack of social engagement, sleep problems, and other psychological and physical health problems. This work helps the organization and in an education system to and the present student educational experience. Based on this organization and participation can easily take decision in the engineering studies.

REFERENCES

Analytics, T. (n.d.). Retrieved from https://analytics.twitter.com

Arnold, K. E., & Pistilli, M. D. (2012). Course Signals at Purdue: Using Learning Analytics to Increase Student Success.*Proc. Second Int'l Conf. Learning Analytics and Knowledge*, (pp. 267-270). doi:10.1145/2330601.2330666

Baker, R., & Yacef, K. (2009). The State of Educational Data Mining in 2009: *A Review and Future Visions. J. Educational Data Mining, 1*(1), 3–17.

Davidov, D., Tsur, O., & Rappoport, A. (2010). Enhanced Sentiment Learning Using Twitter Hashtags and Smileys.*Proc. 23rd Int'l Conf. Computational Linguistics: Posters.*

DiMicco, J. M., & Millen, D. R. (2007). Identity Management: Multiple Presentations of Self in Facebook. *Proc. the Int'l ACM Conf. Supporting Group Work.* doi:10.1145/1316624.1316682

Go, A., Bhayani, R., & Huang, L. (2009). *Twitter Sentiment Classification Using Distant Supervision.* CS224N Project Report.

Hu, T., Tang, & Liu. (2013). Exploiting Social Relations for Sentiment Analysis in Micro blogging. In *Proceedings of the 6th ACM International Conference on Web Search and Data Mining.* ACM.

Ito, Horst, Bittanti, boyd, Herr-Stephenson, Lange, … Tripp. (2008). *Living and Learning with New Media: Summary of Findings from the Digital Youth Project.* The John D. and Catherine T. MacAuthur Foundation.

Jiliang, T., & Jie, L., & Huan. (2014). Recommendation in Social Media - Recent Advances and New Frontiers. In *Proceedings of the 20th ACM SIGKDD Conference on Knowledge Discovery and Data Mining.* ACM.

Kaplan, A. M., & Haenlein, M. (2010). Users of the world, unite! The challenges and opportunities of social media. *Business Horizons, 53*(1), 59–68. doi:10.1016/j.bushor.2009.09.003

Pearson, E. (2009). All the World Wide Webs a Stage: The Performance of Identity in Online Social Networks. *First Monday, 14*(3), 1–7. doi:10.5210/fm.v14i3.2162

Siemens, G., & Baker. (2012). Learning Analytics and Educational Data Mining: Towards Communication and Collaboration.*Proc. Second Int'l Conf. Learning Analytics and Knowledge*, (pp. 252-254). doi:10.1145/2330601.2330661

Social Media Mining. (n.d.). Retrieved from https://en.wikipedia.org/wiki/Social_media_mining

Vorvoreanu, M., & Clark, Q. (2010). Managing Identity Across Social Networks. *Proc. Poster Session at the ACM Conf. Computer Supported Cooperative Work.*

Vorvoreanu, M., Clark, Q. M., & Boisvenue, G. A. (2012). Online Identity Management Literacy for Engineering and Technology Students. *J. Online Eng. Education, 3*(1).

KEY TERMS AND DEFINITIONS

Bayes Classifier: Influence of one event occurrence on the probability of another event is called as conditional probability. From the probability theory, Bayes theorem, allows us to calculate the conditional probability for given problem.

Data Mining: Data Mining is that the analysis step of the knowledge Discovery in Databases method.

Educational Data Mining: Educational data mining are approaches emerging in present educational systems.

Multi-label Classifier: M3L is a state-of-the-art multi-label classifier. Different from the one-versus all heuristic, which assumes label independence, this classifier takes label correlation into consideration.

Naive Bayes classifier: Naive Bayes classifiers are highly scalable, requiring a number of parameters linear in the number of variables (features/predictors) in a learning problem. Suppose if there are more than one attribute then best classifier to be used is Naïve Bayes since all the attributes which are coming from different classes are independent of each other while they are mined from twitter.

R: R is a open source programming language and environment for statistical computing and graphics. R is an integrated suite of software facilities for data manipulation, calculation and graphical display.

Social Media Mining: Social media mining is the process of representing, analyzing, and extracting actionable patterns and trends from raw social media data.

Social Media: Social media is the "group of internet-based applications that build on the ideological and technological foundations of Web 2.0, and that allow the creation and exchange of user-generated content|".

Support Vector Machine (SVM): Support Vector Machines are supervised learning models with associated learning algorithms that analyze data used for classification and regression analysis. An SVM model is a representation of the examples as points in space, mapped so that the examples of the separate categories are divided by a clear gap that is as wide as possible. New examples are then mapped into that same space and predicted to belong to a category based on which side of the gap they fall on.

Weka: Weka is a tool which is collection of machine learning algorithms for data mining techniques.

Chapter 14
Some Other Applications in Community Graph under the Preview of Social Graph Using Graph–Mining Techniques

Bapuji Rao
iNurture Education Solutions Private Limited, India

Sasmita Mishra
IGIT, India

Saroja Nanda Mishra
IGIT, India

ABSTRACT

The retrieval of sub-graph from a large graph in structured data mining is one of the fundamental tasks for analyze. Visualization and analyze large community graph are challenging day by day. Since a large community graph is very difficult to visualize, so compression is essential. To study a large community graph, compression technique may be used for compression of community graph. There should not be any loss of information or knowledge while compressing the community graph. Similarly to extract desired knowledge of a particular sub-graph from a large community graph, then the large community graph needs to be partitioned into smaller sub-community graphs. The partition aims at the edges among the community members of dissimilar communities in a community graph. Sometimes it is essential to compare two community graphs for similarity which makes easier for mining the reliable knowledge from a large community graph. Once the similarity is done then the necessary mining of knowledge can be extracted from only one community graph rather than from both which leads saving of time.

DOI: 10.4018/978-1-5225-1877-8.ch014

INTRODUCTION

Day by day the applications on graphs are increasing rapidly leading to increase in size and complexities of graph. To represent a large community graph in the memory is a very challenging and rather difficult task. The direct visualization of such a large community graph is beyond human capability. The visualization can be achieved by compressing a large community graph into a smaller one which ultimately contains all the information's related to the nodes of the community graph. Representation and compressing of such kind of community graph without knowledge loss presents a new challenge to graph mining. One issue in this direction is that, the huge community graph may severely restrict the application of existing pattern mining technologies. The compressed community graph should conserve the characteristics of the original community graph. So that visualization becomes easier and the process of knowledge extraction can be carried out more efficiently and easily. Graph compression problem can be addressed by clustering algorithms, as group members have similar characteristics and can be represented by super nodes. Similar work is done by graph partitioning algorithms by Fjallstrom (1998) and Elsner (1997), which can be used to detect hidden community structures. Most of these algorithms are based on the distance matrix, and do not focus on the structure of the original graph. Another feasible technique is to construct a small graph consisting of a set of the most important nodes and edges. Much literature has discussed how to rank the centrality of nodes and edges by Newman et al (2004) and Gert (1966). Another technique is the information-theoretic technique by Navlakha et al (2008) which can construct both lossless and lossy compressed graph representations. Such representation has two parts. The first one being the graph summary that captures the important communities and relationships in the original community graph and the second one is set of edge corrections which help to re-create the original community graph from a compressed community graph. The analysis of complex networks has become a hot research topic in the field of data mining. One of the examples is social network's community network. Communities, also known as clusters, are often referred to as vertices with a high density of connections among them and seldom connected with the rest of the graph by Girvan et al (2002). Community detection provides valuable information about the structural properties of the network by Boccaletti et al (2006) and Girvan et al (2002), the interactions among the agents of a network by Blondel et al (2008) or the role the agents develop inside the network Wang et al (2010). Scalable Community Detection (SCD) by WWW (2014) detects disjoint communities in undirected and un-weighted networks by maximizing WCC, which is proposed community metric. Weighted Community Clustering (WCC) is a metric based on triangle structures in a community. A community (a module or a cluster) can be thought as a group of nodes with more interactions amongst its members than between its members and the remainder of the network by Girvan et al (2002). Such groups of nodes (communities) are interpreted as organizational units in social networks by Feld (1981) and Simmel (1964). The authors use graph theory's some important techniques to solve the problem of partitioning a community graph to minimize the number of edges or links that connect different community by Rajaraman et al (2011). The aim of partitioning a community graph to sub-community graphs is to detect similar vertices which form a sub-community graph. For example, considering Facebook is a very large social graph. It can be partitioned into sub-graphs, and each sub-group should belong to a particular characteristics. Such cases the authors require graph partitions. In this partition, it is not mandatory that each sub-group contain similar number of members. A partition of a community graph is to divide into clusters, such that each similar vertex belongs to one cluster. Here a cluster means a particular community. A graph arises in many situations like web graph of documents, a social network graph of friends, a road-map graph of cities.

Graph mining has grown rapidly for the last two decades due to the number and the size of graphs has been growing exponentially (with billions of nodes and edges), and from it the authors want to extract much more complicated information. Graph similarity has numerous applications in social networks, image processing, biological networks, chemical compounds, and computer vision, and therefore it has suggested many algorithms and similarity measures. Graph similarity is that "a node in one graph is similar to a node in another graph if their neighborhoods are similar" by Koutra et al (2011).

LITERATURE SURVEY

Greedy algorithm by Navlakha et al (2008) is to iteratively group two nodes with the highest cost reduction. The Greedy algorithm has three phases: Initialization, Iterative merging and Output. In the initialization phase, the cost reduction S for all pairs of nodes will be computed. In each round of merging phase, the globally best pair of nodes will be chosen, so node u and v will be removed from V_S, and a new node W will be added into V_S. In the output phase, the graph summary edge set, E_S, and the edge corrections, C, will be constructed. The Greedy algorithm can construct a much higher-level compressed graph for a given graph. In the literature, we find different community detection algorithms which follow different strategies. Among this one of the community detection algorithms is maximizing modularity by Newman et al (2004). It has been reported that modularity has resolution limits by Bagrow (2012) and Fortunato et al (2007). Modularity is unable to detect small and well defined communities in a large graph. Its maximization make sets in a tree-like structure, which cannot be considered as communities. A multilevel approach has been proposed which constructs graphs with hundreds of millions of objects by Blondel et al (2008), but the quality of its results decreases considerably as long as the size of the graph increases by Lancichinetti (2009). Random walk is a tool on which several community detection algorithms can be grouped together in one area. This strategy is the main idea used in Walktrap by Pons et al (2006). Another algorithm based on random walks is Infomap by Rosvall et al (2008). According to the comparison performed by Lancichinetti (2009), Infomap stands as one of the best community detection algorithms. A recently proposed algorithm is BigClam by Yang et al (2013). This algorithm is based on computing an affiliation of vertices to communities that maximizes an objective function using non negative matrix factorization. In Rajaraman et al (2011), the partition in a graph takes place at the edge where almost equal partition of graph is detected. Such cut makes almost two equal sub-graphs having same number of nodes and the cut is said to be best cut. In Barnes (1982), a graph G = (N, E) is an undirected graph having nodes N and edges E. It partitions the graph G into k-disjoint subsets. So the number of edges in E that connect different subsets is minimal. This partition method is generally used in a linear programming transportation problem. In Ford et al (1956), a directed graph with three types of nodes i.e., source and sink, and the remaining nodes are called intermediate. Each edge with a positive integer is considered its flow capacity. This graph partition is related to transportation problem. In this the cut is made in such a way that the maximum flow must be achieved from source node to sink node. The efficient heuristic procedure Kernighan et al (1970) for partitioning any arbitrary graphs, which is effective in finding limited number of partitions. This method is generally used in electronic circuit construction. So that it minimizes the number of inter connections between boards. To identify the parallelism in a problem by partitioning its data and task among the processors by Pothen (1997) is modeled as graph partitioning problem in which the vertices of a graph are divided into a specified number of subsets such that few edges join two vertices in different subsets. In Ravasz et al (2002), it explains about the hierarchical organization of modularity in metabolic networks which is once again considered as multi-level networks. Such networks are partitioned based on some special nodes which control the connectivity to the remaining nodes of the network. After partition, it forms cluster of nodes each treated as one sub-graph. Graphs are general object model; graph similarity has been studied in many fields. Similarity measures for graphs have been used in systems for shape retrieval by Huet et al (1999), object recognition by Kubicka et al (1990) or face recognition by Wiskott et al (1997). For all those measures, graph features specific to the graphs in the application, are exploited in order to define graph similarity. Examples of such features are given one to one mapping between the vertices of different graphs or the requirement that all graphs are of the same order. A very common similarity measure for graphs is the edit distance. It uses the same principle as the well known edit distance for strings by Levenshtein (1966) and Wagner et al (1974). The idea is to determine the minimal number of insertions and deletions of vertices and edges to make the compared graphs isomorphic. Sanfeliu et al (1983) extended this principle to attributed graphs, by introducing vertex relabeling as a third basic operation beside insertions and deletions. In Cook et al (2000), the measure is used for data mining in a graph. The key idea behind the feature extraction method is that similar graphs probably share certain properties, such as degree distribution, diameter, and Eigen values by Watts (1999). After extracting these features, a similarity measure by Cha (2007) is applied in order to assess the similarity between the aggregated statistics and, equivalently, the similarity between the graphs. In iterative method "two nodes are similar if their neighborhoods are also similar". In each iteration, the nodes exchange similarity scores and this process ends when convergence is achieved. A successful algorithm belong to this category is the similarity flooding algorithm by Melnik et al (2002) applies in database schema matching; which solves the "matching" problem, and attempts to find the correspondence between the nodes of two given graphs. Another successful algorithm is SimRank by Jeh et al (2002), which measures the self-similarity of a graph, i.e., it assesses the similarities between all pairs of nodes in one graph. Furthermore, another successful recursive method related to graph similarity and matching is the algorithm proposed by Zager et al (2008). This method introduces the idea of coupling the similarity scores of nodes and edges in order to compute the similarity between two graphs. A new method to measure the similarity of attributed graphs proposed in Kriegel et al (2003). This method solves the problems mentioned in similarity measures for attributed graphs and is useful in the context of large databases of structured objects. First BP-based algorithm implemented for graph similarity by Koutra et al (2011) uses the original BP algorithm as it is proposed by Yedidia et al (2003). This algorithm is naive and runs in $O(n^2)$ time.

PROPOSED ALGORITHM OF COMMUNITY GRAPH COMPRESSION

Algorithm Community_Graph_Compression()

Algorithm conventions by Lipschutz (Tata McGraw-Hill)

```
// Global Declarations
//n: Number of Communities.
//NCM[1:n, 1:2]: Holds community number and number of community members of
each //community of order nX2.
//tcm: To count total number of community members.
```

```
//CMM[1: tcm+1, 1: tcm+1] : Adjacency matrix of Community Members of order //
(tcm+1)X(tcm+1).
//CCM[1: n, 1: n]: Adjacency matrix of Compressed Community Graph of order nXn.
//CEC[1: n] : To count number of edges between similar community.
i.    [Read Community Data]
      Call Read_Community_Data( )
ii.   [Generate and assign every members code]
      Call Assign_Community_Member_Codes( )
iii.  [Creation of adjacency matrix of all the members]
      Call Community_Member_Matrix( )
iv.   [Counting edges in the same sub-community graph]
      Call Same_Community_Edge_Detection( )
v.    [Counting edges between dissimilar sub-community graph]
      Call Dissimilar_Community_Edge_Detection( )
vi.   [Show the compressed community graph]
      Call Compressed_Community_Matrix_Display( )
vii.  Exit
```

PROCEDURE TO READ COMMUNITY DATA

Procedure Read_Community_Data()

```
i. Set tcm := 0.
i. Read Number of communities as 'n'.
ii. Read Community details such as community code and number of members of
each community, and assign to the matrix NCM[ ][ ].
iii. Repeat For I := 1, 2,......., n:
       tcm := tcm + NCM[I][2].
     End For
iv. Return
```

PROCEDURE TO ASSIGN COMMUNITY MEMBER CODES

Procedure Assign_Community_Member_Codes()

```
i.    Set K := 1.
ii.   Repeat For I :=1, 2,......., n:
         Repeat For J := 1, 2,......, NCM[I][2]:
                (a) Set CMM[1][K+1] :=  J.
                (b) Set CMM[K+1][1] :=  J.
                (c) K := K + 1.
             End For
```

```
        End For
iii. Return
```

PROCEDURE TO CREATE COMMUNITY MEMBER MATRIX

Procedure Community_Member_Matrix()

```
i. Get the edge data of all the community members.
ii. Store the above data in the matrix CMM[ ][ ].
iii. Return
```

PROCEDURE TO DETECT SAME COMMUNITY MEMBERS' EDGE

Procedure Same_Community_Edge_Detection()

```
i. Set d:=1, s:=0.
ii. Repeat For i:=1,2,….., n:
        (a) s := s + NCM[i][1].
        (b) Repeat For j := d, d+1,….s:
                Repeat For k := d, d+1,…..,s:
                    [Check for Edge at CMM[j+1][k+1] ]
                    If (CMM[j+1][k+1]=1)
                    Then
                            CCM[i+1][i+1] := CCM[i+1][i+1] + 1.
                        Else
                                Set d := s.
                        End If
                End For
            End For
        End For
iii. Return
```

PROCEDURE TO DETECT DISSIMILAR COMMUNITY MEMBERS' EDGE

Procedure Dissimilar_Community_Edge_Detection()

```
i. Set a := 1, b := NCM[1][2], c := b, d := b.
ii. Repeat For i :=2, 3, ….,(n+1):
        (a) d := d + NCM[i][2].
        (b) Call Addition (i-1, a, b, c, d).
        (c) a := b.
```

```
        (d) b := b + NCM[i][2].
        (e) c := d.
    End For
iii. Return
```

PROCEDURE TO COUNT EDGES BETWEEN DISSIMILAR COMMUNITY MEMBERS

Procedure Addition (p, a, b, c, d)

```
a, b: Variables holds the row-side initial and final index value.
c, d:  Variables holds the column-side initial and final index value.
P: Variable holds the initial index of matrix CCM[ ][ ].
i.  Set x := c, y := d.
ii. Set k := p+1.
iii. Repeat For i := a, a+1,…..,b:
        (a) Set k := p+1.
        (b) Repeat For j := c, c+1, ……,d:
                (b.1) [Check edge between dissimilar community members]
                        If(CMM[i+1][j+1]=1)
        Then
            (b.1.1) [Counting dissimilar community edges row-side and assign-
ment]
                        CCM[p+1][k+1]:= CCM[p+1][k+1] + 1.
            (b.1.2) [Counting dissimilar community edges column-side and as-
signment]
                        CCM[k+1][p+1]:= CCM[k+1][p+1] + 1.
                        End If
                (b.2) k := k+1.
                (b.3) If(d<tcm)
                        Then
                                (b.3.1) Set c := d.
                                (b.3.2) d := d + NCM[k][2].
                                (b.3.3) Goto Step (b).
                        End If
                (b.4) Set c := x.
                (b.5) Set d := y.
            End For
        End For
iv. Return
```

PROCEDURE TO DISPLAY COMPRESSED COMMUNITY MATRIX

Procedure Compressed_Community_Matrix_Display()

```
i. [Assign CEC[ ] array to CCM[ ][ ] matrix]
   Repeat For i :=1, 2 ,......,n:
         CCM[i][i] := CEC[i].
   End For
ii. Repeat For i := 1, 2,.......,n:
        Repeat For j := 1, 2,........,n:
             Display CCM[i][j].
        End For
    End For
iii. Return
```

The proposed algorithm consists of six procedures. Procedure–I allows to read the details about number of communities and number of community members of all communities. The data related to community and their edges are read from two data files namely "commun1.txt" and "graph.dat". Procedure–II generates and assigns community member codes. Procedure–III creates the community adjacency matrix. Procedure–IV detects and counts number of edges in a particular sub-community graph and assign to the array CEC[ ]. Procedure–V detects and counts number of edges among dissimilar sub-community graphs and assign to the matrix CCM[ ][ ]. Procedure–VII assigns CEC[ ] array diagonally to the matrix CCM[ ][ ]. And finally displays the compressed community adjacency matrix. From it we can draw the compressed community graph.

EXAMPLE

Let us consider a community graph by Rao et al (ICCIC 2014), Rao et al (ICHPCA 2014), Rao et al (2014), Rao et al (2015), Rao et al (2015), and Mitra et al (2013) with 23 number of community members belonging to four types of communities shown in "Figure 1". The community C_1, C_2, C_3, and C_4 have community members $\{C_{11}, C_{12}, C_{13}, C_{14}, C_{15}, C_{16}\}$, $\{C_{21}, C_{22}, C_{23}, C_{24}, C_{25}\}$, $\{C_{31}, C_{32}, C_{33}, C_{34}\}$, and $\{C_{41}, C_{42}, C_{43}, C_{44}, C_{45}, C_{46}, C_{47}, C_{48}\}$ respectively. The authors aim is to compress the above community graph. The dotted line circle indicates grouping or clustering of community members of same community which is shown in "Figure 1". To represent in memory, the authors have created an adjacency matrix of order 24X24 which is shown in "Figure 2". The gray color filled boxes indicate the adjacency matrices for the communities C_1, C_2, C_3, and C_4. So the authors have counted these edges and assigned to the array called CEC[ ].The black color filled boxes indicate the edges between the community members of dissimilar communities. So we have counted these edges and assigned to matrix called CCM[ ][ ]. Then we have assigned the values from CEC[ ] to the diagonal position of CCM[ ][ ] which is the indication of self edges. So the final matrix is called as compressed community adjacency matrix which is shown in "Figure 3".

Figure 1.

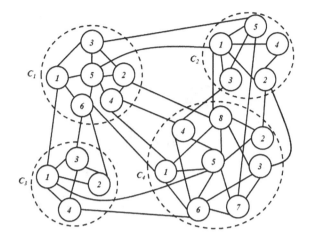

Finally the authors can visualize the compressed community graph from the compressed community adjacency matrix which is shown in "Figure 4". Self-edge or Self-loop or cycle is the indication of number of edges belonging to a particular community. For community C_1, C_2, C_3, and C_4 the total numbers of edges are 18, 12, 10, and 28 respectively. It indicates of self-edge or self-loop or cycle. Hence the authors say that the proposed community graph in "Figure 1" has been successfully compressed to a compressed community graph which is shown in "Figure 4". Finally the compressed community graph has been drawn successfully from the compressed community adjacency matrix which is shown in "Figure 3".

Figure 2.

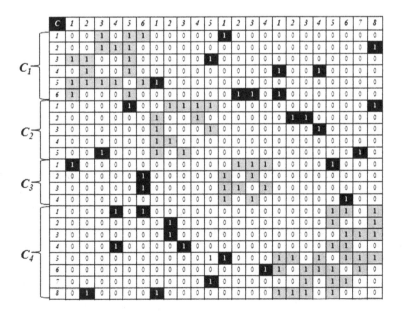

C	1	2	3	4	5	6	1	2	3	4	5	1	2	3	4	1	2	3	4	5	6	7	8
1	0	0	1	0	1	1	1	0	0	0	0	1	0	0	0	0	0	0	0	0	0	0	0
2	0	0	1	1	1	1	0	0	0	0	0	0	0	0	0	0	0	0	0	0	0	0	1
3	1	1	0	0	1	0	0	0	0	0	0	1	0	0	0	0	0	0	0	0	0	0	0
4	0	1	0	0	1	0	0	0	0	0	0	0	0	0	0	1	0	0	1	0	0	0	0
5	1	1	1	1	0	1	1	1	0	0	0	0	0	0	0	0	0	0	0	0	0	0	0
6	1	0	0	0	1	0	0	0	0	0	0	1	1	0	1	0	0	0	0	0	0	0	1
1	0	0	0	0	1	0	0	0	1	1	1	1	0	0	0	0	0	0	0	0	0	0	1
2	0	0	0	0	0	0	0	1	0	0	1	0	0	0	0	0	1	1	0	0	0	0	0
3	0	0	0	0	0	0	0	1	0	0	0	1	0	0	0	0	0	0	1	0	0	0	0
4	0	0	0	0	0	0	0	1	1	0	0	0	0	0	0	0	0	0	0	0	0	0	0
5	0	0	1	0	0	0	0	1	0	1	0	0	0	0	0	0	0	0	0	0	0	1	0
1	1	0	0	0	0	0	0	0	0	0	0	0	1	1	1	0	0	0	0	1	0	0	0
2	0	0	0	0	0	0	1	0	0	0	0	1	0	1	0	0	0	0	0	0	0	0	0
3	0	0	0	0	0	0	1	0	0	0	0	1	1	0	1	0	0	0	0	0	0	0	0
4	0	0	0	0	0	0	0	0	0	0	0	1	0	1	0	0	0	0	0	0	1	0	0
1	0	0	0	0	1	0	1	0	0	0	0	0	0	0	0	0	0	0	0	1	1	0	1
2	0	0	0	0	0	0	0	0	0	1	0	0	0	0	0	0	0	0	0	1	0	0	1
3	0	0	0	0	0	0	0	0	0	1	0	0	0	0	0	0	0	0	0	1	1	1	1
4	0	0	0	0	1	0	0	0	0	0	1	0	0	0	0	0	0	0	0	1	1	0	0
5	0	0	0	0	0	0	0	0	0	0	0	1	1	0	0	0	0	0	1	0	1	1	1
6	0	0	0	0	0	0	0	0	0	0	0	0	0	0	0	1	1	0	1	1	1	0	1
7	0	0	0	0	0	0	0	0	0	0	0	1	0	0	0	0	0	0	1	0	1	1	0
8	0	1	0	0	0	0	0	1	0	0	0	0	0	0	0	1	1	1	0	1	0	0	0

Figure 3.

			Community Codes		
		C_1	C_2	C_3	C_4
	C_1	18	2	3	4
Community Codes	C_2	2	12	0	5
	C_3	3	0	10	2
	C_4	4	5	2	28

Edges of similar community members of community

Figure 4.

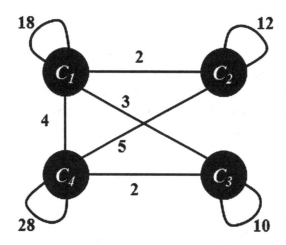

EXPERIMENTAL RESULT

To evaluate the performance of the proposed algorithm, the authors have considered two dataset files for the example of community graph shown in "Figure 1". The 1st dataset file "COMMUN1.TXT" depicted in "Figure 5", which contains the details of community graph such as total number of communities, community numbers (codes), and total number of community members belong to each community. Similarly the 2nd dataset file "DATA.TXT" depicted in "Figure 6", which contains the edge data of community members of all the communities. Indication of 1 means an edge between the community members and 0 means there is on edge. Upon inputting the above two dataset files, the procedure Read_Community_Data() assigns community numbers (codes) and total number of community members in the matrix NCM[n][2] from the dataset file "COMMUN1.TXT". The procedures Assign_Community_Member_Codes() assigns the community codes to the matrix CMM[tcm+1][tcm+1] from the matrix NCM[n][2]. Finally, the procedure community_Member_Matrix() reads edge data from the data file "DATA.TXT" and assigns to the matrix CMM[tcm+1][tcm+1]. The procedures Same_Community_Edge_Detection()

and Dissimilar_Community_Edge_Detection() uses the matrix CMM[][] to create the resultant matrix CCM[][] which holds the edge details of the compressed community matrix. Finally, the procedure Compressed_Community_Matrix_Display() displays the resultant matrix CCM[][] as compressed community matrix. The algorithm was written in C++ and compiled with TurboC++ and run on Intel Core I5-3230M CPU +2.60 GHz Laptop with 4GB memory running MS-Windows 7. The community graph's compression result is depicted in "Figure 7", "Figure 8", and "Figure 9" respectively.

Finally, the authors have drawn the compressed community graph from "Figure 9" which is depicted in "Figure 4".

Figure 5.

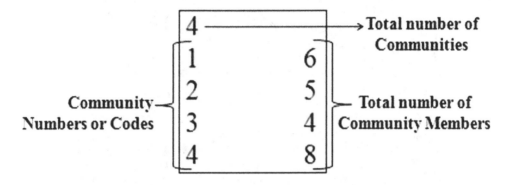

Figure 6.

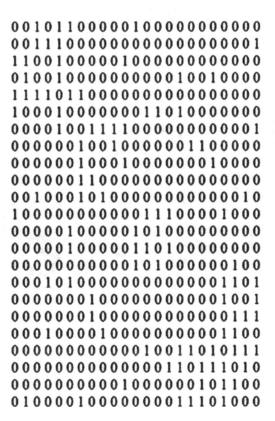

Figure 7.

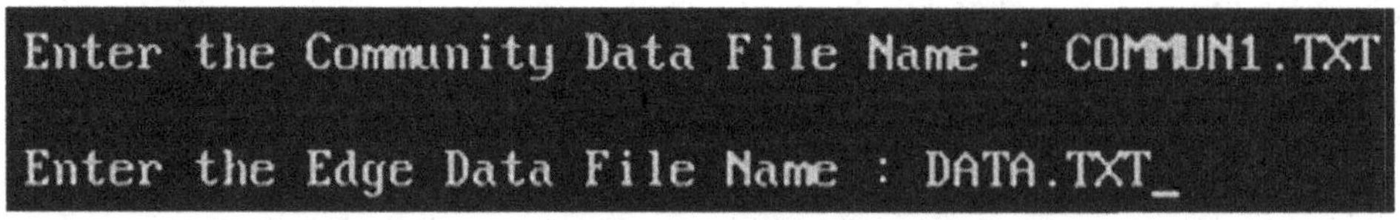

Enter the Community Data File Name : COMMUN1.TXT
Enter the Edge Data File Name : DATA.TXT_

Figure 8.

C	1	2	3	4	5	6	1	2	3	4	5	1	2	3	4	1	2	3	4	5	6	7	8
1	0	0	1	0	1	1	0	0	0	0	0	1	0	0	0	0	0	0	0	0	0	0	0
2	0	0	1	1	1	0	0	0	0	0	0	0	0	0	0	0	0	0	0	0	0	0	1
3	1	1	0	0	1	0	0	0	0	0	1	0	0	0	0	0	0	0	0	0	0	0	0
4	0	1	0	0	1	0	0	0	0	0	0	0	0	0	0	1	0	0	1	0	0	0	0
5	1	1	1	1	0	1	1	0	0	0	0	0	0	0	0	0	0	0	0	0	0	0	0
6	1	0	0	0	1	0	0	0	0	0	0	0	1	1	0	1	0	0	0	0	0	0	0
1	0	0	0	0	1	0	0	1	1	1	1	0	0	0	0	0	0	0	0	0	0	0	1
2	0	0	0	0	0	0	1	0	0	1	0	0	0	0	0	0	1	1	0	0	0	0	0
3	0	0	0	0	0	0	1	0	0	0	1	0	0	0	0	0	0	0	1	0	0	0	0
4	0	0	0	0	0	0	1	1	0	0	0	0	0	0	0	0	0	0	0	0	0	0	0
5	0	0	1	0	0	0	1	0	1	0	0	0	0	0	0	0	0	0	0	0	0	1	0
1	1	0	0	0	0	0	0	0	0	0	0	0	1	1	1	0	0	0	0	1	0	0	0
2	0	0	0	0	0	1	0	0	0	0	0	1	0	1	0	0	0	0	0	0	0	0	0
3	0	0	0	0	0	1	0	0	0	0	0	1	1	0	1	0	0	0	0	0	0	0	0
4	0	0	0	0	0	0	0	0	0	0	0	1	0	1	0	0	0	0	0	0	1	0	0
1	0	0	0	1	0	1	0	0	0	0	0	0	0	0	0	0	0	0	0	1	1	0	1
2	0	0	0	0	0	0	0	1	0	0	0	0	0	0	0	0	0	0	0	1	0	0	1
3	0	0	0	0	0	0	0	1	0	0	0	0	0	0	0	0	0	0	0	0	1	1	1
4	0	0	0	1	0	0	0	0	1	0	0	0	0	0	0	0	0	0	0	1	1	0	0
5	0	0	0	0	0	0	0	0	0	0	0	0	1	0	0	1	1	0	1	0	1	1	1
6	0	0	0	0	0	0	0	0	0	0	0	0	0	0	1	1	0	1	1	1	0	1	0
7	0	0	0	0	0	0	0	0	0	0	1	0	0	0	0	0	0	1	0	1	1	0	0
8	0	1	0	0	0	0	1	0	0	0	0	0	0	0	0	1	1	1	0	1	0	0	0

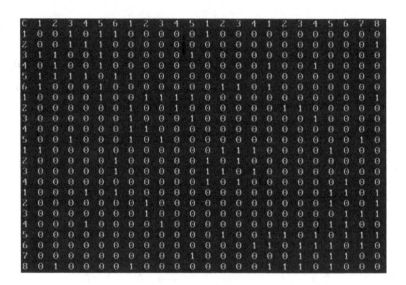

Figure 9.

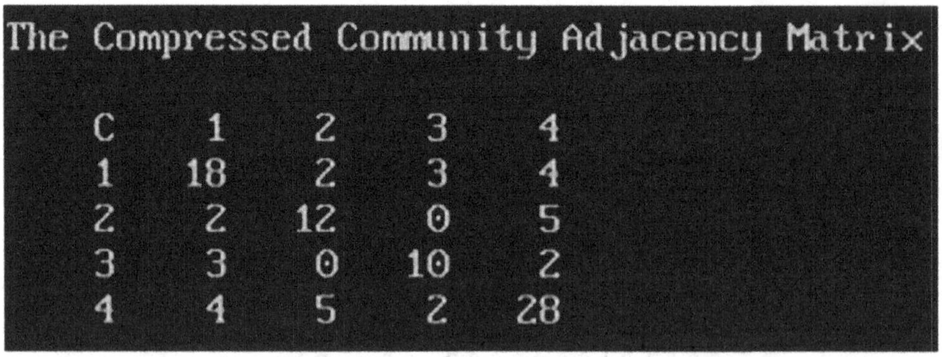

The Compressed Community Adjacency Matrix

C	1	2	3	4
1	18	2	3	4
2	2	12	0	5
3	3	0	10	2
4	4	5	2	28

PROPOSED ALGORITHM FOR EXTRACTION OF SUB-COMMUNITY GRAPH FROM COMPRESSED COMMUNITY GRAPH

Algorithm SCE_CCG()

Algorithm conventions by Lipschutz (Tata McGraw-Hill)

```
// Global Declarations
// Cno: Community number of community sub-graph to extract.
// n: Number of communities.
// TCM: To store total number of community members.
// CN[n][3]: Matrix to hold community numbers, total community members, and
actual edges
// of community.
// CCAM[n][n]: Compressed community adjacency matrix of order nXn.
// EAM[TCM+1][TCM+1]: Expanded adjacency matrix of order (TCM+1)X(TCM+1).
// CCDATA.TXT: Dataset to contain number of edges (similar and dissimilar com-
munity
// members).
// CDATA.TXT: Dataset to contain number of communities, community numbers, and
total
// number of community members.
// EdgeData.TXT: Dataset to contain edge data between the community members.
{
 // opening 1st data file for reading
 open("CDATA.TXT");
 read(n);  // total communities
 i:=1;
 while(Not EOF())
 do
 {
   read(CN[i][1]);
   read(CN[i][2]);
   i:=i+1;
 }
 close("CDATA.TXT");
 // opening 2nd data file for reading
 open("CCDATA.TXT");
 for i:=1 to n do
   for j:=1 to n do
   {
     read(CCAM[i][j]);
   }
 close("CCDATA.TXT");
```

```
// Calculate number of edges using CCAM[ ][ ] matrix and assign at 3rd column
of CN[ ][ ]
 for i:=1 to n do
       CN[i][3] := CCAM[i][i]/2;
// Find total number of community members by using the matrix CN[ ][ ]
TCM:=0;
    for i:=1 to n do
        TCM := TCM + CN[i][2];
// Assign Community numbers to 1st row and 1st column of matrix EAM[ ][ ] ]
k:=2;
     for i:=1 to n do
        for j:=1 to CN[i][2] do
       {
          EAM[1][k] := (CN[i][1]*10) + j;
          EAM[k][1] := (CN[i][1]*10) + j;
          k:=k+1;
          }
Call Show_Matrix(EAM, TCM);
// Edge creation for both the community members
open("EdgeData.TXT");
while(Not EOF())
do
{
  read(rnode);
  read(cnode);
for i:=2 to (TCM+1) do
   if (EAM[i][1]=rnode) then
   {
      for j:=2 to (TCM+1) do
         if (EAM[1][j]=cnode) then
        {
          EAM[i][j]:=1;  // row side edge
          EAM[j][i]:=1;  // column side edge
          break;
          }
     }
close("EdgeData.TXT");
// Display the Expanded Community Adjacency Matrix EAM[ ][ ]
Call Show_Matrix(EAM, TCM);
output("Enter Community Number");
read(Cno);
// Searching Cno and display
Call Sub_Community_Matrix_Extraction (Cno);
}
```

PROCEDURE TO SHOW SUB-COMMUNITY ADJACENCY MATRIX

Procedure Show_Sub_Community_Matrix (Lb, Ub, Cno)

```
// Lb, Ub: Holds the lower bound and upper bound index of community number Cno.
// order: Number of community members in  community Cno.
// sub_mat[order+1][order+1]: To assign the edge details of community Cno.
{
    for i:=1 to n do
      if(Cno=CN[i][1]) { order:=CN[i][2]; break; }
  for i:=1 to (order+1) do
   for j:=1 to (order+1) do
      sub_mat[i][j]:=0;
// community number assignment at 1st row and column of sub_mat[][]
    for i:=1 to order do
    {
      sub_mat[1][i+1] := (Cno*10) + i;
      sub_mat[i+1][1] := (Cno*10) + i;
    }
 // assignment of sub-community matrix from EAM[][] to sub_mat[][]
 row:=2;
 for  i:=Lb to Ub do
 {
    col:=2;
  for  j:=Lb to Ub do
  {
    sub_mat[row][col] := EAM[i][j];
    col:=col+1;
  }
    row:=row+1;
 }
 // display sub_mat[][]
 for i:=1 to (order+1) do
   for j:=1 to (order+1) do
    if(i=1 and j=1) then output("C");
    else output(sub_mat[i][j]);
}
```

PROCEDURE TO DISPLAY COMMUNITY ADJACENCY MATRIX

Procedure Show_Matrix (mat, n)

```
// mat[n][n]: Matrix to store the sub-community adjacency matrix of order nXn.
{
  for i:=1 to n do
  {
    for j:=1 to n do
      if(i=1 and j=1) then output("C");
      else output(mat[i][j]);
    }
}
```

PROCEDURE TO EXTRACT THE PARTICULAR SUB-COMMUNITY MATRIX FROM THE EXPANDED COMMUNITY MATRIX

Procedure Sub_Community_Matrix_Extraction (Cno)

```
// Cno: Community number for extraction of sub-community adjacency matrix.
{
    Flag:=0;  Lb:=1; Ub:=1;
    for i:=1 to TCM do
      if (Cno = EAM[1][i+1]/10)
      {
         if (Flag = 0) then {   Flag:=1;   Lb:= i;  }
         Ub := i;
       }
    // Extract Cno Sub-Community Adjacency Matrix
    if (Flag=1)
        Call Show_Sub_Community_Matrix(Lb, Ub, Cno);
      else
        output("Community not found in the Expanded Community Matrix");
}
```

EXAMPLE

The authors have considered a compressed community graph by Boccaletti et al (2006) depicted in "Figure 10". It has four sets of communities namely C_1, C_2, C_3, and C_4. It has five numbers of edges having its weight, which is said to be the connectivity between community members of dissimilar communities. Between community members of community C_1 and C_2, there are two numbers of connectivity or edges. Similarly between community C_2 and C_4, there are 5 numbers of connectivity or edges. Every community

Figure 10.

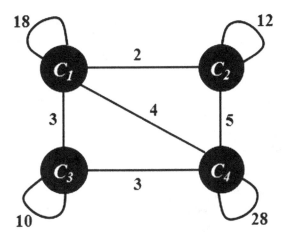

has its own loop or cycle with its own weight. Such loop or cycle of community is said to be the self-loop or cycle. The self-loop or cycle is the total number of edges or connectivity among the community members of a particular community. For community C_1, the self-loop with weight is 18. It means there are 18 numbers of undirected edges among its available community members. While compression of a large community graph into a compressed community graph, one has to preserve the information such as actual number of community members and its connectivity which is shown in "Figure 12". Using number of community members and the number of edges or connectivity, one can expand a compressed community graph to the expanded one by preserving all its information without any loses of data. The authors say this type of graph as weighted undirected graph with self-loops or cycles.

The above graph can be represented in memory using graph techniques as a square matrix which only consists of weights of edges and self-loops or cycles. Its weighted adjacency matrix is shown in "Figure 11" and considered as a compressed community adjacency matrix. The principal diagonal cells of adjacency matrix contain weights of every community's self-loop or cycle. The remaining cells fill with the edges weight between the communities. The expansion of compressed graph can be done with the help of actual number of community members and number of edges among them by using the data available in "Figure 12". By finding the total number of community members from "Figure 12", one can find the actual order of the expanded community adjacency matrix. In the proposed compressed graph, the total numbers of community members are 23 (6 + 5 + 4 + 8). So the order of expanded community adjacency matrix is 23X23. After applying the proposed algorithm on the expanded adjacency matrix, the authors have found the final form of expanded community adjacency matrix which is shown in "Figure 13". The gray filled **1** indicates the edges among the community members of a particular community. The black filled **1** indicates the edges among the community members of dissimilar communities. Once the final expanded community adjacency matrix has been constructed, we can able to draw the expanded community graph which is shown in "Figure 14".

Finally the desired community sub-graph can be extracted from "Figure 14". For this purpose, the authors try to detect the desired community in the expanded community adjacency matrix for extraction. After applying the procedure Sub_Community_Graph_Extraction (4) on "Figure 13", the authors have successfully detected community 4 and its extracted adjacency matrix is shown in "Figure 15". Finally using "Figure 15", the authors have constructed the sub-community graph for community 4 which is shown in "Figure 16".

Figure 11.

Figure 12.

Community Members Edges of Particular Community

Community Names

	C_1	C_2	C_3	C_4
C_1	18	2	3	4
C_2	2	12	0	5
C_3	3	0	10	2
C_4	4	5	2	28

Community Names

C	N	Edges
1	6	18/2 = 9
2	5	12/2 = 6
3	4	10/2 = 5
4	8	28/2 = 14

Figure 13.

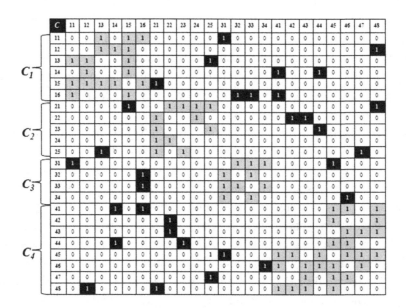

Figure 14.

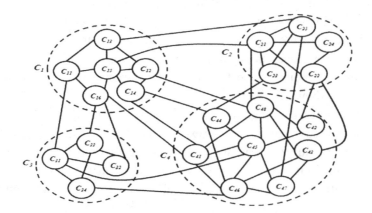

Figure 15.   *Figure 16.*

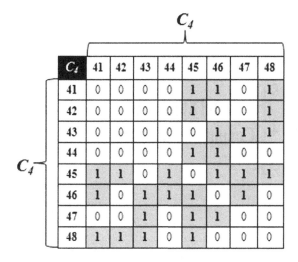

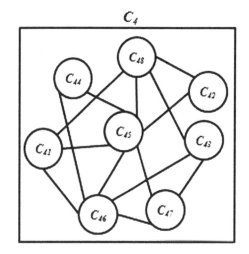

EXPERIMENTAL RESULT

The proposed algorithm's performance is evaluated by considering three dataset files of the example of compressed community graph. The 1st dataset file "CDATA.TXT" depicted in "Figure 17", which contains total number of communities, community numbers (codes), and total number of community members belong to each community. The 2nd dataset file "CCDATA.TXT" depicted in "Figure 18", which contains the details of community's edge details i.e. total number of edges of the members of the communities as well as total number of edges among the members of different communities. Finally, the 3rd dataset file "EdgeData.TXT" depicted in "Figure 19", which contains the node details such as "from node" and "to node" where the actual edge is present. The data from dataset file "CDATA.TXT" are read and assigned to the matrix CN[n][3]. The data from dataset file "CCDATA.TXT" are read and assigned to the matrix CCAM[n][n]. Similarly the data from dataset file "EdgeData.TXT" are assigned to the matrix EAM[TCM+1][TCM+1]. The procedure Show_Matrix(EAM, TCM)for displaying of expanded adjacency matrix from the matrix EAM[TCM+1][TCM+1]. The procedure Sub_Community_Matrix_Extraction(Cno) for extraction of community number Cno's sub-community matrix from the expanded adjacency matrix EAM[TCM+1][TCM+1]. After extraction the community number Cno's sub-community matrix by calling the procedure Show_Sub_Community_Matrix(Lb, Ub, Cno).

The algorithm was written in C++ and compiled with TurboC++ and run on Intel Core I5-3230M CPU +2.60 GHz Laptop with 4GB memory running MS-Windows 7. The datasets "CCDATA.TXT", "CDATA.TXT", and "EdgeData.TXT" are input to the algorithm which is depicted in "Figure 20".The compressed community graph's result is depicted in "Figure 21", "Figure 22", and "Figure 23" respectively.

The authors have drawn the compressed community graph from "Figure 23" which is depicted in "Figure 10".

Figure 17.

Figure 18.

18	2	3	4
2	12	0	5
3	0	10	2
4	5	2	28

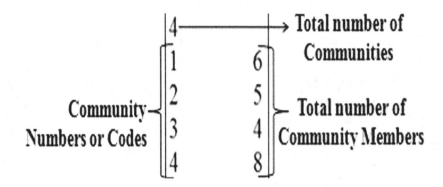

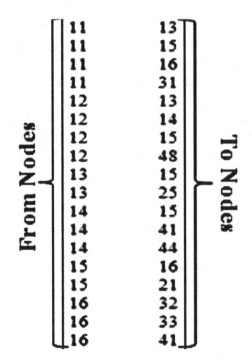

Figure 19.

Figure 20.

```
Enter Compressed Community Data File Name : CCDATA.TXT


Enter Community Data File Name : CDATA.TXT


Enter Community Member Edge DataFile : EdgeData.TXT
```

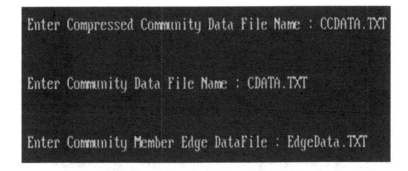

Figure 21.

```
Compressed Community Adjacency Matrix

18    2    3    4
 2   12    0    5
 3    0   10    2
 4    5    2   28

Community Data Matrix

 1    6    9
 2    5    6
 3    4    5
 4    8   14
```

Figure 22.

C	11	12	13	14	15	16	21	22	23	24	25	31	32	33	34	41	42	43	44	45	46	47	48
11	0	0	1	0	1	1	0	0	0	0	0	1	0	0	0	0	0	0	0	0	0	0	0
12	0	0	1	1	1	0	0	0	0	0	0	0	0	0	0	0	0	0	0	0	0	0	1
13	1	1	0	0	1	0	0	0	0	0	1	0	0	0	0	0	0	0	0	0	0	0	0
14	0	1	0	0	1	0	0	0	0	0	0	0	0	0	0	1	0	0	1	0	0	0	0
15	1	1	1	1	0	1	1	0	0	0	0	0	0	0	0	0	0	0	0	0	0	0	0
16	1	0	0	0	1	0	0	0	0	0	0	0	1	1	0	1	0	0	0	0	0	0	0
21	0	0	0	0	1	0	0	1	1	1	1	0	0	0	0	0	0	0	0	0	0	0	1
22	0	0	0	0	0	0	1	0	0	1	0	0	0	0	0	0	1	1	0	0	0	0	0
23	0	0	0	0	0	0	1	0	0	0	1	0	0	0	0	0	0	0	1	0	0	0	0
24	0	0	0	0	0	0	1	1	0	0	0	0	0	0	0	0	0	0	0	0	0	0	0
25	0	0	1	0	0	0	1	0	1	0	0	0	0	0	0	0	0	0	0	0	0	1	0
31	1	0	0	0	0	0	0	0	0	0	0	0	1	1	1	0	0	0	0	1	0	0	0
32	0	0	0	0	0	1	0	0	0	0	0	1	0	1	0	0	0	0	0	0	0	0	0
33	0	0	0	0	0	1	0	0	0	0	0	1	1	0	1	0	0	0	0	0	0	0	0
34	0	0	0	0	0	0	0	0	0	0	0	1	0	1	0	0	0	0	0	0	1	0	0
41	0	0	0	1	0	1	0	0	0	0	0	0	0	0	0	0	0	0	0	1	1	0	1
42	0	0	0	0	0	0	0	1	0	0	0	0	0	0	0	0	0	0	0	1	0	0	1
43	0	0	0	0	0	0	0	1	0	0	0	0	0	0	0	0	0	0	0	0	1	1	1
44	0	0	0	1	0	0	0	0	1	0	0	0	0	0	0	0	0	0	0	1	1	0	0
45	0	0	0	0	0	0	0	0	0	0	0	1	0	0	0	1	1	0	1	0	1	1	1
46	0	0	0	0	0	0	0	0	0	0	0	0	0	0	1	1	0	1	1	1	0	1	0
47	0	0	0	0	0	0	0	0	0	0	1	0	0	0	0	0	0	1	0	1	1	0	0
48	0	1	0	0	0	0	1	0	0	0	0	0	0	0	0	1	1	1	0	1	0	0	0

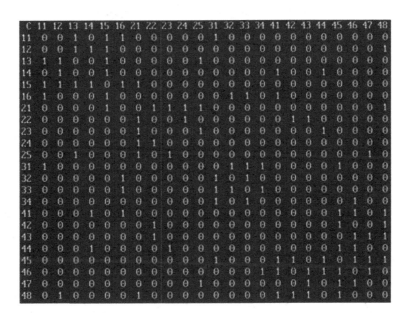

Figure 23.

```
Enter Community Number From [ 1  2  3  4  ] : 4

Sub-Community:-4 Adjacency Matrix

C4   41   42   43   44   45   46   47   48
41    0    0    0    0    1    1    0    1
42    0    0    0    0    1    0    0    1
43    0    0    0    0    0    1    1    1
44    0    0    0    0    1    1    0    0
45    1    1    0    1    0    1    1    1
46    1    0    1    1    1    0    1    0
47    0    0    1    0    1    1    0    0
48    1    1    1    0    1    0    0    0
```

GRAPH PARTITIONS

When a graph is divided into two sets of nodes by removing the edges that connect nodes in different sets should be minimized. While cutting the graph into two sets of nodes so that both the sets contain approximately equal number of nodes or vertices by Rajaraman et al (2011).

In "Figure 24" graph G_1 has seven nodes $\{V_1, V_2, V_3, V_4, V_5, V_6, V_7\}$. After cutting into two parts approximately equal in size, the first partition has nodes $\{V_1, V_2, V_3, V_4\}$ and the second partition has nodes $\{V_5, V_6, V_7\}$. The cut consists of only the edge (V_3, V_5) and the size of edge is 1. In "Figure 25" graph G2 has eight nodes $\{V_1, V_2, V_3, V_4, V_5, V_6, V_7, V_8\}$. Here two edges, (V_3, V_7) and (V_2, V_6) are used to cut the graph into two parts of equal size rather than cutting at the edge (V_5, V_8). The partition at the edge (V_5, V_8) is too small. So the authors reject the cut and choose the best one for cut consisting of edges (V_2, V_6) and (V_3, V_7), which partitions the graph into two equal sets of nodes $\{V_1, V_2, V_3, V_4\}$ and $\{V_5, V_6, V_7, V_8\}$. A good cut always balance the size of cut itself against the sizes of the sets of created cut by Rajaraman et al (2011). For this normalized cut method is being used. First it has to define the volume of set of nodes or vertices V which is denoted as Vol (V) is the number of edges with at least one end in the set of nodes or vertices V. Let us partition the nodes of a graph into two disjoint sets say A

Figure 24.

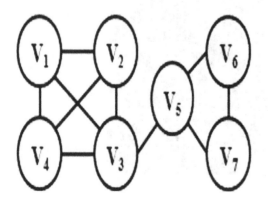

Figure 25.

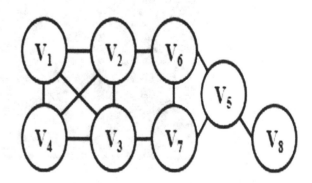

and B. So the Cut (A, B) is the number of edges from the disjoint set A to connect a node in the disjoint set B. The formula for normalized cut values for disjoint sets A and B = Cut (A, B)/Vol (A) + Cut (A, B)/Vol (B). Partition of graph means a division in clusters, such that similar kinds of vertices belong to a particular cluster by Rajaraman et al (2011). In a real world vertices may share among different communities. When a graph is divided into overlapping communities then it is called a cover. To partition a graph having different levels of structure at different scales by Ravasz et al (2002), the partitions can be ordered hierarchically. So in this situation cluster plays an important role. Each cluster displays the community structure independently, which consists of set of smaller communities. Partitioning of a graph means dividing the vertices in a group of predefined size. So the frequently used vertices are often combined together to form a cluster by using some techniques. Many algorithms perform a partition of graph by means of bisecting the graph. Iterative bisection method is employed to partition a graph into more than two clusters and this algorithm is called as Kernighan-Lin by Kernighan et al (1970). Another popular bisection method is the spectral bisection method by Barnes (1982), is completely based on the properties of spectrum of the Laplacian matrix. This algorithm is considered as quiet fast. According to Ford et al (1956) theorem that the minimum cut between any two vertices U and V of a graph G, is any minimum number of subset of edges whose deletion would separate U from V, and carries maximum flow from U to V across the graph G. The algorithms of Goldberg et al (1988), Flake et al (2000), and Flake et al (2002) are used to compute maximum flows in graphs during cut operation. Some other popular methods for graph partition are level-structure partition, the geometric algorithm, and multilevel algorithms by Ravasz et al (2002).

PROPOSED ALGORITHM

Algorithm Community_Graph_Partition()

Algorithm Convention by Horowitz et al (1998)

```
// Community_Data.Txt: Contains total number of communities, community numbers
// (codes), total number of community members, and the community IDs.
// Edge_Data.Txt: Contains from community members and to community members ID.
// n: To assign total communities.
// tcm: To assign total community members.
// NCM[n][100]: To assign the community code and number of community members.
// CMM[tcm+1][tcm+1]: To assign the community member codes and the edge values
i.e. 0 or 1 //between the community members.
{
Read_Community_Data("Community_Data.Txt");
Community_Member_Matrix("Edge_Data.Txt");
Assign_Community_Member_Codes( );
// writing community member matrix before partition in text file "CommunityMa-
trix.Txt"
Write_Community_Matrix("CommunityMatrix.Txt");
a:=1; b:=0;  // row-side initial and final index
```

```
c:=1; d:=0;  // column-side initial and final index
for i:=1 to n do
{
    b:=b + NCM[i][2];
    for j:=1 to n do
    {
     d:=d + NCM[j][2];
     // 'i' is the row-side community code and 'j' is the column-side commu-
nity code
     Community_Graph_Partition(i, a, b, j, c, d);
     c := (d+1);
    }
    a:=(b+1);
    c:=1;
    d:=0;
}
// writing community member matrix after partition in file "PartitionCommuni-
tyMatrix.Txt"
Write_Community_Matrix("PartitionCommunityMatrix.Txt");
s:=0;
for i:=1 to n do
{
// writing community code NCM[i][1]'s adjacency matrix in text file "NCM[i]
[1].Txt"
s:=s+NCM[i][2];
Write_Sub_Community_Matrix(s, NCM[i][1]);
}
}
```

PROCEDURE TO READ COMMUNITY DATA OF COMMUNITY GRAPH

Procedure Read_Community_Data(DataFileName)

```
{
open(DataFileName); // opening for reading
// reading total number of community codes from DataFileName
read(n);
// reading 'n' community details such as community code, number of community
members,
// and community member codes
```

```
for i:=1 to n do
{
   read(NCM[i][1], NCM[i][2]);
   tcm:=tcm+NCM[i][2];
       for j:=1 to NCM[i][2] do
           read(NCM[i][j+2]);
   }
close(DataFileName);
//assign actual codes in the matrix CMM[][]
k := 2;
for i:=1 to n do
   for j:=1 to NCM[i][2] do
     {
         CMM[k][1]:=CMM[1][k]:=NCM[i][j+2];
         k:=k+1;
     }
}
```

PROCEDURE TO GENERATE AND ASSIGN COMMUNITY CODES IN COMMUNITY MEMBER MATRIX

Procedure Assign_Community_Member_Codes()

```
{
 k := 2;
 for i:=1 to n do
 {
    for j:=1 to NCM[i][2] do
   {
       if (NCM[i][j+2]>=1 && NCM[i][j+2]<=9) then Pro:=10;
       if (NCM[i][j+2]>=10 && NCM[i][j+2]<=99) then Pro:=100;
       if (NCM[i][j+2]>=100 && NCM[i][j+2]<=999) then Pro:=1000;

    CMM[1][k] := CMM[k][1] := (NCM[i][0]*Pro) + NCM[i][j+2];
    k:=k+1;
     }
   }
}
```

PROCEDURE TO CREATE COMMUNITY MEMBER MATRIX BY READING FROM NODE AND TO NODE DATA FROM FILE

Procedure Community_Member_Matrix(DataFileName)

```
{
  open(DataFileName); // opening for reading
 // reading from community code and to community code from 'DataFileName' and
assign to
 // the matrix CMM[][]
  while(Not EOF())
  do
   {
     // assign from community code to node1 and to community code to node2
     read(node1, node2);
     //row-side community code's index detection
     for i:=1 to tcm do
        if(CMM[i+1][1]=node1) then break;
     //column-side community code's index detection
     for j:=1 to tcm do
        if (CMM[1][j+1]=node2) then break;
     //Assign 1 to CMM[i+1][j+1]'s position
      CMM[i+1][j+1]:=CMM[j+1][i+1]:=1;
   }
    close(DataFileName);
}
```

PROCEDURE TO WRITE COMMUNITY MEMBER MATRIX IN TEXT FILE BEFORE AND AFTER PARTITION

Procedure Write_Community_Matrix(FileName)

```
{
  // opening file for writing community adjacency matrix from CMM[][]
  open(FileName);
  for i:=1 to (tcm+1) do
  {
    for j:=1 to (tcm+1) do
    {
       if(i=1 and j=1) then write("CCode");
       else write(CMM[i][j]);
```

```
      }
   }
      close(FileName);
}
```

PROCEDURE TO WRITE SUB-COMMUNITY MATRICES IN TEXT FILES

Procedure Write_Sub_Community_Matrix(size, code)

```
{
  x:=2; //static kind
  count := x;
  FileName:=code + ".Txt";
  open(FileName); // opening for writing
  for i:=count to size do
 {
    if (CMM[i][1]>=1 and CMM[i][1]<=9) then div1:=1;
    if (CMM[i][1]>=10 and CMM[i][1]<=99) then div1:=10;
    if (CMM[i][1]>=100 and CMM[i][1]<=999) then div1:=100;
    if (CMM[i][1]>=1000 and CMM[i][1]<=9999) then div1:=1000;
    if (CMM[i][1]>=10000 and CMM[i][1]<=99999) then div1:=10000;
    for j:=count to size do
   {
      if (CMM[1][j]>=1 and CMM[1][j]<=9) then div2:=1;
      if (CMM[1][j]>=10 and CMM[1][j]<=99) then div2:=10;
      if (CMM[1][j]>=100 and CMM[1][j]<=999) then div2:=100;
      if (CMM[1][j]>=1000 and CMM[1][j]<=9999) then div2:=1000;
      if (CMM[1][j]>=10000 and CMM[1][j]<=99999) then div2:=10000;
      if (code>=10) then {div1:=div1/10;  div2:=div2/10;}  // only for double
digit code
      if (i = count and j = count) then write("C", code);
      else if (i = count and j ≠ count) then write(CMM[1][j] mod div2);
      else if (i ≠ count and j = count) then write(CMM[i][1] mod div1);
      else write(CMM[i][j]);
   }
      x:=x+1;
  }
      x:=x-1;
      close(FileName);
}
```

PROCEDURE FOR PARTITIONING COMMUNITY GRAPH

Procedure Community_Graph_Partition(RC, ri, rf, CC, ci, cf)

```
// RC: Row-side community code,   CC: Column-side community code
// ri, rf: Row-side initial and final index
// ci, cf: Column-side initial and final index
{
    for i:=ri to rf do
    {
      if (CMM[i+1][1]>=1 and CMM[i+1][1]<=9) then div1:=1;
      if (CMM[i+1][1]>=10 and CMM[i+1][1]<=99) then div1:=10;
      if (CMM[i+1][1]>=100 and CMM[i+1][1]<=999) then div1:=100;
      if (CMM[i+1][1]>=1000 and CMM[i+1][1]<=9999) then div1:=1000;
      if (CMM[i+1][1]>=10000 and CMM[i+1][1]<=99999) then div1:=10000;
      if (RC>=10) then div1:=div1/10;
      for j:=ci to cf do
      {
        if (CMM[1][j+1]>=1 and CMM[1][j+1]<=9) then div2:=1;
        if (CMM[1][j+1]>=10 and CMM[1][j+1]<=99) then div2:=10;
        if (CMM[1][j+1]>=100 and CMM[1][j+1]<=999) then div2:=100;
        if (CMM[1][j+1]>=1000 and CMM[1][j+1]<=9999) then div2:=1000;
        if (CMM[1][j+1]>=10000 and CMM[1][j+1]<=99999) then div2:=10000;
        if (CC>=10) then div2:=div2/10;
        num1:=CMM[i+1][1]/div1;   num2:=CMM[1][j+1]/div2;
        if (num1≠num2) then
            //cut-off edge between communities of different group of communi-
ties
            CMM[i+1][j+1]:=0;
      }
    }
}
```

The proposed algorithm has three phases. Phase-I is to read data from the text file "Community_Data.Txt" which contains total number of communities, community numbers (codes), total number of community members, and the community IDs. Then the community member matrix, CMM[][] is assigned with the edge data (i.e. 0s and 1s) from the text file "Edge_Data.Txt" which contains "from community members" and "to community members" ID. Finally, it starts generating and assigning community member codes in the community member matrix, CMM[][]. So Phase-1 is about the formation of community member matrix, CMM[][] with the necessary edge data is filled and later it is used for manipulation. Phase-II is to write the community member matrix data in a text file before partition. The procedure Community_Graph_Partition() is to locate the community members edge between the dissimilar communities whose value is 1 (i.e., edge) in the community member matrix, CMM[][]. These 1s are assigned with 0s in the community member matrix which leads to cut-off the edges between the community members of dissimilar communities. The community member matrix, CMM[][] is said to be the partitioned community member matrix and then it is to be written in a text file. So Phase-2 is about writing the actual community matrix in a text file, partitioning the community matrix, and writing the partitioned community member matrix in a text file. Finally, Phase-III is to write 'n' number of sub-community matrices from partitioned community member matrix, CMM[][] in 'n' corresponding text files.

EXAMPLE

The authors have proposed a community graph by Rao et al (ICHPCA 2014) and Rao et al (ICCIC 2014) with twenty two community members from four different communities $\{C_1, C_2, C_3, C_4\}$ depicted in "Figure 26". Here the authors partition the graph into four sub-community graphs of communities $\{C_1, C_2, C_3, C_4\}$. The black lines indicate the edge between the community members of similar communities. Similarly the blue lines indicate the edge between the community members of dissimilar communities. Further the authors represent this graph in memory in an adjacency matrix form depicted in "Figure 27".

The black filled boxes indicate the edge between the community members of dissimilar communities depicted in "Figure 27". So these edges need to cut. Once such edges are cut successfully, then the original community graph is said to be partitioned into so many sub-community graphs. To do so the authors assign 0 over 1 in the adjacency matrix of the community graph which leads to cut-off and depicted in "Figure 28". It indicates that there is no edge between those community members across the dissimilar communities. Finally the authors have retrieved four different adjacency matrices for the communities C_1, C_2, C_3, and C_4 from "Figure 28" and depicted in "Figure 29". For C_1 the community members are $\{11, 12, 13, 14, 15, 16\}$. Hence C_1 community's Id is 1 which is prefixed the community members. Similarly for C_2, C_3, and C_4 the community members are $\{21, 22, 23, 24, 25\}$, $\{31, 32, 33, 34\}$, and $\{41, 42, 43, 44, 45, 46, 47, 48\}$ respectively. Similarly for community C_2, C_3, and C_4, their community members are prefixed with the Ids 2, 3, and 4 respectively. Finally the adjacency matrix of community graph has four sub-community adjacency matrices. The authors have successfully constructed four sub-community graphs depicted in "Figure 30" from these four sub-community adjacency

Figure 26.

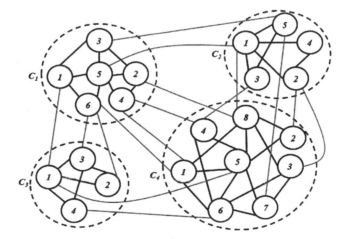

matrices. The proposed method is a different one from Rajaraman et al (2011), Barnes (1982), Ford et al (1956), Kernighan et al (1970), Pothen (1997), and Ravasz et al (2002) and it is about to partitioning a community graph into sub-community graphs. The community graph's nodes are labeled with a number. Further the community members of similar kind are prefixed with same community Id. So based on community Id, the edge between the community members could be of similar kind or dissimilar kind. When the community Id of two community members is different than that edge is considered as dissimilar kind community members' edge and such edges are to be cut by assigning 0. But the similar kind community members' edges remain intact. After partition, similar kinds of community members' graph are considered as sub-community graphs. The proposed method is completely based on graph theoretic concepts. Further the time complexity of the proposed algorithm is $O(n^3)$.

Figure 27.

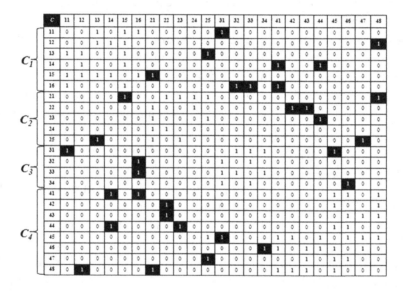

Figure 28.

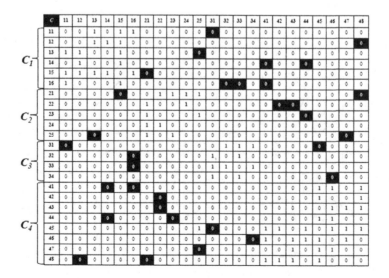

Figure 29.

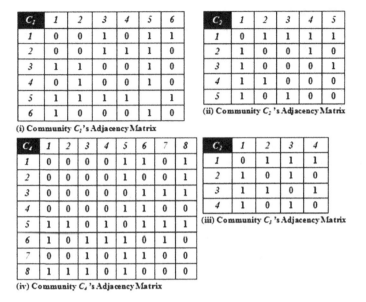

C_1	1	2	3	4	5	6
1	0	0	1	0	1	1
2	0	0	1	1	1	0
3	1	1	0	0	1	0
4	0	1	0	0	1	0
5	1	1	1	1	0	1
6	1	0	0	0	1	0

(i) Community C_1's Adjacency Matrix

C_2	1	2	3	4	5
1	0	1	1	1	1
2	1	0	0	1	0
3	1	0	0	0	1
4	1	1	0	0	0
5	1	0	1	0	0

(ii) Community C_2's Adjacency Matrix

C_4	1	2	3	4	5	6	7	8
1	0	0	0	0	1	1	0	1
2	0	0	0	0	1	0	0	1
3	0	0	0	0	0	1	1	1
4	0	0	0	0	1	1	0	0
5	1	1	0	1	0	1	1	1
6	1	0	1	1	1	0	1	0
7	0	0	1	0	1	1	0	0
8	1	1	1	0	1	0	0	0

(iv) Community C_4's Adjacency Matrix

C_3	1	2	3	4
1	0	1	1	1
2	1	0	1	0
3	1	1	0	1
4	1	0	1	0

(iii) Community C_3's Adjacency Matrix

Figure 30.

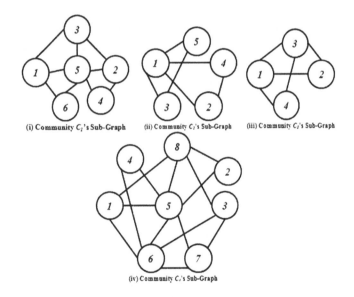

(i) Community C_1's Sub-Graph   (ii) Community C_2's Sub-Graph   (iii) Community C_3's Sub-Graph

(iv) Community C_4's Sub-Graph

EXPERIMENTAL RESULTS

The network of American football games between Division IA Colleges during regular season fall 2000, as compiled by Girvan et al (2002). The authors have considered the above benchmark example of football team community graph with twelve groups $\{C_1, C_2, C_3, C_4, C_5, C_6, C_7, C_8, C_9, C_{10}, C_{11}, C_{12}\}$ and 115 football teams for partitioning to form twelve sub-community graphs depicted in "Figure 31". The similar grouped football teams are circled in a dotted line. The edge between the footballs teams of dissimilar football group are shown with color lines. So the edge represent a match is played between those pair of football teams. Each node has values that indicate to which group the football team (node) belongs. The values are as follows: 1=Atlantic Coast, 2=Big East, 3=Big Ten, 4=Big Twelve, 5=Conference USA, 6=Independents, 7=Mid American, 8=Mountain West, 9=Pacific Ten, 10=South Eastern, 11=Sun Belt and 12=Western Athletic.

Example

There are total 115 football teams. Each team is treated as a node and each node is assigned with ID ranging from 1 to 115. These 115 football teams are distributed among twelve numbers of groups. Group–1 has nine numbers of football teams and the football team IDs are 2, 26, 34, 38, 46, 90, 104, 106, and 110. Similarly Group–2 to Group–12 has total number of football teams are 8, 11, 12, 10, 5, 13, 8, 10, 12, 7, and 10 respectively. These details are stored in a text file called "Community_Data.Txt" and considered as first dataset to the proposed algorithm and depicted in "Figure 32". The edges between "from football team ID" and "to football team ID" are stored in a text file called "Edge_Data.Txt" and depicted in "Figure 33". This text file is considered as the second dataset to the proposed algorithm.

Upon inputting the datasets to the experiment, the algorithm's Read_Community_Data ("Community_Data.Txt") procedure read the details of community data such as total number of communities, community numbers (or codes), total number of community members, and the community IDs. The procedure Community_Member_Matrix("Edge_Data.Txt") read the details such as "from community members ID" and "to community members ID". Using the above data available, the community member matrix, CMM[][] was assigned with the edge data (i.e., 0s and 1s). Then the procedure Assign_Community_Member_Codes() generated community member codes and assigned to community member matrix, CMM[][]. Before and after partition the community member matrix, these two matrices were written in two text files as results and depicted in "Figure 34" and "Figure35". After partition the community member matrix by

Figure 31.

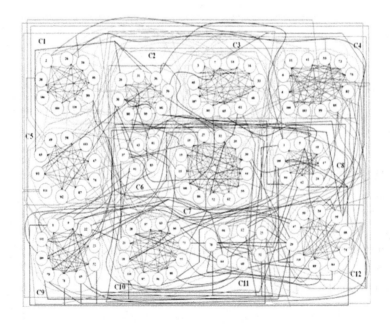

Figure 32.

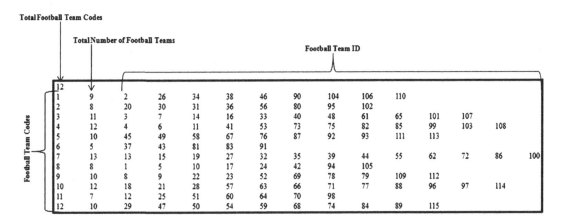

Code	Total	ID	ID	ID	ID	ID	ID	ID	ID	ID	ID	ID	ID	ID
1	9	2	26	34	38	46	90	104	106	110				
2	8	20	30	31	36	56	80	95	102					
3	11	3	7	14	16	33	40	48	61	65	101	107		
4	12	4	6	11	41	53	73	75	82	85	99	103	108	
5	10	45	49	58	67	76	87	92	93	111	113			
6	5	37	43	81	83	91								
7	13	13	15	19	27	32	35	39	44	55	62	72	86	100
8	8	1	5	10	17	24	42	94	105					
9	10	8	9	22	23	52	69	78	79	109	112			
10	12	18	21	28	57	63	66	71	77	88	96	97	114	
11	7	12	25	51	60	64	70	98						
12	10	29	47	50	54	59	68	74	84	89	115			

Figure 33.

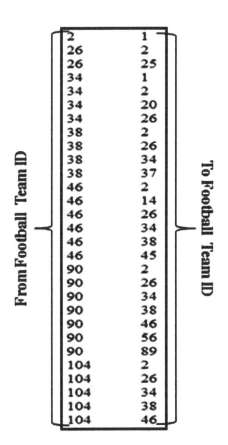

the procedure Community_Graph_Partition(), twelve numbers of sub-community matrices were created and written to twelve text files as results and depicted from "Figure 36", "Figure 37", "Figure 38", "Figure 39", "Figure 40", "Figure 41", "Figure 42", "Figure 43", "Figure 44", "Figure 45", "Figure 46", "Figure 47". The algorithm was written in C++ and compiled with DevC++. The experiment was run on Intel Core I5-3230M CPU + 2.60 GHz Laptop with 4GB memory running MS-Windows 7.

Result

After partitioning football team graph, twelve text files namely "1.txt" to "12.txt" were formed and depicted from "Figure 36" to "Figure 47". By using these twelve text files, the authors have drawn twelve sub-community graphs of football teams namely C_1 to C_{12} and depicted in "Figure 48".

Figure 34.

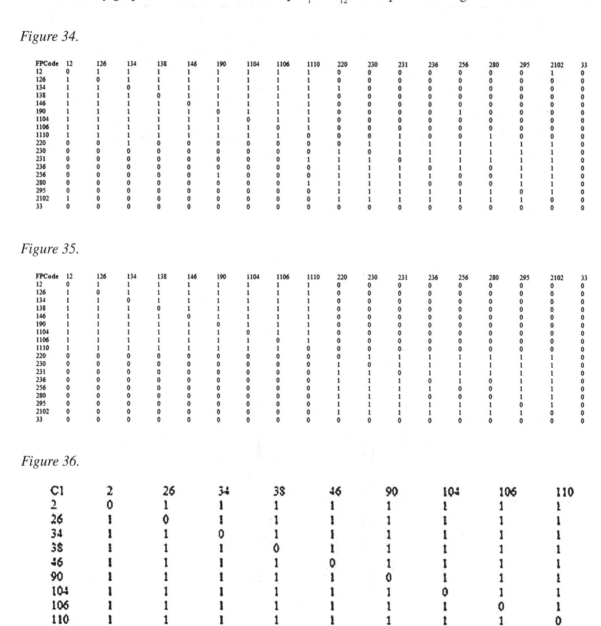

FPCode	12	126	134	138	146	190	1104	1106	1110	220	230	231	236	256	280	295	2102	33
12	0	1	1	1	1	1	1	1	1	0	0	0	0	0	0	0	1	0
126	1	0	1	1	1	1	1	1	1	0	0	0	0	0	0	0	0	0
134	1	1	0	1	1	1	1	1	1	1	0	0	0	0	0	0	0	0
138	1	1	1	0	1	1	1	1	1	0	0	0	0	0	0	0	0	0
146	1	1	1	1	0	1	1	1	1	0	0	0	0	0	0	0	0	0
190	1	1	1	1	1	0	1	1	1	0	0	0	0	1	0	0	0	0
1104	1	1	1	1	1	1	0	1	1	0	0	0	0	0	0	0	0	0
1106	1	1	1	1	1	1	1	0	1	0	0	0	0	0	0	0	0	0
1110	1	1	1	1	1	1	1	1	0	0	0	1	0	0	1	0	0	0
220	0	0	1	0	0	0	0	0	0	0	1	1	1	1	1	1	1	0
230	0	0	0	0	0	0	0	0	0	1	1	1	1	1	1	1	1	0
231	0	0	0	0	0	0	0	0	0	1	1	0	1	1	1	1	1	0
236	0	0	0	0	0	0	0	0	0	1	1	1	0	1	0	1	1	0
256	0	0	0	0	0	1	0	0	0	1	1	1	1	0	0	1	1	0
280	0	0	0	0	0	0	0	0	1	1	1	1	1	0	0	1	1	0
295	0	0	0	0	0	0	0	0	0	1	1	1	1	1	1	0	1	0
2102	1	0	0	0	0	0	0	0	0	1	1	1	1	1	1	1	0	0
33	0	0	0	0	0	0	0	0	0	0	0	0	0	0	0	0	0	0

Figure 35.

FPCode	12	126	134	138	146	190	1104	1106	1110	220	230	231	236	256	280	295	2102	33
12	0	1	1	1	1	1	1	1	1	0	0	0	0	0	0	0	0	0
126	1	0	1	1	1	1	1	1	1	0	0	0	0	0	0	0	0	0
134	1	1	0	1	1	1	1	1	1	0	0	0	0	0	0	0	0	0
138	1	1	1	0	1	1	1	1	1	0	0	0	0	0	0	0	0	0
146	1	1	1	1	0	1	1	1	1	0	0	0	0	0	0	0	0	0
190	1	1	1	1	1	0	1	1	1	0	0	0	0	0	0	0	0	0
1104	1	1	1	1	1	1	0	1	1	0	0	0	0	0	0	0	0	0
1106	1	1	1	1	1	1	1	0	1	0	0	0	0	0	0	0	0	0
1110	1	1	1	1	1	1	1	1	0	0	0	0	0	0	0	0	0	0
220	0	0	0	0	0	0	0	0	0	0	1	1	1	1	1	1	1	0
230	0	0	0	0	0	0	0	0	0	1	0	1	1	1	1	1	1	0
231	0	0	0	0	0	0	0	0	0	1	1	0	1	1	1	1	1	0
236	0	0	0	0	0	0	0	0	0	1	1	1	0	1	0	1	1	0
256	0	0	0	0	0	0	0	0	0	1	1	1	1	0	0	1	1	0
280	0	0	0	0	0	0	0	0	0	1	1	1	0	0	0	1	1	0
295	0	0	0	0	0	0	0	0	0	1	1	1	1	1	1	0	1	0
2102	0	0	0	0	0	0	0	0	0	1	1	1	1	1	1	1	0	0
33	0	0	0	0	0	0	0	0	0	0	0	0	0	0	0	0	0	0

Figure 36.

C1	2	26	34	38	46	90	104	106	110
2	0	1	1	1	1	1	1	1	1
26	1	0	1	1	1	1	1	1	1
34	1	1	0	1	1	1	1	1	1
38	1	1	1	0	1	1	1	1	1
46	1	1	1	1	0	1	1	1	1
90	1	1	1	1	1	0	1	1	1
104	1	1	1	1	1	1	0	1	1
106	1	1	1	1	1	1	1	0	1
110	1	1	1	1	1	1	1	1	0

Figure 37.

C2	20	30	31	36	56	80	95	102
20	0	1	1	1	1	1	1	1
30	1	0	1	1	1	1	1	1
31	1	1	0	1	1	1	1	1
36	1	1	1	0	1	0	1	1
56	1	1	1	1	0	0	1	1
80	1	1	1	0	0	0	1	1
95	1	1	1	1	1	1	0	1
102	1	1	1	1	1	1	1	0

Figure 38.

C3	3	7	14	16	33	40	48	61	65	101	107
3	0	1	1	1	0	0	1	1	1	1	1
7	1	0	0	0	1	1	1	1	1	1	1
14	1	0	0	1	1	1	0	1	1	1	1
16	1	0	1	0	1	1	1	1	0	1	1
33	0	1	1	1	0	1	1	0	1	1	1
40	0	1	1	1	1	0	1	1	0	1	1
48	1	1	0	1	1	1	0	1	1	1	0
61	1	1	1	1	0	1	1	0	1	0	1
65	1	1	1	0	1	0	1	1	0	1	1
101	1	1	1	1	1	1	1	0	1	0	0
107	1	1	1	1	1	1	0	1	1	0	0

Figure 39.

C4	4	6	11	41	53	73	75	82	85	99	103	108
4	0	1	0	1	1	1	1	1	1	0	1	0
6	1	0	1	0	1	0	1	1	1	1	0	1
11	0	1	0	0	0	1	1	1	1	1	1	1
41	1	0	0	0	1	1	1	1	0	1	1	1
53	1	1	0	1	0	1	1	0	1	1	1	0
73	1	0	1	1	1	0	1	1	0	0	1	1
75	1	1	1	1	1	1	0	0	1	0	1	0
82	1	1	1	1	0	1	0	0	1	1	0	1
85	1	1	1	0	1	0	1	1	0	1	0	1
99	0	1	1	1	1	0	0	1	1	0	1	1
103	1	0	1	1	1	1	1	0	0	1	0	1
108	0	1	1	1	0	1	0	1	1	1	1	0

Figure 40.

C5	45	49	58	67	76	87	92	93	111	113
45	0	1	1	1	1	1	1	0	0	1
49	1	0	1	1	1	1	1	1	0	0
58	1	1	0	0	1	1	1	1	0	1
67	1	1	0	0	1	1	1	1	0	1
76	1	1	1	1	0	1	0	1	0	1
87	1	1	1	1	1	0	0	1	0	0
92	1	1	1	1	0	0	1	0	0	1
93	0	1	1	1	1	1	1	0	0	1
111	0	0	0	0	0	0	0	0	0	0
113	1	0	1	1	1	0	1	1	0	0

Figure 41.

C6	37	43	81	83	91
37	0	0	0	0	0
43	0	0	0	0	0
81	0	0	0	1	0
83	0	0	1	0	0
91	0	0	0	0	0

Figure 42.

C7	13	15	19	27	32	35	39	44	55	62	72	86	100
13	0	1	1	1	0	1	1	1	0	0	0	1	0
15	1	0	0	1	0	0	1	1	1	0	1	1	1
19	1	0	0	0	1	1	1	0	1	1	1	0	1
27	1	1	0	0	0	1	1	1	0	1	0	1	0
32	0	0	1	0	0	1	0	1	1	1	1	1	1
35	1	0	1	1	1	0	0	0	1	1	1	0	1
39	1	1	1	1	0	0	0	1	1	0	1	1	0
44	1	1	0	1	1	0	1	0	0	1	0	1	0
55	0	1	1	0	1	1	1	0	0	1	1	0	1
62	0	0	1	1	1	1	0	1	1	0	1	0	1
72	0	1	1	0	1	1	1	0	1	1	0	0	1
86	1	1	0	1	1	0	1	1	0	0	0	0	1
100	0	1	1	0	1	1	0	0	1	1	1	1	0

Figure 43.

CS	1	5	10	17	24	42	94	105
1	0	1	1	1	1	1	1	1
5	1	0	1	1	1	1	1	1
10	1	1	0	1	1	1	1	1
17	1	1	1	0	1	1	1	1
24	1	1	1	1	0	1	1	1
42	1	1	1	1	1	0	1	1
94	1	1	1	1	1	1	0	1
105	1	1	1	1	1	1	1	0

Figure 44.

C9	8	9	22	23	52	69	78	79	109	112
8	0	1	1	1	0	1	1	1	1	1
9	1	0	1	1	1	1	1	1	0	1
22	1	1	0	1	1	1	1	0	1	1
23	1	1	1	0	1	1	1	1	1	0
52	0	1	1	1	0	1	1	1	1	1
69	1	1	1	1	1	0	0	1	1	1
78	1	1	1	1	1	0	0	1	1	1
79	1	1	0	1	1	1	1	0	1	1
109	1	0	1	1	1	1	1	1	0	1
112	1	1	1	0	1	1	1	1	1	0

Figure 45.

C10	18	21	28	57	63	66	71	77	88	96	97	114
18	0	1	1	0	1	1	0	0	1	1	1	1
21	1	0	0	0	1	1	1	1	1	0	1	1
28	1	0	0	1	1	1	1	1	0	1	1	0
57	0	0	1	0	1	1	1	1	1	1	1	0
63	1	1	1	1	0	0	1	1	1	1	0	0
66	1	1	1	1	0	0	1	0	1	0	1	1
71	0	1	1	1	1	1	0	1	0	1	0	1
77	0	1	1	1	1	0	1	0	0	1	1	1
88	1	1	0	1	1	1	0	0	0	1	1	1
96	1	0	1	1	1	0	1	1	1	0	0	1
97	1	1	1	1	0	1	0	1	1	0	0	1
114	1	1	0	0	0	1	1	1	1	1	1	0

Figure 46.

C11	12	25	51	60	64	70	98
12	0	1	1	0	0	1	1
25	1	0	1	0	0	1	0
51	1	1	0	0	0	1	0
60	0	0	0	0	1	0	1
64	0	0	0	1	0	0	1
70	1	1	1	0	0	0	0
98	1	0	0	1	1	0	0

Figure 47.

C12	29	47	50	54	59	68	74	84	89	115
29	0	0	0	0	0	0	0	0	0	0
47	0	0	1	1	0	1	1	1	1	1
50	0	1	0	1	0	1	1	1	1	1
54	0	1	1	0	0	1	1	1	1	1
59	0	0	0	0	0	0	0	0	1	1
68	0	1	1	1	0	0	1	1	1	1
74	0	1	1	1	0	1	0	1	1	1
84	0	1	1	1	0	1	1	0	1	1
89	0	1	1	1	1	1	1	1	0	1
115	0	1	1	1	1	1	1	1	1	0

PROPOSED METHOD FOR SIMILARITY BETWEEN TWO COMMUNITY GRAPHS

In the literature survey the authors have studied thoroughly the existing methods for checking similarity of two graphs. In this paper the authors have proposed graph mining techniques for checking of similarity between two community graphs. Further the authors have proposed a community graph which is depicted in "Figure 49". For similarity measure of two community graphs, the authors have first compressed both the community graphs. Then the compressed community graphs are used for comparison for similarity. The authors have adopted the compression of large community graph to smaller one technique can be seen in Rao et al (2015).

Figure 48.

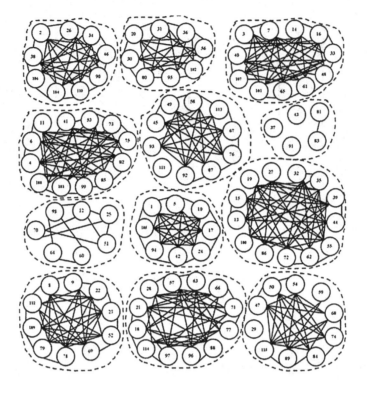

Figure 49.

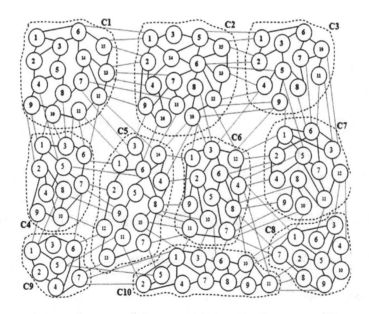

The authors have proposed a village community graph having ten communities namely C_1 to C_{10}, and the total number of community members is 118. The black color edge represents the edge among the community members of similar communities. Whereas the blue color edge represents the edge among the community members of dissimilar communities. To compress the community graph to a smaller one depicted in "Figure 49", the authors have adopted the logic from Rao et al (2015). The compressed community graph is depicted in "Figure 50". Then its corresponding adjacency matrix is represented in the memory which is depicted in "Figure 51". In this weighted adjacency matrix, the self-loop of community has some weight which is considered as total number of edges among the community members of that particular community. Similarly the edge between the pair of communities is considered as the total number of edges between the community members of dissimilar communities. For this proposed approach, the authors have considered "Figure 49" community graph as the principle community graph

Figure 50.

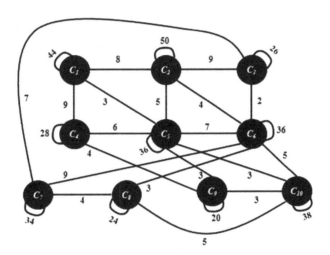

Figure 51.

		C_1	C_2	C_3	C_4	C_5	C_6	C_7	C_8	C_9	C_{10}
	C_1	44	8	0	9	3	0	0	0	0	0
	C_2	8	50	9	0	5	4	0	0	0	0
	C_3	0	9	26	0	0	2	7	0	0	0
	C_4	9	0	0	28	6	0	0	0	4	0
	C_5	3	5	0	6	36	7	0	0	3	3
	C_6	0	4	2	0	7	36	9	3	0	5
	C_7	0	0	7	0	0	9	34	4	0	0
	C_8	0	0	0	0	0	3	4	24	0	5
	C_9	0	0	0	4	3	0	0	0	20	3
	C_{10}	0	0	0	0	3	5	0	5	3	38

Community Members Edges of Particular Community / Community Codes

for comparison with six more community graphs namely CG_2 to CG_7. Before comparison these six community graphs i.e., CG_2 to CG_7's adjacency matrices are compressed and represented in the memory. Finally, the principle community graph CG_1's compressed adjacency matrix is compared with all the six community graphs i.e., CG_2 to CG_7's compressed adjacency matrices for similarity check. The details of all the seven community graphs, CG_1 to CG_7 are considered as datasets for the proposed algorithm is listed in Table 1.

PROPOSED ALGORITHM

Algorithm Community_Graph_Similarity ()

Algorithm Convention by Horowitz et al (Galgotia Publications)

```
//CG1, CG2: Given two community graphs with 'n1' and 'n2' number of community
members.
//tcm1, tcm2: To assign total community members of community graphs CG1 and
CG2.
//NCM1[n1][2], NCM2[n2][2]: Matrices to hold community member's community num-
ber and //number of community //members of CG1 and CG2.
//CMM1[tcm1+1][tcm1+1], CMM2[tcm2+1][tcm2+1]: Adjacency matrices of CG1 and
CG2.
//CCM1[n1][n1], CCM2[n2][n2]: Adjacency matrices of compressed community graphs
of  CG1 and //CG2.
//commun1.txt, commun2.txt: Text file contains number of communities, and com-
munity code and //their total number of  community members of CG1 and CG2.
//data1.txt, data2.txt: Text file contains edge details of CG1 and CG2.
//flag: To assign the similarity check value from 0 to 3.
{
  n1:=RCD (NCM1, "commun1.txt");  // CG1 details
  n2:=RCD (NCM2, "commun2.txt");  // CG2 details
  tcm1:=ACMC (NCM1, n1, CMM1, CCM1);
  tcm2:=ACMC (NCM2, n2, CMM2, CCM2);
  CMMatrix (CMM1, tcm1, "data1.txt");
  CMMatrix (CMM2, tcm2, "data2.txt");
  SCED (NCM1, n1, CMM1, CCM1);
  SCED (NCM2, n2, CMM2, CCM2);
  DCED (NCM1, n1, CMM1, tcm1, CCM1);
  DCED (NCM2, n2, CMM2, tcm2, CCM2);
  flag:=CS (CCM1, n1, CCM2, n2);
if(flag=0) then write("Both the Community Graphs are not Similar");
if(flag=1) then write("Both the Community Graphs are Similar");
if(flag=2) then write("Both the Community Graphs are Similar on Similar Edg-
es");
```

```
if(flag=3) then write("Both the Community Graphs are Similar on Dissimilar
Edges");
}
```

PROCEDURE FOR COMMUNITY DATA READ

Procedure RCD (NCM, FileName)

```
// n: To assign number of communities.
// cc: To assign community code.
// tcm: To assign total community members
{
    open(FileName);
    read(n);
    for i:=2 to (n+1) do
    {
       read(cc, tcm);
       NCM[i-1][1]:=cc;
       NCM[i-1][2]:=tcm;
     }
     close(FileName);
     return(n);
}
```

PROCEDURE FOR ASSIGNMENT OF COMMUNITY MEMBER CODES

Procedure ACMC (NCM, n, CMM, CCM)

```
// k: index variable, tcm: to count total community members
{
   k:=2;
   tcm:=0;
 for i:=1 to n do
 {
    tcm:=tcm+NCM[i][2];
   for j:=1 to NCM[i][2] do // assignment of community codes in community mem-
ber matrix
   {
      CMM[1][k]:=CMM[k][1]:=j;
      k:=k+1;
   }
 }
```

```
//assignment of community codes in compressed community matrix CCM[][]
   for i:=2 to (n+1) do
   {
      CCM[i][1]:= CCM[1][i]:= NCM[i-1][1];
    }
    return(tcm);
}
```

PROCEDURE FOR COMMUNITY MEMBER MATRIX CREATION

Procedure CMMatrix (CMM, tcm, FileName)

```
{
   open(FileName);
   i:=2;
   j:=2;
   while (i ≠ (tcm+1)) do
   {
      read(data);
      if (j=(tcm+1)) then { i:=i+1;    j:=2; }
      CMM[i][j]:=data;
      j:=j+1;
    }
      close(FileName);
}
```

PROCEDURE FOR SAME COMMUNITY EDGE DETECTION

Procedure SCED (NCM, n, CMM, CCM)

```
{
   d:=1;
   s:=0;
  for i:=1 to n do
  {
      s:= s + NCM[i][2];
        for j:=d to s do
          for k:=d to s do
      if (CMM[j+1][k+1]=1) then
         CCM[i+1][i+1]:=CCM[i+1][i+1]+1;   //check for edge at CMM[j+1][k+1]
      d:=s;
```

```
   }
}
```

PROCEDURE FOR COUNTING DISSIMILAR EDGES

Procedure DCED (NCM, n, CMM, tcm, CCM)

```
{
   a:=1;
   b:=NCM[1][2];
   c:=b;
   d:=b;
   for i:=2 to (n+1) do
   {
      d:= d + NCM[i][2];
      // to count dissimilar communities edges
      Count_Edge (i-1, a, b, c, d, NCM, CMM, tcm, CCM);
      a:=b;
      b:=b + NCM[i][2];
      c:=d;
   }
}
```

PROCEDURE TO COUNT DISSIMILAR COMMUNITIES EDGES

Procedure Count_Edge (p, a, b, c, d, NCM, CMM, tcm, CCM)

```
// a, b: Initial and final index of row.
// c, d: Initial and final index of column.
// p: Initial index of CCM[][].
{
   x:= c;
   y:=d;
   k:=p+1;
   for i:=a to b do
   {
       k:=p+1;
   Smiley:
      for j:=c to d do
   if(CMM[i+1][j+1]=1) then
 {
CCM[p+1][k+1]:=CCM[p+1][k+1]+1;    // row-side dissimilar community edges
```

```
counting
CCM[k+1][p+1]:=CCM[k+1][p+1]+1;    // column-side dissimilar community edges
counting
 }
      k:=k+1;
      if(d<tcm) then
     {
         c:=d;
         d:=d+NCM[k][2];
         goto Smiley;
     }
      c:=x;
      d:=y;
    }
}
```

PROCEDURE FOR SIMILARITY CHECK BETWEEN COMMUNITY MATRICES

Procedure CS (CCM1, n1, CCM2, n2)

```
{
    flag:=flag1:=flag2:=count:=0;
    if(n1 ≠ n2) then return(0); // both the community graphs are dissimilar
    else
    {
       // arrange both matrices in ascending order
       Arrange(CCM1, n1);
       Arrange(CCM2, n2);

       // check for dissimilar communities
      for i:=2 to (n1+1) do
        for j:=2 to (n2+1) do
           if(CCM1[1][i]=CCM2[1][j]) then count:=count+1;
       if(count=n1) then flag:=1; else flag:=0;
       // check for same communities
       if(flag=1) then
       {
          // check for same number of edges of each communities
          for i:=2 to (n1+1) or (n2+1) do
              if(CCM1[i][i] ≠ CCM2[i][i]) then
              {
                   flag1:=1;
                   break;
```

```
               }
        // check for different number of edges among communities
           for i:=2 to (n1+1) do
              for j:=2 to (n2+1) do
                 if(j>i) then
                     if(CCM1[i][j] ≠ CCM2[i][j])  then
                     {
                         flag2:=1;
                         break;
                     }
        if(flag1=1 and flag2=1) then return(0);   // same number communities
but different
                                                          // num-
ber of similar and dissimilar edges
        else if(flag1=0 and flag2=1) then return(2);   // similarity on similar
edges
        else if(flag1=1 and flag2=0) then return(3);   // similarity on dissim-
ilar edges
        else return(1);            // same number of similar and dissimilar edges
     }
    else
          return(0);         // number of communities same but not its community
codes (numbers)
     }
}
```

PROCEDURE FOR SORTING OF COMPRESSED COMMUNITY MATRIX

Procedure Arrange (mat, n)

```
// t[]: temporary array for swap.
{
// row-side community code arrangement
    for i:=2 to n do
      for j:=i+1 to (n+1) do
        if(mat[i][1]>mat[j][1]) then
           for k:=1 to (n+1) do
           {
             t[k]:=mat[i][k];
             mat[i][k]:=mat[j][k];
             mat[j][k]:=t[k];
           }
// column-side community code arrangement
```

```
for i:=2 to n do
  for j:=i+1 to (n+1) do
    if(mat[1][i]>mat[1][j]) then
      for k:=1 to (n+1) do
      {
        t[k]:=mat[k][i];
        mat[k][i]:=mat[k][j];
        mat[k][j]:=t[k];
      }
}
```

The proposed algorithm has three phases. Phase-1 is to open for reading four dataset files. The dataset files "commun1.txt" and "commun2.txt" for reading number of communities, and community code and their total number of community members of two community graphs CG_1 and CG_2, and assign to the matrices NCM1[][] and NCM2[][] respectively. Similarly two more dataset files "data1.txt" and "data2.txt" for reading edge details of two community graphs CG_1 and CG_2, and assign to the matrices CMM1[][] and CMM2[][] respectively. So Phase-1 is about read data and creation of community member matrices, and creation of initial form of compressed community matrices. Phase-2 for counting edges of community members of same communities by calling procedure SCED() and counting edges of community members of dissimilar communities by calling procedure DCED(). Using procedures SCED() and DCED(), the compressed community adjacency matrices CCM1[][] and CCM2[][] are assigned with the edge values and self loop values. Finally, Phase-3 for comparison of both the compressed community matrices by calling procedure CS(). Further, it returns a numerical value i.e., from 0 to 3. So based on the numerical value, the similarities of both of community graphs are judged. The numerical value 1 for similarity; whereas values 0, 2, and 3 for no similarity between communities graph CG_1 and CG_2.

EXPLANATION AND EXPERIMENTAL RESULTS

To evaluate the performance of the proposed algorithm, the authors have considered seven community graphs namely CG_1 to CG_7, where 1st community graph CG_1 is considered as principle community graph for comparison with the remaining six community graphs for finding similarities. For the seven examples of community graphs, two sets of dataset files were created for each example of community graphs. The 1st dataset file contains community graph details such as number of communities, community number, and number of community members. So for the seven community graphs, these dataset files are from "datacom1.txt" to "datacom7.txt". Similarly the 2nd dataset file contains community graphs edge details i.e., edge between community members which only consist of 1s and 0s. So for the seven community graphs, these dataset files are from "dataedg1.txt" to "dataedg7.txt". These fourteen dataset file details are depicted in "Table I". The algorithm was written in C++ and compiled with TurboC++ and run on Intel Core I5-3230M CPU +2.60 GHz Laptop with 4GB memory running MS-Windows 7. The comparison results of CG_1 with CG_2 to CG_7 are depicted from "Figure 54" to "Figure 65". The datasets for community graphs CG_1 to CG_7 are in text files from "datacom1.txt" to "datacom7.txt". The "datacom1.txt" is depicted in "Figure 52", which contains the total number of communities, community numbers, and total number of community members. Similarly the datasets for community graphs CG_1

to CG$_7$ are in text files from "dataedg1.txt" to "dataedg7.txt". The "dataedg1.txt" is depicted in "Figure 53", which contains the edge details i.e., 0s (no edge) and 1s (edge) between the community members of similar communities as well as dissimilar communities of the community graphs. The authors have studied the existing techniques of Koutra et al (2011), Melnik et al (2002), Jeh et al (2002), Zager et al (2008), and Kriegel et al (2003) for graph similarity. In Koutra et al (2011) method, two graphs G$_1$(N$_1$, E$_1$) and G$_2$(N$_2$, E$_2$), with possibly different number of nodes and edges for similarity check, then adopting belief propagation (BP) into the proposed method for finding similarity between two graphs which finally returns a similarity value i.e., a real number between 0 and 1.

In Melnik et al (2002) method, the matching of two graphs based on a fixed point computation. It takes two graphs as input, which is preferably a schema or catalog or other data structures for similarity check. Finally, it produces the result as mapping between the corresponding nodes of the graphs. Depending on the matching goal, a sub-set of the mapping is chosen using some filtering methods. Moreover, it allows the user to adjust the results if it is necessary. In Jeh et al (2002) method, to find

Figure 52.

Sl. No.	Community Graphs	Communities	Total Communities	Total Community Members	Number of Edges	Community Data File Name	Community Member Edge File Name
1.	CG$_1$	C$_1$ to C$_{10}$	10	118	435	datacom1.txt	dataedg1.txt
2.	CG$_2$	C$_1$ to C$_{10}$	10	118	466	datacom2.txt	dataedg2.txt
3.	CG$_3$	C$_1$ to C$_{10}$	10	118	439	datacom3.txt	dataedg3.txt
4.	CG$_4$	C$_1$ to C$_{10}$	10	118	471	datacom4.txt	dataedg4.txt
5.	CG$_5$	C$_3$ to C$_8$ C$_{10}$ to C$_{13}$	10	118	434	datacom5.txt	dataedg5.txt
6.	CG$_6$	C$_1$ to C$_{12}$	12	118	515	datacom6.txt	dataedg6.txt
7.	CG$_7$	C$_1$ to C$_{10}$	10	118	435	datacom7.txt	dataedg7.txt

Figure 53.

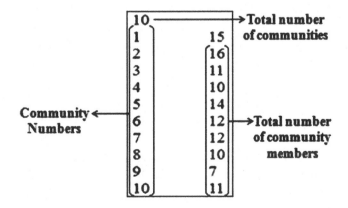

269

Figure 54.

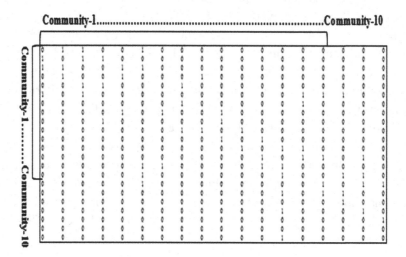

similarity between two objects based on their relationships. Two objects are said to be similar, if they are related to similar objects. This similarity measure is called SimRank. This method is based on simple graph-theoretic model. In Zager et al (2008) method, it is a node-edge coupling i.e., two graph elements is similar if their neighborhoods are similar. So edge score is constructed "when an edge in G_1 is like an edge in G_2 if their respective source and terminal nodes are similar". This is called edge similarity. In Kriegel et al (2003) method, attributed graphs are considered as a natural model for the structured data. The authors proposed a new similarity measure between two attributed graphs, called "matching distance". The matching distance is calculated by sum of the cost for each edge matching. The proposed method in this paper is different from the above existing methods. In the proposed method two community graphs with possibly equal number of nodes (communities) and different number of edges for similarity check. Each node (community) is labeled with a unique community number. Based on the community number of node, the similarity measure takes place by considering the weight of self loop of community as well as the weight of edge between the communities. After similarity between two community graphs, it finally returns a similarity value i.e., a number from 0 to 3. Based on this number, the similarity of two community graphs can be judged. The proposed algorithm has capable of showing similarity and five different ways of dissimilarity. The five different dissimilarities are similar on dissimilar edges, similar on similar edges, communities same but different edges, communities not same, and number of communities are different. Moreover, the proposed method is completely based on labeled community graphs and simple graph-theoretic model. So the authors conclude that the proposed community graph similarity is completely different from the above existing methods as well as it is simple and fast since the time complexity is $O(n^3)$.

COMPARISON OF CG_1 AND CG_2

In community graph CG_1, the community codes (numbers) are $\{C_1, C_2, C_3, C_4, C_5, C_6, C_7, C_8, C_9, C_{10}\}$ with total community members are $\{15, 16, 11, 10, 14, 12, 12, 10, 7, 11\}$. The total number of edges belonging to same community codes member are $\{44, 50, 26, 28, 36, 36, 34, 24, 20, 38\}$. Similarly, the

Figure 55.

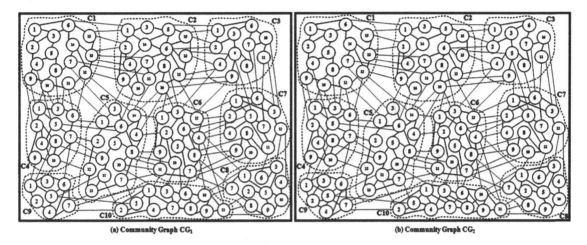

(a) Community Graph CG₁   (b) Community Graph CG₂

Figure 56.

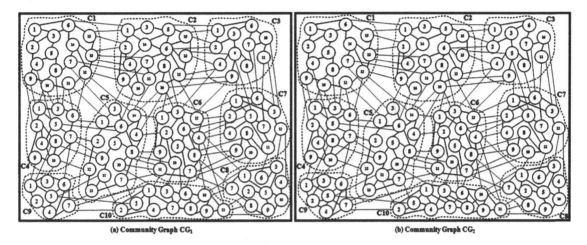

total number of edges belonging to dissimilar community codes member are C_1-C_2:8, C_1-C_4:9, C_1-C_5:3, C_2-C_3:9, C_2-C_5:5, C_2-C_6:4, C_3-C_6:2, C_3-C_7:7, C_4-C_5:6, C_4-C_9:4, C_5-C_6:7, C_5-C_9:3, C_5-C_{10}:3, C_6-C_7:9, C_6-C_8:3, C_6-C_{10}:5, C_7-C_8:4, C_8-C_{10}:5, and C_9-C_{10}:3. In community graph CG_2, the community codes (numbers) are $\{C_1, C_2, C_3, C_4, C_5, C_6, C_7, C_8, C_9, C_{10}\}$ with total community members are $\{15, 16, 11, 10, 14, 12, 12, 10, 7, 11\}$. The total number of edges belonging to same community codes member are $\{44, 46, 24, 32, 42, 42, 38, 28, 26, 46\}$. Similarly, the total number of edges belonging to dissimilar community codes member are C_1-C_2:8, C_1-C_4:9, C_1-C_5:3, C_2-C_3:9, C_2-C_5:5, C_2-C_6:4, C_3-C_6:2, C_3-C_7:7, C_4-C_5:6, C_4-C_9:4,

C_5-C_6:7, C_5-C_9:3, C_5-C_{10}:3, C_6-C_7:9, C_6-C_8:3, C_6-C_{10}:5, C_7-C_8:4, C_8-C_{10}:5, and C_9-C_{10}:3. The comparison takes place on community graph CG_1 and CG_2's community codes and number of edges belonging to dissimilar community codes member since these two is same. So finally the algorithm shows as "Both the Community Graphs are Similar on Dissimilar Edges".

COMPARISON OF CG_1 AND CG_3

In community graph CG_1, the community codes (numbers) are $\{C_1, C_2, C_3, C_4, C_5, C_6, C_7, C_8, C_9, C_{10}\}$ with total community members are $\{15, 16, 11, 10, 14, 12, 12, 10, 7, 11\}$. The total number of edges belonging to same community codes member are $\{44, 50, 26, 28, 36, 36, 34, 24, 20, 38\}$. Similarly, the total number of edges belonging to dissimilar community codes member are C_1-C_2:8, C_1-C_4:9, C_1-C_5:3, C_2-C_3:9, C_2-C_5:5, C_2-C_6:4, C_3-C_6:2, C_3-C_7:7, C_4-C_5:6, C_4-C_9:4, C_5-C_6:7, C_5-C_9:3, C_5-C_{10}:3, C_6-C_7:9, C_6-C_8:3, C_6-C_{10}:5, C_7-C_8:4, C_8-C_{10}:5, and C_9-C_{10}:3. In community graph CG_3, the community codes (numbers) are $\{C_1, C_2, C_3, C_4, C_5, C_6, C_7, C_8, C_9, C_{10}\}$ with total community members are $\{15, 16, 11, 10, 14, 12, 12, 10, 7, 11\}$. The total number of edges belonging to same community codes member are $\{44, 50, 26, 28, 36, 36, 34, 24, 20, 38\}$. Similarly, the total number of edges belonging to dissimilar community codes member are C_1-C_2:7, C_1-C_4:7, C_1-C_5:3, C_2-C_3:10, C_2-C_5:6, C_2-C_6:4, C_3-C_6:3, C_3-C_7:7, C_4-C_5:6, C_4-C_9:4, C_5-C_6:8, C_5-C_9:3, C_5-C_{10}:3, C_6-C_7:9, C_6-C_8:3, C_6-C_{10}:7, C_7-C_8:4, C_8-C_{10}:5, and C_9-C_{10}:3. The comparison takes place on community graph CG_1 and CG_3's community codes and number of edges belonging to similar community codes member since these two is same. So finally the algorithm shows as "Both the Community Graphs are Similar on Similar Edges".

Figure 57.

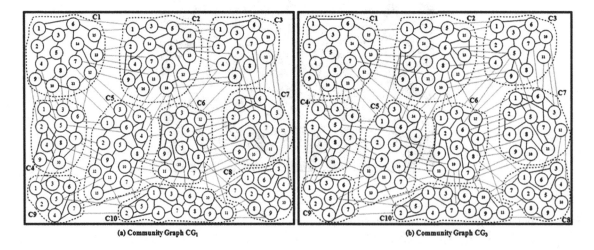

(a) Community Graph CG₁   (b) Community Graph CG₃

Figure 58.

```
< Enter 1st Community Graph's Details >

Enter the Community Data File Name :  datacom1.txt

Enter the Edge Data File Name :  dataedg1.txt

< Enter 2nd Community Graph's Details >

Enter the Community Data File Name :  datacom3.txt

Enter the Edge Data File Name :  dataedg3.txt

Press Any Key to see the 1st Compressed Adjacency Matrix

1st Compressed Community Graph's Adjacency Matrix

C    1    2    3    4    5    6    7    8    9   10
1   44    8    0    9    3    0    0    0    0    0
2    8   50    9    0    5    4    0    0    0    0
3    0    9   26    0    0    2    7    0    0    8
4    9    0    0   28    6    0    0    0    1    0
5    3    5    0    6   36    7    0    0    3    3
6    0    4    2    0    7   36    9    3    0    5
7    0    0    7    0    0    9   34    4    0    0
8    0    0    0    0    0    3    4   24    0    5
9    0    0    0    4    3    0    0    0   20    3
10   0    0    0    0    3    5    0    5    3   38

Press Any Key to see the 2nd Compressed Adjacency Matrix

2nd Compressed Community Graph's Adjacency Matrix

C    1    2    3    4    5    6    7    8    9   10
1   44    7    0    7    3    0    0    0    0    0
2    7   50   10    0    6    4    0    0    0    0
3    0   10   26    0    0    3    7    0    0    0
4    7    0    0   28    6    0    0    0    5    0
5    3    6    0    6   36    8    0    0    3    3
6    0    4    3    0    8   36    9    3    0    7
7    0    0    7    0    0    9   34    4    0    0
8    0    0    0    0    0    3    4   24    0    5
9    0    0    0    5    3    0    0    0   20    3
10   0    0    0    0    3    7    0    5    3   38

Press Any Key to Compare Both Compressed Adjacency Matrices

Both the Community Graphs are Similar on Similar Edges
```

COMPARISON OF CG_1 AND CG_4

In community graph CG_1, the community codes (numbers) are $\{C_1, C_2, C_3, C_4, C_5, C_6, C_7, C_8, C_9, C_{10}\}$ with total community members are $\{15, 16, 11, 10, 14, 12, 12, 10, 7, 11\}$. The total number of edges belonging to same community codes member are $\{44, 50, 26, 28, 36, 36, 34, 24, 20, 38\}$. Similarly, the total number of edges belonging to dissimilar community codes member are C_1-C_2:8, C_1-C_4:9, C_1-C_5:3,

Figure 59.

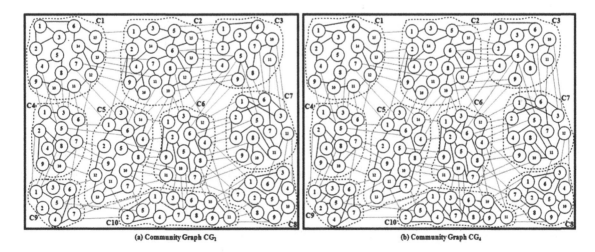

(a) Community Graph CG_1 (b) Community Graph CG_4

Figure 60.

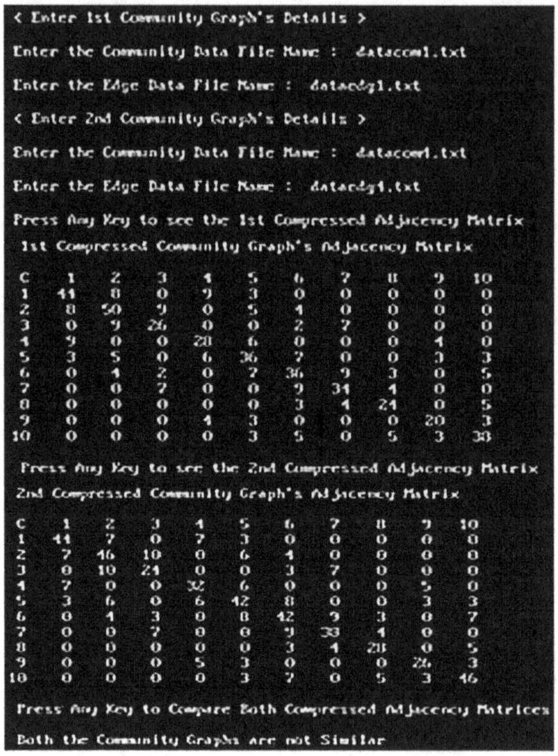

C_2-C_3:9, C_2-C_5:5, C_2-C_6:4, C_3-C_6:2, C_3-C_7:7, C_4-C_5:6, C_4-C_9:4, C_5-C_6:7, C_5-C_9:3, C5-C_{10}:3, C_6-C_7:9, C_6-C_8:3, C_6-C_{10}:5, C_7-C_8:4, C_8-C_{10}:5, and C_9-C_{10}:3. In community graph CG_4, the community codes (numbers) are $\{C_1, C_2, C_3, C_4, C_5, C_6, C_7, C_8, C_9, C_{10}\}$ with total community members are {15, 16, 11, 10, 14, 12, 12, 10, 7, 11}. The total number of edges belonging to same community codes member are {44, 46, 24, 32, 42, 42, 38, 28, 26, 46}. Similarly, the total number of edges belonging to dissimilar community codes member are C_1-C_2:7, C_1-C_4:7, C_1-C_5:3, C_2-C_3:10, C_2-C_5:6, C_2-C_6:4, C_3-C_6:3, C_3-C_7:7, C_4-C_5:6, C_4-C_9:5, C_5-C_6:8, C_5-C_9:3, C_5-C_{10}:3, C_6-C_7:9, C_6-C_8:3, C_6-C_{10}:7, C_7-C_8:4, C_8-C_{10}:5, and C_9-C_{10}:3. The comparison takes place on community graph CG_1 and CG_4's number of edges belonging to similar community codes member and number of edges belonging to dissimilar community codes member since these two are not same. So finally the algorithm shows as "Both the Community Graphs are not Similar".

COMPARISON OF CG_1 AND CG_5

In community graph CG_1, the community codes (numbers) are $\{C_1, C_2, C_3, C_4, C_5, C_6, C_7, C_8, C_9, C_{10}\}$ with total community members are {15, 16, 11, 10, 14, 12, 12, 10, 7, 11}. The total number of edges belonging to same community codes member are {44, 50, 26, 28, 36, 36, 34, 24, 20, 38}. Similarly, the total number of edges belonging to dissimilar community codes member are C_1-C_2:8, C_1-C_4:9, C_1-C_5:3, C_2-C_3:9, C_2-C_5:5, C_2-C_6:4, C_3-C_6:2, C_3-C_7:7, C_4-C_5:6, C_4-C_9:4, C_5-C_6:7, C_5-C_9:3, C_5-C_{10}:3, C_6-C_7:9, C_6-C_8:3, C_6-C_{10}:5, C_7-C_8:4, C_8-C_{10}:5, and C_9-C_{10}:3. In community graph CG_5, the community codes (numbers) are $\{C_3, C_5, C_{10}, C_4, C_6, C_8, C_{11}, C_7, C_{12}, C_{13}\}$ with total community members are {15, 16, 11, 10, 14,

Figure 61.

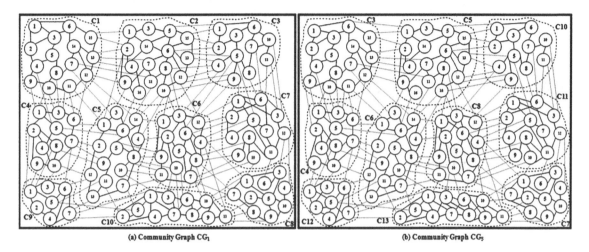

(a) Community Graph CG₁ 　　　　　　　　　　　　　　(b) Community Graph CG₅

Figure 62.

```
< Enter 1st Community Graph's Details >

Enter the Community Data File Name :  datacom1.txt

Enter the Edge Data File Name :  dataedg1.txt

< Enter 2nd Community Graph's Details >

Enter the Community Data File Name :  datacom5.txt

Enter the Edge Data File Name :  dataedg5.txt

Press Any Key to see the 1st Compressed Adjacency Matrix
1st Compressed Community Graph's Adjacency Matrix

 C    1    2    3    4    5    6    7    8    9   10
 1   44    8    0    9    3    0    0    0    0    0
 2    8   50    9    0    5    4    0    0    0    0
 3    0    9   26    0    0    2    7    0    0    0
 4    9    0    0   28    6    0    0    0    4    0
 5    3    5    0    6   36    7    0    0    3    3
 6    0    4    2    0    7   36    9    3    0    5
 7    0    0    7    0    0    9   34    4    0    0
 8    0    0    0    0    0    3    4   24    0    5
 9    0    0    0    4    3    0    0    0   20    3
10    0    0    0    0    3    5    0    5    3   38

Press Any Key to see the 2nd Compressed Adjacency Matrix
2nd Compressed Community Graph's Adjacency Matrix

 C    3    5   10    4    6    8   11    7   12   13
 3   44    8    0    8    3    0    0    0    0    0
 5    8   50    9    0    5    4    0    0    0    0
10    0    9   26    0    0    2    7    0    0    0
 4    8    0    0   28    6    0    0    0    4    0
 6    3    5    0    6   36    7    0    0    3    3
 8    0    4    2    0    7   36    9    3    0    5
11    0    0    7    0    0    9   34    4    0    0
 7    0    0    0    0    0    3    4   24    0    5
12    0    0    0    4    3    0    0    0   20    3
13    0    0    0    0    3    5    0    5    3   38

Press Any Key to Compare Both Compressed Adjacency Matrices

Both the Community Graphs are not Similar
```

12, 12, 10, 7, 11}. The total number of edges belonging to same community codes member are {44, 50, 26, 28, 36, 36, 34, 24, 20, 38}. Similarly, the total number of edges belonging to dissimilar community codes member are C_3-C_5:8, C_3-C_4:8, C_3-C_6:3, C_5-C_{10}:9, C_5-C_6:5, C_5-C_8:4, C_{10}-C_8:2, C_{10}-C_{11}:2, C_4-C_6:6, C_4-C_{12}:4, C_6-C_8:7, C_4-C_{12}:3, C_6-C_{13}:3, C_8-C_{11}:9, C_8-C_7:3, C_8-C_{13}:5, C_{11}-C_7:4, C_7-C_{13}:5, and C_{12}-C_{13}:3. The comparison takes place on community graph CG_1 and CG_5's community codes. Since the community codes of community graphs CG_1 and CG_5 are not same. So the algorithm shows as "Both the Community Graphs are not similar".

COMPARISON OF CG_1 AND CG_6

In community graph CG_1, the community codes (numbers) are $\{C_1, C_2, C_3, C_4, C_5, C_6, C_7, C_8, C_9, C_{10}\}$ with total community members are $\{15, 16, 11, 10, 14, 12, 12, 10, 7, 11\}$. The total number of edges belonging to same community codes member are $\{44, 50, 26, 28, 36, 36, 34, 24, 20, 38\}$. Similarly, the total number of edges belonging to dissimilar community codes member are C_1-C_2:8, C_1-C_4:9, C_1-C_5:3, C_2-C_3:9, C_2-C_5:5, C_2-C_6:4, C_3-C_6:2, C_3-C_7:7, C_4-C_5:6, C_4-C_9:4, C_5-C_6:7, C_5-C_9:3, C_5-C_{10}:3, C_6-C_7:9, C_6-C_8:3, C_6-C_{10}:5, C_7-C_8:4, C_8-C_{10}:5, and C_9-C_{10}:3. In community graph CG_6, the community codes (numbers) are $\{C_1, C_2, C_3, C_4, C_5, C_6, C_7, C_8, C_9, C_{10}, C_{11}, C_{12}\}$ with total community members are $\{15, 16, 11, 10, 14, 12, 12, 10, 7, 11, 9, 11\}$. The total number of edges belonging to same community codes member are $\{44, 50, 26, 28, 36, 36, 34, 24, 20, 38, 26, 38\}$. Similarly, the total number of edges belonging to dissimilar community codes member are C_1-C_2:8, C_1-C_4:8, C_1-C_5:3, C_2-C_3:9, C_2-C_5:5, C_2-C_6:4, C_3-C_6:2, C_3-C_7:7, C_4-C_5:6, C_4-C_9:4, C_5-C_6:7, C_5-C_9:3, C_5-C_{10}:3, C_6-C_7:9, C_6-C_8:3, C_6-C_{10}:5, C_7-C_8:4, C_8-C_{10}:5, C_8-C_{12}:2, C_9-C_{10}:3, C_9-C_{11}:2, C_{10}-C_{11}:4, C_{10}-C_{12}:4, and C_{11}-C_{12}:5. The comparison takes place on community graph CG_1 and CG_6's community codes. Since the number of community codes of community graphs CG_1 and CG_6 are not same. So the algorithm shows as "Both the Community Graphs are not similar."

Figure 63.

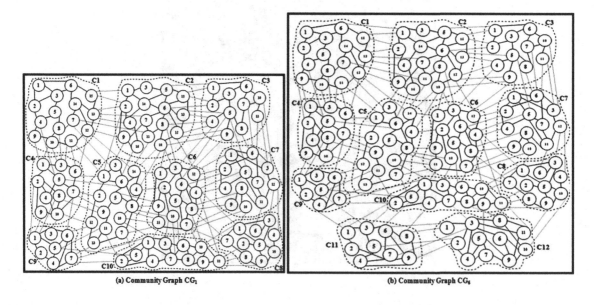

(a) Community Graph CG_1 (b) Community Graph CG_6

Figure 64.

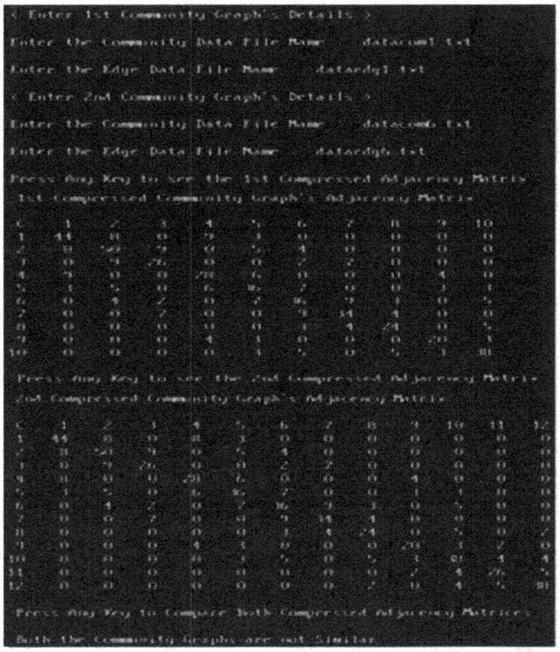

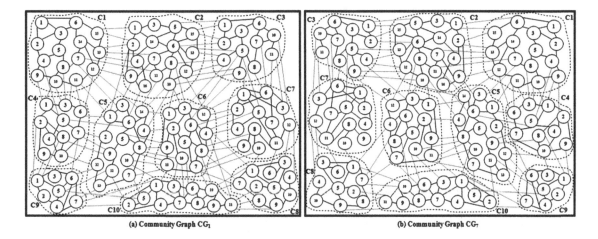

COMPARISON OF CG₁ AND CG₇

In community graph CG_1, the community codes (numbers) are $\{C_1, C_2, C_3, C_4, C_5, C_6, C_7, C_8, C_9, C_{10}\}$ with total community members are $\{15, 16, 11, 10, 14, 12, 12, 10, 7, 11\}$. The total number of edges belonging to same community codes member are $\{44, 50, 26, 28, 36, 36, 34, 24, 20, 38\}$. Similarly, the total number of edges belonging to dissimilar community codes member are C_1-C_2:8, C_1-C_4:9, C_1-C_5:3, C_2-C_3:9, C_2-C_5:5, C_2-C_6:4, C_3-C_6:2, C_3-C_7:7, C_4-C_5:6, C_4-C_9:4, C_5-C_6:7, C_5-C_9:3, C_5-C_{10}:3, C_6-C_7:9, C_6-C_8:3, C_6-C_{10}:5, C_7-C_8:4, C_8-C_{10}:5, and C_9-C_{10}:3. In community graph CG_7, the community codes (numbers) are

Figure 65.

(a) Community Graph CG₁

(b) Community Graph CG₇

Figure 66.

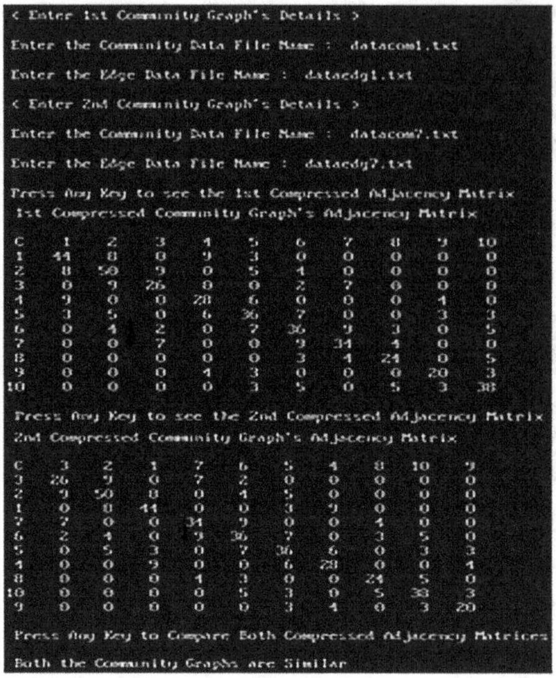

$\{C_3, C_2, C_1, C_7, C_6, C_5, C_4, C_8, C_{10}, C_9\}$ with total community members are $\{11, 16, 15, 12, 12, 14, 10, 10, 11, 7\}$. The total number of edges belonging to same community codes member are $\{26, 50, 44, 34, 36, 36, 28, 24, 38, 20\}$. Similarly, the total number of edges belonging to dissimilar community codes member are C_3-C_2:9, C_3-C_7:7, C_3-C_6:2, C_2-C_1:8, C_2-C_6:4, C_2-C_5:5, C_1-C_5:3, C_1-C_4:9, C_7-C_6:9, C_7-C_8:4, C_6-C_5:7, C_6-C_8:3, C_6-C_{10}:5, C_5-C_4:6, C_5-C_{10}:3, C_5-C_9:3, C_4-C_9:4, C_8-C_{10}:5, and C_{10}-C_9:3. The comparison takes place on community graph CG_1 and CG_7's community codes. Since the community codes of community graphs CG_1 and CG_7 are same. Then the comparison takes place on number of edges belonging to similar community codes member and number of edges belonging to dissimilar community codes member. So finally the algorithm shows as "Both the Community Graphs are Similar".

The chapter algorithms are designed on the basic principle of graph theory, since graph theory is the essential concept related to any network representation as graphs. To represent any network in memory, it requires a matrix. So matrix is the fundamental concept of mathematics. Based on this, the authors have designed this chapter algorithm by using fundamental concepts of graphs and matrices. Hence the readers can easily understand. In the result area of all the four algorithms, the output has been explained in details. This technique has not been tried by any other researcher earlier in a community network. Hence the authors have tried their level best by adopting the graph and matrix techniques to make easier and understandable to the readers.

CONCLUSION

The initial section of chapter explains the definitions and notations on graph theory, and followed by literature surveys. The first section discusses on compression of large village community graph using proposed graph mining techniques. Visualization and analyzing large community graph are challenging and to process a large community graph, compression techniques may be used. There should not be any loss of information or knowledge while compressing the community graph. For this the authors have proposed a similar technique for compressing the large community graphs, which is suitable for carrying out steps of graph mining. The second section focuses on retrieval of sub-community graphs from a compressed community graph using graph mining techniques. Community detection is important as it constitutes a significant role for analysis of a large community graph by enabling and selecting the desired sub-community graph. Community detection is important as it constitutes a significant role for analysis of a large community graph by enabling and selecting the desired sub-community graph. For this the authors have proposed an algorithm to extract a sub-community graph from a compressed community graph after expanding it to a large community graph for analysis using graph mining techniques. The third section focuses on partitioning community graph into sub-community graphs. For this the authors have proposed an algorithm using graph mining techniques. To run the algorithm, the authors have considered a benchmark dataset of football teams as input. The fourth and final section discusses about the similarity between two community graphs. Graph similarity technique is helpful in the fields of shape retrieval, object recognition, face recognition and many more fields. For this purpose the authors have proposed an algorithm for similarity check of two community graphs using graph mining techniques. All the four algorithms proposed in this chapter were implemented using C++ programming language. The outcomes of the algorithms were satisfactory.

REFERENCES

Bagrow, J. P. (2012). *Are communities just bottlenecks? Trees and treelike networks have high modularity*. CoRR, abs/1201.0745.

Barabasi, A. L., & Oltvai, Z. N. (2004). Network biology: Understanding the cells functional organization. *Nature Reviews. Genetics*, *5*(2), 101–113. doi:10.1038/nrg1272 PMID:14735121

Barnes, E. R. (1982). Algebraic Discrete Methods 3. *SIAM Journal*, *4*, 541–550.

Blondel, V. D., Guillaume, J. L., Lambiotte, R., & Lefebvre, E. (2008). *Fast unfolding of communities in large networks*. JSTAT.

Boccaletti, S., Latora, V., Moreno, Y., Chavez, M., & Hwang, D. U. (2006). Complex networks: Structure and dynamics. *Physics Reports*, *424*(4), 175–308. doi:10.1016/j.physrep.2005.10.009

Cha, S.-H. (2007). Comprehensive survey on distance/similarity measures between probability density functions. *International Journal of Mathematical Models and Methods in Applied Sciences*, *1*(4), 300–307.

Cook, D. J., & Holder, L. B. (2000). Graph-based data mining. *Proceedings of IEEE Intelligent Systems*, *15*, 32–41. doi:10.1109/5254.850825

Elsner, U. (1997). *Graph partitioning - A survey.* Technical Report SFB393/97-27. Technische University at Chemnitz.

Feld, S. L. (1981). The focused organization of social ties. *American Journal of Sociology, 86*(5), 1015–1035. doi:10.1086/227352

Fjallstrom, P.O. (1998). Algorithms for graph partitioning: A Survey. *Linkoping Electronic Articles in Computer and Information Science, 3.*

Flake, G. W., Lawrence, S., & Giles, C. L. (2000). Efficient identification of web communities. In *Proceedings of Sixth ACM SIGKDD International Conference on Knowledge Discovery and Data Mining* (pp. 150-160). ACM Press. doi:10.1145/347090.347121

Flake, G. W., Lawrence, S., Giles, C. L., & Coetzee, F. M. (2002). Computer Vision and Pattern Recognition. *IEEE Computer, 35*(3), 66–70. doi:10.1109/2.989932

Ford, L. R., & Fulkerson, D. R. (1956). A Simple Algorithm for Finding Maximal Network Flows and an Application to the Hitchcock Problem. *Canadian Journal of Mathematics, 8*, 399–404. doi:10.4153/CJM-1956-045-5

Fortunato, S., & Barthelemy, M. (2007). Resolution limit in community detection. *Proceedings of the National Academy of Sciences of the United States of America, 104*(1), 36–41. doi:10.1073/pnas.0605965104 PMID:17190818

Gert, S. (1966). The centrality index of a graph. *Psychometrika, 31*(4), 581–603. doi:10.1007/BF02289527 PMID:5232444

Girvan, M., & Newman, M. E. J. (2002). Community structure in social and biological networks. *Proceedings of the National Academy of Sciences of the United States of America, 99*(12), 7821–7826. doi:10.1073/pnas.122653799 PMID:12060727

Goldberg, A. V., & Tarjan, R. E. (1988). A New Approach to the Maximum Flow Problem. *Journal of the ACM, 35*(4), 921–940. doi:10.1145/48014.61051

Horowitz, Sahani, & Rajasekaran. (1998). *Fundamentals of Computer Algorithms.* Galgotia Publications Pvt. Ltd.

Huet, B., Cross, A., & Hancock, E. (1999). Shape retrieval by inexact graph matching. In *Proceedings of IEEE International Conference on Multimedia Computing Systems* (vol. 2, pp. 40–44). IEEE Computer Society Press.

Jeh, G., & Widom, J. (2002). SimRank: A measure of structural-context similarity. In *Proceedings of the eighth ACM SIGKDD International Conference on Knowledge Discovery and Data Mining, KDD '02* (pp. 538–543). doi:10.1145/775047.775126

Kernighan, B. W., & Lin, S. (1970). An Efficient Heuristic Procedure for Partitioning Graph. *The Bell System Technical Journal, 49*(2), 291–307. doi:10.1002/j.1538-7305.1970.tb01770.x

Koutra, Ankur, Aditya, & Jing. (2011). *Algorithms for Graph Similarity and Subgraph Matching.* Retrieved from https://www.cs.cmu.edu/~jingx/docs/DBreport.pdf

Kriegel, H.-P., & Schonauer, S. (2003). Similarity Search in Structured Data. In *Proceedings of 5th International Conference on Data Warehousing and Knowledge Discovery* (pp. 224-233). doi:10.1007/978-3-540-45228-7_23

Kubicka, E., Kubicki, G., & Vakalis, I. (1990). Using graph distance in object recognition. In *Proceedings of ACM Computer Science Conference* (pp. 43–48).

Lancichinetti, A., & Fortunato, S. (2009). Community detection algorithms: A comparative analysis. *Phy. Rev. E*, *80*(5), 056117. doi:10.1103/PhysRevE.80.056117 PMID:20365053

Levenshtein, V. (1966). Binary codes capable of correcting deletions, insertions and reversals. *Soviet Physics, Doklady*, (10), 707–710.

Lipschutz, S. (n.d.). *Schaum's outline of Data Structures*. New Delhi: Tata McGraw-Hill Publishing Company Limited.

Melnik, S., Garcia-Molina, H., & Rahm, E. (2002). Similarity flooding: A versatile graph matching algorithm and its application to schema matching. In *Proceedings of 18th International Conference on Data Engineering* (ICDE 2002).

Mitra, A., Satpathy, S. R., & Paul, S. (2013). Clustering analysis in social network using Covering Based Rough Set. In *Proceedings of Advance Computing Conference* (pp. 476-481). doi:10.1109/IAdCC.2013.6514272

Navlakha, S., Rastogi, R., & Shrivastava, N. (2008). Graph summarization with bounded error. In *Proceedings of the 2008 ACM SIGMOD international conference on Management of data* (pp. 419-432). ACM. doi:10.1145/1376616.1376661

Newman, M. E. J., & Girvan, M. (2004). Finding and evaluating community structure in networks. *Physical Review E: Statistical, Nonlinear, and Soft Matter Physics*, *69*(2), 026113. doi:10.1103/PhysRevE.69.026113 PMID:14995526

Pons, P., & Latapy, M. (2006). Computing communities in large networks using random walks. *Journal of Graph Algorithms Applications*, *10*(2), 191–218. doi:10.7155/jgaa.00124

Pothen, A. (1997). Graph Partitioning Algorithms with Applications to Scientific Computing. Technical Report.

Proceedings of WWW'14 23rd International World Wide Web Conference. (2014). Seoul, South Korea: ACM.

Rajaraman, A., Leskovec, J., & Ullman, J. D. (2011). Mining of Massive Datasets. Cambridge University Press.

Rao, B., & Mitra, A. (2014). An Approach to Merging of two Community Sub-Graphs to form a Community Graph using Graph Mining Techniques. In *Proceedings of 2014 IEEE International Conference on Computational Intelligence and Computing Research* (pp. 460-466). Doi:10.1109/ICCIC.2014.7238392

Rao, B., & Mitra, A. (2014). A new approach for detection of common communities in a social network using graph mining techniques. In *Proceedings of 2014 IEEE International Conference on High Performance Computing and Applications* (pp.1-6). doi:10.1109/ICHPCA.2014.7045335

Rao, B., Mitra, A., & Narayana, U. (2014). An Approach to Study Properties and Behaviour of Social Network Using Graph Mining Techniques. In *Proceedings of DIGNATE 2014: ETEECT 2014* (pp. 13–17).

Rao, B. (2015). An Algorithm for Partitioning Community Graph into Sub-Community Graphs using Graph Mining Techniques. In *Proceedings of 3rd Springer Smart Innovation, Systems and Technologies, ICACNI* (pp. 23–25). Bhubaneswar, India: KIIT University. doi:10.1007/978-81-322-2529-4_1

Rao, B., Mitra, A., & Acharjya, D. P. (2015). A New Approach of Compression of Large Community Graph Using Graph Mining Techniques. In *Proceedings of 3rd ERCICA* (*vol. 1*, pp. 127 – 136). NMIT. Doi:10.1007/978-81-322-2550-8_13

Rao, B., Mitra, A., & Mondal, J. (2015). Algorithm for Retrieval of Sub-Community Graph from a Compressed Community Graph using Graph Mining Techniques. In *Proceedings of 3rd International Conference on Recent Trends in Computing 2015*. SRM University.

Ravasz, E., Somera, A. L., Mongru, D. A., Oltvai, Z. N., & Barabasi, A. L. (2002). Hierarchical Organization of Modularity. *Metabolic Networks. Science*, *297*(5586), 1551–1555. doi:10.1126/science.1073374 PMID:12202830

Rosvall, M., & Bergstrom, C. (2008). Maps of random walks on complex networks reveal community structure. *Proceedings of the National Academy of Sciences of the United States of America*, *105*(4), 1118–1123. doi:10.1073/pnas.0706851105 PMID:18216267

Sanfeliu, A., & Fu, K. S. (1983). A distance measure between attributed relational graphs for pattern recognition. *IEEE Transactions on Systems, Man, and Cybernetics*, *13*(3), 353–362. doi:10.1109/TSMC.1983.6313167

Simmel, G. (1964). *Conflict and the web of group affiliations*. Simon and Schuster.

Tian, Y., Hankins, R., & Patel, J. (2008). Efficient aggregation for graph summarization. In *Proceedings of the 2008 ACM SIGMOD International Conference on Management of data* (pp. 567-580). ACM. doi:10.1145/1376616.1376675

Wagner, R. A., & Fisher, M. J. (1974). The string-to-string correction problem. *Journal of the ACM*, *21*(1), 168–173. doi:10.1145/321796.321811

Wang, Y., Cong, G., Song, G., & Xie, K. (2010). Community-based greedy algorithm for mining top-k influential nodes in mobile social networks. In *Proceedings of SIGKDD* (pp. 1039–1048). ACM. doi:10.1145/1835804.1835935

Watts, D. J. (1999). *Small worlds: the dynamics of networks between order and randomness*. Princeton University Press.

Wiskott, L., Fellous, J. M., Kr¨uger, N., & Von Der Malsburg, C. (1997). Face recognition by elastic bunch graph matching. In *Proceedings of IEEE PAMI* (pp. 775–779). doi:10.1109/ICIP.1997.647401

Yang, J., & Leskovec, J. (2013). Overlapping community detection at scale: a nonnegative matrix factorization approach. In *Proceedings of the Sixth ACM InternationalnConferenceon Web search and data mining* (pp. 587–596). ACM. doi:10.1145/2433396.2433471

Yedidia, J. S., Freeman, W. T., & Weiss, Y. (2003). *Understanding belief propagation and its generalizations*. San Francisco, CA: Morgan Kaufmann Publishers Inc.

Zager, L., & Verghese, G. (2008). Graph similarity scoring and matching. *Applied Mathematics Letters*, *21*(1), 86–94. doi:10.1016/j.aml.2007.01.006

Chapter 15
Social Network Web Mining:
Web Mining Techniques for Online Social Network Analysis

Balamurugan Balusamy
VIT University, India

Vegesna Tarun Sai Varma
VIT University, India

Sohil Sri Mani Yeshwanth Grandhi
VIT University, India

ABSTRACT

Today, social networks are major part of everyone's lives. They provide means to communicate with people across the globe with ease. As of July 2016, there are over 1.71 billion monthly active Facebook users. They generate significant amount of data, which if analysed well will provide us with valuable information. This can be done by analysing the log data collected at the respective social networking service. This chapter focuses on extraction and analysis of Facebook data since it is presently the most used social network. The result of analysis can be used in building decision support systems for an organization to help with the decision making process.

INTRODUCTION

Social Networks have been a major part of everyone's lives since the evolution of the web into Web 2.0 which emphasizes on user-generated content, usability and interoperability. A social network can formally defined as a platform to build social relations among people who share similar interests, backgrounds or real life connections. According to a survey conducted by PewResearchCenter (2015), 72% of American adult internet users use Facebook, as indicated in Table 1. This accounts to about 62% of the entire American adult population.

DOI: 10.4018/978-1-5225-1877-8.ch015

Table 1. Percentage of Social Network Users among American adult Internet Users

Social Network	Internet Users
Facebook	72.00%
Pinterest	31.00%
Instagram	28.00%
LinkedIn	25.00%
Twitter	23.00%

Source: Pew Research Center,March 17-April 12

As there is a huge number of users for Social Networks, there is a lot of data generated. Extracting knowledge from this data can give us a lot of useful information. This is done through social web mining algorithms and techniques. Social Network Mining is a hot research topic since it combines two very interesting research topics: Web Data Mining and Social Network Analysis. Social Network Mining discusses a lot more disciplines than discussed above such as Machine Learning, Network Analysis, Sociology, Ethnography, Statistics and may more. Before we discuss any more Social Network Mining let us see a brief introduction of Web Data Mining.

BACKGROUND: WEB DATA MINING

Overview

Web Mining refers to applying data mining techniques used to extract useful knowledge from patterns on the World Wide Web documents and services. Although Web Mining has deep roots into Data Mining, it converges from Data Mining in a lot of directions. Web Mining also digs into fields like Information Retrieval, Artificial Intelligence, Psychology and Statistics.

Web Mining can be decomposed into the following sub-tasks (Wang, Y., 2000):

- **Resource Discovery:** Refers to retrieving the raw data from the particular web document.
- **Information Extraction:** The task of pre-processing specific information from retrieved Web resources.
- **Generalization:** Discovering general patterns in information retrieved from the target Web document.
- **Analysis:** Analyzing the pattern mined from the document.

Web involves three types of data: data on the Web document (Content), Web user-logs and server-side data (Usage Data) and the HTML tag data(Structure Data).Hence, Web Mining can also be categorized into web content mining, web usage mining and web structure mining respectively.

Web Content Mining

Web content mining is a framework that uses information retrieval, machine learning and data mining techniques for mining the web content data. Web content data is mostly unstructured text data. The unstructured characteristic of the web data forces web content mining to follow a more complicated approach. Web content mining is characterized from two views (Kosala, R., & Blockeel, H., 2000): Information Retrieval View and Database View.

Information Retrieval View and Database View

In information retrieval view, the web document to be mined is taken as a bag of words or vector representation. One of the many methods used to achieve this is Latent Semantic Indexing (LSI) that seeks to transform actual document vectors (bag of words) into a more simplistic form. This is done by reducing the words into their morphological forms. For example, the words "dominating", "domination", "dominated" are taken as their common root word "dominate" and only this word is stored into the document vector. Other techniques used commonly for preprocessing are Text Categorization, Information Extraction and NLP. Information Retrieval View is generally used for unstructured data and semi-structured data. Database view transforms a web document into a database for better information management. This can be achieved by finding the schema for the web document and then building a web warehouse or a virtual database. The database obtained is queried to get the required information from time to time. Database View mainly deals with semi-structured data. Here, semi-structured data refers to data that has some structure but no rigid schema. Web Content Mining focuses on two approaches for organizing the web: Classification and Clustering

Classification and Clustering

Classification is also known as supervised learning or inductive learning in machine learning (Liu, B., 2007). We are given a set of records known as training set. Each record contains set of attributes where one of the attributes is the class. We are interested to predict the value of this discrete class attribute (Srivastava, J., Desikan, P., & Kumar, V., 2002). The objective of supervised learning is to produce a classification/prediction function to predict the class values/labels of unseen or future data using the known knowledge of attributes and class in the training set. This function is called classification model, a predictive model or a classifier as in Figure 1. After a model is learned or built from the training set, it is evaluated using test set (unseen data) to assess the model accuracy.

Clustering is often referred as unsupervised learning. There can be a situation where data has no class attributes. We might want to explore the data and find some intrinsic structures in them. Clustering is one technology for finding such structures (Srivastava, et al., 2002).. Clustering is the process of organizing data instances into groups whose members are similar in some way. These groups are called similarity groups or clusters. A cluster thus is a collection of data instances which are similar to each other and are dissimilar to data instances in other clusters (Liu, B., 2007). We represent these data instances in a r-dimension space, where r is the number of attributes in the data. See Figure 2.

Figure 1. Classification

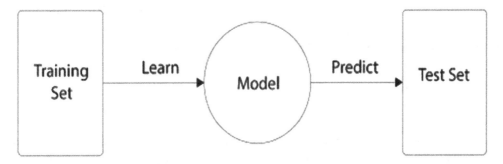

Figure 2. Four clusters of 2-dimensional data set

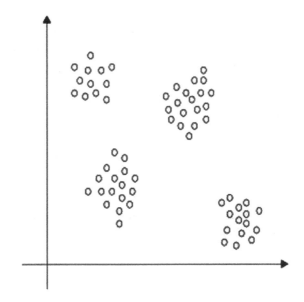

Multimedia Data Mining

Multimedia data mining is a form of web content mining, and refers to mining the content from multimedia web documents. Multimedia data mining is challenging since it requires extraction of knowledge from multimedia like the images from a satellite and videos of eruption of volcanoes on Venus, and not plain text.

Web Structure Mining

Mostly, while retrieving information from a web document, emphasis is given on textual information while the very valuable link information is ignored. The goal of web structure mining is to extract knowledge from the link structure of the hyperlinks at the inter-document level. It is also used to discover the nature of hierarchy in the websites that represent a particular domain, therefore making query processing a lot easier and more efficient. Web structure mining is generally considered to be same as the database view of web content mining. But in the database view of web content mining we are interested in the structure (schema) within the web document (intra-document structure) where as in web structure mining we are interested in the structure of hyperlinks within the web itself (inter-document structure). Web structure mining is inspired a lot from study of social networks and citation analysis.

Social Network Analysis

Social network is the study of actors (people in organization), their interactions and relationship between them. These interactions and relationships can be depicted with a graph or a network. This concept can be extended to Web because Web can be regarded as a virtual social network, where each page can be regarded as a social actor and each hyperlink as a relationship (Liu, B., 2007). There are two main types of social network analysis, centrality and prestige. Both centrality and prestige are measures of degree of prominence of an actor in a social network. Centrality: According to this analysis, important or prominent actors are linked or involved with other actors extensively (Liu, B., 2007). Figure 3 shows a simple example using an undirected graph. Each node is an actor and each link indicates that actors on the two ends of the link can communicate with each other. We can observe that actor i is most central actor as he/she can communicate with most other actors.

There are different types of links or involvements between actors. Thus, several types of centrality are defined on undirected or directed graphs:

- **Degree Centrality:** Central actors are most active actors that have most links or ties with other actors.
- **Closeness Centrality:** This centrality is based on closeness or distance. An actor is central if it can easily interact with all other actors. This means that distance to all other actors should be short. Shortest distance is measured as number of links in a shortest path. The concept is only meaningful for a connected graph.

Figure 3. Social network

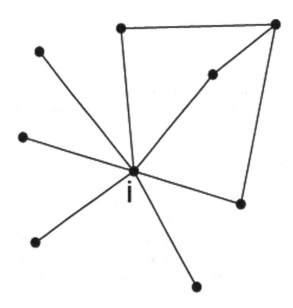

- **Betweenness Centrality:** If two non-adjacent actors j and k want to interact and actor i is on the path between j and k, then i may have some control over their interactions. Betweenness measures this control of i over other pairs of actors. Thus, if i is on the paths of many such interactions, then i is an important actor. This works even when the graph is not connected.
- **Prestige:** It is a refined measure of prominence of an actor than centrality. To compute the prestige of an actor, we only look at the links directed or pointed to the actor (Liu, B., 2007). Hence, the graph should be directed to compute the prestige. We define three prestige measures:
  - **Degree Prestige:** An actor i is considered to be prestigious if it receives many in-links or nominations.
  - **Proximity Prestige:** The degree prestige considers the actors that are adjacent to i. Unlike degree prestige, proximity prestige generalizes it by considering both the actors directly and indirectly linked to actor i.
  - **Rank Prestige:** The most important factor that is considered is prominence of each individual actor in the graph. An actor i chosen by an important person is more prestigious than chosen by a less important person. For example, a company CEO voting for a person is much more important than an employee voting for a person. If one's circle of influence is filled with prestigious actors, then one's own prestige is also high. Thus, one's prestige is affected by the ranks or statuses of other involved actors.

The algorithms that have been proposed to model the Web topology like PageRank and HITS are a major application of the combination of Web structure mining and content mining. Rank prestige forms the basis of most Web page link analysis algorithms, including PageRank and HITS.

PageRank and HITS

The purpose of PageRank and HITS is to calculate the quality rank or relevance of each webpage. Some examples that use these models are Google and Clever system. Some other applications of PageRank and HITS include Web pages categorization and discovering micro-communities on the Web.

PageRank is a static ranking of web pages in the sense that PageRank value is computed for each page off-line and it doesn't depend upon search queries (Liu, B., 2007). As PageRank is based on the measure of prestige in social networks, the PageRank value of each page can be regarded as its prestige. HITS stands for Hypertext Induced Topic Search. Unlike PageRank which is a static ranking algorithm, HITS is a search query dependent. When a search query is issued, HITS expands the relevant pages returned by the search engine and then produces two rankings of expanded set of pages, authority ranking and hub ranking. An authority is a page with many in-links. This page may have good and decent content on the required topic and thus many people trust and link to it. A hub is a page with many out-links. The page serves as an organizer of the information on required topic and points to many good authority pages on the topic. The underlying idea of HITS is that a good hub points to many good authorities and a good authority is pointed to by many good hubs. Thus, authorities and hubs, as shown in Figure 4, have a mutual reinforcement relationship (Liu, B., 2007).

Figure 4. Densely linked authorities and hubs (Bipartite Sub graph)

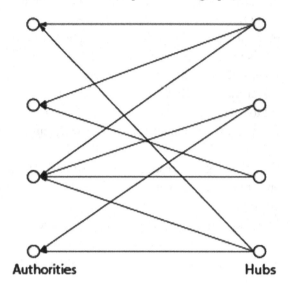

Authorities   **Hubs**

Web Usage Mining

Web usage mining can be defined as application of data mining techniques to discover usage patterns from Web data, to better serve the needs of Internet based applications. Web usage mining differs from web structure mining and web content mining as it reflects user behavior as he/she interacts with the web document (Internet). Because of this, web usage mining is widely used by e-commerce professionals. Analysis of user behavior in web usage mining has led to customization and personalization of a user's web experience. For example, the e-vendor may provide a choice of items to the user based on the items he has browsed recently. Recommendation making is one of the most common applications of knowledge gained from web usage mining. Data mining techniques like classification and clustering are used to segregate users to groups and provide them the required recommendations based on the group allotted. The web usage mining can be classified into two commonly used approaches: The first approach maps the usage data of a web server into relational database tables before the preferred data mining technique is performed. The second approach uses the log data collected directly by using special pre-processing techniques. The typical problem faced here is differentiating between users, server sessions, etc. in the proxy servers. A huge amount of usage data is collected every day. According to a research done several years ago (Srivastava, J., et al., 2002)., it was found that approx. 30GB/day of click-stream data is collected per day at Amazon.com. Hence, most people consider this a breach of privacy. But, without this collection of data, web would not be the user-friendly place it is today.

MAIN FOCUS OF THE CHAPTER

Social network is a term used to describe web-based services that allow individuals to create public/semi-public profile within a domain where they can connect and interact with other users within the network (Adedoyin-Olowe, M., Gaber, M. M., & Stahl, F., 2014). Social networks facilitate the formation and exchange of user-generated content (Chen, Z., Kalashnikov, D. V., & Mehrotra, S., 2009; Adedoyin-

Olowe, M. et al., 2014). In simple words, social network is a graph consisting of nodes and links that represent social relations on social network sites. Social network has gained enormous attention in the last decade. People are becoming more interested in relying on social network for information, news and opinion of other users on diverse subjects (Borgatti, S. P., Everett, M. G., & Freeman, L. C., 2002). Due to this, social network sites are generating massive data. Mining this large amount of data refines it into knowledge. Many people engage themselves in Social Web Mining because the data is rich in patterns (which play a key role in information retrieval). Also, Social Network Mining requires a lot less effort since organizations like Facebook make their API's readily accessible to everyone. This chapter considers its basis as Facebook due to its clean, well-documented API's.

Social Graph

It is a representation of how a user interacts with their social network. It depicts the connections and objects utilized by the user. In other words, it can be defined as the way information is stored about users on database. So when a user joins Facebook, he is more likely to establish connections with other people, applications, like and comment on different posts, update their status and profile. All these actions create a series of relationships or connections between these entities. A Facebook user can generate content by creating posts, uploading photos, videos, building an application, creating his/her own page. Things that are created become objects and user interactions with these objects are connections. Facebook lets us interact with content of other user users and thus establishing connection to their content. So the social graph is representation of all the connections we make in Facebook. It is a way to describe types of connections a person makes creating their own social network. As of 2010, Facebook's social graph is the largest social network dataset in the world ("Social Graph - Wikipedia, the free encyclopedia," 2016; "One Graph To Rule Them All?," 2016) and it contains the largest number of defined relationships between the largest number of people among all websites because it is the most widely used social networking service in the world ("Social Graph - Wikipedia, the free encyclopedia," 2016; "Facebook: No. 1 Globally," 2016). The traditional web applications are different from Facebook applications as Facebook applications are having access to user social data or the social graph as shown in Figure 5. This access is possible through Facebook API's.

Figure 5. Social graph

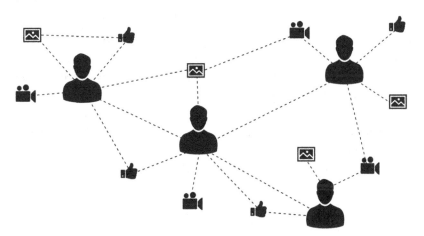

Working with API's

API (Application Program Interface) is a way to access content on the website. API's provide an access to data, feeds, objects, methods and functions within a web site. All the famous social organizations like Facebook, Google, Twitter provide API's for working with their content. This helps to increase the scope and functionality of a web site to a greater extent. Facebook provides many API's to interact with the social graph. Before getting started with Graph API, it is highly advisable to get acquainted with https:// developers.facebook.com. To use Graph API, we need an access token. An access token is a special key which an application needs to call Graph API on behalf of the user. The access token can be obtained by hitting *Get Token*. Now, the Graph API explorer asks us which additional permissions we want to request from the user. If the permissions are granted, the application can access more information about the user.

Graph API

The graph API is the primary way to get the data. We can read, update and delete information in Facebook's graph using this API. This is a JSON based API which means that it can be accessed in standard web browser. This makes it easy to use and traverse the graph. Graph API is an easy way to build expensive queries. The entire Facebook data is represented in the form of graph. A graph is all about two things i.e objects or the nodes and links between them. So every user of the Facebook is represented as a node or an object. The object need not be a user. It could be a page, photo, event. Every object has a unique ID. While using this Graph API Explorer, we are actually making basic HTTP requests to Facebook. We can run these queries directly in the browser ("Graph API," 2016). This makes it really easy to integrate this graph API into any technology that is desired. There are 3 main actions that can be done using Graph API Explorer i.e GET, POST and DELETE. Let us understand these actions in detail.

GET

This is the basic action provided by Graph API Explorer to access any general information. When the user starts to use this tool, he can see that the default get query is *me?fields=id,name*. ("Graph API," 2016). When we hit the submit button, we can see that the response window contains a JSON object that has two fields name and id. This is the object in the graph that represents the user. Here, name and id are the fields on that object. A user is more than just an id and a name. There are two main special query tokens. They are */me* and */app*. Calling */me* is same as calling the graph API with user id. Calling */app* is same as calling graph API with app id for the application that was used to generate the access token. Most of the applications build their requests using */me* and */app* because there is no need of breaking current user's user id into each request made to the graph API. We always need to refine the GET query so as to get the desired information. Sometimes, it's may not be possible to access the desired information because of lack of required permissions. To refine this query, we can select the desired fields and connections. In Figure 6, we can see that we have checked about (which is a field) and likes (which is a connection). We can see the desired result in the response window.

Complex queries can take more time but are highly advantageous. By requesting more data in single HTTP request, we are minimizing the network latency (delay in data communication over a network).

Figure 6. An example of GET query

DELETE

Any Facebook application should ask for minimum number of permissions to complete the desired task. More the number of permissions, less likely are the users to use that application. User can always revoke the granted permissions by using this DELETE functionality. If the user doesn't want the application to access his/her email, the permission can be revoked by giving the query as *me/permissions/email*. ("Graph API," 2016). Refer to Figure 7. In this way, the user has a complete control over data that can be accessed about him.

POST

Many applications that are integrated with Facebook help the user share stories about their activity in these applications back to Facebook. For example, Spotify is one such application that displays the songs on user's timeline. For this, the applications require a special write permission. The required permission is *publish_actions*.Figure 8 shows how to share a link with a message back to Facebook. Here we are making post to the user's feed connection. Make sure that the permission *public_actions*

Figure 7. Using DELETE action to revoke email permission

Figure 8. Publishing a story using POST action

is granted before sharing the link. When the link and message are successfully shared, we get back an id. This id represents the story that has been published to Facebook. Note that the story is an object as well ("Graph API," 2016).

OPEN GRAPH PROTOCOL

When Facebook was launched, the first thing to be focused was identity of a user that described user's name and a profile picture. The next step was allowing users to connect to each other in the social graph. In 2010, Facebook launched the initial version of open graph which allowed people to build their identity by liking objects all over the world (Overland, H. M., 2010). So millions of people started to like different entities. These entities could be anything. They could be games, movies, books, songs etc. But liking objects didn't quite cover everything. For example, instead of just hitting the like button after playing a game, the user can convey that he/she is playing the game. Open graph is a way to give users of application more detail to what they are doing with the application. So to achieve these minute but important details, Facebook launched the very next version of open graph that allowed the user to connect to any object on the web in any desired way. These connections should be organized and arranged in an orderly manner to ensure the best end user experience. To achieve this, Facebook introduced the concept of timeline. Timeline describes a user on a single page and maintains the feeds and activities of the user in a systematic manner. One of the main reasons for Facebook to use open graph is because of its complete cross platform nature. So the actions can be published to the open graph from native applications (that include iOS, android), mobile web and desktop web. So, open graph protocol allows to post rich, structured stories from an application. In Figure 9, we can see that open graph stories have four basic elements ("Open Graph Stories – Sharing",n.d):

1. **Actor:** The person who posts the story.
2. **App:** Every story includes attribution to the app that created it.
3. **Action:** Activity performed by the actor.
4. **Object:** The entity that actor interacts with.

Figure 9. Open graph

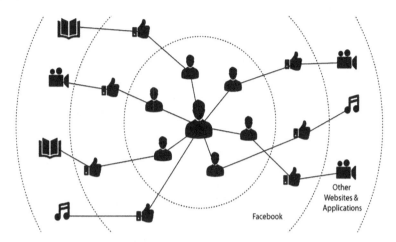

For example, Spotify is one such application that integrates itself with open graph. Spotify floods newsletters with what users have listened to. Facebook users can like, comment or even listen to a particular song in a status update.

Facebook's Open graph allows developers to make any webpage into an object of the Facebook's social graph by injecting RDFa metadata into the webpage. In simple words, Open Graph is a means of opening up the Social Graph to third-party websites and applications like Spotify, IMDB and Rotten Tomatoes. Given here in Figure 10 is an example, which illustrates a page for the movie *Captain America: Civil War* from Rotten Tomatoes. On the right, highlighted in a box we see the 'Like' and 'Share' option. Rotten Tomatoes put this functionality by implementing Open Graph for each of its Web Documents. This helps elevate the Facebook User experience.

Here the metadata is injected by putting additional metadata into the head tag of your webpage. The four required metadata properties in each page are as follows:

- og:title - The title of your webpage (Social Graph object).
- og:type - The type of the object(Ex. Video, Audio or Text).
- og:image - An image url to represent your object(webpage) within the graph.
- og:url - The url of the object to be used as permanent ID in the social graph.

As an example, this is the metadata markup for the rotten tomatoes page given above:

```
<head prefix="og: http://ogp.me/ns#flixstertomatoes: http://ogp.me/ns/apps/
flixstertomatoes#">
    ......
<title>Captain America: Civil War (2016) - Rotten Tomatoes</title>
    ......
<meta property="og:title" content="Captain America: Civil War"/>
<meta property="og:type" content="video.movie"/>
<meta property="og:image" content= "https://resizing.flixster.
```

Figure 10. Implementation of open graph in Rotten Tomatoes

```
com/9RTYLKMD0mAF5ksKYlwffGrk_OI=/488x720/v1.bTsxMTY5MDA3MDtwOzE2OTgwOzIwNDg7ND
g4OzcyMA"/>
<meta property="og:image:width" content="800"/>
<meta property="og:image:height" content="1200"/>
<meta property="og:url" content = "http://www.rottentomatoes.com/m/captain_
america_civil_war/"/>
<meta property="og:description" content="Captain America: Civil War begins the
next wave of Marvel movies with an action-packed superhero blockbuster boast-
ing a decidedly non-cartoonish plot and the courage to explore thought-provok-
ing themes."/>
    ......
</head>
```

Querying the Facebook open Graph is very simple. To do so, just append the metadata property og:url (generally the url of the webpage) to https://graph.facebook.com/ to fetch details about the object. For example, querying https://graph.facebook.com/http://www.rottentomatoes.com/m/captain_america_civil_war/ in your webpage would return:

```
{
  "id": "http://www.rottentomatoes.com/m/captain_america_civil_war/",
```

```
    "shares": 19847
}
```

By appending metadata=1 to the query we can request additional metadata for an object. Here our sample query is:

```
https://graph.facebook.com/
http://www.rottentomatoes.com/m/captain_america_civil_war?metadata=1:
{
"id": "http://www.rottentomatoes.com/m/captain_america_civil_war",
"shares": 19850, "metadata":
{
      "connections": {
       "comments":
       "https://graph.facebook.com/http://www.rottentomatoes.com/
        m/captain_america_civil_war/comments"
            },
             "type": "link_stat"
          }
   }
```

The objects in metadata.connections are the pointers to other nodes in the social graph. Querying this data in the social graph would give us comments data in this case. Each page and user you know is a part of the social graph. You can put in your og:url to access your details (https://graph.facebook. com/<USER_ID>).

Open Graph is continuously evolving as we speak. It got the possibility of semantic web one step closer to reality. The success of open graph has unfolded many opportunities for Facebook and many other companies too.

FACEBOOK QUERY LANGUAGE

FQL is an easy way to access the Open graph with SQL like language. Some advanced queries that are possible with FQL may not be possible with the Graph API. It has some features that are not present in Graph API like the ability to handle multiple queries in a single call ("FQL Overview," 2016). Even though FQL is deprecated after version 2.0, it is highly advisable to know basics of FQL. Figure 11 shows an FQL query to display first and last names of user's friends.

Figure 11. An example of FQL query

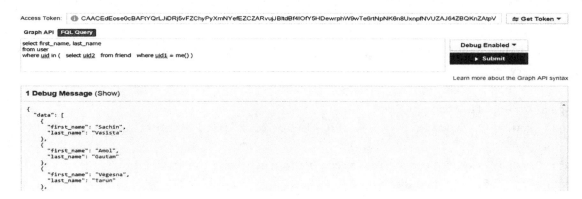

EXTRACTION AND ANALYSIS OF DATA

Analysis of Facebook Pages

A Facebook Page is a public profile mostly created for businesses, brands, celebrities etc. Unlike private profiles of people, Facebook pages do not have 'friends', instead they have 'fans'. Also unlike private profiles which have a limit of 5000 friends, pages have no limit to fans. Facebook pages are a powerful tool and a major part of the Social graph. They let the businesses or brands know their fans with a tool-kit called 'Facebook Page Insights'. Every Facebook user is likely a fan of atleast one Facebook page. Therefore, analyzing facebook pages gives us insights into the companies owning the pages.

Analyzing Facebook's Facebook Page

Since, we have been working on Facebook, let us query the graph API about Facebook India's official page. As mentioned in Section 3.3.2, we query the Facebook page through the URL https://graph.facebook.com/FacebookIndia. The graph API might give an access token error which can be rectified by adding your access token which can be obtained at the Graph API Explorer on https://developers.facebook.com at the end of the URL as https://graph.facebook.com/FacebookIndia?access_token=<ACCESS_TOKEN>. Here, we get the following results:

```
{
    "id": "103274306376166",
    "about": "Millions of people use Facebook everyday to keep up with friends,
upload an unlimited number of photos, share links and videos, and learn more
about the people they meet. Comment Policy: We love your comments, but please
be respectful of others.",
    "birthday": "02/04/2004",
    "can_post": false,
    "category": "Product/Service",
    "checkins": 0,
    "company_overview": "Millions of people use Facebook everyday to keep up
```

with friends, upload an unlimited number of photos, share links and videos, and learn more about the people they meet.\n\nComment Policy: We love your comments, but please be respectful of others. We reserve the right to delete profane, harassing, abusive and spam comments and to block repeat offenders.",
    "cover": {
        "cover_id": "980716155298639",
        "offset_x": 0,
        "offset_y": 9,
        "source": "https://scontent.xx.fbcdn.net/t31.0-8/s720x720/886224_9807161
55298639_5437131099444524727_o.jpg",
        "id": "980716155298639"
    },
    "founded": "February 4, 2004",
    "global_brand_root_id": "1499730620315598",
    "has_added_app": false,
    "is_community_page": false,
    "is_published": true,
    "likes": 171049102,
    "link": "https://www.facebook.com/FacebookIndia/",
    "mission": "Become a fan to learn more about what Facebook is doing in In-
dia",
    "name": "Facebook",
    "parking": {
        "lot": 0,
        "street": 0,
        "valet": 0
    },
    "talking_about_count": 30768,
    "username": "FacebookIndia",
    "website": "http://www.facebook.com",
    "were_here_count": 0
}

The 'likes' and 'talking_about_count' tells us about the page's overall popularity. Here, since the FacebookIndia page is very popular, it has 171049102 likes and 30768 have recently engaged in a discussion about the page. This analysis is a method to understand the popularity of a company. For example, a less famous company like Delberry has 435 likes and 2 talking_about_count while a very famous company like Sony has 7114113 likes and 16395 talking_about_count. Therefore, page analysis can be used to draw comparisons between two competitors. We can also draw the following analyses: Most of us know the business rivalry between MasterCard and Visa. So, let's determine their popularity through Facebook. Now,let's query the graph for likes on their official page.

Visa Page:

```
"name": "Visa",
"likes": 20078903,
```

MasterCard Page:

```
"name": "MasterCard",
"likes": 13822930,
```

Here, we see that Visa page has more likes than MasterCard page. Hence, we can deduce that Visa is more popular than MasterCard. This is backed up by the total equity of the companies: in the year 2015, total equity of Visa is around $30 billion whereas the sales equity of MasterCard is around $6 billion. This might not be true for every pair of competitors in the business realm, as they might not be managing their Facebook page as well as their rival company. This can also be seen in the given analysis as the difference in likes is about 30 percent (6255973 likes) where as the difference in equities is about 80 percent ($24 billion). Through this, we can determine that although the equity of MasterCard is way lower than that of Visa, its popularity is very close to that of Visa in Facebook. This tells us that MasterCard's social campaign is better than Visa page. The Facebook page for the brand NestleIndia has around 8 million likes where as it's product Maggi has about 14 million likes. This might indicate that Nestle in India draws most of its popularity through Maggi.

Analyzing Friendships

As we know, friendships are the first and the most elementary part of the social graph. The concept of friendships can give us insights into things like the special interests of people, how well connected are people in your social network, do you share common interests with your friends and so on. We can check the list of our friends by appending the phrase '*fields=friends*' while querying the Graph API as https://graph.facebook.com/me?fields=friends. You might notice that there are a lot less friends than your actual friends. This is due to their privacy settings (They have not given permissions to Graph API explorer at *developers.facebook.com*). Now, let's analyze the details about our friends. On querying as above, we get:

```
{
    "friends": {
        "data": [
            {
                "name": "Sachin Vasista",
                "id": "1320606388"
            },
            {
                "name": "Amol Gautam",
                "id": "1321929271"
            },
            {
```

```
            "name": "Vegesna Tarun",
            "id": "920095028013248"
        },
        {

            "name": "Lalith Varma",
            "id": "834525739943678"
        },
        {

            "name": "Akhil Reddy",
            "id": "370835546441659"
        },
        {

            "name": "Sai Vasista",
            "id": "1655741264660103"
        }
    ],
    "paging": {
      "cursors": {
          "before": "QVFIUmZAaRXV2NjR6czYxQW9sRVliSE9TUThPeUFJUU1iM0RWYk1Tc-
zZAaQXIzaC1femxKMFc3a1lKSTV1UG8wUzE5dVcZD",
          "after": "QVFIUmR0MGxIb1ZARZAlRjWDdiRmlrZA3NXZA3FFb1pNNmRkcTJwQUY-
wcS1IcTQ3dXFtQkFMLTBoaTR6dERoYTZA3Y1JWWHozelVHUENrUG95TWFXbDFGVURETT1B"
      }
    },
    "summary": {
        "total_count": 352
    }
  },
  "id": "790179194363706"
}
```

Now, as we know the ID's of our friends, we can query the Graph API to know their likes. To query for likes we append the phrase '*fields=likes*' to the Graph URL as above. The likes would be shown as follows:

```
{
  "likes": {
    "data": [
        {
          "name": "Apple Inc.",
          "category": "Company",
          "category_list": [
              {
                  "id": "177721448951559",
```

```
          "name": "Workplace & Office"
       }
    ],
    "id": "105596369475033",
    "created_time": "2016-05-07T08:59:51+0000"
},                           .
{

    "name": "Sony",
    "category": "Company",
    "id": "56232316996",
    "created_time": "2016-04-16T11:19:27+0000"
},
{

    "name": "Paytm",
    "category": "Shopping/Retail",
    "category_list": [
       {
          "id": "200600219953504",
          "name": "Shopping & Retail"
       }
    ],
    "id": "137725316293048",
    "created_time": "2016-04-06T16:08:43+0000"
},
{

    "name": "BuzzFeed Animals",
    "category": "Media/News/Publishing",
    "id": "377382845617050",
    "created_time": "2016-03-22T02:15:13+0000"
},
{

    "name": "Creation Labs",
    "category": "Engineering/Construction",
    "id": "825514724131781",
    "created_time": "2016-03-17T13:09:35+0000"
},
{

    "name": "Kapil sharma",
    "category": "Comedian",
    "id": "534383099925612",
    "created_time": "2016-03-01T15:10:08+0000"
},
{

    "name": "Barack Obama",
```

```
        "category": "Politician",
        "id": "6815841748",
        "created_time": "2016-03-01T15:10:05+0000"
    },
    {
        "name": "Hungry Shark Evolution",
        "category": "App Page",
        "id": "477785905567921",
        "created_time": "2016-01-18T09:16:55+0000"
    },
    {
        "name": "Rowan Atkinson",
        "category": "Author",
        "id": "111954258821685",
        "created_time": "2016-01-06T07:43:54+0000"
    },
    {
        "name": "FRIENDS (TV Show)",
        "category": "TV Show",
        "id": "22577904575",
        "created_time": "2015-12-07T16:54:02+0000"
    },
    {
        "name": "Rockstar Games",
        "category": "Games/Toys",
        "id": "51752540096",
        "created_time": "2015-11-20T17:20:44+0000"
    },
    {
        "name": "Grand Theft Auto V",
        "category": "Games/Toys",
        "id": "473819899309541",
        "created_time": "2015-11-20T17:20:42+0000"
    }
],
"paging": {
    "cursors": {
        "before": "MTA1NTk2MzY5NDc1MDMz",
        "after": "NDczODE5ODk5MzA5NTQx"
    },
    "next": "https://graph.facebook.com/v2.0/790179194363706/likes?access_
token=EAACEdEose0cBADr0femTZCiwv6hCvi1ud0ZAk1qNiHchPn1e40s860yGVhgRrk7xdRFBdsd
cuGdwsLDZCCzoY7vVeqZC9b8aG0WaHFmYeghwoBJiRIFZC1vMWQgnVBAsqPEt8yZA4gm8wSE6NOYGc
7EmE1Uou7BP0yQYNaiUN9WAZDZD&pretty=1&limit=25&after=NDczODE5ODk5MzA5NTQx"
```

```
      }
    },
    "id": "790179194363706"
}
```

By querying the likes of several people among our friend list, we can know the mutual likes among friends, family and so on. On performing this for a large community of people, we can know the things people of a same area prefer, good restaurants and places to visit in a city. As we know by now, there are unlimited possibilities and applications for querying the social graph.

Extraction and Analysis Using Netvizz

We use a tool called Netvizz that can be used to extract information from different sections of Facebook platform. The tool is readily available as a Facebook application that is mainly used for research purposes. The outputs can be analyzed in any standard software. The current version of *Netvizz v1.25* is designed to work with *Facebook's API v2.2.* The tool is mainly focused on extracting data from groups and pages (Rieder, B., 2013). Let us consider an example of a Facebook group "Apple Fans Deutschland" which is an open group. Since, this is an open group, Netvizz doesn't require *user_groups* permission and can directly retrieve data from this group. According to Rieder, B. (2013) the group data module of Netvizz creates the following from a group:

- A tabular file (tsv) that lists different metrics for each post. Refer to Figure 12.
- A tabular file (tsv) that lists basic stats per day for the period covered by the selected posts.
- A tabular file (tsv) that contains the text of user comments (anonymized).
- A bipartite graph file in gdf format that shows posts, users (anonymized), and connections between the two. A user is connected to a post if she commented or liked it.
- A monopartite graph file in gdf format that shows interactions between users (anonymized). Connections are made through liking or commenting on a post. Refer to Figure 13.

In Figure 12, we can observe that the field *post_publisher* is kept anonymous as it is a sensitive information that cannot be disclosed with available permissions.

Figure 12. List of different metrics for each post

	A	B	C	D	E	F	G	H	I	J
1	type	from_id	from_nam	post_mes	picture	link	link_dom	post_publ	post_publ	post_publ
2	link	14dae223	e5b87a88	Halllo App	https://ex	http://m.i	m.redcooi	2016-05-0	1.46E+09	########
3	status	8a527396	438be18cf	Hej Was sollte man eher als E-Reader nut				2016-05-0	1.46E+09	########
4	status	59bcf13c4	248d9d37	Ich habe eine Cd zu iTunes hinzugefÃ¼gt.				2016-05-0	1.46E+09	########
5	status	568891354	974740f77	Servus Leute_ ich bin 21 und komme vom				2016-05-0	1.46E+09	########
6	status	08bf8f14e	23116d26	Hallo Ihr Alle_ ich bin neu hier und kÃ¶n				2016-05-0	1.46E+09	########
7	link	f86541c33	d6563272	Ist das bei	https://ex	http://ww	clipfish.de	2016-05-0	1.46E+09	########
8	photo	49656754	11bc6b8a	FÃ¤llt irge	https://sc	https://w	facebook.	2016-05-0	1.46E+09	########
9	status	3a601cb61	459ec5117	Moin Apple Fans_ gibt es irgendwie die N				2016-05-0	1.46E+09	########
10	status	9df60685e	cc1df47b7	Moin zusammen_ wie sagt man Siri das si				2016-05-0	1.46E+09	########
11	status	083ebaa1	1c8030a29	#siri - ha ... Fragt Siri mal_ wie das Musiks				2016-05-0	1.46E+09	########
12	status	7c6b2ca84	ed6eb71d	Moin und Servus! Bin am Ã¼berlegen ne				2016-05-0	1.46E+09	########
13	status	489d63b6	4077ac72a	Guten Abend_ KÃ¶nnt ihr mir eine Joysti				2016-05-0	1.46E+09	########
14	status	514b35b9	7d9e81db	Mac Book 12 am LadegerÃ¤t lassen Ã¼be				2016-05-0	1.46E+09	########
15	link	9321e675	380277c55ce40e5472		https://ex	http://ww	appgefahr	2016-05-0	1.46E+09	########
16	status	91c418e4	041abc73c	Hi_ ich wollte heute mal die hotline anru				2016-05-0	1.46E+09	########
17	photo	efe4c8567	dd63747c	iPHONE SI	https://sc	https://w	facebook.	2016-05-0	1.46E+09	########
18	status	85a8597e	9d795459	Hallo Zusammen Ich wollte Bilder auf eir				2016-05-0	1.46E+09	########
19	status	1d23a549	cd92523cc	Moinsen Leute! Ich mÃ¶chte heute mal a				2016-05-0	1.46E+09	########
20	status	30b89a01	45478b8e	Hi kennt ihr ne Video App wo man beim a				2016-05-0	1.46E+09	########
21	photo	8710b303	3d658a00	Warum sir	https://sc	https://w	facebook.	2016-05-0	1.46E+09	########
22	status	6a22fd4d2	0f5eb2b4	Okay... ich bin offensichtlich ein DAU unc				2016-05-0	1.46E+09	########
23	status	1fc80d2ff	95af57708	Kann mir jemand helfen musik von Ã-tun				2016-05-0	1.46E+09	########
24	status	a17edee5	6dfb7e58	Moin Leute_ Habe nun endlich ne_n MAC				2016-05-0	1.46E+09	########
25	link	443de260	ac3672951	http://ww	https://ex	http://ww	techradar	2016-05-0	1.46E+09	########

	K	L	M	N	O	P	Q	R	S	T	U
1	likes	likes_cou	comment	comment	comment	comment	shares	comment_	engagem	post_id	post_
2	0	0	4	4	3	1	0	0	4	329560737	http:
3	0	0	12	12	12	0	0	3	15	329560737	http:
4	0	0	0	0	0	0	0	0	0	329560737	http:
5	19	19	23	23	10	13	0	7	49	329560737	http:
6	0	0	8	8	4	4	0	5	13	329560737	http:
7	0	0	0	0	0	0	0	0	0	329560737	http:
8	7	7	21	21	14	7	0	17	45	329560737	http:
9	0	0	0	0	0	0	0	0	0	329560737	http:
10	0	0	0	0	0	0	0	0	0	329560737	http:
11	0	0	2	2	2	0	0	0	2	329560737	http:
12	1	1	34	34	27	7	0	10	45	329560737	http:
13	0	0	5	5	2	3	0	0	5	329560737	http:
14	0	0	27	27	7	20	0	2	29	329560737	http:
15	0	0	0	0	0	0	0	0	0	329560737	http:
16	1	1	8	5	4	1	0	3	9	329560737	http:
17	0	0	0	0	0	0	0	0	0	329560737	http:
18	0	0	12	12	12	0	0	1	13	329560737	http:
19	3	3	24	24	21	3	0	33	60	329560737	http:
20	1	1	0	0	0	0	0	0	1	329560737	http:
21	0	0	7	7	4	3	0	2	9	329560737	http:
22	0	0	5	5	5	0	0	1	6	329560737	http:
23	0	0	2	2	2	0	0	0	2	329560737	http:
24	0	0	7	7	5	2	0	7	14	329560737	http:
25	0	0	0	0	0	0	0	0	0	329560737	http:

Figure 13. Monopartite graph that shows interactions between user

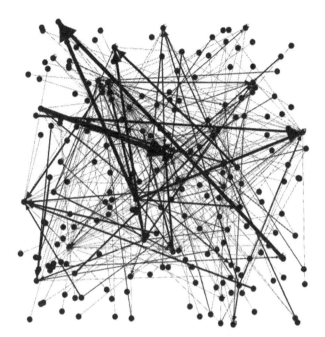

Figure 13 shows different nodes and connections where each node is a user and connections are established between the users based on their likes and comments on a post. We can further analyze important metrics like average degree, average weighted degree, graph density, modularity from this graph. They play a key role in social network web mining. Figure 14 is an example that depicts the prestige of a user in the graph.

As we discussed earlier, Prestige is a refined measure of prominence of an actor. In Figure 14, we can see many links are directed to a user from many other users. This clearly says that this user is important and has good prestige in this group. This is a small example to calculate prestige of a user. In the same way, we can see that values of other important metrics are computed from this graph in Figure 14. Each and every metric plays an important role in mining any data. We can also mine the page data in the same way we mined the group data using Netvizz.

SOCIAL NETWORK MINING IN DECISION SUPPORT SYSTEMS

The last decade has seen a lot of advancements in the field of Decision Support Systems. A decision support system is a computer-based information system that supports business or organizational decision-making activities. Mining the social networks can provide us with a vast amount of information to help the organization take vital decisions. Let us see few applications: An important example is applications of opinion mining in Decision Support Systems. People can post reviews and rate anything on website in present world. It could be a blog, product on E-Commerce site, website, web service etc. This is commonly known as user generated content or user generated media. Three Mining Tasks of Evaluative Texts:

Figure 14. An example to depict prestige of a user

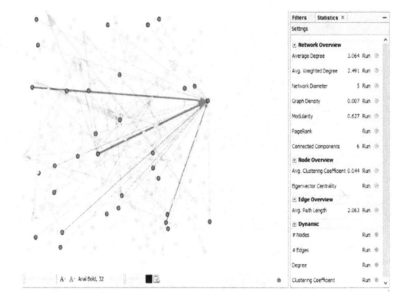

1. **Sentiment Classification:** System classified whether a review is positive or negative. No details are discovered about the likes and dislikes of the product.
2. **Feature Based Opinion Mining and Summarization:** Here, positive and negative features of entity are focused. The entity can be an organization, product, web service etc.
3. **Comparative Sentence and Relation Mining:** Here we compare one object against other similar projects.

Classification Based on Sentiment Analysis

The algorithm described here is based on the work of Turney which is designed to classify customer reviews. The steps involved are as follows:

Step 1: The algorithm makes use of parts of speech tagging (POS). The algorithm extracts phrases containing adjectives or adverbs as they are good indicators of subjectivity and opinions.

Step 2: Then Semantic Orientation (SO) is devised using extracted above extracted phases. The semantic/opinion orientation (SO) of a phrase is computed based on its association with the positive reference word "excellent" and its association with the negative reference word "poor". The probabilities are calculated by issuing queries to a search engine and collecting the number of hits.

Step 3: The algorithm then computes average SO of all phrases. If SO holds a positive value, the review is classified as "recommended" and "not recommended" otherwise.

The next example describes a scenario where social network mining could be used for a DSS in which a customer approaches a company and receives bad service from an employee of the company. Now, the customer might provide bad reviews on the company through a social network. Now, the organization may deploy a decision support system which mines the reviews on the company from the social network and converts them into a database or a spreadsheet and a graph which gives the performance of the company. Now, the manager can analyze the data provided by decision support system, as seen in Figure 15, and take the respective action on the employee (Saguna, S., Zaslavsky, A., & Paris, C., 2012.).

Another important example for applications of opinion mining in Decision Support System is introduction of Facebook reactions in the year 2016. The main reason is that not every post is likable ("Facebook Reactions, the Totally Redesigned Like Button, Is Here | WIRED," 2016). So, Facebook focused on the sentiments its users expressed the most. We can see the reactions in Fig 16. Analyzing these user reactions can give us better details about the post. This analyzed data can be used by Decision Support System to achieve the desired goal.

CONCLUSION

The chapter identifies various web mining techniques for online social networking analysis. This chapter mainly focuses on Facebook due to its clean, well-documented API's. A significant effort is made to explain the systematic functioning of social graph and open graph protocol. The chapter explains the importance of API's and the techniques to extract the desired information using them. There is a growing importance to analyze social networks as they can reveal priceless information. This information is used by many organizations and enterprises in the process of decision making. This entire process of analysis is presented in the chapter. The importance of results of this analysis is reflected in the process of decision making.

Figure 15. Social network mining in DSS

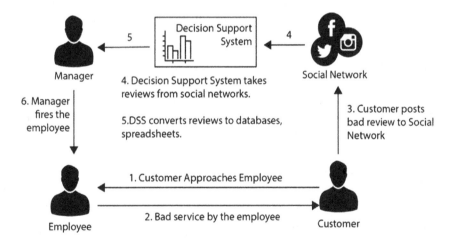

Figure 16. Reactions introduced by Facebook

REFERENCES

Adedoyin-Olowe, M., Gaber, M. M., & Stahl, F. (2014). A survey of data mining techniques for social network analysis. *Journal of Data Mining & Digital Humanities*.

Borgatti, S. P., Everett, M. G., & Freeman, L. C. (2002). *Ucinet for Windows: Software for social network analysis*. Academic Press.

Chakrabarti, S. (2002). *Mining the Web: Discovering knowledge from hypertext data*. Elsevier.

Chen, Z., Kalashnikov, D. V., & Mehrotra, S. (2009). Exploiting context analysis for combining multiple entity resolution systems. In *Proceedings of the 2009 ACM SIGMOD International Conference on Management of data*(pp. 207-218). ACM. doi:10.1145/1559845.1559869

Cooley, R., Mobasher, B., & Srivastava, J. (1997). Web mining: Information and pattern discovery on the world wide web. In Tools with Artificial Intelligence, 1997. *Proceedings., Ninth IEEE International Conference on* (pp. 558-567). IEEE.

DSS-Wikipedia, the free encyclopedia. (2016). Retrieved April, 2016 from https://en.wikipedia.org/wiki/Decision_support_system

Duggan, M. (2015). *The Demographics of Social Media Users*. Retrieved May, 2016 from http://www.pewinternet.org/2015/08/19/the-demographics-of-social-media-users/

Facebook: No. 1 Globally. Business Week. (2008). Retrieved April 9, 2016 from http://www.businessweek.com/technology/content/aug2008/tc20080812_853725.htm

Facebook Pages for marketing your business | Facebook for Business. (n.d.). Retrieved April, 2016 https://www.facebook.com/business/products/pages

FQL Overview. (n.d.). Retrieved May, 2016 from https://developers.facebook.com/docs/technical-guides/fql/

Galitsky, B. A., Dobrocsi, G., de la Rosa, J. L., & Kuznetsov, S. O. (2011, July). Using generalization of syntactic parse trees for taxonomy capture on the web. In *International Conference on Conceptual Structures* (pp. 104-117). Springer Berlin Heidelberg. doi:10.1007/978-3-642-22688-5_8

Graph API. (n.d.). Retrieved May,2016 from https://developers.facebook.com/docs/graph-api/

Kosala, R., & Blockeel, H. (2000). Web mining research: A survey. *ACM Sigkdd Explorations Newsletter*, *2*(1), 1–15. doi:10.1145/360402.360406

Liu, B. (2007). *Web data mining: exploring hyperlinks, contents, and usage data*. Springer Science & Business Media.

Markov, Z., & Larose, D. T. (2007). *Data mining the Web: uncovering patterns in Web content, structure, and usage*. John Wiley & Sons. doi:10.1002/0470108096

MasterCard - Wikipedia, the free encyclopedia. (2016). Retrieved March, 2016 https://en.wikipedia.org/wiki/MasterCard

One Graph To Rule Them All? (n.d.). AVC. Retrieved April 11, 2016 from http://avc.com/2010/04/one-graph-to-rule-them-all/

Open Graph Stories – Sharing. (n.d.). Retrieved May, 2016 from https://developers.facebook.com/ docs/sharing/opengraph

Overland, H. M. (2010). *What is Facebook Open Graph? Search Engine People.* Retrieved May, 2016 from http://www.searchenginepeople.com/blog/what-is-facebook-open-graph.html

Rieder, B. (2013). Studying Facebook via data extraction: the Netvizz application. In *Proceedings of the 5th Annual ACM Web Science Conference*(pp. 346-355). ACM. doi:10.1145/2464464.2464475

Rouse, M. (2010). *What is Facebook page? - Definition from WhatIs.com.* Retrieved in April, 2016 from http://whatis.techtarget.com/definition/Facebook-page

Russell, M. A. (2013). *Mining the Social Web: Data Mining Facebook, Twitter, LinkedIn, Google+, GitHub, and More.* O'Reilly Media, Inc.

Saguna, S., Zaslavsky, A., & Paris, C. (2012). *Context-Aware Twitter Validator (CATVal) a system to validate credibility and authenticity of Twitter content for use in decision support systems.* Fusing Decision Support Systems into the Fabric of the Context.

Social Graph - Wikipedia, the free encyclopedia. (n.d.). Retrieved May, 2016 from https://en.wikipedia.org/wiki/Social_graph

Srivastava, J., Desikan, P., & Kumar, V. (2002). Web mining: Accomplishments and future directions. In *National Science Foundation Workshop on Next Generation Data Mining* (NGDM'02) (pp. 51-69).

Stinson, L. (2016). *Facebook Reactions, the Totally Redesigned Like Button, Is Here | WIRED.* Retrieved May, 2016 from http://www.wired.com/2016/02/facebook-reactions-totally-redesigned-like-button/

The Open Graph Protocol. (2014). Retrieved April, 2016 from http://ogp.me/

Van Wel, L., & Royakkers, L. (2004). Ethical issues in web data mining. *Ethics and Information Technology*, 6(2), 129–140. doi:10.1023/B:ETIN.0000047476.05912.3d

Visa Inc. - Wikipedia, the free encyclopedia. (2016). Retrieved in March, 2016 from https://en.wikipedia.org/wiki/Visa_Inc

Wang, Y. (2000). *Web mining and knowledge discovery of usage patterns.* Cs 748T Project, 1-25.

KEY TERMS AND DEFINITIONS

Decision Support System: Decision Support System is a set of related computer programs and the data required to assist with analysis and decision-making within an organization.

Open Graph Protocol: The Open Graph protocol enables any web page to become a rich object in a social graph. For instance, this is used on Facebook to allow any web page to have the same functionality as any other object on Facebook.

Social Graph: Social graph is a representation of the interconnection of relationships in an online social network.

Web Content Mining: Web content mining is the mining, extraction and integration of useful data, information and knowledge from Web page content.

Web Mining: Web Mining is the application of data mining techniques to discover patterns from the World Wide Web.

Web Structure Mining: Web structure mining is the process of using graph theory to analyze the node and connection structure of a web site.

Web Usage Mining: Web Usage Mining is the application of data mining techniques to discover interesting usage patterns from Web data in order to understand and better serve the needs of Web-based applications.

Section 5
Developing Data and Text Mining Systems

Chapter 16
Data Mining and Data Warehousing:
Introduction to Data Mining and Data Warehousing

Sathiyamoorthi V
Sona College of Technology, India

ABSTRACT

It is generally observed throughout the world that in the last two decades, while the average speed of computers has almost doubled in a span of around eighteen months, the average speed of the network has doubled merely in a span of just eight months! In order to improve the performance, more and more researchers are focusing their research in the field of computers and its related technologies. Data Mining is one such research area. It extracts useful information the huge amount of data present in the database. The discovered knowledge can be applied in various application areas such as marketing, fraud detections and customer retention. It discovers implicit, previously unknown and potentially useful information out of datasets. Recent trend in data mining include web mining where it discover knowledge from web based information to improve the page layout, structure and its content.

INTRODUCTION

Data mining is the process of nontrivial extraction of implicit, previously unknown and potentially useful information from the raw data present in the large database (Jiawei et al. 2006). It is also known as Knowledge Discovery in Databases (KDD). Data mining techniques can be applied upon various data sources to improve the value of the existing information system. When implemented on high performance client and server system, data mining tools can analyze large databases to deliver highly reliable results. It is also described that the data mining techniques can be coupled with relational database engines (Jiawei et al. 2006). Data mining differs from the conventional database retrieval in the fact that it extracts hidden information or knowledge that is not explicitly available in the database, whereas database retrieval

DOI: 10.4018/978-1-5225-1877-8.ch016

extracts the data that is explicitly available in the databases through some query language. Based on the fact that, a certain degree of intelligence is incorporated in the system, data mining could further be viewed as a branch of artificial intelligence and thus, it could be treated as an intelligent database manipulation system. Dunham et al. (2006) have explained that data mining is an interdisciplinary field that incorporates concepts and techniques from several disciplines such as statistics, neural networks and machine learning in the process of knowledge discovery. Data warehousing is the location where it stores subject oriented and task relevant data for an organization decision support system. It contains data that are most important and relevant to decision making process. Hence, this chapter describes the functionality of data mining and data warehousing system with its applications. Also, it focuses on Web mining where it addresses the issues and challenges present in it. Finally, it describes the integration technique where data mining and data warehousing system can be combined for an effective functionality. As data mining is an interdisciplinary field, it uses algorithms and techniques from various fields such as statistics, machine learning, artificial intelligence, neural networks and database technology. The most commonly used methods that assist in data mining tasks are (Jiawei et al. 2006) given below:

- **Artificial Neural Networks (ANN):** A non-linear predictive model comprises of different layers namely input, hidden and output layers that learn through training and resemble biological neural network in a structure.
- **Decision Tree:** A tree structure comprises of nodes and branches and represents a set of decisions. A node in decision tree represents conditions and branches of outcome. These decisions generate rules for the classifications of a dataset. Specific decision tree method includes classification and regression trees.
- **Genetic Algorithm (GA):** This Evolutionary optimization technique uses operators such as genetic combination, mutation, and natural selection in a design-based concept of evolution. This can be applied to optimization problem that either maximize or minimize the given objective function.
- **Nearest Neighbor Method:** A technique that classifies each record in a dataset based on a combination of the classes of 'k' records that are most similar to its historical dataset. Sometimes called as the K-Nearest Neighbor (KNN) technique.
- **Rule Induction:** This is the extraction of useful if-then rules from the dataset.

BACKGROUND

It is described that data mining can be viewed as a crucial step in knowledge discovery process which is shown in Figure 1. It is composed of various phases such as:

- Pre-processing
- Data Mining
- Pattern Extraction
- Pattern Evaluation
- Knowledge Presentation

The data preprocessing phase devises the data to be in a format that are suitable for further data mining operations. Data cleaning removes noise, inconsistent data, and irrelevant data that are present in the data sources. Since the input database could be composed of data that arrives from multiple sources, data integration is employed to integrate data from those sources. Data mining phase identifies the specific data mining tasks that employs intelligent methods and extracts knowledge. The resulting knowledge or patterns are evaluated for usability in the pattern evaluation phase. The last step of KDD process is the presentation of discovered knowledge in a user friendly and user understandable format referred to as the knowledge presentation phase (Jiawei et al. 2006). Data mining system could be categorized into the following dimensions (Jiawei et al. 2006):

- **Kinds of Databases to be Mined**
  - This includes whether it uses relational, transactional, object-oriented, object-relational, active, spatial, time-series, text, multi-media, heterogeneous, legacy, WWW and so on.
- **Kinds of Knowledge to be Discovered**
  - This includes whether it applies characterization, discrimination, association, classification, clustering, and trend, deviation and outlier analysis and so on.
- **Kinds of Techniques Utilized**
  - This includes type of techniques it employed such as database oriented, data warehouse, machine learning, statistics, visualization, neural network and so on.
- **Kinds of Applications Adapted**
  - This includes application areas such as retail, telecommunication, banking, fraud analysis, stock market analysis; Web mining, Web log analysis and so on.

Data Mining Tasks Classification

In general, data mining tasks can be broadly classified into either descriptive or predictive (Jiawei et al. 2006). Descriptive data mining tasks are those that provide description or characterization of properties of the input database. Predictive data mining tasks are those that provide inference on input data to arrive at hidden knowledge and to make interesting and useful predictions. Some of the data mining tasks and its categorization are given below:

- Classification [Predictive]
- Clustering [Descriptive]
- Association Rule Mining [Descriptive]
- Sequential Pattern Discovery [Descriptive]
- Regression [Predictive]
- Deviation Detection [Predictive]

Data sources for mining knowledge can vary depending on the type of data present in the database. Typical data sources are:

- Spatial data base
- Text database
- Multimedia database

Figure 1. Steps in KDD process

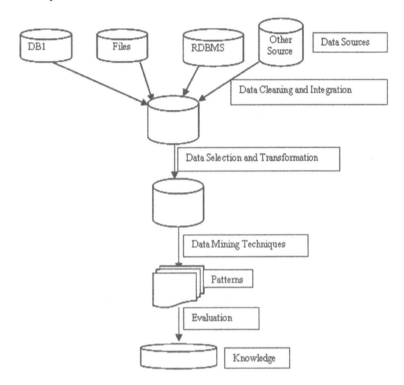

- Web database
- Relational database
- Bioinformatics like DNA database
- Time series database and so on

As mentioned earlier, data mining is an interdisciplinary field which utilizes the domain knowledge, skills, tools and techniques from several other fields such as Database, Data Statistics, Machine Learning, Information Retrieval, Data Visualization and other disciplines as well which is shown in Figure 2.

DATA MINING TASKS

Classification

It is one of the data mining techniques used for data analysis and used to construct the classification model. It is used to predict future trends analysis. It is also known as supervised learning.

The classification models used to predict categorical class labels whereas and prediction models predict continuous valued. For example, classification model for bank is used to classify bank loan applications as either safe or risky one. A prediction model is used to predict the potential customers who will buy computer equipment given their income and occupation. Some other examples of data analysis task of classification are given below:

Figure 2. Data mining as interdisciplinary field   *Figure 3. Data mining task classification*

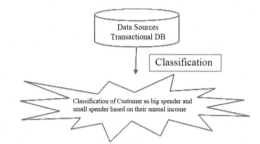

- A bank loan officer wants to analyze the data in order to predict which loan applicant is risky or which are safe.
- A marketing manager at a company needs to analyze a customer with a given profile, who will buy a new computer as shown in Figure 3.

In both the cases, a model is constructed to predict the categorical labels. These labels are risky or safe for loan application and yes or no for marketing data.

Working Principles

It is the task of building a model that describe and distinguish data class of an object. This is used to predict class label for an object where class label information is not available (Jiawei et al. 2006). It is an example of learning from samples. The first phase called model construction is also referred to as training phase, where a model is built based on the features present in the training data. This model is then used to predict class labels for the testing data, where class label information is not available. A test set is used to determine the accuracy of the model. Usually, the given data set is divided into training and test sets, with training set used to construct the model and test set used to validate it. Decision trees are commonly used to represent classification models. A decision tree is similar to a flowchart like structure where every node represents a test on an attribute value and branches denote a test outcome and tree leaves represent actual classes. Other standard representation techniques include K-nearest neighbor, Bayesians classification algorithm, if-then rules and neural networks (Jiawei et al. 2006). It is also known as supervised learning process. Effectiveness of prediction depends on training dataset used to train the model. The classification is two steps process:

Phase I: Building the Classifier (Training Phase)
Phase II: Using Classifier (Testing Phase)

Training Phase

This is the first step in classification and in this step a classification algorithm is used to construct the classifier model shown in Figure 5. The model is built from the training dataset which contain tuples called records with the associated class labels. Each tuple presents in the training dataset is called as category or class. Consider that training dataset of a bank_loan schema contains value for the following attributes:

\<Name, Age, Income, Loan_decision\>

and class label here is Loan_decision and possible class label are risky, safe and low_risky. Say for an example, classification algorithm uses ID 3 then classification model is the decision tree which is shown below Figure 4. A decision tree is a tree that includes a root node, branches and leaf nodes. Each internal node denotes a test on an attribute, each branch denotes the outcome of the test, and each leaf node holds a class label. The node without parent is the root node. Nodes without children is called leaf node and it represents the outcome. Once the decision tree was built, then it uses the IF-THEN rules on nodes present in the node to find the class label of a tuple in the testing dataset. It may be following six rules are derived from the above tree:

1. If Age=young and Income=low then Loan_decision= risky
2. If Age=Senior and Income=low then Loan_decision= risky
3. If Age=Middle_Aged and Income=low then Loan_decision= risky
4. If Age=young and Income=High then Loan_decision= Safe
5. If Age=Middle_Aged and Income=High then Loan_decision=Safe
6. If Age=Senior and Income=High then Loan_decision= Low_risky

Once the model is built then next step is testing the classifier using some sample testing dataset which is shown in Figure 4. Here, the testing dataset is used to measure the accuracy of classification model shown in Figure 6. There are two different metrics such as precision and recall used for measuring accuracy of a classification model.

Testing Phase

Refer to Figure 6 for an illustration of the testing phase.

Figure 4. Decision tree

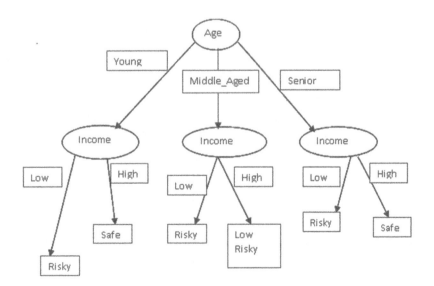

Figure 5. Training Process of Classification

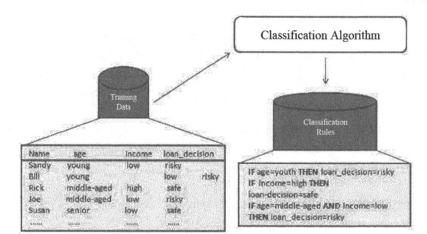

Figure 6. Testing Process of Classification

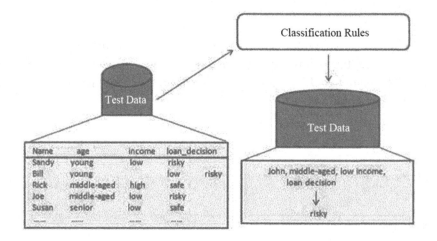

Prediction

Data mining is an analytic process designed to explore data for consistent patterns or systematic relationships among variables and then to validate the findings by applying the detected patterns to new subsets of data. (Jiawei et al. 2006) uncover that the predictive data mining is the most common type of data mining and it has the most direct business applications. An example is shown in Figure 7. The process of predictive data mining task consists of three stages:

1. Data exploration
2. Model building
3. Deployment

Data Exploration usually starts with data preparation which may involve data cleaning, data transformations, selecting subsets of records and feature selection. Feature selection is one of the important operations in the exploration process. It is defined as reducing the numbers of variables to a manageable range if the datasets are with large number of variables performing some preliminary feature selection operations. Then, a simple choice of straightforward predictors for a regression model is used to elaborate exploratory analyses. The most widely used graphical and statistical method is exploratory data analysis. Model building and validation steps involve considering various models and choosing the best one based on their predictive performance. Deployment is the final step which involves selecting the best model in the previous step and applying it to a new data in order to generate predictions or estimates of the expected outcome.

Both classification and prediction are used for data analysis but there exists some issues dealing with preparing the data for data analysis. It involves the following activities:

- **Data Cleaning:** Data cleaning involves removing the noisy, incomplete and inconsistent data and methods for handling missing values of an attribute. The noisy data is removed by applying smoothing techniques such as binning and then problem of missing values is handled by replacing a missing value with most commonly occurring value for that attribute or replacing missing value by mean value of that attribute or replacing the missing value by global constant and so on.
- **Relevance Analysis:** Datasets may also have some irrelevant attributes and hence correlation analysis is performed to know whether any two given attributes are related or not. All irrelevant attributes are removed.
- **Normalization:** Normalization involves scaling all values for given attribute in order to make them fall within a small specified range. Ex. Min_Max normalization.
- **Generalization:** It is data generalization method where data at low levels are mapped to some higher level there by reducing the number of values of an attributes. For this purpose, we can use the concept hierarchies. An example is shown in Figure 8.

Figure 7. Data mining task prediction

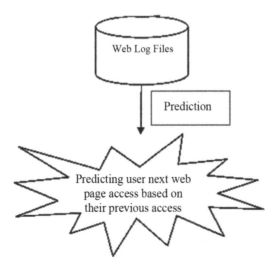

Figure 8. Generalization of days

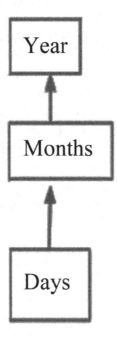

Clustering

Clustering is the process of grouping of objects into classes of similar objects based on some similarity measures between them (Sathiyamoorthi & Murali Baskaran 2011b). It is unsupervised leaning method. Each cluster can be represented as one group and while performing cluster analysis, first partition objects into groups based on the similarity between them and then assign the class labels to those groups. The main difference between clustering and classification is that, clustering is adaptable to changes and helps select useful features that distinguish objects into different groups. An example of clustering is shown in Figure 9.

Figure 9. Data mining task clustering

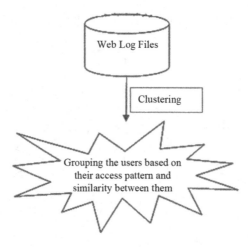

Applications of Cluster Analysis

- Clustering is used in many different applications such as market research, pattern recognition, data analysis and image processing.
- It helps marketing manager to discover distinct potential buyers from the customer base. Also, it helps in characterizing the customer groups based on their purchasing patterns and select target audience for the current products.
- In biology department, it helps to deriving plant and animal taxonomy, categorizing genes with similar functionalities and gaining insight into structures inherent to populations and so on.
- In spatial database application, it helps in identification of areas of similar land and groups the houses in a city based on the house type, house value, and geographic location and so on.
- In web based application, it helps in categorizing the similar documents on the web for information retrieval.
- It used in outlier detection applications such as detection of credit card fraud and fraud transaction and so on.
- In general, in data mining clustering acts as a tool for gaining knowledge about distribution of data and observes characteristics of each cluster.

Issues Related to Clustering

- **Scalability:** Clustering algorithms should be scalable and can handle large databases.
- **Ability to Deal with Different Kinds of Attributes:** clustering algorithms should be in such a way that it should be capable of handling different kinds of data such as numerical data, categorical, and binary data and so on.
- **Discovery of Clusters with Attribute Shape:** Clustering algorithms should be capable of producing clusters of arbitrary shape using different measures.
- **High Dimensionality:** Clustering algorithm should be designed in such way that it should be capable of handling both low as well as high dimensional data.
- **Ability to Deal with Noisy Data:** Data sources may contain noisy, missing or erroneous data. So presence of these data may leads too poor quality clusters. Hence clustering algorithm should be designed in such way that it should handle noisy, missing and error data and produce high quality clusters.
- **Interpretability:** The results of clustering should be readable, interpretable, comprehensible into different form and useful to the end users.

Types of Clustering

- Partitioning Method
- Hierarchical Method
- Density-based Method
- Grid-Based Method
- Model-Based Method
- Constraint-based Method

Partitioning Method

Given a database of 'n' objects and then the partitioning algorithm groups the objects into 'k' partition where k ≤ n. Each group should have at least one object. Also, objects in the same group should satisfy the following criteria:

- Each group contains at least one object.
- Each object must belong to exactly one group.
- Objects within clusters are highly similar and objects present in the different clusters are highly dissimilar.
- Kmeans algorithm is the most popular algorithm in this category. It works as follows.
- For a given number of partitions (say K), the Kmeans partitioning will create an initial partitioning representing K clusters using some distance measure.
- Then it uses the iterative technique to improve the partitioning by moving objects from one group to other. The problem with Kmeans algorithm is that K (number of partition) value is fixed before executing cluster and it does not change.
- Another algorithm is Kmedoid which is an improvement of Kmeans algorithm and provides better performance.

Hierarchical Clustering

In this method, it tries to create a hierarchical decomposition of given objects into various groups. There are two approaches used here for decomposition:

1. Agglomerative Approach
2. Divisive Approach

In agglomerative approach, clustering starts with each object forming a different group. Then, it keeps on merging the objects that are close to one another into groups. It repeats it until all of the groups are merged into one or until the termination condition holds. It is also known as bottom-up approach. In divisive approach, clustering starts with all the objects representing a single cluster as a root. In each iteration, it tries to split the cluster into smaller clusters having similar i.e. objects that are close to one another. It proceeds towards down and split the cluster until each object in one cluster or the termination condition holds. This method is inflexible means that once a merging or splitting is done then it cannot be undone. It is also known as top-down approach.

Density-Based Clustering

It is based on the concept of density i.e. each clusters should have minimum number of data objects within the cluster radius. Here a cluster is continuing growing as long as the density in the neighborhood exceeds some threshold.

Grid-Based Clustering

In this clustering, the objects together form a grid. The object space is quantized into finite number of cells that form a grid structure. The main advantage of this approach is that it produces the cluster faster and takes less processing time.

Model-Based Clustering

In this approach, a model is used to build each cluster and find the best fit of data object for a given clusters. This method locates the clusters by using the density function. It reflects spatial distribution of the data objects among the clusters. It determines the number of clusters based on statistics, taking outlier or noise into account. Also, it yields robust clustering algorithm.

Constraint-Based Clustering

In this approach, the clustering is performed by incorporating the user and application constraints or requirements. Here, a constraint is the user expectation or the properties of desired clustering results. It is so interactive since constraints provide an interactive way of communication with the clustering process. Constraints can be specified by the user or by the application.

Association Rule Mining

As defined by (Jiawei et al. 2006), an association rule identifies the collection of data attributes that are statistically related to one another. The association rule mining problem can be defined as follows: Given a database of related transactions, a minimal support and confidence value, find all association rules whose confidence and support are above the given threshold. In general, it produces a dependency rule that predicts an object based on the occurrences of other objects. An association rule is of the form X->Y where X is called antecedent and Y is called consequent. There are two measures that assist in identification of frequent items and generate rules from it. One such measure is confidence which is the conditional probability of Y given X, $Pr(Y|X)$, and the other is support which is the prior probability of X and Y, $Pr(X and Y)$ (Jiawei et al 2006). It can be classified into either single dimensional association rule or multidimensional association rule based on number of predicates it contains (Jiawei et al. 2006). It can be extended to better fit in the application domains like genetic analysis and electronic commerce and so on. Aprior algorithm, FP growth algorithm and vertical data format are some of the standard algorithm used to identify the frequent items present in the large data set (Jiawei et al. 2006). Association rule mining is shown in Figure 10.

Algorithms used for association rule mining are given below:

- Aprior algorithm
- FP-Growth
- Vertical Data format algorithm

Figure 10. Data mining task association rule

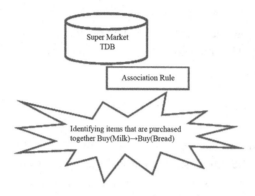

APPLICATIONS OF DATA MINING

Data mining applications include (Sathiyamoorthi & Murali Baskaran 2010b):

- **Market Basket Analysis and Management**
  - Helps in determining customer purchase pattern i.e. what kind of consumer going to buy what kind of products.
  - Helps in finding the best products for different consumers. Here prediction is a data mining technique used to find the users interests based on available data.
  - Performs correlations analysis between product and sales.
  - Helps in finding clusters of consumers who share the same purchase characteristics such as user interests, regular habits, and monthly income and so on.
  - Is used in analyzing and determining customer purchasing pattern.
  - Provides multidimensional analysis on user data and support various summary reports.
- **Corporate Analysis and Risk Management in Industries**
  - It performs cash flow analysis and prediction, contingent claim analysis to evaluate assets.
  - Where it summarizes and compares the resource utilization i.e. how much resources are allocated and how much are currently available. it, helps in production planning and control system
  - Current trend analysis where it monitors competitors and predict future market directions.
- **Fraud Detection or Outlier Detection**
  - It is also known as outlier analysis which is used in the fields of credit card analysis and approval and telecommunication industry to detect fraudulent users.
  - In communication department, it helps in finding the destination of the fraud call, time duration of the fraud call, at what time the user made a call and the day or week of the calls and so on.
  - It helps in analyzing the patterns that are deviating from the normal behavior called outlier.
- **Spatial and Time Series Data Analysis**
  - For predicting stock market trends and bond analysis
  - Identifying areas that shares similar characteristics

- **Image Retrieval and Analysis**
  - Image segmentation and classification
  - Face recognition and detection
- **Web Mining**
  - Web content mining
  - Web structure mining
  - Web log mining

The most emerging research area is Web mining which is discussed in the next section.

WEB MINING

In today's Internet scenario, WWW plays a significant role in retrieving and sharing information. Hence, WWW becomes a huge repository of data. As a result, it is difficult for data analyst or end users to analyze the entire data and to discover some useful information. To overcome these troubles, data mining can be applied for knowledge discovery in WWW. To discover knowledge from Web, Web mining is used. Web mining is broadly categorized into three major areas such as Web Content Mining; Web Structure Mining and Web Log Mining or Web Usage Mining (Srivastava et al. 2000; Zaiane 2000). Web Content Mining is the part of Web Mining which focuses on the raw information available in Webpages (Kosala & Blockeel 2000). Data source mainly consists of textual data present in the Webpages. Mining is based on content categorization and content ranking of Web pages. Web Structure Mining is a Web Mining task which deals with the structure of the Websites. The data source consists of structural information present in Webpages that are hyperlinks. The mining includes link-based categorization of Webpages, ranking of Webpages through a combination of content and structure (Brin & Pange 1998), and reverse engineering of Website models. Web Usage Mining (WUM) is another Web Mining task which describes knowledge discovery from Web server log files. The source data mainly consist of the raw text file that is stored in Web server when a user accesses the Webpage. It might be represented either in Common Log Format (CLF) or in Extended Common Log Format (ECLF). It includes Web personalization, adaptive Websites, and user modeling. In this research work, WUM is used to optimize the existing Web caching technique. It is noted that Research in Web Usage Mining started in late 1990's according to Srivastava et al. (2000), Mobasher et al. (2002), Cyrus et al (1997) and Feng et al. (2009). Web Usage Mining is also known as Web log mining wherein it relies on the information present in the Web log file produced by the Web servers. Web log files are raw text file which needs certain preprocessing methods before applying the data mining techniques. Hence, the next subsection gives an overview of Web log mining and its applications.

Web Log Mining

Who's coming to your site? What are they doing there? Where are they coming from? Answers to these questions are recorded in raw log file. It provides necessary information to enhance the performance of WWW. Web usage mining, an application of data mining technique is used to discover pattern from Web sources. These discovered patterns are used to understand and to serve the need of Web-based system in a better way. Hence, prior to applying data mining techniques, Web log files require certain kind of preprocessing activities that must be performed on raw text file called Web server log. Web usage mining is defined as the automatic discovery of useful patterns from Web server log (Sathiyamoorthi, 2016). In this, knowledge discovery process and pattern analysis focus on Web user access data. The browsing behaviors exhibited by different users are captured in access log by the server. Most systems use log data as their data source. In this thesis, the usage data represents the access log recorded in proxy server that records information about user navigation to different Websites. The basic steps involved in WUM are (Sathiyamoorthi & Murali Baskaran 2011a):

1. Data Collection
2. Data Preprocessing
3. Pattern Extraction
4. Pattern Analysis and Visualization
5. Pattern Applications

Data sources used for WUM can be collected from three different locations (Srivastva et al. 2000) as is given below:

- **Server-Level:** It stores data about the requests that are activated by different clients. It keeps track of multiple users' interest on a single Website. The main drawback is that log files must be secured since it contains some sensitive information about the users. Further, it does not contain information about cached pages.
- **Client-Level:** The browser itself will send some information to a repository regarding the user's access. This is achieved by using an adhoc browsing application or through client-side applications that can run on standard Web browsers. It requires the design team to develop special software and deploy it along with the end users' browsers.
- **Proxy-level:** It collects the information about user's browsing behavior and recorded at proxy server log. It keeps track of multiple users' interest on several Websites. It is used only by the users whose requests are passed through the proxy.

NEED FOR DATA PRE-PROCESSING

In the present internet scenario, there has been barely credible growth of Web in terms of users and Webpages. It is vital for the Website owners to better understand their customer's need; provide better services and to improve the Website quality. Due to these reasons, a huge amount of data related to the users interactions with the Websites were recorded in the Web server access log (Navin et al. 2011). Thus, Web access log plays a predominant role to predict the user access pattern, by pre-fetching and caching of Web data for better performance. Web log files contain raw data, which needs certain kind of pre-processing activities prior to data mining techniques. Most of the recorded data present in the Web log are irrelevant and incomplete to accomplish data mining tasks. Hence, the task in Web usage mining is data pre-processing activities which prepares data for data mining tasks. On Web usage data, different data mining techniques such as association rule, clustering, classification and so on can be applied in order to discover hidden patterns. This discovered knowledge is useful in applications such as System improvement, Website modification, Business intelligence, etc. The following section presents a detailed research works on Web log mining.

RESEARCH PROGRESS IN WEB LOG MINING

Many researchers have focused on Web Usage Mining in recent years (Srivastava et al. 2000; Mobasher et al. 2002; Sathiyamoorthi & Muralibaskaran 2013). Web mining is concerned as extracting knowledge from Web data (Etizoni 1996). It can be categorized into different areas as follow; Web content mining, Web structure mining and Web usage mining. Web usage mining is the application of data mining techniques to large Web data repositories (Cooley et al. 1997). Data is collected in the Web server whenever user accesses the Website and is represented in standard formats. The standard log format called Common Log File (CLF) consists of IP address, access date and time, request method (GET or POST), URL of page accessed, transfer protocol, success return code or in Extended Common Log File (ECLF) format (Cooley et al. 1999). As raw data collected from the Web server is incomplete and also limited fields are required for pattern discovery, preprocessing is necessary to discover access pattern. Once the raw log data is preprocessed, different data mining techniques like statistical analysis, association rules, sequential mining and clustering can be applied to discover patterns. The basic steps in data preprocessing are user identification, page identification, session identification and page view identification (Cooley et al. 1999). The authors have also proposed some heuristics to deal with the difficulties involved in these tasks. Joshi and Krishnapuram (2000) have compared time-based and referrer-based heuristics for session identification process. The authors also state that a heuristic-based approach depends on the Website design and on the length of visit. Fu et al. (2000) have discussed the possibility of merging and analyzing multiple server log files. Various techniques have been used from the fields like statistics, machine learning, data mining and pattern recognition in order to discover patterns from Web usage log (Cooley et al 1999). Data mining tools have also been widely used to analyze and perform statistical analysis such as most visited Webpages, average daily hits, etc. These tools are mainly used to analyze Web traffic and server loads. Joshi and Krishnapuram (2000) have used association rules to discover patterns where it considers each URL as an item and identifies the relationships between them with the given support and confidence value. The sequential analysis is used by Fu et al (2000), to predict the user's future access, based on the past access sequence. Another data mining technique called clustering is used to form clusters based on the similarity present in the user access pattern by Srivastva et al (2000). In yet another work (Berendt et al. 2002), the authors have compared time-based and referrer-based heuristics for visits reconstruction. Marquardt et al (2004) have developed and used the Web usage mining application that is specific to e-learning domain.

APPLICATIONS OF WEB USAGE MINING

Web Usage Mining has been considered with great importance and hence many researchers have started focusing on this for better Web utilization. The significance of this research work can be better realized through the following research scope and findings. Web Usage Mining is well explained by Facca and Lanzi (2005), Srivastava et al (2000). Both of them have described it in their research and business communities' perspective. Web personalization is a technique which delivers personalized Web content depending on the user profile or user needs. It includes, a recommender system explained (Jaczynski & Trousse 1998, Mobasher et al. 2000) and an adaptive Website (Velasquez et al. 2004; De et. al 2004).

A recommender system suggests possible links to the user based on the access history. The adaptive Website is the one which adapts itself for each user visiting the Website in order to deliver the personalized content. Personalization is achieved by keeping track of the previously accessed Webpages for E-Commerce applications (Pirolli et al. 1996). The appearance of a Website, in terms of both content and structure, is the most important factor to be considered in many applications like product catalog for E-Commerce. Web usage mining provides detailed information regarding user behavior and it can help Website designers to redesign their Website based on it. In adaptive Website (Anderson 2002; Perkowitz & Etzioni 1998), the structure of a Website changes dynamically based on the user access patterns discovered from server logs. Site improvement may be achieved either by modifying the logical structure or the physical structure of the Website depending on the access patterns of the Website users. Some of the important works related to web usage mining is tabulated below with its merits and demerits.

RESEARCH WORKS ON WEB PREFETCHING

Response time and performance are the two important factors that play major role in determining user satisfaction (Sathiyamoorthi & Murali Baskaran 2012a). This is mainly helpful for services like Web-based applications, databases and networks, etc. Similar qualities are been expected from the users of Web services. To enhance the performance, Web log mining could provide the key to understand Web traffic behavior by developing policies for Web caching and network transmission (Anderson et al. 2002).

Web caching represents another possibility for improving the quality of a Website as the pages are delivered to the users in a faster way (Podlipnig & Boszormenyi 2003). Users are less likely to spend time on a slow Website. By using the results of a WUM system, a Web caching system turns capable to predict the user's next request by loading it into a cache. Thus, the speed of page retrieval from a Website is improved as the user will not wait for the page to be loaded from the server. Information about how customers use a Website is central for the marketers of retailing business. Alex and Mulvenna (1998), Srivastava et al (2000) have discussed a knowledge discovery process to discover marketing intelligence from Web data(Sathiyamoorthi & Murali Baskaran 2012b). Some of the research work on web usage mining is tabulated in Table 1. From this, it is also observed that both the techniques would improve the performance by reducing server load and latency in accessing Webpages. However, if the Web caching and pre-fetching approaches are integrated inefficiently then this might causes huge network traffic; increase in Web server load in addition to the inefficient use of cache space (Waleed et al. 2011). Hence, the pre-fetching approach should be designed carefully in order to overcome the above said limitations. Therefore, the importance of Web usage mining to optimize the existing Web cache performance has been realized.

Table 1. Literature support for formulation of research problem

S. No.	Base papers	Authors	Issue and Inference
1	Web user clustering and its application to pre-fetching using ART neural networks	Rangarajan et al (2004)	It presents a pre-fetching approach based on ART1 neural network. It does not address the issues while integrating Web caching and Web pre-fetching
2	Integrating Web caching and Web pre-fetching in Client-Side Proxies	Teng et al (2005)	Have proposed pre-fetching approach based on association rule. They have proposed an innovative cache replacement policy called (Integration of Web Caching and Pre-fetching (IWCP). They have categorized Web objects into implied and non-implied objects.
3	A clustering-based pre-fetching scheme on a Web cache environment	Pallis et al (2008)	Proposed a graph-based pre-fetching technique. Have used DG for pre-fetching. It is based on association rule and it is controlled by support and confidence. Moreover they have used traditional policies in Web cache environment and didn't address issues while integrating these two.
4	Intelligent Client-side Web Caching Scheme Based on Least Recently Used Algorithm and Neuro-Fuzzy System	Ali and Shamsuddin (2009)	It uses the neuro-fuzzy system to classify a Web object into cacheable or un-cacheable objects. It has LRU algorithm in cache to predict Web objects that may be re-accessed later. Training process requires long time and extra computational cost. It ignored the factors such as cost and size of the objects in the cache replacement policy
5	A survey of Web cache replacement strategies	Podlipnig and Böszörmenyi (2003)	The authors have reviewed and presented an overview of various page replacement policies. It is observed that GDSF perform better in Web cache environment. They also have presented merits and demerits of various page replacement policies.
6	A Keyword-Based Semantic Pre-fetching Approach in Internet News Services	Ibrahim and Xu (2004)	It predicts users' future access based on semantic preferences of past retrieved Web documents. It is implemented on Internet news services. The semantic preferences are identified by analyzing keywords present in the URL of previously accessed Web. It employs a neural network model over the keyword set to predict user future requests.
7	A Survey of Web Caching and Pre-fetching	Waleed et al (2011)	The authors have discussed and reviewed various Web caching and Web pre-fetching techniques. It is observed that most of the pre-fetching techniques discussed here were focusing on single user which will ultimately reduce server performance if number of users increase. Moreover, in recent year's data mining plays a major role in Web pre-fetching areas and most of the data mining-based approach uses association rule mining.

DATA WAREHOUSE

A data warehouse contains a subject oriented, integrated, time variant and nonvolatile data for organizational effective decision-making. It supports analytical reporting, structured, ad hoc queries and decision making. It has the following characteristics:

- **Subject Oriented**
  - Means that it containing relevant and useful data for timely decision making under different sections
- **Integrated**
  - It is an integrated data source which collects data from various heterogeneous data sources such as relational databases, flat files and mapped under a unified schema.
- **Time Variant**
  - It contains current and up-to-date historical data.

- **Non-volatile**
  - ○ It is permanently stored data i.e. data is not removed when database modification such as insertion or deletion. The data warehouse is separated from the organizational database thereby it reduces the frequent changes. Any changes in the operational database are not reflected to the data warehouse.

DATA WAREHOUSE CONSTRUCTION

The process of building data warehouse consists of following steps and shown in Figure 11.

1. **Data collection:** where data are collected from various data sources which are geographically distributed across the world
2. **Data cleaning:** where it removes noise, irrelevant and inconsistent data present in the collected data
3. **Data integration:** where it integrates various data sources into a single unified schema and provide a consistent view of data warehouse
4. **Data transformation:** formatting the data in accordance to the data warehouse schema and architecture

Figure 11. Data warehouse construction

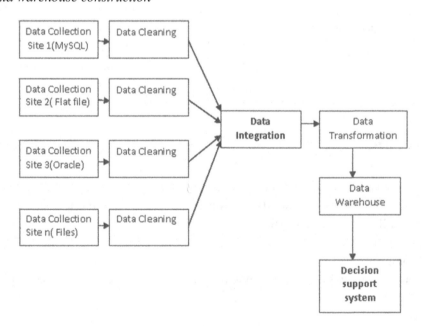

COMMUNICATION BETWEEN DATA WAREHOUSE AND DATA SOURCES

To communicate with the various heterogeneous data sources, the following two approaches are used:

1. Query Driven Approach
2. Update Driven Approach

Query-Driven Approach

In this approach, mediators are used on the top of many heterogeneous data sources for transforming the data between the data warehouse and the client data source. These mediators are acting as an intermediatory for data communication to bridge communication gap between the client and data warehouse.

*   When a query is issued to data sources, the mediator retrieves the metadata from the local data source that is used to translate the given query into the query that is appropriate to execute in that local source.
*   Then, the translated query is send to the query processor engine which executes the query and retrieves the data from that source.
*   Finally, resultant data are collected from various data sources and merged then transformed for the original query.
*   The main drawback of this approach is that it takes longer time to communicate with different data sources and to get actual data from there. If there is any communication delay or problem with the computer network, then retrieval of data is impossible. So, it is not suitable for timely decision making system and hence rarely used.

Update-Driven Approach

In this update-driven approach, rather than issuing a query to various heterogeneous data sources to collect the data on demand basis, the information from multiple heterogeneous data sources are pushed and combined under unified schema called as data warehouse. It uses processes called data cleaning, integration and transformation in advance. Here, the data is collected and stored in a place called data warehouse well in advance. Further, it is used for direct querying and analysis of data by the top level manager to make an effective decision. Also, it contains up-to-date information for decision making.

*   It is suitable for quick and timely decision making and provides high performance.
*   Communication delay and network problems can be avoided in transferring data.
*   Quick feedback to all the departments is possible

INTEGRATION OF DATA MINING SYSTEM WITH A DATA WAREHOUSE SYSTEM

Various integration strategies are possible which are based on whether it uses the underlying concepts or functionality of the underlying database or data warehouse system. Based on this, it is classified as follows:

- **Non-Coupling:** Data mining system is not integrated with any of the database or the data warehouse system components and all are working as independent parts. Hence, there is no communication with the other system. It is mainly used for designing new data mining system which focuses on research and development of various data mining techniques for knowledge discovery. Most of the scientists are using this type of system.
- **No Coupling:** Data mining system does not utilize functionalities of a data mining or data warehousing system. It only fetches the data from a particular data source called files, processes it by using some data mining techniques and then stores the results in another file. Here, typical data source will be the operating system files which are used for storing input and output.
- **Loose Coupling:** The data mining system may use some of the functionalities of an underlying database and data warehouse system. It fetches the data from the particular database or from data warehouse and then process it using data mining system. It stores the results back to the database or in the warehouse for future reference.
- **Semi–Tight Coupling:** The data mining system is coupled with the database or the warehouse for fetching and storing the data. In addition to that, an efficient implementation of a few data mining task primitives can be derived from the underlying database.
- **Tight Coupling:** The data mining system is smoothly integrated into the database or data warehouse system. Also, data mining is treated as one of the subsystems and used as one of the functional component of an information processing system. It fully dependent on data warehouse or data base for their functionalities.

Figure 12 shows the integration of data mining system with data warehousing in an organization. The organizational decision support system uses the data mining techniques to make an effective and timely decision. In Figure 12, data mart is a component that contains data that is specific to the given department (Sathiyamoorthi & Murali Baskaran 2010b).

FUTURE RESEARCH DIRECTIONS

As the user datasets containing the privacy information should not be exposed to the outside world then privacy preserving data mining techniques can be applied in order to hide some personal information about the users. Also, evolutionary optimization techniques can be applied in order to optimize the data mining system further. Moreover, a hybrid approach out of existing algorithms can be tried out for the process that requires two or more techniques. Data mining system can also be used to extend the performance of Content Distribution Network (CDN) server and Enterprise Resource Planning (ERP) system for an effective content distribution and decision making process. This system can also be used in the application areas where Web search, access and retrieval are involved, such as Predicting user purchase pattern of commodities in E-Commerce Website, redesigning of a site according to user interest. Nowadays, big data is a field that is emerging rapidly and lot of research work is progressing in this field.

Figure 12. Integration of data warehouse with data mining system

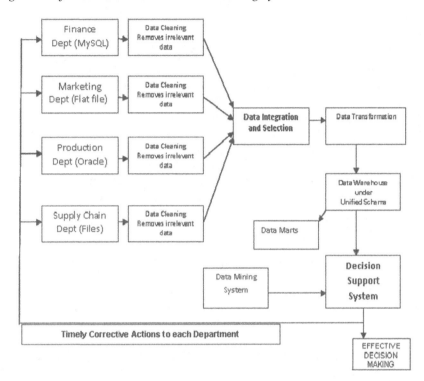

CONCLUSION

Due to the presence of huge volume of data and noisy data, it is impossible for a human being to analyze and retrieve some useful knowledge out of it. Hence, data mining plays a vital role in knowledge discovery from huge datasets. From this extensive survey, it is understood that data mining plays a vital role and helps in discovering knowledge from huge dataset. This chapter discussed the basic concepts, techniques and importance of data mining in KDD process and the construction of a data warehousing system. Also, it narrated and underlined the importance of certain data mining techniques in various fields or domains like web mining. Though data is retrieved from data sources, they need to undergo a data preprocessing step where removal of irrelevant and inconsistent content takes place. Hence, data preprocessing was discussed. Through the preprocessing approach, data is prepared for data mining tasks. This chapter also gave an overview of Web mining and its applications in order to improve the website performance.

REFERENCES

Ali, W., & Shamsuddin, S. M. (2009). Intelligent Client-Side Web Caching Scheme Based on Least Recently Used Algorithm and Neuro-Fuzzy System. In *Sixth International Symposium on Neural Networks,* (LNCS). Springer-Verlag Berlin Heidelberg. doi:10.1007/978-3-642-01510-6_9

Anderson, C. R. (2002). *A Machine Learning Approach to Web Personalization* (Ph.D. Thesis). University of Washington.

Berendt, B., Mobasher, B., Nakagawa, M., & Spiliopoulou, M. (2002). The Impact of Site Structure and User Environment and Session Reconstruction in Web usage analysis. In *Proceedings of the forth Web KDD 2002 workshop at the ACM – SIGKDD Conference on Knowledge Discovery in Databases (KDD 2002)*.

Brin, S., & Pange, L. (1998). The Anatomy of a Large-scale Hyper Textual Web Search Engine. *Computer Networks and ISDN Systems, 30*(1-7), 107–117. doi:10.1016/S0169-7552(98)00110-X

Cooley, R., Bamshed, M., & Srinivastava, J. (1997). Web Mining: Information and Pattern Discovery on the World Wide Web. In *International conference on Tools with Artificial Intelligence*. Newport Beach, CA: IEEE. doi:10.1109/TAI.1997.632303

Cooley, R., Mobasher, B., & Srinivastaa, J. (1999). Data Preparation for Mining World Wide Web Browsing Patterns. *Journal of knowledge and Information Systems,* 78-85.

Cyrus, S., Zarkessh, A. M., Jafar, A., & Vishal, S. (1997). Knowledge discovery from Users Web Page Navigation. In *Workshop on Research Issues in Data Engineering*. Retrieved from www.tutorialspoint. com/data_mining/notes

De, P. B., Aroyo, L., & Chepegin, V. (2004). The Next Big Thing: Adaptive Web-Based Systems. *Journal of Digital Information, 5*(1), 22–30.

Dunham, M. H. (2006). *Data Mining Introductory and Advanced Topics* (1st ed.). Pearson Education.

Etizoni, O. (1996). The World Wide Web: Quagmire or Gold Mine. *Communications of the ACM, 39*(2), 65–68. doi:10.1145/240455.240473

Facca, F.M., & Lanzi, P. L. (2005). Mining Interesting Knowledge from Web logs: A Survey. *International Journal of Data and Knowledge Engineering, 53*(3), 225-241.

Feng, W., Man, S., & Hu, G. (2009). *Markov Tree Prediction on Web Cache Pre-fetching. In Software Engineering, Artificial Intelligence (SCI)* (Vol. 209, pp. 105–120). Berlin: Springer-Verlag.

Fu, Y., Sandhu, K., & Shih, M. (2000). A Generalization-Based Approach to Clustering of Web Usage Sessions. In *Proceedings of the KDD Workshop on Web Mining*. Springer.

Ibrahim, T. I., & Xu, C. Z. (2004). A Keyword-Based Semantic Pre-fetching Approach in Internet News Services. *IEEE Transactions on Knowledge and Data Engineering, 16*(5), 601–611. doi:10.1109/TKDE.2004.1277820

Jaczynski, M., & Trousse, B. (1998). WWW Assisted Browsing by Reusing Past Navigations of a Group of Users. In *Proceedings of the Advances in Case-Based Reasoning, Forth European Workshop* (LNCS). Dublin, Ireland: Springer.

Jiawei, H., Micheline, K., & Jian, P. (2006). *Data Mining Concepts and Techniques*. Pearson Education.

Joshi, A., & Krishnapuram, R. (2000). On Mining Web Access Logs. In *ACM SIGMOD Workshop on Research Issues in Data Mining and Knowledge Discovery*, (pp. 63- 69).

Koskela, T.J., Heikkonen, & Kaski, K. (2003). Web cache optimization with nonlinear model using object feature. *Computer Networks Journal, 43*(6), 805-817.

Marquardt, C., Becker, K., & Ruiz, D. (2004). A Pre-processing Tool for Web Usage Mining in the Distance Education Domain. In *Proceedings of the International Database Engineering and Application Symposium (IDEAS)*, (pp. 78-87).

Mobasher, B., Dai, H., Luo, T., & Nakagawa, M. (2002). Discovery and Evaluation of Aggregate Usage Profiles for Web Personalization. *Data Mining and Knowledge Discovery, 6*(1), 61–82. doi:10.1023/A:1013232803866

Navin, K., Tyagi, & Solanki, A.K. (2011). Analysis of Server Log by Web Usage Mining for Website Improvement. *International Journal of Computer Science Issues, 7*(4).

Pallis, G., Vakali, A., & Pokorny, J. (2008). A Clustering-Based Pre-Fetching Scheme on A Web Cache Environment. ACM Journal Computers and Electrical Engineering, 34(4).

Perkowitz, M., & Etzioni, O. (1998). Adaptive Web Sites: Automatically Synthesizing Web Pages. *IAAI '98: Proceedings of the Fifteenth National/Tenth International Conference on Artificial Intelligence/ Innovative Applications of Artificial Intelligence*, (pp. 727-732).

Pirolli, P., Pitkow, J., & Ramna, R. (1996). Extracting Usable Structure from the Web. In CHI – 96.

Podlipnig, S., & Boszormenyi, L. (2003). A Survey of Web Cache Replacement Strategies. *ACM Computing Surveys, 35*(4), 374–398. doi:10.1145/954339.954341

Rangarajan, S.K., Phoha, V.V., Balagani, K., Selmic, R.R., & Iyengar S.S. (2004). Web User Clustering and its Application to Pre-fetching using ART Neural Networks. *IEEE Computer*, 45-62.

Sathiyamoorthi, V. (2016). A Novel Cache Replacement Policy for Web Proxy Caching System Using Web Usage Mining. *International Journal of Information Technology and Web Engineering, 11*(2), 12–20. doi:10.4018/IJITWE.2016040101

Sathiyamoorthi, V., & Murali Bhaskaran, V. (2010a). Data Preparation Techniques for Mining World Wide Web through Web Usage Mining-An Approach. *International Journal of Recent Trends in Engineering, 2*(4), 1–4.

Sathiyamoorthi, V., & Murali Bhaskaran, V. (2010b). Data Mining for Intelligent Enterprise Resource Planning System. *International Journal of Recent Trends in Engineering, 2*(3), 1–4.

Sathiyamoorthi, V., & Murali Bhaskaran, V. (2011a). Improving the Performance of Web Page Retrieval through Pre-Fetching and Caching. *European Journal of Scientific Research, 66*(2), 207–217.

Sathiyamoorthi, V., & Murali Bhaskaran, V. (2011b). Data Pre-Processing Techniques for Pre-Fetching and Caching of Web Data through Proxy Server. *International Journal of Computer Science and Network Security, 11*(11), 92-98.

Sathiyamoorthi, V., & Murali Bhaskaran, V. (2012a). A Novel Approach for Web Caching through Modified Cache Replacement Algorithm. *International Journal of Engineering Research and Industrial Applications*, *5*(1), 241–254.

Sathiyamoorthi, V., & Murali Bhaskaran, V. (2012b). Optimizing the Web Cache Performance by Clustering Based Pre-Fetching Technique Using Modified ART1. *International Journal of Computers and Applications*, *44*(1), 51–60.

Sathiyamoorthi, V., & Murali Bhaskaran, V. (2013). Novel Approaches for Integrating MART1 Clustering based Pre-Fetching Technique with Web Caching. *International Journal of Information Technology and Web Engineering*, *8*(2), 18–32. doi:10.4018/jitwe.2013040102

Srivastava, J., Cooley, R., Deshpande, M., & Tan, P. N. (2000). Web Usage Mining: Discovery and Applications of Usage Patterns from Web Data. *SIGKDD Explorations*, *1*(2), 12–23. doi:10.1145/846183.846188

Teng, W., Chang, C., & Chen, M. (2005). Integrating Web Caching and Web Pre-fetching in Client-Side Proxies. *IEEE Transactions on Parallel and Distributed Systems*, *16*(5), 444–455. doi:10.1109/TPDS.2005.56

Velasquez, J., Bassi, A., Yasuda, H., & Aoki, T. (2004). Mining Web Data to Create Online Navigation Recommendations. In *Proceedings of the Fourth IEEE International Conference on Data Mining (ICDM)*. doi:10.1109/ICDM.2004.10019

Waleed, A., Siti, M. S., & Abdul, S. I. (2011). A Survey of Web Caching and Pre--fetching. International Journal on Advances in Soft Computing and Application, 3(1).

Zaiane, O. (2000). Web Mining: Concepts, Practices and Research. In *Proc. SDBD, Conference Tutorial Notes*.

KEY TERMS AND DEFINITIONS

Association Rule: Given a database of related transactions, a minimal support and confidence value, it will find all association rules whose confidence and support are above the given threshold. In general, it produces a dependency rule that predicts an object based on the occurrences of other objects.

Classification: It is the process of building a model that describes the class for an object. The main purpose of this model is, to predict the class label of an object. Classification model is built based on the training datasets and tested using testing datasets where testing datasets contain objects whose class label are unknown or to be predicted.

Clustering: Cluster analysis refers to grouping of objects that are similar to each other. Here objects that are highly similar form a cluster. Here various measures are used to find the similarity between objects.

Data Cleaning: it is the process of removing irrelevant, inconsistent and incomplete attribute values from the dataset. It is used to select task relevant data from huge dataset.

Data Mining: It is also known as knowledge Discovery in Database (KDD) is the process of extracting implicit, previously unknown and potentially useful information out of database.

Data Warehousing: A data warehouse contains a subject oriented, integrated, time variant and nonvolatile data for organizational effective decision-making.

Normalization: Normalization involves scaling all values for given attribute in order to make them fall within a small specified range.

Outlier Analysis: it is used to predict an object that deviates from the group of objects called outlier. It is mainly used in fraud detection.

Prediction: It is used to predict unknown value from the given set of data. Regression analysis is a statistical methodology that is used to predict numeric value which is based on either linear regression or non-linear regression.

Chapter 17
Text Mining:
Current Trends and Applications

Kijpokin Kasemsap
Suan Sunandha Rajabhat University, Thailand

ABSTRACT

This chapter reveals the overview of text mining; text mining, patent analysis, and keyword selection; text mining and sentiment analysis in modern marketing; text mining applications in the biomedical sciences; and the multifaceted applications of text mining. Text mining is an advanced technology utilized in business, marketing, biomedical sciences, education, and operations. Text mining offers a solution to many problems, drawing on techniques concerning information retrieval, natural language processing, information extraction, and knowledge management. Through text mining, information can be extracted to derive summaries for the words contained in the documents. Text mining has the potential to increase the research base available to business and society and to enable business to utilize the research base more effectively. Economic and societal benefits of text mining include cost savings, productivity gains, innovative new service development, new business models, and new medical treatments.

INTRODUCTION

There is a tremendous growth in the volume of online text documents from networked resources, such as the Internet, digital libraries, and company-wide intranets (Kim, 2009). Many text mining approaches are based on words in the texts (Loh, Wives, Lichtnow, & de Oliveira, 2009). Text mining deals with how to extract the latent knowledge from the unstructured textual descriptions (Yoon, Park, & Coh, 2014). Text mining requires the highly scalable algorithms to meet the overall performance demands (Indurkhya, 2015) and facilitates the identification of relevant literature, its rapid categorization, and its summarization (Thomas, McNaught, & Ananiadou, 2011). Text mining has adopted certain techniques from the more general field of data analysis, including sophisticated methods for analyzing relationships among highly formatted data, such as numerical data or data with a relatively small fixed number of possible values (Kao et al., 2012).

DOI: 10.4018/978-1-5225-1877-8.ch017

Text mining can be broadly defined as a knowledge-intensive process in which a user interacts with a document collection over time by using a combination of analysis tools (Cheney, 2015). The good text knowledge representation model should contain rich text semantics and should automatically construct with a lower complexity (Zhang, Luo, He, & Cai, 2013). Text mining involves six main phases (i.e., business understanding, data understanding, data preparation, modeling, evaluation, and deployment). Perovšek et al. (2016) indicated that text mining can be distinguished from general data mining by special procedures applied in the data preparation phase, where unstructured or poorly structured text needs to be converted into organized data, structured as a table of instances (rows) described by attributes (columns).

This chapter aims to bridge the gap in the literature on the thorough literature consolidation of text mining. The extensive literature of text mining provides a contribution to practitioners and researchers by describing the trends and applications of text mining in order to maximize the technological impact of text mining in the digital age.

Background

Texts are written in natural language, carrying out implicit knowledge, and ambiguities (Cherfi, Napoli, & Toussaint, 2009). Text mining, also known as text data mining or text analytics, is considered as a subfield of data mining research (Perovšek et al., 2016) and continues to expand as mass volumes of unstructured data (Karl, Wisnowski, & Rushing, 2015). Data mining is the process of applying these computational methods in showing unknown data formats in large data sets (Kasemsap, 2015) and provides a set of techniques of artificial intelligence which can be used to increase the efficiency of data mining methods (Guerrero et al., 2014). Data mining brings the new direction on business planning from the last decades (Klepac & Berg, 2015) and is utilized to discover patterns and relationships in the data in order to help make better business decisions (Kasemsap, 2016a).

Text mining tasks include the activities of search engines, such as assigning texts to one or more categories (i.e., text categorization), grouping similar texts together (i.e., text clustering), finding the subject of discussions (i.e., concept/entity extraction), finding the tone of a text (i.e., sentiment analysis), summarizing documents, and learning relations between entities described in a text (i.e., entity relation modeling) (Truyens & van Eecke, 2014). Text mining techniques include text categorization, summarization, topic detection, concept extraction, search and retrieval, and document clustering (Hashimi, Hafez, & Mathkour, 2015). Text categorization concerns of classifying documents into some categories according to their contents, characteristics, and properties (Yang, Lee, & Hsiao, 2015). When documents are properly categorized, documents in a cluster should have a common theme (Yang et al., 2015).

The applications of text mining include various disciplines, ranging from biomedicine to legal, business intelligence, and security (Truyens & van Eecke, 2014). Text mining applications enhance novel thinking (Segers & de Vries, 2003), develop artificial intelligence (Falkenhainer, Forbus, & Gentner, 1986), and create valuable knowledge for more effective knowledge management (Xu & Luo, 2009). Text mining seeks to extract the useful information from data sources through the identification and exploration of interesting patterns (Cheney, 2015) and helps individual efficiently analyze a large number of texts (Yamada, Kato, & Hirokawa, 2013). As more reliable tools are developed for text analysis, it is important to capture the text information for an analysis that was unavailable within conventional text analysis approaches (Fujii, Iwayama, & Kando, 2007).

IMPORTANT PERSPECTIVES ON TEXT MINING

This section emphasizes the overview of text mining; text mining, patent analysis, and keyword selection; text mining and sentiment analysis in modern marketing; text mining applications in the biomedical sciences; and the multifaceted applications of text mining.

Overview of Text Mining

With the growth of the World Wide Web, the applications of text mining (e.g., web search engines) have become commonplace (Chew, 2009). Text mining is regarded as a process to find the unknown and useful patterns from a large text repository (Jin, Jeong, & Yoon, 2015). These patterns can become the important intelligence for decision making (Tseng, Lin, & Lin, 2007). Text mining deals with the construction of models and patterns from text resources, aiming at solving several tasks, such as text categorization and clustering, taxonomy construction, and sentiment analysis (Feldman & Sanger, 2007). Most of text mining tools assume that keywords can be used to label the important content of documents, and thus the operation for knowledge discovery can be executed on the labels of documents (Feldman & Hirsh, 1997). Text mining provides a set of labels on each document and discovery operations are performed on the labels (Yoon et al., 2014).

Text mining and natural language processing are the fast growing areas of research, with numerous applications in business, science, and creative industries (Perovšek, Kranjc, Erjavec, Cestnik, & Lavrac, 2016). Due to the growing amount of digital information stored in natural language, systems that automatically process text are significant and useful (Serrano, 2009). Natural language processing tasks are identical for many text mining applications (Mandl, 2015) and include four important engines, namely string matching engine, syntactic engine, concept engine, and semantic engine (Guerrero, León, Monedero, Biscarri, & Biscarri, 2014).

The typical metrics used to evaluate the performance of text classification algorithms are accuracy, precision, and recall (Rivera, Minsker, Work, & Roth, 2014). Regarding the text classification of news articles, accuracy refers to the percentage of correctly classified news articles out of the total number of classified articles (i.e., correct and incorrect classified articles). Within a label, precision refers to the proportion of correctly classified articles to the total number of articles classified under that label. Recall is the percentage of all news articles corresponding to the label that were classified with that label (Rivera et al., 2014). Text clustering is the unsupervised learning paradigm where clustering methods try to identify the inherent groupings of the text documents so that clusters are produced in which clusters exhibit both the high intra-cluster similarity and the low inter-cluster similarity (Shehata, Karray, & Kamel, 2010).

Business intelligence involves creating any type of data visualization that provides the insight into a business for the purpose of making a decision or taking an action (Kasemsap, 2016b). Three major techniques for text mining in business intelligence include term extraction, information extraction, and link analysis (Sullivan, 2004). Term extraction, the most basic technique, identifies key terms and logical entities, such as the names of organizations, locations, dates, and monetary amounts. Information extraction builds on terms extracted from text to identify the basic relationships, such as the roles of different companies in a merger or the promotion of a chemical reaction by an enzyme. Link analysis combines multiple relationships to establish the multistep models of complex processes, such as metabolic pathways (Sullivan, 2004).

Organizations establish new capabilities concerning the analysis of data and texts to create the necessary information (Penteado & Boutin, 2008). One of the most important text mining tasks that exploits ontological resources consists of the mapping of concepts to terms in textual sources (e.g., named entity recognition, and semantic indexing) and the expansion of queries in information retrieval (Jimeno-Yepes, Berlanga-Llavori, & Rebholz-Schuchmann, 2010). Ontologies represent domain knowledge that improves user interaction and interoperability between applications (Jimeno-Yepes et al., 2010).

Text Mining, Patent Analysis, and Keyword Selection

Patent documents include bibliographical information, such as application date, filing date, assignees and inventors, as well as the invention details covered by the corresponding patent (Yoon & Park, 2004). Patent documents are recognized as the important sources for evaluating the technological strength and corporate research and development (R&D) performance (Li, Wang, & Hong, 2009). Technological information extracted from patent data is utilized in various data analysis techniques and in developing the text mining tools (Murphy et al., 2014).

Patent data is semi-structured, and technological contents are easy to extract utilizing the text mining tools (Kang, Na, Kim, & Lee, 2007). Most of terms used in patent documents are technical in nature, making it more likely that keywords have only single meanings, so the problems associated with text mining approaches are expected to be relatively less severe in patent data than other applications (Lee, Yoon, & Park, 2009). The text mining-based patent analysis with WordNet or latent semantic analysis enables to establish the word ontologies by indicating the synonyms of a set of keywords (Murphy et al., 2014).

Regarding text mining, the automatic extraction of major keywords from patent documents is utilized in the technology management contexts (Dou, Leveille, Manullang, & Dou, 2005). In keyword-based studies, researchers have commonly tried to achieve their study goals through analyses using sets of keywords extracted from patent documents (Yoon, Lee, & Lee, 2010). Selecting the keywords that represents the patent's technological concept is the critical process in patent analysis as modeling bibliographic data is significant in bibliometric analysis (Ferrara & Salini, 2012). The importance of keyword selection has been recognized not only in the field of patent analysis research, but also in the text mining applications (Clifton, Cooley, & Rennie, 2004).

Applying text mining techniques to patent analysis enables to provide the technological details, implications, and trends regarding patent selection (Tseng et al., 2007). Seo et al. (2016) indicated that patent analysis-based studies tend to focus on the technology-oriented issue since the patents deal with the technological contents. Patent citations, which are linked to the patenting procedure itself, capture only the knowledge flows, thus underestimating the actual extent of knowledge flows (Lukach & Plasmans, 2005). In order to overcome the drawback of citation based approach, text mining, using textual data to discover useful pattern, can be applied along with citation analysis (No, An, & Park, 2015).

Co-word analysis is mainly utilized to explore the concept network in different fields since the nature of words, on which co-word analysis is based, can act as the important carrier of knowledge (van Raan & Tijssen, 1993). Words and co-occurrences of words cover a much broader domain than citations (Leydesdorff, 1989). Words occur not only as indicators of links among documents but also internally within documents. Thus, the text data can be used to measure the amount of knowledge transferred by measuring text similarities between patents while patent citation is used to measure a path of knowledge flows (No et al., 2015).

Text Mining and Sentiment Analysis in Modern Marketing

Web-generated opinions in blogs and social networks have recently become a valuable resource for mining the sentiments for the purpose of customer relationship management, public opinion tracking, and text filtering (Zhang, Zeng, Li, Wang, & Zuo, 2009). An opinion is considered as a statement in which the opinion holder makes a specific claim about a topic using a certain sentiment (Kim & Hovy, 2004). Online opinions can be analyzed using sentiment analysis (Mostafa, 2013). Sentiment analysis can be viewed as an automated knowledge discovery technique that aims at finding the hidden patterns in a large number of reviews, blogs, or tweets (Mostafa, 2013). Sentiment analysis deals with detecting the general sentiment that is available in online resources and social media to understand how people feel about the topic (Nassirtoussi, Aghabozorgi, Wah, & Ngo, 2015). To calculate the sentiment score, the sentiment obtained from the text is compared to a lexicon or a dictionary to determine the strength of the sentiment (Balahur, Mihalcea, & Montoyo, 2014).

Sentiment analysis techniques have been utilized in many applications, such as extracting suggestions from consumers' product reviews (Vishwanath & Aishwarya, 2011), classifying consumers' positive and negative product reviews (Turney, 2002), detecting the Internet hotspots (Li & Wu, 2010), tracking political opinions (Thomas, Pang, & Lee, 2006), determining consumers' dissatisfaction with online advertising campaigns (Qiu et al., 2010), tracking emotions in e-mails (Mohammad, 2012), predicting stock market movements (Wong, Xia, Xu, Wu, & Li, 2008), and differentiating between informative and emotional social media content (Denecke & Nejdi, 2009).

Regarding product reviews, Blair-Goldensohn et al. (2008) utilized the Google Maps data as the input in order to analyze consumer sentiments toward hotels, department stores and restaurants. Yi et al. (2003) developed a sentiment analyzer to evaluate consumers' opinions regarding digital camera features through online text reviews in order to extract consumers' sentiments concerning the important features of digital cameras, such as resolution and picture quality. Hu and Liu (2004) applied the machine learning methods to extract and summarize consumers' sentiments related to several electronic products, including digital cameras, and cellular phones. Abrahams et al. (2015) employed text mining techniques to detect online consumer complaints regarding several automotive models. Consumer sentiments can be used to categorize and prioritize vehicle defects through text mining (Abrahams et al., 2015).

Text Mining Applications in the Biomedical Sciences

Text mining is a flexible technology that can be applied to various tasks in biology and medicine (Pletscher-Frankild, Palleja, Tsafou, Binder, & Jensen, 2015) and is useful when dealing with the abundant biomedical information and they have been applied to various topics of biomedical field (Xie, Ding, & Wu, 2015). By adding meaning to text, text mining techniques produce a much more structured analysis of textual knowledge than do simple word searches, and can provide powerful tools for knowledge discovery in biomedicine (Ananiadou, 2009).

Text mining has evolved into the specialized field in the biomedical sciences where text processing and machine learning techniques are combined with mining of biological pathways and gene expression databases (Fleuren & Alkema, 2015). Text mining can assist in the analysis and interpretation of large-scale biomedical data, helping biologists gain the confirmation of hypothesized relationships between biological entities (Ailem, Role, Nadif, & Demenais, 2016). Extracting disease–gene associations from text is an obvious case for text mining, and disease–gene associations have indeed previously been extracted by the generalized co-occurrence-based text mining systems (Tsuruoka, Miwa, Hamamoto, Tsujii, & Ananiadou, 2011).

Text mining of biomedical literature has supported the development of biomedical knowledge bases, which are actively used by the research community (Jimeno-Yepes et al., 2010). These databases have contributed in the development of methods to perform text mining-related tasks, such as entity recognition and relation extraction (Yepes & Berlanga, 2015). Recognizing named entities and concepts, such as genes and diseases, in text is the basis for the biomedical applications of text mining (Jensen, Saric, & Bork, 2006). Named entity recognition (NER) is divided into two subtasks, namely recognition and normalization (also known as identification or grounding), the former being to recognize the words of interest and the latter being to map them to the correct identifiers in databases or ontologies (Pletscher-Frankild et al., 2015).

The main challenges in NER are the poor standardization of names and the fact that a name of a gene or disease may have other meanings (Chen, Liu, & Friedman, 2005). To recognize names in text, many systems thus make use of rules that look at the features of names themselves, such as capitalization and word endings, as well as contextual information from nearby words. In early methods, the rules were hand-crafted (Fukuda, Tamura, Tsunoda, & Takagi, 1998), whereas newer methods make use of machine learning (Settles, 2005), relying on the availability of manually annotated text corpora. Text mining techniques try to automate the extraction of interconnected proteins through their coexistence in sentences, abstracts or paragraphs within text corpuses (Papanikolaou, Pavlopoulos, Theodosiou, & Iliopoulos, 2015). This can be done by searching for co-occurrences between gene names (Blaschke, Hoffmann, Oliveros, & Valencia, 2001) in public repositories and online resources.

Proteins are the molecules that facilitate the most biological processes in a cell (Papanikolaou et al., 2015). At a systems biology level, the correct identification of protein–protein interactions (PPIs) is of importance for the understanding of the complex mechanisms in a cell (Papanikolaou et al., 2015). Non text-mining prediction methods for PPIs can vary concerning strategy they follow to infer the putative interactions. Those methods can be categorized depending on whether prediction is based on protein sequence, protein structure, genomic context, homology, experimental profiles, and literature-derived associations (Lees, Heriche, Morilla, Ranea, & Orengo, 2011). Regarding sequences, prediction tools use text mining-related artificial intelligence and machine learning approaches to predict protein interactions through their sequence or structural characteristics (Shen et al., 2007), such as shared binding partners (Pazos, Helmer-Citterich, Ausiello, & Valencia, 1997), domains (Chen & Liu, 2005), or neighboring residues (Ben-Hur & Noble, 2005).

Multifaceted Applications of Text Mining

Since text is the most readily available form of information around, text mining has a high potential value and wide applications (Liew, Adhitya, & Srinivasan, 2014), such as text clustering (Ahmad & Khanum, 2010), information retrieval (Vashishta & Jain, 2011), knowledge transfer and integration (Kriegel, Kroger, & Zimek, 2009), topic tracking (Patel & Sharma, 2014), summarization, categorization, clustering, and concept linkage (Patel & Sharma, 2014), information visualization and question answering (Don et al., 2007), emotional contents of texts in online social networks (Shelke, 2014), and data processing (Zhai, Velivelli, & Yu, 2004). Once the information has been selected through text mining, connections must be established between diverse data (Piedra, Ferrer, & Gea, 2014). This process is called integration and is essential for generating new knowledge (Piedra et al., 2014).

Nowadays, text mining approach is utilized in the technology management fields (Noh, Jo, & Lee, 2015). Text mining-based approaches have also been applied in technology management to exploit technological documents (Yoon et al., 2014). With the development of text mining algorithms that allow the extraction of information from the text, it is possible to find the indications of the projects' nature and likelihood to experience cost overruns (Williams & Gong, 2014). The text mining analysis indicated that there are words and word pairs that can be associated with the different levels of cost overruns, particularly for projects completed near the low bid amount and for projects with large cost overruns (Williams & Gong, 2014).

Text mining application is represented as a complex workflow with multiple phases, where individual workflow nodes support the Big Data-related MapReduce computations (Goncalves, Assuncao, & Cunha, 2013). Bug severity is the degree of impact that a defect has on the development or operation of the system, and can be classified into different levels based on their impact on the system (Chaturvedi & Singh, 2012). Various researchers have attempted text mining techniques in predicting the severity of bugs, detection of duplicate bug reports, and assignment of bugs to the suitable fixer for its adjustment (Chaturvedi & Singh, 2012). However, performance evaluation is required for text mining system development and comparison (Suominen, 2009).

The profiles of R&D projects are summarized through indicating the linkages between them (Porter, Kongthon, & Lu, 2002), and technology trends and developments can be analyzed using text mining approach (Watts & Porter, 1997). Text mining has the potential to identify the new opportunities for technology development by generating technology or patent maps (Zhu & Porter, 2002). Kostoff et al. (2004) developed an approach, whereas text mining can be used to apply the disruptive technologies, proposing the concept of disruptive technology roadmaps. Text mining can enhance science and technology roadmaps through bibliometric analysis, such as co-word and co-citation analysis (Kostoff & Schaller, 2001).

Text mining can be used by investigating overall referred words, or through the use of specific dictionary words (Moro, Cortez, & Rita, 2015), toward discovering knowledge from textual databases by isolating the bits of information from large amounts of text, identifying relationships among documents (Durfee, 2008). Text mining technology is used for plagiarism and authorship attribution, text summarization, and deception detection (Durfee, 2008). Without a strong data analysis tool, an abundance of data is still poor in information (Dirsehan, 2016).

Text mining is widely used in the fields of knowledge management and customer relationship management (Yoon et al., 2014). Dai et al. (2011) proposed MinEdec, a decision-support model that combines two competitive intelligence analysis methods, namely the Five Forces analysis and a SWOT (strength, weakness, opportunity, and threat) analysis, with various text mining technologies. Godbole and Roy (2008) deployed a text mining solution in the service industry settings, specifically in the call centers, and focused on the application of customer satisfaction analysis in the call centers. Text mining as a way to segment customers can result in predictive models that are as good as or better than models developed using only structured data (Ramsey & Bapna, 2016).

Yang et al. (2014) indicated that linguamatics I2E (Interactive Information Extraction) is the text mining platform that uses natural language processing, combined with taxonomies, to provide a highly interactive output (in Excel). The linguamatics I2E is claimed to provide effective and efficient methods performing text mining in context in extracting and analyzing patent information to answer business-critical questions. The I2E is highly scalable, allowing for the queries of huge amounts of text using large taxonomies that may include both concepts and synonyms (Yang et al., 2014).

With the staggering amount of textual information available online, about every aspect of every conceivable topic, the necessity to develop specialized text-mining systems rapidly emerges (Nassirtoussi, Aghabozorgi, Wah, & Ngo, 2014). Web text mining is the process of using unstructured web-type text documents and examining it in an attempt to find the implicit patterns hidden in the web text documents (Yu, Wang, & Lai, 2009). Through text mining, computational advertising utilizes information on web-browsing activity and additional covariates to select advertisements toward user (Soriano, Au, & Banks, 2013).

FUTURE RESEARCH DIRECTIONS

The classification of the extensive literature in the domains of text mining will provide the potential opportunities for future research. Through text mining, businesses apply the information extracted to competitive advantage, improving and producing new products and services. Big data contains the very large sets of data that are produced by people using the Internet, and that can only be stored, understood, and utilized with the help of special tools and methods (Kasemsap, 2016c). Business process modeling is the documentation of a business system using a combination of text and graphical notation (Kasemsap, 2016d). Business process management is the development and control of processes used in a company, department, and project to ensure they are effective (Kasemsap, 2017a).

Information retrieval has considerably changed with the expansion of the Internet and the advent of modern and inexpensive graphical user interfaces and mass storage devices (Kasemsap, 2017b). Supply chain networks are the integrated patterns of processes utilized within a facility and over distribution connections, adding value to customers by improving the delivery and manufacturing of products (Kasemsap, 2016e). Firms in the supply chain networks must integrate process activities internally and with other firms in the network through information system (Kasemsap, 2017c). Social media is the website and application considered as collectively constituting a medium by which people share messages, photographs, and other information, especially in online communities (Kasemsap, 2017d). An examination of linkages among text mining, big data, business process modeling, business process management, information retrieval, information system, and social media would seem to be viable for future research efforts.

CONCLUSION

This chapter highlighted the overview of text mining; text mining, patent analysis, and keyword selection; text mining and sentiment analysis in modern marketing; text mining applications in the biomedical sciences; and the multifaceted applications of text mining. The purpose of text mining is to process unstructured (textual) information, extract meaningful numeric indices from the text, and make the information contained in the text accessible to various data mining algorithms. Through text mining, information can be extracted to derive summaries for the words contained in the document or to compute summaries for the document based on the words contained in them. The ability to automatically extract information gained from text mining cuts down the time spent on ensuring the coverage of domain knowledge in the literature review process.

Text mining is an advanced technology utilized in business, marketing, biomedical sciences, education, and operations. Businesses utilize data and text mining to analyze customer and competitor data to improve competitiveness toward identifying emerging trends, exploring consumer preferences, and investigating and competitor developments; the pharmaceutical industry mines patents and research articles to improve drug discovery; within academic research, mining and analytics of large data sets are delivering efficiencies and new knowledge in areas as diverse as biological science, particle physics, and communications.

Text mining encourages innovation and growth through organizing additional value from the public research base. Economic and societal benefits of text mining include cost savings, productivity gains, innovative new service development, new business models, and new medical treatments. Text mining offers a solution to many problems, drawing on techniques concerning information retrieval, natural language processing, information extraction, and knowledge management. Text mining has the potential to increase the research base available to business and society and to enable business to utilize the research base more effectively.

REFERENCES

Abrahams, A. S., Fan, W., Wang, G. A., Zhang, Z. J., & Jiao, J. (2015). An integrated text analytic framework for product defect discovery. *Production and Operations Management*, *24*(6), 975–990. doi:10.1111/poms.12303

Ahmad, R., & Khanum, A. (2010). Document topic generation in text mining by using cluster analysis with EROCK. *International Journal of Computer Science & Security*, *4*(2), 176–182.

Ailem, M., Role, F., Nadif, M., & Demenais, F. (2016). Unsupervised text mining for assessing and augmenting GWAS results. *Journal of Biomedical Informatics*, *60*, 252–259. doi:10.1016/j.jbi.2016.02.008 PMID:26911523

Ananiadou, S. (2009). Text mining for biomedicine. In V. Prince & M. Roche (Eds.), *Information retrieval in biomedicine: Natural language processing for knowledge integration* (pp. 1–9). Hershey, PA: IGI Global. doi:10.4018/978-1-60566-274-9.ch001

Balahur, A., Mihalcea, R., & Montoyo, A. (2014). Computational approaches to subjectivity and sentiment analysis: Present and envisaged methods and applications. *Computer Speech & Language*, *28*(1), 1–6. doi:10.1016/j.csl.2013.09.003

Ben-Hur, A., & Noble, W. S. (2005). Kernel methods for predicting protein-protein interactions. *Bioinformatics (Oxford, England)*, *21*(Suppl. 1), i38–i46. doi:10.1093/bioinformatics/bti1016 PMID:15961482

Blair-Goldensohn, S., Hannan, K., McDonald, R., Neylon, T., Reis, G., & Reynar, J. (2008). *Building a sentiment summarizer for local service reviews*. Paper presented at the 2nd International Workshop on NLP Challenges in the Information Explosion Era (NLPIX 2008), Beijing, China.

Blaschke, C., Hoffmann, R., Oliveros, J. C., & Valencia, A. (2001). Extracting information automatically from biological literature. *Comparative and Functional Genomics*, *2*(5), 310–313. doi:10.1002/cfg.102 PMID:18629239

Chaturvedi, K. K., & Singh, V. (2012). An empirical comparison of machine learning techniques in predicting the bug severity of open and closed source projects. *International Journal of Open Source Software and Processes*, *4*(2), 32–59. doi:10.4018/jossp.2012040103

Chen, L., Liu, H., & Friedman, C. (2005). Gene name ambiguity of eukaryotic nomenclatures. *Bioinformatics (Oxford, England)*, *21*(2), 248–256. doi:10.1093/bioinformatics/bth496 PMID:15333458

Chen, X. W., & Liu, M. (2005). Prediction of protein-protein interactions using random decision forest framework. *Bioinformatics (Oxford, England)*, *21*(24), 4394–4400. doi:10.1093/bioinformatics/bti721 PMID:16234318

Cheney, D. (2015). Big Data, text mining, and news content: Where is the Big Data? In W. Gibbs & J. McKendrick (Eds.), *Contemporary research methods and data analytics in the news industry* (pp. 133–151). Hershey, PA: IGI Global. doi:10.4018/978-1-4666-8580-2.ch008

Cherfi, H., Napoli, A., & Toussaint, Y. (2009). A conformity measure using background knowledge for association rules: Application to text mining. In Y. Zhao, C. Zhang, & L. Cao (Eds.), *Post-mining of association rules: Techniques for effective knowledge extraction* (pp. 100–115). Hershey, PA: IGI Global. doi:10.4018/978-1-60566-404-0.ch006

Chew, P. A. (2009). Multilingual text mining. In J. Wang (Ed.), *Encyclopedia of data warehousing and mining* (2nd ed., pp. 1380–1385). Hershey, PA: IGI Global. doi:10.4018/978-1-60566-010-3.ch213

Clifton, C., Cooley, R., & Rennie, J. (2004). TopCat: Data mining for topic identification in a text corpus. *IEEE Transactions on Knowledge and Data Engineering*, *16*(8), 949–964. doi:10.1109/TKDE.2004.32

Dai, Y., Kakkonen, T., & Sutinen, E. (2011). MinEDec: A decision-support model that combines text mining technologies with two competitive intelligence analysis methods. *International Journal of Computer Information Systems and Industrial Management Applications*, *3*, 165–173.

Denecke, K., & Nejdi, W. (2009). How valuable is medical social media data? Content analysis of the medical web. *Information Sciences*, *179*(12), 1870–1880. doi:10.1016/j.ins.2009.01.025

Dirsehan, T. (2016). An application of text mining to capture and analyze eWOM: A pilot study on tourism sector. In S. Rathore & A. Panwar (Eds.), *Capturing, analyzing, and managing word-of-mouth in the digital marketplace* (pp. 168–186). Hershey, PA: IGI Global. doi:10.4018/978-1-4666-9449-1.ch010

Don, A., Zheleva, E., Gregory, M., Tarkan, S., Auvil, L., Clement, T.,... Plaisant, C. (2007). *Discovering interesting usage patterns in text collections: Integrating text mining with visualization*. Paper presented at the 16th ACM Conference on Information and Knowledge Management (CIKM 2007), Lisbon, Portugal. doi:10.1145/1321440.1321473

Dou, H., Leveille, V., Manullang, S., & Dou, J. M. Jr. (2005). Patent analysis for competitive technical intelligence and innovative thinking. *Data Science Journal*, *4*, 209–236. doi:10.2481/dsj.4.209

Durfee, A. (2008). Text mining. In G. Garson & M. Khosrow-Pour (Eds.), *Handbook of research on public information technology* (pp. 592–603). Hershey, PA: IGI Global. doi:10.4018/978-1-59904-857-4.ch054

Falkenhainer, B., Forbus, K. D., & Gentner, D. (1986). *The structure-mapping engine*. Paper presented at the 5th National Conference on Artificial Intelligence (AAAI 1986), Philadelphia, PA.

Feldman, R., & Hirsh, H. (1997). Exploiting background information in knowledge discovery from text. *Journal of Intelligent Information Systems*, *9*(1), 83–97. doi:10.1023/A:1008693204338

Feldman, R., & Sanger, J. (2007). *Text mining handbook: Advanced approaches in analyzing unstructured data*. New York, NY: Cambridge University Press.

Fleuren, W. C. M., & Alkema, W. (2015). Application of text mining in the biomedical domain. *Methods (San Diego, Calif.)*, *74*, 97–106. doi:10.1016/j.ymeth.2015.01.015 PMID:25641519

Fujii, A., Iwayama, M., & Kando, N. (2007). Introduction to the special issue on patent processing. *Information Processing & Management*, *43*(5), 1149–1153. doi:10.1016/j.ipm.2006.11.004

Fukuda, K., Tamura, A., Tsunoda, T., & Takagi, T. (1998). *Toward information extraction: Identifying protein names from biological papers* Paper presented at the Pacific Symposium on Biocomputing (PSB 1998), Maui, HI.

Godbole, S., & Roy, S. (2008). *Text to intelligence: Building and deploying a text mining solution in the services industry for customer satisfaction analysis*. Paper presented at the 2008 IEEE International Conference on Services Computing (SCC 2008), Hololulu, HI. doi:10.1109/SCC.2008.99

Goncalves, C., Assuncao, L., & Cunha, J. C. (2013). Flexible MapReduce workflows for cloud data analytics. *International Journal of Grid and High Performance Computing*, *5*(4), 48–64. doi:10.4018/ijghpc.2013100104

Guerrero, J. I., León, C., Monedero, I., Biscarri, F., & Biscarri, J. (2014). Improving knowledge-based systems with statistical techniques, text mining, and neural networks for non-technical loss detection. *Knowledge-Based Systems*, *71*, 376–388. doi:10.1016/j.knosys.2014.08.014

Guerrero, J. I., Monedero, Í., Biscarri, F., Biscarri, J., Millán, R., & León, C. (2014). Detection of non-technical losses: The project MIDAS. In B. Tripathy & D. Acharjya (Eds.), *Advances in secure computing, Internet services, and applications* (pp. 140–164). Hershey, PA: IGI Global. doi:10.4018/978-1-4666-4940-8.ch008

Hashimi, H., Hafez, A., & Mathkour, H. (2015). Selection criteria for text mining approaches. *Computers in Human Behavior*, *51*, 729–733. doi:10.1016/j.chb.2014.10.062

Hu, M., & Liu, B. (2004). *Mining and summarizing customer reviews*. Paper presented at the 10th ACM SIGMOD International Conference on Knowledge Discovery and Data Mining (KDD 2004), Seattle, WA. doi:10.1145/1014052.1014073

Indurkhya, N. (2015). Emerging directions in predictive text mining. *Wiley Interdisciplinary Reviews: Data Mining and Knowledge Discovery*, *5*(4), 155–164.

Jensen, L. J., Saric, J., & Bork, P. (2006). Literature mining for the biologist: From information retrieval to biological discovery. *Nature Reviews. Genetics*, *7*(2), 119–129. doi:10.1038/nrg1768 PMID:16418747

Jimeno-Yepes, A., Berlanga-Llavori, R., & Rebholz-Schuchmann, D. (2010). Applications of ontologies and text mining in the biomedical domain. In F. Gargouri & W. Jaziri (Eds.), *Ontology theory, management and design: Advanced tools and models* (pp. 261–283). Hershey, PA: IGI Global. doi:10.4018/978-1-61520-859-3.ch012

Jin, G., Jeong, Y., & Yoon, B. (2015). Technology-driven roadmaps for identifying new product/market opportunities: Use of text mining and quality function deployment. *Advanced Engineering Informatics*, *29*(1), 126–138. doi:10.1016/j.aei.2014.11.001

Kang, I. S., Na, S. H., Kim, J., & Lee, J. H. (2007). Cluster-based patent retrieval. *Information Processing & Management*, *43*(5), 1173–1182. doi:10.1016/j.ipm.2006.11.006

Kao, A., Poteet, S., Wu, J., Ferng, W., Tjoelker, R., & Quach, L. (2012). Latent semantic analysis for text mining and beyond. In L. Yan & Z. Ma (Eds.), *Intelligent multimedia databases and information retrieval: Advancing applications and technologies* (pp. 253–280). Hershey, PA: IGI Global. doi:10.4018/978-1-61350-126-9.ch015

Karl, A., Wisnowski, J., & Rushing, W. H. (2015). A practical guide to text mining with topic extraction. *Wiley Interdisciplinary Reviews: Computational Statistics*, *7*(5), 326–340. doi:10.1002/wics.1361

Kasemsap, K. (2015). The role of data mining for business intelligence in knowledge management. In A. Azevedo & M. Santos (Eds.), *Integration of data mining in business intelligence systems* (pp. 12–33). Hershey, PA: IGI Global. doi:10.4018/978-1-4666-6477-7.ch002

Kasemsap, K. (2016a). Multifaceted applications of data mining, business intelligence, and knowledge management. *International Journal of Social and Organizational Dynamics in IT*, *5*(1), 57–69. doi:10.4018/IJSODIT.2016010104

Kasemsap, K. (2016b). The fundamentals of business intelligence. *International Journal of Organizational and Collective Intelligence*, *6*(2), 12–25. doi:10.4018/IJOCI.2016040102

Kasemsap, K. (2016c). Mastering big data in the digital age. In M. Singh & D. G. (Eds.), Effective big data management and opportunities for implementation (pp. 104–129). Hershey, PA: IGI Global. doi:10.4018/978-1-5225-0182-4.ch008

Kasemsap, K. (2016d). The roles of business process modeling and business process reengineering in e-government. In J. Martins & A. Molnar (Eds.), *Handbook of research on innovations in information retrieval, analysis, and management* (pp. 401–430). Hershey, PA: IGI Global. doi:10.4018/978-1-4666-8833-9.ch015

Kasemsap, K. (2016e). Encouraging supply chain networks and customer loyalty in global supply chain. In N. Kamath & S. Saurav (Eds.), *Handbook of research on strategic supply chain management in the retail industry* (pp. 87–112). Hershey, PA: IGI Global. doi:10.4018/978-1-4666-9894-9.ch006

Kasemsap, K. (2017a). Mastering business process management and business intelligence in global business. In M. Tavana, K. Szabat, & K. Puranam (Eds.), *Organizational productivity and performance measurements using predictive modeling and analytics* (pp. 192–212). Hershey, PA: IGI Global. doi:10.4018/978-1-5225-0654-6.ch010

Kasemsap, K. (2017b). Mastering web mining and information retrieval in the digital age. In A. Kumar (Ed.), *Web usage mining techniques and applications across industries* (pp. 1–28). Hershey, PA: IGI Global. doi:10.4018/978-1-5225-0613-3.ch001

Kasemsap, K. (2017c). Advocating information system, information integration, and information sharing in global supply chain. In G. Jamil, A. Soares, & C. Pessoa (Eds.), *Handbook of research on information management for effective logistics and supply chains* (pp. 107–130). Hershey, PA: IGI Global. doi:10.4018/978-1-5225-0973-8.ch006

Kasemsap, K. (2017d). Mastering social media in the modern business world. In N. Rao (Ed.), *Social media listening and monitoring for business applications* (pp. 18–44). Hershey, PA: IGI Global. doi:10.4018/978-1-5225-0846-5.ch002

Kim, H. (2009). Text mining methods for hierarchical document indexing. In J. Wang (Ed.), *Encyclopedia of data warehousing and mining* (2nd ed., pp. 1957–1965). Hershey, PA: IGI Global. doi:10.4018/978-1-60566-010-3.ch299

Kim, S., & Hovy, E. (2004). *Determining the sentiment of opinions*. Paper presented at the International Conference on Computational Linguistics (COLING 2004), East Stroudsburg, PA.

Klepac, G., & Berg, K. L. (2015). Proposal of analytical model for business problems solving in Big Data environment. In J. Girard, D. Klein, & K. Berg (Eds.), *Strategic data-based wisdom in the Big Data era* (pp. 209–228). Hershey, PA: IGI Global. doi:10.4018/978-1-4666-8122-4.ch012

Kostoff, R. N., Boylan, R., & Simons, G. R. (2004). Disruptive technology roadmaps. *Technological Forecasting and Social Change*, *71*(1/2), 141–159. doi:10.1016/S0040-1625(03)00048-9

Kostoff, R. N., & Schaller, R. R. (2001). Science and technology roadmaps. *IEEE Transactions on Engineering Management*, *48*(2), 132–143. doi:10.1109/17.922473

Kriegel, H. P., Kroger, P., & Zimek, A. (2009). Clustering high-dimensional data: A survey on subspace clustering, pattern-based clustering, and correlation clustering. *ACM Transactions on Knowledge Discovery from Data*, *3*(1), 1–58. doi:10.1145/1497577.1497578

Lee, S., Yoon, B., & Park, Y. (2009). An approach to discovering new technology opportunities: Keyword-based patent map approach. *Technovation*, *29*(6), 481–497. doi:10.1016/j.technovation.2008.10.006

Lees, J. G., Heriche, J. K., Morilla, I., Ranea, J. A., & Orengo, C. A. (2011). Systematic computational prediction of protein interaction networks. *Physical Biology*, *8*(3), 035008. doi:10.1088/1478-3975/8/3/035008 PMID:21572181

Leydesdorff, L. (1989). Words and co-words as indicators of intellectual organization. *Research Policy*, *18*(4), 209–223. doi:10.1016/0048-7333(89)90016-4

Li, N., & Wu, D. (2010). Using text mining and sentiment analysis for online forums hotspot detection and forecast. *Decision Support Systems*, *48*(2), 354–368. doi:10.1016/j.dss.2009.09.003

Li, Y. R., Wang, L. H., & Hong, C. F. (2009). Extracting the significant-rare keywords for patent analysis. *Expert Systems with Applications: An International Journal*, *36*(3), 5200–5204. doi:10.1016/j.eswa.2008.06.131

Liew, W. T., Adhitya, A., & Srinivasan, R. (2014). Sustainability trends in the process industries: A text mining-based analysis. *Computers in Industry*, *65*(3), 393–400. doi:10.1016/j.compind.2014.01.004

Loh, S., Wives, L. K., Lichtnow, D., & de Oliveira, J. P. (2009). Concept-based text mining. In M. Song & Y. Brook Wu (Eds.), *Handbook of research on text and web mining technologies* (pp. 346–358). Hershey, PA: IGI Global. doi:10.4018/978-1-59904-990-8.ch021

Lukach, R., & Plasmans, J. (2005). International knowledge flows from and into a small open economy: Patent citation analysis. In A. Spithoven & P. Teirlinck (Eds.), *Beyond borders: Internationalisation of R&D and policy implications for small open economies* (pp. 331–357). Amsterdam, The Netherlands: Elsevier.

Mandl, T. (2015). Text mining. In M. Khosrow-Pour (Ed.), *Encyclopedia of information science and technology* (3rd ed., pp. 1923–1930). Hershey, PA: IGI Global. doi:10.4018/978-1-4666-5888-2.ch185

Mohammad, S. (2012). From once upon a time to happily ever after: Tracking emotions in mail and books. *Decision Support Systems*, *53*(4), 730–741. doi:10.1016/j.dss.2012.05.030

Moro, S., Cortez, P., & Rita, P. (2015). Business intelligence in banking: A literature analysis from 2002 to 2013 using text mining and latent Dirichlet allocation. *Expert Systems with Applications: An International Journal*, *42*(3), 1314–1324. doi:10.1016/j.eswa.2014.09.024

Mostafa, M. M. (2013). More than words: Social networks' text mining for consumer brand sentiments. *Expert Systems with Applications: An International Journal*, *40*(10), 4241–4251. doi:10.1016/j.eswa.2013.01.019

Murphy, J., Fu, K., Otto, K., Yang, M., Jensen, D., & Wood, K. (2014). Function based design-by-analogy: A functional vector approach to analogical search. *Journal of Mechanical Design*, *136*(10), 101102. doi:10.1115/1.4028093

Nassirtoussi, A. K., Aghabozorgi, S., Wah, T. Y., & Ngo, D. C. L. (2014). Text mining for market prediction: A systematic review. *Expert Systems with Applications: An International Journal*, *41*(16), 7653–7670. doi:10.1016/j.eswa.2014.06.009

Nassirtoussi, A. K., Aghabozorgi, S., Wah, T. Y., & Ngo, D. C. L. (2015). Text mining of news-headlines for FOREX market prediction: A multi-layer dimension reduction algorithm with semantics and sentiment. *Expert Systems with Applications: An International Journal*, *42*(1), 306–324. doi:10.1016/j.eswa.2014.08.004

No, H. J., An, Y., & Park, Y. (2015). A structured approach to explore knowledge flows through technology-based business methods by integrating patent citation analysis and text mining. *Technological Forecasting and Social Change*, *97*, 181–192. doi:10.1016/j.techfore.2014.04.007

Noh, H., Jo, Y., & Lee, S. (2015). Keyword selection and processing strategy for applying text mining to patent analysis. *Expert Systems with Applications: An International Journal*, *42*(9), 4348–4360. doi:10.1016/j.eswa.2015.01.050

Papanikolaou, N., Pavlopoulos, G. A., Theodosiou, T., & Iliopoulos, I. (2015). Protein–protein interaction predictions using text mining methods. *Methods (San Diego, Calif.)*, *74*, 47–53. doi:10.1016/j.ymeth.2014.10.026 PMID:25448298

Patel, R., & Sharma, G. (2014). A survey on text mining techniques. *International Journal of Engineering and Computer Science, 3*(5), 5621–5625.

Pazos, F., Helmer-Citterich, M., Ausiello, G., & Valencia, A. (1997). Correlated mutations contain information about protein-protein interaction. *Journal of Molecular Biology, 271*(4), 511–523. doi:10.1006/jmbi.1997.1198 PMID:9281423

Penteado, R., & Boutin, E. (2008). Creating strategic information for organizations with structured text. In H. do Prado & E. Ferneda (Eds.), *Emerging technologies of text mining: Techniques and applications* (pp. 34–53). Hershey, PA: IGI Global. doi:10.4018/978-1-59904-373-9.ch002

Perovšek, M., Kranjc, J., Erjavec, T., Cestnik, B., & Lavrac, N. (2016). TextFlows: A visual programming platform for text mining and natural language processing. *Science of Computer Programming, 121*, 128–152. doi:10.1016/j.scico.2016.01.001

Piedra, D., Ferrer, A., & Gea, J. (2014). Text mining and medicine: Usefulness in respiratory diseases. *Archivos de Bronconeumologia, 50*(3), 113–119. PMID:24507559

Pletscher-Frankild, S., Palleja, A., Tsafou, K., Binder, J. X., & Jensen, L. J. (2015). DISEASES: Text mining and data integration of disease–gene associations. *Methods (San Diego, Calif.), 74*, 83–89. doi:10.1016/j.ymeth.2014.11.020 PMID:25484339

Porter, A. L., Kongthon, A., & Lu, J. C. (2002). Research profiling: Improving the literature review. *Scientometrics, 53*(3), 351–370. doi:10.1023/A:1014873029258

Qiu, G., He, X., Zhang, F., Shi, Y., Bu, J., & Chen, C. (2010). DASA: Dissatisfaction-oriented advertising based on sentiment analysis. *Expert Systems with Applications: An International Journal, 37*(9), 6182–6191. doi:10.1016/j.eswa.2010.02.109

Ramsey, G., & Bapna, S. (2016). Text mining to identify customers likely to respond to cross-selling campaigns: Reading notes from your customers. *International Journal of Business Analytics, 3*(2), 33–49. doi:10.4018/IJBAN.2016040102

Rivera, S. J., Minsker, B. S., Work, D. B., & Roth, D. (2014). A text mining framework for advancing sustainability indicators. *Environmental Modelling & Software, 62*, 128–138. doi:10.1016/j.envsoft.2014.08.016

Segers, N., & de Vries, B. (2003). *The idea space system: Words as handles to a comprehensive data structure*. Paper presented at the 10th International Conference on Computer Aided Architectural Design Futures (CADfutures 2003), Tainan, Taiwan.

Seo, W., Yoon, J., Park, H., Coh, B. Y., Lee, J. M., & Kwon, O. J. (2016). Product opportunity identification based on internal capabilities using text mining and association rule mining. *Technological Forecasting and Social Change, 105*, 94–104. doi:10.1016/j.techfore.2016.01.011

Serrano, J. I. (2009). Document indexing techniques for text mining. In J. Wang (Ed.), *Encyclopedia of data warehousing and mining* (2nd ed., pp. 716–721). Hershey, PA: IGI Global. doi:10.4018/978-1-60566-010-3.ch111

Settles, B. (2005). ABNER: An open source tool for automatically tagging genes, proteins, and other entity names in text. *Bioinformatics (Oxford, England)*, *21*(14), 3191–3192. doi:10.1093/bioinformatics/bti475 PMID:15860559

Shehata, S., Karray, F., & Kamel, M. (2010). Concept-based mining model. In A. Ali & Y. Xiang (Eds.), *Dynamic and advanced data mining for progressing technological development: Innovations and systemic approaches* (pp. 57–69). Hershey, PA: IGI Global. doi:10.4018/978-1-60566-908-3.ch004

Shelke, N. M. (2014). Approaches of emotion detection from text. *International Journal of Computer Science and Information Technology Research*, *2*(2), 123–128.

Shen, J., Zhang, J., Luo, X., Zhu, W., Yu, K., Chen, K., & Jiang, H. et al. (2007). Predicting protein-protein interactions based only on sequences information. *Proceedings of the National Academy of Sciences of the United States of America*, *104*(11), 4337–4341. doi:10.1073/pnas.0607879104 PMID:17360525

Soriano, J., Au, T., & Banks, D. (2013). Text mining in computational advertising. *Statistical Analysis and Data Mining*, *6*(4), 273–285. doi:10.1002/sam.11197

Sullivan, D. (2004). Text mining in business intelligence. In M. Raisinghani (Ed.), *Business intelligence in the digital economy: Opportunities, limitations and risks* (pp. 98–110). Hershey, PA: Idea Group Publishing. doi:10.4018/978-1-59140-206-0.ch006

Suominen, H. (2009). Performance evaluation measures for text mining. In M. Song & Y. Brook Wu (Eds.), *Handbook of research on text and web mining technologies* (pp. 724–747). Hershey, PA: IGI Global. doi:10.4018/978-1-59904-990-8.ch041

Thomas, J., McNaught, J., & Ananiadou, S. (2011). Applications of text mining within systematic reviews. *Research Synthesis Methods*, *2*(1), 1–14. doi:10.1002/jrsm.27 PMID:26061596

Thomas, M., Pang, B., & Lee, L. (2006). *Get out the vote: Determining support or opposition from congressional floor-debate transcripts*. Paper presented at the 2006 Conference on Empirical Methods in Natural Language Processing (EMNLP 2006), Sydney, Australia. doi:10.3115/1610075.1610122

Truyens, M., & van Eecke, P. (2014). Legal aspects of text mining. *Computer Law & Security Report*, *30*(2), 153–170. doi:10.1016/j.clsr.2014.01.009

Tseng, Y. H., Lin, C. J., & Lin, Y. I. (2007). Text mining techniques for patent analysis. *Information Processing & Management*, *43*(5), 1216–1247. doi:10.1016/j.ipm.2006.11.011

Tsuruoka, Y., Miwa, M., Hamamoto, K., Tsujii, J., & Ananiadou, S. (2011). Discovering and visualizing indirect associations between biomedical concepts. *Bioinformatics (Oxford, England)*, *27*(13), i111–i119. doi:10.1093/bioinformatics/btr214 PMID:21685059

Turney, P. (2002). *Thumbs up or thumbs down? Semantic orientation applied to unsupervised classification of reviews*. Paper presented at the 40th Annual Meeting of the Association for Computational Linguistics (ACL 2002), Philadelphia, PA.

van Raan, A. F. J., & Tijssen, R. J. W. (1993). The neural net of neural network research. *Scientometrics*, *26*(1), 169–192. doi:10.1007/BF02016799

Vashishta, S., & Jain, Y. K. (2011). Efficient retrieval of text for biomedical domain using data mining algorithm. *International Journal of Advanced Computer Science and Applications*, 2(4), 77–80. doi:10.14569/IJACSA.2011.020412

Vishwanath, J., & Aishwarya, S. (2011). User suggestions extraction from customer reviews. *International Journal on Computer Science and Engineering*, 3(3), 1203–1206.

Watts, R. J., & Porter, A. L. (1997). Innovation forecasting. *Technological Forecasting and Social Change*, 56(1), 25–47. doi:10.1016/S0040-1625(97)00050-4

Williams, T. P., & Gong, J. (2014). Predicting construction cost overruns using text mining, numerical data and ensemble classifiers. *Automation in Construction*, 43, 23–29. doi:10.1016/j.autcon.2014.02.014

Wong, K., Xia, Y., Xu, R., Wu, M., & Li, W. (2008). Pattern-based opinion mining for stock market trend prediction. *International Journal of Computer Processing of Languages*, 21(4), 347–361. doi:10.1142/S1793840608001949

Xie, B., Ding, Q., & Wu, D. (2015). Text mining on big and complex biomedical literature. In B. Wang, R. Li, & W. Perrizo (Eds.), *Big data analytics in bioinformatics and healthcare* (pp. 21–45). Hershey, PA: IGI Global. doi:10.4018/978-1-4666-6611-5.ch002

Xu, S., & Luo, X. (2009). Current issues and future analysis in text mining for information security applications. In H. Rahman (Ed.), *Social and political implications of data mining: Knowledge management in e-government* (pp. 165–177). Hershey, PA: IGI Global. doi:10.4018/978-1-60566-230-5.ch010

Yamada, Y., Kato, K., & Hirokawa, S. (2013). Text mining for analysis of interviews and questionnaires. In *Data mining: Concepts, methodologies, tools, and applications* (pp. 1390–1406). Hershey, PA: IGI Global. doi:10.4018/978-1-4666-2455-9.ch072

Yang, H. C., Lee, C. H., & Hsiao, H. W. (2015). Incorporating self-organizing map with text mining techniques for text hierarchy generation. *Applied Soft Computing*, 34, 251–259. doi:10.1016/j.asoc.2015.05.005

Yang, Y. Y., Klose, T., Lippy, J., Barcelon-Yang, C. S., & Zhang, L. (2014). Leveraging text analytics in patent analysis to empower business decisions: A competitive differentiation of kinase assay technology platforms by I2E text mining software. *World Patent Information*, 39, 24–34. doi:10.1016/j.wpi.2014.09.002

Yepes, A. J., & Berlanga, R. (2015). Knowledge based word-concept model estimation and refinement for biomedical text mining. *Journal of Biomedical Informatics*, 53, 300–307. doi:10.1016/j.jbi.2014.11.015 PMID:25510606

Yi, J., Nasukawa, T., Bunescu, R., & Niblack, W. (2003). *Sentiment analyzer: Extracting sentiments about a given topic using natural language-processing techniques*. Paper presented at the 2003 3rd IEEE International Conference on Data Mining (ICDM 2003), Melbourne, FL. doi:10.1109/ICDM.2003.1250949

Yoon, B., Lee, S., & Lee, G. (2010). Development and application of a keyword-based knowledge map for effective R&D planning. *Scientometrics*, 85(3), 803–820. doi:10.1007/s11192-010-0294-5

Yoon, B., Park, I., & Coh, B. Y. (2014). Exploring technological opportunities by linking technology and products: Application of morphology analysis and text mining. *Technological Forecasting and Social Change*, 86, 287–303. doi:10.1016/j.techfore.2013.10.013

Yoon, B., & Park, Y. (2004). A text-mining-based patent network: Analytical tool for high-technology trend. *The Journal of High Technology Management Research, 15*(1), 37–50. doi:10.1016/j.hitech.2003.09.003

Yu, L., Wang, S., & Lai, K. K. (2009). A multi-agent neural network system for web text mining. In M. Song & Y. Brook Wu (Eds.), *Handbook of research on text and web mining technologies* (pp. 201–226). Hershey, PA: IGI Global. doi:10.4018/978-1-59904-990-8.ch013

Zhai, C., Velivelli, A., & Yu, B. (2004). *A cross-collection mixture model for comparative text mining.* Paper presented at the 10th ACM SIGKDD International Conference on Knowledge Discovery and Data Mining (KDD 2004), Seattle, WA. doi:10.1145/1014052.1014150

Zhang, C., Zeng, D., Li, J., Wang, F., & Zuo, W. (2009). Sentiment analysis of Chinese documents: From sentence to document level. *Journal of the American Society for Information Science and Technology, 60*(12), 2474–2487. doi:10.1002/asi.21206

Zhang, J., Luo, X., He, X., & Cai, C. (2013). Text semantic mining model based on the algebra of human concept learning. In Y. Wang (Ed.), *Cognitive informatics for revealing human cognition: Knowledge manipulations in natural intelligence* (pp. 221–236). Hershey, PA: IGI Global. doi:10.4018/978-1-4666-2476-4.ch014

Zhu, D., & Porter, A. L. (2002). Automated extraction and visualization of information for technological intelligence and forecasting. *Technological Forecasting and Social Change, 69*(5), 495–506. doi:10.1016/S0040-1625(01)00157-3

ADDITIONAL READING

Abdous, M., & He, W. (2011). Using text mining to uncover students' technology-related problems in live video streaming. *British Journal of Educational Technology, 42*(1), 40–49. doi:10.1111/j.1467-8535.2009.00980.x

Akkoyun, O., & Careddu, N. (2015). Mine simulation for educational purposes: A case study. *Computer Applications in Engineering Education, 23*(2), 286–293. doi:10.1002/cae.21598

Anwar, T., & Abulaish, M. (2014). A social graph based text mining framework for chat log investigation. *Digital Investigation, 11*(4), 349–362. doi:10.1016/j.diin.2014.10.001

Atkinson, J. (2007). Intelligent text mining: Putting evolutionary methods and language technologies together. In X. Zha (Ed.), *Artificial intelligence and integrated intelligent information systems: Emerging technologies and applications* (pp. 88–113). Hershey, PA: Idea Group Publishing. doi:10.4018/978-1-59904-249-7.ch006

Bhat, S. Y., & Abulaish, M. (2013). Analysis and mining of online social networks: Emerging trends and challenges. *Wiley Interdisciplinary Reviews: Data Mining and Knowledge Discovery, 3*(6), 408–444. doi:10.1002/widm.1105

Boussalis, C., & Coan, T. G. (2016). Text-mining the signals of climate change doubt. *Global Environmental Change, 36*, 89–100. doi:10.1016/j.gloenvcha.2015.12.001

Cerrito, P. (2010). Text mining and patient severity clusters. In P. Cerrito (Ed.), *Text mining techniques for healthcare provider quality determination: Methods for rank comparisons* (pp. 287–340). Hershey, PA: IGI Global. doi:10.4018/978-1-60566-752-2.ch008

Chen, Y. L., Liu, Y. H., & Ho, W. L. (2013). A text mining approach to assist the general public in the retrieval of legal documents. *Journal of the American Society for Information Science and Technology, 64*(2), 280–290. doi:10.1002/asi.22767

Choi, S., Kim, H., Yoon, J., Kim, K., & Lee, J. Y. (2013). An SAO-based text-mining approach for technology roadmapping using patent information. *R & D Management, 43*(1), 52–74. doi:10.1111/j.1467-9310.2012.00702.x

Choudhary, S. P., & Vidyarthi, D. (2015). A simple method for detection of metamorphic malware using dynamic analysis and text mining. *Procedia Computer Science, 54*, 265–270. doi:10.1016/j.procs.2015.06.031

Dařena, F., & Žižka, J. (2015). Revealing groups of semantically close textual documents by clustering: Problems and possibilities. In J. Žižka & F. Dařena (Eds.), *Modern computational models of semantic discovery in natural language* (pp. 71–111). Hershey, PA: IGI Global. doi:10.4018/978-1-4666-8690-8.ch004

Gurulingappa, H., Toldo, L., Rajput, A. M., Kors, J. A., Taweel, A., & Tayrouz, Y. (2013). Automatic detection of adverse events to predict drug label changes using text and data mining techniques. *Pharmacoepidemiology and Drug Safety, 22*(11), 1189–1194. doi:10.1002/pds.3493 PMID:23935003

He, W., Chee, T., Chong, D., & Rasnick, E. (2012). Using bibliometrics and text mining to explore the trends of e-marketing literature from 2001 to 2010. *International Journal of Online Marketing, 2*(1), 16–24. doi:10.4018/ijom.2012010102

Ishikiriyama, C. S., Miro, D., & Gomes, C. F. S. (2015). Text mining business intelligence: A small sample of what words can say. *Procedia Computer Science, 55*, 261–267. doi:10.1016/j.procs.2015.07.044

Kim, J. M., & Jun, S. (2015). Graphical causal inference and copula regression model for apple keywords by text mining. *Advanced Engineering Informatics, 29*(4), 918–929. doi:10.1016/j.aei.2015.10.001

Klepac, G., & Velić, M. (2015). Natural language processing as feature extraction method for building better predictive models. In J. Žižka & F. Dařena (Eds.), *Modern computational models of semantic discovery in natural language* (pp. 141–166). Hershey, PA: IGI Global. doi:10.4018/978-1-4666-8690-8.ch006

Lam, H. T., Mörchen, F., Fradkin, D., & Calders, T. (2014). Mining compressing sequential patterns. *Statistical Analysis and Data Mining, 7*(1), 34–52. doi:10.1002/sam.11192

Lucas, N. (2009). Discourse processing for text mining. In V. Prince & M. Roche (Eds.), *Information retrieval in biomedicine: Natural language processing for knowledge integration* (pp. 222–254). Hershey, PA: IGI Global. doi:10.4018/978-1-60566-274-9.ch012

McArthur, D., & Crompton, H. (2012). Understanding public-access cyberlearning projects using text mining and topic analysis. *Journal of the American Society for Information Science and Technology*, *63*(11), 2146–2152. doi:10.1002/asi.22663

Narock, T., Zhou, L., & Yoon, V. (2013). Semantic similarity of ontology instances using polarity mining. *Journal of the American Society for Information Science and Technology*, *64*(2), 416–427. doi:10.1002/asi.22769

Oh, S., & Park, M. S. (2013). Text mining as a method of analyzing health questions in social Q&A. *Proceedings of the American Society for Information Science and Technology*, *50*(1), 1–4. doi:10.1002/meet.14505001130

Porter, A. L., Guo, Y., & Chiavatta, D. (2011). Tech mining: Text mining and visualization tools, as applied to nanoenhanced solar cells. *Wiley Interdisciplinary Reviews: Data Mining and Knowledge Discovery*, *1*(2), 172–181. doi:10.1002/widm.7

Qi, Y. (2009). Text mining in bioinformatics: Research and application. In M. Song & Y. Brook Wu (Eds.), *Handbook of research on text and web mining technologies* (pp. 748–757). Hershey, PA: IGI Global. doi:10.4018/978-1-59904-990-8.ch042

Raja, U., & Tretter, M. J. (2011). Classification of software patches: A text mining approach. *Journal of Software Maintenance and Evolution: Research and Practice*, *23*(2), 69–87. doi:10.1002/smr.468

Saldana-Perez, A. M., & Moreno-Ibarra, M. (2016). Traffic analysis based on short texts from social media. *International Journal of Knowledge Society Research*, *7*(1), 63–79. doi:10.4018/IJKSR.2016010105

Segall, R. S., & Zhang, Q. (2009). A survey of selected software technologies for text mining. In P. Tiako (Ed.), *Software applications: Concepts, methodologies, tools, and applications* (pp. 1164–1181). Hershey, PA: IGI Global. doi:10.4018/978-1-60566-060-8.ch068

Tackett, J. A. (2011). Using text mining to monitor employee e-mail. *Journal of Corporate Accounting & Finance*, *22*(4), 15–22. doi:10.1002/jcaf.20685

Vazquez, M., Krallinger, M., Leitner, F., & Valencia, A. (2011). Text mining for drugs and chemical compounds: Methods, tools and applications. *Molecular Informatics*, *30*(6/7), 506–519. doi:10.1002/minf.201100005 PMID:27467152

Wang, H., Wu, J., Yuan, S., & Chen, J. (2016). On characterizing scale effect of Chinese mutual funds via text mining. *Signal Processing*, *124*, 266–278. doi:10.1016/j.sigpro.2015.05.018

Warrer, P., Hansen, E. H., Juhl-Jensen, L., & Aagaard, L. (2012). Using text-mining techniques in electronic patient records to identify ADRs from medicine use. *British Journal of Clinical Pharmacology*, *73*(5), 674–684. doi:10.1111/j.1365-2125.2011.04153.x PMID:22122057

Yang, H., & Lee, C. (2009). Topic maps generation by text mining. In J. Wang (Ed.), *Encyclopedia of data warehousing and mining* (2nd ed., pp. 1979–1984). Hershey, PA: IGI Global. doi:10.4018/978-1-60566-010-3.ch302

Yu, C. H., DiGangi, S. A., & Jannasch-Pennell, A. (2011). Using text mining for improving student experience management in higher education. In P. Tripathi & S. Mukerji (Eds.), *Cases on innovations in educational marketing: Transnational and technological strategies* (pp. 196–213). Hershey, PA: IGI Global. doi:10.4018/978-1-60960-599-5.ch012

Zhou, Y., Tong, Y., Gu, R., & Gall, H. (2016). Combining text mining and data mining for bug report classification. *Journal of Software: Evolution and Process*, 28(3), 150–176. doi:10.1002/smr.1770

Žižka, J., & Dařena, F. (2015). Semantics-based document categorization employing semi-supervised learning. In J. Žižka & F. Dařena (Eds.), *Modern computational models of semantic discovery in natural language* (pp. 112–140). Hershey, PA: IGI Global. doi:10.4018/978-1-4666-8690-8.ch005

KEY TERMS AND DEFINITIONS

Artificial Intelligence: The area of computer science that emphasizes the creation of intelligent machines that work and react like humans.

Business Intelligence: The use of computing technologies for the identification, discovery, and analysis of business data, such as sales revenue, products, and costs.

Data Mining: The process of analyzing the hidden patterns of data according to the different perspectives for categorization into useful information.

Information: The data that is accurate and organized for a specific purpose.

Knowledge Management: The discipline with processes involving the comprehensive gathering of information or knowledge, its organization, development and analysis, and sharing it with the goal of effective utilization.

Natural Language Processing: The method to translate between computer and human languages.

Text Mining: The type of data mining applied to the unstructured data.

Unstructured Data: The data that does not have a recognizable structure.

Compilation of References

Ababneh, M., Almanasreh, A. M., & Amasha, H. (2009). Design of digital controllers for uncertain chaotic systems using fuzzy logic. *Journal of the Franklin Institute*, *346*(6), 543–556. doi:10.1016/j.jfranklin.2009.02.002

Abrahams, A. S., Fan, W., Wang, G. A., Zhang, Z. J., & Jiao, J. (2015). An integrated text analytic framework for product defect discovery. *Production and Operations Management*, *24*(6), 975–990. doi:10.1111/poms.12303

Acharjee, U. (2006). *Personalized and Artificial Intelligence Web Caching and Pre-fetching* (Master thesis). University of Ottawa, Canada.

Acharyya, S., & Ghosh, J. (2003). Context-sensitive modeling of web- surfing behaviour using concept trees. In *Proceedings of the 5th WEBKDD Workshop*.

Adedoyin-Olowe, M., Gaber, M. M., & Stahl, F. (2014). A survey of data mining techniques for social network analysis. *Journal of Data Mining & Digital Humanities*.

Adriaana, P., & Zantinge, D. (2002). *Data Mining*. Pearson Education Asia.

Agarwal, C. C. (2004). On leveraging user access patterns for topic specific crawling. *Data Mining and Knowledge Discovery*, *9*(2), 123–145. doi:10.1023/B:DAMI.0000031633.76754.d3

Agrawal, R., Imielinski, T., & Swami, A. N. (1993). Mining association rules between sets of items in large databases. In P. Buneman (Ed.), *Proceedings of the 1993 ACM-SIGMOD International Conference on Management of Data* (pp. 207–216). doi:10.1145/170035.170072

Ahmad, R., & Khanum, A. (2010). Document topic generation in text mining by using cluster analysis with EROCK. *International Journal of Computer Science & Security*, *4*(2), 176–182.

Ailem, M., Role, F., Nadif, M., & Demenais, F. (2016). Unsupervised text mining for assessing and augmenting GWAS results. *Journal of Biomedical Informatics*, *60*, 252–259. doi:10.1016/j.jbi.2016.02.008 PMID:26911523

Alavi, M., & Dufner, D. (2005). Technology-mediated collaborative learning: A research perspective. In S. R. Hiltz & R. Goldman (Eds.), *Learning together online: Research on asynchronous learning networks* (pp. 191–213). Mahwah, NJ: Lawrence Erlbaum.

Ali, W., & Shamsuddin, S. M. (2009). Intelligent Client-Side Web Caching Scheme Based on Least Recently Used Algorithm and Neuro-Fuzzy System. In *Sixth International Symposium on Neural Networks,* (LNCS). Springer-Verlag Berlin Heidelberg. doi:10.1007/978-3-642-01510-6_9

Ali, W., & Shamsuddin, S. M. (2009). Intelligent Client-Side Web Caching Scheme Based on Least Recently Used Algorithm and Neuro-Fuzzy System. *The Sixth International Symposium on Neural Networks (ISNN 2009)*, (LNCS). Springer-Verlag Berlin Heidelberg.

Allen, R. B. (1990). *User Models: Theory, Method, Practice. International J. Man-Machine Studies.*

Altingovde, I. S., & Ulusoy, O. (2004). Exploiting interclass rules for focussed crawling. *IEEE Intelligent Systems, 19*(6), 66–73. doi:10.1109/MIS.2004.62

Analytics, T. (n.d.). Retrieved from https://analytics.twitter.com

Analyzing Website Speed. (n.d.). Retrieved from www.GTMetrix.com

Ananiadou, S. (2009). Text mining for biomedicine. In V. Prince & M. Roche (Eds.), *Information retrieval in biomedicine: Natural language processing for knowledge integration* (pp. 1–9). Hershey, PA: IGI Global. doi:10.4018/978-1-60566-274-9.ch001

Anderson, C. R. (2002). *A Machine Learning Approach to Web Personalization* (Ph.D. Thesis). University of Washington.

Anderson, T., & Elloumi, F. (2008). *Theory and Practice of online Learning.* Athabasca University Digitization Portal. Retrieved from http://cde.athabascau.ca/online_book/

Andujar, J. M., & Barragan, A. J. (2005). A methodology to design stable nonlinear fuzzy control systems. *Fuzzy Sets and Systems, 154*(2), 157–181. doi:10.1016/j.fss.2005.03.006

Ansari, S., Kohavi, R., Mason, L., & Zheng, Z. (2001). Integrating e-commerce and data mining: Architecture and challenges.*Proceedings of the 2001 IEEE International Conference on Data Mining.* IEEE Computer Society. doi:10.1109/ICDM.2001.989497

Arnold, K. E., & Pistilli, M. D. (2012). Course Signals at Purdue: Using Learning Analytics to Increase Student Success. *Proc. Second Int'l Conf. Learning Analytics and Knowledge,* (pp. 267-270). doi:10.1145/2330601.2330666

Arnott, D., & Pervan, G. (2008). Eight key issues for the decision support systems discipline. *Decision Support Systems, 44*(3), 657–672. doi:10.1016/j.dss.2007.09.003

Arzanian, B., Akhlaghian, F., & Moradi, P. (2010). A Multi-Agent Based Personalized Meta-Search Engine Using Automatic Fuzzy Concept Networks. In *Proceedings of Third International Conference on Knowledge Discovery and Data Mining*(pp. 208- 211). Phuket, Thailand: IEEE. doi:10.1109/WKDD.2010.95

Athas, W. C., & Seitz, C. L. (1988). Multicomputers: Message-passing concurrent computers. *Computer, 21*(8), 9–24. doi:10.1109/2.73

Baba, N., & Suto, H. (2000). Utilization of artificial neural networks and the TD-learning method for constructing intelligent decision support system. *European Journal of Operational Research, 122*(2), 501–508. doi:10.1016/S0377-2217(99)00250-7

Back, T., Hammel, U., & Schwefel, H. P. (1997). Evolutionary computation: Comments on the history and current state. *IEEE Transactions on Evolutionary Computation, 1*(1), 3–17. doi:10.1109/4235.585888

Bagrow, J. P. (2012). *Are communities just bottlenecks? Trees and treelike networks have high modularity.* CoRR, abs/1201.0745.

Baker, R. S., & Inventado, P. S. (2014). Educational data mining and learning analytics. In J. A. Larusson & B. White (Eds.), *Learning analytics: from research to practice* (pp. 61–75). New York: Springer.

Baker, R., & Yacef, K. (2009). The State of Educational Data Mining in 2009: *A Review and Future Visions. J. Educational Data Mining, 1*(1), 3–17.

Balahur, A., Mihalcea, R., & Montoyo, A. (2014). Computational approaches to subjectivity and sentiment analysis: Present and envisaged methods and applications. *Computer Speech & Language*, *28*(1), 1–6. doi:10.1016/j.csl.2013.09.003

Balamash, A., & Krunz, M. (2004). An Overview of Web Caching Replacement Algorithms. *IEEE Communications Surveys and Tutorials*, *6*(2), 44–56. doi:10.1109/COMST.2004.5342239

Bamshad, M. (2007). *Data Mining for Web Personalization*. Heidelberg, Germany: LCNS, Springer-Verleg Berlin.

Barabasi, A. L., & Oltvai, Z. N. (2004). Network biology: Understanding the cells functional organization. *Nature Reviews. Genetics*, *5*(2), 101–113. doi:10.1038/nrg1272 PMID:14735121

Barab, S. A., & Duffy, T. (2012). From practice fields to communities of practice. In D. Jonassen & S. Land (Eds.), *Theoretical foundation of learning environments* (pp. 29–65). New York: Routledge.

Baraglia, R., & Silvestri, F. (2007). Dynamic personalization of web sites without user intervention. *Communications of the ACM*, *50*(2), 63–67. doi:10.1145/1216016.1216022

Bari, P., & Chawan, P. M. (2013). Web usage mining. *Journal of Engineering. Computers & Applied Sciences*, *2*(6), 34–38.

Barnes, E. R. (1982). Algebraic Discrete Methods 3. *SIAM Journal*, *4*, 541–550.

Barnes, J. (1984). Cognitive Biases and Their Impact on Strategic Planning. *Strategic Management Journal*, *5*(2), 129–137. doi:10.1002/smj.4250050204

Baron, J. (1998). *Thinking and deciding*. Cambridge, UK: Cambridge University Press.

BBC. (2005). *Web enjoys year of biggest growth, Online*. Accessed on 05/2008 from *http://news.bbc.co.uk/2/hi/technology/4325918.stm

Beach, R., Muhlemann, A. P., Price, D. H. R., Paterson, A., & Sharp, J. A. (2000). A review of manufacturing flexibility. *European Journal of Operational Research*, *122*(2), 41–57. doi:10.1016/S0377-2217(99)00062-4

Bedi, P., & Chawla, S. (2008). Improving information retrieval precision using query log mining and information scent. *Journal of Information Technology*, *6*(4), 584–588.

Bedi, P., & Chawla, S. (2009). Use of fuzzy rough set attribute reduction in high scent web page recommendations. In *Rough Sets* (pp. 192–200). Fuzzy Sets, Data Mining and Granular Computing, Springer Berlin Heidelberg. doi:10.1007/978-3-642-10646-0_23

Bedi, P., & Chawla, S. (2010). Agent based information retrieval system using information scent. *Journal of Artificial Intelligence*, *3*(4), 220–238. doi:10.3923/jai.2010.220.238

Ben-Hur, A., & Noble, W. S. (2005). Kernel methods for predicting protein-protein interactions. *Bioinformatics (Oxford, England)*, *21*(Suppl. 1), i38–i46. doi:10.1093/bioinformatics/bti1016 PMID:15961482

Berendt, B., Mobasher, B., Nakagawa, M., & Spiliopoulou, M. (2002). The Impact of Site Structure and User Environment and Session Reconstruction in Web usage analysis. In *Proceedings of the forth Web KDD 2002 workshop at the ACM – SIGKDD Conference on Knowledge Discovery in Databases (KDD 2002)*.

Berendt, B., Mobasher, B., Nakagawa, M., & Spiliopoulou, M. (2002). The impact of site structure and user environment on session reconstruction in web usage analysis.*Proceedings of the 4th WebKDD 2002 Workshop, at the ACMSIGKDD Conference on Knowledge Discovery in Databases*.

Bergeron, P. (1996). Information resources management. *Annual Review of Information Science & Technology*, *31*, 263–300.

Berners-Lee, T., Hendler, J., & Lassila, O. (2001). The Semantic Web. Scientific American Magazine; Retrieved March 26, 2008.

Berners-Lee, T. (2000). *Weaving the Web – The Past, Present and Future of the World Wide Web by its Inventor*. Texere.

Berners-Lee, T., Weitzner, D. J., Hall, W., OHara, K., Shadbolt, N., & Hendler, J. A. (2006). A Framework for Web Science. *Foundations and Trends in Web Science*, *1*(1), 1–130. doi:10.1561/1800000001

Berry, F. (1997). Explaining managerial acceptance of expert systems. *Public Productivity and Management Review*, *20*(3), 323–335. doi:10.2307/3380981

Berry, F., Berry, W., & Foster, S. (1998). The determinants of success in implementing an expert system in state government. *Public Administration Review*, *58*(4), 293–305. doi:10.2307/977559

Best, D. P. (2010). The future of information management. *Records Management Journal*, *20*(1), 61–71. doi:10.1108/09565691011039834

Biancalana, C., & Micarelli, A. (2009). Social tagging in query expansion: A new way for personalized web search. In *Proceedings of International Conference on Computational Science and Engineering*, (Vol 4, pp. 1060-1065), Vancouver, BC: IEEE. doi:10.1109/CSE.2009.492

Bianchini, M., Gori, M., & Scarselli, F. (2005). Inside pagerank. *ACM Transactions on Internet Technology*, *5*(1), 92–128. doi:10.1145/1052934.1052938

Biggs, J. B., & Collis, K. F. (1982). *Evaluating the quality of learning: The SOLO taxonomy (Structure of the Observed Learning Outcome)*. London: Academic Press.

Birukov, A., Blanzieri, E., & Giorgini, P. (2005). Implicit: An agent-based recommendation system for web search. In *Proceedings of the fourth international joint conference on Autonomous agents and multiagent systems* (pp. 618-624). ACM.

Black, P., & Wiliam, D. (1998). *Inside the black box: raising standards through classroom assessment*. London: GL Assessment.

Black, P., & Wiliam, D. (2003). In praise of educational research: Formative assessment. *British Educational Research Journal*, *29*(5), 623–637. doi:10.1080/0141192032000133721

Blair-Goldensohn, S., Hannan, K., McDonald, R., Neylon, T., Reis, G., & Reynar, J. (2008). *Building a sentiment summarizer for local service reviews*. Paper presented at the 2nd International Workshop on NLP Challenges in the Information Explosion Era (NLPIX 2008), Beijing, China.

Blanzieri, E., Giorgini, P., Massa, P., & Recla, S. (2001). Implicit culture for multi-agent interaction support. In *International Conference on Cooperative Information Systems* (pp. 27-39). Springer Berlin Heidelberg. doi:10.1007/3-540-44751-2_4

Blaschke, C., Hoffmann, R., Oliveros, J. C., & Valencia, A. (2001). Extracting information automatically from biological literature. *Comparative and Functional Genomics*, *2*(5), 310–313. doi:10.1002/cfg.102 PMID:18629239

Blondel, V. D., Guillaume, J. L., Lambiotte, R., & Lefebvre, E. (2008). *Fast unfolding of communities in large networks*. JSTAT.

Bloom, B. S. (1956). *Taxonomy of educational objectives*. London: Longman.

Bloomberg, J. (2013, January 17) *The Big Data Long Tail*. Retrieved from http://www.devx.com/blog/the-big-data-long-tail.html/

Boccaletti, S., Latora, V., Moreno, Y., Chavez, M., & Hwang, D. U. (2006). Complex networks: Structure and dynamics. *Physics Reports*, *424*(4), 175–308. doi:10.1016/j.physrep.2005.10.009

Boreisha, Y., & Myronovych, O. (2005a). Knowledge Navigation and Evolutionary Prototyping in E-Learning Systems. *Proceedings of the E-Learn 2005 World Conference on E-Learning in Corporate, Government, Healthcare, and Higher Education.*

Boreisha, Y. (2001). Internet-Based Data Warehousing. *Proceedings of SPIE Internet-Based Enterprise Integration and Management*, *4566*, 102–108. doi:10.1117/12.443132

Boreisha, Y. (2002). Database Integration Over the Web. *Proceedings of the International Conference on Internet Computing, IC'02.*

Boreisha, Y., & Myronovych, O. (2003). Data-Driven Web Sites. *WSEAS Transactions on Computers*, *2*(1), 79–83.

Boreisha, Y., & Myronovych, O. (2005b). Web Services-Based Virtual Data Warehouse as an Integration and ETL Tool. *Proceedings of the 2005 International Symposium on Web Services and Applications, ISWS'05.*

Boreisha, Y., & Myronovych, O. (2007). Web-Based Decision Support Systems in Knowledge Management and Education. *Proceedings of the 2007 International Conference on Information and Knowledge Engineering, IKE'07.*

Borgatti, S. P., Everett, M. G., & Freeman, L. C. (2002). *Ucinet for Windows: Software for social network analysis.* Academic Press.

Borges, J., & Levene, M. (2000). Data mining of user navigation patterns. In *Web usage analysis and user profiling.* Springer Berlin Heidelberg.

Bouidghaghen, O., Tamine, L., & Boughanem, M. (2011, June). Personalizing mobile web search for location sensitive queries. In *12th International Conference on Mobile Data Management*, (vol. 1, pp. 110-118). IEEE. doi:10.1109/MDM.2011.52

Breese, J. S., & Heckerman, D. (1998). Empirical analysis of predictive algorithms for collaborative filtering. In *Proceedings of the Fourteenth conference on Uncertainty in artificial intelligence (UAI'98).*

Breitman, K. K., Truszkowski, & Felicissiomo. (2006). The automatic semantic desktop; Helping users copy with information system and complexity. In *Proceedings of IEEE International workshop*, (pp. 156-162).

Breitman, K., Casanova, M., & Truszkowski, W. (2006). *Semantic Web.* Concepts.

Brickell, J., Dhillon, I. S., & Modha, D. S. (2007). *Adaptive website design using caching algorithm. Advances in Web Mining and Web Usage Analysis* (Vol. 4811, pp. 1–20). Springer. doi:10.1007/978-3-540-77485-3_1

Brickley, D., & Guha, R. V. (2003). *Resource Description Framework (RDF) Schema specification 1.0: RDF Schema.* W3C Working Draft.

Brindley, J. E., Walti, C., & Blaschke, L. M. (2009). Creating effective collaborative learning groups in an online environment. *The International Review of Research in Open and Distributed Learning*, *10*(3), 1–18. doi:10.19173/irrodl.v10i3.675

Brin, S., & Pange, L. (1998). The Anatomy of a Large-scale Hyper Textual Web Search Engine. *Computer Networks and ISDN Systems*, *30*(1-7), 107–117. doi:10.1016/S0169-7552(98)00110-X

Broder, A. (2002). A taxonomy of web search. *ACM Sigir Forum, 36*(2), 3-10.

Brookhart, S. M., Moss, C. M., & Long, B. A. (2010). Teacher inquiry into formative assessment practices in remedial reading classrooms. *Assessment in Education: Principles, Policy & Practice*, *17*(1), 41–58. doi:10.1080/09695940903565545

Brusilovsky, P. (2007). *The Adaptive Web*. doi:10.1007/978-3-540-72079-9

Brustoloni, J. C. (1991). *Autonomous Agents: Characterization and Requirements*. Technical Report CMU-CS-91-204. School of Computer Science, Carnegie Mellon University.

Buckland, M., & Plaunt, C. (1994). On the construction of selection systems. *Library Hi Tech*, *12*(4), 15–28. doi:10.1108/eb047934

Buettner, R. (2014). A Framework for Recommender Systems in Online Social Network Recruiting: An Interdisciplinary Call to Arms.*47th Annual Hawaii International Conference on System Sciences*. Big Island, HI: IEEE. doi:10.1109/HICSS.2014.184

Bussmann, S., & Demazeau, Y. (1994). An agent model combining reactive and cognitive capabilities. In *Proceedings of the IEEE/RSJ/GI International Conference on Intelligent Robots and Systems 94* (vol. 3, pp. 2095-2102). Munich: IEEE.

Carman, M. J., Crestani, F., Harvey, M., & Baillie, M. (2010). Towards query log based personalization using topic models. In *Proceedings of the 19th ACM international conference on Information and knowledge management*, (pp.1849-1852). ACM. doi:10.1145/1871437.1871745

Catledge, L. D., & Pitkow, J. E. (1995). Characterizing browsing strategies in the World Wide Web. *Computer Networks and ISDN Systems*, *27*(6), 1065–1073. doi:10.1016/0169-7552(95)00043-7

Cearley, D., Burke, B., & Walker, M. (2016). *Top 10 Strategic Technology Trends for 2016*. Gartner, Inc.

Celic, S., & Tan, O. (2005). Determination of preconsolidation pressure with artificial neural network. *Civil Engineering and Environmental Science*, *22*(4), 217–231. doi:10.1080/10286600500383923

Cerrada, M., Cardillo, J., Aguilar, J., & Faneite, R. (2007). Agents-based design for fault management systems in industrial processes. *Computers in Industry*, *58*(4), 313–328. doi:10.1016/j.compind.2006.07.008

Chakrabarti, S. (2002). *Mining the Web: Discovering knowledge from hypertext data*. Elsevier.

Chakrabarti, S., Dom, B., & van de Berg, M. (1999). Focussed crawling: A new approach to topic specific web resource discovery.*Proceedings of the 8th World Wide Web Conference*. Elsevier.

Chan, F. T. S., Jiang, B., & Tang, N. K. H. (2000). The development of intelligent decision support tools to aid the design of flexible manufacturing systems. *International Journal of Production Economics*, *65*(1), 73–84. doi:10.1016/S0925-5273(99)00091-2

Chang, B., Chang, C. W., & Wu, C. H. (2011). Fuzzy DEMATEL method for developing supplier selection criteria. *Expert Systems with Applications: An International Journal*, *38*(3), 1850–1858. doi:10.1016/j.eswa.2010.07.114

Chang, G., Healy, M. J., McHugh, J. A. M., & Wang, J. T. L. (2001). *Mining the World Wide Web: An Information Search Approach*. Kluwer Academic Publishers. doi:10.1007/978-1-4615-1639-2

Cha, S.-H. (2007). Comprehensive survey on distance/similarity measures between probability density functions. *International Journal of Mathematical Models and Methods in Applied Sciences*, *1*(4), 300–307.

Chaturvedi, K. K., & Singh, V. (2012). An empirical comparison of machine learning techniques in predicting the bug severity of open and closed source projects. *International Journal of Open Source Software and Processes*, *4*(2), 32–59. doi:10.4018/jossp.2012040103

Chau, M., Zeng, D., Chen, H., Huang, M., & Hendriawan, D. (2003). Design and evaluation of a multi-agent collaborative Web mining system. *Decision Support Systems*, *35*(1), 167–183. doi:10.1016/S0167-9236(02)00103-3

Chawla, S., & Bedi, P. (2008a). Personalized web search using information scent. In *Innovations and Advanced Techniques in Systems, Computing Sciences and Software Engineering* (pp. 483–488). Springer Netherlands. doi:10.1007/978-1-4020-8735-6_90

Chawla, S., & Bedi, P. (2008b). Query expansion using information scent.*International Symposium on Information Technology*(vol. 3, pp 1-8). Kuala Lumpur: IEEE.

Chawla, S., & Bedi, P. (2008c). Finding Hubs and Authorities using Information Scent to Improve the Information Retrieval precision. In *Proceedings of International Conference on Artificial Intelligence* (pp. 185-191).

Chawla, S., & Bedi, P. (2008d). Improving information retrieval precision by finding related queries with similar information need using information scent.*First International Conference on Emerging Trends in Engineering and Technology* (pp 486-491). Nagpur, Maharashtra: IEEE. doi:10.1109/ICETET.2008.23

Chen, Liu, Liu, Pu, & Ma. (2003). *Building a Web Thesaurus form Web Link Structure*. SIGIR 2003, Toronto, Canada.

Chen, Ororbia II, & Giles. (2015). *ExpertSeer: a Keyphrase Based Expert Recommender for Digital Libraries*. in arXiv preprint 2015.

Cheney, D. (2015). Big Data, text mining, and news content: Where is the Big Data? In W. Gibbs & J. McKendrick (Eds.), *Contemporary research methods and data analytics in the news industry* (pp. 133–151). Hershey, PA: IGI Global. doi:10.4018/978-1-4666-8580-2.ch008

Cheng, P. S., & Chang, P. (1998). Transforming corporate information into value through data warehousing and data mining. *Aslib Proceedings*, *50*(5), 109–113. doi:10.1108/eb051492

Chen, H., Gou, L., Zhang, X., & Giles Collabseer, C. (2011). A search engine for collaboration discovery. In *ACM/IEEE Joint Conference on Digital Libraries (JCDL)*.

Chen, L., Liu, H., & Friedman, C. (2005). Gene name ambiguity of eukaryotic nomenclatures. *Bioinformatics (Oxford, England)*, *21*(2), 248–256. doi:10.1093/bioinformatics/bth496 PMID:15333458

Chen, L., & Sycara, K. (1998). WebMate: A personal agent for browsing and searching. In *Proceedings of the second international conference on Autonomous agents* (pp. 132-139). New York: ACM. doi:10.1145/280765.280789

Chen, S. G., & Lin, Y. K. (2009). On performance evaluation of ERP systems with fuzzy mathematics. *Expert Systems with Applications: An International Journal*, *36*(3), 6362–6367. doi:10.1016/j.eswa.2008.08.078

Chen, T. (2007). Obtaining the Optimal Cache Document Replacement Policy for the Caching System of an EC Website. *European Journal of Operational Research*, *181*(2), 828–835. doi:10.1016/j.ejor.2006.05.034

Chen, T. Y., Chen, Y. M., Lin, C. J., & Chen, P. Y. (2010). A fuzzy trust evaluation method for knowledge sharing in virtual enterprises. *Computers & Industrial Engineering*, *59*(4), 853–864. doi:10.1016/j.cie.2010.08.015

Chen, X. W., & Liu, M. (2005). Prediction of protein-protein interactions using random decision forest framework. *Bioinformatics (Oxford, England)*, *21*(24), 4394–4400. doi:10.1093/bioinformatics/bti721 PMID:16234318

Chen, X., & Zhang, X. (2002). Popularity-based PPM: An effective Web pre-fetching technique for high accuracy and low storage. In *Proceedings of the International Conference on Parallel Processing*, (pp. 296-304). doi:10.1109/ICPP.2002.1040885

Chen, Z., Kalashnikov, D. V., & Mehrotra, S. (2009). Exploiting context analysis for combining multiple entity resolution systems. In *Proceedings of the 2009 ACM SIGMOD International Conference on Management of data*(pp. 207-218). ACM. doi:10.1145/1559845.1559869

Cherfi, H., Napoli, A., & Toussaint, Y. (2009). A conformity measure using background knowledge for association rules: Application to text mining. In Y. Zhao, C. Zhang, & L. Cao (Eds.), *Post-mining of association rules: Techniques for effective knowledge extraction* (pp. 100–115). Hershey, PA: IGI Global. doi:10.4018/978-1-60566-404-0.ch006

Chew, P. A. (2009). Multilingual text mining. In J. Wang (Ed.), *Encyclopedia of data warehousing and mining* (2nd ed., pp. 1380–1385). Hershey, PA: IGI Global. doi:10.4018/978-1-60566-010-3.ch213

Chi, E. H., Pirolli, P., & Pitkow, J. (2000). The scent of a site: A system for analyzing and predicting information scent, usage, and usability of a web site. In *Proceedings of the SIGCHI Conference on Human Factors in Computing Systems* (pp. 161-168). New York: ACM.

Chi, E. H., Pirolli, P., Chen, K., & Pitkow, J. (2001). Using information scent to model user information needs and actions and the Web. In *Proceedings of the SIGCHI conference on Human factors in computing systems* (pp. 490-497). New York: ACM. doi:10.1145/365024.365325

Chi, E. H., Rosien, A., Supattanasiri, G., Williams, A., Royer, C., Chow, C., & Cousins, S. (2003). The bloodhound project: automating discovery of web usability issues using the InfoScentπ simulator. In *Proceedings of the SIGCHI conference on Human factors in computing systems* (pp 505-512). New York: ACM. doi:10.1145/642611.642699

Chiong, R., & Jovanovic, J. (2012). Collaborative learning in online study groups: An evolutionary game theory perspective. *Journal of Information Technology Education: Research, 11*, 81–101.

Clements, D. H., & Nastasi, B. K. (1992). Computers and early childhood education. In M. Gettinger, S. N. Elliott, & T. R. Kratochwill (Eds.), *Preschool and early childhood treatment directions* (pp. 187–246). London: Lawrence Erlbaum Associates.

Clifton, C., Cooley, R., & Rennie, J. (2004). TopCat: Data mining for topic identification in a text corpus. *IEEE Transactions on Knowledge and Data Engineering, 16*(8), 949–964. doi:10.1109/TKDE.2004.32

Coakes, E., Merchant, K., & Lehaney, B. (1997). The use of expert systems in business transformation. *Management Decision, 35*(1), 53–57. doi:10.1108/00251749710160197

Cobb, J., & ElAarag, H. (2008). Web Proxy Cache Replacement Scheme based on Back-Propagation Neural Network. *Journal of Systems and Software, 81*(9), 1539–1558. doi:10.1016/j.jss.2007.10.024

Coley, D. A. (1999). *An introduction to genetic algorithms for scientists and engineers.* Singapore: World Scientific Publishing. doi:10.1142/3904

Collins-Thompson, K., Bennett, P. N., White, R. W., de la Chica, S., & Sontag, D. (2011). Personalizing web search results by reading level. In *Proceedings of the 20th ACM international conference on Information and knowledge management* (pp. 403-412). New York: ACM. doi:10.1145/2063576.2063639

Cook, D. J., & Holder, L. B. (2000). Graph-based data mining. *Proceedings of IEEE Intelligent Systems, 15*, 32–41. doi:10.1109/5254.850825

Cooley, R. (2000). *Web Usage Mining: Discovery and Usage of Interesting Patterns from Web Data* (Ph.D. Thesis). University of Minnesota, Computer Science & Engineering.

Cooley, R. W. (2000). *Web usage mining: discovery and application of interesting patterns from web data* (Doctoral dissertation). University of Minnesota.

Cooley, R., Mobasher, B., & Srinivastaa, J. (1999). Data Preparation for Mining World Wide Web Browsing Patterns. *Journal of knowledge and Information Systems,* 78-85.

Cooley, R., Mobasher, B., & Srivastava, J. (1997). Web mining: Information and pattern discovery on the world wide web. In Tools with Artificial Intelligence, 1997. *Proceedings., Ninth IEEE International Conference on* (pp. 558-567). IEEE.

Cooley, R., Mobasher, B., & Srivastava, J. (1997). Web Mining: Information and Pattern Discovery on the Word Wide Web.*Proceedings ICTAI*. doi:10.1109/TAI.1997.632303

Cooley, R., Mobasher, B., & Srivastava, J. (1999). Data preparation for mining World Wide Web browsing patterns. *Knowledge and Information Systems*, *1*(1), 5–32. doi:10.1007/BF03325089

Cooley, R., Tan, P.-N., & Srivastava, J. (2000). *Discovery of interesting usage patterns from web data. Web Usage Analysis and User Profiling* (Vol. 1836, pp. 163–182). San Diego, CA: Springer. doi:10.1007/3-540-44934-5_10

Crescenzi, V., Merialdo, P., & Missier, P. (2005). Clustering Web pages based on their structures. *Data & Knowledge Engineering*, *54*(3), 279–299. doi:10.1016/j.datak.2004.11.004

Crotty, M. (1998). *The foundations of social research: meaning and perspective in the research process*. London: Sage.

Crunk, J., & North, M. M. (2007). Decision support systems and artificial intelligence technologies in aid of information systems based marketing. *International Management Review*, *3*(2), 61–67.

Cyrus, S., Zarkessh, A. M., Jafar, A., & Vishal, S. (1997). Knowledge discovery from Users Web Page Navigation. In *Workshop on Research Issues in Data Engineering*. Retrieved from www.tutorialspoint.com/data_mining/notes

Cyrus, S., Zarkessh, A. M., Jafar, A., & Vishal, S. (1997). Knowledge discovery from Users Web Page Navigation. In *Workshop on Research Issues in Data Engineering*.

Cyzyowicz, J., Kranakis, E., Krizanc, D., Pelc, A., & Vargas Martin, M. (2003). Enhancing hyperlink structure for improving web performance. *Journal of Web Engineering*, *1*(2), 93–127.

Dai, Y., Kakkonen, T., & Sutinen, E. (2011). MinEDec: A decision-support model that combines text mining technologies with two competitive intelligence analysis methods. *International Journal of Computer Information Systems and Industrial Management Applications*, *3*, 165–173.

Dansdan, A., Tsioutsiouliklis, K., & Velipasaoglu, E. (2009). *Web search engine metrics for measuring user satisfaction*. Retrieved from http://dasdan.net/ali/www2009/web-search-metrics-tutorial-www09-part6a.pdf

Daoud, M., Tamine-Lechani, L., & Boughanem, M. (2008). Using a graph- based ontological user profile for personalizing search. In *Proceedings of the 17th ACM conference on Information and knowledge management*(pp 1495-1496). New York: ACM. doi:10.1145/1458082.1458352

Daskalaki, S., Kopanas, I., Goudara, M., & Avouris, N. (2003). Data mining for decision support on customer insolvency in telecommunications business. *European Journal of Operational Research*, *2003*(2), 239–255. doi:10.1016/S0377-2217(02)00532-5

Davidov, D., Tsur, O., & Rappoport, A. (2010). Enhanced Sentiment Learning Using Twitter Hashtags and Smileys. *Proc. 23rd Int'l Conf. Computational Linguistics: Posters*.

De la Rosa, J. L., Oller, A., Vehí, J., & Puyol, J. (1997). Soccer team based on agent-oriented programming. *Robotics and Autonomous Systems*, *21*(2), 167–176. doi:10.1016/S0921-8890(97)00024-9

Decker, S., & Frank, M. (2004). The social semantic desktop. In *Proceeding of the WWW 2004 Workshop Application Design, Development and Implementation Issues in the Semantic Web*.

Deitel, P. J., & Deitel, H. M. (2008). *Internet and World Wide Web. How to Program* (4th ed.). Prentice Hall.

Denecke, K., & Nejdi, W. (2009). How valuable is medical social media data? Content analysis of the medical web. *Information Sciences, 179*(12), 1870–1880. doi:10.1016/j.ins.2009.01.025

De, P. B., Aroyo, L., & Chepegin, V. (2004). The Next Big Thing: Adaptive Web-Based Systems. *Journal of Digital Information, 5*(1), 22–30.

Dey, P. K. (2001). Decision support system for risk management: A case study. *Management Decision, 39*(8), 634–649. doi:10.1108/00251740110399558

DiMicco, J. M., & Millen, D. R. (2007). Identity Management: Multiple Presentations of Self in Facebook. *Proc. the Int'l ACM Conf. Supporting Group Work.* doi:10.1145/1316624.1316682

Dimitrijevic, & Bosnjak. (2010). Discovering interesting association rules in the web log usage data. *Interdisciplinary Journal of Information, Knowledge, and Management, 5*, 191–207.

Dirsehan, T. (2016). An application of text mining to capture and analyze eWOM: A pilot study on tourism sector. In S. Rathore & A. Panwar (Eds.), *Capturing, analyzing, and managing word-of-mouth in the digital marketplace* (pp. 168–186). Hershey, PA: IGI Global. doi:10.4018/978-1-4666-9449-1.ch010

Domenech, J., Pont-Sanju, A., Sahuquillo, J., & Gil, J. A. (2010). *Evaluation, Analysis and Adaptation of Web Pre-fetching Techniques in Current Web. In Web-Based Support Systems* (pp. 239–271). London: Springer.

Don, A., Zheleva, E., Gregory, M., Tarkan, S., Auvil, L., Clement, T., . . . Plaisant, C. (2007). *Discovering interesting usage patterns in text collections: Integrating text mining with visualization.* Paper presented at the 16th ACM Conference on Information and Knowledge Management (CIKM 2007), Lisbon, Portugal. doi:10.1145/1321440.1321473

Dou, H., Leveille, V., Manullang, S., & Dou, J. M. Jr. (2005). Patent analysis for competitive technical intelligence and innovative thinking. *Data Science Journal, 4*, 209–236. doi:10.2481/dsj.4.209

Dou, Z., Song, R., Wen, J. R., & Yuan, X. (2009). Evaluating the effectiveness of personalized web search. *IEEE Transactions on Knowledge and Data Engineering, 21*(8), 1178–1190. doi:10.1109/TKDE.2008.172

DSS-Wikipedia, the free encyclopedia. (2016). Retrieved April, 2016 from https://en.wikipedia.org/wiki/Decision_support_system

Duggan, M. (2015). *The Demographics of Social Media Users.* Retrieved May, 2016 from http://www.pewinternet.org/2015/08/19/the-demographics-of-social-media-users/

Dumbill, E. (2013). Big data, cool kids: Making sense of the hype-cycle scuffle.*Proceedings from the O'Reilly Strata Conference.*

Dunham, M. H. (2006). *Data Mining Introductory and Advanced Topics* (1st ed.). Pearson Education.

Dunham, M. H. (2006). *Data mining: Introductory and advanced topics.* Pearson Education.

Durfee, A. (2008). Text mining. In G. Garson & M. Khosrow-Pour (Eds.), *Handbook of research on public information technology* (pp. 592–603). Hershey, PA: IGI Global. doi:10.4018/978-1-59904-857-4.ch054

Durkin, J. (1994). *Expert systems: Design and development.* New York, NY: Prentice Hall.

Eirinaki, M., & Vazirgiannis, M. (2003). Web mining for web personalization. *ACM Transactions on Internet Technology, 3*(1), 1–27. doi:10.1145/643477.643478

ElAarag, H., & Romano, S. (2009). Improvement of the neural network proxy cache replacement strategy.*Proceedings of the 2009 Spring Simulation Multiconference.*

EL-Korany, A., & EL-Bahnasy, K. (2009). A multi-agent framework to facilitate knowledge sharing. *Journal of Artificial Intelligence*, *2*(1), 17–28. doi:10.3923/jai.2009.17.28

Elsner, U. (1997). *Graph partitioning - A survey*. Technical Report SFB393/97-27. Technische University at Chemnitz.

Etzioni, O. (1996). The World Wide Web: Quagmire or Gold Mine. *Communications of the ACM*, *39*(11), 65–68. doi:10.1145/240455.240473

Etzioni, O., & Perkowitz, M. (1997). Adaptive websites: An AI challenge.*Proceedings of the 15th International Joint Conference on Artificial Intelligence*. Morgan Kaufmann.

Etzioni, O., & Perkowitz, M. (2000). Towards adaptive web sites: Conceptual framework and case study. *Artificial Intelligence*, *118*(1-2), 245–275. doi:10.1016/S0004-3702(99)00098-3

Facca, F.M., & Lanzi, P. L. (2005). Mining Interesting Knowledge from Web logs: A Survey. *International Journal of Data and Knowledge Engineering*, *53*(3), 225-241.

Facca, F., & Lanzi, P. (2005). Mining interesting knowledge from weblogs: A survey. *Data Mining and Knowledge Discovery*, *53*(5), 225–241.

Facebook Pages for marketing your business | Facebook for Business. (n.d.). Retrieved April, 2016 https://www.facebook.com/business/products/pages

Facebook: No. 1 Globally. Business Week. (2008). Retrieved April 9, 2016 from http://www.businessweek.com/technology/content/aug2008/tc20080812_853725.htm

Falkenhainer, B., Forbus, K. D., & Gentner, D. (1986). *The structure-mapping engine*. Paper presented at the 5th National Conference on Artificial Intelligence (AAAI 1986), Philadelphia, PA.

Fan, L., Cao, P., & Jacobson, Q. (1999). Web Pre-fetching between Low-Bandwidth Clients and Proxies: Potential and Performance. In *Proceedings of the Joint International Conference on Measurement and Modeling of Computer Systems (SIGMETRICS'99)*.

Fan, L., Cao, P., Lin, W., & Jacobson, Q. (1999).Web prefetching between low- bandwidth clients and proxies: Potential and performance.*Proceedings of the ACM SIGMETRICS International Conference on Measurement and Modeling of Computer Systems*. ACM Press. doi:10.1145/301464.301557

Feldman, R., & Hirsh, H. (1997). Exploiting background information in knowledge discovery from text. *Journal of Intelligent Information Systems*, *9*(1), 83–97. doi:10.1023/A:1008693204338

Feldman, R., & Sanger, J. (2007). *Text mining handbook: Advanced approaches in analyzing unstructured data*. New York, NY: Cambridge University Press.

Feld, S. L. (1981). The focused organization of social ties. *American Journal of Sociology*, *86*(5), 1015–1035. doi:10.1086/227352

Felfernig, A., & Isak, K. (2007). The VITA Financial Services Sales Support Environment. In AAAI/IAAI 2007, (pp. 1692-1699).

Feng, W., Man, S., & Hu, G. (2009). *Markov Tree Prediction on Web Cache Pre-fetching. In Software Engineering, Artificial Intelligence (SCI)* (Vol. 209, pp. 105–120). Berlin: Springer-Verlag.

Ferguson, R. (2012). Learning analytics: Drivers, developments and challenges. *International Journal of Technology Enhanced Learning*, *4*(5-6).

Fernandez, M., Wegerif, R., Mercer, N., & Drummond, S. R. (2001). Re-conceptualizing "scaffolding" and the zone of proximal develoopment in the context of symmetrical collaborative learning. *Journal of Classroom Interaction*, *36*(2), 40–54.

Festa, P. (2003). *Personalized websites are driving customers away*. Accessed on 03/2007 from *http://networks.silicon.com/webwatch/0,39024667,10006394,00.htm

Fidalgo-Blanco, A., Sein-Echaluce, M. L., Garcia-Penalvo, F. J., & Conde, M. A. (2015). Using learning analytics to improve teamwork assessment. *Computers in Human Behavior*, *47*, 149–156. doi:10.1016/j.chb.2014.11.050

Fikes, R; Horrocks, I. (2003). OWL-QL – A Language for Deductive Query Answering on the Semantic Web. *KSL*.

Fitzpatrick, L., & Dent, M. (1997). Automatic feedback using past queries: social searching? *ACM SIGIR Forum*, *31*(SI), 306-313.

Fjallstrom, P.O. (1998). Algorithms for graph partitioning: A Survey. *Linkoping Electronic Articles in Computer and Information Science*, 3.

Flake, G. W., Lawrence, S., & Giles, C. L. (2000). Efficient identification of web communities. In *Proceedings of Sixth ACM SIGKDD International Conference on Knowledge Discovery and Data Mining* (pp. 150-160). ACM Press. doi:10.1145/347090.347121

Flake, G. W., Lawrence, S., Giles, C. L., & Coetzee, F. M. (2002). Computer Vision and Pattern Recognition. *IEEE Computer*, *35*(3), 66–70. doi:10.1109/2.989932

Fleuren, W. C. M., & Alkema, W. (2015). Application of text mining in the biomedical domain. *Methods (San Diego, Calif.)*, *74*, 97–106. doi:10.1016/j.ymeth.2015.01.015 PMID:25641519

Flores-Mendez, R. A. (1999). Towards a standardization of multi-agent system frameworks. *Crossroads*, *5*(4), 18–24. doi:10.1145/331648.331659

Ford, L. R., & Fulkerson, D. R. (1956). A Simple Algorithm for Finding Maximal Network Flows and an Application to the Hitchcock Problem. *Canadian Journal of Mathematics*, *8*, 399–404. doi:10.4153/CJM-1956-045-5

Fortunato, S., & Barthelemy, M. (2007). Resolution limit in community detection. *Proceedings of the National Academy of Sciences of the United States of America*, *104*(1), 36–41. doi:10.1073/pnas.0605965104 PMID:17190818

FQL Overview. (n.d.). Retrieved May, 2016 from https://developers.facebook.com/docs/technical-guides/fql/

Franklin, S., & Graesser, A. (1996). Is it an Agent, or just a Program?: A Taxonomy for Autonomous Agents. In *Intelligent agents III agent theories, architectures, and languages* (pp. 21–35). Springer Berlin Heidelberg.

French, S., & Turoff, M. (2007). Decision Support Systems. *Communications of the ACM*, *50*(3), 39–40. doi:10.1145/1226736.1226762

Freund, E., & Buxbaum, H. J. (1993). A new approach to multi agent systems control in robot-based flexible manufacturing work cells. In *Proceedings of the 1993 IEEE/RSJ International Conference on Intelligent Robots and Systems*(vol. 3, pp 2015-2022). Yokohama: IEEE. doi:10.1109/IROS.1993.583909

Fu, Y., Sandhu, K., & Shih, M. (2000). A Generalization-Based Approach to Clustering of Web Usage Sessions. In *Proceedings of the KDD Workshop on Web Mining*. Springer.

Fujii, A., Iwayama, M., & Kando, N. (2007). Introduction to the special issue on patent processing. *Information Processing & Management*, *43*(5), 1149–1153. doi:10.1016/j.ipm.2006.11.004

Fukuda, K., Tamura, A., Tsunoda, T., & Takagi, T. (1998). *Toward information extraction: Identifying protein names from biological papers* Paper presented at the Pacific Symposium on Biocomputing (PSB 1998), Maui, HI.

Fu, L. (1994). *Neural networks in computer intelligence.* New York, NY: McGraw–Hill.

Galitsky, B. A., Dobrocsi, G., de la Rosa, J. L., & Kuznetsov, S. O. (2011, July). Using generalization of syntactic parse trees for taxonomy capture on the web. In *International Conference on Conceptual Structures* (pp. 104-117). Springer Berlin Heidelberg. doi:10.1007/978-3-642-22688-5_8

Gandhi, M., Jeyebalan, K., Kallukalam, J., Rapkin, A., Reilly, P., & Widodo, N. (2004). *Web Research Infrastructure Project Final Report.* Cornell University.

Gao, Y., Gu, Y., & Li, T. (2009). *Evaluation approach on enterprise integrated business efficiency based on ANN-QPSO.* Paper presented at the 2nd International Conference on Information Management, Innovation Management and Industrial Engineering (ICIII 2009), Xi'an, China. doi:10.1109/ICIII.2009.398

Gao, Q., Xi, S. M., & Im Cho, Y. (2013). A multi-agent personalized ontology profile based user preference profile construction method. In *44th International Symposium on Robotics (ISR)*(pp 1-4). IEEE.

Gartner, Inc. (2016) *What Is Big Data?* Retrieved from http://www.gartner.com/it-glossary/big-data

Gauch, S., Chaffee, J., & Pretschner, A. (2003). Ontology-based personalized search and browsing. *International Journal Web Intelligence and Agent Systems, 1*(3-4), 219-234.

Gedov, V., Stolz, C., Neuneier, R., Skubacz, M., & Seipel, D. (2004). Matching web site structure and content. In *Proceedings of the 13th International World Wide Web Conference on Alternate Track Papers & Posters* (pp 286-287). New York: ACM.

Gerstel, O., Kutten, S., Laber, E. S., Matichin, R., Peleg, D., Pessoa, A. A., & Souza, C. (2007). Reducing human interactions in Web directory searches. *ACM Transactions on Information Systems, 25*(4), 20, es. doi:10.1145/1281485.1281491

Gert, S. (1966). The centrality index of a graph. *Psychometrika, 31*(4), 581–603. doi:10.1007/BF02289527 PMID:5232444

Ghazanfar, PrüGel-Bennett, & Szedmak. (n.d.). Kernel-Mapping Recommender system algorithms. *Information Sciences, 208*, 81–104. doi:10.1016/j.ins.2012.04.012

Ghosh, R., & Dekhil, M. (2009, April). Discovering user profiles. In *Proceedings of the 18th international conference on World wide web*(pp 1233-1234). ACM. doi:10.1145/1526709.1526944

Girvan, M., & Newman, M. E. J. (2002). Community structure in social and biological networks. *Proceedings of the National Academy of Sciences of the United States of America, 99*(12), 7821–7826. doi:10.1073/pnas.122653799 PMID:12060727

Glance, N. S. (2001). Community search assistant. In *Proceedings of the 6th international conference on Intelligent user interfaces*(pp. 91-96). New York: ACM.

Glover, E., Tsioutisiouliklis, K., Lawrence, S., Pennock, D., & Flake, G. (2002). Using Web Structure for Classifying and Describing Web Pages.*Proceedings of WWW2002.* doi:10.1145/511446.511520

Go, A., Bhayani, R., & Huang, L. (2009). *Twitter Sentiment Classification Using Distant Supervision.* CS224N Project Report.

Godbole, S., & Roy, S. (2008). *Text to intelligence: Building and deploying a text mining solution in the services industry for customer satisfaction analysis.* Paper presented at the 2008 IEEE International Conference on Services Computing (SCC 2008), Hololulu, HI. doi:10.1109/SCC.2008.99

Godoy, D., & Amandi, A. (2006). *Modeling user interests by conceptual clustering, Information Systems* (Vol. 31). Elsevier Science Ltd.

Goker, A., & He, D. (2000a). Analysing Web search logs to determine session boundaries for user-oriented learning. *Proceedings of the International Conference on Adaptive Hypermedia and Adaptive Web-based Systems.* doi:10.1007/3-540-44595-1_38

Goker, A., & He, D. (2000b). Detecting session boundaries from Web user logs.*Proceedings of the 22nd Annual Colloquium on Information Retrieval Research*, (pp. 57–66).

Goker, A., He, D., & Harper, D. (2002). Combining evidence for automatic web session identification. *Information Processing & Management*, *38*(5), 727–742. doi:10.1016/S0306-4573(01)00060-7

Goldberg, A. V., & Tarjan, R. E. (1988). A New Approach to the Maximum Flow Problem. *Journal of the ACM*, *35*(4), 921–940. doi:10.1145/48014.61051

Goncalves, C., Assuncao, L., & Cunha, J. C. (2013). Flexible MapReduce workflows for cloud data analytics. *International Journal of Grid and High Performance Computing*, *5*(4), 48–64. doi:10.4018/ijghpc.2013100104

Good, N., Schafer, B., Konstan, J., Borchers, A., Sarwar, B., Herlocker, J., & Riedl, J. (1999). Combining collaborative filtering with personal agents for better recommendation.*Proceedings of the 16th National Conference on Artificial Intelligence.* American Association for Artificial Intelligence.

Grandon, G. (1996). Expert systems usage: Task challenge and intrinsic motivation. *Management Information Systems Quarterly*, *20*(3), 301–329. doi:10.2307/249658

Graph API. (n.d.). Retrieved May,2016 from https://developers.facebook.com/docs/graph-api/

Gress, C. L., Fior, M., Hadwin, A. F., & Winne, P. H. (2010). Measurement and assessment in computer-supported collaborative learning. *Computers in Human Behavior*, *26*(5), 806–814. doi:10.1016/j.chb.2007.05.012

Gubbi, J., Buyya, R., Marusic, S., & Palaniswamia, M. (2013). *Internet of Things: A Vision, Architectural Elements and Future directions in Future Generation Computer Systems.* Cornell University. Retrieved from https://arxiv.org/ftp/arxiv/papers/1207/1207.0203.pdf

Guerlain, S., Brown, D. E., & Mastrangelo, C. (2000). *Intelligent decision support systems.* Paper presented at the 2000 IEEE International Conference on Systems, Man, and Cybernetics (SMC 2000), Nashville, TN.

Guerrero, J. I., León, C., Monedero, I., Biscarri, F., & Biscarri, J. (2014). Improving knowledge-based systems with statistical techniques, text mining, and neural networks for non-technical loss detection. *Knowledge-Based Systems*, *71*, 376–388. doi:10.1016/j.knosys.2014.08.014

Guerrero, J. I., Monedero, Í., Biscarri, F., Biscarri, J., Millán, R., & León, C. (2014). Detection of non-technical losses: The project MIDAS. In B. Tripathy & D. Acharjya (Eds.), *Advances in secure computing, Internet services, and applications* (pp. 140–164). Hershey, PA: IGI Global. doi:10.4018/978-1-4666-4940-8.ch008

Guessoum, Z., & Dojat, M. (1996). *A real-time agent model in an asynchronous-object environment.* Springer Berlin Heidelberg.

Guimaraes, T., Yoon, Y., & Clevenson, A. (1997). Empirically testing ES success factors in business process reengineering. *International Journal of Production Economics*, *50*(2/3), 245–259. doi:10.1016/S0925-5273(97)00044-3

Gulati, P., & Sharma, A. K. (2010). Ontology Driven Query Expansion for Better Image Retrieval. *International Journal of Computers and Applications*, *5*(10), 33–37. doi:10.5120/946-1324

Guo, J., Kešelj, V., & Gao, Q. (2005). Integrating web content clustering into web log association rule mining. In *Advances in Artificial Intelligence* (pp. 182–193). Springer Berlin Heidelberg. doi:10.1007/11424918_19

Gupta, Goel, Lin, Sharma, Wang, & Zadeh. (n.d.). WTF: The who-to-follow system at Twitter. In *Proceedings of the 22nd International Conference on World Wide Web.*

Hadavandi, E., Ghanbari, A., Shahanaghi, K., & Abbasian, S. (2011). Tourist arrival forecasting by evolutionary fuzzy systems. *Tourism Management, 32*(5), 1196–1203. doi:10.1016/j.tourman.2010.09.015

Halpin, H; Tuffield, M. (2010). *A Standards-based, Open and Privacy-aware Social Web.* W3C Social Web Incubator Group Report. W3C Incubator Group Report.

Han & Kamber. (n.d.). *Data Mining: Concepts and Techniques.* Morgan Kaufmann.

Han, J., Kamber, M., & Pei, J. (2011). *Data Mining: Concepts and Techniques.* New Delhi: Morgan Kaufmann.

Hashimi, H., Hafez, A., & Mathkour, H. (2015). Selection criteria for text mining approaches. *Computers in Human Behavior, 51,* 729–733. doi:10.1016/j.chb.2014.10.062

Hassani, M., & Stewart, D. B. (1997). A Mechanism for Communicating in Dynamically Reconfigurable Embedded Systems. In *Proceedings of High Assurance Software Engineering Workshop,* (pp. 215-220). IEEE. doi:10.1109/HASE.1997.648069

Hayes-Roth, B., Washington, R., Ash, D., Hewett, R., Colinot, A., Vina, A., & Seiviur, A. (1982). Guardian: A Prototype Intelligent Agent for Intensive-Care Monitoring. *Artificial Intelligence in Medicine, 4*(2), 165–185. doi:10.1016/0933-3657(92)90052-Q

Haykin, S. (1994). *Neural networks: A comprehensive foundation.* Englewood Cliffs, NJ: Prentice Hall.

Heckman, R. (1998). Planning to solve the "skill problem" in the virtual information management organization. *International Journal of Information Management, 18*(1), 3–16. doi:10.1016/S0268-4012(97)00036-4

Heer, J., & Chi, E. H. (2001). Identification of web user traffic composition using multi-modal clustering and information scent. In *Proceedings of the Workshop on Web Mining,SIAM Conference on Data Mining* (pp. 51-58).

Heer, J., & Chi, E. H. (2002). Separating the swarm: categorization methods for user sessions on the web. In *Proceedings of the SIGCHI Conference on Human factors in Computing Systems* (pp. 243-250). New York: ACM. doi:10.1145/503376.503420

Hengshan, W., Cheng, Y., & Hua, Z. (2006). Design and Implementation of a Web Usage Mining Model Based on FPgrowth and Prefixspan. Communications of the IIMA, 6(2).

Hewitt, C. (1977). Viewing Control Structures as Patterns of Passing Messages. *Artificial Intelligence, 8*(3), 323–364. doi:10.1016/0004-3702(77)90033-9

Hitzler, P; Krotzsch, M; Rudolph, S. (2009). *Foundation of Semantic Web Technologies.* CRS Press Taylor & Francis Group, A Chapman & Hall Book.

Holsapple, C., & Whinston, A. (1987). *Business expert systems.* New York, NY: McGraw–Hill.

Hong, J. I., Heer, J., Waterson, S., & Landay, J. A. (2001). WebQuilt: A proxy-based approach to remote web usability testing. *ACM Transactions on Information Systems, 19*(3), 263–285. doi:10.1145/502115.502118

Hopgood, A. A. (1993). *Knowledge-based systems for engineers and scientists.* Boca Raton, FL: CRC Press, Inc.

Horowitz, Sahani, & Rajasekaran. (1998). *Fundamentals of Computer Algorithms.* Galgotia Publications Pvt. Ltd.

Hou, J., & Zhang, Y. (2003). Effectively finding relevant web pages from linkage information. *IEEE Transactions on Knowledge and Data Engineering, 15*(4), 940–951. doi:10.1109/TKDE.2003.1209010

Hrastinski, S. (2008). What is online learner participation? A literature review. *Computers & Education, 51*(4), 1755–1765. doi:10.1016/j.compedu.2008.05.005

Hrastinski, S. (2009). A theory of online learning as online participation. *Computers & Education, 52*(1), 78–82. doi:10.1016/j.compedu.2008.06.009

Hron, A., & Friedrich, H. F. (2003). A review of web-based collaborative learning: Factors beyond technology. *Journal of Computer Assisted Learning, 19*(1), 70–79. doi:10.1046/j.0266-4909.2002.00007.x

Hu, M., & Liu, B. (2004). *Mining and summarizing customer reviews.* Paper presented at the 10th ACM SIGMOD International Conference on Knowledge Discovery and Data Mining (KDD 2004), Seattle, WA. doi:10.1145/1014052.1014073

Hu, T., Tang, & Liu. (2013). Exploiting Social Relations for Sentiment Analysis in Micro blogging. In *Proceedings of the 6th ACM International Conference on Web Search and Data Mining.* ACM.

Huang, W., & Li, B. (2011). An improved method for the computation of PageRank. In *International Conference on Mechatronic Science, Electric Engineering and Computer*(pp. 2191-2194). Jilin: IEEE. doi:10.1109/MEC.2011.6025926

Huang, Y. F., & Hsu, J. M. (2008). Mining Web Logs to Improve Hit Ratios of Pre-fetching and Caching. *Knowledge-Based Systems, 21*(1), 62–69. doi:10.1016/j.knosys.2006.11.004

Huet, B., Cross, A., & Hancock, E. (1999). Shape retrieval by inexact graph matching. In *Proceedings of IEEE International Conference on Multimedia Computing Systems* (vol. 2, pp. 40–44). IEEE Computer Society Press.

Ibrahim, T. I., & Xu, C. Z. (2000). Neural Nets based Predictive Pre-fetching to Tolerate WWW Latency. In *Proceedings of the 20th International Conference on Distributed Computing Systems.* IEEE.

Ibrahim, T. I., & Xu, C. Z. (2004). A Keyword-Based Semantic Pre-fetching Approach in Internet News Services. *IEEE Transactions on Knowledge and Data Engineering, 16*(5), 601–611. doi:10.1109/TKDE.2004.1277820

Inamdar, S. A., & Shinde, G. N. (2008). An agent based intelligent search engine system for web mining. *Research, Reflections and Innovations in Integrating ICT in Education,* (pp. 1062-1065).

Indurkhya, N. (2015). Emerging directions in predictive text mining. *Wiley Interdisciplinary Reviews: Data Mining and Knowledge Discovery, 5*(4), 155–164.

Ishak, W. H. W., Ku-Mahamud, K. R., & Morwawi, N. M. (2011). Conceptual model of intelligent decision support system based on naturalistic decision theory for reservoir operation during emergency situation. *International Journal of Civil & Environmental Engineering, 11*(2), 6–11.

Ito, Horst, Bittanti, boyd, Herr-Stephenson, Lange, ... Tripp. (2008). *Living and Learning with New Media: Summary of Findings from the Digital Youth Project.* The John D. and Catherine T. MacAuthur Foundation.

Jackson, P. (1998). *Introduction to expert systems.* Harlow, UK: Addison–Wesley.

Jaczynski, M., & Trousse, B. (1998). WWW Assisted Browsing by Reusing Past Navigations of a Group of Users. In *Proceedings of the Advances in Case-Based Reasoning, Forth European Workshop* (LNCS). Dublin, Ireland: Springer.

Jafarkarimi, Sim, & Saadatdoost. (2012, June). A Naïve Recommendation Model for Large Databases. *International Journal of Information and Education Technology.*

Janca, P. C. (1995). *Pragmatic application of information agents.* BIS Strategic Report.

Jang, J. S. R., & Sun, C. T. (1995). Neuro-fuzzy modeling and control. *Proceedings of the IEEE, 83*(3), 378–406. doi:10.1109/5.364486

Janjua, N. K., & Hussain, F. K. (2012). Web@IDSS: Argumentation-enabled web-based IDSS for reasoning over incomplete and conflicting information. *Knowledge-Based Systems, 32*, 9–27. doi:10.1016/j.knosys.2011.09.009

Jansen, B., & Spink, A. (2006). How are we searching the web? a comparison of nine search engine query logs. *Information Processing & Management, 42*.

Jantan, H., Hamdan, A. R., & Othman, Z. A. (2010). Intelligent techniques for decision support system in human resource management. In G. Devlin (Ed.), *Decision support systems: Advances* (pp. 261–276). Rijeka, Croatia: InTech. doi:10.5772/39401

Jayaraman, V., & Srivastava, R. (1996). Expert systems in production and operations management: Current applications and future prospects. *International Journal of Operations & Production Management, 16*(12), 27–44. doi:10.1108/01443579610151742

Jeh, G., & Widom, J. (2002). SimRank: A measure of structural-context similarity. In *Proceedings of the eighth ACM SIGKDD International Conference on Knowledge Discovery and Data Mining, KDD '02* (pp. 538–543). doi:10.1145/775047.775126

Jennings, N. R. (1996). Software agents. *IEEE Review*, 17-20.

Jensen, L. J., Saric, J., & Bork, P. (2006). Literature mining for the biologist: From information retrieval to biological discovery. *Nature Reviews. Genetics, 7*(2), 119–129. doi:10.1038/nrg1768 PMID:16418747

Jiang, X.-M., Song, W.-G., & Zeng, H.-J. (2005). *Applying associative relationship on the clickthrough data to improve web search. Advances in Information Retrieval* (Vol. 3408, pp. 475–486). Springer.

Jianhan, Z. (2002). Using Markov Chains for Link Prediction in Adaptive Web Sites. *SoftWare* 2002. *LNCS, 2311*, 60–73.

Jian, Y., Wen, J.-R., & Hong-Jiang, Z. (2002). Query clustering using user logs. *ACM Transactions on Information Systems, 20*(1), 59–81. doi:10.1145/503104.503108

Jiawei, H., Micheline, K., & Jian, P. (2006). *Data Mining Concepts and Techniques*. Pearson Education.

Jiliang, T., & Jie, L., & Huan. (2014). Recommendation in Social Media - Recent Advances and New Frontiers. In *Proceedings of the 20th ACM SIGKDD Conference on Knowledge Discovery and Data Mining*. ACM.

Jimeno-Yepes, A., Berlanga-Llavori, R., & Rebholz-Schuchmann, D. (2010). Applications of ontologies and text mining in the biomedical domain. In F. Gargouri & W. Jaziri (Eds.), *Ontology theory, management and design: Advanced tools and models* (pp. 261–283). Hershey, PA: IGI Global. doi:10.4018/978-1-61520-859-3.ch012

Jin, G., Jeong, Y., & Yoon, B. (2015). Technology-driven roadmaps for identifying new product/market opportunities: Use of text mining and quality function deployment. *Advanced Engineering Informatics, 29*(1), 126–138. doi:10.1016/j.aei.2014.11.001

Joshi, A., & Krishnapuram, R. (2000). On Mining Web Access Logs. In *ACM SIGMOD Workshop on Research Issues in Data Mining and Knowledge Discovery*, (pp. 63- 69).

Kahraman, C., Kaya, I., & Cevikcan, E. (2011). Intelligence decision systems in enterprise information management. *Journal of Enterprise Information Management, 24*(4), 360–379. doi:10.1108/17410391111148594

Kahraman, C., Oztaysi, B., Sari, I. U., & Turanoglu, E. (2014). Fuzzy analytic hierarchy process with interval type-2 fuzzy sets. *Knowledge-Based Systems, 59*, 48–57. doi:10.1016/j.knosys.2014.02.001

Kang, I. S., Na, S. H., Kim, J., & Lee, J. H. (2007). Cluster-based patent retrieval. *Information Processing & Management, 43*(5), 1173–1182. doi:10.1016/j.ipm.2006.11.006

Kanooni, A. (2009). *Organizational factors affecting business and information technology alignment: A structural equation modeling analysis* (Ph.D. dissertation). Capella University.

Kao, A., Poteet, S., Wu, J., Ferng, W., Tjoelker, R., & Quach, L. (2012). Latent semantic analysis for text mining and beyond. In L. Yan & Z. Ma (Eds.), *Intelligent multimedia databases and information retrieval: Advancing applications and technologies* (pp. 253–280). Hershey, PA: IGI Global. doi:10.4018/978-1-61350-126-9.ch015

Kaplan, A. M., & Haenlein, M. (2010). Users of the world, unite! The challenges and opportunities of social media. *Business Horizons, 53*(1), 59–68. doi:10.1016/j.bushor.2009.09.003

Karl, A., Wisnowski, J., & Rushing, W. H. (2015). A practical guide to text mining with topic extraction. *Wiley Interdisciplinary Reviews: Computational Statistics, 7*(5), 326–340. doi:10.1002/wics.1361

Karsak, E. E., & Ozogul, C. O. (2009). An integrated decision making approach for ERP system selection. *Expert Systems with Applications: An International Journal, 36*(1), 660–667. doi:10.1016/j.eswa.2007.09.016

Kasemsap, K. (2016c). Mastering big data in the digital age. In M. Singh & D. G. (Eds.), Effective big data management and opportunities for implementation (pp. 104–129). Hershey, PA: IGI Global. doi:10.4018/978-1-5225-0182-4.ch008

Kasemsap, K. (2015a). Implementing enterprise resource planning. In M. Khosrow-Pour (Ed.), *Encyclopedia of information science and technology* (3rd ed., pp. 798–807). Hershey, PA: IGI Global. doi:10.4018/978-1-4666-5888-2.ch076

Kasemsap, K. (2015b). The role of information system within enterprise architecture and their impact on business performance. In M. Wadhwa & A. Harper (Eds.), *Technology, innovation, and enterprise transformation* (pp. 262–284). Hershey, PA: IGI Global. doi:10.4018/978-1-4666-6473-9.ch012

Kasemsap, K. (2015c). The role of customer relationship management in the global business environments. In T. Tsiakis (Ed.), *Trends and innovations in marketing information systems* (pp. 130–156). Hershey, PA: IGI Global. doi:10.4018/978-1-4666-8459-1.ch007

Kasemsap, K. (2015d). The role of data mining for business intelligence in knowledge management. In A. Azevedo & M. Santos (Eds.), *Integration of data mining in business intelligence systems* (pp. 12–33). Hershey, PA: IGI Global. doi:10.4018/978-1-4666-6477-7.ch002

Kasemsap, K. (2015e). The role of radio frequency identification in modern libraries. In S. Thanuskodi (Ed.), *Handbook of research on inventive digital tools for collection management and development in modern libraries* (pp. 361–385). Hershey, PA: IGI Global. doi:10.4018/978-1-4666-8178-1.ch021

Kasemsap, K. (2016a). Multifaceted applications of data mining, business intelligence, and knowledge management. *International Journal of Social and Organizational Dynamics in IT, 5*(1), 57–69. doi:10.4018/IJSODIT.2016010104

Kasemsap, K. (2016a). The fundamentals of business intelligence. *International Journal of Organizational and Collective Intelligence, 6*(2), 12–25. doi:10.4018/IJOCI.2016040102

Kasemsap, K. (2016b). The fundamentals of neuroeconomics. In B. Christiansen & E. Lechman (Eds.), *Neuroeconomics and the decision-making process* (pp. 1–32). Hershey, PA: IGI Global. doi:10.4018/978-1-4666-9989-2.ch001

Kasemsap, K. (2016c). The roles of knowledge management and organizational innovation in global business. In G. Jamil, J. Poças-Rascão, F. Ribeiro, & A. Malheiro da Silva (Eds.), *Handbook of research on information architecture and management in modern organizations* (pp. 130–153). Hershey, PA: IGI Global. doi:10.4018/978-1-4666-8637-3.ch006

Kasemsap, K. (2016d). The roles of business process modeling and business process reengineering in e-government. In J. Martins & A. Molnar (Eds.), *Handbook of research on innovations in information retrieval, analysis, and management* (pp. 401–430). Hershey, PA: IGI Global. doi:10.4018/978-1-4666-8833-9.ch015

Kasemsap, K. (2016d). The roles of lifelong learning and knowledge management in global higher education. In P. Ordóñez de Pablos & R. Tennyson (Eds.), *Impact of economic crisis on education and the next-generation workforce* (pp. 71–100). Hershey, PA: IGI Global. doi:10.4018/978-1-4666-9455-2.ch004

Kasemsap, K. (2016e). The roles of e-learning, organizational learning, and knowledge management in the learning organizations. In E. Railean, G. Walker, A. Elçi, & L. Jackson (Eds.), *Handbook of research on applied learning theory and design in modern education* (pp. 786–816). Hershey, PA: IGI Global. doi:10.4018/978-1-4666-9634-1.ch039

Kasemsap, K. (2016f). Encouraging supply chain networks and customer loyalty in global supply chain. In N. Kamath & S. Saurav (Eds.), *Handbook of research on strategic supply chain management in the retail industry* (pp. 87–112). Hershey, PA: IGI Global. doi:10.4018/978-1-4666-9894-9.ch006

Kasemsap, K. (2017a). Advocating problem-based learning and creative problem-solving skills in global education. In C. Zhou (Ed.), *Handbook of research on creative problem-solving skill development in higher education* (pp. 351–377). Hershey, PA: IGI Global. doi:10.4018/978-1-5225-0643-0.ch016

Kasemsap, K. (2017b). Mastering web mining and information retrieval in the digital age. In A. Kumar (Ed.), *Web usage mining techniques and applications across industries* (pp. 1–28). Hershey, PA: IGI Global. doi:10.4018/978-1-5225-0613-3.ch001

Kasemsap, K. (2017c). Advocating information system, information integration, and information sharing in global supply chain. In G. Jamil, A. Soares, & C. Pessoa (Eds.), *Handbook of research on information management for effective logistics and supply chains* (pp. 107–130). Hershey, PA: IGI Global. doi:10.4018/978-1-5225-0973-8.ch006

Kasemsap, K. (2017d). Mastering social media in the modern business world. In N. Rao (Ed.), *Social media listening and monitoring for business applications* (pp. 18–44). Hershey, PA: IGI Global. doi:10.4018/978-1-5225-0846-5.ch002

Kasemsap, K. (2017e). Mastering business process management and business intelligence in global business. In M. Tavana, K. Szabat, & K. Puranam (Eds.), *Organizational productivity and performance measurements using predictive modeling and analytics* (pp. 192–212). Hershey, PA: IGI Global. doi:10.4018/978-1-5225-0654-6.ch010

Kaya, A. (2009). Residual and fully softened strength evaluation of soils using artificial neural networks. *Geotechnical and Geological Engineering*, 27(2), 281–288. doi:10.1007/s10706-008-9228-x

Kaya, C. C., Zhang, G., Tan, Y., & Mookerjee, V. S. (2009). An Admission-Control Technique for Delay Reduction in Proxy Caching. *Decision Support Systems*, 46(2), 594–603. doi:10.1016/j.dss.2008.10.004

Keen, P. (1980). Decision support systems: a research perspective. Cambridge, MA: Center for Information Systems Research, Alfred P. Sloan School of Management. Retrieved from http://hdl.handle.net/1721.1/47172

Kernighan, B. W., & Lin, S. (1970). An Efficient Heuristic Procedure for Partitioning Graph. *The Bell System Technical Journal*, 49(2), 291–307. doi:10.1002/j.1538-7305.1970.tb01770.x

Khalil, F., Li, A. J., & Wang, H. (2009). Integrated Model for Next Page Access Prediction. Int. *J. Knowledge and Web Intelligence*, 1(2), 48–80. doi:10.1504/IJKWI.2009.027925

Kildisas, V. (2001). Intelligent decision support system for environmental management. *Environmental Research, Engineering and Management*, 2(16), 69–75.

Kim, J. Y., Collins-Thompson, K., Bennett, P. N., & Dumais, S. T. (2012). Characterizing web content, user interests, and search behavior by reading level and topic. In *Proceedings of the fifth ACM international conference on Web search and data mining* (pp. 213-222). New York: ACM. doi:10.1145/2124295.2124323

Kim, S., & Hovy, E. (2004). *Determining the sentiment of opinions*. Paper presented at the International Conference on Computational Linguistics (COLING 2004), East Stroudsburg, PA.

Kim, H. (2009). Text mining methods for hierarchical document indexing. In J. Wang (Ed.), *Encyclopedia of data warehousing and mining* (2nd ed., pp. 1957–1965). Hershey, PA: IGI Global. doi:10.4018/978-1-60566-010-3.ch299

Kim, J. H., Shim, H. S., Kim, H. S., Jung, M. J., Choi, L. H., & Kim, J. O. (1997). A cooperative multi-agent system and its real time application to robot soccer. In *Proceedings of IEEE International Conference on Robotics and Automation*(vol. 1, pp. 638-643). Albuquerque, NM: IEEE. doi:10.1109/ROBOT.1997.620108

Klayman, J., & Schoemaker, P. (1993). Thinking about the future: A cognitive perspective. *Journal of Forecasting*, *12*(2), 161–186. doi:10.1002/for.3980120208

Kleinberg, J. M. (1999). Authoritative sources in a hyperlinked environment. *Journal of the ACM*, *46*(5), 604–632. doi:10.1145/324133.324140

Kleinberg, J., & Lawrence, S. (2001). The Structure of the Web. *Science*, *294*(5548), 1849–1850. doi:10.1126/science.1067014 PMID:11729296

Klepac, G., & Berg, K. L. (2015). Proposal of analytical model for business problems solving in Big Data environment. In J. Girard, D. Klein, & K. Berg (Eds.), *Strategic data-based wisdom in the Big Data era* (pp. 209–228). Hershey, PA: IGI Global. doi:10.4018/978-1-4666-8122-4.ch012

Kobbacy, K. A. H., & Vadera, S. (2011). A survey of AI in operations management from 2005 to 2009. *Journal of Manufacturing Technology Management*, *22*(6), 706–733. doi:10.1108/17410381111149602

Koenemann, J., & Belkin, N. J. (1996). A case for interaction: a study of interactive information retrieval behavior and effectiveness. In *Proceedings of the SIGCHI conference on human factors in computing systems* (pp. 205-212). New York: ACM. doi:10.1145/238386.238487

Konar, A. (2005). *Computational intelligence: Principles, techniques and applications*. Berlin, Germany: Springer–Verlag. doi:10.1007/b138935

Kosala & Blockeel. (2000). Web mining research: A survey. *Newsletter of the Special Interest Group (SIG) on Knowledge Discovery and Data Mining*. ACM.

Kosala, R., & Blockeel, H. (2000). Web mining research: A survey. *ACM Sigkdd Explorations Newsletter*, *2*(1), 1–15. doi:10.1145/360402.360406

Koskela, T.J., Heikkonen & Kaski, K. (2003). Web cache optimization with nonlinear model using object feature. *Computer Networks Journal*, *43*(6), 805-817.

Koskela, T.J., Heikkonen, & Kaski, K. (2003). Web cache optimization with nonlinear model using object feature. *Computer Networks Journal*, *43*(6), 805-817.

Kostoff, R. N., Boylan, R., & Simons, G. R. (2004). Disruptive technology roadmaps. *Technological Forecasting and Social Change*, *71*(1/2), 141–159. doi:10.1016/S0040-1625(03)00048-9

Kostoff, R. N., & Schaller, R. R. (2001). Science and technology roadmaps. *IEEE Transactions on Engineering Management*, *48*(2), 132–143. doi:10.1109/17.922473

Kotsiantis, S., & Kanellopoulos, D. (2006). Association Rules Mining: A Recent Overview. *International Transactions on Computer Science and Engineering*, *32*(1), 71–82.

Koutra, Ankur, Aditya, & Jing. (2011). *Algorithms for Graph Similarity and Subgraph Matching*. Retrieved from https://www.cs.cmu.edu/~jingx/docs/DBreport.pdf

Kriegel, H.-P., & Schonauer, S. (2003). Similarity Search in Structured Data. In *Proceedings of 5th International Conference on Data Warehousing and Knowledge Discovery* (pp. 224-233). doi:10.1007/978-3-540-45228-7_23

Kriegel, H. P., Kroger, P., & Zimek, A. (2009). Clustering high-dimensional data: A survey on subspace clustering, pattern-based clustering, and correlation clustering. *ACM Transactions on Knowledge Discovery from Data*, *3*(1), 1–58. doi:10.1145/1497577.1497578

Krishnamurthy, B., & Rexforrd, J. (2001). *Web Protocols and Practice: HTTP/1.1, Networking Protocols, Caching and Traffic Measurement*. Addison-Wesley.

Kroeger, T. M., Long, D. D. E., & Mogul, J. C. (1997). Exploring the Bounds of Web Latency Reduction from Caching and Pre-fetching. *Proceedings of the USENDC Symposium on Internet Technology and Systems*, (pp. 13-22).

Kubicka, E., Kubicki, G., & Vakalis, I. (1990). Using graph distance in object recognition. In *Proceedings of ACM Computer Science Conference* (pp. 43–48).

Kumar, K. (2013). Towards Web 3.0: An Application oriented approach. *IOSR Journal of Computer Engineering*, *15*(5), 50-53.

Kumar, K., & Rao, R. (2009a). Semantic Extension of Syntactic table data. *International Journal of Systems and Technologies*.

Kumar, K., & Rao, R. (2009b). TBL2RDF: Html Table To RDF Translator. *International Journal of Web Applications*.

Kumar, C., & Norris, J. B. (2008). A New Approach for a Proxy-level Web Caching Mechanism. *Decision Support Systems, Elsevier*, *46*(1), 52–60. doi:10.1016/j.dss.2008.05.001

Kune, R., Konugurthi, P. K., Agarwal, A., Rao Chillarige, R., & Buyya, R. (2011). *The Anatomy of Big Data Computing*. Cornell University. Retrieved from https://arxiv.org/pdf/1509.01331

Kuo, R. J., Chen, C. H., & Hwang, Y. C. (2001). An intelligent stock trading decision support system through integration of genetic algorithm based fuzzy neural network and artificial neural network. *Fuzzy Sets and Systems*, *118*(2), 21–45. doi:10.1016/S0165-0114(98)00399-6

Kuo, T. C., Wu, H. H., & Shieh, J. I. (2009). Integration of environmental considerations in quality function deployment by using fuzzy logic. *Expert Systems with Applications: An International Journal*, *36*(3), 7148–7156. doi:10.1016/j.eswa.2008.08.029

Kwon, O., Yoo, K., & Suh, E. (2005). UbiDSS: A proactive intelligent decision support system as an expert system deploying ubiquitous computing technologies. *Expert Systems with Applications*: An International Journal, *28*(1), 149–161. doi:10.1016/j.eswa.2004.08.007

Lai, K. K., & Shi, J. (2015). An intelligence system based on social web mining and its application in health care in Hong Kong. *AFIN 2015: The Seventh International Conference on Advances in Future Internet* (pp. 42-46). Venice, Italy: IARIA.

Lai, Y. C., & Ng, W. S. (2011). Nurturing information literacy of early childhood teachers through web-based collaborative learning activities. *Hong Kong Journal of Early Childhood*, *10*(1), 77–83.

Lan, B., Bressan, S., Ooi, B. C., & Tan, K. L. (2000). Rule-Assisted Pre-fetching in Web-Server Caching. In *Proceedings of the 9th International Conference on Information and Knowledge Management.*

Lancichinetti, A., & Fortunato, S. (2009). Community detection algorithms: A comparative analysis. *Phy. Rev. E, 80*(5), 056117. doi:10.1103/PhysRevE.80.056117 PMID:20365053

Langley, P. (1999). User modeling in adaptive interfaces.*Proceedings of the 7th International Conference on User Modeling. Springer New York, Inc.*

Larusson, J. A., & White, B. (2016). *Learning analytics: from research to practice.* New York: Springer.

Laudon, K., & Laudon, J. (2002). Management Information Systems Managing the Digital Firm (7th ed.). Pearson Prentice-Hall.

Laudon, K. C., & Laudon, J. P. (2004). *Management information system.* Upper Saddle River, NJ: Prentice Hall.

Laudon, K. C., & Laudon, J. P. (2006). *Management Information Systems. In Managing the Digital Farm* (pp. 428–508). Prentice Hall.

Lee, Yang, & Park. (2007). *Discovery of Hidden Similarity on Collaborative Filtering to Overcome Sparsity Problem.* Discovery Science.

Lee, C. K. M., Ho, W., Ho, G. T. S., & Lau, H. C. W. (2011). Design and development of logistics workflow systems for demand management with RFID. *Expert Systems with Applications: An International Journal, 38*(5), 5428–5437. doi:10.1016/j.eswa.2010.10.012

Lee, H. K., An, B. S., & Kim, E. J. (2009). Adaptive Pre-fetching Scheme Using Web Log Mining in Cluster-Based Web Systems.*IEEE International Conference on Web Services (ICWS)*, (pp. 903-910).

Lee, J. G., & Lee, E. S. (1997). VEMA: Multi-Agent System for Electronic Commerce on Interne, Design of Computing Systems: Cognitive Considerations. In *Proceedings of the Seventh International Conference on Human-Computer Interaction*(vol. 1, pp. 19-22).

Lee, J. K., & Lee, W. (1997). Intelligent agent based contract process in electronic commerce: UNIK-AGENT approach. In *Proceedings of the Thirtieth Hawaii International Conference on System Sciences*(vol. 4, pp. 230-241). Wailea, HI: IEEE. doi:10.1109/HICSS.1997.663394

Lee, J.-H., & Shiu, W.-K. (2004). An adaptive website system to improve efficiency with web mining techniques. *Advanced Engineering Informatics, 18*(3), 129–142. doi:10.1016/j.aei.2004.09.007

Lee, S., Yoon, B., & Park, Y. (2009). An approach to discovering new technology opportunities: Keyword-based patent map approach. *Technovation, 29*(6), 481–497. doi:10.1016/j.technovation.2008.10.006

Lees, J. G., Heriche, J. K., Morilla, I., Ranea, J. A., & Orengo, C. A. (2011). Systematic computational prediction of protein interaction networks. *Physical Biology, 8*(3), 035008. doi:10.1088/1478-3975/8/3/035008 PMID:21572181

Leeuwen, A., Janssen, J., Erkens, G., & Brekelmans, M. (2015). Teacher regulation of cognitive activities during student collaboration: Effects of learning analytics. *Computers & Education, 90*, 80–94. doi:10.1016/j.compedu.2015.09.006

Lera-Lopez, F., Faulin, J., Juan, A. A., & Cavaller, V. (2010). Monitoring students' activity and performance in online higher education: A European perspective. In A. A. Juan, T. Daradoumis, F. Xhafa, S. Caballe, & J. Faulin (Eds.), *Monitoring and assessment in online collaborative environments: Emergent computational technologies for e-learning support* (pp. 131–148). New York: Information Science Reference. doi:10.4018/978-1-60566-786-7.ch008

Leung, K. W. T., Lee, D. L., & Lee, W. C. (2010). Personalized web search with location preferences. In *26thInternational Conference on Data Engineering*(pp. 701-712). IEEE.

Levenshtein, V. (1966). Binary codes capable of correcting deletions, insertions and reversals. *Soviet Physics, Doklady*, (10), 707–710.

Leydesdorff, L. (1989). Words and co-words as indicators of intellectual organization. *Research Policy, 18*(4), 209–223. doi:10.1016/0048-7333(89)90016-4

Lieberman, H. (1995). Letizia: An agent that assists web browsing. *IJCAI, 1995*(1), 924–929.

Lieberman, H. (1995). Letizia: An agent that assists Web browsing.*Proceedings of the International Joint Conference on Artificial Intelligence*. Morgan Kaufmann.

Lieberman, H., Dyke, N. V., & Vivacqua, A. S. (1999). Let's Browse: A collaborative Web browsing agent. *Proceedings of the 1999 International Conference on Intelligent User Interfaces*. ACM Press. doi:10.1145/291080.291092

Liew, W. T., Adhitya, A., & Srinivasan, R. (2014). Sustainability trends in the process industries: A text mining-based analysis. *Computers in Industry, 65*(3), 393–400. doi:10.1016/j.compind.2014.01.004

Li, L., Yang, Z., & Kitsuregawa, M. (2009). Rank optimization of personalized search. *Information and Media Technologies, 4*(3), 666–671.

Li, N., & Wu, D. (2010). Using text mining and sentiment analysis for online forums hotspot detection and forecast. *Decision Support Systems, 48*(2), 354–368. doi:10.1016/j.dss.2009.09.003

Lipschutz, S. (n.d.). *Schaum's outline of Data Structures*. New Delhi: Tata McGraw-Hill Publishing Company Limited.

Littleton, K., & Hakkinen, P. (1999). Learning together: Understanding the processes of computer-based collaborative learning. In P. Dillenbourg (Ed.), *Collaborative learning: cognitive and computational approaches* (pp. 20–30). Oxford: Elsevier.

Liu, Q. (2009). *Web Latency Reduction with Pre-fetching* (Ph.D Thesis). University of Western Ontario, London, Canada.

Liu, B. (2007). *Web data mining: exploring hyperlinks, contents, and usage data*. Springer Science & Business Media.

Liu, C., & Itoh, Y. (2001). Information technology applications for bridge maintenance management. *Logistics Information Management, 14*(5/6), 393–400. doi:10.1108/EUM0000000006251

Liu, F., Yu, C., & Meng, W. (2004). Personalized web search for improving retrieval effectiveness. *IEEE Transactions on Knowledge and Data Engineering, 16*(1), 28–40. doi:10.1109/TKDE.2004.1264820

Li, Y. R., Wang, L. H., & Hong, C. F. (2009). Extracting the significant-rare keywords for patent analysis. *Expert Systems with Applications: An International Journal, 36*(3), 5200–5204. doi:10.1016/j.eswa.2008.06.131

Loh, S., Wives, L. K., Lichtnow, D., & de Oliveira, J. P. (2009). Concept-based text mining. In M. Song & Y. Brook Wu (Eds.), *Handbook of research on text and web mining technologies* (pp. 346–358). Hershey, PA: IGI Global. doi:10.4018/978-1-59904-990-8.ch021

Loon, T. S., & Bharghavan, V. (1997). Alleviating the Latency and Bandwidth Problems in WWW Browsing. In *Proceedings of the USENIX Symposium on Internet Technologies and Systems (USITS)*.

Lopez-Ortega, O., & Villar-Medina, I. (2009). A multi-agent system to construct production orders by employing an expert system and a neural network. *Expert Systems with Applications: An International Journal, 36*(2), 2937–2946. doi:10.1016/j.eswa.2008.01.070

Lourenco, A., & Belo, O. (2006). Catching web crawlers in the act. *Proceedings of the 6th International Conference on Web Engineering*. ACM.

Lu, F. Q., Huang, M., & Wang, X. W. (2010). *Partners' risk level considered CDDM model for risk management of virtual enterprise*. Paper presented at the 4th International Conference on Management and Service Science (MASS 2010), Wuhan, China. doi:10.1109/ICMSS.2010.5577219

Lu, F. Q., Huang, M., Ching, W. K., Wang, X. W., & Sun, X. L. (2009). *Multi-swarm particle swarm optimization based risk management model for virtual enterprise*. Paper presented at the 1st ACM/SIGEVO Summit on Genetic and Evolutionary Computation (GEC 2009), Shanghai, China. doi:10.1145/1543834.1543886

Lukach, R., & Plasmans, J. (2005). International knowledge flows from and into a small open economy: Patent citation analysis. In A. Spithoven & P. Teirlinck (Eds.), *Beyond borders: Internationalisation of R&D and policy implications for small open economies* (pp. 331–357). Amsterdam, The Netherlands: Elsevier.

Lv, Y., Sun, L., Zhang, J., Nie, J. Y., Chen, W., & Zhang, W. (2006). An iterative implicit feedback approach to personalized search. In *Proceedings of the 21st International Conference on Computational Linguistics and the 44th annual meeting of the Association for Computational Linguistics* (pp. 585-592). Association for Computational Linguistics. doi:10.3115/1220175.1220249

MacPhail, A., & Halbert, J. (2010). We had to do intelligent thinking during recent PE: Students and teachers experiences of assessment for learning in post-primary physical education. *Assessment in Education: Principles, Policy & Practice, 17*(1), 23–39. doi:10.1080/09695940903565412

Madana Kumar Reddy, C. (2009). Operating Systems Made easy. New Delhi: University Science Press.

Madana Kumar Reddy, C. (2016). Reliability and Scalability of Service Oriented Architecture in web services: Signature verification. IGI Global.

Madani, O., & DeCoste, D. (2005). Contextual recommender problems [extended abstract]. In *Proceedings of the 1st international workshop on Utility-based data mining* (pp. 86-89). New York: ACM. doi:10.1145/1089827.1089838

Maedche, A. (2002). *Ontology Learning for the Semantic Web*. New York: Springer Science and Business Media. doi:10.1007/978-1-4615-0925-7

Malhotra, P., Burstein, F., Fisher, J., McKemmish, S., Anderson, J., & Manaszewicz, R. (2003). *Brest cancer knowledge on-line portal: An intelligent decision support system perspective*. Paper presented at the 14th Australasian Conference on Information Systems (ACIS 2003), Perth, Australia.

Mandl, T. (2015). Text mining. In M. Khosrow-Pour (Ed.), *Encyclopedia of information science and technology* (3rd ed., pp. 1923–1930). Hershey, PA: IGI Global. doi:10.4018/978-1-4666-5888-2.ch185

Marakas, G. M. (2003). *Decision support systems in the 21st century*. Upper Saddle River, NJ: Prentice Hall.

Markatos, E. P., & Chronaki, C. E. (1998). A Top-10 Approach to Pre-fetching on the Web. In *Proceedings of INET Geneva*.

Markovsky, I. (2012). *Low-Rank Approximation: Algorithms, Implementation, Applications*. Springer. doi:10.1007/978-1-4471-2227-2

Markov, Z., & Larose, D. T. (2007). *Data mining the Web: uncovering patterns in Web content, structure, and usage*. John Wiley & Sons. doi:10.1002/0470108096

Marquardt, C., Becker, K., & Ruiz, D. (2004). A Pre-processing Tool for Web Usage Mining in the Distance Education Domain. In *Proceedings of the International Database Engineering and Application Symposium (IDEAS)*, (pp. 78-87).

Martinez, O., & Botella, F. (n.d.). *Building E-Commerce Web Applications: Agent and Ontology-based Interface Adaptivity.* Operations Research Center, University Miguel Hernández of Elche, Avda. Universidad.

Masand, Spiliopoulou, Srivastava, & Zaiane. (Eds.). (2002). *Proceedings of WebKDD2002 –Web Mining for Usage Patterns and User Profiles.* Retrieved from http://db.cs.ualberta.ca/webkdd02/

Masseglia, F., Poncelet, P., & Teisseire, M. (2003). Using data mining techniques on Web access logs to dynamically improve hypertext structure. *SIGWEB Newsletter, 8*(3), 13–19. doi:10.1145/951440.951443

MasterCard - Wikipedia, the free encyclopedia. (2016). Retrieved March, 2016 https://en.wikipedia.org/wiki/MasterCard

Matsatsinis, N. F., & Siskos, Y. (1999). MARKEX: An intelligent decision support system for product development decisions. *European Journal of Operational Research, 113*(2), 336–354. doi:10.1016/S0377-2217(98)00220-3

Matthijs, N., & Radlinski, F. (2011). Personalizing web search using long term browsing history. In *Proceedings of the fourth ACM international conference on Web search and data mining* (pp. 25-34). New York: ACM. doi:10.1145/1935826.1935840

Mazzoni, E., & Gaffuri, P. (2010). Monitoring activitiy in e-learning: A quantitative model based on web tracking. In A. A. Juan, T. Daradoumis, F. Xhafa, S. Caballe, & J. Faulin (Eds.), *Monitoring and assessment in online collaborative environments: Emergent computational technologies for e-learning support* (pp. 111–130). New York: Information Science Reference. doi:10.4018/978-1-60566-786-7.ch007

McGovern, G. (2003). *Why personalization hasn't worked.* Accessed on 03/2007 from http://www.gerrymcgovern.com/nt/2003/nt 2003 10 20 personalization.htm

McLeod, R., & Schell, G. (2006). *Management Information Systems* (10th ed.). Prentice Hall.

McLoughlin, C., & Marshall, L. (2000). Scaffolding: A model for learner support in an online teaching enviornment. In A. Herrmann & M. M. Kulski (Eds.), *Flexible futures in tertiary teaching.Proceedings of the 9th Annual Teaching Learning Forum.* Perth: Curtin University of Technology.

Mehrdad, J. (2008). Web User Navigation Pattern Mining Approach Based on Graph Partitioning Algorithm. *Journal of Theoretical and Applied Information Technology.*

Meirong, T., & Xuedong, C. (2010). Application of Agent-based Web Mining in E-business. *Second International Conference on Intelligent Human-Machine Systems and Cybernetic.* Retrieved from http://www.websiteoptimization.com

Melnik, S., Garcia-Molina, H., & Rahm, E. (2002). Similarity flooding: A versatile graph matching algorithm and its application to schema matching. In *Proceedings of 18th International Conference on Data Engineering* (ICDE 2002).

Melville & Sindhwani. (2010). Recommender Systems. In Encyclopedia of Machine Learning. Academic Press.

Menczer, F. (2003). Complementing search engines with online web mining agents. *Decision Support Systems, 35*(2), 195–212. doi:10.1016/S0167-9236(02)00106-9

Mitchell, T., Joachims, T., & Freitag, D. (1997). Web watcher: A tour guide for the world wide web.*Proceeding of the 15th International Joint Conference on Artificial Intelligence.* Morgan Kaufmann.

Mitra, A., Satpathy, S. R., & Paul, S. (2013). Clustering analysis in social network using Covering Based Rough Set. In *Proceedings of Advance Computing Conference* (pp. 476-481). doi:10.1109/IAdCC.2013.6514272

Mittal, A., & Sethi, S. (2015).A Review on Personalization Techniques, *Proceedings of National Conference on Innovative Trends in Computer Science Engineering (pp.*123-125).

Moawad, I. F., Talha, H., Hosny, E., & Hashim, M. (2012). Agent-based web search personalization approach using dynamic user profile. *Egyptian Informatics Journal, 13*(3), 191–198. doi:10.1016/j.eij.2012.09.002

Mobasher, B., Cooley, R., & Srivastava, J. (1999). Creating adaptive web sites through usage-based clustering of URLs. *Proceedings of the 1999 Workshop on Knowledge and Data Engineering Exchange*. IEEE Computer Society.

Mobasher, B., Cooley, R., & Srivastava, J. (2000). Automatic personalization based on web usage mining. *Communications of the ACM, 43*(8), 142–151. doi:10.1145/345124.345169

Mobasher, B., Dai, H., Luo, T., & Nakagawa, M. (2002). Discovery and Evaluation of Aggregate Usage Profiles for Web Personalization. *Data Mining and Knowledge Discovery, 6*(1), 61–82. doi:10.1023/A:1013232803866

Mohammad, S. (2012). From once upon a time to happily ever after: Tracking emotions in mail and books. *Decision Support Systems, 53*(4), 730–741. doi:10.1016/j.dss.2012.05.030

Mokbel, M., Bao, J., Eldawy, A., Levandoski, J., & Sarwat, M. (2011). Personalization, socialization, and recommendations in location-based services 2.0. In *5th International VLDB workshop on Personalized access, Profile Management and context awareness in Databases (PersDB)*.

Montazemi, A. R., & Gupta, K. M. (1997). On the effectiveness of cognitive feedback from an interface agent. *Omega, 25*(6), 643–658. doi:10.1016/S0305-0483(97)00028-5

Monteiro, T., Daniel, R. B., & Anciaux, D. (2007). Multi-site coordination using a multi-agent system. *Computers in Industry, 58*(4), 367–377. doi:10.1016/j.compind.2006.07.005

Mooney, R. J., & Roy, L. (1999). Content-based book recommendation using learning for text categorization. In *Workshop Recom. Sys. Algo. and Evaluation.*

Moro, S., Cortez, P., & Rita, P. (2015). Business intelligence in banking: A literature analysis from 2002 to 2013 using text mining and latent Dirichlet allocation. *Expert Systems with Applications: An International Journal, 42*(3), 1314–1324. doi:10.1016/j.eswa.2014.09.024

Morris, M. R., Teevan, J., & Bush, S. (2008). Enhancing collaborative web search with personalization: groupization, smart splitting, and group hit-highlighting. In *Proceedings of the conference on Computer supported cooperative work*, (pp. 481-484). ACM. doi:10.1145/1460563.1460640

Mostafa, M. M. (2013). More than words: Social networks' text mining for consumer brand sentiments. *Expert Systems with Applications: An International Journal, 40*(10), 4241–4251. doi:10.1016/j.eswa.2013.01.019

Motiwalla, L., & Fairfield-Sonn, J. (1998). Measuring the impact of expert systems. *Journal of Business and Economic Studies, 4*, 10–17.

Müller, J.-P., & Pischel, M. (1994). Modelling Reactive Behaviour in Vertically Layered Agent Architectures. In *Proceedings of the Eleventh European Conference on A* (pp. 709-713).

Murat Ali Bayir. (n.d.). *A New Reactive Method for Processing Web Usage Data*. Retrieved from http://etd.lib.metu.edu.tr/upload/12607323/index.pdf

Murphy, J., Fu, K., Otto, K., Yang, M., Jensen, D., & Wood, K. (2014). Function based design-by-analogy: A functional vector approach to analogical search. *Journal of Mechanical Design, 136*(10), 101102. doi:10.1115/1.4028093

Nanopoulos, A., Katsaros, D., & Manolopoulos, Y. (2003). A Data Mining Algorithm for Generalized Web Pre-fetching. *IEEE Transactions on Knowledge and Data Engineering, 15*(5), 1155–1169. doi:10.1109/TKDE.2003.1232270

Nassirtoussi, A. K., Aghabozorgi, S., Wah, T. Y., & Ngo, D. C. L. (2014). Text mining for market prediction: A systematic review. *Expert Systems with Applications: An International Journal, 41*(16), 7653–7670. doi:10.1016/j.eswa.2014.06.009

Nassirtoussi, A. K., Aghabozorgi, S., Wah, T. Y., & Ngo, D. C. L. (2015). Text mining of news-headlines for FOREX market prediction: A multi-layer dimension reduction algorithm with semantics and sentiment. *Expert Systems with Applications: An International Journal, 42*(1), 306–324. doi:10.1016/j.eswa.2014.08.004

Nauman, M., & Khan, S. (2007). Using personalized web search for enhancing common sense and folksonomy based intelligent search systems.*International Conference on Web Intelligence*(pp. 423-426). Fremont, CA: IEEE. doi:10.1109/WI.2007.44

Navin, K., Tyagi, & Solanki, A.K. (2011). Analysis of Server Log by Web Usage Mining for Website Improvement. *International Journal of Computer Science Issues, 7*(4).

Navlakha, S., Rastogi, R., & Shrivastava, N. (2008). Graph summarization with bounded error. In *Proceedings of the 2008 ACM SIGMOD international conference on Management of data* (pp. 419-432). ACM. doi:10.1145/1376616.1376661

Nestorov, S., Abiteboul, S., & Motwani, R. (1998). Extracting Schema from Semistructured Data. In ACM SIGMOD. doi:10.1145/276305.276331

Netcraft. (2008). *Web server survey*. Accessed on 05/2008 from http://news.netcraft.com/archives/web server survey.html

Newman, M. E. J., & Girvan, M. (2004). Finding and evaluating community structure in networks. *Physical Review E: Statistical, Nonlinear, and Soft Matter Physics, 69*(2), 026113. doi:10.1103/PhysRevE.69.026113 PMID:14995526

Nielsen, J. (2006). *Quantitative studies: how many users to test?*. Retrieved from http://www.useit.com

Nielsen, J. (1993). *Usability engineering*. London: Academic Press.

Niu, D., & Gu, X. (2007). *Application of HGPSOA in electric power system material purchase and storage optimization*. Paper presented at the 16th International Conference on Service Systems and Service Management (ICSSSM 2007), Chengdu, China. doi:10.1109/ICSSSM.2007.4280283

Noda, I., Matsubara, H., Hiraki, K., & Frank, I. (1998). Soccer server: A tool for research on multiagent systems. *Applied Artificial Intelligence, 12*(2-3), 233–250. doi:10.1080/088395198117848

No, H. J., An, Y., & Park, Y. (2015). A structured approach to explore knowledge flows through technology-based business methods by integrating patent citation analysis and text mining. *Technological Forecasting and Social Change, 97*, 181–192. doi:10.1016/j.techfore.2014.04.007

Noh, H., Jo, Y., & Lee, S. (2015). Keyword selection and processing strategy for applying text mining to patent analysis. *Expert Systems with Applications: An International Journal, 42*(9), 4348–4360. doi:10.1016/j.eswa.2015.01.050

Nwankwo, S., Obidigbo, B., & Ekwulugo, F. (2002). Allying for quality excellence: Scope for expert systems in supplier quality management. *International Journal of Quality & Reliability Management, 19*(2), 187–205. doi:10.1108/02656710210413516

O'Donnell, A. M., & Hmelo-Silver, C. E. (2013). Introduction: What is collaborative learning? An overview. In *The international handbook of collaborative learning* (pp. 1–15). New York: Routledge.

Olston, C., & Chi, E. H. (2003). ScentTrails: Integrating browsing and searching on the Web. *ACM Transactions on Computer-Human Interaction, 10*(3), 177–197. doi:10.1145/937549.937550

One Graph To Rule Them All? (n.d.). AVC. Retrieved April 11, 2016 from http://avc.com/2010/04/one-graph-to-rule-them-all/

Open Graph Stories – Sharing. (n.d.). Retrieved May, 2016 from https://developers.facebook.com/docs/sharing/opengraph

Oriezy, P., Gorlick, M. M., Taylor, R. N., Heimbigner, D., Johnson, G., Medvidovic, N., & Wolf, A. L. et al. (1999). An Architecture-Based Approach to Self-Adaptive Software. *IEEE Intelligent Systems*, *14*(3).

Overland, H. M. (2010). *What is Facebook Open Graph? Search Engine People.* Retrieved May, 2016 from http://www.searchenginepeople.com/blog/what-is-facebook-open-graph.html

Ozmutlu, S., & Cavdur, F. (2005). Neural network applications for automatic new topic identification. *Online Information Review*, *29*(1), 34–53. doi:10.1108/14684520510583936

Padmanabhan, V. N., & Mogul, J. C. (1996). Using Predictive Pre-fetching to Improve World Wide Web Latency. *ACM Computer Communication Review*, *26*(3), 23–36. doi:10.1145/235160.235164

Page, L., Brin, S., Motwani, R., & Winograd, T. (1998). *The PageRank citation ranking: Bringing order to the web.* Technical report. Stanford Digital Library Technologies Project. Accessed from citeseer.ist.psu.edu/page98pagerank.html

Page, L., Brin, S., Motwani, R., & Winograd, T. (1998). *The Page Rank Citation Ranking: Bring Order to the Web.* Technical Report. Stanford University.

Page, L., Brin, S., Motwani, R., & Winograd, T. (1999). *The PageRank citation ranking: bringing order to the web.* Technical Report. Stanford InfoLab.

Palleti, P., Karnick, H., & Mitra, P. (2007). Personalized web search using probabilistic query expansion. In *Proceedings of the 2007 IEEE/WIC/ACM International Conferences on Web Intelligence and Intelligent Agent Technology- Workshops* (pp. 83-86). Washington, DC: IEEE Computer Society.

Pallis, G., Vakali, A., & Pokorny, J. (2008). A Clustering-Based Pre-Fetching Scheme on A Web Cache Environment. ACM Journal Computers and Electrical Engineering, 34(4).

Palma-dos-Reis, A., & Zahedi, F. M. (1999). Designing personalized intelligent financial support systems. *Decision Support Systems*, *26*(1), 31–47. doi:10.1016/S0167-9236(99)00027-5

Palpanas, T., & Mendelzon, A. (1999). Web Pre-fetching using Partial Match Prediction. In *Proceedings of the 4th International Web Caching Workshop*.

Pal, S. K., & Mitra, S. (1992). Multilayer perception, fuzzy sets, and classification. *IEEE Transactions on Neural Networks*, *3*(5), 683–697. doi:10.1109/72.159058 PMID:18276468

Pandey, S. C., & Dutta, A. (2013). Role of knowledge infrastructure capabilities in knowledge management. *Journal of Knowledge Management*, *17*(3), 435–453. doi:10.1108/JKM-11-2012-0365

Pandia, Pani, & Padhi, Panigrahy, & Ramakrishna. (2011). A Review of Trends in Research on Web Mining. *International Journal of Instrumentation Control and Automation*, *1*(1), 37–41.

Pannu, M., Anane, R., & James, A. (2013). Hybrid profiling in information retrieval. *17th International Conference on Computer Supported Cooperative Work in Design* (pp. 84-91). Whistler, BC: IEEE.

Pantaleon, M. E., & Saiz, E. E. (2010). Proposal of a set of reports for students' tracking and assessing in e-learning platforms. In A. A. Juan, T. Daradoumis, F. Xhafa, S. Caballe, & J. Faulin (Eds.), *Monitoring and assessment in online collaborative environments: Emergent computational technologies for e-learning support* (pp. 235–261). New York: Information Science Reference. doi:10.4018/978-1-60566-786-7.ch013

Pan, X., Wang, Z., & Gu, X. (2007). Context-based adaptive personalized web search for improving information retrieval effectiveness. *International Conference on Wireless Communications, Networking and Mobile Computing* (pp. 5427-5430). Shanghai: IEEE. doi:10.1109/WICOM.2007.1329

Paola, B.c(2007). Web Usage Mining Using Self Organized Maps. *International Journal of Computer Science and Network Security, 7*(6).

Papanikolaou, N., Pavlopoulos, G. A., Theodosiou, T., & Iliopoulos, I. (2015). Protein–protein interaction predictions using text mining methods. *Methods (San Diego, Calif.), 74*, 47–53. doi:10.1016/j.ymeth.2014.10.026 PMID:25448298

Park, H. I., & Kim, Y. T. (2011). Prediction of strength of reinforced lightweight soil using an artificial neural network. *Engineering Computations: International Journal for Computer-Aided Engineering and Software, 28*(5), 600–615. doi:10.1108/02644401111141037

Patel, R., & Sharma, G. (2014). A survey on text mining techniques. *International Journal of Engineering and Computer Science, 3*(5), 5621–5625.

Pavlov, D., Manvoglu, E., Giles, L., & Pennock, D. (2004). Collaborative filtering with maximum entropy. *IEEE Intelligent Systems, 19*(6), 40–48. doi:10.1109/MIS.2004.59

Pazos, F., Helmer-Citterich, M., Ausiello, G., & Valencia, A. (1997). Correlated mutations contain information about protein-protein interaction. *Journal of Molecular Biology, 271*(4), 511–523. doi:10.1006/jmbi.1997.1198 PMID:9281423

Pearson, E. (2009). All the World Wide Webs a Stage: The Performance of Identity in Online Social Networks. *First Monday, 14*(3), 1–7. doi:10.5210/fm.v14i3.2162

Pei, C., & Irani, S. (1997). Cost-Aware WWW Proxy Caching Algorithms. In *Proceedings of the USENIX Symposium on Internet Technologies and Systems*, (pp. 193-206).

Peng, W. C., & Lin, Y. C. (2006). Ranking web search results from personalized perspective. *The 8th IEEE International Conference on E-Commerce Technology and The 3rd IEEE International Conference on Enterprise Computing, E-Commerce, and E- Services* (pp. 12-12). San Francisco, CA: IEEE.

Peng, X., Niu, Z., Huang, S., & Zhao, Y. (2012). Personalized web search using clickthrough data and web page rating. *Journal of Computers, 7*(10), 2578–2584. doi:10.4304/jcp.7.10.2578-2584

Penteado, R., & Boutin, E. (2008). Creating strategic information for organizations with structured text. In H. do Prado & E. Ferneda (Eds.), *Emerging technologies of text mining: Techniques and applications* (pp. 34–53). Hershey, PA: IGI Global. doi:10.4018/978-1-59904-373-9.ch002

Perkowitz, M., & Etzioni, O. (1997). *Adaptive sites: Automatically learning from user access patterns. Technical report.* Department of Computer Science and Engineering, University of Washington.

Perkowitz, M., & Etzioni, O. (1998). Adaptive Web Sites: Automatically Synthesizing Web Pages. *IAAI '98: Proceedings of the Fifteenth National/Tenth International Conference on Artificial Intelligence/Innovative Applications of Artificial Intelligence*, (pp. 727-732).

Perovšek, M., Kranjc, J., Erjavec, T., Cestnik, B., & Lavrac, N. (2016). TextFlows: A visual programming platform for text mining and natural language processing. *Science of Computer Programming, 121*, 128–152. doi:10.1016/j.scico.2016.01.001

Persico, D., Pozzi, F., & Sarti, L. (2010). A model for monitoring and evaluating CSCL. In A. A. Juan, T. Daradoumis, F. Xhafa, S. Caalle, & J. Faulin (Eds.), *Monitoring and assessment in online collaborative environments: Emergent computational technologies for e-learning support* (pp. 149–170). Hershey, PA: Information Science Reference. doi:10.4018/978-1-60566-786-7.ch009

Pessoa, Laber, & Souza. (2004). Efficient algorithms for the hotlink assignment problem: The worst case search. *Proceedings of the International Symposium on Algorithms and Computation.*

Piedra, D., Ferrer, A., & Gea, J. (2014). Text mining and medicine: Usefulness in respiratory diseases. *Archivos de Bronconeumologia, 50*(3), 113–119. PMID:24507559

Pierrakos, D., Paliouras, G., Papatheodorou, C., & Spyropoulos, C. D. (2003). Web usage mining as a tool for personalization: A survey. *User Modeling and User-Adapted Interaction, 13*(4), 311–372. doi:10.1023/A:1026238916441

Pirolli, P. (2006). The use of proximal information scent to forage for distal content on the World Wide Web. Adaptive Perspectives on Human-Technology Interaction: Methods and Modfiles for Cognitive Engineering and Human-Computer Interaction (pp. 247-266).

Pirolli, P., & Fu, W. T. (2003). SNIF-ACT: A model of information foraging on the World Wide Web. In User modeling. Springer Berlin Heidelberg.

Pirolli, P., Pitkow, J., & Ramna, R. (1996). Extracting Usable Structure from the Web. In CHI – 96.

Pirolli, P. (1997). Computational models of information scent-following in a very large browsable text collection. In *Proceedings of the ACM SIGCHI Conference on Human factors in computing systems*(pp. 3-10). New York: ACM. doi:10.1145/258549.258558

Pirolli, P., & Card, S. K. (1999). Information foraging. *Psychological Review, 106*(4), 643–675. doi:10.1037/0033-295X.106.4.643

Pirolli, P., Card, S. K., & Van Der Wege, M. M. (2003). The effects of information scent on visual search in the hyperbolic tree browser. *ACM Transactions on Computer-Human Interaction, 10*(1), 20–53. doi:10.1145/606658.606660

Pirolli, P., Pitkow, J., & Rao, R. (1996). Silk from a sow's ear: Extracting usable structures from the Web.*Proceedings of the 1996 Conference on Human Factors in Computing Systems (CHI-96).* doi:10.1145/238386.238450

Pitkow, J. (1997). *In search of reliable usage data on the WWW. In Computer Networks and ISDN Systems* (Vol. 29, pp. 1343–1355). Santa Clara, CA: Elsevier Science.

Pitkow, J., & Pirolli, P. (1999). Mining Longest Repeating Subsequences to Predict World Wide Web Surfing.*Proceedings USENIX Symposium on Internet Technologies and Systems* (USITS).

Pletscher-Frankild, S., Palleja, A., Tsafou, K., Binder, J. X., & Jensen, L. J. (2015). DISEASES: Text mining and data integration of disease–gene associations. *Methods (San Diego, Calif.), 74*, 83–89. doi:10.1016/j.ymeth.2014.11.020 PMID:25484339

Podlipnig, S., & Boszormenyi, L. (2003). A Survey of Web Cache Replacement Strategies. *ACM Computing Surveys, 35*(4), 374–398. doi:10.1145/954339.954341

Pol, K., Patil, N., Patankar, S., & Das, C. (2008). A Survey on Web Content Mining and extraction of Structured and Semistructured data.*First International Conference on Emerging Trends in Engineering and Technology*(pp. 543-546). Nagpur, Maharashtra: IEEE. doi:10.1109/ICETET.2008.251

Pons, P., & Latapy, M. (2006). Computing communities in large networks using random walks. *Journal of Graph Algorithms Applications*, *10*(2), 191–218. doi:10.7155/jgaa.00124

Porter, A. L., Kongthon, A., & Lu, J. C. (2002). Research profiling: Improving the literature review. *Scientometrics*, *53*(3), 351–370. doi:10.1023/A:1014873029258

Pota, M., Exposito, M., & de Pietro, G. (2014). Fuzzy partitioning for clinical DSSs using statistical information transformed into possibility-based knowledge. *Knowledge-Based Systems*, *67*, 1–15. doi:10.1016/j.knosys.2014.06.021

Pothen, A. (1997). Graph Partitioning Algorithms with Applications to Scientific Computing. Technical Report.

Power, D. J., & Sharda, R. (2007). Model-driven decision support systems: Concepts and research directions. *Decision Support Systems*, *43*(3), 1044–1061. doi:10.1016/j.dss.2005.05.030

Pretorius, M. (2008). When Porters generic strategies are not enough: Complementary strategies for turnaround situations. *The Journal of Business Strategy*, *29*(6), 19–28. doi:10.1108/02756660810917200

Proceedings of WWW'14 23rd International World Wide Web Conference. (2014). Seoul, South Korea: ACM.

Pujari, R. K. (n.d.). Data mining Techniques. *Universities Press*.

Purandare, P. (2002). Web Mining: A Key to Improve Business On Web.*IADIS European Conference Data Mining*.

Qian, Z., Huang, G. H., & Chan, C. W. (2004). Development of an intelligent decision support system for air pollution control at coal-fired power plants. *Expert Systems with Applications*: An International Journal, *26*(3), 335–356. doi:10.1016/j.eswa.2003.09.005

Qiu, G., He, X., Zhang, F., Shi, Y., Bu, J., & Chen, C. (2010). DASA: Dissatisfaction-oriented advertising based on sentiment analysis. *Expert Systems with Applications: An International Journal*, *37*(9), 6182–6191. doi:10.1016/j.eswa.2010.02.109

Qiu, R. G., Tang, Y., & Xu, Q. (2006). Integration design of material flow management in an e-business manufacturing environment. *Decision Support Systems*, *42*(2), 1104–1115. doi:10.1016/j.dss.2005.10.005

Quintero, A., Konare, D., & Pierre, S. (2005). Prototyping an intelligent decision support system for improving urban infrastructures management. *European Journal of Operational Research*, *162*(3), 654–672. doi:10.1016/j.ejor.2003.10.019

Raghavan, V. V., & Sever, H. (1995). On the reuse of past optimal queries. In *Proceedings of the 18th annual international ACM SIGIR conference on Research and development in information retrieval*(pp. 344-350). New York: ACM. doi:10.1145/215206.215381

Rajaraman, A., Leskovec, J., & Ullman, J. D. (2011). Mining of Massive Datasets. Cambridge University Press.

Ramsey, G., & Bapna, S. (2016). Text mining to identify customers likely to respond to cross-selling campaigns: Reading notes from your customers. *International Journal of Business Analytics*, *3*(2), 33–49. doi:10.4018/IJBAN.2016040102

Rangarajan, S.K., Phoha, V.V., Balagani, K., Selmic, R.R., & Iyengar S.S. (2004). Web User Clustering and its Application to Pre-fetching using ART Neural Networks. *IEEE Computer*, 45-62.

Rangarajan, S. K., Phoha, V. V., Balagani, K., Selmic, R. R., & Iyengar, S. S. (2004). *Web User Clustering and its Application to Pre-fetching using ART Neural Networks*. IEEE Computer.

Rangarajan, S., Phoha, V., Balagani, K., Selmic, R., & Iyengar, S. (2004). Adaptive neural network clustering of Web users. *Computer*, *37*(4), 34–40. doi:10.1109/MC.2004.1297299

Rao & ValliKumari. (2010). An Enhanced Pre-Processing Research Framework For Web Log Data Using A Learning Algorithm. *NeTCoM 2010, CSCP 01*. Retrieved September 10, 2016 from https://en.wikipedia.org/wiki/

Rao, B., & Mitra, A. (2014). A new approach for detection of common communities in a social network using graph mining techniques. In *Proceedings of2014IEEE International Conference on High Performance Computing and Applications* (pp.1-6). doi:10.1109/ICHPCA.2014.7045335

Rao, B., & Mitra, A. (2014). An Approach to Merging of two Community Sub-Graphs to form a Community Graph using Graph Mining Techniques. In *Proceedings of 2014 IEEE International Conference on Computational Intelligence and Computing Research* (pp. 460-466). Doi:10.1109/ICCIC.2014.7238392

Rao, B., Mitra, A., & Acharjya, D. P. (2015). A New Approach of Compression of Large Community Graph Using Graph Mining Techniques. In *Proceedings of 3rd ERCICA* (*vol. 1*, pp. 127 – 136). NMIT. Doi:10.1007/978-81-322-2550-8_13

Rao, B., Mitra, A., & Mondal, J. (2015). Algorithm for Retrieval of Sub-Community Graph from a Compressed Community Graph using Graph Mining Techniques. In *Proceedings of 3rd International Conference on Recent Trends in Computing 2015*. SRM University.

Rao, B., Mitra, A., & Narayana, U. (2014). An Approach to Study Properties and Behaviour of Social Network Using Graph Mining Techniques. In *Proceedings of DIGNATE 2014: ETEECT 2014* (pp. 13–17).

Rao, B. (2015). An Algorithm for Partitioning Community Graph into Sub-Community Graphs using Graph Mining Techniques. In *Proceedings of 3rd Springer Smart Innovation, Systems and Technologies, ICACNI* (pp. 23–25). Bhubaneswar, India: KIIT University. doi:10.1007/978-81-322-2529-4_1

Rastegari, H., & Shamsuddin, S. M. (2010). Web search personalization based on browsing history by artificial immune system. *International Journal of Advances in Soft Computing and Its Applications, 2*(3), 282-301.

Ravasz, E., Somera, A. L., Mongru, D. A., Oltvai, Z. N., & Barabasi, A. L. (2002). Hierarchical Organization of Modularity. *Metabolic Networks. Science, 297*(5586), 1551–1555. doi:10.1126/science.1073374 PMID:12202830

Rehman, S., & Marouf, L. (2004). Human resources for information management operations in Kuwaiti corporate companies. *Information Management & Computer Security, 12*(2), 191–201. doi:10.1108/09685220410530825

Rennie, J., & Srebro, N. (2005). Fast Maximum Margin Matrix Factorization for Collaborative Prediction (PDF).*Proceedings of the 22nd Annual International Conference on Machine Learning*. ACM Press.

Rieder, B. (2013). Studying Facebook via data extraction: the Netvizz application. In *Proceedings of the 5th Annual ACM Web Science Conference*(pp. 346-355). ACM. doi:10.1145/2464464.2464475

Rivera, S. J., Minsker, B. S., Work, D. B., & Roth, D. (2014). A text mining framework for advancing sustainability indicators. *Environmental Modelling & Software, 62*, 128–138. doi:10.1016/j.envsoft.2014.08.016

Rizzi, A. A., Gowdy, J., & Hollis, R. L. (1997). Agile assembly architecture: An agent based approach to modular precision assembly systems. *IEEE International Conference on Robotics and Automation* (vol. 2, pp. 1511-1516). Albuquerque, NM: IEEE. doi:10.1109/ROBOT.1997.614353

Roschelle, J., & Teasley, S. D. (1995). The construction of shared knowledge in collaborative problem solving. In *Computer-supported collaborative learning* (pp. 69–97). Berlin: Springer. doi:10.1007/978-3-642-85098-1_5

Rosenschein, S. J., & Kaelbling, L. P. (1995). A Situated View of Representation and Control. *Artificial Intelligence, 73*(1-2), 149–173. doi:10.1016/0004-3702(94)00056-7

Rosvall, M., & Bergstrom, C. (2008). Maps of random walks on complex networks reveal community structure. *Proceedings of the National Academy of Sciences of the United States of America*, *105*(4), 1118–1123. doi:10.1073/pnas.0706851105 PMID:18216267

Rouse, M. (2010). *What is Facebook page? - Definition from WhatIs.com*. Retrieved in April, 2016 from http://whatis.techtarget.com/definition/Facebook-page

Rovai, A. (2002). Building sense of community at a distance. *International Review of Research in Open and Distance Learning*, *3*(1), 1–16. doi:10.19173/irrodl.v3i1.79

Rubin, J. (1994). *Handbook of usability testing: How to plan, design, and conduct effective tests*. Wiley.

Russell, M. A. (2013). *Mining the Social Web: Data Mining Facebook, Twitter, LinkedIn, Google+, GitHub, and More*. O'Reilly Media, Inc.

Russell, M. A. (2013). *Mining the social web: Data mining Facebook, Twitter, LinkedIn, Google+, GitHub, and more*. O'Reilly Media.

Russell, S. J., & Norvig, P. (2003). *Artificial Intelligence: A modern approach*. Upper Saddle River, NJ: Prentice Hall.

Saguna, S., Zaslavsky, A., & Paris, C. (2012). *Context-Aware Twitter Validator (CATVal) a system to validate credibility and authenticity of Twitter content for use in decision support systems*. Fusing Decision Support Systems into the Fabric of the Context.

Sajjad, A., & Slobodan, P. S. (2006). An intelligent decision support system for management of floods. *Water Resources Management*, *20*(3), 391–410. doi:10.1007/s11269-006-0326-3

Sakthipriya, C., Srinaganya, G., & Sathiaseelan, J. G. (2015). An analysis of recent trends and challenges in web usage mining applications. *International Journal of Computer Science and Mobile Computing*, *4*(4), 41–48.

Salamon, T. (2011). *Design of agent-based models*. Repin, Czech Republic: Bruckner Publishing.

Salem, M. (2005). The Use of Strategic Planning Tools and Techniques in Saudi Arabia: An Empirical study. *International Journal of Management*, *22*(3), 376-395, 507.

Sam Anahory, S., & Dennis Murray, D. (2006). Data Warehousing in the real World A practice; Guide for Building Decision Support Systems. Pearson Education.

Sandahl, Z., & Sandahl, K. (2003). Potential advantages of Semantic Web for Internet commerce. In *Proceedings of the International Conference on Enterprise Information Systems (ICEIS)*.

Sandeep, S. (2010). Discovering Potential User Browsing Behaviors Using Custom-Built Apriori Algorithm. *International Journal of Computer Science & Information Technology, 2*(4).

Sanfeliu, A., & Fu, K. S. (1983). A distance measure between attributed relational graphs for pattern recognition. *IEEE Transactions on Systems, Man, and Cybernetics*, *13*(3), 353–362. doi:10.1109/TSMC.1983.6313167

Saravanakumar, K., & Deepa, K. (2011). Alternate query construction agent for improving web search result using wordnet.*International Conference on Computational Intelligence and Communication Networks (pp.*117-120). IEEE. doi:10.1109/CICN.2011.23

Sarwar, B., Karypis, G., Konstan, J., & Riedl, J. (2000). *Application of Dimensionality Reduction in Recommender System: A Case Study*. Academic Press.

Sathiyamoorthi, V., & Murali Bhaskaran, V. (2011b). Data Pre-Processing Techniques for Pre-Fetching and Caching of Web Data through Proxy Server. *International Journal of Computer Science and Network Security, 11*(11), 92-98.

Sathiyamoorthi, V. (2016). A Novel Cache Replacement Policy for Web Proxy Caching System Using Web Usage Mining. *International Journal of Information Technology and Web Engineering, 11*(2), 1–12. doi:10.4018/IJITWE.2016040101

Sathiyamoorthi, V., & Murali Bhaskaran, V. (2010a). Data Preparation Techniques for Mining World Wide Web through Web Usage Mining-An Approach. *International Journal of Recent Trends in Engineering, 2*(4), 1–4.

Sathiyamoorthi, V., & Murali Bhaskaran, V. (2010b). Data mining for intelligent enterprise resource planning system. *International Journal of Recent Trends in Engineering, 2*(3), 1–4.

Sathiyamoorthi, V., & Murali Bhaskaran, V. (2010b). Data Mining for Intelligent Enterprise Resource Planning System. *International Journal of Recent Trends in Engineering, 2*(3), 1–4.

Sathiyamoorthi, V., & Murali Bhaskaran, V. (2011a). Improving the Performance of Web Page Retrieval through Pre-Fetching and Caching. *European Journal of Scientific Research, 66*(2), 207–217.

Sathiyamoorthi, V., & Murali Bhaskaran, V. (2012). Optimizing the Web Cache performance by Clustering Based Pre-Fetching Technique Using Modified ART1. *International Journal of Computers and Applications, 44*(1), 51–60.

Sathiyamoorthi, V., & Murali Bhaskaran, V. (2012a). A Novel Approach for Web Caching through Modified Cache Replacement Algorithm. *International Journal of Engineering Research and Industrial Applications, 5*(1), 241–254.

Sathiyamoorthi, V., & Murali Bhaskaran, V. (2012b). Optimizing the Web Cache Performance by Clustering Based Pre-Fetching Technique Using Modified ART1. *International Journal of Computers and Applications, 44*(1), 51–60.

Sathiyamoorthi, V., & Murali Bhaskaran, V. (2013). Novel Approaches for Integrating MART1 Clustering Based Pre-Fetching Technique with Web Caching. *International Journal of Information Technology and Web Engineering, 8*(2), 18–32. doi:10.4018/jitwe.2013040102

Sauermann, L., Sebastian, T., & Linux, M. (2008). Case Study: KDE 4.0 Semantic Desktop Search and Tagging. Academic Press.

Scott, V. M., & Fuente, M. (2008). Whats the problem? L2 learners use of the L1 during consciousness-raising, form-focused tasks. *Modern Language Journal, 92*(1), 100–103. doi:10.1111/j.1540-4781.2008.00689.x

Segers, N., & de Vries, B. (2003). *The idea space system: Words as handles to a comprehensive data structure.* Paper presented at the 10th International Conference on Computer Aided Architectural Design Futures (CADfutures 2003), Tainan, Taiwan.

Selker, T. (1994). COACH: A teaching agent that learns. *Communications of the ACM, 37*(7), 92–99. doi:10.1145/176789.176799

Seo, W., Yoon, J., Park, H., Coh, B. Y., Lee, J. M., & Kwon, O. J. (2016). Product opportunity identification based on internal capabilities using text mining and association rule mining. *Technological Forecasting and Social Change, 105,* 94–104. doi:10.1016/j.techfore.2016.01.011

Serrano, J. I. (2009). Document indexing techniques for text mining. In J. Wang (Ed.), *Encyclopedia of data warehousing and mining* (2nd ed., pp. 716–721). Hershey, PA: IGI Global. doi:10.4018/978-1-60566-010-3.ch111

Sethi, S., & Dixit, A. (2015). Design of personalised search system based on user interest and query structuring. In *2nd International Conference on Computing for Sustainable Global Development* (pp. 1346-1351). IEEE.

Settles, B. (2005). ABNER: An open source tool for automatically tagging genes, proteins, and other entity names in text. *Bioinformatics (Oxford, England)*, *21*(14), 3191–3192. doi:10.1093/bioinformatics/bti475 PMID:15860559

Shahrabi, J., Hadavandi, E., & Esfandarani, M. S. (2013). Developing a hybrid intelligent model for constructing a size recommendation expert system in textile industries. *International Journal of Clothing Science and Technology*, *25*(5), 338–349. doi:10.1108/IJCST-04-2012-0015

Shardanand, U., & Maes, P. (1995). Social information filtering: malgorithms for automating "word of mouth". *Proceedings of ACM Conference on Human Factor in Computing Systems*. ACM Press. doi:10.1145/223904.223931

Shehata, S., Karray, F., & Kamel, M. (2010). Concept-based mining model. In A. Ali & Y. Xiang (Eds.), *Dynamic and advanced data mining for progressing technological development: Innovations and systemic approaches* (pp. 57–69). Hershey, PA: IGI Global. doi:10.4018/978-1-60566-908-3.ch004

Shelke, N. M. (2014). Approaches of emotion detection from text. *International Journal of Computer Science and Information Technology Research*, *2*(2), 123–128.

Shen, J., Zhang, J., Luo, X., Zhu, W., Yu, K., Chen, K., & Jiang, H. et al. (2007). Predicting protein-protein interactions based only on sequences information. *Proceedings of the National Academy of Sciences of the United States of America*, *104*(11), 4337–4341. doi:10.1073/pnas.0607879104 PMID:17360525

Shim, J. P., Warkentin, M., Counrtney, J. F., Power, D. J., Sharda, R., & Carlsson, C. (2002). Past, present, and future of decision support technology. *Decision Support Systems*, *33*(2), 111–126. doi:10.1016/S0167-9236(01)00139-7

Shoham, Y. (1997). Agent Oriented Programming: A Survey. In J. M. Bradshaw (Ed.), *Software Agents*. Menlo Park, CA: MIT Press.

Sieg, A., Mobasher, B., & Burke, R. (2007a). Web search personalization with ontological user profiles. In *Proceedings of the sixteenth ACM conference on Conference on information and knowledge management* (pp. 525-534). New York: ACM. doi:10.1145/1321440.1321515

Sieg, A., Mobasher, B., & Burke, R. (2007b). Ontological user profiles for representing context in web search. In *Proceedings of the 2007 IEEE/WIC/ACM International Conferences on Web Intelligence and Intelligent Agent Technology-Workshops* (pp. 91-94). Washington, DC: IEEE Computer Society.

Siemens, G. (2012). Learning analytics: envisioning a research discipline and a domain of practice. *Proceedings of the 2nd International Conference on Learning Analytics and Knowledge* (pp. 4-8). New York: ACM. doi:10.1145/2330601.2330605

Siemens, G., & Baker. (2012). Learning Analytics and Educational Data Mining: Towards Communication and Collaboration. *Proc. Second Int'l Conf. Learning Analytics and Knowledge*, (pp. 252-254). doi:10.1145/2330601.2330661

Simmel, G. (1964). *Conflict and the web of group affiliations*. Simon and Schuster.

Singh, B., & Singh, H. K. (2010). Web data mining research: a survey. *IEEE International Conference on Computational Intelligence and Computing Research* (pp. 1-10). Coimbatore: IEEE.

Sirola, M. (1996). A Rule-Based Agent Model for Process Automation. In *Proceedings of the IASTED/ISMM International Conference Modelling and Simulation* (pp 213-215).

Smith, D. C., Cypher, A., & Spohrer, J. (1994). KidSim: Programming agents without a programming language. *Communications of the ACM*, *37*(7), 54–67. doi:10.1145/176789.176795

Smyth, B. (2007). A community-based approach to personalizing web search. *Computer*, *40*(8), 42–50. doi:10.1109/MC.2007.259

Social Graph - Wikipedia, the free encyclopedia. (n.d.). Retrieved May, 2016 from https://en.wikipedia.org/wiki/Social_graph

Social Media Mining. (n.d.). Retrieved from https://en.wikipedia.org/wiki/Social_media_mining

So, H.-J., & Brush, T. A. (2008). Student perceptions of collaborative learning, social presence and satisfaction in a blended learning environment: Relationships and critical factors. *Computers & Education, 51*(1), 318–336. doi:10.1016/j. compedu.2007.05.009

Soriano, J., Au, T., & Banks, D. (2013). Text mining in computational advertising. *Statistical Analysis and Data Mining, 6*(4), 273–285. doi:10.1002/sam.11197

Speretta, M., & Gauch, S. (2005). Personalized search based on user search histories.*IEEE/WIC/ACM International Conference on Web Intelligence*(pp. 622-628). IEEE. doi:10.1109/WI.2005.114

Sprague, R. (1980). A Framework for the Development of Decision Support Systems. *Management Information Systems Quarterly, 4*(4), 1–25. doi:10.2307/248957

SPSS. (2008). *Predictive web analytics*. Accessed on 04/2008 from http://www.spss.com/pwa/index.html

Sreedhar, G. (2016). *Design solutions for improving website quality and effectiveness*. IGI Global.

Sreedhar, G. (2016). Identifying and Evaluating Web Metrics for Assuring the Quality of Web Designing. In Design Solutions for Improving Website Quality and Effectiveness (pp. 1-23). Hershey, PA: Information Science Publishing (an imprint of IGI Global).

Srikant, R., & Yang, Y. (2001). Mining web logs to improve website organization.*Proceedings of the 10th international conference on World Wide Web*. ACM Press. doi:10.1145/371920.372097

Srivastava, J., Desikan, P., & Kumar, V. (2002). Web mining: Accomplishments and future directions. In *National Science Foundation Workshop on Next Generation Data Mining* (NGDM'02) (pp. 51-69).

Srivastava. Desikan, J. P., & Kumar, V. (2002). Web Mining: *Accomplishments and Future Directions. National Science Foundation Workshop on Next Generation Data Mining*.

Srivastava, J., Cooley, R., Deshpande, M., & Tan, P. N. (2000). Web Usage Mining: Discovery and Applications of Usage Patterns from Web Data. *ACM SIGKDD Explorations Newsletter, 1*(2), 12–23. doi:10.1145/846183.846188

Staab, S., & Studer, R. (2009). *Handbook on Ontologies*. Berlin: International Handbooks on Information Systems, Springer Science and Business Media. doi:10.1007/978-3-540-92673-3

Stermsek, G., Strembeck, M., & Neumann, G. (2007). User Profile Refinement Using Explicit User Interest Modeling. GI Jahrestagung, 1, 289-293.

Stinson, L. (2016). *Facebook Reactions, the Totally Redesigned Like Button, Is Here | WIRED*. Retrieved May, 2016 from http://www.wired.com/2016/02/facebook-reactions-totally-redesigned-like-button/

Sugiyama, K., Hatano, K., & Yoshikawa, M. (2004). Adaptive web search based on user profile constructed without any effort from users. In *Proceedings of the 13th international conference on World Wide Web*(pp. 675-684). New York: ACM. doi:10.1145/988672.988764

Sujatha, N., & Iyakutty, K. (2010). Refinement of Web usage Data Clustering from K-means with Genetic Algorithm. *European Journal of Scientific Research, 42*(3), 464-476.

Sullivan, D. (2004). Text mining in business intelligence. In M. Raisinghani (Ed.), *Business intelligence in the digital economy: Opportunities, limitations and risks* (pp. 98–110). Hershey, PA: Idea Group Publishing. doi:10.4018/978-1-59140-206-0.ch006

Sundin, S., & Braban-Ledoux, C. (2001). Artificial Intelligence–Based Decision Support Technologies in Pavement Management. *Computer-Aided Civil and Infrastructure Engineering*, *16*(2), 143–157. doi:10.1111/0885-9507.00220

Sun, J. T., Zeng, H. J., Liu, H., Lu, Y., & Chen, Z. (2005). Cubesvd: a novel approach to personalized web search. In *Proceedings of the 14th international conference on World Wide Web* (pp. 382-390). New York: ACM. doi:10.1145/1060745.1060803

Suominen, H. (2009). Performance evaluation measures for text mining. In M. Song & Y. Brook Wu (Eds.), *Handbook of research on text and web mining technologies* (pp. 724–747). Hershey, PA: IGI Global. doi:10.4018/978-1-59904-990-8.ch041

Supyuenyong, V., & Islam, N. (2006). Knowledge Management Architecture: Building Blocks and Their Relationships. *Technology Management for the Global Future*, *3*, 1210–1219.

Swanepoel, K. T. (2004). Decision support system: Real-time control of manufacturing processes. *Journal of Manufacturing Technology Management*, *15*(1), 68–75. doi:10.1108/09576060410512338

Taherizadeh, S., & Moghadam, N. (2012). Integrating Web content mining into Web usage mining for finding patterns and predicting users' behaviors. *International Journal of Information Science and Management*, *7*(1), 51–66.

Tai, W. S., & Chen, C. T. (2009). A new evaluation model for intellectual capital based on computing with linguistic variable. *Expert Systems with Applications: An International Journal*, *36*(2), 3483–3488. doi:10.1016/j.eswa.2008.02.017

Takács, G., Pilászy, I., Németh, B., & Tikk, D. (2009, March). Scalable Collaborative Filtering Approaches for Large Recommender Systems. *Journal of Machine Learning Research*, *10*, 623–656.

Tan, P.-N., & Kumar, V. (2002). Discovery of web robot sessions based on their navigational patterns. *Data Mining and Knowledge Discovery*, *6*(1), 9–35. doi:10.1023/A:1013228602957

Taylor, J. (2012). *Decision Management Systems: A Practical Guide to Using Business Rules and Predictive Analytics*. Boston, MA: Pearson Education.

Teevan, J., Alvarado, C., Ackerman, M. S., & Karger, D. R. (2004). The perfect search engine is not enough: a study of orienteering behavior in directed search. In *Proceedings of the SIGCHI conference on Human factors in computing systems* (pp. 415-422). New York: ACM. doi:10.1145/985692.985745

Teng, W., Chang, C., & Chen, M. (2005). Integrating Web Caching and Web Pre-fetching in Client-Side Proxies. *IEEE Transactions on Parallel and Distributed Systems*, *16*(5), 444–455. doi:10.1109/TPDS.2005.56

The Open Graph Protocol. (2014). Retrieved April, 2016 from http://ogp.me/

Thomas, M., Pang, B., & Lee, L. (2006). *Get out the vote: Determining support or opposition from congressional floor-debate transcripts*. Paper presented at the 2006 Conference on Empirical Methods in Natural Language Processing (EMNLP 2006), Sydney, Australia. doi:10.3115/1610075.1610122

Thomas, J., McNaught, J., & Ananiadou, S. (2011). Applications of text mining within systematic reviews. *Research Synthesis Methods*, *2*(1), 1–14. doi:10.1002/jrsm.27 PMID:26061596

Tian, W., Choi, B., & Phoha, V. V. (2002). An Adaptive Web Cache Access Predictor Using Neural Network. *Proceedings of the 15th international conference on Industrial and engineering applications of artificial intelligence and expert systems: developments in applied artificial intelligence*, (LNCS). Springer-Verlag. doi:10.1007/3-540-48035-8_44

Tian, Y., Hankins, R., & Patel, J. (2008). Efficient aggregation for graph summarization. In *Proceedings of the 2008 ACM SIGMOD International Conference on Management of data* (pp. 567-580). ACM. doi:10.1145/1376616.1376675

Trastour, D., Bartolini, C., & Preist, C. (2002). Semantic web support for the business-to-business e-commerce lifecycle. In *Proceedings of the 11th international conference on World Wide Web*, (pp. 89-98). ACM. doi:10.1145/511446.511458

Trentin, G. (2009). Using a wiki to evaluate individual contribution to a collaborative learning project. *Journal of Computer Assisted Learning, 25*(1), 43–55. doi:10.1111/j.1365-2729.2008.00276.x

Truyens, M., & van Eecke, P. (2014). Legal aspects of text mining. *Computer Law & Security Report, 30*(2), 153–170. doi:10.1016/j.clsr.2014.01.009

Tseng, Y. H., Lin, C. J., & Lin, Y. I. (2007). Text mining techniques for patent analysis. *Information Processing & Management, 43*(5), 1216–1247. doi:10.1016/j.ipm.2006.11.011

Tsuruoka, Y., Miwa, M., Hamamoto, K., Tsujii, J., & Ananiadou, S. (2011). Discovering and visualizing indirect associations between biomedical concepts. *Bioinformatics (Oxford, England), 27*(13), i111–i119. doi:10.1093/bioinformatics/btr214 PMID:21685059

Turban, E., Aronson, J. E., & Liang, T. P. (2005). *Decision support systems and intelligent systems*. Upper Saddle River, NJ: Prentice Hall.

Turban, E., Aronson, J. E., Liang, T. P., & Sharda, R. (2007). *Decision support and business intelligence systems*. Upper Saddle River, NJ: Prentice Hall.

Turban, E., Volonio, L., McLean, E., & Wetherbe, J. (2009). *Information technology for management: Transforming organizations in the digital economy*. New York, NY: John Wiley & Sons.

Turner, R. M., Turner, E. H., Wagner, T. A., Wheeler, T. J., & Ogle, N. E. (2001). Using explicit, a priori contextual knowledge in an intelligent web search agent. In *International and Interdisciplinary Conference on Modeling and Using Context* (pp. 343-352). Springer Berlin Heidelberg. doi:10.1007/3-540-44607-9_26

Turney, P. (2002). *Thumbs up or thumbs down? Semantic orientation applied to unsupervised classification of reviews*. Paper presented at the 40th Annual Meeting of the Association for Computational Linguistics (ACL 2002), Philadelphia, PA.

Tyagi, N., & Sharma, S. (2012). Weighted Page rank algorithm based on number of visits of Links of web page. *International Journal of Soft Computing and Engineering*.

U.S. Department of Education, Office of Educational Technology. (2012). Enhancing teaching and learning through educational data mining and learning analytics: An issue brief. Washington, DC: Author.

Vakili-Ardebili, A., & Boussabaine, A. H. (2007). Application of fuzzy techniques to develop an assessment framework for building design eco-drivers. *Building and Environment, 42*(11), 3785–3800. doi:10.1016/j.buildenv.2006.11.017

van de Water, H., & van Peet, H. P. (2006). A decision support model based on the analytic hierarchy process for the make or buy decision in manufacturing. *Journal of Purchasing and Supply Management, 12*(5), 258–271. doi:10.1016/j.pursup.2007.01.003

van Raan, A. F. J., & Tijssen, R. J. W. (1993). The neural net of neural network research. *Scientometrics, 26*(1), 169–192. doi:10.1007/BF02016799

Van Wel, L., & Royakkers, L. (2004). Ethical issues in web data mining. *Ethics and Information Technology, 6*(2), 129–140. doi:10.1023/B:ETIN.0000047476.05912.3d

Vashishta, S., & Jain, Y. K. (2011). Efficient retrieval of text for biomedical domain using data mining algorithm. *International Journal of Advanced Computer Science and Applications*, 2(4), 77–80. doi:10.14569/IJACSA.2011.020412

Velasquez, J., Bassi, A., Yasuda, H., & Aoki, T. (2004). Mining Web Data to Create Online Navigation Recommendations. In *Proceedings of the Fourth IEEE International Conference on Data Mining (ICDM)*. doi:10.1109/ICDM.2004.10019

Venketesh, P., & Venkatesan, R. (2009). A Survey on Applications of Neural Networks and Evolutionary Techniques in Web Caching. *IETE Technical Review*, 26(3), 171–180. doi:10.4103/0256-4602.50701

Verma, N., Malhotra, D., Malhotra, M., & Singh, J. (2015). E-commerce website ranking using semantic web mining and neural computing. *Procedia Computer Science*, 45, 42–51. doi:10.1016/j.procs.2015.03.080

Viademonte, S., & Burstein, F. (2006). *From knowledge discovery to computational intelligence: A framework for intelligent decision support systems*. London, UK: Springer–Verlag.

Vinodh, S., & Kumar, C. D. (2012). Development of computerized decision support system for leanness assessment using multi grade fuzzy approach. *Journal of Manufacturing Technology Management*, 23(4), 503–516. doi:10.1108/17410381211230457

Visa Inc. - Wikipedia, the free encyclopedia. (2016). Retrieved in March, 2016 from https://en.wikipedia.org/wiki/Visa_Inc

Vishwanath, J., & Aishwarya, S. (2011). User suggestions extraction from customer reviews. *International Journal on Computer Science and Engineering*, 3(3), 1203–1206.

Vonderwell, S., & Zachariah, S. (2005). Factors that influence participation in online learning. *Journal of Research on Technology in Education*, 38(2), 213–230. doi:10.1080/15391523.2005.10782457

Vorvoreanu, M., & Clark, Q. (2010). Managing Identity Across Social Networks. *Proc. Poster Session at the ACM Conf. Computer Supported Cooperative Work*.

Vorvoreanu, M., Clark, Q. M., & Boisvenue, G. A. (2012). Online Identity Management Literacy for Engineering and Technology Students. *J. Online Eng. Education*, 3(1).

Vygotsky, L. S. (1978). *Mind in Society: The development of higher psychological processes*. Cambridge, MA: Harvard University Press.

Wagner, R. A., & Fisher, M. J. (1974). The string-to-string correction problem. *Journal of the ACM*, 21(1), 168–173. doi:10.1145/321796.321811

Waiman, C., Leung, L. C., & Tam, P. C. F. (2005). An intelligent decision support system for service network planning. *Decision Support Systems*, 39(3), 415–428. doi:10.1016/j.dss.2003.09.007

Waleed, A., Siti M.S. & Abdul S.I. (2011). A Survey of Web Caching and Prefetching. *Int. J. Advance. Soft Comput. Appl.*, 3(1).

Waleed, A., Siti, M. S., & Abdul, S. I. (2011). A Survey of Web Caching and Pre--fetching. International Journal on Advances in Soft Computing and Application, 3(1).

Wang, Y. (2000). *Web mining and knowledge discovery of usage patterns*. Cs 748T Project, 1-25.

Wang, G. T., & Pi-lian, H. E. (2005). *Web Log Mining by an Improved AprioriAll Algorithm* (Vol. 4). World Academy of Science, Engineering and Technology.

Wang, J. (1999). A Survey of Web Caching Schemes for the Internet. *ACM Comp. Commun. Review*, 29(5), 36–46. doi:10.1145/505696.505701

Wang, W. P. (2010). A fuzzy linguistic computing approach to supplier evaluation. *Applied Mathematical Modelling*, *34*(10), 3130–3141. doi:10.1016/j.apm.2010.02.002

Wang, Y., Cong, G., Song, G., & Xie, K. (2010). Community-based greedy algorithm for mining top-k influential nodes in mobile social networks. In *Proceedings of SIGKDD* (pp. 1039–1048). ACM. doi:10.1145/1835804.1835935

Watts, D. J. (1999). *Small worlds: the dynamics of networks between order and randomness*. Princeton University Press.

Watts, R. J., & Porter, A. L. (1997). Innovation forecasting. *Technological Forecasting and Social Change*, *56*(1), 25–47. doi:10.1016/S0040-1625(97)00050-4

Wavish, P. (1996). Situated action approach to implementing characters in computer games. *Applied Artificial Intelligence*, *10*(1), 53–74. doi:10.1080/088395196118687

Weber, I., & Castillo, C. (2010, July). The demographics of web search. In *Proceedings of the 33rd international ACM SIGIR conference on Research and development in information retrieval* (pp. 523-530). ACM.

WebTrend. (2008). *Webtrends visitor intelligence*. Accessed on 04/2008 from http://www.webtrends.com/Products/WebTrendsVisitorIntelligence.aspx

Wei, Y. Z., Moreau, L., & Jennings, N. R. (2003). Recommender systems: A market-based design. In *Proceedings of the second international joint conference on Autonomous agents and multiagent systems*(pp. 600-607). ACM. doi:10.1145/860575.860671

Wenger, E. (1998). *Communities of practice: Learning, meaning, and identity*. Cambridge, UK: Cambridge University Press. doi:10.1017/CBO9780511803932

Wessels & Duane. (2001). Web Caching. O'Reilly Publication.

Wexelblat, A., & Maes, P. (1999). Footprints: History-rich tools for information foraging.*Proceedings of the SIGCHI Conference on Human Factors in Computing Systems*. ACM Press.

Weyns, D., Omicini, A., & Odell, J. (2007). Environment as a first-class abstraction in multiagent systems. *Autonomous Agents and Multi-Agent Systems*, *14*(1), 5–30. doi:10.1007/s10458-006-0012-0

Williams, H., Li, F., & Whalley, J. (2000). Interoperability and electronic commerce: A new policy framework for evaluating strategic options. *Journal of Computer-Mediated Communication*, *5*(3).

Williams, T. P., & Gong, J. (2014). Predicting construction cost overruns using text mining, numerical data and ensemble classifiers. *Automation in Construction*, *43*, 23–29. doi:10.1016/j.autcon.2014.02.014

Winston, P. H. (1992). *Artificial Intelligence*. Addison-Wesley.

Wiskott, L., Fellous, J. M., Kr¨uger, N., & Von Der Malsburg, C. (1997). Face recognition by elastic bunch graph matching. In *Proceedings of IEEE PAMI* (pp. 775–779). doi:10.1109/ICIP.1997.647401

Wong, A. K. Y. (2006). Web Cache Replacement Policies: A Pragmatic Approach. *IEEE Network*, *20*(1), 28–34. doi:10.1109/MNET.2006.1580916

Wong, K., Xia, Y., Xu, R., Wu, M., & Li, W. (2008). Pattern-based opinion mining for stock market trend prediction. *International Journal of Computer Processing of Languages*, *21*(4), 347–361. doi:10.1142/S1793840608001949

Wooldridge, M. (2002). *An introduction to multiagent systems*. New York, NY: John Wiley & Sons.

Wu, J. Y. (2010). *Computational intelligence-based intelligent business intelligence system: Concept and framework.* Paper presented at the 2nd International Conference on Computer and Network Technology (ICCNT 2010), Bangkok, Thailand. doi:10.1109/ICCNT.2010.23

Xiao, J., Zhang, Y., Jia, X., & Li, T. (2001). Measuring Similarity of Interests for Clustering Web-users. *12th Australasian Database Conference (ADC)*, (pp. 107-114).

Xiao, Y., & Lucking, R. (2008). The impact of two types of peer assessment on students performance and satisfaction within a wiki environment. *The Internet and Higher Education, 11*(3-4), 186–193. doi:10.1016/j.iheduc.2008.06.005

Xie, B., Ding, Q., & Wu, D. (2015). Text mining on big and complex biomedical literature. In B. Wang, R. Li, & W. Perrizo (Eds.), *Big data analytics in bioinformatics and healthcare* (pp. 21–45). Hershey, PA: IGI Global. doi:10.4018/978-1-4666-6611-5.ch002

Xing, W., Wadholm, B., & Goggins, S. (2014). Learning analytics in CSCL with a focus on assessment: an exploratory study of activity theory-informed cluster analysis. *LAK '14 Proceedings of the Fourth International Conference on Learning Analytics and Knowledge* (pp. 59-67). New York: ACM.

Xing, W., Wadholm, R., Petakovic, E., & Goggins, S. (2015). Group learning assessment: Developing a theory-informed analytics. *Journal of Educational Technology & Society, 18*(2), 110–128.

Xirogiannis, G., Chytas, P., Glykas, M., & Valiris, G. (2008). Intelligent impact assessment of HRM to the shareholder value. *Expert Systems with Applications: An International Journal, 35*(4), 2017–2031. doi:10.1016/j.eswa.2007.08.103

Xu, L., Mo, H., Wang, K., & Tang, N. (2006). Document Clustering Based on Modified Artificial Immune Network. Rough Sets and Knowledge Technology, 4062, 516-521.

Xu, S., Jiang, H., & Lau, F. C. M. (2011). Mining user dwell time for personalized web search re-ranking. *International Joint Conference on Artificial Intelligence, 22*(3), 2367.

Xu, S., & Luo, X. (2009). Current issues and future analysis in text mining for information security applications. In H. Rahman (Ed.), *Social and political implications of data mining: Knowledge management in e-government* (pp. 165–177). Hershey, PA: IGI Global. doi:10.4018/978-1-60566-230-5.ch010

Yamada, Y., Kato, K., & Hirokawa, S. (2013). Text mining for analysis of interviews and questionnaires. In *Data mining: Concepts, methodologies, tools, and applications* (pp. 1390–1406). Hershey, PA: IGI Global. doi:10.4018/978-1-4666-2455-9.ch072

Yang, Q., Zhang, H., & Li, T. (2001). Mining Web Logs for Prediction Models in WWW Caching and Pre-Fetching. *Proceedings of the 7th ACM International Conference on Knowledge Discovery and Data Mining*, (pp. 473-478).

Yang, C., Hsu, H., & Hung, J. C. (2006). A Web Content Suggestion System for Distance Learning. *Tamkang Journal of Science and Engineering, 9*(3), 243.

Yang, H. C., Lee, C. H., & Hsiao, H. W. (2015). Incorporating self-organizing map with text mining techniques for text hierarchy generation. *Applied Soft Computing, 34*, 251–259. doi:10.1016/j.asoc.2015.05.005

Yang, J., & Leskovec, J. (2013). Overlapping community detection at scale: a nonnegative matrix factorization approach. In *Proceedings of the Sixth ACM InternationalnConferenceon Web search and data mining* (pp. 587–596). ACM. doi:10.1145/2433396.2433471

Yang, Q., Li, T., & Wang, K. (2004). Building Association-Rule Based Sequential Classifiers for Web-Document Prediction. *Journal of Data Mining and Knowledge Discovery, 8*(3), 253–273. doi:10.1023/B:DAMI.0000023675.04946.f1

Yang, S. L., & Li, T. F. (2002). Agility evaluation of mass customization product manufacturing. *Journal of Materials Processing Technology*, *129*(1/3), 640–644. doi:10.1016/S0924-0136(02)00674-X

Yang, Y. Y., Klose, T., Lippy, J., Barcelon-Yang, C. S., & Zhang, L. (2014). Leveraging text analytics in patent analysis to empower business decisions: A competitive differentiation of kinase assay technology platforms by I2E text mining software. *World Patent Information*, *39*, 24–34. doi:10.1016/j.wpi.2014.09.002

Yedidia, J. S., Freeman, W. T., & Weiss, Y. (2003). *Understanding belief propagation and its generalizations*. San Francisco, CA: Morgan Kaufmann Publishers Inc.

Yelland, N. (2005). The future is now: A review of the literature on the use of computers in early childhood education (1994-2004). *AACE Journal*, *13*(3), 201–232.

Yepes, A. J., & Berlanga, R. (2015). Knowledge based word-concept model estimation and refinement for biomedical text mining. *Journal of Biomedical Informatics*, *53*, 300–307. doi:10.1016/j.jbi.2014.11.015 PMID:25510606

Yi, J., Nasukawa, T., Bunescu, R., & Niblack, W. (2003). *Sentiment analyzer: Extracting sentiments about a given topic using natural language-processing techniques*. Paper presented at the 2003 3rd IEEE International Conference on Data Mining (ICDM 2003), Melbourne, FL. doi:10.1109/ICDM.2003.1250949

Yoon, B., Lee, S., & Lee, G. (2010). Development and application of a keyword-based knowledge map for effective R&D planning. *Scientometrics*, *85*(3), 803–820. doi:10.1007/s11192-010-0294-5

Yoon, B., Park, I., & Coh, B. Y. (2014). Exploring technological opportunities by linking technology and products: Application of morphology analysis and text mining. *Technological Forecasting and Social Change*, *86*, 287–303. doi:10.1016/j.techfore.2013.10.013

Yoon, B., & Park, Y. (2004). A text-mining-based patent network: Analytical tool for high-technology trend. *The Journal of High Technology Management Research*, *15*(1), 37–50. doi:10.1016/j.hitech.2003.09.003

Yu. (2004). A Web-Based Consumer- Oriented Intelligent Decision Support System for Personalized E-Services. ACM International Conference Proceeding Series, 60, 429-437.

Yu, B., & Singh, M. P. (2002). An agent-based approach to knowledge management. In *Proceedings of the eleventh international conference on Information and knowledge management*(pp. 642-644). ACM.

Yu, L., Wang, S., & Lai, K. K. (2009). A multi-agent neural network system for web text mining. In M. Song & Y. Brook Wu (Eds.), *Handbook of research on text and web mining technologies* (pp. 201–226). Hershey, PA: IGI Global. doi:10.4018/978-1-59904-990-8.ch013

Zadeh, L. A. (1965). Fuzzy sets. *Information and Control*, *8*(3), 338–353. doi:10.1016/S0019-9958(65)90241-X

Zadeh, L. A. (1973). Outline of a new approach to the analysis of complex systems and decision processes. *IEEE Transactions on Systems, Man, and Cybernetics*, *3*(1), 28–44. doi:10.1109/TSMC.1973.5408575

Zadeh, L. A. (1975). The concept of a linguistic variable and its application to approximate reasoning. *Information Sciences*, *8*(3), 199–249. doi:10.1016/0020-0255(75)90036-5

Zadeh, L. A. (1996). Fuzzy logic equals computing with words. *IEEE Transactions on Fuzzy Systems*, *4*(2), 103–111. doi:10.1109/91.493904

Zager, L., & Verghese, G. (2008). Graph similarity scoring and matching. *Applied Mathematics Letters*, *21*(1), 86–94. doi:10.1016/j.aml.2007.01.006

Zaiane, O. (2000). Web Mining: Concepts, Practices and Research. In *Proc. SDBD, Conference Tutorial Notes.*

Zhai, C., Velivelli, A., & Yu, B. (2004). *A cross-collection mixture model for comparative text mining.* Paper presented at the 10th ACM SIGKDD International Conference on Knowledge Discovery and Data Mining (KDD 2004), Seattle, WA. doi:10.1145/1014052.1014150

Zhang, C., Zeng, D., Li, J., Wang, F., & Zuo, W. (2009). Sentiment analysis of Chinese documents: From sentence to document level. *Journal of the American Society for Information Science and Technology, 60*(12), 2474–2487. doi:10.1002/asi.21206

Zhang, J., Luo, X., He, X., & Cai, C. (2013). Text semantic mining model based on the algebra of human concept learning. In Y. Wang (Ed.), *Cognitive informatics for revealing human cognition: Knowledge manipulations in natural intelligence* (pp. 221–236). Hershey, PA: IGI Global. doi:10.4018/978-1-4666-2476-4.ch014

Zhao, K., & Yu, X. (2011). A case based reasoning approach on supplier selection in petroleum enterprises. *Expert Systems with Applications: An International Journal, 38*(6), 6839–6847. doi:10.1016/j.eswa.2010.12.055

Zhijie, B., Zhimin, G., & Yu, J. (2009). A Survey of Web Pre-fetching. *Journal of Computer Research and Development, 46*(2), 202–210.

Zhu, D., & Porter, A. L. (2002). Automated extraction and visualization of information for technological intelligence and forecasting. *Technological Forecasting and Social Change, 69*(5), 495–506. doi:10.1016/S0040-1625(01)00157-3

Zhu, Z., Xu, J., Ren, X., Tian, Y., & Li, L. (2007). Query Expansion Based on a Personalized Web Search Model. *Third International Conference on Semantics, Knowledge and Grid* (pp. 128-133). Shan Xi: IEEE. doi:10.1109/SKG.2007.83

About the Contributors

G. Sreedhar is working as an Associate Professor in the Department of Computer Science, Rashtiya Sanskrit Vidyapeetha (Deemed University), Tirupati, India since 2001. G. Sreedhar received his Ph.D in Computer Science and Technology from Sri Krishnadevaraya University, Anantapur, India in the year 2011. He has over 15 years of Experience in Teaching and Research in the field of Computer Science. He published more than 15 research papers related to web engineering in reputed international journals. He published 4 books from reputed international publications and he presented more than 15 research papers in various national and international conferences. He handled research projects in computer science funded by University Grants Commission, Government of India. He is a member in various professional bodies like academic council, board of studies and editorial board member in various international journals in the field of computer science, Information Technology and other related fields. He has proven knowledge in the field of Computer Science and allied research areas.

* * *

Balamurugan Balusamy had completed his B.E(computer science) from Bharathidasan University and M.E(computer Science) from Anna University.He completed his Ph.D. in cloud security domain specifically on access control techniques.He has published papers and chapters in several renowned journals and conferences.

A. Anandarja Chari is working as Emeritus Professor in Department of OR &SQC, Rayalaseema University, Kurnool. He has over 30 years of teaching and research experience in the field of OR&SQC, Mathematics, Computer Science and related fields.

Sohil Grandhi is Studying B.Tech (IT) in VIT University.He has done several projects in the Data Science domain.His research interests are Cloud computing and Big data.

Kijpokin Kasemsap received his BEng degree in Mechanical Engineering from King Mongkut's University of Technology, Thonburi, his MBA degree from Ramkhamhaeng University, and his DBA degree in Human Resource Management from Suan Sunandha Rajabhat University. Dr. Kasemsap is a Special Lecturer in the Faculty of Management Sciences, Suan Sunandha Rajabhat University, based in Bangkok, Thailand. Dr. Kasemsap is a Member of the International Association of Engineers (IAENG), the International Association of Engineers and Scientists (IAEST), the International Economics Development and Research Center (IEDRC), the International Association of Computer Science and Information Technology (IACSIT), the International Foundation for Research and Development (IFRD), and the International Innovative Scientific and Research Organization (IISRO). Dr. Kasemsap also serves on the International Advisory Committee (IAC) for the International Association of Academicians and Researchers (INAAR). Dr. Kasemsap is the sole author of over 250 peer-reviewed international publications and book chapters on business, education, and information technology.

Raghvendra Kumar is working as Assistant Professor in Computer Science and Engineering Department at L.N.C.T Group of College Jabalpur, M.P. India. He received B. Tech. in Computer Science and Engineering from SRM University Chennai (Tamil Nadu), India, in 2011, M. Tech. in Computer Science and Engineering from KIIT University, Bhubaneswar, (Odisha) India in 2013, and pursuing Ph.D. in Computer Science and Engineering from Jodhpur National University, Jodhpur (Rajasthan), India. He has published many research papers in international journal including IEEE and ACM. He attends many national and international conferences and also He Received best paper award in IEEE 2013 for his research work in the field of distributed database in Tamil Nadu. His researches areas are Computer Networks, Data Mining, cloud computing and Secure Multiparty Computations, Theory of Computer Science and Design of Algorithms. He authored many computer science books in field of Data Mining, Robotics, Graph Theory, Turing Machine, Cryptography, Security Solutions in cloud computing and Privacy Preservation.

Saroja Nanda Mishra is currently working as Professor and Head of the Department of Computer Science, Engg. & Applications at Indira Gandhi Institute of Technology (IGIT), Sarang, Dhenkanal, Odisha, India. He has published more than 70 papers in International Journals and National Journals of repute. His research area focuses on fractal graphics, fractal geometry and internet data analysis. He has more than 25 years of teaching and research experiences. Many students obtained PhD degree and are continuing their PhD and M. Tech research work under his guidance.

Sasmita Mishra is currently working as Associate Professor in the Department of Computer Science, Engg. & Applications at Indira Gandhi Institute of Technology, Sarang, Dhenkanal, Odisha, India. She has published more than 80 papers in International Journals and National Journals of repute. Her research area focuses on multidimensional database, spatial data analysis and fractal & its applications. She has more than 25 years of teaching and research experiences. She is guiding many PhD and MTech scholars for their research work.

G. Vishnu Murthy obtained Doctorate in Computer Science & Engineering from Jawaharlal Nehru Technological University, has 18 years teaching experience at under graduate and post graduate level. He is presently working as professor in Computer Science, CACR Laboratory, Anurag Group of Institutions. He has published 20 papers in reputed/peer reviewed international journals. His areas of research interest are Array Grammars, Big Data Analytics and Web Usage Mining.

Venkata Naresh received his M.Tech(CSE) from JNTUH. He is pursuing PhD from VFSTR university. He published several papers in IEEE, Scopus, EI Compendex and Web of Science journals. His research interests are Image processing, Cloud computing and data mining.

Wing Shui Ng has extensive involvement in computer education in Hong Kong. In addition to the experience to serve as the Panel Head of computer subjects and the person in charge of Information Technology in Education Committee in schools, he was seconded to Technology Education Section of Curriculum Development Institute of Education Bureau to develop New Senior Secondary Information and Communication Technology Curriculum, to participate in school-based curriculum development, to organize teacher training programmes and to serve as a speaker in educational seminars. He also contributed his expertise to serve as a reviewer of Computer Education Textbook Review Panel and as a setter as well as the marker of public examination papers for Hong Kong Examinations and Assessment Authority. Moreover, he was appointed as the Subject Expert Adviser in an advisory study on computer curriculum in Hong Kong. Other than his involvement in computer education, he has substantial experience in school administration by the experiences of serving as the School Development Officer in Education Bureau and a member of School Administrative Council. Currently, Dr. Ng devotes his efforts for training and assessing pre-service and in-service teachers as well as conducting educational research in The Education University of Hong Kong. He also dedicates effort to serve as a speaker and a member of publication and promotion committee in a number of international conferences, as well as to serve as a reviewer of international journals. His research areas include Information Technology in Education and Assessment for Learning.

Alberto Ochoa Ortiz-Zezzatti (BS '94–Eng. Master '00; PhD '04-Postdoctoral Researcher '06 & Industrial Postdoctoral Research '09) joined the Juarez City University in 2008. He participates in the organization of several International Conferences. He has review of four important Journals from Elsevier: highlighting Applied Soft Computing and Computers in Human Behavior. His research interests include ubiquitous compute, evolutionary computation, natural processing language, social modeling, anthropometrics characterization and Social Data Mining. In May 2016 begin a Sabbatical internship year in Barcelona Supercomputing Center with a project related with simulation of human stampedes and refugee boat sinking improved with Artificial Intelligence. Actually has Level 2 in SNI membership at Conacyt.

Priyanka Pandey is working as Assistant Professor in Computer Science and Engineering Department at L.N.C.T Group of College Jabalpur, M.P. India. She received B.E. in Information Technology from TIE Tech (RGPV University), Jabalpur, MP, India, in 2013, M. Tech. in Computer Science and Engineering from TIE Tech (RGPV University), Jabalpur, MP, India. She published many research papers in international journal and conferences including IEEE. She attends many national and international conferences, her researches areas are Computer Networks, Data Mining, wireless network and Design of Algorithms.

Prasant Kumar Pattnaik, Ph.D. (Computer Science), Fellow IETE, Senior Member IEEE is Professor at the School of Computer Engineering, KIIT University, Bhubaneswar. He has more than a decade of teaching research experience. Dr. Pattnaik has published numbers of Research papers in peer reviewed international journals and conferences. His researches areas are Computer Networks, Data Mining, cloud computing, Mobile Computing. He authored many computer science books in field of Data Mining, Robotics, Graph Theory, Turing Machine, Cryptography, Security Solutions in Cloud Computing, Mobile Computing and Privacy Preservation.

A. V. Krishna Prasad working as a Professor in Department of Computer Science and Engineering at KL University. He completed his Ph.D in Computer Science from Sri Venkateswara University, Tirupati in 2012. He is an Editorial Board Member and Reviewer for several International Journals. He published several papers in national and international journals. His Interested Research areas are Mining, Big Data and Analytics.

Thendral Puyalnithi has completed Bachelor of Engineering in Electrical and Electronics in PSG College of Technology and Master of Engineering in Software Systems in BITS Pilani. He worked as Senior Software Engineer for 3 years. He is currently pursuing PhD in Computer Science and his technical area of interest is in data mining, soft computing, machine learning.

Bapuji Rao is currently pursuing PhD (CSE) from Biju Patnaik University of Technology (BPUT), Rourkela, Odisha, India. He received M.Tech (Computer Science) from Berhampur University, Berhampur, Odisha, India. He has published 13 papers in International Conferences which includes IEEE-5, Springer-3, Elsevier-1, and McGraw-Hill-1. A book chapter titled "Graph Mining and Its Applications in Studying Community Based Graph under the Preview of Social Network" in Product Innovation through Knowledge Management and Social Media Strategies, IGI Global, USA. His Current Research area focuses on Graph Mining, Social Network, Data Mining, Opinion Mining, and Multi-Layer Graph.

M. Varaprasad Rao obtained Doctorate in Computer Science & Engineering, has 16 years teaching experience at under graduate and post graduate level. He is presently working as professor in Computer Science, Centre for Advanced Computational Research Laboratory, Anurag Group of Institutions. He has published 12 papers in reputed/peer reviewed international journals. His areas of research interest are Security, Data Mining, Data Analytics and Recommended Systems.

C. Madana Kumar Reddy received his Bachelors Degree in Computer Science from Sri Krishnadevaraya University, India in 1995. Masters Degree in Computer Applications from S Sri Krishnadevaraya University, India in 1998. M.Phil Degree in Computer Science from Madurai Kamaraj University, India in 2005. Ph.D. Degree from Computer Science from Dravidian University, Kuppam, India. in 2016. He is currently working as Associate Professor in the Department of Computer Applications in Annamacharya Institute of Technology and Sciences, Rajampet. He is having over 18 Years of Teaching Experience. He has published his papers in various national and international conferences. Presently he is Heading the Department of Computer Applications in Annamacharya Institute of Technologies and Sciences, Rajampet, Kadapa Dt, India. Several of his speeches are broadcast through All India Radio, Kurnool. Completed his Doctoral research in Computer Science under the guidance of Dr A. Rama Mohan Reddy, Professor of CSE, SV University, Tirupati.

V. Sathiyamoorthi is currently working as an Associate Professor in Computer Science and Engineering Department at Sona College of Technology, Salem, Tamil Nadu, India. He was born on June 21, 1983, at Omalur in Salem District, Tamil Nadu, India. He received his Bachelor of Engineering degree in Information Technology from Periyar University, Salem with First Class. He obtained his Master of Engineering degree in Computer Science and Engineering from Anna University, Chennai with Distinction and secured 30th University Rank.He received his Ph.D degree from Anna University, Chennai in Web

Mining. His areas of specialization include Web Usage Mining, Data Structures, Design and Analysis of Algorithm and Operating System. He has published five papers in International Journals and eight papers in various National and International conferences. He has also participated in various National level Workshops and Seminars conducted by various reputed institutions.

Madhu Viswanatham V has completed Master of Computer Applications, Master of Technology in Information Technology and PhD in Computer Science. His area of interests lies in Information Security, Cryptography, Computer Networks, Machine learning and Data Mining. He has published technical works in many International Journals and in Conferences.

Vegesna Tarun Sai Varma is Studying B.Tech (IT) in VIT University.He has done several projects in the Data Science domain. His research interests are Cloud computing and Big data.

Index

A

B

C

D

E

F

H